The Rise and Fall of the
Confederate Government

JEFFERSON DAVIS

THE RISE AND
CONFEDERATE

FALL OF THE GOVERNMENT

Abridged for the Modern Reader

Foreword by Earl Schenck Miers

GLOUCESTER, MASS.

PETER SMITH

1971

Collier Books is a division of The Crowell-Collier Publishing Company.

First Edition, 1961
This edition is reprinted, 1971, by arrangement with
The Macmillan Company

JEFFERSON DAVIS, soldier, planter, politician, and President of the Confederacy, was born in Kentucky on June 3, 1808. A graduate of West Point, Davis served as a lieutenant in the Army for seven years before becoming a cotton planter in Mississippi. In 1844 Davis was elected to Congress but resigned soon thereafter to become Colonel of the First Mississippi Rifles during the Mexican War. A severe wound abruptly ended Davis' military career but enhanced his political career. In 1847 Davis went to the United States Senate to fill a vacancy created by the death of Jesse Speight. Davis was elected in 1850 to serve a full term but resigned the following year to run, unsuccessfully as it turned out, for the Mississippi governorship. A term as Secretary of War in Franklin Pierce's Cabinet was followed by Davis' return to the Senate in 1857, where he was recognized as one of the most ardent spokesmen of the Southern cause. As President of the Confederate States of America, Davis was an integral part of the Civil War. After Lee's surrender at Appomattox, Davis fled southward, hoping to maintain a semblance of organized resistance. He was soon captured but was never brought to trial. In the years following his release from prison, Davis was in constant demand as a speaker and writer. In addition to *The Rise and Fall of the Confederate Government* he wrote *A Short History of the Confederacy*. Jefferson Davis, an apologist for the Confederacy to the end of his days, died in New Orleans on December 6, 1889.

Contents

Part Three / Secession and Confederation

Part Four / The War

Foreword

I.

"CAPTURE OR kill Jefferson Davis, the rebel ex-President," stated the orders given to Lieutenant Colonel B. D. Pritchard when he led his regiment of Federal soldiers out of Macon, Georgia on May 7, 1865. Three days later, in the damp, chilly dawn, Pritchard and his cavalry found Davis and his party encamped near the little town of Irwinville. Defiantly, the Confederate President stood his ground as a Federal trooper advanced.

"He leveled his carbine at me," Davis recalled later for the New York *Herald,* "but I expected, if he fired, he would miss me, and my intention was in that event to put my hand under his foot, tumble him off on the other side, spring into the saddle, and attempt to escape. My wife, who had been watching, ran forward and threw her arms around me. Success depended on instantaneous action, and, recognizing that the opportunity had been lost, I turned back . . ."

For the politicians who now dominated the North, this little scene on a Georgia crossroads at morning on May 10, 1865 brought to a climax the War Between the States. At long last the radical Republicans had bagged the "villain" of the bloodiest civil war the world ever had known, and the terrible vengefulness that such Northerners felt was expresed by the Chicago *Tribune*: ". . . We hold if that most guilty and infamous of men is suffered to escape the penalties he has earned, there is not a murderer, a robber, or a perjurer in all the land and who may not with propriety plead the leniency that was extended to him, as a reason why all punishment should cease, and why stabbing, poisoning, arson and robbery should be considered offences no more. . . ." The editors of *Harper's Weekly* were equally bloodthirsty: "Jefferson Davis must be tried for treason. If convicted he must be sentenced. If sentenced he must be executed."

At the time of Davis's apprehension the North still grieved for Abraham Lincoln, struck down by an assassin's bullet a month before; but as time went on that suffering could not excuse the North's shameful behavior toward its old foe. Even the Confederate leader's confinement in a dank casemate of Fortress Monroe might have been justified as an act of military expediency; but when Davis was manacled and made to endure the humiliations of a common felon of the Dark Ages a wave of revulsion swept the civilized world. Andrew Johnson continued to insist that Davis had committed crimes "worse than murder" and therefore should be hanged; but British publicists reminded Lincoln's successor that the same charge could be brought against such opponents of constituted authority as Cromwell and Washington, Kossuth and Garibaldi.

With splendid dignity, Jefferson Davis withstood the abuses heaped upon him. In the memoirs that follow he dismisses these months of degradation briefly, paying tribute to the "bitter tears . . . shed by the gentle" because of the "needless torture" to which he was subjected. What he could never quite forgive was "the mental agony" his Northern captors also inflicted: "It was long before I was permitted to hear from my wife and children, and this, and things like this, was the power which education added to savage cruelty."

As the months piled into years saner minds began to gain influence in the North. Among those who spoke out boldly was Chief Justice Salmon P. Chase; the captivity of the Confederate President had been a national misfortune, in Chase's judgment; now to go further and place him on trial would amount to a national tragedy. Others like Cornelius Vanderbilt and Horace Greeley signed a bond for $100,000 to secure the release of their one-time adversary; and in May, 1867 the doors of Fortress Monroe swung open and Jefferson Davis again became a free man.

II.

How badly the Northern politicians had blundered in confining the Confederate President in a dismal bastion became clear when Jefferson Davis arrived in Richmond. Not since the first days of the Confederacy had the South cheered so wildly. Forgotten entirely were those bitter April days of 1865 when Lee surrendered at Appomattox and Davis, in flight with his Cabinet, had been blamed for all the heartbreak and humiliation that had befallen his countrymen. Instead the Confederate President emerged from Fortress Monroe a martyr—once more the bold, beloved, noble leader of the South. Foe and friend alike rallied to his side in that moment of emotional release; he was again the spirit of a cause that had not deserved to lose—again, the grand old man of unbending will whose face had called them to rebellion every time they licked a postage stamp. On June 1, General Robert E. Lee, now a college president in Lexington, Virginia, spoke for the majority of fellow Southerners in a warm-hearted letter:

"*My Dear Mr. Davis:* You can conceive better than I can express the misery which your friends have suffered from your long imprisonment, and the other afflictions incident thereto. To no one has this been more painful than to me, and the impossibility of affording relief has added to my distress. Your release has lifted a load from my heart which I have not words to tell. My daily prayer to the great Ruler of the world is that He may shield you from all future harm, guard you from evil, and give you that peace which the world cannot take away. That the rest of your days may be triumphantly happy is the sincere and earnest wish of

"Your most obedient, faithful friend and servant,

"R. E. Lee."

How like the gentle Lee were these kind expressions—Lee who stood stanchly by Davis through every trial of war and peace! From the first months of the Confederacy an opposition to Davis existed—in and out of Congress, in and out of the army—but no anti-Davis movement ever received the least comfort from Lee. Even in the last dying weeks of the Confederacy, when Davis's enemies sought to make Lee dictator, the Virginian had been unapproachable. It was not in Lee's character to forget how Davis had sustained him after his first failure in western Virginia; or how, when Lee had offered to resign his command after Gettysburg, Davis had advised: "There has been nothing which I have found to require a greater effort of patience than to bear the criticisms of the ignorant, who pronounce everything a failure which does not equal their expectations or desires, and can see no good result which is not in line of their own imaginings."

Unyielding devotion to the Southern cause held these two men together; others could argue that the Confederacy could have found a more capable executive but Lee, first and last, was satisfied with the heart of Jefferson Davis. Yet, heaven knows, those who were less generous in judging the Confederate President were not without their justification. An obstinate man, quick to take umbrage at personal criticism, socially aloof, contemptuous of public opinion, a poor judge of people who failed to see faults in his pets or virtues in his opponents, tactless, too given to fussing with small details —all these epithets, unfortunately, could be applied on occasion to Jefferson Davis. "He is as vain as a peacock, as ambitious as the Devil," declared South Carolina's influential James Henry Hammond, in appraising Davis; and Robert G. H. Kean, Chief of the Bureau of War, wrote in his diary in late November, 1862: "I am coming to Mr. [Frank G.] Ruffin's opinion. He says he used to think Jefferson Davis a *mule,* but a *good mule.* He has come to think him a jackass." By then Robert Barnwell Rhett, wielder of Charleston opinion, was calling the President "not only a dishonest man but a liar."

But Jefferson Davis was neither. Nor was he, despite the croaking of his critics, an ineffectual administrator. True, he had his run-ins with the Confederate Congress over such sobering issues as conscription and the exemption laws, finance, suspension of the writ of habeas corpus and the impressment of supplies, yet the political waters in which he waded were shallow compared to the tidal waves that inundated Lincoln. True, he was too often a meddler in details which should have been entrusted to subordinates, and as a result secretaries sometimes shuttled in and out of his Cabinet like trains trying to keep a schedule, but mediocre men largely filled his official family and it is conjectural whether he could have found any much better. True, his quarrels with General Joseph E. Johnston amounted at times to a personal vendetta, but both were at fault and Johnston, unlike Lee, was too easily made the prey of the anti-Davis forces led by Louis T. Wigfall of Texas. Richmond in those years thrived on jealousy, intrigue, fault-finding and whistling up a chimney; even lifelong friends like Lydia Johnston and Varina Davis would finally come to a social sword's point, worn down by the bickering between husband-general and husband-President, until Lydia hoped that the general would resign rather than throw away his life serving under that "wicked man."

In this brittle atmosphere more than luck explained the survival of Jefferson Davis. His service in the United States Senate and as Secretary of War under Franklin Pierce had given him a sound understanding of government. As a slaveowner he had given extraordinary freedom to his own charges so that when he supported the "peculiar institution" with stubborn pride it was not the voice of Simon Legree who spoke. His occasional irritability, and even his social stand-offishness, stemmed in no small measure from the attacks of facial neuralgia that often made him a very sick man, yet his mind never wavered from its purpose and his heart never yielded its conviction of justice in the Southern cause. After First Manassas, speaking at the Spottswood Hotel, he offered the South that test of character which he set for himself: "Never be haughty to the humble, or humble to the haughty."

Early in 1865, Jefferson Davis proposed arming the slaves, giving his enemies a point of attack around which they could rally. In the phrase of the time, he had cooked his goose, and when, within a few short weeks, the war ended there were few who really cared whether he made his escape. But his imprisonment in chains touched the hearts of all who sorrowed for the defeated South. Richmond cheered and cried and heaped its affection upon him when in 1867 he returned from Fortress Monroe. A troubled decade followed, filled with travel abroad and two unsuccessful business ventures, until he came to look upon himself as "a citizen of no land under the sun;" then in the spring of 1877, when the azaleas were in flame and the wisteria sparkled, he found refuge at last at Beauvoir, a fine mansion facing the Gulf of Mexico about halfway between Gulfport and Biloxi.

III.

JEFFERSON DAVIS was sixty-nine when he came to live at Beauvoir; for a dozen years he would find here the contentment of mind and heart for which he had so long been searching. His surroundings certainly helped, for as an example of a gracious Louisiana plantation-home Beauvoir represented a spectacular achievement. The original owner and builder was James Brown, a prosperous planter of Madison County, who imported his slate from England, cut his cypress in Back Bay swamp, and had his slaves hand-make the bricks for foundation and chimneys. Decorators and carpenters, brought from New Orleans, accounted for the perfect styling that so appealed to Davis's love for neatness. Among the great good fortunes of his life was the fact that by 1877 the ownership of Beauvoir had passed to Sarah Anne Dorsey, a girlhood friend of the President's wife.

East of the plantation stood the little cottage where Jefferson Davis wrote *The Rise and Fall of the Confederate Government,* and pleasant indeed were the surroundings where he toiled for three years on his long, thoughtful, and often moving justification of secession and the war. The room, a great tourist attraction today, has charm, order, simplicity, the mark of the man whose memory it cherishes. The book shelves, visitors are told, Davis built with the help of a servant. The portrait of Franklin Pierce to the left of the clock on the mantle was a gift from the President whom Davis served as Secretary of War; the portrait on the right depicts Senator Jesse Speight, whose death in 1847 created the vacancy in the Senate to which Davis was appointed by the governor of Mississippi.

The President's literary habits were as orderly as his cottage-studio. When he had a passage in mind he dictated —first to Mrs. Dorsey and later to his wife after her return from Europe in 1878. He was still a prodigious worker, sparing neither himself nor his helper, so that he finished his book at four o'clock one morning after eight hours of dictation. Yet it seems a safe conjecture that neither amanuensis ever complained over these long hours—or ever questioned the disputatious tone of his work—or ever doubted that his hostility toward critics like Confederate Vice-President Alexander H. Stephens, Joseph E. Johnston and William Tecumseh Sherman (all these memoirs preceded his own) deserved anything less than the retributive scorn he leveled at them. A gifted Southern historian, Bell Irvin Wiley, contends that the obvious "prejudices and antipathies" which Davis revealed in *The Rise and Fall of the Confederate Government* must be regarded as among the book's most commendable qualities since these biases are so easily detected. The point is well taken—but with one reservation. On July 4, 1861, in a special message to Congress, Abraham Lincoln said:

"It might seem, at first thought, to be of little difference whether the present movement at the South be called 'secession' or 'rebellion.' The movers, however, will understand the difference. At the beginning, they knew they could never raise their treason to any respectable magnitude, by any name which implies *violation* of law. They knew their people possessed as much of moral sense, as much of devotion to law and order, and as much pride in, and reverence for, the history, and government, of their common country, as any other civilized, and patriotic people. They knew they could make no advancement directly in the teeth of these strong and noble sentiments. Accordingly they commenced by an insidious debauching of the public mind. They invented an ingenious sophism, which, if conceded, was followed by perfectly logical steps, through all the incidents, to the complete destruction of the Union. The sophism itself is, that any state of the Union may, *consistently* with the national Constitution, and therefore *lawfully,* and *peacefully*, withdraw from the Union, without the consent of the Union, or of any other state. The little disguise that the supposed right is to be exercised only for just cause, themselves to be the sole judge of its justice, is too thin to merit any notice."

To read *The Rise and Fall of the Confederate Government* without remembering this paragraph by Mr. Lincoln is to miss the essential dispute which divided North and South, and created civil war between them, and led Mr. Davis in the end to state *his* case with force and spirit.

IV.

A FINE marble arch, erected in 1917 by the Mississippi Division of the United Daughters of the Confederacy, today welcomes the visitor to Beauvoir. As an American (of Southern or Northern origin) strolls under the great old liveoaks with their festoons of moss, he cannot but marvel at how completely the human heart forgives and history sentimentalizes. Today no one would guess that Jefferson Davis came to Beauvoir "a citizen of no land under the sun;" or that Mrs. Dorsey felt constrained to stipulate in her will: "If Davis should not survive me, I give all that I have bequeathed to him to his youngest daughter Varina. I do not intend to share in the ingratitude of my country toward the man who is in my eyes the highest and noblest in existence."

"Even a child's disapproval discomposed him," Varina Davis once said in describing her husband's sensitivity. But he could feel for others. When Grant was dying at Mount McGregor the Boston *Globe* asked its New Orleans correspondent to obtain a statement from Jefferson Davis. The Confederate President replied: "Though he invaded our country, it was with an open hand and, as far as I know, he abetted neither arson nor pillage, and has since the war, I believe, showed no malignity to Confederates either of the military or civil service. Therefore, instead of seeking to disturb the quiet of his closing hours, I would, if it were in my power, contribute to the peace of his mind and the comfort of his body."

On December 6, 1889, Jefferson Davis died suddenly in New Orleans. Already the New South was beginning to rise from the ashes of the war, and a Southern poet sang:

> After all,
> One country, brethren! We must rise or fall
> With the Supreme Republic. We must be
> The makers of her immortality,—
> Her freedom, fame,
> Her glory or her shame:
> Liegemen to God and fathers of the free!

Lost Cause or New Opportunity? Such was the thought Davis had pondered finally when writing this book.

EARL SCHENCK MIERS

Edison, New Jersey
June, 1961

Preface

THE OBJECT of this work has been from historical data to show that the Southern States had rightfully the power to withdraw from a Union into which they had, as sovereign communities, voluntarily entered; that the denial of that right was a violation of the letter and spirit of the compact between the States; and that the war waged by the Federal Government against the seceding States was in disregard of the limitations of the Constitution, and destructive of the principles of the Declaration of Independence.

The author, from his official position, may claim to have known much of the motives and acts of his countrymen immediately before and during the war of 1861–'65, and he has sought to furnish material for the future historian, who, when the passions and prejudices of the day shall have given place to reason and sober thought, may, better than a contemporary, investigate the causes, conduct, and results of the war.

The incentive to undertake the work now offered to the public was the desire to correct misapprehensions created by industriously circulated misrepresentations as to the acts and purposes of the people and the General Government of the Confederate States. By the reiteration of such unappropriate terms as "rebellion" and "treason," and the asseveration that the South was levying war against the United States, those ignorant of the nature of the Union, and of the reserved powers of the States, have been led to believe that the Confederate States were in the condition of revolted provinces, and that the United States were forced to resort to arms for the preservation of their existence. To those who knew that the Union was formed for specific enumerated purposes, and that the States had never surrendered their sovereignty, it was a palpable absurdity to apply to them, or to their citizens when obeying their mandates, the terms "rebellion" and "treason"; and, further, it is shown in the following pages that the Confederate States, so far from making war or seeking to destroy the United States, as soon as they had an official organ, strove earnestly, by peaceful recognition, to equitably adjust all questions growing out of the separation from their late associates.

Another great perversion of truth has been the arraignment of the men who participated in the formation of the Confederacy and who bore arms in its defense, as the instigators of a controversy leading to disunion. Sectional issues appear conspicuously in the debates of the Convention which framed the Federal Constitution, and its many compromises were designed to secure an equilibrium between the sections, and to preserve the interests as well as the liberties of the several States. African servitude at that time was not confined to a section, but was numerically greater in the South than in the North, with a tendency to its continuance in the former and cessation in the latter. It therefore thus early presents itself as a disturbing element, and the provisions of the Constitution, which were known to be necessary for its adoption, bound all the States to recognize and protect that species of property. When at a subsequent period there arose in the Northern States an antislavery agitation, it was a harmless and scarcely noticed movement until political demagogues seized upon it as a means to acquire power. Had it been left to pseudo-philanthropists and fanatics, most zealous where least informed, it never could have shaken the foundations of the Union and have incited one section to carry fire and sword into the other. That the agitation was political in its character, and was clearly developed as early as 1803, it is believed has been established in these pages. To preserve a sectional equilibrium and to maintain the equality of the States was the effort on one side, to acquire empire was the manifest purpose on the other. This struggle began before the men of the Confederacy were born; how it arose and how it progressed it has been attempted briefly to show. Its last stage was on the question of territorial governments; and, if in this work it has not been demonstrated that the position of the South was justified by the Constitution and the equal rights of the people of all the States, it must be because the author has failed to present the subject with a sufficient degree of force and clearness.

In describing the events of the war, space has not permitted, and the loss of both books and papers has prevented, the notice of very many entitled to consideration, as well for the humanity as the gallantry of our men in the unequal combats they fought. These numerous omissions, it is satisfactory to know, the official reports made at the time and the subsequent contributions which have been and are being published by the actors, will supply more fully and graphically than could have been done in this work.

Usurpations of the Federal Government have been presented, not in a spirit of hostility, but as a warning to the people against the dangers by which their liberties are beset. When the war ceased, the pretext on which it had been waged could no longer be alleged. The emancipation proclamation of Mr. Lincoln, which, when it was issued, he humorously admitted to be a nullity, had acquired validity by the action of the highest authority known to our institutions—the people assembled in their several State Conventions. The soldiers of the Confederacy had laid down their arms, had in good faith pledged themselves to abstain from further hostile operations, and had peacefully dispersed to their homes; there could not, then, have been further dread of them by the Government of the United States. The plea of necessity could, therefore, no longer exist for hostile demonstration against the people and States of the deceased Confederacy. Did vengeance, which stops at the grave, subside? Did real peace and the restoration of the States to their former rights and positions follow, as was promised on the restoration of the Union? Let the recital of the invasion of the reserved powers of the States, or the people, and the perversion of the republican form of government guaranteed to each State by the Constitution, answer the question. For the deplorable fact of the war, for the cruel manner in which it was waged, for the sad physical and yet sadder moral results it produced, the reader of these pages, I hope, will admit that the South, in the forum of conscience, stands fully acquitted.

Much of the past is irremediable; the best hope for a restoration in the future to the pristine purity and fraternity of the Union, rests on the opinions and character of the men who are to succeed this generation: that they may be suited to that blessed work, one, whose public course is ended, invokes them to draw their creed from the fountains of our political history, rather than from the lower stream, polluted as it has been by self-seeking place-hunters and by sectional strife.

THE AUTHOR

Introduction

A DUTY to my countrymen; to the memory of those who died in defense of a cause consecrated by inheritance, as well as sustained by conviction; and to those who, perhaps less fortunate, staked all, and lost all, save life and honor, in its behalf, has impelled me to attempt the vindication of their cause and conduct. For this purpose I have decided to present an historical sketch of the events which preceded and attended the struggle of the Southern States to maintain their existence and their rights as sovereign communities—the creators, not the creatures, of the General Government.

The social problem of maintaining the just relation between constitution, government, and people, has been found so difficult, that human history is a record of unsuccessful efforts to establish it. A government, to afford the needful protection and exercise proper care for the welfare of a people, must have homogeneity in its constituents. It is this necessity which has divided the human race into separate nations, and finally has defeated the grandest efforts which conquerors have made to give unlimited extent to their domain. When our fathers dissolved their connection with Great Britain, by declaring themselves free and independent States, they constituted thirteen separate communities, and were careful to assert and preserve, each for itself, its sovereignty and jurisdiction.

At a time when the minds of men are straying far from the lessons our fathers taught, it seems proper and well to recur to the original principles on which the system of government they devised was founded. The eternal truths which they announced, the rights which they declared *"unalienable,"* are the foundation-stones on which rests the vindication of the Confederate cause.

He must have been a careless reader of our political history who has not observed that, whether under the style of "United Colonies" or "United States," which was adopted after the Declaration of Independence, whether under the articles of Confederation or the compact of Union, there everywhere appears the distinct assertion of State sovereignty, and nowhere the slightest suggestion of any purpose on the part of the States to consolidate themselves into one body. Will any candid, well-informed man assert that, at any time between

1776 and 1790, a proposition to surrender the sovereignty of the States and merge them in a central government would have had the least possible chance of adoption? Can any historical fact be more demonstrable than that the States did, both in the Confederation and in the Union, retain their sovereignty and independence as distinct communities, voluntarily consenting to federation, but never becoming the fractional parts of a nation? That such opinions should find adherents in our day, may be attributable to the natural law of aggregation; surely not to a conscientious regard for the terms of the compact for union by the States.

In all free governments the constitution or organic law is supreme over the government, and in our Federal Union this was most distinctly marked by limitations and prohibitions against all which was beyond the expressed grants of power to the General Government. In the foreground, therefore, I take the position that those who resisted violations of the compact were the true friends, and those who maintained the usurpation of undelegated powers were the real enemies of the constitutional Union.

PART ONE

ORIGINS

Chapter 1

The Question of Slavery

INASMUCH as questions growing out of the institution of
negro servitude will occupy a conspicuous place in what is
to follow, it is important that the reader should have a right
understanding of the true nature and character of those
questions. No subject has been more generally misunderstood
or more persistently misrepresented. The institution itself has
ceased to exist in the United States; the misconceptions which
have prevailed are likely to be perpetuated unless corrected
before they become crystallized.

It is well known that, at the time of the adoption of the
Federal Constitution, African servitude existed in all the
States with the single exception of Massachusetts, in which
it had, perhaps, very recently ceased to exist. The slaves,
however, were numerous in the Southern, and very few in
the Northern, States. This diversity was occasioned by differences of climate, soil, and industrial interests—not in any
degree by moral considerations, which at that period were
not recognized as an element in the question. It was simply
because negro labor was more profitable in the South than
in the North that the importation of negro slaves had been,
and continued to be, chiefly directed to the Southern ports.
For the same reason slavery was abolished by the States of
the Northern section (though it existed in several of them for
more than fifty years after the adoption of the Constitution),
while the importation of slaves into the South continued to
be carried on by Northern merchants and Northern ships,
without interference in the traffic from any quarter, until it
was prohibited by the spontaneous action of the Southern
States themselves.

The Constitution expressly forbade any interference by
Congress with the slave-trade—or, to use its own language,
with the "migration or importation of such persons" as any

of the States should think proper to admit—"prior to the year 1808." During the intervening period of more than twenty years, the matter was exclusively under the control of the respective States. Nevertheless, every Southern State, without exception, either had already enacted, or proceeded to enact, laws forbidding the importation of slaves. Virginia was the first of all the States, North or South, to prohibit it, and Georgia was the first to incorporate such a prohibition in her organic Constitution.

Two petitions for the abolition of slavery and the slave-trade were presented February 11 and 12, 1790, to the very first Congress convened under the Constitution. The House of Representatives determined "that Congress have no authority to interfere in the emancipation of slaves, or in the treatment of them within any of the States"; and, that no authority existed to prohibit the migration or importation of such persons as the States might think proper to admit, "prior to the year 1808." So distinct and final was this statement of the limitations of the authority of Congress considered to be that, when a similar petition was presented two or three years afterward, the Clerk of the House was instructed to return it to the petitioner.

In 1807, Congress, availing itself of the very earliest moment at which the constitutional restriction ceased to be operative, passed an act prohibiting the importation of slaves into any part of the United States from and after the first day of January, 1808. In the House of Representatives there were one hundred and thirteen (113) yeas to five (5) nays; and it is a significant fact, as showing the absence of any sectional division of sentiment at that period, that the five dissentients were divided as equally as possible between the two sections: two of them were from Northern and three from Southern States.

The slave-trade had thus been finally abolished some months before the birth of the author of these pages, and has never since had legal existence in any of the United States. The question of the maintenance or extinction of the system of negro servitude, already existing in any State, was one exclusively belonging to such State. It is obvious, therefore, that no subsequent question, legitimately arising in Federal legislation, could properly have any reference to the merits or the policy of the institution itself.

No moral nor sentimental considerations were really involved in either the earlier or later controversies which so long agitated and finally ruptured the Union. They were simply struggles between different sections, with diverse institutions and interests.

It is absolutely requisite, in order to a right understanding of the history of the country, to bear these truths clearly in mind. The phraseology of the period referred to will otherwise be essentially deceptive. The antithetical employment of such terms as *freedom* and *slavery,* or "anti-slavery" and "pro-slavery," with reference to the principles and purposes of contending parties or rival sections, has had immense influence in misleading the opinions and sympathies of the world. The idea of freedom is captivating, that of slavery repellent to the moral sense of mankind in general. It is easy, therefore, to understand the effect of applying the one set of terms to one party, the other to another, in a contest which had no just application whatever to the essential merits of freedom or slavery. Southern statesmen may perhaps have been too indifferent to this consideration—in their ardent pursuit of principles, overlooking the effects of phrases.

This is especially true with regard to that familiar but most fallacious expression, "the extension of slavery." To the reader unfamiliar with the subject, or viewing it only on the surface, it would perhaps never occur that, as used in the great controversies respecting the Territories of the United States, it does not, never did, and never could, imply the addition of a single slave to the number already existing. The question was merely whether the slaveholder should be permitted to go, with his slaves, into territory (the common property of all) into which the non-slaveholder could go with *his* property of any sort. There was no proposal nor desire on the part of the Southern States to reopen the slave-trade, which they had been foremost in suppressing, or to add to the number of slaves. It was a question of the distribution, or dispersion, of the slaves, rather than of the "extension of slavery." Removal is not extension. Indeed, if emancipation was the end to be desired, the dispersion of the negroes over a wider area among additional Territories, eventually to become States, and in climates unfavorable to slave labor, instead of hindering, would have promoted this object by diminishing the difficulties in the way of ultimate emancipation.

The distinction here defined between the distribution, or dispersion, of slaves and the extension of slavery—two things altogether different, although so generally confounded—was early and clearly drawn under circumstances and in a connection which justify a fuller notice.

Virginia, it is well known, in the year 1784, ceded to the United States—then united only by the original Articles of Confederation—her vast possessions northwest of the Ohio, from which the great States of Ohio, Indiana, Michigan, Illinois, Wisconsin, and part of Minnesota, have since been formed. In 1787—before the adoption of the Federal Constitution—the celebrated "Ordinance" for the government of this Northwestern Territory was adopted by the Congress, with the full consent, and indeed at the express instance, of Virginia. This Ordinance included six definite "Articles of compact between the original States and the people and States in the said Territory," which were to "for ever remain unalterable unless by common consent." The sixth of these articles ordains that "there shall be neither slavery nor involuntary servitude in the said Territory, otherwise than in the punishment of crimes whereof the party shall have been duly convicted."

In December, 1805, a petition of the Legislative Council and House of Representatives of the Indiana Territory—then comprising all the area now occupied by the States of Indiana, Illinois, Michigan, and Wisconsin—was presented to Congress. The prayer of these petitions was for a *suspension* of the sixth article of the Ordinance, so as to permit the introduction of slaves into the Territory. The whole subject was referred to a select committee of seven members, consisting of representatives from Virginia, Ohio, Pennsylvania, South Carolina, Kentucky, and New York, and the delegate from the Indiana Territory.

On the 14th of the ensuing February (1806), this committee made a report favorable to the prayer of the petitioners, and recommending a suspension of the prohibitory article for ten years. In their report the committee proceeded to say:

The suspension of this article is an object almost universally desired in that Territory. It appears to your committee to be a question entirely different from that between slavery and freedom, inasmuch as it would merely occasion the removal of persons, already slaves from one part of the country to another.

No final action seems to have been taken on the subject before the adjournment of Congress, but it was brought forward at the next session in a more imposing form. On the 20th of January, 1807, the Speaker laid before the House of Representatives a letter from Governor Harrison, inclosing certain resolutions formally and *unanimously* adopted by the Legislative Council and House of Representatives of the Indiana Territory, in favor of the suspension of the sixth article of the Ordinance and the introduction of slaves into the Territory, which they say would "meet the approbation of at least nine tenths of the good citizens of the same."

These resolutions were submitted to a committee drawn, like the former, from different sections of the country, which again reported favorably. Their report was sustained by the House, and a resolution to suspend the prohibitory article was adopted. The proposition failed, however, in the Senate, and there the matter seems to have been dropped.

· The allusion which has been made to the Ordinance of 1787, renders it proper to notice the argument put forward during the discussion of the Missouri question that the Ordinance afforded a precedent in support of the claim of a power in Congress to determine the question of the admission of slaves into the Territories, and in justification of the prohibitory clause applied in 1820 to a portion of the Louisiana Territory.

The difference between the Congress of the Confederation and that of the Federal Constitution is so broad that the action of the former can, in no just sense, be taken as a precedent for the latter. The Congress of the Confederation represented the States in their sovereignty, each delegation having one vote, so that all the States were of equal weight in the decision of any question. It had legislative, executive, and in some degree judicial powers, thus combining all departments of government in itself.

On the other hand, the Congress of the Constitution is only the legislative department of the General Government, with powers strictly defined and expressly limited to those delegated by the States. It is further held in check by an executive and a judiciary, and consists of two branches, each having peculiar and specified functions.

If, then, it be admitted—which is at least very questionable —that the Congress of the Confederation had rightfully the power to exclude slave property from the territory northwest of the Ohio River, that power must have been derived from its character as an assemblage of the sovereign States; not from the Articles of Confederation, in which no indication of the grant of authority to exercise such a function can be found. The Congress of the Constitution is expressly prohibited from the assumption of any power not distinctly and specifically delegated to it as the legislative branch of an organized government. What was questionable in the former case, therefore, becomes clearly inadmissible in the latter.

But there is yet another distinction to be observed. The States, owners of what was called the Northwestern Territory, were component members of the Congress which adopted the Ordinance for its government, and gave thereto their full and free consent. The Ordinance may, therefore, be regarded as virtually a treaty between the States which ceded and those which received that extensive domain. In the other case, Missouri and the whole region affected by the Missouri Compromise, were parts of the territory acquired from France under the name of Louisiana; and, as it requires two parties to make or amend a treaty, France and the Government of the United States should have coöperated in any amendment of the treaty by which Louisiana had been acquired, and which guaranteed to the inhabitants of the ceded territory "all the rights, advantages, and immunities of citizens of the United States," and "the free enjoyment of their liberty, property, and the religion they profess."

The basis of sectional controversy was the question of the balance of political power. In its earlier manifestations this was undisguised. The purchase of the Louisiana Territory from France in 1803, and the subsequent admission of a portion of that Territory into the Union as a State, afforded one of the earliest occasions for the manifestation of sectional jealousy, and gave rise to the first threats, or warnings (which proceeded from New England), of a dissolution of the Union. Yet, although negro slavery existed in Louisiana, no pretext was made of that as an objection to the acquisition. The ground of opposition is frankly stated in a letter of that period from one Massachusetts statesman to another—"that the influence of *our* part of the Union must be diminished by the acquisition of more weight at the other extremity." *

Some years afterward (in 1819-'20) occurred the memorable contest with regard to the admission into the Union of Missouri, the second State carved out of the Louisiana Territory. The controversy arose out of a proposition to attach to the admission of the new State a proviso prohibiting slavery or involuntary servitude therein. The vehement discussion that ensued agitated the whole country. The restriction was

* Cabot to Pickering, who was then Senator from Massachusetts.—(See "Life and Letters of George Cabot," by H. C. Lodge, p. 334.)

adopted, by a vote almost strictly sectional, in the House of Representatives. It failed in the Senate through the firm resistance of the Southern, aided by a few patriotic and conservative Northern, members of that body. The admission of the new State, without any restriction, was finally accomplished by the addition to the bill of a section forever prohibiting slavery in all that portion of the Louisiana Territory lying north of thirty-six degrees and thirty minutes, north latitude, except Missouri—by implication leaving the portion south of that line open to settlement either with or without slaves.

This provision, as an offset to the admission of the new State without restriction, constituted the celebrated Missouri Compromise. It was reluctantly accepted by a small majority of the Southern members. Nearly half of them voted against it, under the conviction that it was unauthorized by the Constitution, and that Missouri was entitled to determine the question of herself, as a matter of right, not of bargain or concession.

The question of the right or wrong of the institution of slavery was in no wise involved in the sectional controversies. They were essentially struggles for sectional equality or ascendancy—for the maintenance or the destruction of that balance of power or equipoise between North and South, which was early recognized as a cardinal principle in our Federal system.

Chapter 2

Compromise of 1850;
Fugitive Slave Act;
Mississippi Political Life

THE FIRST SESSION of the Thirty-first Congress (1849–'50) was a memorable one. The recent acquisition from Mexico of New Mexico and California required legislation by Congress. In the Senate the bills reported by the Committee on Territories were referred to a select committee, of which Mr. Clay, the distinguished Senator from Kentucky, was chairman. From this committee emanated the bills which, taken together, are known as the compromise measures of 1850.

With some others, I advocated the division of the newly acquired territory by an extension to the Pacific Ocean of the Missouri Compromise line of thirty-six degrees and thirty minutes north latitude. However objectionable it may have been in 1820 to adopt that political line as expressing a geographical definition of different sectional interests, and however it may be condemned as the assumption by Congress of a function not delegated to it, it is to be remembered that the act had received such recognition and *quasi*-ratification by the people of the State as to give it a value which it did not originally possess.

The refusal to divide the territory acquired from Mexico by an extension of the line of the Missouri Compromise to the Pacific was a consequence of the purpose to admit California as a State of the Union before it had acquired the requisite population. The inconsistency of the argument against the extension of the line was exhibited in the division of the Territory of Texas by that parallel, and payment to the State of money to secure her consent to the partition of her domain. In the case of Texas, the North had everything to gain and nothing to lose by the application of the practice of geographical compromise on an arbitrary line. In the case of California, the conditions were reversed; the South might have been the gainer and the North the loser by a recognition of the same rule.

The compensation which it was alleged that the South received was a more effective law for the rendition of fugitives from service or labor. It was reasonably argued that, as the Legislatures of fourteen of the States had enacted what were termed "personal liberty laws," which forbade the coöperation of State officials in the rendition of fugitives from service and labor, it became necessary that the General Government should provide the requisite machinery for the execution of the law. The result proved what might have been anticipated —that those communities which had repudiated their constitutional obligations, which had nullified a previous law of Congress and had murdered men who came peacefully to recover their property, would evade or obstruct, so as to render practically worthless, *any* law that could be enacted for that purpose. In the exceptional cases in which it might be executed, the event would be attended with such conflict between the State and Federal authorities as to produce consequent evils greater than those it was intended to correct.

I had been reëlected by the Legislature of Mississippi and entered upon a new term of service in the Senate on March 4, 1851.

On my return to Mississippi in 1851, the subject chiefly agitating the public mind was that of the "compromise" measures of the previous year. Consequent upon these was a proposition for a convention of delegates, from the people of the Southern States respectively, to consider what steps ought to be taken for their future peace and safety, and the preservation of their constitutional rights. There was diversity of opinion with regard to the merits of the measures referred to, but the disagreement no longer followed the usual lines of party division. They who saw in those measures the forerunner of disaster to the South had no settled policy beyond a convention, the object of which should be to devise new and more effectual guarantees against the perils of usurpation. They were unjustly charged with a desire to destroy the Union—a feeling entertained by few, very few, if by any, in Mississippi, and avowed by none.

There were many, however, who held that the principles of the Declaration of Independence, and the purposes for which the Union was formed, were of higher value than the mere Union itself. Independence existed before the compact of union between the States; and, if that compact should be broken in part, and therefore destroyed in whole, it was hoped that the liberties of the people in the States might still be preserved. Those who were most devoted to the Union of the Constitution might, consequently, be expected to resist most sternly any usurpation of undelegated power, the effect of which would be to warp the Federal Government from its proper character, and, by sapping the foundation, to destroy the Union of the States.

My recent reëlection to the United States Senate had conferred upon me for six years longer the office which I preferred to all others. I could not, therefore, be suspected of desiring a nomination for any other office from the Democratic Convention, the meeting of which was then drawing near. Having, as a Senator of the State, freely participated in debate on the measures which were now exciting so much interest in the public mind, it was very proper that I should visit the people in different parts of the State and render an account of my stewardship.

My devotion to the Union of our fathers had been so often and so publicly declared; I had, on the floor of the Senate, so defiantly challenged any question of my fidelity to it; my services, civil and military, had now extended through so long a period, and were so generally known—that I felt quite assured that no whisperings of envy or ill will could lead the people of Mississippi to believe that I had dishonored their trust by using the power they had conferred on me to destroy the Government to which I was accredited. Then, as afterward, I regarded the separation of the States as a great, though not the greatest, evil.

I returned from my tour among the people at the time appointed for the meeting of the nominating convention of the Democratic (or State-Rights) party. A proposition was made, in the committee on nominations, that I should be invited to become a candidate [for Governor]. I consented to be announced, and immediately resigned from the United States Senate. I was defeated, but the majority of more than seven thousand votes, that had been cast a short time before against the party with which I was associated, was reduced to less than one thousand.

In this canvass, both before and after I became a candidate, no argument or appeal of mine was directed against the perpetuation of the Union. Believing, however, that the signs of the time portended danger to the South from the usurpation by the General Government of undelegated powers, I counseled that Mississippi should enter into the proposed meeting of the people of the Southern States, to consider what could and should be done to insure our future safety, frankly stating my conviction that, unless such action were taken then, sectional rivalry would engender greater evils in the future, and that, if the controversy was postponed, "the last opportunity for a peaceful solution would be lost, then the issue would have to be settled by blood."

Happy in the peaceful pursuits of a planter, the time passed pleasantly away until my retirement was interrupted by an invitation to take a place in the Cabinet of Mr. Pierce, who had been elected to the Presidency of the United States in November, 1852. Although warmly attached to Mr. Pierce, personal reasons led me to decline the offer. This was followed by an invitation to attend the ceremony of his inauguration, which took place on the 4th of March, 1853. While in Washington, on this visit, I was induced by public considerations to reconsider my determination and accept the office of Secretary of War. The public records of that period will best show how the duties of that office were performed.

Chapter 3

Kansas-Nebraska Bill; The Abolitionists; Southern Injuries

THE ORGANIZATION of the Territory of Kansas was the first question that gave rise to exciting debate after my return to the Senate. The celebrated Kansas-Nebraska Bill had become a law [in May 1854] during the Administration of Mr. Pierce. Its purpose was declared in the bill itself to be to carry into practical operation the "propositions and principles established by the compromise measures of 1850." It was not the first step taken toward the repeal of the conditions or obligations expressed or implied by the establishment, in 1820, of the politico-sectional line of thirty-six degrees and thirty minutes. That compact had been virtually abrogated, in 1850, by the refusal of the representatives of the North to apply it to the territory then recently acquired from Mexico. The "Missouri Compromise," therefore, was not repealed by that bill—its virtual repeal by the legislation of 1850 was recognized as an existing fact, and it was declared to be "inoperative and void."

It was added that the "true intent and meaning" of the act was "not to legislate slavery into any Territory or State, nor to exclude it therefrom, but to leave the people thereof perfectly free to form and regulate their domestic institutions in their own way, subject only to the Constitution of the United States."

From the terms of this bill, it is evident that its purpose was to leave the Territories equally open to the people of all the States, with every species of property recognized by any of them; to permit climate and soil to determine the current of immigration, and to secure to the people themselves the right to form their own institutions according to their own will, as soon as they should aquire the right of self-government; that is to say, as soon as their numbers should entitle them to organize themselves into a State. The claim, afterward advanced by Mr. Douglas and others, that this declaration was intended to assert the right of the first settlers of a Territory, in its inchoate, rudimental, dependent, and transitional condition, to determine the character of its institutions, constituted the doctrine popularly known as "squatter sov-

36

ereignty." Its assertion led to the dissensions which ultimately resulted in a rupture of the Democratic party.

Sectional rivalry, the deadly foe of the "domestic tranquillity" and the "general welfare," now interfered, with gigantic efforts, to prevent that free migration which had been promised. Societies were formed in the North to supply money and send emigrants into the new Territories; and a famous preacher [Henry Ward Beecher], addressing a body of those emigrants, charged them to carry with them to Kansas "the Bible and Sharpe's rifles." The latter were of course to be leveled against the bosoms of their Southern brethren who might migrate to the same Territory, but the use to be made of the Bible in the same fraternal enterprise was left unexplained by the reverend gentleman.

The war-cry employed to train the Northern mind for the deeds contemplated by the agitators was "No extension of slavery!" Was this sentiment real or feigned? The number of slaves (as has already been clearly shown) would not have been increased by their transportation to new territory. The climate of Kansas and Nebraska was altogether unsuited to the negro, and the soil was not adapted to those productions for which negro labor could be profitably employed. If, then, any negroes had been transported to those Territories, they would have been such as were bound by personal attachment mutually existing between master and servant, which would have rendered it impossible for the former to consider the latter as property convertible into money. As white laborers, adapted to the climate and its products, flowed into the country, negro labor would have inevitably become a tax to those who held it, and their emancipation would have followed that condition, as it has in all the Northern States, old or new—Wisconsin furnishing the last example. It may, therefore, be reasonably concluded that the "war-cry" was employed by the artful to inflame the minds of the less informed and less discerning; that it was adopted in utter disregard of the means by which negro emancipation might have been peaceably accomplished in the Territories, and with the sole object of obtaining sectional control and personal promotion by means of popular agitation.

The success attending this artifice was remarkable. To such an extent was it made available, that Northern indignation was aroused on the absurd accusation that the South had destroyed "that sacred instrument, the compromise of 1820." The internecine war which raged in Kansas for several years was substituted for the promised peace under the operation of the natural laws regulating migration to new countries.

In these scenes of strife were trained the incendiaries who afterward invaded Virginia under the leadership of John Brown; and at this time germinated the sentiments which led men of high position to sustain, with their influence and their money, this murderous incursion into the South.

Diversity of interests and of opinions among the States of the Confederation had in the beginning presented great difficulties in the way of the formation of a more perfect union. The compact was the result of compromise between the States, at that time generally distinguished as navigating and agricultural, afterward as Northern and Southern. When the first census was taken, in 1790, there was but little numerical difference in the population of these two sections, and (including States about to be admitted) there was also an exact equality in the number of States. Each section had, therefore, the power of self-protection, and might feel secure against any danger of Federal aggression. If the disturbance of that equilibrium had been the consequence of natural causes, and the government of the whole had continued to be administered strictly for the general welfare, there would have been no ground for complaint of the result.

Under the old Confederation the Southern States had a large excess of territory. The acquisition of Louisiana, of Florida, and of Texas, afterward greatly increased this excess. The generosity and patriotism of Virginia led her, before the adoption of the Constitution, to cede the Northwest Territory to the United States. The "Missouri Compromise" surrendered to the North all the newly acquired region not included in the State of Missouri, and north of the parallel of thirty-six degrees and a half. The northern part of Texas was in like manner given up by the compromise of 1850; and the North, having obtained, by those successive cessions, a majority in both Houses of Congress, took to itself all the territory acquired from Mexico. Thus, by the action of the General Government, the means were provided permanently to destroy the original equilibrium between the sections.

Nor was this the only injury to which the South was subjected. Under the power of Congress to levy duties on imports, tariff laws were enacted for the protection against foreign competition of domestic manufactures. The effect of this was to impose the main burden of taxation upon the Southern people, who were consumers and not manufacturers, not only by the enhanced price of imports, but indirectly by the consequent depreciation in the value of exports, which were chiefly the products of Southern States. Nor was this all: a reference to the annual appropriations will show that the disbursements made were as unequal as the burdens borne—the inequality in both operating in the same direction.

These causes all combined to direct immigration to the Northern section; and with the increase of its preponderance appeared more and more distinctly a tendency in the Federal Government to pervert functions delegated to it, and to use them with sectional discrimination against the minority.

The sectional policy brought to its support the passions that spring from man's higher nature, but which, like all passions, if misdirected and perverted, become hurtful and, it may be, destructive. Thus, by the activity of the propagandists of abolitionism, and the misuse of the sacred word Liberty, they recruited from the ardent worshipers of that goddess such numbers as gave them in many Northern States the balance of power between the two great political forces that stood arrayed against each other. Fanaticism, to which is usually accorded sincerity as an extenuation of its mischievous tenets, affords the best excuse to be offered for the original abolitionists, but that can not be conceded to the political associates who joined them for the purpose of acquiring power; with them it was but hypocritical cant, intended to deceive.

Chapter 4

Growth of the Republican Party, 1856-1860; "Squatter Sovereignty"

THE STRIFE in Kansas and the agitation of the territorial question in Congress and throughout the country continued during nearly the whole of Mr. Buchanan's Administration, finally culminating in a disruption of the Union. Meantime the changes, or modifications, which had occurred or were occurring in the great political parties, were such as may require a word of explanation.

The *names* adopted by political parties in the United States have not always been strictly significant of their principles. The old Federal party inclined to nationalism, or consolidation, rather than federalization, of the States. On the other hand, the fundamental idea of the Democratic party was that of the sovereignty of the States and the federal, or confederate, character of the Union. The Whig, which succeeded the old Federal party, though by no means identical with it, was, in the main, favorable to a strong central government, therein antagonizing the transatlantic traditions connected with its name. The "Know-Nothing," or "American," party, which sprang into existence on the decadence of the Whig organization, based upon opposition to the alleged overgrowth of the political influence of naturalized foreigners and of the Roman Catholic Church, had but a brief duration, and after the Presidential election of 1856 declined as rapidly as it had arisen.

At the period to which this narrative has advanced, the "Free-Soil," which had now assumed the title of "Republican" party, had grown to a magnitude which threatened speedily to obtain entire control of Government. Based, as has been shown, upon sectional rivalry and opposition to the growth of the Southern equally with the Northern States of the Union, it had absorbed within itself not only the abolitionists, but other diverse and heterogeneous elements of opposition to the Democratic party. In the House of Representatives of the Thirty-sixth Congress, which met in December, 1859, neither party had a decided majority, the balance of power being held by a few members still adhering to the virtually extinct Whig and "American," or Know-Nothing, organizations. More than eight weeks were spent in the election of a Speaker; and a so-called "Republican" was finally elected by a majority of one vote. The Senate continued to be decidedly Democratic, though with an increase of the so-called "Republican" minority.

Contributing to the rapid growth of the so-called Republican party after the elections of the year 1857 was the dissension among the Democrats, occasioned by the introduction of the doctrine called by its inventors and advocates "popular sovereignty," or "non-intervention," but more generally and more accurately known as "squatter sovereignty."

[Its origin is generally attributed to General Cass, who is supposed to have suggested it in some general expressions of his celebrated "Nicholson letter," written in December, 1847.] But it was not until after the passage of the Kansas-Nebraska Bill, in 1854, that [this doctrine] was fully developed under the plastic and constructive genius of the Hon. Stephen A. Douglas, of Illinois. The leading part which that distinguished Senator had borne in the authorship and advocacy of the Kansas-Nebraska Bill had aroused against him a violent storm of denunciation in the State which he represented and other Northern States. He met it very manfully in some respects, defended his action resolutely, but in so doing was led to make such concessions of principle and to attach such an interpretation to the bill as would have rendered it practically nugatory—a thing to keep the promise of peace to the ear and break it to the hope.

The Constitution expressly confers upon Congress the power to admit new States into the Union, and also to "dispose of and make all needful rules and regulations respecting the territory or other property belonging to the United States." Under these grants of power, the uniform practice of the Government had been to provide executive, legislative, and judicial departments of government for such Territories during their temporary and provisional period of pupilage; to delegate to these governments such authority as might be expedient—subject always to the supervision and controlling government of the Congress. Finally, on the attainment by the Territory of sufficient strength and population for self-government, to receive it into the Union on a footing of entire equality with the original States—sovereign and self-governing. All this is no more inconsistent with the true principles of "popular sovereignty," properly understood, than the temporary subjection of a minor to parental control is inconsistent with the doctrines of the Declaration of Independence.

The usual process of transition from a territorial condition to that of a State was, in the first place, by an act of Congress authorizing the inhabitants to elect representatives for a convention to form a State Constitution, which was then submitted to Congress for approval and ratification. On such ratification the supervisory control of Congress was withdrawn, and the new State authorized to assume its sovereignty, and the inhabitants of the Territory became citizens of a State. The entire control of Congress over the whole subject of territorial government had never been questioned in earlier times. Necessarily conjoined with the *power* of this protectorate, was of course the *duty* of exercising it for the safety of the persons and property of all citizens of the United States, permanently or temporarily resident in any part of the domain belonging to the States in common.

Logically carried out, the new theory of "popular sovereignty" would apply to the first adventurous pioneers settling in the wilderness before the organization of any Territorial government by Congress, as well as afterward. If "sovereignty" is inherent in a thousand or five thousand persons, there can be no valid ground for denying its existence in a dozen, as soon as they pass beyond the limits of the State governments. The advocates of this novel doctrine, however, if rightly understood, generally disavowed any claim to its application prior to the organization of a territorial government.

The Territorial Legislatures were the mere agents of Congress, exercising an authority subject to Congressional supervision and control—an authority conferred only for the sake of convenience, and liable at any time to be revoked and annulled. Yet it is proposed to recognize in these provisional, subordinate, and temporary legislative bodies, a power not possessed by Congress itself. This is to claim that the creature is endowed with an authority not possessed by the creator, or that the stream has risen to an elevation above that of its source.

Furthermore, in contending for a power in the Territorial Legislatures permanently to determine the fundamental, social, and political institutions of the Territory, and thereby virtually to prescribe those of the future State, the advocates of "popular sovereignty" were investing those dependent and subsidiary bodies with powers far above any exercised by the

Legislatures of the fully organized and sovereign States. The authority of the State Legislatures is limited, both by the Federal Constitution and by the respective State Constitutions from which it is derived. This latter limitation did not and could not exist in the Territories.

Strange as it may seem, a theory founded on fallacies so flimsy and leading to conclusions so paradoxical was advanced by eminent and experienced politicians, and accepted by many persons, both in the North and in the South. The terms "popular sovereignty" and "non-intervention" were plausible, specious, and captivating to the public ear. Too many lost sight of the elementary truth that political sovereignty does not reside in unorganized or partially organized masses of individuals, but in the people of regularly and permanently constituted States. As to the "non-intervention" proposed, it meant merely the abnegation by Congress of its duty to protect the inhabitants of the Territories subject to its control.

The raid into Virginia under John Brown—already notorious as a fanatical partisan leader in the Kansas troubles—occurred in October, 1859, a few weeks before the meeting of the Thirty-sixth Congress. Insignificant in itself and in its immediate results, it afforded a startling revelation of the extent to which sectional hatred and political fanaticism had blinded the conscience of a class of persons in certain States of the Union; forming a party steadily growing stronger in numbers, as well as in activity. Sympathy with its purposes or methods was earnestly disclaimed by the representatives of all parties in Congress; but it was charged, on the other hand, that it was only the natural outgrowth of doctrines and sentiments which for some years had been freely avowed on the floors of both Houses. A committee of the Senate made a long and laborious investigation of the facts, with no very important or satisfactory results. In their final report, June 15, 1860, this Committee said:

It [the incursion] was simply the act of lawless ruffians, under the sanction of no public or political authority, distinguishable only from ordinary felonies by the ulterior ends in contemplation by them, and by the fact that the money to maintain the expedition and the large armament . . . had been . . . furnished by the citizens of other States of the Union. . . . If the several States . . . do not hold it incumbent on them . . . to guard in future by appropriate legislation against occurrences similar to the one here inquired into, the Committee can find no guarantee elsewhere for the security of peace between the States of the Union.

On February 2, 1860, the author submitted, in the Senate of the United States, a series of resolutions, afterward slightly modified to read as follows:

1. *Resolved,* That, in the adoption of the Federal Constitution, the States . . . acted severally as free and independent sovereignties, delegating a portion of their powers to be exercised by the Federal Government for the increased security of each against dangers, *domestic* as well as foreign; and that any intermeddling by any one or more States, or by a combination of their citizens, with the domestic institutions of the others, . . . with the view to their disturbance or subdivision, is in violation of the Constitution, and . . . tends to weaken and destroy the Union itself.

2. *Resolved,* That negro slavery, as it exists in fifteen States of this Union, composes an important portion of their domestic institutions, . . . existing at the adoption of the Constitution, and that no change of opinion or feeling on the part of the non-slaveholding States of the Union in relation to this institution can justify them or their citizens in . . . attacks thereon, with a view to its overthrow. . . .

3. *Resolved,* . . . That it is . . . the duty of the Senate . . . to resist all attempts to discriminate either in relation to persons or property in the Territories . . . so as to give advantages to the citizens of one State which are not equally assured to those of every other State.

4. *Resolved,* That neither Congress not a territorial Legislature . . . possesses power to annul or impair the constitutional right of any citizen of the United States to take his slave property into the common Territories. . . .

5. *Resolved,* That if . . . the judiciary and executive authority do not possess means to insure adequate protection to constitutional rights in a Territory, and if the Territorial government shall fail or refuse to provide the necessary remedies for that purpose, it will be the duty of Congress to supply such deficiency.

6. *Resolved,* That the inhabitants of a territory . . . when they rightfully form a Constitution to be admitted as a State into the Union, may then, for the first time, decide . . . whether slavery, as a domestic institution, shall be maintained or prohibited . . . ; and they shall be received into the Union with or without slavery, as their Constitution may prescribe at the time of their admission.

7. *Resolved,* That the provision of the Constitution for the rendition of fugitives from service or labor, . . . and that the laws of 1793 and 1850, which were enacted to secure its execution . . . should be . . . maintained by all who enjoy the benefits of our

compact of union; and that all acts of . . . to . . . nullify the requirements of that provision . . . , are . . . subversive of the Constitution, and revolutionary in their effect.

After a protracted and earnest debate, these resolutions were adopted *seriatim*, on the 24th and 25th of May, by a decided majority of the Senate.

Chapter 5

The Election of Abraham Lincoln

IT MAY NOT BE out of place here to refer to the fact that the grievances which led to [the American Revolution] were directly inflicted upon the Northern colonies. Those of the South had no material cause of complaint; but, actuated by sympathy for their Northern brethren, and a devotion to the principles of civil liberty and community independence which were set forth in the Declaration of Independence, they made common cause with their neighbors.

By the exclusion of the South, in 1820, from all that part of the Louisiana purchase lying north of the parallel of thirty-six degrees thirty minutes, and not included in the State of Missouri; by the extension of that line of exclusion to embrace the territory acquired from Texas; and by the appropriation of *all* the territory obtained from Mexico under the Treaty of Guadalupe Hidalgo, both north and south of that line, it may be stated that the North had monopolized to herself more than three fourths of all that had been added to the domain of the United States since the Declaration of Independence.

The effects of discriminating duties upon imports have been referred to in a former chapter. [So, too, was] the power of the majority section employed to appropriate to itself an unequal share of the public disbursements. These combined causes—the possession of more territory, more money, and a wider field for the employment of special labor—all served to attract immigration; and, with increasing population, the greed grew by what it fed on.

This became distinctly manifest when the so-called "Republican" Convention assembled in Chicago, on May 16, 1860, to nominate a candidate for the Presidency. It was a purely sectional body. There were a few delegates present, representing an insignificant minority in the "border States," Delaware, Maryland, Virginia, Kentucky, and Missouri; but not one from any State south of the celebrated political line of thirty-six degrees thirty minutes. It had been the invariable usage with nominating conventions of all parties to select candidates for the Presidency and Vice-Presidency, one from the North and the other from the South; but this assemblage nominated Mr. Lincoln, of Illinois, for the first office, and the second, Mr. Hamlin, of Maine—both Northerners. Mr. Lincoln had publicly announced that the Union "could not permanently endure, half slave and half free." The resolutions adopted contained some carefully worded declarations, well adapted to deceive the credulous who were opposed to hostile aggressions upon the rights of the States. In order to accomplish this purpose, they were compelled to create a fictitious issue, in denouncing what they described as "the new dogma that the Constitution, of its own force, carries slavery into any or all of the Territories of the United States"—a "dogma" which had never been held or declared by anybody, and which had no existence outside of their own assertion.

Meantime, the Democratic party had held a convention, composed as usual of delegates from all the States. They met in Charleston, South Carolina, on April 23d, but an unfortunate disagreement rendered a nomination impracticable. Both divisions of the Convention adjourned, and met again in Baltimore in June. Then, having finally failed to come to an agreement, they separated and made their respective nominations apart. Mr. Douglas, of Illinois, was nominated by the friends of the doctrine of "popular sovereignty."

The Convention representing the conservative, or State-Rights, wing of the Democratic party, on the first ballot, unanimously made choice of John C. Breckinridge, of Kentucky, then Vice-President of the United States. The resolutions of each of these two conventions denounced the action and policy of the Abolition party, as subversive of the Constitution, and revolutionary in their tendency.

Another convention was held in Baltimore [May 19, 1860] by those who still adhered to the old Whig party, reenforced by the remains of the "American" organization. This Convention also consisted of delegates from all the States, and, repudiating all geographical and sectional issues, pledged itself "to . . . defend, . . . those great principles of public liberty and national safety against all enemies at home and abroad." Its nominees were Messrs. John Bell, of Tennessee, and Edward Everett, of Massachusetts.

The people of the United States now had four rival tickets presented to them by as many contending parties, whose respective positions may be briefly recapitulated as follows:

1. The "Constitutional-Union" party, led by Bell, which ignored the territorial controversy altogether, and contented

with a simple declaration of adherence to "the Constitu-
, the Union, and the enforcement of the laws."

. The party of "popular sovereignty," headed by Douglas,
which affirmed the right of the people of the Territories, in their
territorial condition, to determine their own organic institutions, independently of the control of Congress.

3. The State-Rights party, supporting Breckinridge, who
held that the Territories were open to citizens of all the
States, with their property. At the same time they asserted
the right of the people of a Territory, on emerging from their
territorial condition to that of a State, to determine what
should then be their domestic institutions, subject only to the
limitations prescribed by the Constitution of the United States.

4. The so-called "Republicans," presenting the names of
Lincoln and Hamlin, who held, in the language of one of their
leaders [Horace Greeley], that "slavery can exist only by
virtue of municipal law"; that there was "no law for it in the
Territories, and no power to enact one"; and that Congress
was "bound to prohibit it in or exclude it from any and
every Federal Territory."

On the vital question underlying the whole controversy—
that is, whether the Federal Government should be a Government of the whole for the benefit of all its equal members,
or a sectional Government for the benefit of a part—the first
three of the parties above described were in substantial accord
as against the fourth. If they could or would have acted
unitedly, they could certainly have carried the election, and
averted the catastrophe which followed. Nor were efforts
wanting to effect such a union.

Mr. Bell, the Whig candidate, was not ambitious to the
extent of coveting the Presidency, and he was profoundly impressed by the danger which threatened the country. Mr.
Breckinridge had not anticipated, and it may safely be said
did not eagerly desire, the nomination. Each of them authorized me to say that he was willing to withdraw, if an arrangement could be effected by which the divided forces of the
friends of the Constitution could be concentrated upon some
one more generally acceptable than either of the three who
had been presented to the country. When I made this announcement to Mr. Douglas, he replied that the scheme proposed
was impracticable, because his friends, mainly Northern
Democrats, if he were withdrawn, would join in the support
of Mr. Lincoln, rather than of any one that should supplant
him (Douglas).

It needed but little knowledge of the *status* of parties in the several States to foresee a probable defeat if the conservatives were to continue divided into three parts, and the aggressives were to be held in solid column. But angry passions, which are always bad counselors, had been aroused, and hopes were still cherished, which proved to be illusory. The result was the election, by a minority, of a President whose avowed principles were necessarily fatal to the harmony of the Union.

Of 303 *electoral* votes, Mr. Lincoln received 180, but of the *popular* suffrage of 4,676,853 votes, which the electors represented, he obtained only 1,866,352—something over a third of the votes. This discrepancy was owing to the system of voting by "general ticket"—that is, casting the State votes as a unit, whether unanimous or nearly equally divided. Thus, in New York, the total popular vote was 675,156, of which 362,646 were cast for the so-called Republican (or Lincoln) electors, and 312,510 against them. New York was entitled to 35 electoral votes. Divided on the basis of the popular vote, 19 of these would have been cast for Mr. Lincoln, and 16 against him. But under the "general ticket" system the entire 35 votes were cast for the Republican candidates, thus giving them not only the full strength of the majority in their favor, but that of the great minority against them superadded. So of other Northern States, in which the small majorities on one side operated with the weight of entire unanimity, while the virtual unanimity in the Southern States, on the older side, counted nothing more than a mere majority would have done.

The manifestations which followed this result, in the Southern States, did not proceed, as has been unjustly charged, from chagrin at their defeat in the election, or from any personal hostility to the President-elect, but from the fact that they recognized in him the representative of a party professing principles destructive to "their peace, their prosperity, and their domestic tranquility." The long-suppressed fire burst into frequent flame, but it was still controlled by that love of the Union which the South had illustrated in every battlefield, from Boston to New Orleans. Few, if any, then doubted the right of a State to withdraw its grants delegated to the Federal Government, or, in other words, to secede from the Union; but in the South this was generally regarded as the remedy of last resort, to be applied only when ruin or dishonor was the alternative. The Presidential election occurred in November, 1860. Most of the State Legislatures convened soon afterward in regular session. In some cases special sessions were convoked for the purpose of calling State Conventions to be elected expressly for the purpose of taking such action as should be considered needful and proper under the existing circumstances. The consent of the respective States to the formation of the Union had been given through such conventions, and it was only by the same authority that it could properly be revoked. The time required for this deliberate and formal process precludes the idea of hasty or passionate action, and none who admit the primary power of the people to govern themselves can consistently deny its validity and binding obligation upon every citizen of the several States. Not only was there ample time for calm consideration among the people of the South, but for due reflection by the General Government and the people of the Northern States.

President Buchanan was in the last year of his administration. His freedom from sectional asperity, his long life in the public service, and his peace-loving and conciliatory character, were all guarantees against his precipitating a conflict between the Federal Government and any of the States; but the feeble power that he possessed in the closing months of his term to mold the policy of the future was painfully evident. Like the sages and patriots who had preceded him in the high office that he filled, he believed that "our Union rests upon public opinion, and can never be cemented by the blood of its citizens shed in civil war." (Message of December 3, 1860.)

Ten years before, Mr. Calhoun, addressing the Senate with that sincere desire to avert the danger of disunion which those who knew him best never doubted, had asked the emphatic question, "How can the Union be saved?" He answered his question thus:

There is but one way by which it can be [saved] with any certainty; and that is by a full and final settlement, on the principles of justice, of all the questions at issue between the sections. . . .
Can this be done? Yes, easily! Not by the weaker party; . . . but by the stronger. . . . But will the North agree to do this? . . . I will say, she can not refuse . . . without exposing herself to the charge that her love of power and aggrandizement is far greater than her love of the Union.

During the ten years that intervened between the date of this speech and the message of Mr. Buchanan cited above, the progress of sectional discord and the tendency of the stronger section to unconstitutional aggression had been fearfully rapid. With very rare exceptions, there were none in 1850 who claimed the right of the Federal Government to apply co-coercion to a State. In 1860 men had grown to be familiar with threats of driving the South into submission to any act that the Government might see fit to perform. During the canvass of that year, demonstrations had been made by *quasi*-military organizations in various parts of the North, which looked unmistakably to purposes widely different from those enunciated in the preamble to the Constitution.

Well-informed men still remembered that, in the Convention which framed the Constitution, a proposition was made to authorize the employment of force against a delinquent State, on which Mr. Madison remarked that "the use of force against a State would look more like a declaration of war than an infliction of punishment, and would probably be considered by the party attacked as a dissolution of all previous compacts by which it might have been bound." The Convention expressly refused to confer the power proposed, and the clause was lost. While, therefore, in 1860, many violent men, appealing to passion and the lust of power, were inciting the multitude, and preparing Northern opinion to support a war waged against the Southern States in the event of their secession, there were others who took a different view of the case. Notable among such was the "New York Tribune," which had been the organ of the abolitionists, and which now declared that, "if the cotton States wished to withdraw from the Union, they should be allowed to do so"; that "any attempt to compel them to remain, by force, would be contrary to the principles of the Declaration of Independence and to the fundamental ideas upon which human liberty is based"; and that, "if the Declaration of Independence justified the secession from the British Empire of three millions of subjects in 1776, it was not seen why it would not justify the secession of five millions of Southerners from the Union in 1861." Again, it was said by the same journal that, "sooner than compromise with the South and abandon the Chicago platform," they would "let the Union slide." Taunting expressions were freely used—as, for example, "If the Southern people wish to leave the Union, we will do our best to forward their views."

All this was quite consistent with the oft-repeated declaration that the Constitution was a "covenant with hell," which stood as the caption of a leading abolitionist paper of Boston. That signs of coming danger so visible, evidences of hostility so unmistakable, disregard of constitutional obligations so wanton, taunts and jeers so bitter and insulting, should serve to increase excitement in the South, was a consequence flowing as much from reason and patriotism as from sentiment. He must have been ignorant of human nature who did not expect such a tree to bear fruits of discord and division.

Chapter 6

The Triumph of Sectionalism

IN NOVEMBER, 1860, after the result of the Presidential election was known, the Governor of Mississippi invited the Senators and Representatives of the State in Congress, to meet him for consultation as to the character of the message he should send to the [State] Legislature when assembled.

While holding, in common with my political associates, that the right of a State to secede was unquestionable, I differed from most of them as to the probability of our being permitted peaceably to exercise the right. The knowledge acquired by the administration of the War Department for four years, and by the chairmanship of the Military Committee of the Senate at two different periods had shown me the entire lack of preparation for war in the South. The foundries and armories were in the Northern States, and there were stored all the new and improved weapons of war. In the arsenals of the Southern States were to be found only arms of the old and rejected models. The South had no manufactories of powder, and no navy to protect our harbors, no merchant-ships for foreign commerce. It was evident to me, therefore, that, if we should be involved in war, the odds against us would be far greater than what was due merely to our inferiority in population. Believing that secession would be the precursor of war between the States, I was consequently slower and more reluctant than others, who entertained a different opinion, to resort to that remedy.

The popular movement in the South was tending steadily and rapidly toward the secession of those known as "planting States"; yet, when Congress assembled on December 3, 1860, the representatives of the people of all those States took their seats in the House, and they were all represented in the Senate, except South Carolina, whose Senators had tendered their resignation to the Governor immediately on the announcement of the result of the Presidential election. Hopes were still cherished that the Northern leaders would appreciate the impending peril, and would address themselves to the purpose of devising means to allay the indignation, and quiet the apprehensions of their Southern brethren. But the

53

debates of that session manifest, on the contrary, the arrogance of a triumphant party, and the determination to reap to the uttermost the full harvest of a party victory.

Mr. Crittenden, of Kentucky, the oldest and one of the most honored members of the Senate [a life-long Whig who supported the Bell-Everett ticket in 1860], introduced into that body a joint resolution proposing certain amendments to the Constitution—among them the restoration and incorporation into the Constitution of the geographical line of the Missouri Compromise, with other provisions, which it was hoped might be accepted as the basis for an adjustment of the difficulties rapidly hurrying the Union to disruption. But action upon his proposition was postponed on one pretext or another, until the last day of the session—when seven States had already withdrawn from the Union and established a confederation of their own—and it was then defeated by a majority of one vote.

Meantime, among other propositions made in the Senate were two introduced early in the session. One of these was a resolution offered by Mr. Powell, of Kentucky, which had taken the following form:

Resolved, That so much of the President's message as relates to the present agitated and distracted condition of the country, and the grievances between the slaveholding and the non-slaveholding States, be referred to a special committee of thirteen members, and that said committee be instructed to inquire into the present condition of the country, and report by bill or otherwise.

The other was a resolution offered by Mr. Green, of Missouri:

Resolved, That the Committee on the Judiciary be instructed to inquire into the propriety of providing by law for establishing an armed police force at all necessary points along the line separating the slaveholding States from the non-slaveholding States, for the purpose of maintaining the general peace between those States, of preventing the invasion of one State by citizens of another, and also for the efficient execution of the fugitive-slave laws.

The resolution of Mr. Powell was eventually adopted on the 18th of December, and on the 20th the Committee was appointed. Five were Southern men; three were Northern Democrats, or Conservatives; five, Northern "Republicans." The Southern members declared their readiness to accept any terms that would secure the honor of the Southern States and guarantee their future safety. The Northern Democrats and Mr. Crittenden generally coöperated with the State-Rights Democrats of the South; but the so-called "Republican" Senators of the North rejected every proposition which might satisfy the Southern people, and check the progress of the secession movement. After fruitless efforts, continued for some ten days, the Committee determined to announce their inability to attain any satisfactory conclusion. This report was made on the 31st of December—the last day of that memorable and fateful year, 1860.

Subsequently, on the floor of the Senate, Mr. Douglas, who had been a member of the Committee, called upon the opposite side to state what they were willing to do. He pressed the point that, as they had rejected every overture made by the friends of peace, it was now incumbent upon *them* to make a positive and affirmative declaration of their purposes.

Mr. Seward, of New York, was a member of that Committee—the man who, in 1858, had announced the "irrepressible conflict," and who, in the same year, speaking for abolitionism, had said: "It has driven you back in California and in Kansas; it will invade your soil." He was to be the Secretary of State in the incoming Administration, and was very generally regarded as the "power behind the throne." He was present in the Senate, but made no response to Mr. Douglas's demand.

Meantime the efforts for an adjustment made in the House of Representatives had been equally fruitless. A committee of thirty-three members—one from each State of the Union— charged with a duty similar to that imposed upon the Committee of Thirteen in the Senate had been alike unsuccessful in coming to any agreement. It is true that, a few days afterward, they submitted a majority and two minority reports, and that the report of the majority was ultimately adopted by the House; but, even if this action had been unanimous, and had been taken in due time, it would have been practically futile on account of its absolute failure to provide or suggest any solution of the territorial question, which was the vital point in controversy.

No wonder, then, that, under the shadow of the failure of every effort in Congress to find any common ground on which the sections could be restored to amity, the close of the year should have been darkened by a cloud in the firmament, which had lost even the silver lining so long seen, or thought to be seen, by the hopeful.

Chapter 7

Northern Precedents for Secession

THE CONVENTION of South Carolina had already (on the 20th of December, 1860) unanimously adopted an ordinance revoking her delegated powers and withdrawing from the Union. Her representatives, on the following day, retired from their seats in Congress. The people of the other planting States, [who] had been only waiting in the lingering hope that some action might be taken by Congress to avert the necessity for action similar to that of South Carolina, were now making their final preparations for secession. This was generally admitted to be an unquestionable right appertaining to their sovereignty as States, and the only *peaceable* remedy that remained.

In the prior history of the country, repeated instances are found of the assertion of this right, and of a purpose entertained at various times to put it in execution. Notably is this true of Massachusetts and other New England States. The acquisition of Louisiana, in 1803, had created much dissatisfaction in those States, for the reason, expressed by an eminent citizen of Massachusetts,* that "the influence of our [the Northeastern] part of the Union must be diminished by the acquisition of more weight at the other extremity." The project of a separation was freely discussed, with no intimation, in the records of the period, of any idea among its advocates that it could be regarded as treasonable or revolutionary.

Colonel Timothy Pickering, an officer of the war of the Revolution, afterward Secretary of State in the Cabinet of General Washington, and, still later, a representative of the State of Massachusetts in the Senate of the United States, was one of the leading secessionists of his day. Writing to a friend, on the 24th of December, 1803, he says:

I will not yet despair. I will rather anticipate *a new confederacy*, exempt from the corrupt and corrupting influence and oppression of the aristocratic democrats of the South. There will be (and our children, at farthest, will see it) a separation. The white and black population will mark the boundary.†

* George Cabot, who had been United States Senator from Massachusetts for several years during the Administration of Washington.
† See "Life of Cabot," p. 491; letter of Pickering to Higginson.

In another letter, written a few weeks afterward (January 29, 1804), speaking of what he regarded as wrongs and abuses perpetrated by the then existing Administration, he thus expresses his views of the remedy to be applied:

The principles of our Revolution point to the remedy—a separation. That this can be accomplished, and without spilling one drop of blood, I have little doubt. . . .

I do not believe in the practibility of a long-continued Union. A *Northern Confederacy* would unite congenial characters and present a fairer prospect of public happiness; while the Southern States, having a similarity of habits, might be left to "manage their own affairs in their own way." If a separation were to take place, our mutual wants would render a friendly and commercial intercourse inevitable. The Southern States would require the naval protection of the *Northern Union,* and the products of the former would be important to the navigation and commerce of the latter. . . .

It [the separation] must begin in Massachusetts. The proposition would be welcomed in Connecticut; and could we doubt of New Hampshire? But New York must be associated; and how is her concurrence to be obtained? She must be made the center of the Confederacy. Vermont and New Jersey would follow of course, and Rhode Island of necessity.

Substituting South Carolina for Massachusetts; Virginia for New York; Georgia, Mississippi, and Alabama, for New Hampshire, Vermont, and Rhode Island; Kentucky for New Jersey, etc., etc., we find the suggestions of 1860-'61 only a reproduction of those thus outlined nearly sixty years earlier.

In 1811, on the bill for the admission of Louisiana as a State of the Union, the Hon. Josiah Quincy, a member of Congress from Massachusetts, said:

If this bill passes, it is my deliberate opinion that it is virtually a dissolution of this Union; that it will free the States from their moral obligation; and as it will be the right of all, so it will be the duty of some, definitely to prepare for a separation—amicably if they can, violently if they must.

Mr. Poindexter, delegate from what was then the Mississippi Territory, took exception to these expressions of Mr. Quincy, and called him to order. The Speaker sustained Mr. Poindexter, and decided that the suggestion of a dissolution of the Union was out of order. An appeal was taken from this decision, *and it was reversed.* It is to be remembered that these men—Cabot, Pickering, Quincy, and others—were not Democrats, misled by extreme theories of State rights, but leaders and expositors of the highest type of "Federalism, and of a strong central Government." This fact gives their support of the right of secession the greater significance.

The celebrated Hartford Convention assembled in December, 1814. It consisted of delegates chosen by the Legislatures of Massachusetts, Rhode Island, and Connecticut, with an irregular or imperfect representation from New Hampshire and Vermont, convened for the purpose of considering the grievances complained of by those States in connection with the war with Great Britain. They sat with closed doors, and the character of their deliberations and discussions has not been authentically disclosed. It was generally understood, however, that the chief subject of their considerations was the question of the withdrawal of the States they represented from the Union. The decision, as announced in their published report, was adverse to the expediency of such a measure at that time, and under the then existing conditions; but they proceeded to indicate the circumstances in which a dissolution of the Union might become expedient, and the mode in which it should be effected; and their theoretical plan of separation corresponds very nearly with that actually adopted by the Southern States nearly fifty years afterward. They say:

If the Union be destined to dissolution by reason of the multiplied abuses of bad administration, it should, if possible, be the work of peaceable times and deliberate consent. Some *new form of confederacy* should be substituted among those States which shall intend to maintain a federal relation to each other. . . . Whenever it shall appear that the causes are radical and permanent, a separation by equitable arrangement will be preferable to an alliance by constraint among nominal friends, but real enemies.

The obloquy which has attached to the members of the Hartford Convention has resulted mainly because it was a recognized effort to paralyze the arm of the Federal Government while engaged in a war. Time, which has mollified passion, and revealed many things not then known, has largely modified the first judgment passed on the proceedings and purposes of the Hartford Convention; and, but for the circumstances of existing war which surrounded it, they might have been viewed as political opinions merely, and have received justification instead of censure.

Again, in 1844-'45 the measures taken for the annexation of Texas evoked remonstrances, accompanied by threats of a dissolution of the Union from the Northeastern States. The Legislature of Massachusetts, in 1844, adopted a resolution, declaring, in behalf of that State, that "the Commonwealth of Massachusetts, faithful to the compact between the people of the United States, . . . is sincerely anxious for its preservation; but that it is determined, as it doubts not the other States are, *to submit to undelegated powers in no body of men on earth";* and that "the project of the annexation of Texas, unless arrested on the threshold, *may tend to drive these States into a dissolution of the Union."*

It is evident, therefore, that the people of the South, in the crisis which confronted them in 1860, had no lack either of precept or of precedent for their instruction and guidance in the teaching and the example of our brethren of the North and East. The only practical difference was, that the North threatened and the South acted.

Chapter 8

The Dred Scott Case

THE TRUTH REMAINS intact and incontrovertible, that the existence of African servitude was in no wise the cause of the conflict, but only an incident. In the later controversies that arose, however, its effect in operating as a lever upon the passions, prejudices, or sympathies of mankind, was so potent that it has been spread, like a thick cloud, over the whole horizon of historic truth.

The institution of negro servitude was a matter entirely subject to the control of the States. No power was ever given to the General Government to interfere with it, but an obligation was imposed to protect it. Its existence and validity were distinctly recognized by the Constitution in at least three places:

First, in that part of the second section of the first article which prescribes that "representatives and direct taxes shall be apportioned among the several States which may be included within this Union, according to their respective members, which shall be determined by adding to the whole number of free persons, including those bound to service for a term of years, and, excluding Indians not taxed, three fifths of all other persons." *"Other* persons" than *"free* persons" and those "bound to service for a term of years" must, of course, have meant those permanently bound to service.

Secondly, it was recognized by the ninth section of the same article, which provided that "the migration or importation of such persons as any of the States now existing shall think proper to admit shall not be prohibited by Congress prior to the year one thousand eight hundred and eight." This was a provision inserted for the protection of the interests of the slave-trading New England States.

In the third place, it was specially recognized, and an obligation imposed upon every State, not only to refrain from interfering with it in any other State, but in certain cases to aid in its enforcement, by that clause, or paragraph, of the second section of the fourth article which provides as follows:

No person held to service or labor in one State, under the laws thereof, escaping into another, shall, in consequence of any law or regulation therein, be discharged from such service or labor, but shall be delivered up on claim of the party to whom such service or labor may be due.

The President and Vice-President of the United States, every Senator and Representative in Congress, the members of every State Legislature, and "all executive and judicial officers, both of the United States and of the several States," were required to take an oath to support the Constitution containing these provisions. It is easy to understand how those who considered them in conflict with the "higher law" of religion or morality might refuse to take such an oath or hold such an office, but it is impossible to reconcile with the obligations of honor or honesty the conduct of those who, having taken such an oath, made use of the powers and opportunities of the offices held under its sanctions to nullify its obligations and neutralize its guarantees. The halls of Congress afforded the vantage-ground from which assaults were made upon these guarantees. The Legislatures of various Northern States enacted laws to hinder the execution of the provisions made for the rendition of fugitives from service; State officials lent their aid to the work of thwarting them; and city mobs assailed the officers engaged in the duty of enforcing them.

It was not the passage of the "personal liberty laws," it was not the circulation of incendiary documents, it was not the raid of John Brown, it was not the operation of unjust and unequal tariff laws, nor all combined, that constituted the intolerable grievance, but it was the systematic and persistent struggle to deprive the Southern States of equality in the Union—generally to discriminate in legislation against the interests of their people; culminating in their exclusion from the Territories, the common property of the States, as well as by the infraction of their compact to promote domestic tranquillity.

The question with regard to the Territories has been discussed in the foregoing chapters, and the argument need not be repeated. There was, however, one feature of it which has not been specially noticed, although it occupied a large share of public attention at the time, and constituted an important element in the case. This was the action of the Federal judiciary thereon, and the manner in which it was received.

In 1854 the well-known "Dred Scott case" came before the Supreme Court of the United States, involving the whole question of the *status* of the African race and the rights of citizens of the Southern States to migrate to the Territories, temporarily or permanently, with their slave property, on a footing of equality with the citizens of other States with *their* property of any sort. All parties had united in declaring that a decision by the Supreme Court of the United States would be accepted as final. After long and patient consideration of the case, in 1857, the decision of the Court was delivered by Chief-Justice Taney, seven of the nine judges who composed the Court, concurring in it. The salient points established by this decision were:

1. That persons of the African race were not, and could not be, acknowledged as "part of the people," or citizens, under the Constitution of the United States;

2. That Congress had no right to exclude citizens of the South from taking their negro servants, as any other property, into any part of the common territory, and that they were entitled to claim its protection therein;

3. And, finally, as a consequence of the principle just above stated, that the Missouri Compromise of 1820, in so far as it prohibited the existence of African servitude north of a designated line, was unconstitutional and void. (It will be remembered that it had already been declared "inoperative and void" by the Kansas-Nebraska Bill of 1854.)

Instead of accepting the decision of this then august tribunal as conclusive of a controversy that had so long disturbed the peace and was threatening the perpetuity of the Union, it was flouted, denounced, and utterly disregarded by the Northern agitators, and served only to stimulate the intensity of their sectional hostility.

What resource for justice—what assurance of tranquillity—what guarantee of safety—now remained for the South? Still forbearing, still hoping, still striving for peace and union, we waited until a sectional President, nominated by a sectional convention, elected by a sectional vote—and that the vote of a minority of the people—was about to be inducted into office, under the warning of his own distinct announcement that the Union could not permanently endure "half slave and half free"; meaning thereby that it could not continue to exist in the condition in which it was formed and its Constitution adopted. The leader of his party, who was to be the chief of his Cabinet, was the man who had first proclaimed an "irrepressible conflict" between the North and the South, and who had declared that abolitionism, having triumphed in the Territories, would proceed to the invasion of the States. Even then the Southern people did not finally despair until the temper of the triumphant party had been tested in Congress and found adverse to any terms of reconciliation consistent with the honor and safety of all parties.

No alternative remained except to seek the security out of the Union which they had vainly tried to obtain within it.

PART TWO

THE CONSTITUTION

Chapter 1

Background of the Constitutional Convention

WHEN CERTAIN AMERICAN COLONIES of Great Britain, each acting for itself, although in concert with the others, determined to dissolve their political connection with the mother-country, they sent their representatives to a general Congress of those colonies, and through them made a declaration that the colonies were, and of right ought to be, "free and independent States." As such they contracted an alliance for their "common defense," successfully resisted the effort to reduce them to submission, and secured the recognition by Great Britain of their separate independence; each State being distinctly recognized under its own name—not as one of a group or nation. That this was not merely a foreign view is evident from the second of the "Articles of Confederation" between the States, adopted subsequently to the Declaration of Independence, which is in these words: "Each State retains its sovereignty, freedom, and independence, and every power, jurisdiction, and right, which is not by this Confederation expressly delegated to the United States in Congress assembled."

These "Articles of Confederation and Perpetual Union between the States," as they were styled in their title, were adopted by eleven of the original States in 1778, and by the other two in the course of the three years next ensuing, and continued in force until 1789. During this period the General Government was vested in the Congress alone, in which each State, through its representatives, had an equal vote in the determination of all questions whatever. The Congress exercised all the executive as well as legislative powers delegated by the States. Provision was made for the creation, by the Congress, of courts having a certain specified jurisdiction in admiralty and maritime cases, and for the settlement of controversies between two or more States in a mode specifically prescribed.

The Government thus constituted was found inadequate and it became requisite to reorganize it. The first idea of such reorganization arose from the necessity of regulating the commercial intercourse of the States with one another and with foreign countries, and also of making some provision for payment of the debt contracted during the war for independence, the Congress, on the 21st of February 1787, adopted the following resolution:

> *Resolved,* That, in the opinion of Congress, it is expedient that, on the second Monday in May next, a convention of delegates, who shall have been appointed by the several States, be held at Philadelphia, for the sole and express purpose of revising the Articles of Confederation, and reporting to Congress and the several Legislatures such alterations and provisions therein as shall, when agreed to in Congress and confirmed by the States, render the Federal Constitution adequate to the exigencies of Government and the preservation of the Union.

The Legislatures of the various States, with the exception of Rhode Island, adopted and proceeded to act upon by the appointment of delegates. The instructions given to these delegates in all cases conformed to the [resolution] which [has] been quoted, and in one case imposed an additional restriction or limitation.

The General Assembly of Virginia enacted: "That seven commissioners be appointed by joint ballot of both Houses of Assembly, who, or any three of them, are hereby authorized, as deputies from this Commonwealth, to meet such deputies as may be appointed and authorized by other States, to assemble in convention at Philadelphia, and to join with them in devising and discussing *all such alterations and further provisions as may be necessary to render the Federal Constitution adequate to the exigencies of the Union, and in reporting such an act for that purpose to the United States in Congress, as, when agreed to by them, and duly confirmed by the several States,* will effectually provide for the same."

The Council and Assembly of New Jersey, the General Assembly of Pennsylvania, the General Assembly of North Carolina, the Legislature of South Carolina, the General Assembly of Georgia, the Assembly of New York, the General Court of Massachusetts, the General Assembly Court of Connecticut, the General Court of New Hampshire, and the General Assembly of Maryland similarly appointed delegates and instructed them in like manner.

The instructions given to the deputies of Delaware were substantially in accord with the others but the following proviso was added: "So, always, and provided, that such alterations or further provisions do not extend to that part of the fifth article of the Confederation of the said States which declares that, '*in determining questions in the United States in Congress assembled, each State shall have one vote.*'"

From an examination and comparison of the enactments and instructions, we may derive certain conclusions:

1. In the first place, the delegates to the Convention of 1787 represented, not *the people of the United States* in mass, as has been most absurdly contended by some political writers, but *the people* of the several States, *as States*—just as in the Congress of that period—Delaware, with her sixty thousand inhabitants, having entire equality with Pennsylvania, which had more than four hundred thousand, or Virginia, with her seven hundred and fifty thousand.

2. The object for which they were appointed was not to organize a *new* Government, but "solely and expressly" to amend the "Federal Constitution" already existing; in other words, "to revise the Articles of Confederation," and to suggest such "alterations" or additional "provisions" as should be deemed necessary to render them "adequate to the exigencies of the Union."

3. The term "Federal Constitution," or its equivalent, "Constitution of the Federal Government," was as freely and familiarly applied to the system of government established by the Articles of Confederation—undeniably a league or compact between States expressly retaining their sovereignty and independence—as to that amended system which was substituted for it by the Constitution that superseded those articles.

4. The functions of the delegates to the Convention were, of course, only to devise, deliberate, and discuss. No validity could attach to any action taken, unless and until it should be afterward ratified by the several States.

Chapter 2

The Convention Meets

WHEN THE CONVENTION met in Philadelphia, in May, 1787, it soon became evident that the work before it would involve more radical changes in the "Federal Constitution" than had at first been contemplated. Under the Articles of Confederation the General Government was obliged to rely upon the governments of the several States for the execution of its enactments. Except its own officers and employees, and in time of war the Federal army and navy, it could exercise no control upon individual citizens. With regard to the States, no compulsory or coercive measures could be employed to enforce its authority, in case of opposition or indifference to its exercise. This last was a feature of the Confederation which it was not desirable nor possible to change, and no objection was made to it; but it was generally admitted that some machinery should be devised to enable the General Government to exercise its legitimate functions by means of a mandatory authority operating directly upon the individual citizens within the limits of its constitutional powers.

Beyond the common ground of a recognition of this necessity, there was a wide diversity of opinion among the members of the Convention. Luther Martin, a delegate from Maryland, classifies these differences as constituting three parties in the Convention:

One party, whose object and wish it was to abolish and annihilate all State governments, and to bring forward one General Government . . . of a monarchical nature, under certain restrictions and limitations. Those who openly avowed this sentiment were, it is true, but few; yet it is equally true that there was a considerable number, who did not openly avow it, who were . . . considered as being in reality favorers of that sentiment. . . .

The second party . . . wished to establish such a system as could give their own States undue power and influence in the government over the other States.

A third party was what I considered truly federal and republican. This party was nearly equal in number with the other two, and was composed of the delegates from Connecticut, New York, New Jersey, Delaware, and in part from Maryland. . . . This party was for taking our present federal system as the basis of their proceedings, and, as far as experience had shown that other powers were necessary to the Federal Government, to give those powers.

In his account of the second party above described, Mr. Martin refers to those representatives of the larger States who wished to establish a numerical basis of representation in the Congress, instead of the equal representation of the States (whether large or small) which existed under the Articles of Confederation. There was naturally much dissatisfaction on the part of the greater States—Virginia, Pennsylvania, North Carolina, and Massachusetts—whose population at that period exceeded that of all the others combined, but which, in the Congress, constituted less than one third of the voting strength. On the other hand, the smaller States were tenacious of their equality in the Union. This difference gave more trouble than any other question that came before the Convention, and for some time threatened to hinder any final agreement. It was ultimately settled by a compromise. Provision was made for the representation of the people of the States in one branch of the Federal Legislature (the House of Representatives) in proportion to their numbers; in the other branch (the Senate), for the equal representation of the States as such. The perpetuity of this equality was furthermore guaranteed by a stipulation that no State should ever be deprived of its equal suffrage in the Senate without its own consent. This compromise required no sacrifice of principle on either side, and no provision of the Constitution has in practice proved more entirely satisfactory.

Early in the session of the Convention a series of resolutions was introduced by Mr. Edmund Randolph, of Virginia, embodying a proposed plan of government, which were considered in committee of the whole House, and formed the basis of a protracted discussion. The first of these resolutions was in these words:

Resolved, That it is the opinion of this committee that a national Government ought to be established, consisting of a supreme legislative, executive, and judiciary.

This was followed by other resolutions—twenty-three in all . . . in which the word "national" occurred twenty-six times.

The day after the report of the committee was made, Mr. Ellsworth, of Connecticut, moved to strike out the words "national Government" in the resolution above quoted, and to insert the words "Government of the United States." He wished also the plan to go forth as an amendment of the Articles of Confederation. That is to say, he wished to avoid even the appearance of undertaking to form a *new* government, instead of reforming the old one, which was the proper object of the Convention. This motion was agreed to without opposition, and the word "national" was stricken out wherever it occurred, and nowhere makes its appearance in the Constitution finally adopted. The prompt rejection, after introduction, of this word "national," is obviously much more expressive of the intent and purpose of the authors of the Constitution than its mere absence from the Constitution would have been.

Continuing their great work of revision and reorganization, the Convention proceeded to construct the framework of a government for the Confederacy, strictly confined to certain specified and limited powers, but complete in all its parts, legislative, executive, and judicial, and provided with the means for discharging all its functions without interfering with the "sovereignty, freedom, and independence" of the constituent States.

All this might have been done without going beyond the limits of their commission "to revise the Articles of Confederation," and to consider and report such "alterations and provisions" as might seem necessary to "render the Federal Constitution adequate to the exigencies of government and the preservation of the Union." A serious difficulty, however, was foreseen. The thirteenth and last of the aforesaid articles had this provision: "The Articles of this Confederation *shall be inviolably observed by every State, and the union shall be perpetual; nor shall any alteration, at any time hereafter, be made in any of them,* unless such alteration be agreed to in a Congress of the United States, and be afterward confirmed by the Legislatures of *every State."*

It is obvious, from an examination of the records, that the original idea in calling a Convention was, that their recommendations should take the course prescribed by this article— first, a report to the Congress, and then, if approved by that body, a submission to the various Legislatures for final action. There was no reason to apprehend the non-concurrence of Congress, in which a mere majority would determine the question; but the consent of the Legislatures of *"every State"* was requisite in order to final ratification, and there was serious reason to fear that this consent could not be obtained. Rhode Island, as we have seen, had declined to send any representatives to the Convention; of the three delegates from New York, two had withdrawn; and other indications of dissatisfaction had appeared. In case of the failure of a single Legislature to ratify, the labors of the Convention would go for naught. The danger of a total frustration of their efforts was imminent.

In this emergency the Convention took the responsibility of transcending the limits of their instructions, and recommending a procedure which was in direct contravention of the letter of the Articles of Confederation. This was the introduction of a provision into the new Constitution, that the ratification of *nine* States should be sufficient for its establishment among themselves. In order to validate this provision, it was necessary to refer it to authority higher than that of Congress and the State Legislatures—that is, to the PEOPLE of the States, assembled, by their representatives, in convention. Hence it was provided, by the seventh and last article of the new Constitution, that "the ratification of the *Conventions* of nine States" should suffice for its establishment "between the States so ratifying the same."

Mr. Madison, in the "Federalist," says: "It has been heretofore noted among the defects of the Confederation, that in many of the States it had received no higher sanction than a mere legislative ratification." This objection would of course have applied with greater force to the proposed Constitution, which provided for additional grants of power from the States, and the conferring of larger and more varied powers upon a General Government, which was to act upon individuals instead of States, if the question of its confirmation had been submitted merely to the several State Legislatures. Hence the obvious propriety of referring it to the respective *people* of the States in their sovereign capacity, as provided in the final article of the Constitution.

In this article provision was deliberately made for the *secession* (if necessary) of a part of the States from a union which, when formed, had been declared "perpetual," and its terms and articles to be "inviolably observed by every State."

The only possible alternative to the view here taken of the seventh article of the Constitution, as a provision for the secession of any nine States, and the formation of an amended or "more perfect union" with one another, is to regard it as a provision for the continuance of the old Union, or Confederation, under altered conditions, by the majority which should accede to them, with a recognition of the right of the recusant minority to withdraw, secede, or stand aloof. The idea of compelling any State or States to enter into or to continue in union with the others by *coercion,* is as absolutely excluded under the one supposition as under the other —with reference to one State or a minority of States, as well as to a majority. The article declares that "the ratification of the Conventions of nine States shall be sufficient for the establishment of this Constitution"—not between all, but— *"between the States so ratifying the same."* It is submitted whether a fuller justification of this right of the nine States to form a new Government is not found in the fact of the sovereignty in each of them, making them "a law unto themselves."

Here the attention of the reader may be directed to the refutation, afforded by this article of the Constitution, of that astonishing fiction, which has been put forward by some distinguished writers of later date, that the Constitution was established by the people of the United States "in the aggregate." If such had been the case, the will of a majority, duly ascertained and expressed, would have been binding upon the minority. No such idea existed in its formation. It was not even established by the *States in the aggregate,* nor was it proposed that it should be. It was submitted for the acceptance of each separately, the time and place at their own option, so that the dates of ratification did extend from December 7, 1787, to May 29, 1790. The long period required for these ratifications makes manifest the absurdity of the assertion, that it was a decision by the votes of one people, or one community, in which a majority of the votes cast determined the result.

Chapter 3

Ratification

THE AMENDED SYSTEM of union, or confederation (the terms are employed indiscriminately and interchangeably by the statesmen of that period), devised by the Convention of 1787, and embodied in the Constitution, was now to be acted on by the people of the several States. This they did in the highest and most majestic form in which the sanction of organized communities could be given or withheld, through conventions of delegates chosen expressly for the purpose and clothed with the plenary authority of sovereign people. The action of these conventions was deliberate, cautious, and careful. There was much debate, and no little opposition to be conciliated. Eleven States, however, ratified and adopted the new Constitution within the twelve months immediately following its submission to them. Two of them positively rejected it, and, although they afterward acceded to it, remained outside of the Union in the exercise of their sovereign right, which nobody then denied—North Carolina for nine months, Rhode Island for nearly fifteen, after the new Government was organized and went into operation.

The terms in which this action was expressed by the several States and the declarations with which it was accompanied by some of them are worthy of attention.

Delaware was the first to act. Her Convention met on December 3, 1787, and ratified the Constitution on the 7th. Delaware alone had given special instructions to her deputies in the Convention not to consent to any sacrifice of the principle of equal representation in Congress. The promptness and unanimity of her people in adopting the new Constitution prove very clearly that they did not understand the Constitution, in any of its features, as compromising the "sovereignty, freedom, and independence" which she had so especially cherished. The ratification of their Convention is expressed in these words:

We, the deputies of *the people of the Delaware State,* in convention met, having taken into our serious consideration the Federal Constitution proposed and agreed upon by the deputies of the United States at a General Convention . . . have *approved of, assented to, and ratified and confirmed,* and by these presents do, in virtue of the powers and authority to us given for that purpose, for and in behalf of ourselves and our constituents, fully, freely, and entirely, *approve of, assent to, ratify, and confirm* the said Constitution.

This, and twelve other like acts, gave to the Constitution "all the life and validity it ever had, or could have, as to the thirteen united or associated States."

Pennsylvania acted next (December 12, 1787). In New Jersey the ratification, which took place on the 18th of December, was unanimous. This is no less significant and instructive than the unanimity of Delaware, from the fact that the New Jersey delegation, in the Convention that framed the Constitution, had taken the lead in behalf of the federal, or State-rights, idea, in opposition to that of nationalism, or consolidation. Georgia was next, followed by Connecticut.

In Massachusetts there was a sharp contrast. The people of that State were then—as for a long time afterward—exceedingly tenacious of their State independence and sovereignty. The proposed Constitution was ultimately adopted by a very close vote and then only as accompanied by certain proposed amendments. The most strenuously urged of these was that ultimately adopted (in substance) as the tenth amendment to the Constitution, which was intended to take the place of the second Article of Confederation, as an emphatic assertion of the continued freedom, sovereignty, and independence of the States.

Maryland followed on the 28th of April, and South Carolina on the 23rd of May, in equivalent expressions, the ratification being made "on behalf of *the people of this State.*" But South Carolina, like Massachusetts, accompanied her ordinance of ratification with the following distinct assertion of the principle afterward embodied in the tenth amendment:

This Convention doth also declare that *no section or paragraph* of the said Constitution warrants a construction that *the States do not retain every power not expressly relinquished by them* and vested in the General Government of the Union.

"The delegates of *the people of the State of New Hampshire,*" in convention, on the 21st of June, "in the name and

behalf of *the people of the State of New Hampshire,"* declared their approval and adoption of the Constitution. In
this State, as in South Carolina, it was "explicitly declared
that all powers not expressly and particularly delegated by
the aforesaid Constitution are reserved to the several States."

The debates in the Virginia Convention were long and
animated. Among the members were Madison, Mason, and
Randolph, who had been members of the Convention at
Philadelphia. Mr. Madison was one of the most earnest advocates of the new Constitution, while Mr. Mason was as
warmly opposed to its adoption. It was assailed with great
vehemence at every vulnerable or doubtful point, and was
finally ratified June 26, 1788, by a majority of only ten. In
so doing, however, Virginia demanded certain amendments
and accompanied the demand with the following declaration:

That the powers granted under the Constitution, being derived from the people of the United States, may be resumed by
them, whenever the same shall be perverted to their injury or
oppression, and that every power not granted thereby remains
with them and at their will, etc., etc.

New York, the eleventh State to signify her assent, did so
on July 26, 1788, after an arduous and protracted discussion,
and then by a majority of but three votes.

Accompanying the ratification was a declaration of principles, one paragraph of which runs as follows:

That the powers of government may be *reassumed* by the
people, whensoever it shall become necessary to their happiness;
that every power, jurisdiction, and right, which is not, by the
said Constitution, clearly delegated to the Congress of the United
States, or the departments of the Government thereof, remains
to the people of the several *States,* or to their respective State
governments, to whom they may have been granted the same; and
that those clauses in the said Constitution which declare that
Congress shall not have or exercise certain powers, do not imply
that Congress is entitled to any powers not given by the said
Constitution, but such clauses are to be construed either as exceptions to certain specified powers or as inserted for greater
caution.

The acceptance of these eleven States having been signified
to the Congress, provision was made for putting the new
Constitution in operation.

Meantime, two States were standing, as we have seen,

unquestioned and unmolested, in an attitude of absolute independence. The Convention of North Carolina, on August 2, 1788, had withheld her ratification until action could be taken upon the following resolution adopted by her Convention:

Resolved, That a declaration of rights, asserting and securing from encroachment the great principles of civil and religious liberty, and the unalienable rights of the people, together with amendments to the most ambiguous and exceptionable parts of the said Constitution of government, ought to be laid before Congress and the Convention of the States that shall or may be called for the purpose of amending the said Constitution, for their consideration, previous to the ratification of the Constitution aforesaid on the part of the State of North Carolina.

More than a year afterward, when the newly organized Government had been in operation for nearly nine months, and when North Carolina had good reason to feel assured that the most important provisions of her proposed amendments and "declaration of rights" would be adopted, she acceded to the amended compact.

In Rhode Island on May 29, 1790, when the reorganized Government had been in operation for nearly fifteen months, and when it had become reasonably certain that the amendments thought necessary would be adopted—a convention of the people of Rhode Island acceded to the new Union, and ratified the Constitution.

Chapter 4

The Preamble to the Constitution

THE PREAMBLE to the Constitution proposed by the Convention of 1787 is in these words:

> We, the people of the United States, in order to form a more perfect union, establish justice, insure domestic tranquillity, provide for the common defense, promote the general welfare, and secure the blessings of liberty to ourselves and our posterity, do ordain and establish this Constitution for the United States of America.

The phraseology of this preamble has been generally regarded as the stronghold of the advocates of consolidation. It has been interpreted as meaning that "we, the people of the United States," as a collective body, or as a "nation," in our aggregate capacity, had "ordained and established" the Constitution *over* the States.

This interpretation constituted, in the beginning, the most serious difficulty in the way of the ratification of the Constitution. Patrick Henry, in the very opening of the debate in the Virginia Convention, attacked it vehemently. He said:

> That this is a consolidated government is demonstrably clear; and the danger of such a government is, to my mind, very striking. I have the highest veneration for those gentlemen [its authors]; but, sir, give me leave to demand, What right had they to say, *We, the people?* My political curiosity, exclusive of my anxious solicitude for the public welfare, leads me to ask, Who authorized them to speak the language of *"We, the people,"* instead of *We, the States?* States are the characteristics and the soul of a confederation. If the States be not the agents of this compact, it must be one great consolidated national government of the people of all the States.

The same difficulty arose in other minds and in other conventions.

Mr. Henry's objection was thus answered by Mr. Madison:

> Who are the parties to it [the Constitution]? The people—but *not the people as composing one great body;* but the people as

composing *thirteen sovereignties:* were it, as the gentleman [Mr. Henry] asserts, a consolidated government, the assent of a majority of the people would be sufficient for its establishment, and as a majority have adopted it already, the remaining States would be bound by the act of the majority, even if they unanimously reprobated it: were it such a government as is suggested, it would be now binding on the people of this State, without having had the privilege of deliberating upon it; but, sir, no State is bound by it, as it is, without its own consent. Should all the States adopt it, it will be then a government established by the thirteen States of America, not through the intervention of the Legislatures, but by the people at large. In this particular respect the distinction between the existing and proposed governments is very material. The existing system has been derived from the dependent, derivative authority of the Legislatures of the States, whereas this is derived from the superior power of the people.

The explanation seems to have been as satisfactory as it was simple and intelligible. Mr. Henry, although he fought to the last against the ratification of the Constitution, did not again bring forward this objection. Indeed, we hear no more of the interpretation which suggested it, from that period, for nearly half a century, when it was revived, and has since been employed, to sustain that theory of a "great consolidated national government."

But *we* have access to sources of information, not then available, which make the intent and meaning of the Constitution still plainer. When Mr. Henry made his objection, and Mr. Madison answered it, the journal of the Philadelphia Convention had not been published. That body had sat with closed doors. But the secrecy then covering those proceedings has long since been removed. The manuscript journal, which was intrusted to the keeping of General Washington, has since been published, and we can ascertain the exact significance, of that expression, "We, the people," on which Patrick Henry thought the fate of America might depend, and which has been so grossly perverted in later years from its true intent.

The original language of the preamble, as we find it in the proceedings of August 6, 1787, was as follows:

We, the people of the States of New Hampshire, Massachusetts, Rhode Island and Providence Plantations, Connecticut, New York, New Jersey, Pennsylvania, Delaware, Maryland, Virginia, North Carolina, South Carolina, and Georgia, do ordain, declare, and establish, the following Constitution for the government of ourselves and our posterity.

There can be no question here what was meant: it was *"the people of the States,"* designated by name, that were to "ordain, declare, and establish" the compact of union. There is no ambiguity nor uncertainty in the language; nor was there any difference in the Convention as to the use of it. The preamble, as perfected, was submitted to vote on the next day, and, as the journal informs us, "it passed *unanimously* in the affirmative."

There was no subsequent change of opinion on the subject. The reason for the modification afterward made in the language is obvious. It was found that unanimous ratification of all the States could not be expected, and it was determined, as we have already seen, that the consent of *nine* States should suffice for the establishment of the new compact "between the States so ratifying the same." *Any* nine would be sufficient to put the proposed government in operation as to them, thus leaving the remainder of the thirteen to pursue such course as might be to each preferable. When this conclusion was reached, it became manifestly impracticable to designate beforehand the consenting States by name. The imposing fabric of political delusion, which has been erected on the basis of this simple transaction, disappears before the light of historical record.

Could the authors of the Constitution have foreseen the perversion to be made of their obvious meaning, it might have been prevented by an easy periphrasis—such as, "We, the people of the States hereby united," or something to the same effect. The word "people" in 1787, as in 1880, was, as it is, a collective noun, employed indiscriminately, either as a unit in such expressions as "this people," "a free people," etc., or in a distributive sense, as applied to the citizens or inhabitants of one state or country or a number of states or countries. When the Convention of the colony of Virginia, in 1774, instructed their delegates to the Congress that was to meet in Philadelphia, "to obtain a redress of those grievances, without which *the people of America* can neither be safe, free, nor happy," it was certainly not intended to convey the idea that the people of the American Continent, or even of the British colonies in America, constituted one political community.

In the Declaration of Independence we find instances of

the employment of the singular form for both singular and plural senses—"one people," "a free people," in the former, and "the good people of these colonies" in the latter. Judge Story, in the excess of his zeal in behalf of a theory of consolidation, bases upon this last expression the conclusion that the assertion of independence was the act of *"the whole people of the united colonies"* as a unit; overlooking or suppressing the fact that, in the very same sentence, the colonies declare themselves "free and independent *States*"—not a free and independent *state*—repeating the words "independent States" three times.

If, however, the Declaration of Independence constituted one *"whole people"* of the colonies, then that geographical section of it, formerly known as the colony of Maryland, was in a state of revolt or "rebellion" against the others, as well as against Great Britain, from 1778 to 1781, during which period Maryland refused to ratify or be bound by the Articles of Confederation, which, according to this theory, was binding upon her, as a majority of the "whole people" had adopted it. *A fortiori,* North Carolina and Rhode Island were in a state of rebellion in 1789–'90, while they declined to ratify and recognize the Constitution adopted by the other eleven fractions of this united people. Yet no hint of any such pretension—of any claim of authority over them by the majority—of any assertion of "the supremacy of the Union" —is to be found in any of the records of that period. Yet such a claim has been made the plea to justify a bloody war against that principle of State sovereignty and independence, which was regarded by the fathers of the Union as the corner-stone of the structure and the basis of the hope for its perpetuity.

Chapter 5

Growth of Federal Government and Accretions of Power

IN THE progressive growth of the Government of the United States in power, splendor, patronage, and consideration abroad, men have been led to exalt the place of the *Government* above that of the *States* which *created* it. Those who would understand the true principles of the Constitution can not afford to lose sight of the essential *plurality* of idea invariably implied in the term "United States," wherever it is used in that instrument. No such unit as the United States is ever mentioned therein. We read that "no title of nobility shall be granted by the United States, and no person holding any office of profit or trust under *them* shall, without the consent of Congress, accept," etc. "The President . . . shall not receive, within that period, any other emolument from the United States, or any of *them*." "The laws of the United States, and treaties made or which shall be made under *their* authority," etc. "Treason against the United States shall consist only in levying war against *them,* or in adhering to *their* enemies. The Federal character of the Union is expressed by this very phraseology, which recognizes the distinct integrity of its members, not as fractional parts of one great unit, but as component units of an association. So clear was this to contemporaries, that it needed only to be pointed out to satisfy their scruples.

I am informed, by one who has taken the pains to examine carefully that document that—without including any mention of "the United States" or of "foreign states," and excluding also the amendments—the Constitution, in its original draft, makes mention of the States, *as* States, no less than *seventy* times; and of these *seventy* times, only *three* times in the way of prohibition of the exercise of a power. In fact, it is full of statehood. Leave out all mention of the States—I make no mere verbal point or quibble, but mean the States in their separate, several, distinct capacity—and what would remain would be of less account than the play of the Prince of Denmark with the part of *Hamlet* omitted.

The meaning of the preamble, "We, the people of the

United States . . . . do ordain and establish this Constitution," is ascertained, fixed, and defined by the final article: "The ratification of the conventions of *nine States* shall be sufficient for the *establishment* of this Constitution between *the States so ratifying* the same." If it was already established, what need was there of further establishment? It was not ordained or established at all, until ratified by the requisite number of States. The announcement in the preamble of course had reference to that expected ratification, without which the preamble would have been as void as the body of the instrument.

If, we can conceive, and admit for a moment, the possibility that, when the Constitution was under consideration, the people of the United States were politically "one people" —a collective unit—two deductions are clearly inevitable: In the first place, each geographical division of this great community would have been entitled to vote according to its relative population; and, in the second, the expressed will of the legal majority would have been binding upon the whole. A denial of the first proposition would be a denial of common justice and equal rights; a denial of the second would be to destroy all government and establish mere anarchy.

Now, *neither* of these principles was practiced or proposed or even imagined in the case of the action of the people of the United States (if they were one political community) upon the proposed Constitution. On the contrary, seventy thousand people in the State of Delaware had precisely the same weight—one vote—in its ratification, as seven hundred thousand (and more) in Virginia, or four hundred thousand in Pennsylvania. Would not this have been an intolerable grievance and wrong—would no protest have been uttered against it—if these had been fractional parts of one community of people?

Before the ratification of the Constitution—when there was some excuse for an imperfect understanding or misconception of the terms proposed—Mr. Madison thus answered, in advance, the objections made on the ground of this misconception. He wrote:

That it will be a federal and not a national act, as these terms are understood by objectors—the act of the people, as forming so many independent States, not as forming one aggregate nation—is obvious from this single consideration, that it is to result neither from the decision of a *majority* of the people of the Union nor from that of a *majority* of *the States*. It must result from the *unanimous* assent of the several *States that are parties to it,* differing no otherwise from their ordinary assent than in its being expressed, not by the legislative authority, but by that of the people themselves. Were the people regarded in this transaction as forming one nation, the will of the majority of the whole people of the United States would bind the minority, in the same manner as the majority in each State must bind the minority; and the will of the majority must be determined either by a comparison of the individual votes or by considering the will of the majority of the States as evidence of the will of a majority of the people of the United States. Neither of these has been adopted. Each State, in ratifying the Constitution, is considered as a sovereign body, independent of all others, and only to be bound by its own voluntary act.

Chapter 6

The "New Vocabulary"

I HAVE habitually spoken of the Federal Constitution as a compact, and of the parties to it as sovereign States. These terms should not, and in earlier times would not, have required explanation or vindication. But they have been called in question by the modern school of consolidation. These gentlemen admit that the Government under the Articles of Confederation was a compact. Mr. Webster, in his rejoinder to Mr. Hayne, on the 27th of January, 1830, said:

> When the gentleman says the Constitution is a compact between the States, he uses language exactly applicable to the old Confederation. He speaks as if he were in Congress before 1789. . . . The Confederation was, in strictness, a compact; the States, as States, were parties to it. We had no other General Government. But that was found insufficient and inadequate to the public exigencies. The people were not satisfied with it, and undertook to form a General Government, which should stand on a new basis—not a confederacy, not a league, not a compact between States, but a Constitution.

The distinction drawn between the language proper to a confederation and that belonging to a constitution, as indicating two different ideas, will not bear the test of examination and application to the case of the United States. The former Union was—as Mr. Webster expressly admits—as nobody denies—a compact between States, yet it nowhere "calls itself" "a compact"; the word does not occur in it even the one time that it occurs in the present Constitution, although the contracting or constituent parties are termed "United States" in the one just as in the other.

Mr. Webster is particularly unfortunate in his criticisms upon what he terms the "new vocabulary," in which the Constitution is styled a compact, and the States which ratified it are spoken of as having "acceded" to it. In the same speech, last quoted, he says:

> This word 'accede,' not found either in the Constitution itself or in the ratification of it by any one of the States, has been

chosen for use here, doubtless not without a well-considered purpose. The natural converse of accession is secession; and therefore, when it is stated that the people of the States acceded to the Union, it may be more plausibly argued that they may secede from it. If, in adopting the Constitution, nothing was done but acceding to a compact, nothing would seem necessary, in order to break it up, but to secede from the same compact. But the term is wholly out of place. Accession, as a word applied to political associations, implies coming into a league, treaty, or confederacy, by one hitherto a stranger to it; and secession implies departing from such league or confederacy. The people of the United States have used no such form of expression in establishing the present Government.

In this and similar passages, Mr. Webster virtually concedes that, if the Constitution *were* a compact; if the Union *were* a confederacy; if the States *had,* as States, severally acceded to it—all which propositions he denies—then the sovereignty of the States and their right to secede from the Union would be deducible.

Now, it happens that these very terms—"compact," "confederacy," "accede," and the like—were the terms in familiar use by the authors of the Constitution and their associates with reference to that instrument and its ratification.

Mr. Gerry, of Massachusetts, in the Convention of 1787 said: "If nine out of thirteen States can dissolve *the compact,* six out of nine will be just as able to dissolve *the new one* hereafter."

Mr. Gouverneur Morris, one of the most pronounced advocates of a strong central government, in the Convention, said: "He came here to form *a compact* for the good of Americans. He was ready to do so with all the States. He hoped and believed they all would enter into such a *compact.* If they would not, he would be ready to join with any States that would. But, as the *compact* was to be voluntary, it is vain for the Eastern States to insist on what the Southern States will never agree to." *

Mr. Madison, while inclining to a strong government, said: "In the case of a union of people under one Constitution, the nature *of the* pact has always been understood," etc. †

Mr. Hamilton, in the "Federalist," repeatedly speaks of the new government as a *"confederate republic"* and a *"con-*

---

* "Madison Papers," pp. 1081, 1082.
† Ibid., p. 1184.

federacy," and calls the Constitution a "compact."

General Washington referred to the Constitution as a *compact* or treaty, and repeatedly uses the terms "accede" and "accession," and once the term "secession."

He asks what the opponents of the Constitution in Virginia would do, "if nine other States should *accede* to the Constitution." It is needless to multiply the proofs that abound in the writings of the "fathers" to show that Mr. Webster's "new vocabulary" was the very language they familiarly used. Let two more examples suffice, from authority higher than that of any individual speaker or writer, however eminent—from authority second only, if at all inferior, to that of the text of the Constitution itself—that is, from the acts or ordinances of ratification by the States.

The ratification of Massachusetts is expressed in the following terms:

> The Convention, . . . acknowledging . . . the goodness of the Supreme Ruler . . . in affording . . . the people of the United States . . . an opportunity . . . of entering into an explicit and solemn COMPACT with each other, by assenting to and ratifying a new Constitution . . . do, in the name and in behalf of the people of the Commonwealth of Massachusetts, assent to and ratify the said Constitution for the United States of America.

The ratification of New Hampshire is expressed in precisely the same words. Both distinctly accept it as a *compact* of the States "with each other."

If it were possible that any doubt could still exist, there is one provision in the Constitution which stamps its character as a compact too plainly for cavil or question. The Constitution, which had already provided for the representation of the States in both Houses of Congress, thereby bringing the matter of representation within the power of amendment, in its fifth article contains a stipulation that "no State, without its [own] consent, shall be deprived of its equal suffrage in the Senate." If this is not a compact between the States, the smaller States have no guarantee for the preservation of their equality of representation in the United States Senate. If the obligation of a contract does not secure it, the guarantee itself is liable to amendment, and may be swept away at the will of three fourths of the States, without wrong to any party— for, according to this theory, there is no party of the second part.

Chapter 7

Sovereignty

I THINK it has already been demonstrated that, in this country, the only political community—the only independent corporate unit—through which the people can exercise their sovereignty, is the State. Minor communities—as those of counties, cities, and towns—are merely fractional subdivisions of the State; and these do not affect the evidence that there was not such a political community as the "people of the United States in the aggregate." The States are sovereign, unless they have surrendered or been divested of their sovereignty; and those who deny the proposition have been vainly called upon to point out the process by which they have divested themselves, or have been divested of it, otherwise than by usurpation.

Confounding the sovereign authority of the *people* with the delegated powers conferred by them upon their *governments,* we hear of a Government of the United States "sovereign within its sphere," and of State governments "sovereign in their sphere"; of the surrender by the States of *part* of their sovereignty to the United States, and the like. Now, if there be any one great principle pervading the Federal Constitution, the State Constitutions, the writings of the fathers, the whole American system, it is that *no* government is sovereign—that all governments derive their powers from the people, and exercise them in subjection to the will of the people—not a will expressed in any irregular, lawless, tumultuary manner, but the will of the organized political community, expressed through authorized and legitimate channels. The founders of the American republics never conferred, nor intended to confer, sovereignty upon either their State or Federal Governments.

If, then, the people of the States, in forming a Federal Union, surrendered—or transferred—*part* of their sovereignty, to whom was the transfer made? Not to "the people of the United States in the aggregate"; for there was no such people in existence, and they did not create or constitute such a people by merger of themselves. Not to the Federal Government; for they disclaimed, as a fundamental principle, the sovereignty of any government. There was no such surrender, no such transfer, in whole or in part, expressed or implied. They retained, and intended to retain, their sovereignty in its integrity—undivided and indivisible.

The people inhabiting the territory formerly called the Province of Massachusetts Bay do hereby solemnly and mutually agree with each other to form themselves into a free, *sovereign,* and independent body politic, or State, by the name of *The Commonwealth of Massachusetts.*

New Hampshire, in her Constitution, had identically the same declaration, except as regards the name of the State and the word "State" instead of "Commonwealth."

Mr. Madison, in a speech to the Virginia Convention of 1788, explained that "We, the people," who were to establish the Constitution, were the people of "thirteen SOVEREIGNTIES."

In the "Federalist," he repeatedly employs the term: "Do they [the fundamental principles of the Confederation] require that, in the establishment of the Constitution, the States should be regarded as distinct and independent SOVEREIGNS? They *are* so regarded by the Constitution proposed."

Alexander Hamilton says, in the "Federalist":

It is inherent in the nature of *sovereignty,* not to be amenable to the suit of an individual without its consent. This is the general sense and the general practice of mankind; and the exemption, as one of the attributes of *sovereignty,* is now enjoyed by the government of *every State* in the Union.

Benjamin Franklin advocated equality of suffrage in the Senate as a means of securing "the *sovereignties* of the individual States." Gouverneur Morris, who was one of the warmest advocates in the Convention of a strong central government, spoke of the Constitution as "a *compact,*" and of the parties to it as "each enjoying *sovereign* power." Roger Sherman, of Connecticut, declared that the Government "was instituted by a number of *sovereign States.* These were all eminent members of the Convention which formed the Constitution. There was scarcely a statesman of that period who did not leave on record expressions of the same sort.

It is quite certain that the Constitution would never have received the assent and ratification of Massachusetts, New Hampshire, New York, North Carolina, and perhaps other States, but for a well-grounded assurance that the substance of the tenth amendment would be adopted as soon as the requisite formalities could be complied with. That amendment is in these words:

> The powers not delegated to the United States by the Constitution nor prohibited by it to the States are reserved to the States respectively, or to the people.

The full meaning of this article may not be as clear to us as it was to the men of that period, on account of the confusion of ideas by which the term "people" has since been obscured, and also the ambiguity attendant upon the use of the little conjunction *or,* which has been said to be the most equivocal word in our language, and for that reason has been excluded from indictments in the English courts. The true intent and meaning of the provision, however, may be ascertained from an examination and comparison of the terms in which it was expressed by the various States which proposed it, and whose ideas it was intended to embody.

Massachusetts and New Hampshire, in their ordinances of ratification, each recommended:

> That it be explicitly declared that all powers not expressly delegated by the aforesaid Constitution *are reserved to the several States,* to be by them exercised.

Of course, those stanch republican communities meant *the people of the States*—not their *governments,* as something distinct from their people.

New York expressed herself as follows:

> That the powers of government may be reassumed by the people whenever it shall become necessary to their happiness; that every power, jurisdiction, and right, which is not by the said Constitution clearly delegated to the Congress of the United States, or the departments of the Government thereof, remains to *the people of the several States, or to their respective State governments, to whom they may have granted the same;* and that those clauses in the said Constitution, which declare that Congress shall not have or exercise certain powers, do not imply that Congress is entitled to any powers not given by the said Constitution; but such clauses are to be construed either as exceptions to certain specified powers or as inserted merely for greater caution.

South Carolina, North Carolina, and Rhode Island each expressed similar ideas.

No objection was made from any quarter to the principle thus asserted or to the amendment in which it was finally expressed, although many thought it unnecessary, as being merely declaratory of what would have been sufficiently obvious without it.

Is it compatible with reason to suppose that people so chary of the delegation of specific powers or functions could have meant to surrender or transfer the very basis and origin of all power—their inherent sovereignty—and this, not by express grant, but by implication?

Much has been said of the "prohibition" of the exercise by the States of certain functions of sovereignty; such as, making treaties, declaring war, coining money, etc. It is not a prohibition imposed upon them from without, or from above, by any external or superior power, but is self-imposed by their free consent. The case is strictly analogous to that of individuals forming a mercantile or manufacturing copartnership, who voluntarily agree to refrain, as individuals, from engaging in other pursuits or speculations, which they may think proper to subject to the consent, or intrust to the management of the firm.

The prohibitory clauses of the Constitution are not at all a denial of the full sovereignty of the States, but are merely an agreement among them to exercise certain powers of sovereignty in concert, and not separately and apart.

There is one other provision of the Constitution, which is generally adduced by the friends of centralism as antagonistic to State sovereignty. This is found in the second clause of the sixth article, as follows:

This Constitution, and the laws of the United States which shall be made in pursuance thereof, and all treaties made, or which shall be made, under the authority of the United States, shall be the supreme law of the land; and the judges in every State shall be bound thereby, anything in the Constitution or laws of any State to the contrary notwithstanding.

This enunciation of a principle, which, even if it had not been expressly declared, would have been a necessary deduction from the acceptance of the Constitution itself, has been magnified and perverted into a meaning and purpose entirely foreign to that which plain interpretation is sufficient to discern.

In the first place, it must be remembered that, when the Federal Constitution was formed, each then existing State already had its own Constitution and code of statute laws. It was, no doubt, primarily with reference to these that the provision was inserted, and not in the expectation of future conflicts or discrepancies. Again, it is to be observed that the supremacy accorded to the general laws of the United States is expressly limited to those enacted in conformity with the Constitution, or, to use the exact language, "made in pursuance thereof." Mr. Hamilton, in the "Federalist," calls particular attention to this, saying (and the italics are all his own) "that the laws of the Confederacy, as to the *enumerated* and *legitimate* objects of its jurisdiction, will become the supreme law of the land," and that the State functionaries will coöperate in their observance and enforcement with the General Government, *"as far as its just and constitutional authority extends."*

In the third place, it is not the *Government* of the United States that is declared to be supreme, but the *Constitution* and the laws and treaties made in accordance with it. The proposition was made in the Convention to organize a government consisting of "supreme legislative, executive, and judicial powers," but it was not adopted. Its deliberate rejection is much more significant and conclusive than if it had never been proposed. Correction of so gross an error as that of confounding the Government with the Constitution ought to be superfluous, but so crude and confused are the ideas which have been propagated on the subject, that no misconception seems to be too absurd to be possible. Thus, it has not been uncommon, of late years, to hear, even in the highest places, the oath to support the Constitution, which is taken by both State and Federal officers, spoken of as an oath "to support *the Government*"—an obligation never imposed upon any one in this country, and which the men who made the Constitution, with their recent reminiscences of the Revolution, would have been the last to prescribe. Could any assertion be less credible than that they proceeded to institute another supreme government which it would be treason to resist?

This confusion of ideas pervades the treatment of the whole subject of sovereignty. Mr. Webster has said, and very justly so far as these United States are concerned: "The sovereignty of government is an idea belonging to the other side of the Atlantic. No such thing is known in North America. Our governments are all limited. In Europe sovereignty is of feudal origin, and imports no more than the state of the sovereign. It comprises his rights, duties, exemptions, prerogatives, and powers. But with us all power is with the people. They alone are sovereign, and they erect what governments they please, and confer on them such powers as they please."

But the same intellect, which can so lucidly define the general proposition, seems to be covered by a cloud of thick darkness, when it comes to apply it to the particular case in issue. Thus, a little afterward, we have the following:

There is no language in the whole Constitution applicable to a confederation of States. If the States be parties, as States, what are their rights, and what their respective covenants and stipulations? and where are their rights, covenants, and stipulations expressed? In the Articles of Confederation they did make promises, and did enter into engagements, and did plight the faith of each State for their fulfillment; but in the Constitution there is nothing of that kind. The reason is that, in the Constitution, it is the people who speak and not the States. The people ordain the Constitution, and therein address themselves to the States and to the Legislatures of the States in the language of injunction and prohibition.

The author of such inconsistent ideas falls into the very error which he had just before so distinctly pointed out, in confounding the people of the States with their governments. In the vehemence of his hostility to State sovereignty, he seems—as all of his disciples seem—unable even to comprehend that it means the sovereignty, not of State governments, but of people who make them. With minds preoccupied by the unreal idea of one great people of a consolidated nation, these gentlemen are blinded to the plain and primary truth that the only way in which the people ordained the Constitution was as the people of STATES. When Mr. Webster says that "in the Constitution it is the people who speak, and not the States," he says what is untenable. The States *are* the people. The people do not speak, never have spoken, and never can speak, in their sovereign capacity (without a subversion of our whole system), otherwise than as the people of States.

There are but two modes of expressing their sovereign will known to the people of this country. One is by direct vote— the mode adopted by Rhode Island in 1788, when she rejected the Constitution. The other is the method, more generally pursued, of acting by means of conventions of delegates elected expressly as representatives of the sovereignty of the people. Now, it is not a matter of opinion or theory or speculation, but a plain, undeniable, historical *fact,* that there never has been any act or expression of sovereignty in either of these modes by that imaginary community, "the people of the United States in the aggregate." *Usurpations of power* by the *Government* of the United States, there may have been, and may be again, but there has never been either a sovereign convention or a direct vote of the "whole people" of the United States to demonstrate its existence as a corporate unit.

When the Articles of Confederation were amended, when the new Constitution was substituted in their place and the General Government reorganized, its structure was changed, additional powers were conferred upon it, and thereby subtracted from the powers theretofore exercised by the State governments; but the seat of sovereignty—the source of all those delegated and dependent powers—was not disturbed. There was a new Government or an amended Government— it is entirely immaterial in which of these lights we consider it—but no new PEOPLE was created or constituted. No doubt, the States—the people of the States—if they had been so disposed, might have merged themselves into one great consolidated State, retaining their geographical boundaries merely as matters of convenience. But such a merger must have been distinctly and formally stated, not left to deduction or implication. The monstrous conception of the creation of a new people, invested with the whole or a great part of the sovereignty which had previously belonged to the people of each State, has not a syllable to sustain it in the Constitution, but is built up entirely upon the palpable misconstruction of a single expression in the preamble.

In denying that there is any such collective unit as the people of the United States in the aggregate, of course I am not to be understood as denying that there is such a political organization as the United States, or that there exists, with large and distinct powers, a *Government* of the United States; but it is claimed that the Union, as its name implies, is constituted of States. The Government of the United States derives its existence from the same source, and exercises its functions by the will of the same sovereignty that creates and confers authority upon the State governments. The people of each State are, in either case, the source. The only difference is that, in the creation of the State governments, each sovereign acted alone; in that of the Federal Government, they acted on coöperation with the others. Neither the whole nor any part of their sovereignty has been surrendered to either Government.

To have transferred sovereignty from the people to a Government would have been to have fought the battles of the Revolution in vain—not for the freedom and independence of the States, but for a mere change of masters.

Chapter 8

Sovereignty (continued)

IT HAS been said, in a foregoing chapter, that the authors of the Constitution could scarcely have anticipated the idea of such a community as the people of the United States in one mass. Perhaps this expression needs some little qualification, for there is rarely a fallacy, however stupendous, that is wholly original. A careful examination of the records of the Convention of 1787 exhibits one or perhaps two instances of such a suggestion—both by the same person—and the result in each case is strikingly significant.

The original proposition made concerning the office of President of the United States contemplated his election by the Congress, or, as it was termed by the proposer, "the national Legislature." On the 17th of July, this proposition being under consideration, Mr. Gouverneur Morris moved that the words "national Legislature" be stricken out, and "citizens of the United States" inserted. The proposition was supported by Mr. James Wilson—both of these gentlemen being among the most earnest advocates of centralism in the Convention.

Now, it is not at all certain that Mr. Morris had in view an election by the citizens of the United States "in the aggregate," voting as *one people*. The language of his proposition is entirely consistent with the idea of an election by the citizens of each State, voting separately and independently, though it is ambiguous, and may admit of the other construction. But this is immaterial. The proposition was submitted to a vote, and received the approval of only *one State*—Pennsylvania, of which Mr. Morris and Mr. Wilson were both representatives. *Nine* States voted against it.*

Six days afterward in a discussion of the proposed ratification of the Constitution by Conventions of the people of each State, Mr. Gouverneur Morris—as we learn from Mr. Madison—"moved that the reference of . . . [the proposed Constitution] be made to one General Convention, chosen and authorized by the people, to consider, amend, and establish the same."

Here the issue seems to have been more distinctly made

between the two ideas of people of the States and one people in the aggregate. The fate of the latter is briefly recorded in the two words, "not seconded." Mr. Morris was a man of distinguished ability, great personal influence, and undoubted patriotism, but, out of all that assemblage there was not one to sustain him in the proposition to incorporate into the Constitution that theory which now predominates, the theory on which was waged the late bloody war, which was called a "war for the Union."

The extracts which have been given, from the writings and speeches of the framers of the Constitution and other statesmen of that period, afford ample proof of their almost unanimous accord with the principles which have been established on the authority of the Constitution itself, the acts of ratification by the several States, and other attestations of the highest authority and validity. No statesman of that day would have ventured to risk his reputation by construing an obligation to support the Constitution as an obligation to adhere to the Federal Government.

As to the features of centralism, or nationalism, which they did advocate, all the ability of this little minority of really gifted men failed to secure the incorporation of any one of them into the Constitution, or to obtain their recognition by any of the ratifying States. On the contrary, the very men who had been the leading advocates of such theories, on failing to secure their adoption, loyally accepted the result, and became the ablest and most efficient supporters of the principles which had prevailed. Thus, Mr. Hamilton, in the eighty-first number of the ["Federalist"] replying to apprehensions expressed by some that a State might be brought before the Federal courts to answer as defendant in suits instituted against her, repels the idea in plain and conclusive terms. The italics are my own:

It is inherent in the nature of *sovereignty* not to be amenable to the suit of any individual without its consent. This is the general sense and the general practice of mankind; and the exemption, as one of the *attributes of sovereignty,* is now enjoyed by the government of *every State in the Union.* Unless, therefore, there is *a surrender of this immunity* in the plan of the Convention, *it will remain with the States,* and the danger intimated must be merely ideal. . . . The contracts between *a nation* and individuals are only binding on the conscience of *the sovereign,* and have no pretensions to a compulsive force. They confer no right of action, independent of *the sovereign will.* To what purpose would it be to authorize suits against States for the debts they owe? How could recoveries be enforced? It is evident that it could not be done without *waging war* against the contracting State; and to ascribe to the Federal courts, by mere implication, and in destruction of a preëxisting right of the State governments, a power which would involve such a consequence, would be altogether forced and unwarranted.

In a subsequent number, Mr. Hamilton, replying to the objection that the Constitution contains no bill or declaration of rights, argues that it was entirely unnecessary, because in reality "the people *surrender nothing;* and, as they *retain everything,* they have no need of particular reservations." And again: "I go further, and affirm that bills of rights, in the sense and to the extent they are contended for, are not only unnecessary in the proposed Constitution, but would be absolutely dangerous. They would contain various exceptions to *powers not granted,* and on this very account would afford a colorable pretext to claim more than were granted. For why declare that things shall not be done, which there is no power to do?"

Finally, in the concluding article of the "Federalist," he bears emphatic testimony to the same principles, in the remark that "every Constitution for the United States must inevitably consist of a great variety of particulars, in which *thirteen independent States* are to be accommodated in their interests or opinions of interest . . . Hence the necessity of molding and arranging all the particulars, which are to compose the whole, in such a manner as to satisfy *all the parties* to the compact."

Mr. Madison, in the Philadelphia Convention, had at first held views similar to those of Mr. Hamilton, though more moderate in extent. He, too, however, cordially conformed to the modifications in them made by his colleagues, and was no less zealous and eminent in defending and expounding the Constitution as finally adopted. The evidence of Hamilton and Madison—two of the most eminent of the authors of the Constitution, and the two preeminent contemporary expounders of its meaning—is the most valuable that could be offered for its interpretation. That of all the other statesmen of the period only tends to confirm the same conclusions. The illustrious WASHINGTON, in his correspondence, repeatedly refers to the proposed Union as a "Confederacy" of States, or a "confederated Government," and to the several States as "acceding," or signifying their "accession," to it, in ratifying the Constitution. In a letter written to Benjamin Lincoln, October 26, 1788, he [says], "Whoever shall be found to enjoy the confidence of *the* States so far as to be elected Vice-President," etc.—showing that in the "confederated Government," as he termed it, the States were still to act independently, even in the selection of officers of the General Government. June 28, 1788, he wrote to General Pinckney that New Hampshire "had acceded to the new Confederacy," and, in reference to North Carolina, "I should be astonished if that State should withdraw from the Union."

I shall add but two other citations. They are from speeches of John Marshall, afterward the most distinguished Chief Justice of the United States—who has certainly never been regarded as holding high views of State rights—in the Virginia Convention of 1788. Speaking of the power of the States over the militia:

The State governments did not derive their powers from the General Government; but each government derived its powers from the people, and each was to act according to the powers given it. Would any gentleman deny this? . . . Could any man say that this power was not retained by the States, as they had not given it away? For does not a power remain till it is given away? The State Legislatures had power to command and govern their militia before, and have it still, undeniably, unless there be something in this Constitution that takes it away. . . .

With regard to the power of the Federal judiciary, Mr. Marshall said: "I hope that no gentleman will think that a State can be called at the bar of the Federal court. Is it rational to suppose that the SOVEREIGN POWER shall be dragged before a court?" Authorities to the same effect might be multiplied indefinitely by quotation from nearly all the most eminent statesmen and patriots of that brilliant period.

The principles which have been set forth in the foregoing chapters, although they had come to be considered as peculiarly Southern, were not sectional in their origin. In the beginning and earlier years of our history they were cherished as faithfully and guarded as jealously in Massachusetts and New Hampshire as in Virginia or South Carolina. It was in these principles that I was nurtured. I have frankly proclaimed them during my whole life, always contending against what I believed to be the mistaken construction of the Constitution taught by Mr. Webster and his adherents.

It is satisfactory to know that in the closing year of his life, when looking retrospectively, with judgment undisturbed by any extraneous influence, he uttered views of the Government which are founded on the rock of truth. In his speech at Capon Springs, Virginia, in 1851, he says:

How absurd it is to suppose that, when different parties enter into a compact for certain purposes, either can disregard any one provision, and expect, nevertheless, the other to observe the rest! . . .

I have not hesitated to say, and I repeat, that, if the Northern States refuse, willfully and deliberately, to carry into effect that part of the Constitution which respects the restoration of fugitive slaves, and Congress provides no remedy, the South would no longer be bound to observe the compact. A bargain can not be broken on one side, and still bind the other side.

Chapter 9

The Right of Secession

THE RIGHT OF SECESSION—that subject which, beyond all others, ignorance, prejudice, and political rancor have combined to cloud with misstatements and misapprehensions—is a question easily to be determined in the light of what has already been established with regard to the history and principles of the Constitution. So far from being against the Constitution or incompatible with it, we contend that, if the right to secede is not prohibited to the States, and no power to prevent it expressly delegated to the United States, it remains as reserved to the States or the people, from whom all the powers of the General Government were derived.

We have seen that a number of States, during the war of the Revolution, entered into a partnership with one another, which was not only unlimited in duration, but expressly declared to be a "perpetual union." Yet, when that Union failed to accomplish the purposes for which it was formed, the parties withdrew, separately and independently, one after another, without any question made of their right to do so, and formed a new association. One of the declared objects of this new partnership was to form "a more perfect union." This certainly did not mean more perfect in respect of duration; for the former union had been declared perpetual, and perpetuity admits of no addition. It did not mean that it was to be more indissoluble; for the delegates of the States, in ratifying the former compact of union, had expressed themselves in terms that could scarcely be made more stringent.

The formation of a "more perfect union" was accomplished by the organization of a government more complete in its various branches, legislative, executive, and judicial, and by the delegation to this Government of certain additional powers or functions which had previously been exercised by the Governments of the respective States. There was no abandonment nor modification of the essential principle of a *compact* between sovereigns, which applied to the one case as fully as to the other. The additional powers conferred upon the Federal Government by the Constitution were merely transfers of some of those possessed by the State governments—not subtractions from the reserved and inalienable sovereignty of the political communities which conferred them. It was an amended Union, not a consolidation.

It is a remarkable fact that the very powers of the Federal Government and prohibitions to the States, which are most relied upon by the advocates of centralism as incompatible with State sovereignty, were in force under the old Confederation when the sovereignty of the States was expressly recognized. The exercise of these powers was prohibited to the States under the old compact, "without the consent of the United States in Congress assembled," but no one has claimed that the Confederation had thereby acquired sovereignty.

Entirely in accord with these truths are the arguments of Mr. Madison in the "Federalist," to show that the great principles of the Constitution are substantially the same as those of the Articles of Confederation. He says:

I ask, What are these principles? Do they require that, in the establishment of the Constitution, the States should be regarded as distinct and independent sovereigns? They *are* so regarded by the Constitution proposed. . . . Do these principles, in fine, require that the powers of the General Government should be limited, and that, beyond this limit, the States should be left in possession of their sovereignty and independence? We have seen that, in the new Government as in the old, the general powers are limited; and that the States, in all unenumerated cases, are left in the enjoyment of their sovereign and independent jurisdiction.

"The truth is," he adds, "that the great principles of the Constitution proposed by the Convention may be considered *less as absolutely new, than as the expansion of principles which are found in the Articles of Confederation.*" The present Union owes its very existence to the dissolution, by separate secession of its members, of the former Union, which, as we have thus seen, as to its *organic principles,* rested upon precisely the same foundation. The right to withdraw from the association results, in either case, from the same principles—principles which, I think, have been established on an impregnable basis of history, reason, law, and precedent. The pertinent question that occurs is, Why was so obvious an attribute of sovereignty not expressly renounced if it was intended to surrender it? It certainly existed; it was not surrendered; therefore it still exists. This would be a more natural and rational conclusion than that it has ceased to exist because it is not mentioned.

The simple truth is, that it would have been a very extraordinary thing to incorporate into the Constitution any expess provision for the secession of the States and dissolution of the Union. Its founders undoubtedly desired and hoped that it would be perpetual; against the proposition for power to coerce a State, the argument was that it would be a means, not of preserving, but of destroying, the Union. It was not for them to make arrangements for its termination—a calamity which there was no occasion to provide for in advance. Sufficient for their day was the evil thereof. It was not necessary in the Constitution to affirm the right of secession, because it was an attribute of sovereignty, and the States had reserved all which they had not delegated.

The right of the people of the several States to resume the powers delegated by them to the common agency, was not left without positive and ample assertion, even at a period when it had never been denied. The ratification of the Constitution by Virginia has already been quoted, in which the people of that State, through their Convention, did expressly "declare and make known that the powers granted under the Constitution, being derived from the people of the United States, *may be resumed by them,* whensoever the same shall be perverted to their injury or oppression . . . ." New York and Rhode Island were no less explicit.

These expressions are not mere *obiter dicta.* They are parts of the very acts or ordinances by which these States ratified the Constitution and acceded to the Union. If they are invalid, the ratification itself was invalid, for they are inseparable. By inserting these declarations in their ordinances, Virginia, New York, and Rhode Island, formally, officially, and permanently, declared their interpretation of the Constitution as recognizing the right of secession by the resumption of their grants. By accepting the ratifications with this declaration incorporated, the other States as formally accepted the principle which it asserted.

As there be those who see danger to the perpetuity of the Union in the possession of reserved power by the States, and insist that our fathers did not intend to bind the States together by a compact no better than "a rope of sand," it may be well to examine their position. From what have dangers to the Union arisen? Have they sprung from too great restriction on the exercise of the granted powers, or from the assumption by the General Government of power claimed by implication? The whole record of our Union answers, from the latter only.

Chapter 10

Coercion and the Nature of Allegiance

THE ALTERNATIVE to secession is coercion. That is to say, if no such right as that of secession exists, then it is a wrong; and, by a well settled principle of public law, for every wrong there must be a remedy, which in this case must be the application of force to the State attempting to withdraw from the Union.

Early in the session of the Convention which formed the Constitution, it was proposed to confer upon Congress the power "to call forth the force of the Union against any member of the Union failing to fulfill its duty under the articles thereof." When this proposition came to be considered, Mr. Madison observed that a "union of the States containing such an ingredient seemed to provide for its own destruction. The use of force against a State would look more like a declaration of war than an infliction of punishment, and would probably be considered by the party attacked as a dissolution of all previous compacts by which it might be bound. He moved that the clause be postponed." This motion was adopted *nem. con.*, and the proposition was never again revived. Again, on a subsequent occasion, speaking of an appeal to force, Mr. Madison said: "Was such a remedy eligible? Was it practicable? . . . Any government for the United States, formed on the supposed practicability of using force against the unconstitutional proceedings of the States, would prove as visionary and fallacious as the government of Congress." Every proposition looking in any way to the same or a similar object was promptly rejected by the convention. George Mason, of Virginia, said of such a proposition: "Will not the citizens of the invaded State assist one another, until they rise as one man and shake off the Union altogether?"

Unhappily, our generation has seen that, in the decay of the principles and feelings which animated the hearts of all patriots in that day, this thing has been only too feasible, and that States have permitted themselves to be used as instruments, not merely for the coercion, but for the destruction of the freedom and independence of their sister States.

Edmund Randolph, Governor of Virginia, although the mover of the original proposition to authorize the employment of the forces of the Union against a delinquent member, which had been so signally defeated in the Federal Convention, afterward, in the Virginia Convention, made an eloquent protest against the idea of the employment of force against a State. "What species of military coercion," said he, "could the General Government adopt for the enforcement of obedience to its demands? Either an army sent into the heart of a delinquent State, or blocking up its ports. Have we lived to this, then, that, in order to suppress and exclude tyranny, it is necessary to render the most affectionate friends the most bitter enemies, set the father against the son, and make the brother slay the brother? Is this the happy expedient that is to preserve liberty? Will it not destroy it? If an army be once marched into Virginia, figure to yourselves what the dreadful consequence will be: the most lamentable civil war must ensue."

We have seen already how vehemently the idea of even *judicial* coercion was repudiated by Hamilton, Marshall, and others. The suggestion of *military* coercion was uniformly treated, as in the above extracts, with still more abhorrence. No principle was more fully and firmly settled on the highest authority than that, under our system, there could be no coercion of a State.

Mr. Webster, in his elaborate speech of February 16, 1833, arguing throughout against the sovereignty of the States, and in the course of his argument sadly confounding the ideas of the Federal Constitution and the Federal Government, as he confounds the sovereign people of the States with the State governments, says: "The States *can not* omit to appoint Senators and electors. It is not a matter resting in State discretion or State pleasure. . . . No member of a State Legislature can refuse to proceed, at the proper time, to elect Senators to Congress, or to provide for the choice of electors of President and Vice-President, any more than the members can refuse, when the appointed day arrives, to meet the members of the other House, to count the votes for those officers and ascertain who are chosen." Mr. Hamilton, on the contrary, fresh from the work of forming the Constitution, and familiar with its principles and purposes, said: "It is certainly true that the State Legislatures, by forbearing the appointment of Senators, may destroy the national Government."

It is unnecessary to discuss the particular question on which these two great authorities are thus directly at issue. I do not contend that the State Legislature, of their own will, have a right to forego the performance of any Federal duty imposed upon them by the Constitution. But there is a power beyond and above that of either the Federal or State governments— the power of the people of the State. At the behest of this power, it certainly becomes not only the right, but the duty, of their State Legislature to refrain from any action implying adherence to the Union, or partnership, from which the sovereign has withdrawn.

It is sometimes said that, whatever weight may attach to principles founded on the sovereignty and independence of the original thirteen States, they can not apply to the States of more recent origin—constituting now a majority of the members of the Union—because these are but the offspring or creatures of the Union, and must of course be subordinate and dependent.

This objection would scarcely occur to any instructed mind, though it may possess a certain degree of specious plausibility for the untaught. It is enough to answer that the entire equality of the States, in every particular, is a vital condition of their union. Every new member that has been admitted into the partnership of States came in, as is expressly declared in the acts for their admission, on a footing of perfect equality in every respect with the original members. This equality is as complete as the equality, before the laws, of the son with the father, immediately on the attainment by the former of his legal majority, without regard to the prior condition of dependence and tutelage.

But, with regard to States formed of territory acquired by purchase from France, Spain, and Mexico, it is claimed that, as they were bought by the United States, they belong to the same, and have no right to withdraw at will from an association the property which had been purchased by the other parties.

As for the sordid claim of ownership of States, on account of the money spent for the land which they contain—I can understand the ground of a claim to some interest in the soil, so long as it continues to be public property, but have yet to learn in what way the United States ever became purchaser of the *inhabitants* or of their political rights.

The treaty by which the Louisiana territory was ceded to the United States expressly provided that the inhabitants thereof should be "admitted, as soon as possible, according to the principles of the Federal Constitution, to the enjoyment of all the rights, advantages, and immunities of citizens of the United States." In all other acquisitions of territory the same stipulation is either expressed or implied. Indeed, the denial of the right would be inconsistent with the character of American political institutions.

Another objection made to the right of secession is based upon obscure, indefinite, and inconsistent ideas with regard to *allegiance*. It may be stated thus: that the citizen owes a double allegiance, or a divided allegiance—partly to his State, partly to the United States: that the State can no more release him from his obligations to the Union than the United States can absolve him from his duties to his State. This is the most moderate way in which the objection is put. The extreme centralizers go further, and claim that allegiance to the Union, or, as they generally express it, to *the Government* is paramount, and the obligation to the State only subsidiary—if, indeed, it exists at all.

This latter view, if the more monstrous, is at least the more consistent of the two, for it does not involve the difficulty of a divided allegiance, nor the paradoxical position in which the other places the citizen, in case of a conflict between his State and the other members of the Union, of being necessarily a rebel against the General Government or a traitor to the State of which he is a citizen.

As to *true* allegiance, in the light of the principles which have been established, there can be no doubt with regard to it. The primary, paramount allegiance of the citizen is due to the sovereign only. That sovereign, under our system, is the people—the people of the State to which he belongs. If the sovereign abolishes the State government and ordains and establishes a new one, the obligation of allegiance requires him to transfer his obedience accordingly. If the sovereign withdraws from association with it confederates in the Union, the allegiance of the citizen requires him to follow the sovereign. Any other course is rebellion or treason. His relation to the Union arose from the membership of the State of which he was a citizen, and ceased whenever his State withdrew from it.

Every officer of both Federal and State governments is required to take an oath to support the Constitution, a compact the binding force of which is based upon the sovereignty of all the States. Every such officer is, therefore, virtually sworn to maintain and support the sovereignty of all the States. A little consideration of these plain and irrefutable truths would show how utterly unworthy and false are the vulgar taunts which attribute "treason" to those who, in the late secession of the Southern States, were loyal to the only sovereign entitled to their allegiance, and which still more absurdly prate of the violation of oaths to support *"the Government,"* an oath which nobody ever could have been legally required to take, and which must have been ignorantly confounded with the prescribed oath to support the Constitution.

Nullification and secession are often erroneously treated as if they were one and the same thing. It is true that both ideas spring from the sovereign right of a State to interpose for the protection of its own people, but they are altogether unlike as to both their extent and the character of the means to be employed. The first was a temporary expedient, intended to restrain action until the question at issue could be submitted to a convention of the States. It was a remedy which its supporters sought to apply within the Union; a means to avoid the last resort—separation. If the application for a convention should fail, or if the State making it should suffer an adverse decision, the advocates of that remedy have not revealed what they proposed as the next step—supposing the infraction of the compact to have been of that character which, according to Mr. Webster, dissolved it.

Secession, on the other hand, was the assertion of the inalienable right of a people to change their government, whenever it ceased to fulfill the purposes for which it was ordained and established. Under our form of government, and the cardinal principles upon which it was founded, it should have been a peaceful remedy. The withdrawal of a State from a league has no revolutionary or insurrectionary characteristic. The government of the State remains unchanged as to all internal affairs. It is only its external or confederate relations that are altered. To term this action of a sovereign a "rebellion," is a gross abuse of language. So is the flippant phrase which speaks of it as an appeal to the "arbitrament of the sword." In the late contest, in particular, there was no appeal by the seceding States to the arbitrament of arms. They stood in an attitude of self-defense, and were attacked for merely exercising a right guaranteed by the original terms of the compact. They neither tendered nor accepted any challenge to the wager of battle. The man who defends his house against attack can not with any propriety be said to have submitted the question of his right to it to the arbitrament of arms.

Two moral obligations or restrictions upon a seceding State certainly exist: in the first place, not to break up the partnership without good and sufficient cause; and, in the second, to make an equitable settlement with former associates, and, as far as may be, to avoid the infliction of loss or damage upon any of them. Neither of these obligations was violated or neglected by the Southern States in their secession.

Chapter 11

State Interposition

FROM THE EARLIEST period, it was foreseen by the wisest of our statesmen that a danger to the perpetuity of the Union would arise from the conflicting interests of different sections, and every effort was made to secure each of these classes of interests against aggression by the other. As a proof of this, may be cited the following extract from Mr. Madison's report of a speech made by himself in the Philadelphia Convention on the 30th of June, 1787:

> He admitted that every peculiar interest, whether in any class of citizens or any description of States, ought to be secured as far as possible. Wherever there is danger of attack, there ought to be given a constitutional power of defense. But he contended that the States were divided into different interests, not by their difference of size, but by other circumstances; the most material of which resulted from climate, but principally from the effects of their having or not having slaves. These two causes concurred in forming the great division of interests in the United States. It did not lie between the large and small States; it lay between the Northern and Southern; and, if any defensive power were necessary, it ought to be mutually given to these two interests.

The wise men who formed the Constitution endeavored to prevent the conflicts inevitable from the ascendancy of a sectional or party majority, by so distributing the powers of government that each interest might hold a check upon the other. It was believed that the compromises made with regard to representation would have the effect of giving at an early period a majority in the House of Representatives to the South, while the North would retain the ascendancy in the Senate. Thus it was supposed that the two great sectional interests would be enabled to restrain each other within the limits of purposes and action beneficial to both.

Not at all incompatible with these views and purposes was the recognition of the right of the States to reassume, if occasion should require it, the powers which they had delegated. On the contrary, the maintenance of this right was the surest guarantee of the perpetuity of the Union, and the denial of it sounded the first serious note of its dissolution. The conservative efficiency of *"State interposition,"* for maintenance of the essential principles of the Union against aggression or decadence, is one of the most conspicuous features in the debates of the various State Conventions by which the Constitution was ratified. But for a firm reliance upon it, as a sure resort in case of need, it may safely be said that the Union would never have been formed.

At an early period in the history of the Federal Government, the States of Kentucky and Virginia found reason to reassert this right of state interposition. In the first of the famous resolutions drawn by Mr. Jefferson in 1798, and with some modification adopted by the Legislature of Kentucky in November of that year, it is declared that, "whensoever the General Government assumes undelegated powers, its acts are *unauthoritative, void, and of no force;* that to this compact each State acceded as a State, and is an integral party; that this Government, created by this compact, was not made the exclusive or final judge of the extent of the powers delegated to itself . . . but that . . . *each party has an equal right to judge for itself, as well of infractions as of the mode and measure of redress."*

These, it is true, were only the resolves of two States, and they were dissented from by several other State Legislatures—not so much on the ground of opposition to the general principles asserted as on that of their being unnecessary in their application to the alien and sedition laws, which were the immediate occasion of their utterance.

At a critical and memorable period, the great statesman of South Carolina [John C. Calhoun] invoked this remedy of State interposition against the Tariff Act of 1828, which was deemed injurious and oppressive to his State. There remained at that day enough of the spirit in which the Union had been founded—enough of respect for the sovereignty of States and of regard for the limitations of the Constitution—to prevent a conflict of arms. The compromise of 1833 was adopted, which South Carolina agreed to accept, the principle for which she contended being virtually conceded.

Meantime there had been no lack, as we have already seen, of assertions of the sovereign rights of the States from other quarters. The declaration of these rights by the New England States and their representatives, on the acquisition of Louisiana in 1803, on the admission of the State of that name in 1811-'12, and on the question of the annexation of Texas in 1843-'45, have been referred to in another place.

To these stanch declarations of principles may be added the avowal of John Quincy Adams, in his discourse before the New York Historical Society, in 1839:

. . . If the day should ever come (may Heaven avert it!) when the affections of the people of these States shall be alienated from each other . . . or collision of interests shall fester into hatred, the bonds of political association will not long hold together parties no longer attracted by the magnetism of conciliated interests and kindly sympathies; and *far better will it be for the people of the disunited States to part in friendship with each other than to be held together by constraint.* Then will be the time for reverting to the precedents which occurred at the formation and adoption of the Constitution, to form again a *more perfect Union, by dissolving that which could no longer bind,* and to leave the separated parts to be reunited by the law of political gravitation to the center.

PART THREE

SECESSION AND CONFEDERATION

Chapter 1

Personal Motives and Popular Feelings

WITH THE FAILURE of the Senate Committee of Thirteen to come to any agreement, the last reasonable hope of a pacific settlement of difficulties within the Union was extinguished in the minds of those most reluctant to abandon the effort. The year 1861 opened, as we have seen, upon the spectacle of a general belief, among the people of the planting States, in the necessity of an early secession, as the only possible alternative left them.

It has already been shown that the calmness and deliberation, with which the measures requisite for withdrawal were adopted and executed, afford the best refutation of the charge that they were the result of haste, passion, or precipitation. Still more contrary to truth is the assertion, so often recklessly made and reiterated, that the people of the South were led into secession, against their will and their better judgment, by a few ambitious and discontented politicians.

The truth is, that the Southern people were in advance of their representatives throughout, and that these latter were not agitators or leaders in the popular movement. They were in harmony with its great principles, but their influence, with very few exceptions, was exerted to restrain rather than to accelerate their application, and to allay rather than to stimulate excitement. In that last session of the last Congress that preceded the disruption, Southern Senators, of the class generally considered extremists, served on a committee of pacification, and strove earnestly to promote its objects. Failing in this, they still exerted themselves to prevent the commission of any act that might result in bloodshed.

It is enough to say [for myself] that I always held, and

repeatedly avowed, the principle that a Senator in Congress occupied the position of an ambassador from the State which he represented to the Government of the United States, as well as in some sense a member of the Government; and that, in either capacity, it would be dishonorable to use his powers and privileges for the destruction or for the detriment of the Government to which he was accredited. Acting on this principle, as long as I held a seat in the Senate, my best efforts were directed to the maintenance of the Constitution, the Union resulting from it, and to make the General Government an effective agent of the States for its prescribed purpose. As soon as the paramount allegiance due to Mississippi forbade a continuance of these efforts, I withdrew from the position.

With regard to the forts, arsenals, etc., something more remains to be said. The authorities of the Southern States immediately after, and in some cases a few days before, their actual secession, took possession (in every instance without resistance or bloodshed) of forts, arsenals, custom-houses, and other public property within their respective limits. I do not propose at this time to consider the question of their right to do so; that may be more properly done hereafter. But it may not be out of place briefly to refer to the statement, often made, that the absence of troops from the military posts in the South, which enabled the States so quietly to take such possession, was the result of collusion and prearrangement between the Southern leaders and the Federal Secretary of War, John B. Floyd, of Virginia. It is a sufficient answer to this allegation to state the fact that the absence of troops from these posts, instead of being exceptional, was, and still is, their ordinary condition in time of peace. At the very moment when these sentences are being written (in 1880), although the army of the United States is twice as large as in 1860; although four years of internal war and a yet longer period of subsequent military occupation of the South have habituated the public to the presence of troops in their midst, to an extent that would formerly have been startling if not offensive; although allegations of continued disaffection on the part of the Southern people have been persistently reiterated, for party purposes—yet it is believed that the forts and arsenals in the States of the Gulf are in as defenseless a condition, and as liable to quiet seizure (if any such purpose existed), as in the beginning of the year 1861. During the anxious period of uncertainty and apprehension which ensued [after the possession of public property], the efforts of the Southern Senators in Washington were employed to dissuade (they could not *command*) from any aggressive movement, however justifiable, that might lead to collision. It is believed that by such influence alone a collision was averted; and it is certain that its exercise gave great dissatisfaction at the time to some of the ardent advocates of more active measures. It may be that *they* were right, and that we, who counseled delay and forbearance, were wrong. Certainly, if we could have foreseen the ultimate failure of all efforts for a peaceful settlement, and the perfidy that was afterward to be practiced in connection with them, our advice would have been different.

Certain resolutions, said to have been adopted in a meeting of Senators held on the evening of the 5th of January, have been magnified, by the representations of artful commentators on the events of the period, into something vastly momentous.

The significance of these resolutions was the admission that we could not longer advise delay, and even that was unimportant under the circumstances, for three of the States concerned had taken final action on the subject before the resolutions could have been communicated to them. They recommended the formulation of a confederacy among the seceding States as early as possible after their secession.

It will not be amiss here briefly to state what were my position and feelings at the period now under consideration, as they have been the subject of gross and widespread misrepresentation. It is not only untrue, but absurd, to attribute to me motives of personal ambition to be gratified by a dismemberment of the Union. Much of my life had been spent in the military and civil service of the United States. Whatever reputation I had acquired was identified with their history; and, if future preferment had been the object, it would have led me to cling to the Union as long as a shred of it should remain. If any, judging after the event, should assume that I was allured by the high office subsequently conferred upon me by the people of the Confederate States, the answer to any such conclusion has been made by others, to whom it was well known, before the Confederacy was formed, that I had no desire to be its President. When the suggestion was made to me, I expressed a decided objection, and gave reasons of a public and permanent character against being placed in that position.

Furthermore, I then held the office of United States Senator from Mississippi—one which I preferred to all others. The kindness of the people had three times conferred it upon me, and I had no reason to fear that it would not be given again, as often as desired. So far from wishing to change this position for any other, I had specially requested my friends (some of whom had thought of putting me in nomination for the Presidency of the United States in 1860) not to permit "my name to be used before the Convention for any nomination whatever."

I had been so near the office for four years, while in the Cabinet of Mr. Pierce, that I saw it from behind the scenes, and it was to me an office in no wise desirable. The responsibilities were great; the labor, the vexations, the disappointments, were greater. Those who have intimately known the official and personal life of our Presidents can not fail to remember how few have left the office as happy men as when they entered it.

Chapter 2

Secession of South Carolina;
Garrisoning of Fort Sumter

ON THE SECESSION of South Carolina [December 20, 1860], the condition of the defenses of Charleston Harbor became a subject of anxiety with all parties. Of the three forts in or at the entrance of the harbor, two were unoccupied, but the third (Fort Moultrie) was held by a garrison of but little more than one hundred men under command of Major Robert Anderson, of the First Artillery.

About twelve days before the secession of South Carolina, the representatives in Congress from that State had called on the President to assure him, in anticipation of the secession of the State, that no purpose was entertained by South Carolina to attack, or in any way molest, the forts held by the United States in the harbor of Charleston—at least until opportunity could be had for an amicable settlement of all questions that might arise with regard to these forts and other public property—provided that no reënforcements should be sent, and the military *status* should be permitted to remain unchanged. The South Carolinians understood Mr. Buchanan as approving of this suggestion, although declining to make any formal pledge.

It appears, nevertheless, from subsequent developments, that both before and after the secession of South Carolina preparations were secretly made for reënforcing Major Anderson, in case it should be deemed necessary by the Government at Washington. On the 11th of December instructions were communicated to him, from the War Department, of which the following is the essential part:

You are carefully to avoid every act which would needlessly tend to provoke aggression . . . but you are to hold possession of the forts in this harbor, and, if attacked, you are to defend yourself to the last extremity. The smallness of your force will not permit you, perhaps, to occupy more than one of the three forts, but an attack on, or attempt to take possession of either of them, will be regarded as an act of hostility, and you may then put your command into either of them which you may deem most proper to increase its power of resistance. You are also authorized to take similar defensive steps, whenever you have tangible evidence of a design to proceed to a hostile act.

Immediately after the secession of the State, the Convention of South Carolina deputed three distinguished citizens of that State to proceed to Washington, "to treat with the Government of the United States for the delivery of the forts, magazines, lighthouses, and other real estate, with their appurtenances, within the limits of South Carolina, and also for an apportionment of the public debt, and for a division of all other property held by the Government of the United States, as agent of the confederated States, of which South Carolina was recently a member; and generally to negotiate . . . for the continuance of peace and amity between this Commonwealth and the Government at Washington."

The Commissioners arrived in Washington on the 26th of December. Before they could communicate with the President, however—indeed, on the morning after their arrival—they were startled, and the whole country electrified, by the news that, during the previous night, Major Anderson had "secretly dismantled Fort Moultrie," and removed his command to Fort Sumter, which occupied a more commanding position in the harbor. This movement changed the whole aspect of affairs. It was considered by the Government and people of South Carolina as a violation of the implied pledge of a maintenance of the *status quo;* the remaining forts and other public property were at once taken possession of by the State; and the condition of public feeling became greatly exacerbated. An interview between the President and the Commissioners was followed by a sharp correspondence, which was terminated on the 1st of January, 1861, by the return to the Commissioners of their final communication, with an endorsement stating that it was of such a character that the President declined to receive it. The negotiations were thus abruptly broken off.

The kind relations which had long existed between Mr. Buchanan and myself, had led him, occasionally, to send for me to confer with him on subjects that caused him anxiety, and warranted me in sometimes calling upon him to offer my opinion on matters of special interest or importance. After the removal of the garrison to the stronger and safer position of Fort Sumter, I called upon him again to represent, from my knowledge of the people and the circumstances of the case, how productive the movement would be of discontent, and how likely to lead to collision. One of the vexed questions of the day was, by what authority the collector of the port should be appointed, and the rumor was, that instructions had been given to the commanding officer at Fort Sumter not to allow vessels to pass, unless under clearance from the United States collector. It was easy to understand that, if a vessel were fired upon under such circumstances, it would be accepted as the beginning of hostilities—a result which both he and I desired to avert, as the greatest calamity that could be foreseen or imagined. My opinion was, that the wisest and best course would be to withdraw the garrison altogether from the harbor of Charleston.

The President's objection to this was, that it was his bounden duty to preserve and protect the property of the United States. To this I replied that I would pledge my life that, if an inventory were taken of all the stores and munitions in the fort, and an ordnance-sergeant with a few men left in charge of them, they would not be disturbed. As a further guarantee, I offered to obtain from the Governor of South Carolina full assurance that, in case any marauders should attempt to disturb the property, he would send an adequate guard to protect it.

The President promised me to reflect upon this proposition, and to confer with his Cabinet upon the propriety of adopting it. The result was not communicated to me, but the events which followed proved that the suggestion was not accepted.

Major Anderson, who commanded the garrison, had many ties and associations that bound him to the South. He performed his part like the true soldier that he was; but that it was most painful to him to be charged with the duty of holding the fort as a threat to the people of Charleston is a fact known to many others as well as to myself.

In comparing the past and the present one is profoundly and painfully impressed by the extent to which public opinion has drifted from the landmarks set up by the patriots who formed the Union, and observed by those who administered its government down to the time when war between the States was inaugurated. Mr. Buchanan, the last President of the old school, would as soon have thought of aiding in the establishment of a monarchy among us as of accepting the doctrine of coercing the States into submission to the will of a majority. He yielded a ready assent to the proposition that the cession of a site for a fort lapses, whenever that fort should be employed against the State by which the cession was made, on the familiar principle that any grant for a specific purpose expires when it ceases to be used for that purpose. Whether on this or any other ground, if the garrison of Fort Sumter had been withdrawn in accordance with the spirit of the Constitution, the honor of the United States Government would have been maintained intact, and nothing could have operated more powerfully to quiet the apprehensions and allay the resentment of the people of South Carolina. The influence which such a measure would have exerted upon the States which had not yet seceded, but were then contemplating the adoption of that extreme remedy, would probably have induced further delay; and the mellowing effect of time, with a realization of the dangers to be incurred, might have wrought mutual forbearance.

The ill-advised attempt secretly to throw reënforcements and provisions into Fort Sumter, by means of the steamer Star of the West, resulted in the repulsion of that vessel at the mouth of the harbor, by the authorities of South Carolina, on the morning of the 9th of January. I drove immediately to the Executive mansion, and for the last time appealed to the President to take prompt measures to avert the impending calamity. The result was even more unsatisfactory than that of former efforts had been.

On the same day the special message of the President on the state of the Union was submitted to Congress. This message was accompanied by the *first* letter of the South Carolina Commissioners to the President, with his answer, but of course *not* by their rejoinder, which he had declined to receive.

From the history of Fort Sumter during the remaining period, until the organization of the Confederate Government, it will be seen that the authorities of South Carolina still continued to refrain from any act of aggression or retaliation, under the provocation of the secret attempt to reënforce the garrison, as they had previously under that of its nocturnal transfer from one fort to another.

Another Commissioner (the Hon. I. W. Hayne) was sent to Washington by the Governor of South Carolina, to effect, if possible, an amicable and peaceful transfer of the fort, and settlement of all questions relating to property. This Commissioner remained for nearly a month, endeavoring to accomplish the objects of his mission, but was met only by evasive and unsatisfactory answers, and eventually returned without having effected anything.

There is one passage in the last letter of Colonel Hayne to the President which presents the case of the occupancy of Fort Sumter by the United States troops so clearly and forcibly that it may be proper to quote it:

You say that the fort was garrisoned for our protection, and is held for the same purposes for which it has been ever held since its construction. Are you not aware, that to hold, in the territory of a foreign power, a fortress against her will, avowedly for the purpose of protecting her citizens, is perhaps the highest insult which one government can offer to another? But Fort Sumter was never garrisoned at all until South Carolina had dissolved her connection with your Government. This garrison entered it in the night, with every circumstance of secrecy, after spiking the guns and burning the gun-carriages and cutting down the flag-staff of an adjacent fort, which was then abandoned. South Carolina had not taken Fort Sumter into her own possession, only because of her misplaced confidence in a Government which deceived her.

Thus, during the remainder of Mr. Buchanan's Administration, matters went rapidly from bad to worse. The old statesman, who had, in his earlier career looked steadily to the Constitution, as the mariner looks to the compass, for guidance—retired to private life at the expiration of his term of office, having effected nothing to allay the storm which had been steadily gathering during his administration.

Timid vacillation was then succeeded by unscrupulous cunning; and, for futile efforts, without hostile collision, to impose a claim of authority upon people who repudiated it, were substituted measures which could be sustained only by force.

Chapter 3

Secession of Other States

MISSISSIPPI was the second State to withdraw from the Union, seceded on the 9th of January, 1861. She was quickly followed by Florida on the 10th, Alabama on the 11th, and, in the course of the same month, by Georgia on the 18th, and Louisiana on the 26th. The Conventions of these States (together with that of South Carolina) agreed in designating Montgomery, Alabama, as the place, and the 4th of February as the day, for the assembling of a congress of the seceding States, to which each State Convention appointed delegates.

Telegraphic intelligence of the secession of Mississippi had reached Washington some considerable time before the fact was officially communicated to me. This official knowledge I considered it proper to await before taking formal leave of the Senate. My associates from Alabama and Florida concurred in this view. Accordingly, having received notification of the secession of these three States about the same time, on the 21st of January Messrs. Yulee and Mallory, of Florida, Fitzpatrick and Clay, of Alabama, and myself, announced the withdrawal of the States from which we were respectively accredited, and took leave of the Senate at the same time.

In the action which she then took, Mississippi certainly had no purpose to levy war against the United States, or any of them. As her Senator, I endeavored plainly to state her position in remarks addressed to the Senate in taking leave of the body.

There are some who contend that we should have retained our seats and "fought for our rights in the Union." Could anything be less rational or less consistent than that a Senator, an ambassador from his State, should insist upon representing it in a confederacy from which the State has withdrawn? What was meant by "fighting in the Union" I have never quite understood. If it be to retain a seat in Congress for the purpose of crippling the Government and rendering it unable to perform its functions, I can certainly not appreciate the idea of honor that sanctions the suggestion. Among the advantages claimed for this proposition by its supporters was that of thwarting the President in the appointment of his

Cabinet and other officers necessary for the administration of public affairs. Would this have been to maintain the Union formed by the States? Would such have been the Government which Washington recommended as a remedy for the defects of the original Confederation, the greatest of which was the paralysis of the action of the general agent by the opposition or indifference of the States? Sad as have been the consequences of the war which followed secession—disastrous in its moral, material, and political relations—still we have good cause to feel proud that the course of the Southern States has left no blot nor stain upon the honor and chivalry of their people.

Chapter 4

Good Faith in the South

DURING THE INTERVAL between the announcement by telegraph of the secession of Mississippi and the receipt of the official notification which enabled me to withdraw from the Senate, rumors were in circulation of a purpose, on the part of the United States Government, to arrest members of Congress preparing to leave Washington on account of the secession of the States which they represented. This threat received little attention from those most concerned. Indeed, it was thought that it might not be an undesirable mode of testing the question of the right of a State to withdraw from the Union.

No attempt, however, was made to arrest any of the retiring members; and, after a delay of a few days in necessary preparations, I left Washington for Mississippi, passing through southwestern Virginia, East Tennessee, a small part of Georgia, and north Alabama. A deep interest in the events which had recently occurred was exhibited by the people of these States, and much anxiety was indicated as to the future. Many years of agitation had made them familiar with the idea of separation. Nearly two generations had risen to manhood since it had begun to be discussed as a possible alternative. Few, very few, of the Southern people had ever regarded it as otherwise than as a last resort for escape from evils more intolerable. It was a calamity, which, however threatened, they had still hoped might be averted, or indefinitely postponed, and they had regarded with contempt, rather than anger, the ravings of a party in the North, which denounced the Constitution and the Union, and persistently defamed their brethren of the South.

In the minds of many there was the not unreasonable hope that the secession of six Southern States—certainly soon to be followed by that of others—would so arouse the sober thought and better feeling of the Northern people as to compel their representatives to agree to a Convention of the States, and that such guarantees would be given as would secure to the South the domestic tranquillity and equality in the Union which were assured under the Federal compact.

122

There were others, and they the most numerous class, who considered that the separation would be final, but peaceful. For my own part, while believing that secession was a right, I had never believed that it would be permitted to be peaceably exercised. Very few in the South at that time agreed with me, and my answers to queries were, therefore, unwelcome.

On my arrival at Jackson, the capital of Mississippi, I found that the Convention of the State had made provision for a State army, and had appointed me to the command, with the rank of major-general. After the preparation of the necessary rules and regulations, the division of the State into districts, the apportionment among them of the troops to be raised, and the appointment of officers of the general staff, such measures as were practicable were taken to obtain the necessary arms. The State had few serviceable weapons, and no establishment for their manufacture or repair. This fact (which is true of other Southern States as of Mississippi) is a clear proof of the absence of any desire or expectation of war. If the purpose of the Northern States to make war upon us because of secession had been foreseen, preparation to meet the consequences would have been contemporaneous with the adoption of a resort to that remedy—a remedy the possibility of which had for many years been contemplated. Had the Southern States possessed arsenals, and collected in them the requisite supplies of arms and munitions, such preparation would not only have placed them more nearly on an equality with the North in the beginning of the war, but might, perhaps, have been the best conservator of peace.

It is a satisfaction to know that the calamities which have befallen the Southern States were the result of their credulous reliance on the power of the Constitution, that, if it failed to protect their rights, it would at least suffice to prevent an attempt at coercion, if, in the last resort, they peacefully withdrew from the Union.

Chapter 5

Provisional Congress, Election, and Cabinet

THE CONGRESS of delegates from the seceding States convened at Montgomery, Alabama on the 4th of February, 1861. Their first work was to prepare a provisional Constitution for the new Confederacy, for which the style "Confederate States of America" was adopted. The powers conferred upon them were adequate for the performance of this duty, the immediate necessity for which was obvious and urgent. This Constitution was adopted on the 8th of February, to continue in force for one year, unless superseded at an earlier date by a permanent organization.

On the next day (9th of February) an election was held for the chief executive offices, resulting, as I afterward learned, in my election to the Presidency, with the Hon. Alexander H. Stephens, of Georgia, as Vice-President.

While these events were occurring, having completed the most urgent of my duties at the capital of Mississippi, I had gone to my home, Brierfield, in Warren County, and had begun, in the homely but expressive language of Mr. Clay, "to repair my fences." While thus engaged, notice was received of my election to the Presidency of the Confederate States, with an urgent request to proceed immediately to Montgomery for inauguration.

As this had been suggested as a probable event, and what appeared to me adequate precautions had been taken to prevent it, I was surprised, and, still more, disappointed. I thought myself better adapted to command in the field; and Mississippi had given me the position which I preferred to any other—the highest rank in her army. It was, therefore, that I afterward said, in an address delivered before the Legislature of the State, that the duty to which I was thus called was temporary, and that I expected soon to be with the Army of Mississippi again.

On my way to Montgomery, brief addresses were made at various places, at which there were temporary stoppages of the trains, in response to calls from the crowds assembled at such points. Some of these addresses were grossly misrepresented in sensational reports in Northern newspapers, and were not considered worthy of correction under the pressure of the momentous duties then devolving upon me. These false reports, which represented me as invoking war and threatening devastation of the North, have since been adopted by partisan writers as authentic history. It is a sufficient answer to these accusations to refer to my farewell address to the Senate.

After being inaugurated, I proceeded to the formation of my Cabinet. The unanimity existing among our people made this a much easier and more agreeable task than where the rivalries in the party of an executive have to be consulted and accommodated, often at the expense of the highest capacity and fitness. Unencumbered by any other consideration than the public welfare, having no friends to reward or enemies to punish, it resulted that not one of those who formed my first Cabinet had borne to me the relation of close personal friendship, or had political claims upon me; indeed, with two of them I had no previous acquaintance.

Among others, I chose Mr. Robert Toombs of Georgia for the State Department; Mr. Stephen R. Mallory, of Florida, for Secretary of the Navy; Mr. Judah P. Benjamin, of Louisiana, for Attorney-General; Mr. John H. Reagan, of Texas, for Postmaster-General; Mr. C. G. Memminger, of South Carolina, for Secretary of the Treasury; and Mr. L. P. Walker, of Alabama, for the War Department.

The executive departments having been organized, my attention was first directed to preparation for military defense, for, though I, in common with others, desired to have a peaceful separation, and sent commissioners to the United States Government to effect, if possible, negotiations to that end, I did not hold the common opinion that we would be allowed to depart in peace, and therefore regarded it as an imperative duty to make all possible preparation for the contingency of war.

Chapter 6

Conciliatory Actions of the New Confederacy

THE LEGISLATION of the Confederate Congress furnishes the best evidence of the temper and spirit which prevailed in the organization of the Confederate Government. The very first enactment, made on the 9th of February, 1861—the day after the adoption of the Provisional Constitution—was this:

That all the laws of the United States of America in force and in use in the Confederate States of America on the first day of November last, and not inconsistent with the Constitution of the Confederate States, be and the same are hereby continued in force until altered or repealed by the Congress.

The next act was one continuing in office until the 1st of April next ensuing all officers connected with the collection of customs and the assistant treasurers intrusted with the keeping of the moneys arising therefrom, who were engaged in the performance of such duties within any of the Confederate States, with the same powers and functions which they had been exercising under the Government of the United States.

The Provisional Constitution itself, in the second section of its sixth article, had ordained as follows:

The Government hereby instituted shall take immediate steps for the settlement of all matters between the States forming it and their other late confederates of the United States, in relation to the public property and public debt at the time of their withdrawal from them; these States hereby declaring it to be their wish and earnest desire to adjust everything pertaining to the common property, common liabilities, and common obligations of that Union, upon the principles of right, justice, equity, and good faith.

In accordance with this requirement of the Constitution, the Congress, on the 15th of February—before my arrival at Montgomery—passed a resolution declaring "that it is the sense of this Congress that a commission of three persons be appointed by the President-elect, as early as may be convenient after his inauguration, and sent to the Government of the United States of America, for the purpose of negotiating friendly relations between that Government and the Confederate States of America, and for the settlement of all questions of disagreement between the two Governments, upon principles of right, justice, equity, and good faith."

Persistent efforts were made to inflame the minds of the people of the Northwestern States by representing to them that, in consequence of the separation of the States, they would lose the free navigation of the Mississippi River. At that early period in the life of the Confederacy, the intercourse between the North and South had been so little interrupted, that the agitators, whose vocation it was to deceive the masses of the people, could not have been ignorant that, as early as the 25th of February, 1861, an act was passed by the Confederate Congress, and approved by the President, "to declare and establish the free navigation of the Mississippi River."

By an act approved on the 26th of February, all laws which forbade the employment in the coasting-trade of vessels not enrolled or licensed, and all laws imposing discriminating duties on foreign vessels or goods imported in them, were repealed. These acts and all other indications manifested the well-known wish of the people of the Confederacy to encourage unrestricted commerce with all nations, surely not least with their late associates, the Northern States. Indeed, all the laws enacted during the first session of the Provisional Congress show how consistent were the purposes and actions of its members with their original avowal of a desire peacefully to separate from those with whom they could not live in tranquillity.

Three discreet, well-informed, and distinguished citizens were selected as Commissioners, and accredited to the President of the Northern States, Mr. Lincoln, to the end that by negotiation all questions between the two Governments might be so adjusted as to avoid war, and perpetuate the kind relations which had been cemented by the common trials, sacrifices, and glories of the people of all the States. The nomination of the members of the commission was made on the 25th of February—within a week after my inauguration—and confirmed by Congress on the same day. The Commissioners appointed were Messrs. A. B. Roman, of Louisiana; Martin J. Crawford, of Georgia; and John Forsyth, of Alabama. Mr. Roman had been Governor of his native State. Mr. Crawford had served with distinction in Congress for several years. Mr. Forsyth had been Minister to Mexico under Mr. Pierce and Mr. Buchanan. These gentlemen, moreover, represented the three great parties which had opposed the sectionalism of the so-called "Republicans." Their commissions authorized them, "in the name of the Confederate States, to meet and confer with any person or persons duly authorized by the Government of the United States, being furnished with like power and authority, and with him or them to agree, treat, consult, and negotiate" concerning all matters in which the parties were both interested. No secret instructions were given them, for there was nothing to conceal. The objects of their mission were open and avowed, and its inception and conduct throughout were characterized by frankness and good faith. How this effort was received, how the Commissioners were kept waiting, and, while fair promises were held to the ear, how military preparations were pushed forward for the unconstitutional, criminal purpose of coercing States, let the shameful record of that transaction attest.

Chapter 7

Border States Seek Peace

WHILE THE EVENTS which have been occupying our attention were occurring, the last conspicuous effort was made within the Union to stay the tide of usurpation which was driving the Southern States into secession. This effort was set on foot by Virginia, the General Assembly of which State, on the 19th of January, 1861, adopted a preamble and resolutions, deprecating disunion, and inviting all such States as were willing to unite in an earnest endeavor to avert it to appoint commissioners to meet in Washington, on the 4th of February, "to consider, and, if practicable, agree upon some suitable adjustment." Ex-President John Tyler and four other of the most distinguished citizens of the State were appointed to represent Virginia in the proposed conference. If they could agree with the Commissioners of other States upon any plan of settlement requiring amendments to the Federal Constitution, they were instructed to communicate them to Congress, with a view to their submission to the several States for ratification.

The "border States" in general promptly acceded to this proposition of Virginia, and others followed, so that in the "Peace Congress," which assembled on the 4th, and adjourned on the 27th of February, twenty-one States were eventually represented of which fourteen were Northern, or "non-slaveholding," and seven slaveholding States. The six States which had already seceded were of course not represented; nor were Texas and Arkansas, the secession of which, although not consummated, was obviously inevitable. Michigan, Wisconsin, Minnesota, Oregon, and California also held aloof from the conference.

It is needless to follow the course of the deliberations of the Peace Conference. It included among its members many men of distinction and eminent ability, and some of unquestionable patriotism, from every part of the Union. The venerable John Tyler presided. A plan was finally agreed upon by a majority of the States represented, for certain amendments to the Federal Constitution, which it was hoped might put an end to further contention. In its leading features this plan resembled that of Mr. Crittenden,* which was pending in the Senate, though with some variations, which were regarded as less favorable to the South. It was reported immediately to both Houses of the United States Congress. In the Senate, Mr. Crittenden promptly expressed his willingness to accept it as a substitute for his own proposition, and eloquently urged its adoption. But the arrogance of a sectional majority inflated by recent triumph was too powerful to be allayed by the appeals of patriotism or the counsels of wisdom. The plan of the Peace Conference was treated by the majority with the contemptuous indifference shown to every other movement for conciliation. It was defeated on a vote, as were the Crittenden propositions.

With the failure of these efforts on the eve of the inauguration of Mr. Lincoln, and the accession to power of a party founded on a basis of sectional aggression, expired the last hopes of reconciliation and union.

* See pp. 54-55.

Chapter 8

Reaction in the North

IT IS A GREAT MISTAKE to assume that, at the period under consideration, the Southern States stood alone in the assertion of the principles with regard to the right of secession and the wrong of coercion. Down to the formation of the Confederate Government, the one was distinctly admitted, the other still more distinctly disavowed and repudiated, by many of the leaders of public opinion in the North of both parties—indeed, any purpose of direct coercion was disclaimed by nearly all. If presented at all, it was in the delusive and ambiguous guise of "the execution of the laws" and "protection of the public property."

The "New York Tribune"—the leading organ of the party which triumphed in the election of 1860—had said, soon after the result of that election was ascertained, with reference to secession: "We hold, with Jefferson, to the inalienable right of communities to alter or abolish forms of government that have become oppressive or injurious; and, if the cotton States shall decide that they can do better out of the Union than in it, we insist on letting them go in peace. The right to secede may be a revolutionary right, *but it exists nevertheless;* and we do not see how one party can have *a right to do what another party has a right to prevent.* We must ever resist the asserted right of any State to remain in the Union and nullify or defy the laws thereof: *to withdraw from the Union is quite another matter.* And, whenever a considerable section of our Union shall deliberately resolve to go out, *we shall resist all coercive measures designed to keep her in. We hope never to live in a republic whereof one section is pinned to the residue by bayonets.*"

The "Tribune" was far from being singular among its Northern contemporaries in the entertainment of such views, as Mr. Greeley, its chief editor, has shown by many citations in his book, "The American Conflict." The Albany "Argus," about the same time, said, in language which Mr. Greeley characterizes as "clear and temperate": "We sympathize with and justify the South as far as this: their rights have been invaded to the extreme limit possible within the forms of the

Constitution; and, beyond this limit, their feelings have been insulted and their interests and honor assailed by almost every possible form of denunciation and invective; and, if we deemed it certain that the real *animus* of the Republican party could be carried into the administration of the Federal Government, and become the permanent policy of the nation, we should think that all the instincts of self-preservation and of manhood rightfully impelled them to a resort to revolution and a separation from the Union, and we would applaud them and wish them godspeed in the adoption of such a remedy."

The "New York Herald"—a journal which claimed to be independent of all party influences—about the same period said: "Each State is organized as a complete government, holding the purse and wielding the sword, possessing the right to break the tie of the confederation as a nation might break a treaty, and to repel coercion as a nation might repel invasion. . . . Coercion, if it were possible, is out of the question."

On the 31st of January, 1861—after six States had already seceded—a great meeting was held in the city of New York, to consider the perilous condition of the country. At this meeting ex-Governor Horatio Seymour asked whether "successful coercion by the North is less revolutionary than successful secession by the South? Shall we prevent revolution [he added] by being foremost in overthrowing the principles of our Government, and all that makes it valuable to our people and distinguishes it among the nations of the earth?"

Other distinguished speakers expressed themselves in similar terms—varying somewhat in their estimate of the propriety of the secession of the Southern States, but all agreeing in emphatic and unqualified reprobation of the idea of coercion. A series of conciliatory resolutions was adopted, one of which declares that "civil war will not restore the Union, but will defeat for ever its reconstruction."

At a still later period—some time in the month of February—the "Free Press," a leading paper in Detroit, had the following:

If there shall not be a change in the present seeming purpose to yield to no accommodation of the national difficulties, and if troops shall be raised in the North to march against the people of the South, *a fire in the rear will be opened upon such troops,* which will either stop their march altogether or wonderfully accelerate it.

That these were not expressions of isolated or exceptional sentiment is evident from the fact that they were copied with approval by other Northern journals.

Mr. Lincoln, when delivering his inaugural address, on the 4th of March, 1861, had not so far lost all respect for the consecrated traditions of the founders of the Constitution and for the majesty of the principle of State sovereignty as openly to enunciate the claim of coercion. While arguing against the right to secede, and asserting his intention "to hold, occupy, and possess the property and places belonging to the Government, and collect the duties and imposts," he says that, "beyond what may be necessary for these objects, there will be no invasion, no using of force against or among the people anywhere," and appends to this declaration the following pledge:

Where hostility to the United States shall be so great as to prevent competent resident citizens from holding the Federal offices, there will be no attempt to force obnoxious strangers among the people for that object. While the strict legal right may exist of the Government to enforce the exercise of these offices, the attempt to do so would be so irritating, and so nearly impracticable withal, that I deem it better to forego for the time the uses of such offices.

These extracts will serve to show that the people of the South were not without grounds for cherishing the hope that the separation would, indeed, be as peaceable in fact as it was, on their part, in purpose; that the conservative and patriotic feeling still existing in the North would control the elements of sectional hatred and bloodthirsty fanaticism; and that there would be really "no war."

And here the ingenuous reader may very naturally ask, What became of all this feeling? How was it that, in the course of a few weeks, it had disappeared like a morning mist? Where was the host of men who had declared that an army marching to invade the Southern States should first pass over their dead bodies? No *new* question had arisen—no change in the attitude occupied by the seceding States—no cause for controversy not already existing when these utterances were made. And yet the sentiments which they expressed were so entirely swept away by the tide of reckless fury which soon afterward impelled an armed invasion of the South, that (with a few praiseworthy but powerless exceptions) scarcely a vestige of them was left.

I leave to others to offer, if they can, an explanation of this strange phenomenon. To the student of human nature, however, it may not seem altogether without precedent, when he remembers certain other instances on record of mutations in public sentiment equally sudden and extraordinary. Ten thousand swords that would have leaped from their scabbards —as the English statesman thought—to avenge even a look of insult to a lovely queen, hung idly in their places when she was led to the scaffold in the midst of the vilest taunts and execrations. The case that we have been considering was, perhaps, only an illustration of the general truth that, in times of revolutionary excitement, the higher and better elements are crushed and silenced by the lower and baser—not so much on account of their greater extent, as of their greater violence.

Chapter 9

Confederate Constitution

THE CONSERVATIVE TEMPER of the people of the Confederate States was conspicuously exhibited in the most important product of the early labors of their representatives in Congress assembled. The Provisional Constitution, although prepared only for temporary use, and necessarily in some haste, was so well adapted for the purposes which it was intended to serve, that many thought it would have been wise to continue it in force indefinitely, or at least until the independency of the Confederacy should be assured. The Congress, however, deeming it best that the system of Government should emanate from the people, accordingly, on the 11th of March, prepared the permanent Constitution, which was submitted to and ratified by the people of the respective States.

The Constitution of the United States was the model followed throughout, with only such changes as experience suggested for better practical working or for greater perspicuity. The preamble to both instruments is the same in substance, and very nearly identical in language. The words "We, the people of the United States," in one, are replaced by "We, the people of the Confederate States," in the other; and the gross perversion which has been made of the former expression is precluded in the latter merely by the addition of the explanatory clause, "each State acting in its sovereign and independent character."

The official term of the President was fixed at six instead of four years, and it was provided that he should not be eligible for reëlection. This was in accordance with the original draft of the Constitution of 1787.

The President was empowered to remove officers of his Cabinet, or those engaged in the diplomatic service, at his discretion, but in all other cases removal from office could be made only for cause, and the cause was to be reported to the Senate.

Congress was authorized to provide by law for the admission of Cabinet officers to a seat upon the floor of either House, with the privilege of taking part in the discussion of subjects pertaining to his department. This wise and judicious provision, which would have tended to obviate much delay and misunderstanding, was, however, never put into execution by the necessary legislation.

Protective duties for the benefit of special branches of industry, which had been so fruitful a source of trouble under the Government of the United States, were altogether prohibited. So, also, were bounties from the Treasury, and extra compensation for services rendered by officers, contractors, or employees, of any description.

A vote of two thirds of each House was requisite for the appropriation of money from the Treasury, unless asked for by the chief of a department and submitted to Congress by the President, or for payment of the expenses of Congress, or of claims against the Confederacy judicially established and declared. The President was also authorized to approve any one appropriation and disapprove any other in the same bill.

With regard to the impeachment of Federal officers, it was intrusted, as formerly, to the discretion of the House of Representatives, with the additional provision, however, that, in the case of any judicial or other officer exercising his functions solely within the limits of a particular State, impeachment might be made by the Legislature of such State—the trial in all cases to be by the Senate of the Confederate States.

Any two or more States were authorized to enter into compacts with each other for the improvement of the navigation of rivers flowing between or through them. A vote of two thirds of each House—the Senate voting by States—was required for the admission of a new State.

With regard to amendments of the Constitution, it was made obligatory upon Congress, on the demand of any three States, concurring in the proposed amendment or amendments, to summon a convention of all the States to consider and act upon them, voting by States, but restricted in its action to the particular propositions thus submitted. If approved by such convention, the amendments were to be subject to final ratification by two thirds of the States.

With regard to slavery and the slave-trade, the provisions of this Constitution furnish an effectual answer to the assertion, so often made, that the Confederacy was founded on slavery, that slavery was its "corner-stone," etc. Property in slaves, *already existing,* was recognized and guaranteed, just as it was by the Constitution of the United States; and the rights of such property in the common Territories were protected against any such hostile discrimination as had been attempted in the Union. But the "extension of slavery," in the only practical sense of that phrase, was more distinctly and effectually precluded by the Confederate than by the Federal Constitution. This will be. manifest on a comparison of the provisions of the two relative to the slave-trade. These are found at the beginning of the ninth section of the first article of each instrument. The Constitution of the United States has the following:

The migration or importation of such persons as any of the States now existing shall think proper to admit, shall not be prohibited by the Congress prior to the year one thousand eight hundred and eight; but a tax or duty may be imposed on such importations, not exceeding ten dollars for each person.

The Confederate Constitution, on the other hand, ordained as follows:

1. The importation of negroes of the African race from any foreign country, other than the slaveholding States or Territories of the United States of America, is hereby forbidden; and Congress is required to pass such laws as shall effectually prevent the same.
2. Congress shall also have the power to prohibit the introduction of slaves from any State not a member of, or Territory not belonging to, this Confederacy.

In the case of the United States, the only prohibition is against any interference by Congress with the slave-trade for a term of years, and it was further legitimized by the authority given to impose a duty upon it. The term of years, it is true, had long since expired, but there was still no prohibition of the trade by the Constitution; it was after 1808 entirely within the discretion of Congress either to encourage, tolerate, or prohibit it.

Under the Confederate Constitution, on the contrary, the African slave-trade was *"hereby forbidden,"* positively and unconditionally, from the beginning. The only discretion in the matter intrusted to the Congress was, whether or not to permit the introduction of slaves from any of the United States or their Territories.

Mr. Lincoln, in his inaugural address, had said: "I have no purpose, directly or indirectly, to interfere with the institution of slavery in the States where it exists. I believe I have no lawful right to do so, and I have no inclination to do so."

Now, if there was no purpose on the part of the Government of the United States to interfere with the institution of slavery within its already existing limits—a proposition which permitted its propagation within those limits by natural increase—and inasmuch as the Confederate Constitution precluded any other than the same natural increase, we may plainly perceive the disingenuousness and absurdity of the pretension by which a factitious sympathy has been obtained in certain quarters for the war upon the South, on the ground that it was a war in behalf of freedom against slavery.

(As late as the 22nd of April, 1861, Mr. Seward, United States Secretary of State, in a dispatch to Mr. Dayton, Minister to France, since made public, expressed the views and purposes of the United States Government in the premises as follows. It may be proper to explain that, by what he is pleased to term "the revolution," Mr. Seward means the withdrawal of the Southern States; and that the words italicized are, perhaps, not so distinguished in the original. He says: "The Territories will remain in all respects the same, whether the revolution shall succeed or shall fail. *The condition of slavery in the several States will remain just the same, whether it succeed or fail.* There is not even a pretext for the complaint that the disaffected States are to be conquered by the United States if the revolution fails; for the rights of the States and *the condition of every being in them* will remain subject to exactly the same laws and forms of administration, whether the revolution shall succeed or whether it shall fail. In the one case, the States would be federally connected with the new Confederacy; in the other, they would, as now, be members of the United States; *but their Constitutions and laws, customs, habits, and institutions, in either case, will remain the same.*")

I had no direct part in the preparation of the Confederate Constitution. No consideration of delicacy forbids me, therefore, to say, in closing this brief review of that instrument, that it was a model of wise, temperate, and liberal statesmanship. Intelligent criticism, from hostile as well as friendly sources, has been compelled to admit its excellences, and has sustained the judgment of a popular Northern journal [The New York Herald] which said, a few days after it was adopted and published [March 19, 1861]:

The new Constitution is the Constitution of the United States with various modifications and some very important and most desirable improvements. We are free to say that the invaluable reforms enumerated should be adopted by the United States, with or without a reunion of the seceded States, and as soon as possible. But why not accept them with the propositions of the Confederate States on slavery as a basis of reunion?

Chapter 10

Duplicity in Washington

THE APPOINTMENT of Commissioners to proceed to Washington, for the purpose of establishing friendly relations with the United States has already been mentioned. No time was lost in carrying this purpose into execution. Mr. Martin J. Crawford—first of the Commissioners—arrived in Washington two or three days before the expiration of Mr. Buchanan's term of office as President of the United States.

It may here be mentioned, in explanation of my desire that the commission, or at least a part of it, should reach Washington before the close of Mr. Buchanan's term, that I had received an intimation from him that he would be happy to receive a Commissioner or Commissioners from the Confederate States, and would refer to the Senate any communication that might be made through such a commission.

Mr. Crawford—now a Judge of the Supreme Court of Georgia, and the only surviving member of the commission —in a manuscript account of his recollections, says:

The feverish and emotional condition of affairs soon made the presence of the special Commissioner at Washington known throughout the city. Congress was still, of course, in session; Senators and members of the House of Representatives, excepting those of the Confederate States, who had withdrawn, were in their seats, and the manifestations of anxious care and gloomy forebodings were plainly to be seen on all sides. This was not confined to sections, but existed among the men of the North and West as well as those of the South. . . .

Mr. Buchanan, the President, was in a state of most thorough alarm, not only for his home at Wheatland, but for his personal safety. In the very few days which had elapsed between the time of his promise to receive a Commissioner from the Confederate States and the actual arrival of the Commissioner, he had become so fearfully panic-stricken, that he declined either to receive him or to send any message to the Senate touching the subject-matter of his mission.

The Commissioner had been for several years in Congress before the Administration of Mr. Buchanan, as well as during his official term, and had always been in close political and social relations with him; yet he was afraid of a public visit from him.

He said that he had only three days of official life left, and could incur no further dangers or reproaches than those he had already borne from the press and public speakers of the North.

The intensity of the prevalent feeling increased as the vast crowds, arriving by every train, added fresh material; and hatred and hostility toward our new Government were manifested in almost every conceivable manner.

Another of the Commissioners (Mr. Forsyth) having arrived in Washington on the 12th of March—eight days after the inauguration of Mr. Lincoln, Messrs. Forsyth and Crawford, addressed to Mr. Seward, Secretary of State, a note informing him of their presence, stating the friendly and peaceful purposes of their mission, and requesting the appointment of a day, as early as possible, for the presentation to the President of the United States of their credentials and the objects which they had in view.

No *written* answer to the note of the Commissioners was delivered to them for twenty-seven days after it was written. The paper of Mr. Seward, in reply, without signature or address, dated March 15th was "filed," as he states, on that day, in the Department of State, but a copy of it was not handed to the Commissioners until the 8th of April. But an oral answer had been made to the note of the Commissioners at a much earlier date, for the significance of which it will be necessary to bear in mind the condition of affairs at Charleston and Pensacola.

Fort Sumter was still occupied by the garrison under command of Major Anderson, with no material change in the circumstances since the failure of the attempt made in January to reënforce it by means of the Star of the West. This standing menace at the gates of the chief harbor of South Carolina had been tolerated by the government and people of that State, and afterward by the Confederate authorities, in the abiding hope that it would be removed without a collision of forces. Fort Pickens, on one side of the entrance to the harbor of Pensacola, was also occupied by a garrison of United States troops, while the two forts on the other side were in possession of the Confederates. Communication by sea was not entirely precluded, however, in the case of Fort Pickens; the garrison had been strengthened, and a fleet of Federal men-of-war was lying outside of the harbor. The condition of affairs at these forts—especially at Fort Sumter —was a subject of anxiety with the friends of peace, and the hope of settling by negotiation the questions involved in their occupation had been one of the most urgent motives for the prompt dispatch of the Commissioners to Washington.

The letter of the Commissioners to Mr. Seward was written, as we have seen, on the 12th of March. The oral message, above mentioned, was obtained and communicated to the Commissioners through the agency of two Judges of the Supreme Court of the United States—Justices Nelson, of New York, and Campbell, of Alabama. On the 15th of March they visited the State Department, for the purpose of urging Mr. Seward to reply to the Commissioners, and assure them of the desire of the United States Government for a friendly adjustment. Mr. Seward seems to have objected to an immediate recognition of the Commissioners, on the ground that the state of public sentiment in the North would not sustain it, in connection with the withdrawal of the troops from Fort Sumter, which had been determined on. "The evacuation of Sumter," he said, "is as much as the Administration can bear."

Judge Campbell afterwards reported:* "I concurred in the conclusion that the evacuation of Sumter involved responsibility, and stated that there could not be too much caution in the adoption of measures so as not to shock or to irritate the public sentiment, and that the evacuation of Sumter was sufficient for the present in that direction. I stated that I would see the Commissioners, and I would write to Mr. Davis to that effect. I asked him what I should say as to Sumter and as to Pickens. *He authorized me to say that, before that letter could reach him* [Mr. Davis], *he would learn by telegraph that the order for the evacuation of Sumter had been made.* He said the condition of Pickens was satisfactory, and there would be no change made there." The italics in this extract are my own.

The letter in which this promise was communicated to me has been lost, but it was given in substantially the terms above stated—that the order for the evacuation of the fort would be issued before the letter could reach me. The same assurance was given, on the same day, to the Commissioners. Judge Campbell tells us that Mr. Crawford was slow to consent to refrain from pressing the demand for recognition. "It was only after some discussion and the expression of some objections that he consented" to do so. This consent

* See letter of Judge Campbell to Colonel George W. Munford in "Papers of the Southern Historical Society," appended to "Southern Magazine" for February, 1874.

was clearly one part of stipulation, of which the other part was the pledge that the fort would be evacuated in the course of a few days. Mr. Crawford required the pledge of Mr. Seward to be reduced to writing. The fact that the pledge had been given in his name and behalf was communicated to Mr. Seward the same evening by letter. He was cognizant of, consenting to, and in great part the author of, the whole transaction.

It will be observed that not only the Commissioners in Washington, but the Confederate Government at Montgomery also, were thus assured on the highest authority—that of the Secretary of State of the United States—of the intention of that Government to order the evacuation of Fort Sumter within a few days from the 15th of March, and not to disturb the existing *status* at Fort Pickens. Moreover, this was not the mere statement of a fact, but a *pledge,* given as the consideration of an appeal to the Confederate Government and its Commissioners to refrain from embarrassing the Federal Administration by prosecuting any further claims at the same time. As such a pledge, it was accepted, and, while its fulfillment was quietly awaited, the Commissioners forbore to make any further demand for reply to their note of the 12th of March.

Five days having elapsed in this condition of affairs, the Commissioners in Washington telegraphed Brigadier-General Beauregard, commander of the Confederate forces at Charleston, inquiring whether the fort had been evacuated, or any action taken by Major Anderson indicating the probability of an evacuation. Answer was made to this dispatch, that the fort had not been evacuated, that there were no indications of such a purpose, but that Major Anderson was still working on its defenses. This dispatch was taken to Mr. Seward by Judge Campbell. Two interviews occurred in relation to it, at both of which Judge Nelson was also present. Of the result of these interviews, Judge Campbell states: "The last was full and satisfactory. The Secretary was buoyant and sanguine; he spoke of his ability to carry through his policy with confidence. He accounted for the delay as accidental, and *not involving the integrity of his assurance that the evacuation would take place,* and that I should know whenever any change was made in the resolution in reference to Sumter or to Pickens. I repeated this assurance in writing to Judge Crawford, *and informed Governor Seward in writing what I had said.*"

During all this period of reiterated assurances of a purpose to withdraw the garrison from Fort Sumter, and of excuses for delay on account of the difficulties which embarrassed it, the Government of the United States was assiduously engaged in devising means for furnishing supplies and reënforcements to the garrison, with the view of retaining possession of the fort!

Mr. G. V. Fox, afterward Assistant Secretary of the United States Navy, had proposed a plan for reënforcing and furnishing supplies to the garrison of Fort Sumter in February, during the Administration of Mr. Buchanan. In a letter published in the newspapers since the war, he gives an account of the manner in which the proposition was renewed to the new Administration and its reception by them, as follows:

On the 12th of March I received a telegram from Postmaster-General Blair to come to Washington. . . . Mr. Blair having been acquainted with the proposition I presented to General Scott, under Mr. Buchanan's Administration, sent for me to tender the same to Mr. Lincoln, informing me that Lieutenant-General Scott had advised the President that the fort could not be relieved, and must be given up. . . . I explained the plan to the President. . . .

Finding that there was great opposition to any attempt to relieving Fort Sumter, . . . I judged that my arguments in favor of the practicability of sending in supplies would be strengthened by a visit to Charleston and the fort. The President readily agreed to my visit. . . .

I left Washington on the 19th of March, and, passing through Richmond and Wilmington, reached Charleston on the 21st.

Thus we see that, at the very moment when Mr. Secretary Seward was renewing to the Confederate Government his positive assurance that "the evacuation *would* take place," this emissary was on his way to Charleston to devise measures by means of which this promise might be broken.

On his arrival in Charleston, Mr. Fox tells us that he obtained from Governor Pickens permission to visit Fort Sumter. He fails, in his narrative, to state, what we learn from Governor Pickens himself,* that this permission was obtained "expressly upon the pledge of 'pacific purposes.' " Notwithstanding this pledge, he employed the opportunity afforded by his visit to mature the details of his plan for furnishing supplies and reënforcements to the garrison. He did not, he says, communicate his plan or purposes to Major

* Message to the Legislature of South Carolina, November, 1861.

Anderson, the commanding officer of the garrison, having discernment enough, perhaps, to divine that the instincts of that brave and honest soldier would have revolted at the perfidy of the whole transaction. The result of his visit was, however, that his plan was approved by President Lincoln, and he was sent to New York to make arrangements for putting it in execution.

In a very few days after (says Governor Pickens, in the message quoted above), another confidential agent, Colonel Lamon, was sent by the President [Mr. Lincoln], who informed me that he had come to try and arrange for the removal of the garrison, and . . . asked if a war-vessel could not be allowed to remove them. I replied that no war-vessel could be allowed to enter the harbor on any terms. He said he believed Major Anderson preferred an ordinary steamer, and I agreed that the garrison might be thus removed. He said he hoped to return in a very few days for that purpose.

This, it will be remembered, occurred while Mr. Fox was making active, though secret, preparations for his relief expedition.

Colonel, or Major, Lamon, as he is variously styled in the correspondence, did not return to Charleston, as promised. About the 30th of March a telegram from Governor Pickens was received by the Commissioners in Washington, making inquiry with regard to Colonel Lamon, and the meaning of the protracted delay to fulfill the promise of evacuation. This was fifteen days after the original assurance of Mr. Seward that the garrison would be withdrawn immediately, and ten days after his explanation that the delay was "accidental." The dispatch of Governor Pickens was taken by Judge Campbell to Mr. Seward, who informed Judge Campbell that "the President was concerned about the contents of the telegram—*there was a point of honor involved;* that Lamon had no agency from him, nor title to speak." (This late suggestion of the point of *honor* would seem, under the circumstances, to have been made in a spirit of sarcastic pleasantry, like Sir John Falstaff's celebrated discourse on the same subject.) The only substantial result of the conversation, however, was the written assurance of Mr. Seward, to be communicated to the Commissioners, that "the Government will not undertake to supply Fort Sumter without giving notice to Governor Pickens."

This, it will be observed, was a very material variation

from the positive pledge previously given to the Commissioners, to Governor Pickens, and to myself directly, that the fort was to be forthwith evacuated. Judge Campbell, in his account of the interview, says: "I asked him [Mr. Seward] whether I was to understand that there had been a change in his former communications. His answer was, 'None.'"

About the close of the same week (the first in April), the patience of the Commissioners having now been wellnigh exhausted, and the hostile preparations of the Government of the United States, notwithstanding the secrecy with which they were conducted, having become matter of general rumor, a letter was addressed to Mr. Seward by Judge Campbell, in behalf of the Commissioners, again asking whether the assurances so often given were well or ill founded. To this the Secretary returned answer in writing: *"Faith as to Sumter fully kept. Wait and see."*

This was on the 7th of April. The very next day the following official notification (without date or signature) was read to Governor Pickens and General Beauregard by Mr. Chew, an official of the *State Department,* who said—as did a Captain or Lieutenant Talbot, who accompanied him—that it was from the President of the United States, and delivered by him to Mr. Chew on the 6th—the day *before* Mr. Seward's assurance of *"faith fully kept."*

I am directed by the President of the United States to notify you to expect an attempt will be made to supply Fort Sumter with provisions only; and that, if such an attempt be not resisted, no effort to throw in men, arms, or ammunition, will be made, without further notice, or in case of an attack upon the fort.

Thus disappeared the last vestiges of the plighted faith and pacific pledges of the Federal Government.

In order fully to appreciate the significance of this communication, and of the time and circumstances of its delivery, it must be borne in mind that the naval expedition which had been secretly in preparation for some time at New York was now ready to sail, and might reasonably be expected at Charleston almost immediately after the notification was delivered to Governor Pickens, and before preparation could be made to receive it. Owing to cross-purposes or misunderstandings in the Washington Cabinet, however, and then to the delay caused by a severe storm at sea, this expectation was disappointed, and the Confederate commander at

Charleston had opportunity to communicate with Montgomery and receive instructions for his guidance, before the arrival of the fleet, which had been intended to be a surprise.

In publications made since the war by members of Mr. Lincoln's Cabinet, it has been represented that, during the period of the disgraceful transactions above detailed, there were dissensions and divisions in the Cabinet—certain members of it urging measures of prompt and decided coercion; the Secretary of State favoring a pacific or at least a dilatory policy; and the President vacillating for a time between the two, but eventually adopting the views of the coercionists. In these statements it is represented that the assurances and pledges, given by Mr. Seward to the Confederate Government and its Commissioners, were given on his own authority, and without the consent or approval of the President of the United States. The absurdity of any such attempt to disassociate the action of the President from that of his Secretary, and to relieve the former of responsibility for the conduct of the latter, is too evident to require argument or comment. On one occasion, Judge Campbell informs us that the Secretary, in the midst of an important interview, excused himself for the purpose of conferring with the President, and left his visitor for some time, when the answer was given, avowedly and directly proceeding from the President.

If, however, it were possible to suppose that Mr. Seward was acting on his own responsibility, and practicing a deception upon his own chief, as well as upon the Confederate authorities, it is nevertheless certain that the principal facts were brought to light within a few days after the close of the efforts at negotiation. Yet the Secretary of State was not impeached for the grave offense of undertaking to conduct the most vital transactions that could be brought before the Government of the United States, without the knowledge and in opposition to the will of the President, and for having involved the Government in dishonor, if not in disaster. He was not even dismissed from office, but continued to be the chief officer of the Cabinet and confidential adviser of the President, as he was afterward of the ensuing Administration. No disavowal of his action, no apology nor explanation, was ever made. Politically and legally, the President is unquestionably responsible for the action of any member of his Cabinet, and in this case it is as preposterous to dissever from him the moral, as to relieve him of the legal, responsibility that rests upon the Government of the United States for the systematic series of frauds perpetrated by its authority.

On the other hand, Mr. Seward, throughout the whole negotiation, was fully informed of the views of his colleagues in the Cabinet and of the President. Whatever his real hopes or purposes may have been in the beginning, it is positively certain that long before the end, and while still reiterating his assurances that the garrison would be withdrawn, he knew that it had been *determined,* and that active preparations were in progress, to strengthen it.

It is scarcely necessary to say that the Commissioners had, with good reason, ceased to place any confidence in the promises of the United States Government, before they ceased to be made. On the 8th of April they sent the following dispatch to General Beauregard:

GENERAL G. T. BEAUREGARD: Accounts uncertain, because of the constant vacillation of this Government. We were reassured yesterday that the status of Sumter would not be changed without previous notice to Governor Pickens, but we have no faith in them. The war policy prevails in the Cabinet at this time.
M. J. CRAWFORD

On the same day the announcement made to Governor Pickens through Mr. Chew was made known. The Commissioners immediately applied for a definitive answer to their note of March 12th, which had been permitted to remain in abeyance. The paper of the Secretary of State, dated March 15th, was thereupon delivered to them.

Negotiation was now at an end, and the Commissioners withdrew from Washington. Their last dispatch, before leaving, shows that they were still dependent upon public rumor and the newspapers for information as to the real purposes and preparations of the Federal Administration. It was in these words:

WASHINGTON, *April 10, 1861*
GENERAL G. T. BEAUREGARD: The "Tribune" of to-day declares the main object of the expedition to be the relief of Sumter, and that a force will be landed which will overcome all opposition.
ROMAN, CRAWFORD, AND FORSYTH

Chapter 11

Reduction of Fort Sumter

THE COURSE pursued by the Government of the United States with regard to the forts had not passed without earnest remonstrance from the most intelligent and patriotic of its own friends during this period. In the Senate of the United States, which continued in executive session for several weeks after the inauguration of Mr. Lincoln, it was the subject of discussion. Mr. Douglas, of Illinois—who was certainly not suspected of sympathy with secession, or lack of devotion to the Union—on the 15th of March offered a resolution recommending the withdrawal of the garrisons from all forts within the limits of the States which had seceded, except those at Key West and the Dry Tortugas. Mr. Douglas, in urging the maintenance of *peace* as a motive for the evacuation of the forts, was no doubt aware of the full force of his words. He knew that their continued occupation was virtually a declaration of war.

The General-in-Chief of the United States Army, also, it is well known, urgently advised the evacuation of the forts. But the most striking protest against the coercive measures finally adopted was that of Major Anderson himself. The letter in which his views were expressed has been carefully suppressed in the partisan narratives of that period and wellnigh lost sight of, although it does the highest honor to his patriotism and integrity. It was written on the same day on which the announcement was made to Governor Pickens of the purpose of the United States Government to send supplies to the fort, and is worthy of reproduction here:

FORT SUMTER, S.C., *April 8, 1861*
To Colonel L. Thomas, Adjutant-General United States Army.
COLONEL: I have the honor to report that the resumption of work yesterday (Sunday) at various points on Morris Island, and the vigorous prosecution of it this morning, apparently strengthening all the batteries which are under the fire of our guns, shows that they either have just received some news from Washington which has put them on the *qui vive*, or that they have received orders from Montgomery to commence operations here. I am preparing, by the side of my barbette guns, protection for our

men from the shells which will be almost continually bursting over or in our work.

I had the honor to receive, by yesterday's mail, the letter of the Honorable Secretary of War, dated April 4th, and confess that what he there states surprises me very greatly—following, as it does, and contradicting so positively, the assurance Mr. Crawford telegraphed he was "authorized" to make. I trust that this matter will be at once put in a correct light, as a movement made now, when the South has been erroneously informed that none such would be attempted, would produce most disastrous results throughout our country. It is, of course, now too late for me to give any advice in reference to the proposed scheme of Captain Fox. I fear that its result can not fail to be disastrous to all concerned. . . .

We have not oil enough to keep a light in the lantern for one night. The boats will have to, therefore, rely at night entirely upon other marks. I ought to have been informed that this expedition was to come. Colonel Lamon's remark convinced me that the idea, merely hinted at to me by Captain Fox, would not be carried out.

We shall strive to do our duty, though I frankly say that my heart is not in this war, which I see is to be thus commenced. That God will still avert it, and cause us to resort to pacific means to maintain our rights, is my ardent prayer!

I am, Colonel, very respectfully,

Your obedient servant,

ROBERT ANDERSON

Major, 1st Artillery, commanding

The "relief squadron," as with unconscious irony it was termed, was already under way for Charleston, consisting, according to their own statement, of eight vessels, carrying twenty-six guns and about fourteen hundred men, including the troops sent for reënforcement of the garrison.

These facts became known to the Confederate Government, and it was obvious that no time was to be lost in preparing for, and if possible anticipating the impending assault. The character of the instructions given General Beauregard in this emergency may be inferred from the ensuing correspondence, which is here reproduced from contemporary publications:

CHARLESTON, *April 8th.*

L. P. WALKER, *Secretary of War*

An authorized messenger from President Lincoln just informed Governor Pickens and myself that provisions will be sent to Fort Sumter peaceably, or otherwise by force.

(Signed)   G. T. BEAUREGARD

MONTGOMERY, *10th.*

GENERAL G. T. BEAUREGARD, *Charleston*

If you have no doubt of the authorized character of the agent who communicated to you the intention of the Washington Government to supply Fort Sumter by force, you will at once demand its evacuation, and, if this is refused, proceed, in such a manner as you may determine, to reduce it. Answer.

(Signed)   L. P. WALKER, *Secretary of War*

L. P. WALKER, *Secretary of War*

The demand will be made to-morrow at twelve o'clock.

(Signed)   G. T. BEAUREGARD

HEADQUARTERS PROVISIONAL ARMY, C.S.A.,
CHARLESTON, *S.C., April 11, 1861, 2* P. M.

SIR: The Government of the Confederate States has hitherto forborne from any hostile demonstrations against Fort Sumter, in the hope that the Government of the United States, with a view to the amicable adjustment of all questions between the two Governments, and to avert the calamities of war, would voluntarily evacuate it. There was reason at one time to believe that such would be the course pursued by the Government of the United States; and, under that impression, my Government has refrained from making any demand for the surrender of the fort.

But the Confederate States can no longer delay assuming actual possession of a fortification commanding the entrance of one of their harbors, and necessary to its defense and security.

I am ordered by the Government of the Confederate States to demand the evacuation of Fort Sumter. My aides, Colonel Chesnut and Captain Lee, are authorized to make such demand of you. All proper facilities will be afforded for the removal of yourself and command, together with company arms and property, and all private property, to any post in the United States which you may elect. The flag which you have upheld so long and with so much fortitude, under the most trying circumstances, may be saluted by you on taking it down.

Colonel Chesnut and Captain Lee will, for a reasonable time, await your answer.

I am, sir, very respectfully, your obedient servant,

(Signed)   G. T. BEAUREGARD,
Brigadier-General commanding

MAJOR ROBERT ANDERSON,
Commanding at Fort Sumter, Charleston Harbor, S.C.

HEADQUARTERS FORT SUMTER, S.C., *April 11, 1861*

GENERAL: I have the honor to acknowledge the receipt of your communication demanding the evacuation of this fort; and to say in reply thereto that it is a demand with which I regret that my sense of honor and of my obligations to my Government prevents my compliance.

Thanking you for the fair, manly, and courteous terms proposed, and for the high compliment paid me,

I am, General, Very respectfully, your obedient servant,

(Signed) ROBERT ANDERSON,
Major U. S. Army, commanding

To Brigadier-General G. T. BEAUREGARD,
Commanding Provisional·Army, C.S.A.

MONTGOMERY, *April 11th.*

General BEAUREGARD, *Charleston*

CHARLESTON, *April 11, 1861, 11* P.M.

We do not desire needlessly to bombard Fort Sumter, if Major Anderson will state the time at which, as indicated by him, he will evacuate, and agree that, in the mean time, he will not use his guns against us, unless ours should be employed against Fort Sumter. You are thus to avoid the effusion of blood. If this or its equivalent be refused, reduce the fort as your judgment decides to be most practicable.

(Signed) L. P. WALKER, *Secretary of War*

HEADQUARTERS PROVISIONAL ARMY, *C. S. A.,*
CHARLESTON, *April 11, 1861, 11* P.M.

MAJOR: In consequence of the verbal observations made by you to my aides, Messrs. Chesnut and Lee, in relation to the condition of your supplies, and that you would in a few days be starved out if our guns did not batter you to pieces—or words to that effect—and desiring no useless effusion of blood, I communicated both the verbal observation and your written answer to my Government.

If you will state the time at which you will evacuate Fort Sumter, and agree that in the mean time you will not use your guns against us, unless ours shall be employed against Fort Sumter, we will abstain from opening fire upon you. Colonel Chesnut and Captain Lee are authorized by me to enter into such an agreement with you. You are therefore requested to communicate to them an open answer.

I remain, Major, very respectfully,
Your obedient servant,

(Signed) G. T. BEAUREGARD,
Brigadier-General commanding

Major ROBERT ANDERSON,
Commanding at Fort Sumter, Charleston Harbor, S. C.

HEADQUARTERS FORT SUMTER, S.C., *2.30* A.M., *April 12, 1861*

GENERAL: I have the honor to acknowledge the receipt of your second communication of the 11th instant, by Colonel Chesnut, and to state, in reply, that, cordially uniting with you in the desire to avoid the useless effusion of blood, I will, if provided with the proper and necessary means of transportation, evacuate Fort Sumter by noon on the 15th instant, should I not receive, prior to that time, controlling instructions from my Government, or additional supplies; and that I will not, in the mean time, open my fire upon your forces unless compelled to do so by some hostile act against this fort, or the flag of my Government, by the forces under your command, or by some portion of them, or by the perpetration of some act showing a hostile intention on your part against this fort or the flag it bears.

I have the honor to be, General,

Your obedient servant,

(Signed)   ROBERT ANDERSON,

Major U. S. Army, commanding

To Brigadier-General G. T. BEAUREGARD,
Commanding Provisional Army, C. S. A.

FORT SUMTER, S. C., *April 12, 1861, 3.20 A. M.*

SIR: By authority of Brigadier-General Beauregard, commanding the provisional forces of the Confederate States, we have the honor to notify you that he will open the fire of his batteries on Fort Sumter in one hour from this time.

We have the honor to be, very respectfully,

Your obedient servants,

(Signed)   JAMES CHESNUT, Jr,

Aide-de-camp

(Signed)   STEPHEN D. LEE,

Captain S. C. Army, and Aide-de-camp

Major ROBERT ANDERSON,
United States Army, Commanding Fort Sumter

It is essential to a right understanding of the last two letters to give more than a superficial attention to that of Major Anderson, bearing in mind certain important facts not referred to in the correspondence. Major Anderson had been requested to state the time at which he *would evacuate* the fort, if unmolested, agreeing in the mean time not to use his guns against the city and the troops defending it unless *Fort Sumter* should be first attacked by them. On these conditions General Beauregard offered to refrain from opening fire upon him. In his reply Major Anderson promises to evacuate the fort on the 15th of April, *provided* he should not, before that time, receive "controlling instructions" or "additional supplies" from his Government. He furthermore offers to pledge himself not to open fire upon the Confederates, unless in the mean time compelled to do so by some hostile act against the fort *or the flag of his Government.*

Inasmuch as it was known to the Confederate commander that the "controlling instructions" were already issued, and that the "additional supplies" were momentarily expected; inasmuch, also, as any attempt to introduce the supplies would compel the opening of fire upon the vessels bearing them under the flag of the United States—thereby releasing Major Anderson from his pledge—it is evident that his conditions could not be accepted. It would have been merely, after the avowal of a hostile determination by the Government of the United States, to await an inevitable conflict with the guns of Fort Sumter and the naval forces of the United States in combination; with no possible hope of averting it, unless in the improbable event of a delay of the expected fleet for nearly four days longer. (In point of fact, it arrived off the harbor on the same day, but was hindered by a gale of wind from entering it.) There was obviously no other course to be pursued than that announced in the answer given by General Beauregard.

It should not be forgotten that, during the early occupation of Fort Sumter by a garrison the attitude of which was at least offensive, no restriction had been put upon their privilege of purchasing in Charleston fresh provisions, or any delicacies or comforts not directly tending to the supply of the means needful to hold the fort for an indefinite time.

The forbearance of the Confederate Government, under the circumstances, is perhaps unexampled in history. It was carried to the exteme verge, short of a disregard of the safety of the people who had intrusted to that government the duty of their defense against their enemies. The attempt to represent us as the *aggressors* in the conflict which ensued is as unfounded as the complaint made by the wolf against the lamb in the familiar fable. He who makes the assault is not necessarily he that strikes the first blow or fires the first gun. To have awaited further strengthening of their position by land and naval forces, with hostile purpose now declared, for the sake of having them "fire the first gun," would have been as unwise as it would be to hesitate to strike down the arm of the assailant, who levels a deadly weapon at one's breast, until he has actually fired. After the assault was made by the hostile descent of the fleet, the reduction of Fort Sumter was a measure of defense rendered absolutely and immediately necessary.

Such clearly was the idea of the commander of the Pawnee, when he declined, as Captain Fox informs us, without orders from a superior, to make any effort to enter the harbor, "there to inaugurate civil war." The straightforward simplicity of the sailor had not been perverted by the shams of political sophistry. Even Mr. Horace Greeley, with all his extreme partisan feeling, is obliged to admit that, "whether the bombardment and reduction of Fort Sumter shall or shall not be justified by posterity, it is clear that the Confederacy had no alternative but its own dissolution."

Accordingly to the notice given by General Beauregard, fire was opened upon Fort Sumter at half-past four o'clock on the morning of Friday, the 12th of April, 1861. The fort soon responded. It is not the purpose of this work to give minute details of the military operation, as the events of the bombardment have been often related, and are generally well known, with no material discrepancy in matters of fact among the statements of the various participants. It is enough, therefore, to add that the bombardment continued for about thirty-three or thirty-four hours. The fort was eventually set on fire by shells, after having been partly destroyed by shot. It is a remarkable fact—probably without precedent in the annals of war—that, notwithstanding the extent and magnitude of the engagement, and the amount of damage done to inanimate material in both sides, especially to Fort Sumter, nobody was injured on either side by the bombardment. The only casualty attendant upon the affair was the death of one man and the wounding of several others by the explosion of a gun in the firing of a salute to their flag by the garrison on evacuating the fort the day after the surrender.

A striking incident marked the close of the bombardment. Ex-Senator Louis T. Wigfall, of Texas—a man as generous as he was recklessly brave—when he saw the fort on fire, supposing the garrison to be hopelessly struggling for the honor of its flag, voluntarily and without authority, went under fire in an open boat to the fort, asked for Major Anderson, and insisted that he should surrender a fort which it was palpably impossible that he could hold. Major Anderson agreed to surrender on the same terms and conditions that had been offered him before his works were battered in breach, and the agreement between them to that effect was promptly ratified by the Confederate commander.

The President of the United States, in his message of July

4, 1861, to the Federal Congress convened in extra session, said:

> It is thus seen that the assault upon and reduction of Fort Sumter was in no sense a matter of self-defense on the part of the assailants. They well knew that the garrison in the fort could by no possibility commit aggression upon them. They knew—they were expressly notified—that the giving of bread to the few brave and hungry men of the garrison was all which would on that occasion be attempted, unless themselves, by resisting so much, should provoke more.

Mr. Lincoln well knew that, if the brave men of the garrison were hungry, they had only him and his trusted advisers to thank for it. They had been kept for months in a place where they ought not to have been, contrary to the judgment of the General-in-Chief of his army, contrary to the counsels of the wisest statesmen in his confidence, and the protests of the commander of the garrison. A word from him would have relieved them at any moment in the manner most acceptable to them and most promotive of peaceful results.

But, suppose the Confederate authorities had been disposed to yield, and to consent to the introduction of supplies for the maintenance of the garrison, what assurance would they have had that nothing further would be attempted? What reliance could be placed in any assurances of the Government of the United States after the experience of the attempted *ruse* of the Star of the West and the deceptions practiced upon the Confederate Commissioners in Washington? He says we were "expressly notified" that nothing more "would *on that occasion* be attempted"—the words in italics themselves constituting a very significant though unobtrusive and innocent-looking limitation. But we had been just as expressly notified, long before, that the garrison would be withdrawn. It would be as easy to violate the one pledge as it had been to break the other.

Moreover, the so-called notification was a mere memorandum, without date, signature, or authentication of any kind, sent to Governor Pickens, not by an accredited agent, but by a subordinate employee of the State Department. Like the oral and written pledges of Mr. Seward, given through Judge Campbell, it seemed to be carefully and purposely divested of every attribute that could make it binding and valid, in case its authors should see fit to repudiate it. It was as empty and worthless as the complaint against the Confederate Government based upon it, is disingenuous.

PART FOUR

THE WAR

Chapter 1

The Organization of the Confederate Army

As HERETOFORE STATED, there was a prevailing belief that there would be no war, or, if any, that it would be of very short duration. Therefore the first bill which passed the provisional Congress provided for receiving troops for short periods—as my memory serves, for sixty days. The chairman of the Committee on Military Affairs, the heroic Colonel Bartow, procured a modification from Congress by which the term of service was extended to twelve months.

This first act to provide for the public defense became a law on the 28th of February, 1861, and its fifth section so clearly indicates the opinions and expectations prevailing when the Confederation was formed, that it is inserted here:

That the President be further authorized to receive into the service of this Government such forces now in the service of said States (Confederate States) as may be tendered, or who may volunteer by consent of their State, in such numbers as he may require for any time not less than twelve months unless sooner discharged.

It will be seen that the arms and munitions within the limits of the several States were regarded as entirely belonging to them; that the forces which were to constitute the provisional army could only be drawn from the several States by their consent, and that these were to be organized under State authority and to be received with their officers so appointed; that the lowest organization was to be that of a company and the highest that of a regiment, and that the appoinment of general officers to command these forces was confided to the Government of the Confederate States, should the assembling of large bodies of troops require organization above that of a regiment; and it will also be observed that provision was made for the discharge of the forces so provided for, before the term of service fixed by the law. No one will fail to perceive how little was anticipated a war of the vast proportions and great duration which ensued, and how tenaciously the sovereignty and self-government of the States were adhered to.

The hope of a peaceful solution rapidly diminished, so that we find on the 6th of March that the Congress, "in order to provide speedily forces to repel invasion," etc., authorized the President to employ the militia, and to ask for and accept the services of any number of volunteers, not exceeding one hundred thousand, and to organize companies into battalions, battalions into regiments, and regiments into brigades and divisions. As in the first law, the President was authorized to appoint the commanding officer of such brigades and divisions, the commissions only to endure while the brigades were in service.

On the same day (March 6, 1861) was enacted the law for the establishment and organization of the Army of the Confederate States of America, this being in contradistinction to the provisional army, which was to be composed of troops tendered by the States, as in the first act, and volunteers received, as in the second act, to constitute a provisional army.

Regarding the Army of the United States as belonging neither to a section of the Union nor to the General Government, but to the States conjointly while they remained united, it follows that, when disintegration occurred, the undivided *personnel* composing the army would be left free to choose their future place of service. Therefore, provision was made for securing to officers, who should leave the Army of the United States and join that of the Confederate States, the same relative rank in the latter which they held in the former.

It is a noteworthy fact that the three highest officers in rank were all so indifferent to any question of personal interest, that they had received their appointment before they were aware that it was to be conferred. Each brought from the Army of the United States an enviable reputation, such as would have secured to him, had he chosen to remain in it, any position his ambition could have coveted. These officers were—first, Samuel Cooper, a native of New York, a graduate of the United States Military Academy in 1815, and who served continuously in the army until March 7, 1861, with such distinction as secured to him the appointment of Adjutant-General of the United States Army. Second, Albert Sidney Johnston, a native of Kentucky, a graduate of the United States Military Academy in 1826, served conspicuously in the army until 1834, then served in the army of the Republic of Texas, and then in the United States Volunteers in the war with Mexico. Subsequently he reëntered the United States Army, and for meritorious conduct attained the rank of brevet brigadier-general. After the secession of Texas, his adopted State, he resigned his commission in the United States Army, May 3, 1861, to offer his services to the Confederacy. Third, Robert E. Lee, a native of Virginia, a graduate of the United States Military Academy in 1829, when he was appointed in the Engineer Corps of the United States Army, and served continuously and with such distinction as to secure for him in 1847 brevets of three grades above his corps commission. He resigned from the Army of the United States, April 25, 1861, upon the secession of Virginia, in whose army he served until it was transferred to the Confederate States.

Samuel Cooper was the first of these to offer his services to the Confederacy at Montgomery. Having known him most favorably and intimately as Adjutant-General of the United States Army when I was Secretary of War, the value of his services was considered so great that I invited him to take the position of Adjutant-General of the Confederate Army. The highest grade then authorized by law was that of brigadier-general, and that commission was bestowed upon him.

When General Albert Sidney Johnston reached Richmond, he asked to what duty I would assign him, and, when answered, to serve in the West, he inquired how he was to raise his command, and for the first time learned that he had been nominated and confirmed as a general in the Army of the Confederacy.

The third, General Robert E. Lee, had been commissioned by the State of Virginia as major-general and commander of her army. When that army was transferred to the Confederate States, he was nominated to be brigadier-general in the Confederate Army, but was left for obvious reasons in command of the forces in Virginia. After the seat of government was removed from Montgomery to Richmond, the course of events on the Southern Atlantic coast induced me to direct General Lee to repair thither. Before leaving, he said that, while he was serving in Virginia, he had never thought it needful to inquire about his rank; but now, when about to go into other States and to meet officers with whom he had not been previously connected, he would like to be informed upon that point. Under recent laws, authorizing appointments to higher grades than that of his first commission, he had been appointed a full general; but so wholly had his heart and his mind been consecrated to the public service, that he had not remembered, if he ever knew, of his advancement.

In organizing the bureaus, it was deemed advisable to select, for the chief of each, officers possessing special knowledge of the duties to be performed. The best assurance of that qualification was believed to be service creditably rendered in the several departments of the United States Army before resigning from it. Brevet Lieutenant-Colonel A. C. Myers, who had held many important trusts in the United States Quartermaster's Department, was appointed Quartermaster-General of the Confederacy, with the rank of colonel.

Captain L. B. Northrop, a gallant officer of the United States Dragoons, and who, by reason of a disabling wound had been employed in the subsistence department, was appointed Commissary-General of the Confederate States Army, with the rank of colonel.

Surgeon L. P. Moore, an officer of recognized merit in the United States Medical Department, from which he had resigned to join the Confederacy, was appointed the Surgeon-General of the Confederate States Army. As in the case of other departments, there was in this a want of the stores requisite, as well for the field as the hospital. To supply medicines which were declared by the enemy to be contraband of war, our medical department had to seek in the forest for substitutes, and to add surgical instruments and appliances to the small stock on hand as best they could. It would be quite beyond my power to do justice to the skill and knowledge with which the medical corps performed their arduous task.

In no branch of our service were our needs so great and our means to meet them relatively so small as in the matter of ordnance and ordnance stores. The Chief of Ordnance, General Gorgas, had been an ordnance officer of the United States Army, and resigned to join the Confederacy.

Chapter 2

The Quest for Armaments

ON THE THIRD DAY after my inauguration at Montgomery, an officer of extensive information and high capacity was sent to buy in the market as far as possible, and, furthermore, to make contracts for arms and munitions to be manufactured. Major Huse, found few serviceable arms upon the market; he, however, succeeded in making contracts for the manufacture of large quantities, being in advance of the agents sent from the Northern Government for the same purpose.

The Southern officers of the navy who were in command of United States vessels abroad, under an idea more creditable to their sentiment than to their knowledge of the nature of our constitutional Union, brought the vessels they commanded into the ports of the North, and, having delivered them to the authorities of the United States Government, generally tendered their resignations, and repaired to the States from which they had been commissioned in the navy, to serve where they held their allegiance to be due. The theory that they owed allegiance to their respective States was founded on the fact that the Federal Government was of the States; the sequence was, that the navy belonged to the States, not to their agent the Federal Government; and, when the States ceased to be united, the naval vessels and armament should have been divided among the owners. We were doubly bereft by losing our share of the navy we had contributed to build, and by having it all employed to assail us. The application of the appropriations for the Navy of the United States had been such that the construction of vessels had been at the North, though much of the timber used and other material employed was transported from the South to Northern ship-yards. Therefore, we were without the accessories needful for the rapid supply of naval vessels.

While attempting whatever was practicable at home, we sent a competent officer of the navy to England to obtain there and elsewhere, by purchase or by building, vessels which could be transformed into ships of war.

At the North many had been deceived by the fictions of preparations at the South for the war of the sections, and among ourselves were few who realized how totally deficient the Southern States were in all which was necessary to the active operations of an army, however gallant the men might be, and however able were the generals who directed and led them. From these causes, operating jointly, resulted undue caution at the North and overweening confidence at the South. The habits of our people in hunting, and protecting their stock in fields from the ravages of ferocious beasts, caused them to be generally supplied with the arms used for such purposes. The facility with which individuals traveled over the country led to very erroneous ideas as to the difficulties of transporting an army. The small amount of ammunition required in time of peace gave no measure of the amount requisite for warlike operations, and the products of a country, which insufficiently supplied food for its inhabitants when peaceful pursuits were uninterrupted, would serve but a short time to furnish the commissariat of a large army. It was, of course, easy to foresee that, if war was waged against the seceding States by all of those which remained in the Union, the large supply of provisions which had been annually sent from the Northwest to the South could not, under the altered circumstances, be relied on. That our people did not more immediately turn their attention to the production of food-supplies, may be attributed to the prevailing delusion that secession would not be followed by war. To the able officer then at the head of the commissariat department, Colonel L. B. Northrop, much credit is due for his well-directed efforts to provide both for immediate and prospective wants. Adequate facilities for transportation might have relieved the local want of supplies, especially in Virginia, where the largest bodies of troops were assembled; but, not only were the railroads insufficient in number, but they were poorly furnished with rolling stock, and had been mainly dependent upon Northern foundries and factories for their rails and equipment. Even the skilled operatives of the railroads were generally Northern men, and their desertion followed fast upon every disaster which attended the Confederate arms. The idea that Cotton was king, and would produce foreign intervention, as well as a desire of the Northern people for the return of peace and the restoration of trade, exercised a potent influence in preventing our agriculturists from directing at an early period their capital and labor to the production of food-supplies rather than that of our staple for export. As one after another the illusions vanished, and the material necessities of a great war were recognized by our people, never did patriotic devotion exhibit brighter examples of the sacrifice of self-interest and the abandonment of fixed habits and opinions. If our people had not gone to war without counting the cost, they were, nevertheless, involved in it without means of providing for its necessities. We had no powder-mills, no depots of powder, and beyond the small supply required for sporting purposes, our local traders had no stock on hand. Very little saltpeter was purchasable in our markets. Sulphur had been recently employed in the clarification of sugar-cane juice, and thus a considerable amount of it was found in New Orleans. Prompt measures were taken to secure a supply of sulphur, and parties were employed to obtain saltpeter from the caves, as well as from the earth of old tobacco-houses and cellars; and artificial niter-beds were made to provide for prospective wants. Of soft wood for charcoal there was abundance, and thus materials were procured for the manufacture of gunpowder.

It was our good fortune to secure the services of an able and scientific soldier, General G. W. Rains, who, to a military education, added experience in a large manufacturing establishment, and to him was confided the construction of a powder-mill, and the manufacture of powder, both for artillery and small-arms. Beginning without even instructed workmen, he had, before the close of the war, made what has been pronounced to be the best powder-mill in the world, and in which powder of every variety of grain was manufactured.

In the progress of this work, it is hoped, will be presented not only the magnitude of the obstacles, but the spirit and capacity with which they were encountered by the unseen and much undervalued labors of the officers of the several departments, on whom devolved provision for the civil service, as well as for the armies in the field.

Chapter 3

"Combinations" and Usurpations

IF ANY FURTHER EVIDENCE had been required to show that it was the determination of the Northern people not only to make no concessions to the grievances of the Southern States, but to increase them to the last extremity, it was furnished by the proclamation of President Lincoln, issued on April 15, 1861. This proclamation requires examination, as it was the official declaration, on the part of the Government of the United States, of the war which ensued. In it the President called for seventy-five thousand men to suppress "combinations" opposed to the laws, and obstructing their execution in seven sovereign States which had retired from the Union. The words in which he summoned this force were these: "Whereas the laws of the United States have been for some time past, and now are, opposed, and the execution thereof obstructed, in the States of South Carolina, Georgia, Alabama, Florida, Mississippi, Louisiana, and Texas, by combinations too powerful to be suppressed by the ordinary course of judicial proceedings, or by the powers vested in the marshals by law: Now, therefore, I, Abraham Lincoln, by virtue of the power in me vested by the Constitution and laws," etc.

The power granted in the Constitution is thus expressed: "The Congress shall have power to provide for calling forth the militia to execute the laws of the Union, suppress insurrections, and repel invasions." It was to the Congress, not the Executive, to whom the power was delegated, and thus early was commenced a long series of usurpations of powers inconsistent with the purposes for which the Union was formed.

On December 20, 1960, a State Convention of South Carolina passed "an ordinance to dissolve the union between the State of South Carolina and other States united with her under the compact entitled 'The Constitution of the United States of America.'" About four months afterward, when the State, in union with others which had joined her, had possessed herself of the forts within her limits, which the United States Government had refused to evacuate, President Lincoln issued the above-mentioned proclamation.

The State of South Carolina is designated in the proclamation as a combination. This designation does not recognize the State, or manifest any consciousness of its existence, whereas South Carolina was one of the colonies that had declared her independence, and had been recognized as a sovereign State by Great Britain, the only power to which she had ever owed allegiance.

By designating the State as a "combination," and considering that under such a name it might be in a condition of insurrection, he assumed to have authority to raise a great military force and attack the State. Yet, even if the fact had been as assumed, if an insurrection had existed, the President could not lawfully have derived the power he exercised from such condition of affairs. The provision of the Constitution is as follows: "The United States shall guarantee to every State in this Union a republican form of government, and shall protect each of them against invasion; and, on application of the Legislature, or of the Executive (when the Legislature can not be convened), against domestic violence." So the guarantee availed not at all to justify the act which it was presented to excuse—the fact being that a State, and not an "unlawful combination," was the object of assault. For a State or union of States to attack with military force another State, is to make war. Thus, under a perverted use of language, the Executive at Washington did that which he undeniably had no power to do, under a faithful observance of the Constitution.

To justify himself to Congress and the people, or, rather, before the face of mankind, for this evasion of the Constitution of his country, President Lincoln, in his message to Congress, of July 4, 1861, resorted to the artifice of saying, "It [meaning the proceedings of the Confederate States] presents to the whole family of man the question whether a constitutional republic or democracy—a government of the people by the same people—can, or can not, maintain its territorial integrity against its own domestic foes?"

The answer to this question is very plain. Such a government as ours had no power to maintain its existence any longer than the contracting parties pleased to cohere, because it was founded on the great principle of voluntary federation. A forced union is a political absurdity. No less absurd is President Lincoln's effort to dissever the sovereignty of the people from that of the State; as if there could be a State without a people, or a sovereign people without a State.

But the question which Mr. Lincoln presents "to the whole

family of man" deserves a further notice. He says, "So viewing the issue, no choice was left but to call out the war power of the Government." That is the power to make war against foreign nations, for the Government has no other war power. Planting himself on this position, he commenced the devastation and bloodshed which followed to effect our subjugation.

Nothing could be more erroneous than such views. The Government of the United States is like no other government. It is neither a "constitutional republic or democracy," nor has it ever been thus called. Neither is it a "government of the people by the same people"; but it is known and designated as "the Government of the United States." It is an anomaly among governments. Its authority consists solely of certain powers delegated to it, as a common agent, by an association of sovereign and independent States.

The beginning and the end of all the powers of the Government of the United States are to be found in that instrument of delegation. [Mr. Lincoln] says, "No choice was left but to call out the war power of the Government, and so to resist force employed for its destruction by force for its preservation." But there was no "force employed for its destruction." The assertion is not only incorrect, in stating that force was employed by us, but also in declaring that it was for the destruction of the Government of the United States. On the contrary, we wished to leave it alone. Our separation did not involve its destruction. To such fiction was Mr. Lincoln compelled to resort to give even apparent justice to his cause. He now goes to the Constitution for the exercise of his war power, and here we have another fiction.

On April 19th, four days after the call for troops, President Lincoln issued another proclamation, announcing a blockade of the ports of seven confederated States, which was afterward extended to North Carolina and Virginia. It further declared that all persons who should under their authority molest any vessel of the United States, or the persons or cargo on board, should be treated as pirates. In their efforts to subjugate us, the destruction of our commerce was regarded by the authorities at Washington as a most efficient measure. It was early seen that, although acts of Congress established ports of entry where commerce existed, they might be repealed, and the ports nominally closed or declared to be closed; yet such a declaration would be of no avail unless sustained by a naval force, as these ports were located in territory not subject to the United States. An act was subsequently passed authorizing the President of the United States, in his discretion, to close our ports, but it was never executed.

The scheme of blockade was resorted to, and a falsehood was asserted on which to base it. Mr. Seward writes to Mr. Dallas: "You will say (to Lord John Russell) that, by our own laws and the laws of nature and the laws of nations, this Government has a clear right to suppress insurrection. An exclusion of commerce from national ports which have been seized by insurgents, in the equitable form of blockade, is a proper means to that end." * This is the same doctrine of "combinations" fabricated by the authorities at Washington to serve as the basis of a bloody revolution. Under the laws of nations, separate governments when at war blockade each other's ports. This is decided to be justifiable. But the Government of the United States could not consent to justify its blockade of our ports on this ground, as it would be an admission that the Confederate States were a separate and distinct sovereignty, and that the war was prosecuted only for subjugation. It, therefore, assumed that the withdrawal of the Southern States from the Union was an insurrection.

Was it an insurrection? Within the Union are oppressions and grievances; and the attempt to go out brings war and subjugation. The ambitious and aggressive States obtain possession of the central authority which, having grown strong in the lapse of time, asserts its entire sovereignty over the States. Whichever of them denies it and seeks to retire, is declared to be guilty of insurrection, its citizens are stigmatized as "rebels," as if they had revolted against a master, and a war of subjugation is begun.

Men do not fight to make a fraternal union, neither do nations. These military preparations of the Government of the United States signified nothing less than the subjugation of the Southern States, so that, by one devastating blow, the North might grasp for ever that supremacy it had so long coveted.

To be prepared for self-defense, I called Congress together at Montgomery on April 29th. I stated that there were then in the field, at Charleston, Pensacola, Forts Morgan, Jackson, St. Philip, and Pulaski, nineteen thousand men, and sixteen thousand more were on their way to Virginia; that it was proposed to organize and hold in readiness for instant action an army of one hundred thousand men; and that, if a further force should be needed, Congress would be appealed to for

* Diplomatic correspondence, May 21, 1861.

authority to call it into the field. Finally, that the intent of the President of the United States, already developed, to invade our soil, capture our forts, blockade our ports, and wage war against us, rendered it necessary to raise means to a much larger amount than had been done, to defray the expenses of maintaining independence and repelling invasion.

The message closed with these words: "We protest solemnly, in the face of mankind, that we desire peace at any sacrifice, save that of honor. In independence we seek no conquest, no aggrandizement, no concession of any kind from the States with which we have lately been confederated. All we ask is to be let alone—that those who never held power over us shall not now attempt our subjugation by arms. This we will, we must, resist to the direst extremity. The moment that this pretension is abandoned, the sword will drop from our grasp, and we shall be ready to enter into treaties of amity and commerce than can not but be mutually beneficial. So long as this pretension is maintained, with a firm reliance on that Divine Power which covers with its protection the just cause, we must continue to struggle for our inherent right to freedom, independence, and self-government."

At this session Congress passed acts authorizing the President to use the whole land and naval force to meet the necessities of the war thus commenced; to issue to private armed vessels letters of marque; in addition to the volunteer force authorized to be raised, to accept the services of volunteers, to serve during the war; to receive into the service various companies of the different arms; to make a loan of fifty millions of dollars in bonds and notes; and to hold an election of officers of the permanent Government under the new Constitution. An act was also passed to provide revenue from imports; another, relative to prisoners of war; and such others as were necessary to complete the internal organization of the Government, and establish the administration of public affairs.

In every portion of the country there was exhibited the most patriotic devotion to the common cause. Transportation companies freely tendered the use of their lines for troops and supplies. Requisitions for troops were met with such alacrity that the number offering their services in every instance greatly exceeded the demand and the ability to arm them. Men of the highest official and social position served as volunteers in the ranks. The gravity of age and the zeal of youth rivaled each other in the desire to be foremost in the public defense.

The appearance of the proclamation of the President of the

United States, calling out seventy-five thousand men, was followed by the immediate withdrawal of the States of Virginia, North Carolina, Tennessee, and Arkansas, and their union with the Confederate States. The former State, thus placed on the frontier and exposed to invasion, began to prepare for a resolute defense. Volunteers were ordered to be enrolled and held in readiness in every part of the State. Colonel Robert E. Lee, was on April 22d nominated and confirmed by the State Convention of Virginia as "Commander-in-Chief of the military and naval forces of the Commonwealth."

Already the Northern officer in charge had evacuated Harper's Ferry, after having attempted to destroy the public buildings there. His report says: "I gave the order to apply the torch. In three minutes or less, both of the arsenal buildings, containing nearly fifteen thousand stand of arms, together with the carpenter's shop . . . were in a blaze. There is every reason for believing the destruction was complete." Mr. Simon Cameron, the Secretary of War, on April 22d replied to this report in these words: "I am directed by the President of the United States to communicate to you, and through you to the officers and men under your command at Harper's Ferry Armory, the approbation of the Government of your and their judicious conduct there, and to tender you and them the thanks of the Government for the same." At the same time the ship-yard at Norfolk was abandoned after an attempt to destroy it. About midnight of April 20th, a fire was started in the yard, and before daylight the work of destruction extended to two immense shiphouses, one of which contained the entire frame of a seventy-four-gun ship, and to the long ranges of stores and offices on each side of the entrance. The great ship Pennsylvania was burned, and the frigates Merrimac and Columbus, and the Delaware, Raritan, Plymouth, and Germantown were sunk. A vast amount of machinery, valuable engines, small-arms, and chronometers, was broken up and rendered entirely useless. The value of the property destroyed was estimated at several millions of dollars.

This property had been accumulated and constructed with laborious care and skillful ingenuity during a course of years to fulfill one of the objects of the Constitution, "To provide for the common defense." It had belonged to all the States in common, and to each one equally with the others. If the Confederate States were still members of the Union, as the justification of these acts?
President of the United States asserted, where can he find a

In explanation of his policy to the Commissioners sent to him by the Virginia State Convention, he said, referring to his inaugural address, "As I then and therein said, I now repeat, the power confided in me will be used to hold, occupy, and possess property and places belonging to the Government." Yet he tendered the thanks of the Government to those who applied the torch to destroy this property belonging, as he regarded it, to the Government.

Chapter 4

Baltimore

THE BORDER STATE of Maryland was the outpost of the South on the frontier first to be approached by Northern invasion. The first demonstration against State sovereignty was to be made there, and in her fate were the other slaveholding States of the border to have warning of what they were to expect. She had chosen to be, for the time at least, neutral in the impending war, and had denied to the United States troops the right of way across her domain in their march to invade the Southern States. The Governor (Hicks) avowed a desire, not only that the State should avoid war, but that she should be a means for pacifying those more disposed to engage in combat.

On the 18th of April, 1861, Governor Hicks issued a proclamation declaring, "I assure the people that no troops will be sent from Maryland, unless it may be for the defense of the national capital." On the same day Mayor Brown, of the city of Baltimore, issued a proclamation in which he said, "I can not withhold my expression of satisfaction at [the governor's] resolution that no troops shall be sent from Maryland to the soil of any other State." It will be remembered that the capital was on a site which originally belonged to Maryland, and was ceded by her for a special use, so that troops to defend the capital might be considered as not having been sent out of Maryland. It will be remembered that these proclamations were three days after the requisition made by the Secretary of War on the States which had not seceded for their quota of troops to serve in the war about to be inaugurated against the South. On the next day, viz., the 19th of April, 1861, a body of troops arrived at the railroad depot; the citizens assembled in large numbers, and, though without arms, disputed the passage through the city. They attacked the troops with the loose stones found in the street, which was undergoing repair, and with such determination and violence, that some of the soldiers were wounded, and they fired upon the multitude, killing a few and wounding many.

The police of Baltimore were very active in their efforts to prevent conflict and preserve the peace; they rescued the baggage and munitions of the troops, which had been seized by the multitude; and the rear portion of the troops was, by direction of Governor Hicks, sent back to the borders of the State. The troops who had got through the city took the railroad at the Southern Depot and passed on. The militia of the city was called out, and by evening quiet was restored. During the night, on a report that more Northern troops were approaching the city by railroads, the bridges nearest to the city were destroyed, as it was understood, by orders from the authorities of Baltimore.

On the 20th of April President Lincoln wrote in reply to Governor Hicks and Mayor Brown, saying, "For the future, troops must be brought here, but I make no point of bringing them through Baltimore." On the next day, Mayor Brown and other influential citizens, by request of the President, visited him. The interview took place in presence of the Cabinet and General Scott, and was reported to the public by the Mayor after his return to Baltimore. From that report I make the following extract:

The protection of Washington, he asseverated with great earnestness, was the sole object of concentrating troops there, and he protested that none of the troops brought through Maryland were intended for any purposes hostile to the State, or aggressive as against the Southern States. . . . He called on General Scott for his opinion, which the General gave at great length, to the effect that troops might be brought through Maryland without going through Baltimore, etc. . . . The interview terminated with the distinct assurance, on the part of the President, that no more troops would be sent through Baltimore, unless obstructed in their transit in other directions.

On the 5th of May, the Relay House, at the junction of the Washington and Baltimore and Ohio Railroads, was occupied by United States troops under General Butler, and, on the 13th of the same month, he moved a portion of the troops to Baltimore, and took position on Federal Hill—thus was consummated the military occupation of Baltimore. On the next day, the commanding General issued a proclamation in which he announced his purpose and authority to discriminate between citizens, those who agreed with him being denominated "well disposed," and the others described with many offensive epithets. The initiatory step of the policy subsequently developed was found in one sentence: "Therefore, all manufacturers of arms and munitions of war are hereby requested to report to me forthwith, so that the lawfulness of their occupations may be known and understood, and all misconstruction of their doings avoided."

There soon followed a demand for the surrender of the arms stored by the city authorities in a warehouse. The police commissioners, upon representation that the demand was by order of the President, decided to surrender the arms under protest, and they were accordingly removed to Fort McHenry.

Baltimore was now disarmed. The Army of the United States had control of the city. There was no longer necessity to regard the remonstrance of Baltimore against sending troops through the city, and that more convenient route was henceforth to be employed. George P. Kane, Marshal of the Police of Baltimore, was arrested at home by a military force, and sent to Fort McHenry, and a provost-marshal was appointed by General Banks, who had succeeded to the command. But this was only the beginning of unbridled despotism and a reign of terror. The Mayor and Police Commissioners held a meeting, and, after preparing a protest against the suspension of their functions in the appointment of a provost-marshal, resolved that, while they would do nothing to "obstruct the execution of such measures as Major-General Banks may deem proper to take, on his own responsibility, for the preservation of the peace of the city and of public order, they can not, . . . recognize the right of any of the officers and men of the police force, as such, to receive orders or directions from any other authority than from this Board; and that, in the opinion of the Board, the forcible suspension of their functions suspends at the same time the active operations of the police law." The Provost-Marshal, with the plenary powers conferred upon him, commenced a system of search and seizure, in private houses, of arms and munitions of every description.

On the 1st of July, General Banks announced that, "in pursuance of orders issued from the headquarters at Washington for the preservation of the public peace in this department, I have arrested, and do detain in custody of the United States, the late members of the Board of Police . . . ." If the object had been to preserve order by any proper and legitimate method, the effective means would palpably have been to rely upon men whose influence was known to be great, and whose integrity was certainly unquestionable. Thenceforward, arrests of the most illustrious became the rule. In a land where freedom of speech was held to be an unquestioned right, freedom of thought ceased to exist, and men were incarcerated for opinion's sake.

For no better reason than a vote in favor of certain resolutions, General Banks sent his provost-marshal to Frederick, where the Legislature was in session; a cordon of pickets was placed around the town to prevent any one from leaving it without a written permission from a member of General Banks's staff; police detectives from Baltimore then went into the town and arrested some twelve or thirteen members and several officers of the Legislature, which, thereby left without a quorum, was prevented from organizing, and it performed the only act which it was competent to do, i. e., adjourned. Governor Hicks, whose promises had been so cheering in the beginning of the year, sent his final message to the Legislature on December 3, 1861. In that, referring to the action of the Maryland Legislature at its several sessions before that when the arrest of its members prevented an organization, he wrote, "This continued until the General Government had ample reason to believe it was about to go through the farce of enacting an ordinance of secession, when the treason was summarily stopped by the dispersion of the traitors. . . ." After referring to the elections of the 13th of June and the 6th of November, he says, the people have "declared, in the most emphatic tones, what I have never doubted, that Maryland has no sympathy with the rebellion, and desires to do her full share in the duty of suppressing it." It would be more easy than gracious to point out the inconsistency between his first statements and this last.

Henceforth the story of Maryland is sad to the last degree, only relieved by the gallant men who left their homes to fight the battle of State rights when Maryland no longer furnished them a field on which they could maintain the rights their fathers left them. Though Maryland did not become one of the Confederate States, she was endeared to the people thereof by many most enduring ties.

The accumulation of Northern forces at and near Washington City, made it evident that the great effort of the invasion would be from that point, while assaults of more or less vigor might be expected upon all important places which the enemy, by his facilities for transportation, could reach. The concentration of Confederate troops in Virginia was begun, and they were sent forward as rapidly as practicable to the points threatened with attack.

Chapter 5

First Battle of Manassas (Bull Run)

THE PROVISIONAL CONGRESS, in session at Montgomery, Alabama, on the 21st of May, 1861, resolved "that this Congress will adjourn on Tuesday next, to meet again on the 20th day of July at Richmond, Virginia." The resolution further authorized the President to have the several executive departments, with their archives, removed at such intermediate time as he might determine, and added a proviso that, if any public emergency should "render it impolitic to meet in Richmond," he should call the Congress together at some other place to be selected by him.

The hostile demonstrations of the United States Government against Virginia caused the President, at an early day after the adjournment of Congress, to proceed to Richmond and to direct the executive departments, with their archives, to be removed to that place as soon as could be conveniently done.

On my arrival in Richmond, General R. E. Lee, as commander of the Army of Virginia, was found there, where he had established his headquarters. He possessed my unqualified confidence, both as a soldier and a patriot, and the command he had exercised over the Army of Virginia, before her accession to the Confederacy, gave him that special knowledge which at the time was most needful. As has been already briefly stated, troops had previously been sent from other States of the Confederacy to the aid of Virginia. The forces there assembled were divided into three armies, at positions the most important and threatened: one, under General J. E. Johnston, at Harper's Ferry, covering the valley of the Shenandoah; another, under General P. G. T. Beauregard, at Manassas, covering the direct approach from Washington to Richmond; and the third, under Generals Huger and Magruder, at Norfolk and on the Peninsula between the James and York Rivers, covering the approach to Richmond from the seaboard.

The first and second of these armies, though separated by the Blue Ridge, had such practicable communication with each other as to render their junction possible when the necessity should be foreseen. They both were confronted by forces greatly superior in numbers to their own.

The activity and vigilance of Stuart, afterward so distinguished as commander of cavalry in the Army of Virginia, and the skill and daring of Jackson, soon by greater deeds to become immortal, checked, punished, and embarrassed the enemy in his threatened advances, and his movements became so devoid of a definite purpose that one was at a loss to divine the object of his campaign, unless it was to detain General Johnston with his forces in the Valley of the Shenandoah, while General McDowell, profiting by the feint, should make the real attack upon General Beauregard's army at Manassas. However that may be, the evidence finally became conclusive that the enemy under General McDowell was moving to attack the army under General Beauregard. The contingency had therefore arisen for that junction which was necessary to enable us to resist the vastly superior numbers of our assailant; for, though the most strenuous exertions had been made to reënforce both the Armies of the Shenandoah and of the Potomac, they yet remained far smaller than those of the enemy confronting them, and made a junction of our forces indispensable whenever the real point of attack should be ascertained. For this movement we had the advantage of an interior line, so that, if the enemy should discover it after it commenced, he could not counteract it by adopting the same tactics. The success of this policy depended upon the time of execution; failure would equally result if done too soon or too late. The determination as to which army should be reënforced from the other, and the exact time of the transfer, must have been a difficult problem, as both the generals appear to have been unable to solve it (each asking reënforcement from the other).

When it was seen that the real attack was to be against the position at Manassas, the order was sent to General Johnston to move to that point [whenever "practicable"]. His letters of the 12th and 15th instant expressed his doubts about his power to retire from before the superior force of General Patterson, therefore the word "practicable" was in this connection the equivalent of possible.

As has been heretofore stated, Congress was to assemble on the 20th of July, to hold its first session at the new capital, Richmond, Virginia. My presence on that occasion and the delivery of a message were required by usage and law. After the delivery of the message to Congress on Saturday, the 20th of July, I intended to leave in the afternoon for Manassas, but was detained until the next morning, when I left by rail to confer with the generals on the field. As we approached Manassas Railroad junction, a cloud of dust was visible a short distance to the west of the railroad. It resembled one raised by a body of marching troops, and recalled to my remembrance the design of General Beauregard to make the Rappahannock his second line of defense. It was, however, subsequently learned that the dust was raised by a number of wagons which had been sent to the rear for greater security against the contingencies of the battle. The sound of the firing had now become very distinct, so much so as to leave no doubt that a general engagement had commenced. Though that event had been anticipated as being near at hand, it was both hoped and desired that it would not occur quite so soon, the more so as it was not known whether the troops from the Valley had yet arrived.

On reaching the railroad junction, I found a large number of men, bearing the usual evidence of those who leave the field of battle under a panic. They crowded around the train with fearful stories of a defeat of our army. The railroad conductor announced his decision that the railroad train should proceed no farther. Looking among those who were about us for one whose demeanor gave reason to expect from him a collected answer, I selected one whose gray beard and calm face gave best assurance. He, however, could furnish no encouragement. Our line, he said, was broken, all was confusion, the army routed, and the battle lost. I asked for Generals Johnston and Beauregard; he said they were on the field when he left it. I returned to the conductor and told him that I must go on; that the railroad was the only means by which I could proceed, and that, until I reached the headquarters, I could not get a horse to ride to the field where the battle was raging. He finally consented to detach the locomotive from the train, and, for my accommodation, to run it as far as the army headquarters. In this manner Colonel J. R. Davis, aide-de-camp, and myself proceeded.

At the headquarters we found the Quartermaster-General, W. L. Cabell, and the Adjutant-General, Jordan, of General Beauregard's staff, who courteously agreed to furnish us horses, and also to show us the route. While the horses were being prepared, Colonel Jordan took occasion to advise my aide-de-camp, Colonel Davis, of the hazard of going to the field, and the impropriety of such exposure on my part. The horses were after a time reported ready, and we started to the field. The stragglers soon became numerous, and warnings as to the fate which awaited us if we advanced were not only frequent but evidently sincere.

There were, however, many who turned back, and the wounded generally cheered upon meeting us. I well remember one, a mere stripling, who, supported on the shoulders of a man, who was bearing him to the rear, took off his cap and waved it with a cheer, that showed within that slender form beat the heart of a hero.

As we advanced, the storm of the battle was rolling westward, and its fury became more faint. When I met General Johnston, who was upon a hill which commanded a general view of the field of the afternoon's operations, and inquired of him as to the state of affairs, he replied that we had won the battle. I left him there and rode still farther to the west. Several of the volunteers on General Beauregard's staff joined me, and a command of cavalry, the gallant leader of which, Captain John F. Lay, insisted that I was too near the enemy to be without an escort. We, however, only saw one column near to us that created a doubt as to which side it belonged; and, as we were riding toward it, it was suggested that we should halt until it could be examined with a field-glass. Colonel Chesnut dismounted so as the better to use his glass, and at that moment the column formed into line, by which the wind struck the flag so as to extend it, and it was plainly revealed to be that of the United States.

Our cavalry, though there was present but the squadron previously mentioned, dashed boldly forward to charge. The demonstration was followed by the immediate retreat of what was, I believe, the last, thereabout, of the enemy's forces maintaining their organization, and showing a disposition to dispute the possession of the field of battle. In riding over the ground, it seemed quite possible to mark the line of a fugitive's flight. Here was a musket, there a cartridge-box, there a blanket or overcoat, a haversack, etc., as if the runner had stripped himself, as he went, of all impediments to speed.

As we approached toward the left of our line, the signs of an utter rout of the enemy were unmistakable, and justified the conclusion that the watchword of "On to Richmond!" had been changed to "Off for Washington!"

On the extreme left of our field of operations, I found the troops whose opportune arrival had averted impending disaster, and had so materially contributed to our victory. Some of them had, after arriving at the Manassas Railroad junction, hastened to our left; their brigadier-general, E. K. Smith, was wounded soon after getting into action, and the command of the brigade devolved upon Elzy, by whom it was gallantly and skillfully led to the close of the battle; others, under the command of General (then Colonel) Early, made a rapid march, under the pressing necessity, from the extreme right of our line to and beyond our left, so as to attack the enemy in flank, thus inflicting on him the discomfiture his oblique movement was designed to inflict on us. All these troops and the others near to them had hastened into action without supplies or camp-equipage; weary, hungry, and without shelter, night closed around them where they stood, the blood-stained victors on a hard-fought field.

It was reported to me that some of the troops had been so long without food as to be suffering severe hunger, and that no supplies could be got where they were. I made several addresses to them, all to the effect that their position was that best adapted to a pursuit of the enemy, and that they should therefore remain there; adding that I would go to the headquarters and direct that supplies should be sent to them promptly.

It was then late, and we rode back in the night, say seven miles, to the army headquarters. I had not seen General Beauregard on the field, and did not find him at his quarters when we returned; the promise made to the troops was therefore communicated to a staff-officer, who said he would have the supplies sent out. At a later hour when I met General Beauregard and informed him of what had occurred, he stated that, because of a false alarm which had reached him, he had ordered the troops referred to from the left to the right of our line, so as to be in position to repel the reported movement of the enemy against that flank. That such an alarm should have been credited, and a night march ordered on account of it, shows how little the completeness of the victory was realized.

Chapter 6

First Battle of Manassas
(continued)

At a late hour of the night, I had a conference with Generals Johnston and Beauregard; the Adjutant-General of the latter, Colonel Jordan, was present, and sat opposite to me at the table.

When, after some preliminary conversation, I asked whether any troops had been sent in pursuit of the enemy, I was answered in the negative. Upon further inquiry as to what troops were in the best position for pursuit, and had been least fatigued during the day, General Bonham's brigade was named. I then suggested that he should be ordered in pursuit; a pause ensued, until Colonel Jordan asked me if I would dictate the order. I at once dictated an order for immediate pursuit. Some conversation followed, the result of which was a modification of the order by myself, so that, instead of immediate pursuit, it should be commenced at early dawn. Colonel Jordan spoke across the table to me, saying, "If you will send the order as you first dictated it, the enemy won't stop till he gets into the Potomac."

Impressed with the belief that the enemy was very superior to us, both in numbers and appointments, I had felt apprehensive that, unless pressed, he would recover from the panic under which he fled from the field, rally on his reserves, and renew the contest. Therefore it was that I immediately felt the necessity for a pursuit of the fugitives, and insisted that the troops on the extreme left should retain their position during the night of the 21st. A rainfall, extraordinary for its violence and duration, occurred on the morning of the succeeding day, so that, over places where during the battle one could scarcely get a drink of water, rolled torrents which, in the afternoon of the 22d, it was difficult to cross.

From these and other causes, the troops were scattered to such an extent that but few commands could have been assembled for immediate service. It was well for us that the enemy, instead of retiring in order, so as to be rallied and again brought to the attack, left hope behind, and fled in dismay to seek for safety beyond the Potomac.

Each hour of the day following the battle added to the evidence of a thorough rout of the enemy. Abandoned wagons, stores, guns, caissons, small-arms, and ammunition, proved his complete demoralization. As far as our cavalry went, no hostile force was met, and all the indications favored the conclusion that the purpose of invasion had for the time been abandoned. The victory, though decisive and important, both in its moral and physical effect, had been dearly bought by the sacrifice of the lives of many of our bravest and best.

In the afternoon of the 22d, with a guide I went to visit the wounded, and among them a youth of my family, who, it was reported to me, was rapidly sinking. After driving many miles, and witnessing very painful scenes, but seldom finding the troops in the position where my guide supposed them to be, and always disappointed in not discovering him I particularly sought, I was, at the approach of night, about to abandon the search, when I was directed to the temporary hospital to which the wounded of that command had been removed. It was too late; the soul of the young soldier had just left his body; the corpse lay before me. Around him were many gentle boys, suffering in different degrees from the wounds they had received. One bright, refined-looking youth from South Carolina, severely if not fatally wounded, responded to my expression of sympathy by the heroic declaration that it was "sweet to die for such a cause."

The victory at Manassas was certainly extraordinary, not only on account of the disparity of numbers and the inferiority of our arms, but also because of many other disadvantages under which we labored. We had no disciplined troops, and though our citizens were generally skilled in the use of small-arms, which with their high pride and courage, might compensate for the want of training while in position, these inadequately substituted military instruction when manoeuvres had to be performed under fire, and could not make the old-fashioned musket equal to the long-range, new-model muskets with which the enemy was supplied. The disparity in artillery was still greater, both in the number and kind of guns; but, thanks to the skill and cool courage of the Rev. Captain W. N. Pendleton, his battery of light, smooth-bore guns, manned principally by the youths whose rector he had been, proved more effective in battle than the long-range rifle-guns of the enemy. The character of the ground brought the forces into close contact, and the ricochet of the round balls carried havoc into the columns of the enemy, while the rifle-guns, if they missed their object, penetrated harmlessly into the ground.

The field was very extensive, broken, and wooded. The senior general had so recently arrived that he had no opportunity minutely to learn the ground, and the troops he brought were both unacquainted with the field and with those with whom they had to coöperate. To all this must be added the disturbing fact that the plan of battle, as originally designed, was entirely changed by the movement of the enemy on our extreme left, instead of right and center, as anticipated. The operations, therefore, had to be conducted against the plan of the enemy, instead of on that which our generals had prepared and explained to their subordinate commanders. The promptitude with which the troops moved, and the readiness with which our generals modified their preconceived plans to meet the necessities as they were developed, entitled them to the commendation so liberally bestowed at the time by their countrymen at large.

The 22d, the day after the battle, was spent in following up the line of the retreating foe, and collecting the large supplies of arms, of ammunition, and other military stores. The supplies of the army were on a scale of such luxurious extravagance as to excite the surprise of those accustomed only to our rigid economy. The anticipation of an easy victory had caused many to come to the battle as to a joyous feast, and the signs left behind them of the extent to which they had been disappointed in the entertainment, constituted the staple of many laughable stories, which were not without their value because of the lesson they contained as to the uncertainties of war, and the mortification that usually follows vain boasting. Among the articles abandoned by the enemy in his flight were some which excited a just indignation. They were handcuffs, the fit appendage of a policeman, but not of a soldier who came to meet his foeman hilt to hilt. These were reported to have been found in large numbers; some of them were sent to Richmond.

On the night of the 22d I held a second conference with Generals Johnston and Beauregard. All the revelations of the day were of the most satisfactory character as to the completeness of our victory. The large amount gained of fine artillery, small-arms, and ammunition, all of which were much needed by us, was not the least gratifying consequence of our success.

I propounded to [the generals] the inquiry as to what more it was practicable to do. They concurred as to their inability to cross the Potomac, and to the further inquiry as to an advance to the south side of the Potomac, General Beauregard promptly stated that there were strong fortifications there, occupied by garrisons, which had not been in the battle, and were therefore not affected by the panic which had seized the defeated army. He described those fortifications as having wide, deep ditches, with palisades, which would prevent the escalade of the works. Turning to General Johnston, he said, "They have spared no expense." It was further stated in explanation that we had no sappers and miners, nor even the tools requisite to make regular approaches. If we had possessed both, the time required for such operations would have more than sufficed for General Patterson's army and other forces to have been brought to that locality in such numbers as must have rendered the attempt, with our present means, futile.

This view of the matter rests on the supposition that the fortifications and garrisons described did actually exist, of which there seemed then to be no doubt. If the reports which have since reached us be true, that there were at that time neither fortifications nor troops stationed on the south bank of the Potomac; that all the enemy's forces fled to the north side of the river, and even beyond; that the panic of the routed army infected the whole population of Washington City; and that no preparation was made, or even contemplated, for the destruction of the bridge across the Potomac —then it may have been that our army, following close upon the flying enemy, could have entered and taken possession of the United States capital. These reports, however, present a condition of affairs altogether at variance with the information on which we had to act. Thus it was that an advance to the south bank of the Potomac was not contemplated as the immediate sequence of the victory at Manassas. What discoveries would have been made and what results would have ensued from the establishment of our guns upon the south bank of the river, to open fire upon the capital, are speculative questions.

After the conference of the 22d, I decided to return to Richmond and employ all the power of my office to increase the strength of the army. I left the field of Manassas, proud of the heroism of our troops in battle, and of the conduct of the officers who led them.

From the official reports it appears that the strength of the two armies was: Confederate, 30,167 men of all arms, with 29 guns; Federal, 35,732 men, with a body of cavalry, of which only one company is reported, and a large artillery force not shown in the tabular statement. Of these troops, some on both sides were not engaged in the battle. This, it is believed, was the case to a much larger extent on our side than on that of the enemy. He selected the point of attack, and could concentrate his troops for that purpose, but we were guarding a line of some seven miles front, and therefore widely dispersed.

For the purpose above stated, extracts are herein inserted from a narrative in the "Operations on the Line of Bull Run in June and July, 1861, including the First Battle of Manassas." The name of the author, J. A. Early, will be a sufficient guarantee for the accuracy of the statements, and for the justice of the conclusions announced. He was educated as a soldier; after leaving the army became a lawyer, but, when his country was involved in war with Mexico, he volunteered and served in the regiment of his native State, Virginia. After that war terminated, he returned to the practice of his profession, which he was actively pursuing when the controversy between the sections caused the call of a convention to decide whether Virginia should secede from the Union. He was sent, by the people of the county in which he resided, to represent them in that convention. There he opposed to the last the adoption of the ordinance for secession; but, when it was decided to resort to the remedy of withdrawal from the Union, he at once stepped forth to defend [his State] against a threatened invasion.

On June 19, 1861, I arrived at Manassas Junction and reported to General P. G. T. Beauregard, the Twenty-fourth Virginia Regiment. . . .

On the morning of July 18th, my brigade was moved, by order of General Beauregard, to the left of Camp Walker, on the railroad, and remained there some time. . . .

On falling back, General Ewell, in pursuance of his instructions, had burned the bridges on the railroad over Pope's Run, from Fairfax Station to Union Mills, and while I was at Camp Walker I saw the smoke ascending from the railroad-bridge over Bull Run, which was burned that morning.

The burning of this bridge had not been included in the previous instructions to Ewell, and I have always been at a loss to know why it was now fired. That bridge certainly was not necessary to the enemy for crossing Bull Run, either with his troops or wagons, as that stream was easily fordable at numerous places, both above and below. The bridge was, moreover, susceptible of easy defense, as there were deep cuts leading to it on both sides. The only possible purpose to be subserved by the burning of that bridge would have been the prevention for a short time of the running of trains over it by the enemy, in the event of our defeat, or evacuation of Manassas without a fight. As it was, we were afterward greatly inconvenienced by its destruction. . . .

The attack made on the 18th is described as directed against our right center, and as having been met and repulsed in a manner quite creditable to our raw troops, of whom he writes:

On the 19th they were occupied in the effort to strengthen their position by throwing up the best defenses they could with the implements at hand, which consisted of a very few picks and spades, some rough bowie-knives, and the bayonets of the muskets. . . . The position was a very weak one, as the banks on the opposite side of Bull Run overlooked and commanded those on the south side, which were but a few feet above the water's edge, and there was an open field in rear of the strip of woods on our side of the stream, for a considerable distance up and down it, which exposed all of our movements on that side to observation from the opposite one, as the strip of woods afforded but a thin veil which could be seen through. . . .

About dusk on the 19th, brigade commanders were summoned to a conference at McLean's house by General Beauregard, and he then informed us of the fact that General Johnston had been ordered, at his instance, from the Valley, and was marching to coöperate with us. He stated that Johnston would march directly across the Blue Ridge toward the enemy's right flank, and would probably attack on that flank at dawn the next morning. Before he had finished his statement of the plans he proposed pursuing in the event of Johnston's attack on the enemy's right flank, a party of horsemen rode up in front of the house, and, dismounting, one of them walked in and reported himself as Brigadier-General T. J. Jackson, who had arrived with the advanced brigade of Johnston's troops by the way of Manassas Gap Railroad, and he stated that his brigade was about twenty-five hundred strong. This information took General Beauregard very much by surprise, and, after ascertaining that General Jackson had taken the cars at Piedmont Station, General Beauregard asked him if General Johnston would not march the rest of his command on the direct road, so as to get on the enemy's right flank. General Jackson replied with some little hesitation, and, as I thought at the time, in rather a stolid manner, that he thought not; that he thought the purpose was to transport the whole force by railroad from Piedmont Station. This was the first time I ever saw General Jackson, and my first impressions of him were not very favorable from the manner in which he gave his information. I subsequently ascertained very well how it was that he seemed to know so little, in the presence of the strangers among whom he found himself, of General Johnston's intended movements, and I presume nothing but the fact of General Beauregard being his superior rank, and his being ordered to report to him, could have elicited as much information from him, under the circumstances, as was obtained. After General Jackson had given the information above stated, and received instructions where to put his brigade, he retired, and General Beauregard proceeded to develop fully his plans for the next day. The information received from General Jackson was wholly unexpected, but General Beauregard said he thought Jackson was not correctly informed, and was mistaken; that he was satisfied General Johnston was marching with the rest of his troops and would attack the enemy's right flank early next day as he had before stated. Upon this hypothesis, he directed that when General Johnston's attack began and he had become fully engaged, of which we were to judge from the character of the musketry-fire, we should cross Bull Run from our several positions, and move upon the enemy so as to attack him on his left flank and rear. He said that he had no doubt General Johnston's attack would be a complete surprise to the enemy; that the latter would not know what to think of it; that when he turned to meet that attack, and soon found himself assailed on the other side, he would be still more surprised and would not know what to do; that the effect would become a complete rout—a perfect Waterloo; and that, when the enemy took to flight, we would pursue, cross the Potomac, and arouse Maryland. . . .

During the 20th General Johnston arrived at Manassas Junction by the railroad, and that day we received the order from him assuming command of the combined armies of General Beauregard and himself.

Early on the morning of the 21st (Sunday), we heard the enemy's guns open from the heights north of Bull Run, from which they had opened on the 18th, and I soon received orders for the movement of my brigade. . . .

Upon arriving there (McLean's Ford), I found General Jones had returned to the intrenchments with his brigade, and I was informed by him that General Beauregard had directed that I should join him (General Beauregard) with my brigade. . . . He then asked me if I had received an order from General Beauregard to go to him, and, on my replying in the negative, he informed me that he had such an order for me in a note to him. He sent to one of his staff-officers for the note, and showed it to me. The note was one directing him to fall back behind Bull Run, and was in pencil. At the foot of it were these words: "Send Early to me." This was all the order that I received to move to the left, and it was shown to me a very little after twelve o'clock. . . . Chisholm, who carried the note to Jones, in which was contained the order I received, passed me at McLean's Ford going on to Jones about, or a little after, eleven o'clock. If I had not received the order until 2 P. M., it would have been impossible for me to get on the field at the time I reached it, about 3.30 P. M. Colonel Chisholm informed me that the order was for all the troops to fall back across Bull Run. . . . I was met by Colonel John S. Preston, one of the General's aides, who informed me that General Beauregard had gone where the fighting was, . . . but that General Johnston was just in front, and his directions were that we should proceed to the left, where there was a heavy fire of musketry. . . . When we reached General Johnston, he expressed great gratification at our arrival, but it was very perceptible that his anticipations were not sanguine. He gave me special instructions as to my movements, directing me to clear our lines completely before going to the front. . . . In some fields on the left of our line we found Colonel Stuart with a body of cavalry and some pieces of artillery, belonging, as I understood, to a battery commanded by Lieutenant Beckham. . . . I found Stuart already in position beyond our extreme left, and, as I understood it, supporting and controlling Beckham's guns, which were firing on the enemy's extreme right flank, thus rendering very efficient service. I feel well assured that Stuart had but *two* companies of cavalry with him, as these were all I saw when he afterward went in pursuit of the enemy. As I approached the left, a young man named Saunders came galloping to me from Stuart with the information that the enemy was about retreating, and a request to hurry on. This was the first word of encouragement we had received since we reached the vicinity of the battle. I told the messenger to inform Stuart that I was then moving as rapidly as my men could move; but he soon returned with another message informing me that the other was a mistake, that the enemy had merely retired behind the ridge in front to form a new flanking column, and cautioning me to be on my guard. This last information proved to be correct. It was the last effort of the enemy to extend his right beyond our left, and was met by the formation of my regiments in his front. . . . The hill on which the enemy's troops were was Chinn's Hill, so often referred to in the accounts of this battle, and the one next year, on the same field. . . . An officer came to me in a gallop, and entreated me not to fire on the troops in front, and I was so much impressed by his earnest manner and confident tone, that I halted my brigade on the side of the hill, and rode to the top of it, when I discovered, about a hundred and fifty yards to my right, a regiment bearing a flag which was drooping around the staff in such a manner as not to be distinguishable from the Confederate flag of that day. I thought that, if the one that had been in front of me was a Virginia regiment, this must also be a Confederate one; but one or two shots from Beckham's guns on the left caused the regiment to face about, when its flag unfurled, and I discovered it to be the United States flag. I forthwith ordered my brigade forward, but it did not reach the top of the hill soon enough to do any damage to the retiring regiment, which retreated precipitately down the hill and across the Warrenton Pike. At that time there was very little distinction between the dress of some of the Federal regiments and some of ours. As soon as the misrepresentation in regard to the character of the troops was corrected, my brigade advanced to the top of the hill that had been occupied by the enemy, and we ascertained that his troops had retired precipitately, and a large body of them was discovered in the fields in rear of Dogan's house, and north of the turnpike. Colonel Cocke, with one of his regiments, now joined us, and our pieces of artillery were advanced and fired upon the enemy's columns with considerable effect, causing them to disperse, and we soon discovered that they were in full retreat. . . . When my column was seen by General Beauregard, he at first thought it was a column of the enemy, having received erroneous information that such a column was on the Manassas Gap Railroad. The enemy took my troops, as they approached his right, for a large body of our troops from the Valley; and as my men, moving by flank, were stretched out at considerable length, from weariness, they were greatly over-estimated. We scared the enemy worse than we hurt him. . . .

It was impossible for me to pusue the enemy farther, as well because I was utterly unacquainted with the crossings of the Run and the woods in front, as because most of the men belonging to my brigade had been marching the greater part of the day and were very much exhausted. But pursuit with infantry would have been unavailing, as the enemy's troops retreated with such rapidity that they could not have been overtaken by any other than mounted troops. . . . In my movement after the retreat of the enemy commenced, I passed the Carter house and beyond our line of battle. The enemy had by this time entirely disappeared, and . . . not observing any movement of troops from our line, I halted, with the expectation of receiving further orders. Observing some men near the Carter house, I rode to it, and found some five or six Federal soldiers, who had collected some wounded there of both sides, and among them Colonel Gardner, of the Eighth Georgia Regiment. . . . Just after my return from the house where I saw Colonel Gardner, President Davis, in company with several gentlemen, rode to where my command was, and addressed a few stirring remarks to my regiments, in succession, which received him with great enthusiasm.

I briefly informed Mr. Davis of the orders I had received, and the movements of my brigade, and asked him what I should do under the circumstances. He told me that I had better get my men into line, and wait for further orders. I then requested him to inform Generals Johnston and Beauregard of my position, and my desire to receive orders. . . . While we were talking, we saw a body of troops moving on the opposite side of Bull Run, some distance below us.

Mr. Davis then left me . . . and I moved my brigade some half a mile farther, and formed it in line across the peninsula formed by a very considerable bend in Bull Run above the stone bridge. I put out a line of pickets in front, and my brigade bivouacked in this position for the night. By the time all these dispositions were made it was night, and I then rode back with Captain Gardner over the route I had moved on, as I knew no other, in order to find General Johnston or General Beauregard, so that I might receive orders, supposing that there would be a forward movement early in the morning. I first went to the Lewis house, which I found to be a hospital filled with wounded men; but was unable to get any information about either of the generals. I then rode toward Manassas, and, after going some distance in that direction, I met an officer who inquired for General Johnston, stating that he was on his staff. I informed him that I was looking for General Johnston also, as well as for General Beauregard, and supposed they were at Manassas; but he said that he was just from Manassas, and neither of the generals was there. . . . At about twelve o'clock at night I lay down in the field in rear of my command, on a couple of bundles of wheat in the straw. My men had no rations with them. I had picked up a haversack on the field, which was filled with hard biscuits, and had been dropped by some Yankee in his flight, and out of its contents I made my own supper, distributing the rest among a number of officers who had nothing.

Very early next morning, I sent Captain Gardner to look out for the generals, and get orders for my command. He went to Manassas, and found General Beauregard, who sent orders to me to remain where I was until further orders, and to send for the camp-equipage, rations, etc., of my command. A number of the men spread over the country in the vicinity of the battlefield, and picked up a great many knapsacks, India-rubber cloths, blankets, overcoats, etc., as well as a good deal of sugar, coffee, and other provisions that had been abandoned by the enemy. . . .

After I had received orders showing that there was no purpose to make a forward movement, I rode over a good deal of the field, north of the Warrenton pike, and to some hospitals in the vicinity, in order to see what care was being taken of the wounded. I found a hospital on the Sudley road, back of the field of battle, at which Colonel Jones, of the Fourth Alabama, had been, which was in charge of a surgeon of a Rhode Island regiment, whose name was Harris, I think. I asked him if he had what he wanted for the men under his care, and he told me he would like to have some morphine, of which his supply was short. I directed a young surgeon of our cavalry, who rode up at the time, to furnish the morphine, which he did, from a pair of medical saddle-pockets which he had. Dr. Harris told me that he knew that their troops had had a great deal of coffee and sugar mixed, ready for boiling, of which a good deal had been left at different points near the field, and asked if there would be any objection to his sending out and gathering some of it for the use of the wounded under his charge, as it would be of much service to them. I gave him the permission to get not only that, but anything else that would tend to the comfort of his patients. There did not come within my observation any instance of harsh or unkind treatment of the enemy's wounded; nor did I see any indication of a spirit to extend such treatment to them. . . .

On the night following the battle, when I was looking for Generals Beauregard and Johnston, in riding over and to the rear of the battle-field, I discovered that the greater part of the troops that had been engaged in the battle were in a great state of confusion. I saw companies looking for their regiments, and squads looking for their companies, and they were scattered as far as I went toward Manassas. It was very apparent that no considerable body of those troops that had been engaged on the left could have been brought into a condition next day for an advance toward Washington. . . .

The dispute as to who planned the battle, or commanded on the field, General Johnston or General Beauregard, is a most unprofitable one. The battle which General Beauregard planned was never fought, because the enemy did not move as he expected him to move. The battle which was fought was planned by McDowell, at least so far as the ground on which it was fought was concerned. He made a movement on our left which was wholly unexpected and unprovided for, and we were compelled to fight a defensive battle on that flank, by bringing up reënforcements from other points as rapidly as possible. When Generals Johnston and Beauregard arrived on the field where the battle was actually fought, it had been progressing for some time, with the odds greatly against us. What was required then was to rally the troops already engaged, which had been considerably shattered, and hold the position to which they had been compelled to retire until reënforcements could be brought up. According to the statements of both generals, the command of the troops then on the field was given to General Beauregard, and he continued to exercise it until the close, but in subordination, of course, to General Johnston, as commander-in-chief, while the movements of all the reënforcements as they arrived were unquestionably directed by the latter. According to the statement of both, the movement of Elzey's brigade to the left averted a great danger, and both concur in attributing the turning of the tide of battle to the movement of my brigade against the enemy's extreme right flank. . . .

The attempt to show that the failure to advance was due to the want of transportation and rations for the army is idle. If the Bull Run bridge had not been burned on the 18th, our supplies could have been run to Alexandria, if we could have advanced, as easily as to Manassas, for the enemy had repaired the railroad to Fairfax Station as he moved up, and failed to destroy it when he went back. Moreover, we had abundant transportation at that time for all the purposes of an advance as far as Washington. In my brigade, the two Virginia regiments had about fourteen six-horse wagons each, and that would have furnished enough for the brigade, if the Seventh Louisiana had none. In 1862 we carried into Maryland only enough wagons to convey ammunition, medical supplies, and cooking-utensils, and we started from the battlefield of second Manassas with no rations on hand, being, before we crossed the Potomac, entirely dependent on the country, which, in July, 1861, was teeming with supplies, but in August and September, 1862, was nearly depleted. The pretense, therefore, that the advance in July, 1861, was prevented by the want of transportation and of supplies is wholly untenable.

If universal gratulation at our success inspired an overweening confidence, it also begat increased desire to enter the military service; and, but for our want of arms and munitions, we could have enrolled an army little short of the number of able-bodied men in the Confederate States.

Impressed with the conviction that time would naturally work to our disadvantage, as training was more necessary to make soldiers of the Northern people than of our own; and further, because of their larger population, as well as their greater facility in obtaining recruits from foreign countries, the Administration continued assiduously to exert every faculty to increase the efficiency of the army by addition to its numbers, by improving its organization, and by supplying the needful munitions and equipments. Inactivity is the prolific source of evil to an army, especially if composed of new levies, who, like ours, had hurried from their homes at their country's call. For these, and other reasons more readily appreciated, it was thought desirable that all our available forces should be employed as actively as might be practicable.

Chapter 7

Kentucky; Military Preparations

KENTUCKY DECLARED, in the impending conflict between the States seceding from and those adhering to the Federal Government, that she would hold the position of neutrality. The following correspondence took place in August, between Governor Magoffin, of Kentucky, and President Lincoln— also between the Governor and myself, as President of the Confederate States—relative to the neutrality of the State:

COMMONWEALTH OF KENTUCKY, EXECUTIVE DEPARTMENT,
FRANKFURT, *August 19, 1861*
To his Excellency ABRAHAM LINCOLN, *President of the United States.*

SIR: From the commencement of the unhappy hostilities now pending in this country, the people of Kentucky have indicated an earnest desire and purpose, as far as lay in their power, while maintaining their original political status, to do nothing by which to involve themselves in the war. Up to this time they have succeeded in securing to themselves and to the State peace and tranquillity as the fruits of the policy they adopted. My single object now is to promote the continuance of these blessings to this State.

Until within a brief period the people of Kentucky were quiet and tranquil, free from domestic strife, and undisturbed by internal commotion. They have resisted no law, rebelled against no authority, engaged in no revolution, but constantly proclaimed their firm determination to pursue their peaceful avocations, earnestly hoping that their own soil would be spared the presence of armed troops, and that the scene of conflict would be kept removed beyond the border of their State. By thus avoiding all occasions for the introduction of bodies of armed soldiers, and offering no provocation for the presence of military force, the people of Kentucky have sincerely striven to preserve in their State domestic peace and avert the calamities of sanguinary engagements.

Recently a large body of soldiers have been enlisted in the United States army and collected in military camps in the central portion of Kentucky. This movement was preceded by the active organization of companies, regiments, etc., consisting of men sworn into the United States service, under officers holding commissions from yourself. Ordnance, arms, munitions, and supplies of war are being transported into the State, and placed in large

192

quantities in these camps. In a word, an army is now being organized and quartered within the State, supplied with all the appliances of war, without the consent or advice of the authorities of the State, and without consultation with those most prominently known and recognized as loyal citizens. This movement now imperils that peace and tranquility . . . which, up to this time, they [the people of Kentucky] have so secured to the State. . . .

Now, therefore, as Governor of the State of Kentucky . . . I urge the removal from the limits of Kentucky of the military force now organized and in camp within the State.

I am, very respectfully, your obedient servant,

B. MAGOFFIN

WASHINGTON, August 24, 1861

To his Excellency B. MAGOFFIN, Governor of the State of Kentucky.

SIR: Your letter of the 19th instant, in which you "urge the removal from the limits of Kentucky of the military force now organized and in camp within that State," is received.

I may not possess full and precisely accurate knowledge upon this subject; but I believe it is true that there is a military force in camp within Kentucky, acting by authority of the United States, which force is not very large, and is not now being augmented.

I also believe that some arms have been furnished to this force by the United States.

I also believe this force consists exclusively of Kentuckians, having their camp in the immediate vicinity of their own homes, and not assailing or menacing any of the good people of Kentucky.

In all I have done in the premises, I have acted upon the urgent solicitation of many Kentuckians, and in accordance with what I believed, and still believe, to be the wish of a majority of all the Union-loving people of Kentucky.

While I have conversed on this subject with many of the eminent men of Kentucky, including a large majority of her members of Congress, I do not remember that any one of them, or any other person except your Excellency and the bearers of your Excellency's letter, has urged me to remove the military force from Kentucky, or to disband it. One very worthy citizen of Kentucky did solicit me to have the augmenting of the force suspended for a time.

Taking all the means within my reach to form a judgment, I do not believe it is the popular wish of Kentucky that this force shall be removed beyond her limits; and, with this impression, I must respectfully decline to so remove it.

. . . It is with regret I search for, and can not find, in your not very short letter, any declaration or intimation that you entertain any desire for the preservation of the Federal Union.

Your obedient servant,   A. LINCOLN

COMMONWEALTH OF KENTUCKY, EXECUTIVE DEPARTMENT,
FRANKFORT, *August 24, 1861*

Hon. JEFFERSON DAVIS, *Richmond, Virginia*

SIR: Since the commencement of the unhappy difficulties pending in the country, the people of Kentucky, have indicated a steadfast desire and purpose to maintain a position of strict neutrality between the belligerent parties. They have earnestly striven by their policy to avert from themselves the calamity of war, and protect their own soil from the presence of contending armies. Up to this period they have enjoyed comparative tranquillity and entire domestic peace.

Recently a military force has been enlisted and quartered by the United States authorities within this State. I have on this day addressed a communication and dispatched commissioners to the President of the United States, urging the removal of these troops from the soil of Kentucky, and thus exerting myself to carry out the will of the people in the maintenance of a neutral position. The people of this State desire to be free from the presence of the soldiers of either belligerent, and to that end my efforts are now directed.

Although I have no reason to presume that the Government of the Confederate States contemplate or have ever proposed any violation of the neutral attitude thus assumed by Kentucky, there seems to be some uneasiness felt among the people of some portion of the State, occasioned by the collection of bodies of troops along their southern frontier. In order to quiet this apprehension, and to secure to the people their cherished object of peace, this communication is to present these facts and elicit and authorative assurance that the Government of the Confederate States will continue to respect and observe the position indicated as assumed by Kentucky.

Very respectfully, your obedient servant,

B. MAGOFFIN

RICHMOND, *August 28, 1861*

To Hon. B. MAGOFFIN, *Governor of Kentucky, etc.*

SIR: I have received your letter informing me that "since the commencement of the unhappy difficulties pending in the country, the people of Kentucky have indicated a steadfast desire to maintain a position of strict neutrality between the belligerent parties." . . .

. . . I lose no time in assuring you that the Government of the Confederate States neither desires nor intends to disturb the neutrality of Kentucky. The assemblage of troops in Tennessee, to which you refer, had no other object than to repel the lawless invasion of that State by the forces of the United States, should their Government seek to approach it through Kentucky, without respect for its position of neutrality. That such apprehensions were not groundless has been proved by the course of that Government in the States of Maryland and Missouri, and more recently in Kentucky itself. . . .

In view of the history of the past, it can scarcely be necessary to assure your Excellency that the Government of the Confederate States will continue to respect the neutrality of Kentucky so long as her people will maintain it themselves.

But neutrality, to be entitled to respect, must be strictly maintained between both parties; or, if the door be opened on the one side for the aggressions of one of the belligerent parties upon the other, it ought not to be shut to the assailed when they seek to enter it for purposes of self-defense.

I do not, however, for a moment believe that your gallant State will suffer its soil to be used for the purpose of giving an advantage to those who violate its neutrality and disregard its rights, over others who respect both. . . .

Yours, etc.,   JEFFERSON DAVIS

Movements by the Federal forces in southwestern Kentucky revealed such designs as made it absolutely necessary that General Polk, commanding the Confederate forces in that section, should immediately occupy the town of Columbus, Kentucky; a position of much strategic importance on the Mississippi River, which was doubly important, because it commanded the opposite shore in Missouri, and was the gateway on the border of Tennessee.

Two States of the Confederacy were therefore threatened by the anticipated movement of the enemy to get possession of Columbus.

Major-General Polk, therefore, crossed the State line, took possession of Hickman on September 3rd, and on the 4th secured Columbus. General Grant, who took command at Cairo on September 2d, being thus anticipated, seized Paducah, at the mouth of the Tennessee River, and occupied it in force on the 5th and 6th.

The Legislature of Kentucky passed resolutions and appointed a committee to inquire into the action of General Polk, from which the annexed correspondence resulted:

COLUMBUS, KENTUCKY, *September 9, 1861*
To Major-General POLK, *commanding forces, etc.*

SIR: I have the honor to inclose herewith a resolution of the Senate of Kentucky, adopted by that body upon the reception of the intelligence of the military occupation of Hickman, Chalk Bank, and Columbus, by the Confederate troops under your command. I need not say that the people of Kentucky are profoundly astonished that such an act should have been committed by the Confederates, and especially that they should have been the first to do so with an equipped and regularly organized army.

The people of Kentucky have with great unanimity determined upon a position of neutrality in the unhappy war now being waged. . . .

In obedience to the thrice-repeated will of the people, as expressed at the polls, and in their name, I ask you to withdraw your forces from the soil of Kentucky.

I will say, in conclusion, that all the people of the State await, in deep suspense, your action in the premises.

I have the honor to be, your obedient servant, etc.,

(Signed)   JOHN M. JOHNSON,
Chairman of Committee

COLUMBUS, KENTUCKY, *September 9, 1861*

To J. M. JOHNSON, *Chairman of Committee, Senate of Kentucky*

SIR: I have the honor to acknowledge the receipt of your letter of this date. . . .

. . . I have respectfully to say that, so far as the Confederate forces are concerned, the facts are plain, and shortly stated. The Government which they represent, recognizing as a fundamental principle the right of sovereign States to take such a position as they choose in regard to their relations with other States, was compelled by that principle to concede to Kentucky the right to assume the position of neutrality, which she has chosen in the passing struggle. This it has done on all occasions, and without an exception. . . .

The first and only instance in which the neutrality of Kentucky has been disregarded is that in which the troops under my command . . . took possession of the place I now hold, and so much of the territory between it and the Tennessee line as was necessary for me to pass over in order to reach it. This act finds abundant justification in the history of the concessions granted to the Federal Government by Kentucky ever since the war began, notwithstanding the position of neutrality which she had assumed. . . . That history shows the following among other facts:

. . . She has allowed the seizure in her port (Paducah) of property of citizens of the Confederate States; she has, by her members in the Congress of the United States, voted supplies of men and money to carry on the war against the Confederate States; she has allowed the Federal Government to cut timber from her forests for the purpose of building armed boats for the invasion of the Southern States; she is permitting to be enlisted in her territory, troops, not only of her own citizens, but of the citizens of other States, for the purpose of being armed and used in offensive warfare against the Confederate States. . . . Notwithstanding all these and other acts of a similar character, the Confederate States have continued to respect the attitude which Kentucky had assumed as a neutral, and forborne from reprisals, in the hope that Kentucky would yet enforce respect for her position on the part of the Government of the United States.

Our patient expectation has been disappointed, and it was only when we perceived that this continued indifference to our rights and our safety was about to culminate in the seizure of an important part of her territory by the United States forces for offensive operations against the Confederate States, that a regard for self-preservation demanded of us to seize it in advance. We are here, therefore, not by choice, but of necessity, and as I have had the honor to say, in a communication addressed to his Excellency Governor Magoffin . . . I am prepared to agree to withdraw the Confederate troops from Kentucky, provided she will agree that the troops of the Federal Government be withdrawn simultaneously, with a guarantee (which I will give reciprocally for the Confederate Government) that the Federal troops shall not be allowed to enter nor occupy any part of Kentucky for the future. . . .

> Your obedient servant, etc.,
> LEONIDAS POLK,
> *Major-General commanding*

However willing the government of Kentucky might have been to accede to the proposition of General Polk, the State of Kentucky had no power, moral or physical, to prevent the United States Government from using her soil as best might suit its purposes in the war it was waging for the subjugation of the seceded States. President Lincoln, in his message of the previous July, had distinctly and reproachfully spoken of the idea of neutrality as existing in some of the border States. He said: "To prevent the Union forces passing one way, or the disunion the other, over their soil, would be disunion completed. . . . At a stroke it would take all the trouble off the hands of secession, except only what proceeds from the external blockade."

As far as the truth could be ascertained, a decided majority of the people of Kentucky, especially its southwestern portion, if left to a free choice, would have joined the Confederacy in preference to remaining in the Union. The General Government, little by little, gained power over Kentucky, and then proceeded to outrages regardless of law. Men who had been most honored by the State were seized without warrant, condemned without trial, because they had exercised the privilege of free speech. Members of the Legislature vacated their seats and left the State to avoid arrest, the penalty hanging over them for opinion's sake. Others of great worth and distinction left the land desecrated by despotic usurpation to join the Confederacy.

Meanwhile, Albert Sidney Johnston resigned his commission in the United States Army, and came to Richmond to tender his services to the Confederate States. On the 10th of September, 1861, he was assigned to command our Department of the West, which included the States of Tennessee, Missouri, Arkansas, the Indian country, and the western part of Mississippi.

General Johnston, on his arrival at Nashville, found that men were ready to be enlisted, but the arms and equipments had nearly all been required to fit out the first levies. On the next day after his arrival he wrote to the Governor of Alabama, "I shall beg to rely on your Excellency to furnish us as rapidly as possible, at this point, with every arm it may be in your power to provide—I mean small-arms for infantry and cavalry." The Governor replied, "It is out of the power of Alabama to afford you any assistance in the way of arms." The Governor of Georgia replied similarly to the same request on September 18th. On September 19th General Johnston telegraphed to me: "Thirty thousand stand of arms are a necessity to my command. I beg you to order them, or as many as can be got, to be instantly procured and sent with dispatch." The Secretary of War replied: "The whole number received by us, by that steamer, was eighteen hundred, and we purchased of the owners seventeen hundred and eighty, making in all thirty-five hundred Enfield rifles, of which we have been compelled to allow the Governor of Georgia to have one thousand for arming troops to repel an attack now hourly threatened at Brunswick. Of the remaining twenty-five hundred, I have ordered one thousand sent to you, leaving us but fifteen hundred for arming several regiments now encamped here, and who have been awaiting their arms for several months. . . . We have not an engineer to send you. The whole engineer corps comprises only six captains together with three majors, of whom one is on bureau duty. You will be compelled to employ the best material within your reach, by detailing officers from other corps, and by employing civil engineers."

These details are given to serve as an illustration of the deficiencies existing in every department of the military service in the first years of the war. In this respect much relief came from the well-directed efforts of Governor Harris and the Legislature of Tennessee. A cap-factory, ordnance-shops, and work-shops were established. The powder-mills at Nashville turned out about four hundred pounds a day. Twelve or fourteen batteries were fitted out at Memphis. Laws were passed to impress and pay for the private arms scattered throughout the State, and the utmost efforts were made to collect and adapt them to military uses. The returns make it evident that, during most of the autumn of 1861, fully one half of General Johnston's troops were imperfectly armed, and whole brigades remained without weapons for months.

No less energetic were the measures taken to concentrate and recruit his forces. General Hardee's command was moved from northeastern Arkansas, and sent to Bowling Green, which added four thousand men to the troops there. The regiment of Texan rangers was brought from Louisiana, and supplied with horses and sent to the front. Five hundred Kentuckians joined General Buckner on his advance, and five regiments were gradually formed and filled up. A cavalry company under John H. Morgan was also added. At this time (September, 1861), General Johnston, under the authority granted to him by the Government, made a requisition for thirty thousand men from Tennessee, ten thousand from Mississippi, and ten thousand from Arkansas. The Arkansas troops were directed to be sent to General McCulloch for the defense of their own frontier. The Governor of Mississippi sent four regiments, when this source of supply was closed.

Up to the middle of November only three regiments were mustered in under this call from Tennessee, but, by the close of December, the number of men who joined was from twelve to fifteen thousand. Two regiments, fifteen hundred strong, had joined General Polk.

In Arkansas, five companies and a battalion had been organized, and were ready to join General McCulloch.

A speedy advance of the enemy was now indicated, and an increase of force was so necessary that further delay was impossible. General Johnston, therefore, determined upon a levy *en masse* in his department. He made a requisition on the Governors of Tennessee, Alabama, and Mississippi, to call out every able-bodied member of the militia into whose hands arms could be placed, or to provide a volunteer force large enough to use all the arms that could be procured. In his letters to these Governors, he plainly presents his view of the posture of affairs on December 24th, points out impending dangers, and shows that to his applications the response had not been such as the emergency demanded.

On June 5th General Johnston was reënforced by the brigades of Floyd and Maney from western Virginia. He also sent a messenger to Richmond to ask that a few regiments might be detached from the several armies in the field, and sent to him to be replaced by new levies. He said: "I do not ask that my force shall be made equal to that of the enemy; but, if possible, it should be raised to fifty thousand men." Meantime such an appearance of menace had been maintained as led the enemy to believe that our force was large, and that he might be attacked at any time. Frequent and rapid expeditions through the sparsely settled country gave rise to rumors which kept alive this apprehension.

Chapter 8

Federal Coercion of States

BY THE last clause of the Constitution it was provided that not even to suppress domestic violence could the General Government, on its own motion, send troops of the United States into the territory of one of the States. That section reads thus:

The United States shall guarantee to every State in this Union a republican form of government, and shall protect each of them against invasion, and on application of the Legislature, or of the executive (when the Legislature can not be convened), against domestic violence.

That, instead of an obligation upon the citizens of other States to respond to a call by the President for troops to invade a particular State, it was in April, 1861, deemed a high crime to so use them: reference is here made to the published answers of the Governors of States, which had not seceded, to the requisition made upon them for troops.

Governor Letcher, of Virginia, replied to the order as follows:

. . . I have only to say that the militia of Virginia will not be furnished to the powers at Washington for any such use or purpose as they have in view. Your object is to subjugate the Southern States, and a requisition made upon me for such an object—an object, in my judgment, not within the purview of the Constitution, or the Act of 1795—will not be complied with.

Governor Magoffin, of Kentucky, replied:

Your dispatch is received. In answer, I say emphatically, Kentucky will furnish no troops for the wicked purpose of subduing her sister Southern States.

Governor Harris, of Tennessee, replied:

Tennessee will not furnish a single man for coercion, but fifty thousand, if necessary, for the defense of our rights, or those of our Southern brothers.

Governor Jackson, of Missouri, answered:

Requisition is illegal, unconstitutional, revolutionary, inhuman, diabolical, and can not be complied with.

Governor Rector, of Arkansas, replied:

. . . I have to say that none will be furnished. The demand is only adding insult to injury.

Governor Ellis, of North Carolina, responded:

Your dispatch is received, and, if genuine—which its extraordinary character leads me to doubt—I have to say, in reply, that I regard the levy of troops made by the Administration, for the purpose of subjugating the States of the South, as in violation of the Constitution, and a usurpation of power. I can be no party to this wicked violation of the laws of the country, and to this war upon the liberties of a free people. You can get no troops from North Carolina.

There was great similarity in the condition of Missouri to that of Kentucky. They were both border States, and, by their institutions and the origin of a large portion of their citizens, were identified with the South. Both sought to occupy a neutral position in the impending war, and offered guarantees of peace and order throughout their territory if left free to control their own affairs. Both refused to furnish troops to the United States Government for the purpose of coercing the Southern States. Both, because of their stronger affinity to the South than to the North, were the objects of suspicion, and consequent military occupation by the troops of the United States Government.

Captain Nathaniel Lyon, commanding United States forces at St. Louis, initiated hostilities against the State of Missouri under the following circumstances:

In obedience to the militia law of the State, an annual encampment was directed by the Governor for instruction in tactics. Camp Jackson, near St. Louis, was designated for the encampment in 1861. Here for some days companies of State militia, amounting to about eight hundred men, under command of Brigadier-General D. M. Frost, were being exercised. They presented no appearance of a hostile camp. There were no sentinels to guard against surprise; visitors were freely admitted; it was the picnic-ground for the ladies of the city.

Suddenly, Captain (afterward General) Lyon appeared with an overwhelming force of Federal troops, surrounded this holiday encampment, and demanded an unconditional surrender. Resistance was impracticable, and none was attempted; the militia surrendered, and were confined as prisoners; but prisoners of what? There was no war, and no warrant for their arrest as offenders against the law. While thus disarmed and surrounded, a fire was opened on a portion of [the militia] by [the Federal] troops, and a number of the men put to death, together with several innocent lookers-on, men, women, and children. A large crowd of citizens, men, women, and children, were gathered around, gazing curiously at these strange proceedings, when a volley was fired into them, killing ten and wounding twenty non-combatants, mostly women and children. A reign of terror was at once established, and the most severe measures were adopted by the Federals. . . ."

The massacre at Camp Jackson produced intense excitement throughout the State of Missouri. The Legislature passed several bills for the enrollment and organization of the militia, and to confer special powers upon the Governor of the State. By virtue of these, general officers were appointed, chief of whom was Sterling Price.

Because of the atrocities at St. Louis, and the violent demonstrations consequent upon them, General Price, well known to be what was termed "a Union man," was earnestly solicited by influential citizens to unite with General Harney, of the United States Army, commander of the Department of the West, in a joint effort to restore order and preserve peace. With the sanction of Governor Jackson he proceeded to St. Louis, the headquarters of the Department of the West, and entered into the following agreement:

St. Louis, *May 21, 1861*

The undersigned, officers of the United States Government and of the government of the State of Missouri, for the purpose of removing misapprehension and of allaying public excitement, deem it proper to declare publicly that . . . it has been mutually understood . . . that each of them has no other than a common object, . . . that of restoring peace and good order to the people of the State in subordination to the laws of the General and State governments.

. . . General Price, having full authority over the militia of the State of Missouri, undertakes . . . to direct the whole power of the State officers to maintaining order within the State. . . . General

Harney publicly declares that, this object being assured, he can have no occasion, as he has no wish, to make military movements. . . .

W. S. HARNEY,
Brigadier-General commanding
STERLING PRICE,
Major-General Missouri State Guard

In conformity with this understanding, General Price returned to the capital of the State, and sent to their homes the militia who had been assembled there by the Governor. Those who desired to preserve peace in Missouri had just cause to be gratified at the favorable prospect now presented. Those who desired war had equal ground for dissatisfaction.

A few days after the promulgation of the agreement between General Price and General Harney, the latter was removed from command, as many believed, because of his successful efforts to allay excitement and avoid war.

The principal United States arsenal at the West was that near to St. Louis. To it had been transferred a large number of the altered muskets sent from Springfield, Massachusetts, so that in 1861 the arms in that arsenal were, perhaps, numerically second only to those at Springfield. These arms, by a conjunction of deceptive and bold measures, were removed from the arsenal in Missouri and transported to Illinois.

Not satisfied with removing the public arms from the limits of Missouri, the next step was that, in total disrespect of the constitutional right of the citizens to bear arms for their own defense, and to be free from searches and seizures except by warrants duly issued, the officers of the General Government proceeded to search the houses of citizens in St. Louis, and to seize arms wherever they were found.

Missouri had refused to engage in war against her sister States of the South; therefore she was first to be disarmed, and then to be made the victim of an invasion.

In his endeavor to maintain the peace of the State, and to avert, if possible, from its borders a civil war, Governor Jackson caused the aforementioned agreement to be made with the commander of the Northern forces in the State, by which its peace might be preserved. That officer had been promptly removed by his Government. The Governor then, upon the increase of hostile actions, proposed, at an interview with the new officer commanding the forces of the United States Government, to disband the State Guard, and break up its organization; to disarm all companies that had been armed by the State; to pledge himself not to organize the militia under the military bill; that no arms or munitions of war should be brought into the State; that he would protect the citizens equally in all their rights, regardless of their political opinions; that he would repress all insurrectionary movements within the State; would repel all attempts to invade it, from whatever quarter, and by whomsoever made; and would maintain a strict neutrality and preserve the peace of the State. And, further, if necessary, he would invoke the assistance of the United States troops to carry out the pledges. The only conditions to this proposition made by the Governor were that the United States Government should undertake to disarm the "Home Guard" which it had illegally organized and armed throughout the State, and pledge itself not to occupy with its troops any localities in the State not occupied by them at that time.

In the words of Governor Jackson: "Nothing but the most earnest desire to avert the horrors of civil war from our beloved State could have tempted me to propose these humiliating terms. They were rejected by the Federal officers."

These demanded not only the disorganization and disarming of the State militia and the nullification of the military bill, but they refused to disarm their own "Home Guard," and insisted that the Government of the United States should enjoy an unrestricted right to move and station its troops throughout the State whenever and wherever it might, in the opinion of its officers, be necessary either for the protection of its "loyal subjects" or for the repelling of invasion; and they plainly announced that it was the intention of the Administration to take military occupation of the whole State, and to reduce it, as avowed by General Lyon, to the "exact condition of Maryland."

To provide for such contingency as might be anticipated, Governor Jackson, on the 13th of June, issued a call for fifty thousand volunteers, and Major-General Price took the field in command. In this proclamation Governor Jackson said:

A series of unprovoked and unparalleled outrages has been inflicted on the peace and dignity of this Commonwealth, and upon the rights and liberties of its people, by wicked and unprincipled men professing to act under the authority of the Government of the United States.

The volunteers who were assembled under this proclamation had few arms except their squirrel-rifles and shot-guns, and could scarcely be said to have any military equipments. The brigadier-generals, with such men as they could collect, reported in obedience to their orders at Booneville and Lexington. On the 20th of June, 1861, General Lyon and Colonel F. P. Blair, with an estimated force of seven thousand well-armed troops, having eight pieces of artillery, ascended the Missouri River, and debarked about five miles below Booneville. To oppose them, the Missourians had there about eight hundred men, poorly armed, without a piece of artillery, and but little ammunition. With courage which must be commended at the expense of their discretion, they resolved to engage the enemy, and, after a combat of an hour and a half or more, retired, having inflicted heavy loss upon the enemy, and suffering but little themselves. This first skirmish between the Federal troops and the Missouri militia inspired confidence in their fellow-citizens, and checked the contemptuous terms in which the militia had been spoken of by the enemy. Governor Jackson, with two hundred and fifty to three hundred of the militia engaged in the action at Booneville, started toward the southwestern portion of the State, whither General Price, with a view to draw his army from the base-line of the enemy, the Missouri River, ordered his troops. A junction was effected in Cedar County. The total when assembled was about thirty-six hundred men.

This, then, was the patriot army of Missouri. It was a heterogeneous mass representing every condition of Western life. There were the old and young, the rich and poor, the grave and gay, the planter and laborer, the farmer and clerk, the hunter and boatman, the merchant and woodsman. At least five hundred of these men were entirely unarmed. Many had only the common rifle and shot-gun. None were provided with cartridges or canteens. They had eight pieces of cannon, but no shells, and very few solid shot, or rounds of grape and canister.

Rude and almost incredible devices were made to supply these wants: trace-chains, iron rods, hard pebbles, and smooth stones were substituted for shot; and evidence of the effect of such rough missiles was to be given in the next encounter with the enemy.

Governor Jackson continued his march toward southwestern Missouri. He had received reliable intelligence that he was pursued from the northeast and from the northwest, and he subsequently learned that a column numbering three thousand had been sent out from St. Louis to intercept his retreat, and had arrived at the town of Carthage, immediately in his front. His men, however, cheerfully moved forward, attacked the enemy in position, and, after a severe engagement, routed him, pursued him to a second position, from which he was again driven, falling back to Carthage, where he made his last stand, and, upon being driven from which, continued his retreat all night. Thus, despising the plea of helplessness, and defying the threat of a powerful Government to crush her, Missouri, without arms or other military preparation, dared to make war in defense of the laws and liberties of her people.

The Confederate States, themselves engaged in an unequal struggle for existence, by act of their Congress declared that, if Missouri was engaged in repelling a lawless invasion of her territory, it was their right and duty to aid in resisting such invasion. With small means, compared to their wants, the Confederate Congress, on the 6th of August, appropriated one million dollars to that end.

In the battle after Carthage, Missourians were no longer to be alone. General McCulloch, commanding a brigade of Confederate troops, marched from Arkansas to make a junction with General Price, then threatened with an attack by a large force of the enemy under General Lyon, which was concentrated near Springfield, Missouri. The battle was fiercely contested, but finally won by our troops. In this action General Lyon was killed while gallantly endeavoring to rally his discomfited troops, and lead them to the charge.

After the battle of Springfield, General McCulloch returned with his brigade to his former position in Arkansas. John C. Fremont had been appointed a general, and assigned to the command made vacant by the death of General Lyon. He signalized his entrance upon the duty by a proclamation, confiscating the estates and slave property of "rebels."

On the 10th of September, General Price learned that a detachment of Federal troops was marching from Lexington to Warrensburg, to seize the funds of the bank in that place, in accordance with General Fremont's proclamation. General Price, pressing rapidly forward with his mounted men, arrived about daybreak at Warrensburg, where he learned that the enemy had hastily fled about midnight. He then decided to move with his whole force against Lexington. He found the enemy in strong intrenchments, and well supplied with artillery.

The siege proper commenced on the 18th of September, 1861. On the morning of the 20th General Price ordered a number of bales of hemp to be ranged in a line for a breastwork; when rolled before the men as they advanced, they formed a moving rampart which was proof against shot. On came the hempen breastworks, while Price's artillery continued an effective fire. In the afternoon of the 20th the enemy surrendered. About nine hundred thousand dollars of which the Bank of Lexington had been robbed were recovered. General Price caused the money to be at once returned to the bank.

The expedient of the bales of hemp was a brilliant conception, not unlike that which made Tarik, the Saracen warrior, immortal, and gave his name to the northern pillar of Hercules.

The victories in Missouri which have been noticed, and which so far exceeded what might have been expected from the small forces by which they were achieved, had caused an augmentation of the enemy's troops to an estimated number of seventy thousand. Against these the army of General Price could not hope succesfully to contend; he therefore retired toward the southwestern part of the State.

The want of supplies and transportation compelled him to disband a portion of his troops; with the rest he continued his retreat to Neosho. By proclamation of Governor Jackson, the Legislature had assembled at this place, and had passed the ordinance of secession. If other evidence were wanting, the fact that, without governmental aid, without a military chest, the campaign which has been described had so far been carried on by the voluntary service of the citizens, and the free-will offerings of the people, must be conclusive that the ordinance of secession was the expression of the popular will of Missouri.

Chapter 9

Strategy in Virginia, 1861-1862; The Trent Affair

THE LARGE RESOURCES and full preparation of the United States Government enabled it to girt Virginia as with a wall of fire. It has been shown that she was threatened from the east, from the north, and from the west. The capital of the State and of the Confederacy, Richmond, was the objective point, and on this the march of three columns concentrated. On the east, the advance of the enemy was on several occasions feasible, when we consider the number of his forces at and about Fortress Monroe, in comparison with the small means retained for the defense of the capital. On the north, the most formidable army of the enemy was assembled; to oppose it we had the comparatively small Army of the Potomac. This being regarded as the line on which the greatest danger was apprehended, our efforts were mostly directed toward giving it the requisite strength. Troops, as rapidly as they could be raised and armed, were sent forward for that purpose. From the beginning to the close of the war, we mainly relied for the defense of the capital on its aged citizens, boys too young for service, and the civil employees of the executive departments. On several occasions these were called out to resist an attack. They answered with alacrity, and always bore themselves gallantly, more than once repelling the enemy in the open field. Had it been practicable to do so, it would surely have been proper to keep a large force in reserve for the defense of the capital.

Then, there, and everywhere, our difficulty was the want of arms and munitions of war. Lamentable cries came to us from the West for the supplies which would enable patriotic citizens to defend their homes. The resource upon which the people had so confidently relied, the private arms in the hands of citizens, proved a sad delusion. The simple fact was, the country had gone to war without counting the cost.

Undue elation over our victory at Manassas was followed by dissatisfaction at what was termed the failure to reap the fruits of victory; and rumors, for which there could be no better excuse than partisan zeal, were circulated that the heroes of the hour were prevented from reaping the fruits of the victory by the interference of the President. Naturally there followed another rumor, that the inaction of the victorious army, to which reënforcements continued to be sent, was due to the policy of the President. Though these unjust criticisms weakened the power of the Government to meet its present and provide for its future necessities, I bore them in silence, lest to vindicate myself should injure the public service by turning the public censure to the generals on whom the hopes of the country rested.

Discontent is known to be an attendant of armies lying unemployed in camps, especially, as in our case, when the troops were composed of citizens called from their homes under the idea of a pressing necessity, and with the hope of soon returning to them. Our citizen soldiers were a powerful political element, and their correspondence, finding its way to the people through the press and to the halls of Congress by direct communication with the members, was felt, by its influence both upon public opinion and general legislation. Members of Congress, and notably the Vice-President, contended that men should be allowed to go home and attend to their private affairs while there were no active operations, and that there was no doubt but that they would return whenever there was to be a battle. The experience of war soon taught our people the absurdity of such ideas, and before its close probably none would have uttered them.

A marked characteristic of the Southern people was individuality, and time was needful to teach them that the terrible machine, a disciplined army, must be made of men who had surrendered their freedom of will. Perhaps no army ever more thoroughly knew it than did that which Lee led into Pennsylvania, and none ever had a leader who in his own conduct better illustrated the lesson.

Our largest army in 1861 was that of the Potomac. It had been formed by the junction of the forces under General J. E. Johnston with those under General P. G. T. Beauregard, with such additions as could be hurriedly sent forward to meet the enemy on the field of Manassas. They were combined into brigades and divisions as pressing exigencies required.

By the act of February 28, 1861, the President was authorized to receive companies, battalions, and regiments to form a part of the provisional army of the Confederate States, and, with the advice and consent of Congress, to appoint general officers for them; and by the act of March 6th the

President was to apportion the staff and general officers among the respective States from which the volunteers were received. It will thus be seen that the States generously surrendered their right to preserve for those volunteers the character of State troops and to appoint general officers when furnishing a sufficient number of regiments to require such grade for their command; but, in giving their volunteers to form the provisional army of the Confederacy, it was distinctly suggested that the general officers should be so appointed as to make a just apportionment among the States furnishing the troops.

About the 1st of October, at the request of General Johnston, I went to his headquarters, at Fairfax Court-House, for the purpose of conference. General Johnston called in the two generals next in rank to himself, Beauregard and G. W. Smith. The question for consideration was, What course should be adopted for the future action of the army? And the preliminary inquiry by me was as to the number of the troops there assembled. To my surprise and disappointment, the effective strength was stated to be but little greater than when it fought the battle of the 21st of the preceding July. The frequent reënforcements which had been sent to that army in nowise prepared me for such an announcement. To my inquiry as to what force would be required for the contemplated advance into Maryland, the lowest estimate made by any of them was about twice the number there present for duty. Previous suggestions by the generals in regard to a purpose to advance into Maryland had induced me, when I went to that conference, to take with me some drawings made by the veteran soldier and engineer, Colonel Crozêt, of the falls of the Potomac, to show the feasibility of crossing the river at that point. Very little knowledge of the condition and military resources of the country must have sufficed to show that I had no power to make such an addition to that army without a total disregard of the safety of other threatened positions. It only remained for me to answer that I had not power to furnish such a number of troops; and, unless the militia bearing their private arms should be relied on, we could not possibly fulfill such a requisition until after the receipt of the small-arms which we had early and constantly striven to procure from abroad, and had for some time expected.

The position at Fairfax Court-House though it would answer very well as a point from which to advance, was quite unfavorable for defense; and when I so remarked, the opinion seemed to be that to which the generals had previously arrived. It, therefore, only remained to consider what change of position should be made in the event of the enemy threatening soon to advance. But in the mean time I hoped that something could be done by detachments from the army to effect objects less difficult than an advance against his main force, and particularly indicated the lower part of Maryland, where a small force was said to be ravaging the country and oppressing our friends. Previously, General Johnston's attention had been called to possibilities in the Valley of the Shenandoah, and that these and other like things were not done, was surely due to other causes than "the policy of the Administration."

In November, 1861, reports became current that the enemy were concentrating troops west of the Valley of the Shenandoah with a view to a descent upon it. That vigilant, enterprising, and patriotic soldier, General T. J. Jackson, whose steadiness under fire at the first battle of Manassas had procured for him the *sobriquet* of "Stonewall," was then on duty as district commander of the Shenandoah Valley.

He was a West Virginian; and, though he had not acquired the fame which subsequently shed luster upon his name, he possessed a well-deserved confidence among the people of that region. Ever watchful and daring in the discharge of any duty, he was intensely anxious to guard his beloved mountains of Virginia. This, stimulating his devotion to the general welfare of the Confederacy, induced him to desire to march against the enemy, who had captured Romney. On the 20th of November, 1861, he wrote to the War Department, proposing an expedition to Romney, in western Virginia. It was decided to adopt his proposition, endorsed by the commander of the department, and, to insure success, though not recommended in the endorsement, his old brigade, then in the Army of the Potomac, was selected as part of the command with which he was to make the campaign.

After General Jackson commenced his march, the cold became unexpectedly severe, and, as he ascended into the mountainous region, the slopes were covered with ice, which impeded his progress, the more because his horses were smooth-shod; but his tenacity of purpose, fidelity, and daring triumphed over every obstacle, and he attained his object, drove the enemy from Romney and its surroundings, took possession of the place, and prevented the threatened concentration. Having accomplished this purpose, and being assured that the enemy had abandoned that section of country, he returned with his old brigade to the Valley of the Shenandoah, leaving the balance of his command at Romney. General Loring, the senior officer there present, and many others of the command so left, appealed to the War Department to be withdrawn. Their arguments were, as well as I remember, these: that the troops, being from the South, were unaccustomed to, and unprepared for, the rigors of a mountain winter; that they were strangers to the people of that section; that the position had no military strength, and, at the approach of spring, would be accessible to the enemy by roads leading from various quarters. After some preliminary action, an order was issued from the War Office directing the troops to retire to the Valley.

Soon after the conference at Fairfax Court-House the army withdrew to Centreville, a better position for defense but not for attack. There was a general apprehension at Richmond that the northern frontier of Virginia would be abandoned, and a corresponding earnestness was exhibited to raise the requisite force to enable our army to take the offensive. On the 10th of March I telegraphed to General Johnston: "Further assurance given to me this day that you shall be prompty and adequately reënforced, so as to enable you to maintain your position, and resume first policy when the roads will permit." The first policy was to carry the war beyond our own border.

To further inquiry from General Johnston as to where he should take position, I replied that I would go to his headquarters in the field, and found him on the south bank of the river, to which he had retired, in a position possessing great natural advantages. An elevated bank commanded the north side of the river, overlooking the bridge, and an open field beyond it, across which the enemy must pass to reach the bridge, which, if left standing, was an invitation to seek that crossing. Upon inquiring whether the south bank of the river continued to command the other side down to Fredericksburg, General Johnston answered that he did not know. I then proposed that we should go to Fredericksburg, to inform ourselves upon that point. On arriving at Fredericksburg, a reconnaissance soon manifested that the hills on the opposite side commanded the town and adjacent river-bank, and therefore Fredericksburg could only be defended by an army occupying the opposite hills, for which our force was inadequate. In returning to the house of Mr. Barton, where I was a guest, I found a number of ladies had assembled there to welcome me, and who, with anxiety, inquired as to the result of our reconnaissance. Upon learning that the town was not considered defensible against an enemy occupying the heights on the other side, and that our force was not sufficient to hold those heights against such an attack as might be anticipated, the general answer was, "If the good of our cause requires the defense of the town to be abandoned, let it be done." The purposes of the enemy were then unknown to us. If General Johnston's expectation of a hostile advance in great force should be realized, our course must depend partly upon receiving the reënforcement we had reason to expect from promises previously given and renewed.

No immediate decision could therefore be made, and I returned to Richmond, to wait the further development of the enemy's plans, and to prepare as best we might to counteract them.

The feeling heretofore noticed as arousing in Virginia a determination to resist the abandonment of her northern frontier, and which caused the assurance of reënforcements, bore fruit in the addition of about thirty thousand men, by a draft made by the Governor of the State. These, it is true, were not the disciplined, seasoned troops which were asked for by the generals in the conference at Fairfax Court-House, but they were of such men as often during the war won battles for the Confederacy. The development of the enemy's plans, for which we had to wait, proved that, instead of advancing in force against our position at Centreville, he had, before the retreat of our army commenced, decided to move down the Potomac for a campaign against Richmond, from the Peninsula as a base. The conflagration at Centreville gave notice of its evacuation, and an advance was made as far as Manassas, but, as appears by General McClellan's report, with no more important design than to attack our rear guard, if it should be encountered.

There was an apparent advantage to the enemy in the new base for his operations which was sufficiently illustrated by the events of the last year of the war. Had we possessed an army as large as the enemy supposed, it would have been possible for us at the same time to check his advance from the East and to march against his capital, with fair prospect of capturing it, before the army he had sent against Yorktown could have been brought back for the defense of Washington.

On this as on other occasions he greatly magnified the force we possessed, and on this as on other occasions it required the concentration of our troops successfully to resist a detachment of his. Accepting as a necessity the withdrawal of the main portion of our army from northern Virginia to meet the invasion from the seaboard, it was regretted that earlier and more effective means were not employed for the mobilization of the army, a desirable measure in either contingency of advance or retreat, or at the least that the withdrawal was not so deliberate as to secure the removal of our ordnance, subsistence, and quartermasters' stores, which had been collected on the line occupied in 1861 and the early part of 1862.

The enemy's plans were soon thereafter found to be the invasion of Virginia from the seaboard, and the principal portion of our army was consequently ordered to the Peninsula, between the York River and the James. Thus the northern frontier of Virginia, which, in the first year of the war, had been the main field of skirmishes, combats, and battles, of advance and retreat, and the occupation and evacuation of fortified positions, ceased for a time to tremble beneath the tread of contending armies.

To the foregoing narration of events immediately connected with the efforts of the Confederate Government to maintain its existence at home, may here be properly added an incident bearing on its foreign relations in the first year of the war.

Our efforts for the recognition of the Confederate States by the European powers, in 1861, served to make us better known abroad, to awaken a kindly feeling in our favor, and cause a respectful regard for the effort we were making to maintain the independence of the States which Great Britain had recognized.

On the 8th of November, 1861, an outrage was perpetrated by an armed vessel of the United States, in the forcible detention, on the high-seas, of a British mail steamer, the Trent, on one of her regular trips from one British port to another, and the seizure, on that unarmed vessel, of our Commissioners, Mason and Slidell, who with their secretaries were bound for Europe on diplomatic service. The seizure was made by an armed force against the protest of the Captain of the vessel, and of Commander Williams, R. N., the latter speaking as the representative of her Majesty's Government. The Commissioners only yielded when force, which they could not resist, was used to remove them from the mail-steamer, and convey them to the United States vessel of war.

This outrage was the more marked because the United States had been foremost in resisting the right of "visit and search," and had made it the cause of the War of 1812 with Great Britain.

When intelligence of the event was received in Engand, it excited the greatest indignation among the people; and her Majesty's Government, by naval and other preparations, unmistakably exhibited the purpose to redress the wrong.

The Commissioners and their secretaries had been transported to the harbor of Boston, and imprisoned in its main fortress.

Diplomatic correspondence resulted from this event. The British Government demanded the immediate and unconditional release of the Commissioners "in order that they may again be placed under British protection, and a suitable apology for the aggression which has been committed."

In the mean time, Captain Wilkes, commander of the vessel which had made the visit and search of the Trent, returned to the United States and was received with general plaudit, both by the people and the Government. The House of Representatives passed a vote of thanks, an honor not heretofore bestowed except for some deed deserving well of the country. In the midst of all this exultation at the seizure of our Commissioners on board of a British merchant-ship, came the indignant and stern demand for the restoration of those Commissioners to the British protection from which they had been taken, and an apology for the aggression. It was little to be expected, after such explicit commendation of the act, that the United States Government would accede to the demand; and therefore the War and Navy Departments of the British Government made active provision to enforce it. The United States Secretary of State, after a wordy and ingenious reply to the Minister of Great Britain at Washington City, wrote: "The four persons in question are now held in military custody at Fort Warren, in the State of Massachusetts. They will be cheerfully liberated. Your lordship will please indicate a time and place for receiving them."

Chapter 10

Arming the Confederacy

AT THE BEGINNING of the war the arms within the limits of
the Confederacy were distributed as follows:

		Rifles.	Muskets.
At Richmond (State.......... about		4,000	
Fayetteville, North Carolina.....	"	2,000	25,000
Charleston, South Carolina......	"	2,000	20,000
Augusta, Georgia..............	"	3,000	28,000
Mount Vernon, Alabama......	"	2,000	20,000
Baton Rouge, Louisiana........	"	2,000	27,000
Total...................		15,000	120,000

There were at Richmond about sixty thousand old flint-
muskets, and at Baton Rouge about ten thousand old Hall's
rifles and carbines. At Little Rock, Arkansas, there were a
few thousand stands, and a few at the Texas Arsenal, increasing the aggregate of serviceable arms to about one hundred
and forty-three thousand. Add to these the arms owned by
the several States and by military organizations, and it would
make a total of one hundred and fifty thousand for the use
of the armies of the Confederacy. The rifles were of the caliber .54, known as Mississippi rifles, except those at Richmond
taken from Harper's Ferry, which were of the new-model
caliber .58; the muskets were the old flint-lock, caliber .69,
altered to percussion. There were a few boxes of sabers at
each arsenal, and some short artillery-swords. A few hundred
holster-pistols were scattered about. There were no revolvers.

There was before the war little powder or ammunition of
any kind stored in the Southern States, and this was a relic
of the war with Mexico. It is doubtful if there were a million
of rounds of small-arms cartridges. The chief store of powder
was that captured at Norfolk; there was, besides, a small
quantity at each of the Southern arsenals, in all sixty thousand
pounds, chiefly old cannon-powder. The percussion-caps did
not exceed one quarter of a million, and there was no lead
on hand. There were no batteries of serviceable field-artillery
at the arsenals, but a few old iron guns mounted on Gribeau-

val carriages fabricated about 1812. The States and the volunteer companies did, however, possess some serviceable batteries. But there were neither harness, saddles, bridles, blankets nor other artillery or cavalry equipments.

To furnish one hundred and fifty thousand men, on both sides of the Mississippi, in May, 1861, there were no infantry accoutrements, no cavalry arms or equipments, no artillery, and, above all, no ammunition; nothing save arms, and these almost wholly the old pattern smooth-bore muskets, altered to percussion from flint locks.

Within the limits of the Confederate States the arsenals had been used only as depots, and no one of them, except that at Fayetteville, North Carolina, had a single machine above the grade of a foot-lathe. Except at Harper's Ferry Armory, all the work of preparation of material had been carried on at the North; not an arm, not a gun, not a gun-carriage, and, except during the Mexican War, scarcely a round of ammunition, had for fifty years been prepared in the Confederate States. There were consequently no workmen, or very few, skilled in these parts. Powder, save perhaps for blasting, had not been made at the South. No saltpeter was in store at any Southern point; it was stored wholly at the North. There were no worked mines of lead except in Virginia, and the situation of those made them a precarious dependence. The only cannon-foundry existing was at Richmond. Copper, so necessary for field-artillery and for percussion-caps, was just being obtained in East Tennessee. There was no rolling-mill for bar-iron south of Richmond, and but few blast-furnaces, and these, with trifling exceptions, were in the border States of Virginia and Tennessee.

The first efforts made to obtain powder were by orders sent to the North, which had been early done both by the Confederate Government and by some of the States. These were being rapidly filled when the attack was made on Fort Sumter. The shipments then ceased. Niter was contemporaneously sought for in north Alabama and Tennessee. Between four and five hundred tons of sulphur were obtained in New Orleans, at which place it had been imported for use in the manufacture of sugar. Preparations for the construction of a large powder-mill were promptly commenced by the Government, and two small, private mills in East Tennessee were supervised and improved. On June 1, 1861, there was probably two hundred and fifty thousand pounds only, chiefly of cannon-powder, and about as much niter, which had been imported by Georgia. There were the two powder-mills above mentioned, but we had no experience in making powder, or in extracting niter from natural deposits, or in obtaining it by artificial beds.

For the supply of arms an agent was sent to Europe, who made contracts to the extent of nearly half a million dollars. Some small-arms had been obtained from the North, and also important machinery. The machinery at Harper's Ferry Armory had been saved from the flames by the heroic conduct of the operatives, headed by Mr. Armistead M. Ball, the master armorer. Of the machinery so saved, that for making rifle-muskets was transported to Richmond, and that for rifles with sword-bayonets to Fayetteville, North Carolina. In addition to the injuries suffered by the machinery, the lack of skilled workmen caused much embarrassment. In the mean time the manufacture of small-arms was undertaken at New Orleans and prosecuted with energy, though with limited success.

In field-artillery the manufacture was confined almost entirely to the Tredegar Works in Richmond. Some castings were made in New Orleans, and attention was turned to the manufacture of field and siege artillery at Nashville. A small foundry at Rome, Georgia, was induced to undertake the casting of the three-inch iron rifle, but the progress was very slow. The State of Virginia possessed a number of old four-pounder iron guns which were reamed out to get a good bore, and rifled with three grooves, after the manner of Parrott. The army at Harper's Ferry and that at Manassas were supplied with old batteries of six-pounder guns and twelve-pounder howitzers. A few Parrott guns, purchased by the State of Virginia, were with General Magruder at Big Bethel.

For the ammunition and equipment required for the infantry and artillery, a good laboratory and workshop had been established at Richmond. The arsenals were making preparations for furnishing ammunition and knapsacks; but generally, what little was done in this regard was for local purposes. Such was the general condition of ordnance and ordnance stores in May, 1861.

The progress of development, however, was steady. A refinery of saltpeter was established near Nashville during the summer, which received the niter from its vicinity, and from the caves in East and Middle Tennessee. Some inferior powder was made at two small mills in South Carolina. North Carolina established a mill near Raleigh; and a stamping-mill was put up near New Orleans, and powder made there before the fall of the city. Small quantities were also received through the blockade. It was estimated that on January 1, 1862, there were fifteen hundred seacoast-guns of various caliber in position from Evansport, on the Potomac, to Fort Brown, on the Rio Grande. If their caliber was averaged at thirty-two pounder, and the charge at five pounds, it would, at forty rounds per gun, require six hundred thousand pounds of powder for them. The field-artillery—say three hundred guns, with two hundred rounds to the piece—would require one hundred and twenty-five thousand pounds; and the small-arm cartridges—say ten million—would consume one hundred and twenty-five thousand pounds more, making in all eight hundred and fifty thousand pounds. Deducting two hundred and fifty thousand pounds, supposed to be on hand in various shapes, and the increment is six hundred thousand pounds for the year 1861. Of this, perhaps two hundred thousand pounds had been made at the Tennessee and other mills, leaving four hundred thousand pounds to be supplied through the blockade, or before the beginning of hostilities.

The liability of powder to deteriorate in damp atmospheres results from the impurity of the niter used in its manufacture, and this it is not possible to detect by any of the usual tests. Security, therefore, in the purchase, depends on the reliability of the maker. To us, who had to rely on foreign products and the open market, this was equivalent to no security at all. It was, therefore, as well for this reason as because of the precariousness of thus obtaining the requisite supply, necessary that we should establish a Government powder-mill. It was our good fortune to have a valuable man whose military education and scientific knowledge had been supplemented by practical experience in a large manufactory of machinery, General G. W. Rains. The expectations which his reputation justified, caused him to be assigned to the task of making a great powder-mill, which should alike furnish an adequate supply, and give assurance of its possessing all the requisite supplies. This problem, which, under the existing circumstances, seemed barely possible, was fully solved. Not only was powder made of every variety of grain and exact uniformity in each, but the niter was so absolutely purified that there was no danger of its deterioration in service. Had Admiral Semmes been supplied with such powder, it is demonstrated, by the facts which have since been established, that the engagement between the Alabama and the Kearsarge would have resulted in a victory for the former.

These Government powder-mills were located at Augusta, Georgia, and satisfactory progress was made in the construction during the year. All the machinery, including the very heavy rollers, was made in the Confederate States. Contracts were made abroad for the delivery of niter through the blockade; and, for obtaining it immediately, we resorted to caves, tobacco-houses, cellars, etc. The amount delivered from Tennessee was the largest item in the year's supply, but the whole was quite inadequate to existing and prospective needs.

The consumption of lead was mainly met by the Virginia lead-mines at Wytheville, the yield from which was from sixty to eighty thousand pounds per month. Lead was also collected by agents in considerable quantities throughout the country, and the battle-field of Manassas was closely gleaned, from which much lead was collected. A laboratory for the smelting of other ores was constructed at Petersburg, Virginia, and was in operation before midsummer of 1862.

By the close of 1861, eight arsenals and four depots had been supplied with materials and machinery, so as to be efficient in producing the various munitions and equipments, the want of which had caused early embarrassment. Thus a good deal had been done to produce the needed material of war.

The troops were, however, still very poorly armed and equipped. The old smooth-bore musket was the principal weapon of the infantry; the artillery had mostly the six-pounder gun and the twelve-pounder howitzer; and the cavalry were armed with such various weapons as they could get—sabers, horse-pistols, revolvers, Sharp's carbines, musketoons, short Enfield rifles, Holt's carbines, muskets cut off, etc. Equipments were in many cases made of stout cotton domestic, stitched in triple folds and covered with paint or rubber varnish. But, poor as were the arms, enough of them, such as they were, could not be obtained to arm the troops.

In December, 1861, arms purchased abroad began to come in, and a good many Enfield rifles were in the hands of the troops at the battle of Shiloh. The winter of 1862 was the period when our ordnance deficiencies were most keenly felt. Powder was called for on every hand; and the equipments most needed were those we were least able to supply. The abandonment of the line of the Potomac and the upper Mississippi from Columbus to Memphis did somewhat, however, reduce the pressure for heavy artillery; and, after the fall of 1862, when the powder-mills at Augusta had got into full operation, there was no further inability to meet all requisitions for ammunition. To provide the iron needed for cannon and projectiles, it had been necessary to stimulate by contracts the mining and smelting of its ores.

But it was obviously beyond the power of even the great administrative capacity of the chief of ordnance, General J. Gorgas to add, to his already burdensome labors, the numerous and increasing cares of obtaining the material from which ammunition, arms, and equipments were to be manufactured. On his recommendation a niter and mining bureau was organized, and Colonel St. John, who had been hitherto assigned to duty in connection with procuring supplies of niter and iron, was appointed to be chief of this bureau.

Niter was to be obtained from caves and other like sources, and by the formation of niter-beds, some of which had previously been begun at Richmond. These beds were located at Columbia, South Carolina, Charleston, Savannah, Augusta, Mobile, Selma, and various other points. At the close of 1864 there were two million eight hundred thousand feet of earth collected, and in various stages of nitrification, of which a large proportion was presumed to yield one and a half pound of niter per foot of earth. The whole country was laid off into districts, each of which was under the charge of an officer, who obtained details of workmen from the army, and made his monthly reports. Thus the niter production, in the course of a year, was brought up to something like half of the total consumption. The district from which the most constant yield could be relied on had its chief office at Greensboro, North Carolina, a region which had no niter-caves in it. The niter was obtained from lixiviation of nitrous earth found under old houses, barns, etc. The supervision of the production of iron, lead, copper, and all the minerals which needed development, as well as the manufacture of sulphuric and nitric acids (the latter required for the supply of the fulminate of mercury for percussion-caps), without which the firearms of our day would have been useless, was added to the niter bureau. Such was the progress that, in a short time, the bureau was aiding or managing some twenty to thirty furnaces with an annual yield of fifty thousand tons or more of pig-iron. The lead- and copper-smelting works erected were sufficient for all wants, and the smelting of zinc of good quality had been achieved. The chemical works were placed at Charlotte, North Carolina, to serve as a reserve when the supply from abroad might be cut off.

In equipping the armies first sent into the field, the supply of accessories was embarrassingly scant. There were arms, such as they were, for over one hundred thousand men, but no accoutrements nor equipments, and a meager supply of ammunition. In time the knapsacks were supplanted by haversacks, which the women could make. But soldiers' shoes and cartridge-boxes must be had; leather was also needed for artillery-harness and for cavalry-saddles; and, as the amount of leather which the country could furnish was quite insufficient for all these purposes, it was perforce apportioned among them. Soldiers' shoes were the prime necessity. Therefore, a scale was established, by which first shoes and then cartridge-boxes had the preference; after these, artillery-harness, and then saddles and bridles. To economize leather, the waist and cartridge-box belts were made of prepared cotton cloth stitched in three or four thicknesses. Bridle-reins were likewise so made, and then cartridge-boxes were thus covered, except the flap. Saddle-skirts, too, were made of heavy cotton cloth strongly stitched. To get leather, each department procured its quota of hides, made contracts with the tanners, obtained hands for them by exemptions from the army, got transportation over the railroads for the hides and for supplies. To the varied functions of this bureau was finally added that of assisting the tanners to procure the necessary supplies for the tanneries. A fishery, even, was established on Cape Fear River to get oil for mechanical purposes, and at the same time food for the workmen. In cavalry equipments the main thing was to get a good saddle which would not hurt the back of the horse. For this purpose various patterns were tried, and reasonable success was obtained. One of the most difficult wants to supply in this branch of the service was the horseshoe for cavalry and artillery. The want of iron and of skilled labor was strongly felt. Every wayside blacksmith-shop accessible, especially those in and near the theatre of operations, was employed. These, again, had to be supplied with material, and the employees exempted from service.

It early became manifest that great reliance must be placed on the introduction of articles of prime necessity through the blockaded ports. A vessel, capable of stowing six hundred and fifty bales of cotton, was purchased by the agent in England, and kept running between Bermuda and Wilmington. Some fifteen to eighteen successive trips were made before she was captured. Another was added, which was equally successful. These vessels were long, low, rather narrow, and built for speed. They were mostly of pale sky-color, and, with their lights out and with fuel that made little smoke, they ran to and from Wilmington with considerable regularity. Several others were added, and devoted to bringing in ordnance, and finally general supplies. Depots of stores were likewise made at Nassau and Havana. Another organization was also necessary, that the vessels coming in through the blockade might have their return cargoes promptly on their arrival. These resources were also supplemented by contracts for supplies brought through Texas from Mexico.

The arsenal in Richmond soon grew into very large dimensions, and produced all the ordnance stores that the army required, except cannon and small-arms, in quantities sufficient to supply the forces in the field. The arsenal at Augusta was very serviceable to the armies serving in the south and west, and turned out a good deal of field-artillery complete. The Government powder-mills were entirely successful. The arsenal and workshops at Charleston were enlarged, steam introduced, and good work done in various departments. The arsenal at Mount Vernon, Alabama, was moved to Selma, in that State, where it grew into a large and well-ordered establishment of the first class. Mount Vernon Arsenal was dismantled, and served to furnish lumber and timber for use elsewhere. At Montgomery, shops were kept up for the repair of small-arms and the manufacture of articles of leather. There were many other small establishments and depots.

The chief armories were at Richmond and Fayetteville, North Carolina. The former turned out about fifteen hundred stands per month, and the latter only four hundred per month, for want of operatives. To meet the want of cavalry arms, a contract was made for the construction in Richmond of a factory for Sharp's carbines; this being built, it was then converted into a manufactory of rifle-carbines, caliber .58. Smaller establishments grew up at Asheville, North Carolina, and at Tallahassee, Alabama. A great part of the work of the armories consisted in the repair of arms. In this manner the gleanings of the battle-fields were utilized. Nearly ten thousand stands were saved from the field of Manassas, and from those about Richmond in 1862 about twenty-five thousand excellent arms. All the stock of inferior arms disappeared from the armories during the first two years of the war, and were replaced by a better class of arms, rifled and percussioned. Placing the good arms lost previous to July, 1863, at one hundred thousand, there must have been received from various sources four hundred thousand stands of infantry arms in the first two years of the war.

Among the obvious requirements of a well-regulated service was one central laboratory of sufficient capacity to prepare all ammunition, and thus to secure the vital advantage of absolute uniformity. Authority was therefore granted to concentrate this species of work at Macon, Georgia. Plans of the buildings and of the machinery required were submitted and approved, and the work was begun with energy. The pile of buildings had a façade of six hundred feet, was designed with taste, and comprehended every possible appliance for good and well-organized work. The buildings were nearly ready for occupation at the close of the war, and some of the machinery had arrived at Bermuda. This project preceded that of a general armory for the Confederacy, and was much nearer completion. These, with the admirable powder-mills at Augusta, would have been completed, and with them the Government would have been in a condition to supply arms and ammunition to three hundred thousand men. To these would have been added a foundry for heavy guns at Selma or Brierfield, Alabama, where the strongest cast iron in the country had been made.

General J. Gorgas, the chief of ordnance, closes his excellent monograph [on the arming of the Confederate forces] in the following words:

We began in April, 1861, without an arsenal, laboratory, or powder-mill of any capacity, and with no foundry or rolling-mill, except in Richmond, and, before the close of 1863, or within a little over two years, we supplied them. During the harassments of war, while holding our own in the field defiantly and successfully against a powerful enemy; crippled by a depreciated currency; throttled with a blockade that deprived us of nearly all the means of getting material or workmen; obliged to send almost every able-bodied man to the field; unable to use the slave-labor, with which we were abundantly supplied, except in the most unskilled departments of production; hampered by want of transportation even of the commonest supplies of food; with no stock on hand even of articles such as steel, copper, leather, iron, which we must have to build up our establishments, and in that short period created, almost literally out of the ground, foundries and rolling-mills at Selma, Richmond, Atlanta, and Macon; smelting-works at Petersburg, chemical works at Charlotte, North Carolina; a powder-mill far superior to any in the United States and unsurpassed by any across the ocean; and a chain of arsenals, armories, and laboratories equal in their capacity and their improved appointments to the best of those in the United States, stretching link by link from Virginia to Alabama.

The charge was made early in the war that I was slow in procuring arms and munitions of war from Europe. We were not only in advance of the Government of the United States in the markets of Europe, but the facts presented in the following extracts from a letter of our agent, Caleb Huse, dated December 30, 1861, and addressed to Major C. C. Anderson, will serve to place the matter in its proper light:

LONDON, *December 30, 1861*

DEAR MAJOR: . . . I have now more than enough to load three "Bermudas," and can not ship a package, though I have a steamer off the wharf, all ready to receive her cargo. We are literally fighting two governments here. Government watchmen guard the wharf where our goods are stowed and others in the neighborhood, night and day—and the wharfinger has orders not to ship or deliver, by land or water, any goods marked W. D., without first acquainting the honorable Board of Customs. I have applied myself to ship to Bermuda, offering to give bonds to double the amount of value of the goods, that they should be held in Bermuda, subject to the direction of her Majesty's representative in Bermuda. I . . . have applied for permission to ship to Cardenas, agreeing to hold the goods subject to the order of the Spanish authorities—but all without avail, and our army must suffer for the want of blankets, overcoats, shoes, socks, field forges, arms, and ammunition, which have been collected to an amount more than double that I have yet received.

It is miserable to have to look at the immense pile of packages in the warehouse at St. Andrews Wharf, and not be able to send anything—only read the following: twenty-five thousand rifles; two thousand barrels of powder; five hundred thousand caps; ten thousand friction-tubes; five hundred thousand cartridges; thirteen thousand accoutrements; thirteen thousand knapsacks; thirteen thousand gun-slings; forty-four thousand three hundred and twenty-eight pairs of socks; sixteen thousand four hundred and eighty-four blankets; two hundred and twenty-six saddles; saddlers' tools; artillery-harness; leather, etc. Very truly yours,

CALEB HUSE

Chapter 11

Finances

THE FINANCIAL SYSTEM which had been adopted from necessity proved adequate at this early period to supply all the wants of the Government and of the people. An unexpected and very large increase of expenditures had resulted from the great enlargement of the necessary means of defense. Yet the Government entered on its second year without a floating debt and with its credit unimpaired. The total expenditures of the first year, ending February 1, 1862, amounted to one hundred and seventy million dollars.

A review of the legislation of Congress will clearly present the financial system of the Government. The first action of the Provisional Congress was confined to the adoption of a tariff law, and an act for a loan of fifteen million dollars, with a pledge of a small export duty on cotton, to provide for the redemption of the debt. At the next session, after the commencement of the war, provision was made for the issue of twenty million dollars in Treasury notes, and for borrowing thirty million dollars in bonds. After the purpose of subjugation became manifest by the action of the Congress of the United States, early in July, 1861, and the certainty of a long war was demonstrated, there arose the necessity that a financial system should be devised on a basis sufficiently large for the vast proportions of the approaching contest. The plan then adopted was founded on the theory of issuing Treasury notes, convertible at the pleasure of the holder into eight per cent. bonds, with the interest payable in coin. It was assumed that any tendency to depreciation, which might arise from the over-issue of the currency, would be checked by the constant exercise of the holder's right to fund the notes at a liberal interest, payable in specie. The success of this system depended on the ability of the Government constantly to pay the interest in specie. The measures, therefore, adopted to secure that payment consisted in the levy of an internal tax, termed a war-tax, and the appropriation of the revenue from imports.

The first operation of this plan was quite successful. The interest was paid from the reserve of coin existing in the country, and experience sustained the expectations of those who devised the system.

Wheat, in the beginning of the year 1862, was selling at one dollar and thirty cents per bushel, thus but little exceeding its average price in time of peace. The other agricultural products of the country were at similarly moderate rates, thus indicating that there was no excess of circulation. At the same time the premium on coin had reached about twenty per cent. But it had become apparent that the commerce of our country was threatened with permanent suspension by reason of the conduct of neutral nations, who virtually gave aid to the United States Government by sanctioning its declaration of a blockade. This exceptional cause heightened the premium on specie, because it indicated the exhaustion of our reserve, without the possibility of renewing the supply.

At the inauguration of the permanent Government, in February, 1862, a popular aversion to internal taxation had been so strongly manifested as to indicate its partial failure.

Under all these circumstances the effort was made to avoid the increase in the volume of notes in circulation, by offering inducements to voluntary funding. The measures adopted for that purpose were but partially successful. Meanwhile the intervening exigencies from the fortunes of war permitted no delay. The issues of Treasury notes were increased until, in December, 1863, the currency in circulation amounted to more than six hundred million dollars, or more than three-fold the amount required by the business of the country. The possession of large amounts of Treasury notes led to a desire for investment; and, with a constantly increasing volume of currency, there was an equally constant increase of price in all objects of investment. This effect stimulated purchase by the apparent certainty of profit, and a spirit of speculation was thus fostered, which had so debasing an influence and such ruinous consequences that it became our highest duty to remove the cause by prompt and stringent measures.

I therefore recommended to Congress, in December, 1863, the compulsory reduction of the currency to the amount required by the business of the country, accompanied by a pledge that, under no stress of circumstances, would the amount be increased. I stated that, if the currency was not greatly and promptly reduced, the existing scale of inflated prices would not only continue, but, by the very fact of the large amounts thus made requisite in the conduct of the war, these prices would reach rates still more extravagant, and the whole system would fall under its own weight, rendering the redemption of the debt impossible, and destroying its value in the hands of the holder. If, on the contrary, a funded debt, with interest secured by adequate taxation, could be substituted for the outstanding currency, its entire amount would be made available to the holder, and the Government would be in a condition, beyond the reach of any probable contingency, to prosecute the war to a successful issue.

This recommendation was followed by the passage of the act of February 17, 1864. One of its features is the tax levied on the circulation. Regarding the Government when contracting a debt as the agent of the people, its debt is their debt. As the currency was held exclusively by ourselves, it was obvious that, if each person held Treasury notes in exact proportion to the valuation of his whole estate, each would in fact owe himself the amount of the notes held by him; and, were it possible to distribute the currency among the people in this exact proportion, a tax levied on the currency alone, to an amount sufficient to reduce it to its proper limits, would afford the best of all remedies. Under such circumstances, the notes remaining in the hands of each holder after the payment of his tax would be worth quite as much as the whole sum previously held, for it would have an equal purchasing capacity.

After this law had been in operation for one year, it was manifest that it had the desired effect of withdrawing from circulation the large excess of Treasury notes which had been issued. The chief difficulty apprehended in connection with our finances, up to the close of the war, resulted from the depreciation of our Treasury notes, which was to be attributed to the increasing redundancy in amount and the diminishing confidence in their ultimate redemption.

A system of measures by which to obtain a revenue from direct taxes and duties was commenced at the first session of Congress under the provisional Government. The officers who held any office connected with the collection of the customs, duties, and imposts in the several States of the Confederacy were continued in office with the same powers and subject to the same duties. The tariff laws of the United States were continued in force until they might be altered. The free list was enlarged so as to embrace many articles of necessity; additional ports and places of entry were established; restrictive laws were repealed, and foreign vessels were admitted to the coasting-trade. A lighthouse bureau was organized; a lower rate of duties was imposed on a number of enumerated articles, and an export duty of one eighth of one cent per pound was imposed on all cotton exported in the raw state. At the second session, in May, a complete tariff law was enacted, with a lower scale of duties than had previously existed. On August 19, 1861, a war-tax of fifty cents on each hundred dollars of certain classes of property was levied for the special purpose of paying the principal and interest of the public debt, and of supporting the Government. The different classes of property on which the tax was levied were as follows: real estate of all kinds; slaves; merchandise; bank-stocks; railroad and other corporation stocks; money at interest, or invested by individuals in the purchase of bills, notes, and other securities for money, except the bonds of the Confederate States, and cash on hand, or on deposit; cattle, horses, and mules; gold watches, gold and silver plate, pianos, and pleasure-carriages. There were some exemptions, such as the property of educational, charitable, and religious institutions, and of a head of a family having property worth less than five hundred dollars. An act was passed for the sequestration of the property of alien enemies, as a retaliatory measure, to offset the confiscation act of the United States.

On April 24, 1863, a new act was passed relative to internal or direct taxes. It was designed to reach, as far as practicable, every resource of the country except the capital invested in real estate and slaves, and, by means of an income-tax and a tax in kind on the produce of the soil, as well as by licenses on business occupations and professions, to command resources sufficient for the wants of the country. On June 10, 1864, an act was passed which levied a tax equal to one fifth of the amount of the existing tax upon all subjects of taxation for the year.

Within six months after the passage of the war-tax of August 19, 1861, the popular aversion to internal taxation by the General Government had so influenced the legislation of the several States that only in South Carolina, Mississippi, and Texas were the taxes actually collected from the people. The quotas of the remaining States had been raised by the issue of bonds and State Treasury notes. The public debt of the country was thus actually increased instead of being diminished by the taxation imposed by Congress.

At the first and second sessions of Congress in 1862 no means were provided by taxation for maintaining the Government. The legislation was confined to authorizing further sales of bonds and issues of Treasury notes. An obstacle had arisen against successful taxation. About two thirds of the entire taxable property of the Confederate States consisted in land and slaves. Under the provisional Constitution, which ceased to be in force on February 22, 1862, the power of Congress to levy taxes was not restricted by any other condition than that "all duties, imposts, and excises should be uniform throughout the States of the Confederacy." But in the permanent Constitution, which took effect on the same day (February 22d), it was specially provided that "representatives and direct taxes shall be apportioned among the several States according to their respective numbers, which shall be determined by adding to the whole number of free persons . . . three fifths of all slaves." According to the received construction of the Constitution of the United States, which had been acquiesced in for sixty years, taxes on lands and slaves were direct taxes. In repeating, without modification, in our Constitution this language of the United States Constitution, our Convention necessarily seems to have intended to attach to it the meaning which had been sanctioned by long and uninterrupted acquiescence—thus deciding that taxes on lands and slaves were direct taxes. Our Constitution further ordered that a census should be made within three years after the first meeting of Congress, and that "no capitation or other direct tax shall be laid, unless in proportion to the census or enumeration hereinbefore directed to be taken."

So long as there seemed to be a probability of being able to carry out these provisions of the Constitution fully, and in conformity with the intentions of its authors, there was an obvious difficulty in framing any system of taxation. A law which should exempt from the burden two thirds of the property of the country would be as unfair to the owners of the remaining third as it would be inadequate to meet the requirements of the public service. The urgency of the need, however, was such that, after great embarrassment, the law of April 24, 1863, above mentioned, was framed. Still, a very large proportion of these resources was unavailable for some time, and, the intervening exigencies permitting of no delay, a resort to further issues of Treasury notes became unavoidable.

The foreign debt of the Confederate States at the close of the war was twenty-two hundred thousand pounds. The earliest proposals on which this debt was contracted were issued in London and Paris in March, 1863. The bonds bore interest at seven per cent. per annum, in sterling, payable half-yearly. They were exchangeable at par in sterling, in twenty years, by half-yearly drawings, commencing March 1, 1864. The special security of these bonds was the engagement of the Government to deliver cotton to the holders. Each bond, *at the option of the holder,* was convertible at its nominal amount into cotton at the rate of sixpence sterling for each pound of cotton—say four thousand pounds of cotton for each bond of a hundred pounds, or twenty-five hundred francs; and this could be done at any time not later than six months after the ratification of a treaty of peace between the belligerents. Sixty days after the notice, the cotton was to be delivered, if in a state of peace, at the ports of Charleston, Savannah, Mobile, or New Orleans; if at war, at points in the interior of the country, within ten miles of a railroad, or a stream navigable to the ocean. The delivery was to be made free of all charges, except the export duty of one eighth of one cent per pound. An annual sinking fund of five per cent. was provided for, whereby two and a half per cent. of the bonds unredeemed by cotton should be drawn by a lot half-yearly, so as finally to extinguish the loan in twenty years from the first drawing. The bonds were issued at ninety per cent., payable in installments. The loan soon stood in the London market at five per cent. premium. The amount asked for was three million pounds. The amount of applications in London and Paris exceeded fifteen million pounds.

We should not omit to refer once more to the most prolific source of sectional strife and alienation, which is believed to have been the question of the tariff, or duties upon imports. Its influence extended to and affected subjects with which it was not visibly connected, and finally assumed a form surely not contemplated in the original formation of the Union.

In the Convention which framed the Constitution there prominently appears the purpose of a strict equality in the burdens to be borne, as well as the blessings to be enjoyed, by the people of the several States. For a long time after the formation of the "more perfect Union," but little capital was invested in manufacturing establishments; and, though in the early part of the present century the amount had considerably increased, the products were yet quite insufficient for the necessary supplies of our armies in the War of 1812. Government contracts, high prices, and to some extent, no doubt, patriotic impulses, led to the investment of capital in the articles required for the prosecution of the war. With the restoration of peace and the renewal of commerce, prices naturally declined, and it was represented that the investments made in manufacturing establishments were so unprofitable as to involve the ruin of those who had made them. The Congress of the United States, in 1816, enacted a law to protect from the threatened ruin those of their countrymen who had employed their capital for purposes demanded by the general welfare and common defense. These good intentions were most unfortunate as the beginning of a policy the end of which was fraught with the greatest evils that have ever befallen the Union. By the Constitution of 1789 power was conferred upon Congress—

To lay and collect taxes, duties, imposts, and excises, to pay the debts and provide for the common defense and general welfare of the United States; but all duties, imposts, and excises shall be uniform throughout the United States.

In the exercise of this delegated trust, tariff laws were enacted, and had been in operation to the satisfaction of all parts of the Union, from the organization of the Government down to 1816; but throughout that period all of those laws were based upon the principle of duties for revenue. It was true, and of course it was known, that such duties would give incidental protection to any industry producing an article on which the duty was levied; but, while the money was collected for the purposes enumerated, and the rate kept down to the lowest revenue standard, the consumer had no cause to complain of the indirect benefit received by the manufacturer, and the history of the time shows that it produced no discontent. Not so with the tariff law of 1816: though sustained by men from all sections of the Union, and notably by so strict a constructionist as Mr. Calhoun, there were not wanting those who saw in it a departure from the limitation of the Constitution, and sternly opposed it as the usurpation of a power to legislate for the benefit of a class. For the first time a tariff law had protection for its object, and for the first time it produced discontent. In the law there was nothing which necessarily gave to it or in its terms violated the obligation that duties should be uniform throughout the United States. The fact that it affected the sections differently was due to physical causes—that is, geographical differences. The streams of the Southern Atlantic States ran over wide plains into the sea; their last falls were remote from ocean navigation; and their people, almost exclusively agricultural, resided principally on this plain, and as near to the seaboard as circumstances would permit. In the Northern Atlantic States the highlands approached more nearly to the sea, and the rivers made their last leap near to harbors of commerce. Water-power being relied on before the steam-engine had been made, and ships the medium of commerce before railroads and locomotives were introduced, it followed that the staples of the Southern plains were economically sent to the water-power of the North to be manufactured. This remark, of course, applies to such articles as were not exported to foreign countries, and is intended to explain how the North became the seat of manufactures, and the South remained agricultural. From this it followed that legislation for the benefit of manufacturers became a Northern policy. It was not, as has been erroneously stated, because of the agricultural character of the Southern people, that they were opposed to the policy inaugurated by the tariff act of 1816. This is shown by the fact that anterior to that time they had been the friends of manufacturing industry, without reference to its location. As long as duties were imposed for revenue, so that the object was to supply the common Treasury, it has been cheerfully borne, and the agriculture of one section and the manufacturing of another were properly regarded as hand-maids, and not unfrequently referred to as the means of strengthening and perpetuating the bonds by which the States were united. When duties were imposed, not for revenue, but as a bounty to a particular industry, it was regarded both as unjust and without warrant, expressed or implied, in the Constitution.

Then arose the controversy, quadrennially renewed and with increasing provocation, in 1820, in 1824, and in 1828— each stage intensifying the discontent, arising more from the injustice than the weight of the burden borne. It was not the twenty-shilling ship-money tax, but the violation of Magna Charta, which Hampden and his associates resisted. It was not the stamp duty nor the tea-tax, but the principle involved in taxation without representation, against which our colonial fathers took up arms. So the tariff act in 1828, known at the time as "the bill of abominations," was resisted by Southern representatives, because it was the invasion of private rights in violation of the compact by which the States were united. In the last stage of the proceeding, after the friends of the bill had advocated it as a measure for protecting capital invested in manufacturers, Mr. Drayton, of South Carolina, moved to amend the title so that it should read, "An act to increase the duties upon certain imports, for the purpose of increasing the profits of certain manufacturers," and stated his purpose for desiring to amend the title to be that, upon some case which would arise under the execution of the law, an appeal might be made to the Supreme Court of the United States to test its constitutionality. Those who had passed the bill refused to allow the opportunity to test the validity of a tax imposed for the protection of a particular industry. Though the debates showed clearly enough the purpose to be to impose duties for protection, the phraseology of the law presented it as enacted to raise revenue, and therefore the victims of the discrimination were deprived of an appeal to the tribunal instituted to hear and decide on the constitutionality of a law.

South Carolina, oppressed by onerous duties and stung by the injustice of a refusal to allow her the ordinary remedy against unconstitutional legislation, asserted the right, as a sovereign State, to nullify the law. This conflict between the authority of the United States and one of the States threatened for a time disastrous consequences. Before an actual collision of arms occurred, Congress wisely adopted the compromise act of 1833. By that the fact of protection remained, but the principle of duties for revenue was recognized by a sliding scale of reduction, and it was hoped the question had been placed upon a basis that promised a permanent peace. The party of protective duties, however, came into power about the close of the period when the compromise measure had reached the result it proposed, and the contest was renewed. Contemporaneously with this theory of protective duties, arose the policy of making appropriations from the common Treasury for local improvements. As the Southern representatives were mainly those who denied the constitutional power to make such expenditures, it naturally resulted that the mass of those appropriations were made for Northern works. Now that direct taxes had in practice been so wholly abandoned as to be almost an obsolete idea, and now that the Treasury was supplied by the collection of duties upon imports, two golden streams flowed steadily to enrich the Northern and manufacturing region by the impoverishment of the Southern and agricultural section. In the train of wealth and demand for labor followed immigration and the more rapid increase of population in the Northern than in the Southern States. I do not deny the existence of other causes, such as the fertile region of the Northwest, the better harbors, the greater amount of shipping of the Northeastern States, and the prejudice of Europeans against contact with the negro race; but the causes I have first stated were, I think, the chief, and those only which are referable to the action of the General Government. Discontent therefore was steadily accumulating, and, as stated in the beginning of this chapter, I think was due to class legislation in the form of protective duties and its consequences more than to any or all other causes combined.

Turning from the consideration of this question in its sectional aspect, I now invite attention to its general effect upon the character of our institutions. If the common Treasury of the States had, as under the Confederation, been supplied by direct taxation, who can doubt that a rigid economy would have been the rule of the Government; that representatives would have returned to their tax-paying constituents to justify appropriations for which they had voted by showing that they were required for the general welfare, and were authorized by the Constitution under which they were acting? When the money was obtained by indirect taxation, so that but few could see the source from which it was derived, it readily followed that a constituency would ask, not why the representative had voted for the expenditure of money, but how much he had got for his own district, and perhaps he might have to explain why he did not get more. Is it doubtful that this would lead to extravagance, if not to corruption? Nothing could be more fatal to the independence of the people and the liberties of the States than dependence for support upon the public Treasury, whether it be in the form of subsidies, of bounties, or restrictions on trade for the benefit of special interests.

Chapter 12

Military Laws and Measures

THE AGRICULTURAL PRODUCTS were diminished every year during the war. Its demands diminished the number of cultivators, and their labors were more extensively devoted to graincrops. The amount of the cotton-crop was greatly reduced, and numbers of bales were destroyed when in danger of falling into the hands of the enemy. The manufacturing industry became more extensive than ever before, and in many branches more highly developed.

During the first year of the war the authority granted to the President to call for volunteers in the army for a short period was sufficient to secure all the military force which we could fit out and use advantageously. As it became evident that the contest would be long and severe, better measures of preparation were enacted. I was authorized to call out and place in the military service for three years, unless the war should sooner end, all white men residents of the Confederate States between the ages of eighteen and thirty-five years, and to continue those already in the field until three years from the date of their enlistment. But those under eighteen years and over thirty-five were required to remain ninety days. The term of service being lengthened, the discipline was greatly improved. At the same time, on March 13, 1862, General Robert E. Lee was "charged with the conduct of the military operations of the armies of the Confederacy" under my direction. Nevertheless, the law upon which our success so greatly depended was assailed with unexpected criticism in various quarters. A constitutional question of high importance was raised, which tended to involve the harmony of coöperation, so essential in this crisis, between the General and the State governments. It was advanced principally by the Governor of Georgia, Hon. Joseph E. Brown, and the following extracts are taken from my reply to him, dated

EXECUTIVE DEPARTMENT, RICHMOND, *May 29, 1862*
I propose . . . to set forth somewhat at length my own views on the power of the Confederate Government over its own armies and the militia. . . .

The main . . . purpose for which independent states form unions, or confederations, is to combine the power of the several members in such manner as to form one united force in all relations with foreign powers, whether in peace or in war. Each state, amply competent to administer and control its own domestic government, yet too feeble successfully to resist powerful nations, seeks saftey by uniting with other states in like condition, and by delegating to some common agent the use of the combined strength of all, in order to secure advantageous commercial relations in peace, and to carry on hostilities with effect in war.

Now, the powers delegated by the several States to the Confederate Government, which is their common agent, are enumerated in the eighth section of the Constitution; each power being distinct, specific, and enumerated in paragraphs separately numbered. The only exception is the eighteenth paragraph, which by its own terms is made dependent on those previously enumerated, as follows: "18. To make all laws which shall be necessary and proper for carrying into execution the foregoing powers," etc. . . .

It is impossible to imagine a more broad, ample, and unqualified delegation of the whole war power of each State than is here contained, with the solitary limitation of the appropriations to two years. The States not only gave power to raise money for the common defense, to declare war, to raise and support armies (in the plural), to provide and maintain a navy, to govern and regulate both land and naval forces, but they went further, and covenanted, by the third paragraph of the tenth section, not "to engage in war, unless actually invaded, or in such imminent danger as will not admit of delay."

I know of but two modes of raising armies within the Confederate States, viz., voluntary enlistment and draft, or conscription. I perceive, in the delegation of power to raise armies, no restriction as to the mode of procuring troops. I see nothing which confines Congress to one class of men, nor any greater power to receive volunteers than conscripts into its service. I see no limitation by which enlistments are to be received of individuals only, but not of companies, or battalions, or squadrons, or regiments. I find no limitation of time of service, but only of duration of appropriation. I discover nothing to confine Congress to waging war within the limits of the Confederacy, nor to prohibit offensive war. In a word, when Congress desires to raise an army, and passes a law for that purpose, the solitary question is under the eighteenth paragraph, viz., "Is the law one that is necessary and proper to execute the power to raise armies?"

I would have very little difficulty in establishing to your entire satisfaction that the passage of the law was not only necessary, but that it was absolutely indispensable; that numerous regiments of twelve months' men were on the eve of being disbanded, whose places could not be supplied by raw levies in the face of superior numbers of the foe, without entailing the most disastrous results; that the position of our armies was so critical as to fill the bosom of every patriot with the liveliest apprehension; and that the provisions of this law were effective in warding off a pressing danger. But I prefer to answer your objection on other and broader grounds.

I hold that, when a specific power is granted by the Constitution, like that now in question, "to raise armies," Congress is the judge whether the law passed for the purpose of power is "necessary and proper." . . . The true and only test is to inquire whether the law is intended and calculated to carry out the object; whether it devises and creates an instrumentality for executing the specific power granted; and, if the answer be in the affirmative, the law is constitutional. None can doubt that the conscription law is calculated and intended to "raise armies"; it is, therefore, "necessary and proper" for the execution of that power, and is constitutional, unless it comes in conflict with some other provision of our Confederate compact.

"You express the opinion that this conflict exists, and support your argument by the citation of those clauses which refer to the militia. . . .

What, then, are militia? They can only be created by law. The arms-bearing inhabitants of a State are liable to become its militia, if the law so order; but, in the absence of a law to that effect, the men of a State capable of bearing arms are no more militia than they are seamen.

The Constitution also tells us that militia are not *troops*, nor are they any part of the *land* or *naval forces;* for militia exist in time of peace, and the Constitution forbids the States to keep troops in time of peace, and they are expressly distinguished and placed in a separate category from land or naval forces in the sixteenth paragraph . . . ; and the words *land* and *naval forces* are shown by paragraphs 12, 13, and 14, to mean the Army and Navy of the Confederate States.

Now, if militia are not the citizens taken singly, but a body created by law; if they are not troops; if they are no part of the Army and Navy of the Confederacy, we are led directly to the definition, quoted by the Attorney-General, that militia are "a body of soldiers in a State enrolled for discipline.". . .

The Constitution divides the whole military strength of the States into only two classes of organized bodies: one, the armies of the Confederacy; the other, the militia of the States.

In the delegation of power to the Confederacy, after exhausting the subject of declaring war, raising and supporting armies, and providing a navy, in relation to all which the grant of authority to Congress is *exclusive,* the Constitution proceeds to deal with the other organized body, the militia; and, instead of delegating power to Congress alone, or reserving it to the States alone, the power is divided as follows, viz.: Congress is to have power "to provide for calling forth the militia to execute the laws of the *Confederate* States, suppress insurrections, and *repel invasions.*"

To provide for organizing, arming, and disciplining the militia, and for governing such part of them as may be employed in the service of the Confederate States; *reserving* to *the States respectively the appointment of the officers,* and the *authority of training the militia,* according to the discipline prescribed by Congress. . . .

Congress may call them forth to repel invasion; so may the State, for the power is impliedly reserved of governing all the militia, except the part in actual service of the Confederacy. . . . The delegation of authority over the militia, so far as granted, appears to me to be plainly an *additional* enumerated power intended to strengthen the hands of the Confederate Government in the discharge of its paramount duty, the common defense of the States. . . .

But you add that, "by the grant of power to Congress to raise and support armies without qualification, the framers of the Constitution intended the regular armies of the Confederacy, and not armies composed of the whole militia of all the States."

I must confess myself somewhat at a loss to understand this position. If I am right that the militia is a body of enrolled State soldiers, it is not possible in the nature of things that armies raised by the Confederacy can "be composed of the whole militia of all the States." The militia may be called forth in whole or in part into the Confederate service, but do not thereby become part of the "armies raised" by Congress. They remain militia, and go home when the emergency which provoked their call has ceased. Armies raised by Congress are of course raised out of the *same population* as the militia organized by the States, and to deny to Congress the power to draft a citizen into the army, or to receive his voluntary offer of services, because he is a member of the State militia, is to deny the power to raise an army at all; for, practically, all men fit for service in the army may be embraced in the militia organization of the several States. You seem, however, to suggest, rather than directly to assert, that the conscript law may be unconstitutional, because it comprehends all arms-bearing men between eighteen and thirty-five years; at least, this is an inference which I draw from your expression, "armies composed of the *whole* militia of *all* the States." But it is obvious that, if Congress have power to draft into the armies raised by it any citizens at all (without regard to the fact whether they are, or not, members of militia organizations), the power must be coextensive with the exigencies of the occasion, or it becomes illusory; and the extent of the exigency must be determined by Congress; for the Constitution has left the power without any other check or restriction than the Executive veto. Under ordinary circumstances, the power thus delegated to Congress is scarcely felt by the States. At the present moment, when our very existence is threatened by armies vastly superior in numbers to ours, the necessity for defense has induced a call, not for "the whole militia of all the States," not for any militia, but for men to compose *armies* for the Confederate States.

Surely there is no mystery in this subject. During our whole past history, as well as during our recent one year's experience as a new Confederacy, the militia "have been called forth to repel invasion" in numerous instances, and they never came otherwise than as bodies organized by the States with their company, field, and *general officers;* and, when the emergency had passed, they went home again. I can not perceive how any one can interpret the conscription law as taking away from the States the power to appoint officers to their militia. You observe on this point in your letter that, unless your construction is adopted, "the very object of the States in reserving the power of appointing the officers is defeated, and that portion of the Constitution is not only a nullity, but the whole military power of the States, and the entire control of the militia, with the appointment of the officers, is vested in the Confederate Government, whenever it chooses to call its own action "raising an army," and not "calling forth the militia."

I can only say, in reply to this, that the power of Congress depends on the real nature of the act it proposes to perform, not on the name given to it; and I have endeavored to show that its action is really that of "raising an army," and bears no semblance to "calling forth the militia.". . .

. . . You proceed: "Congress shall have power to *raise armies.* How shall it be done? The answer is clear. In conformity to the provisions of the Constitution, which expressly provides that, when the militia of the States are called forth to *repel invasion,* and employed in the service of the Confederate States, which is now the case, the State shall appoint the officers.

I beg you to observe that the answer which you say is clear is not an answer to the question put. The question is, How are armies to be raised? The answer given is, that, when militia are called upon to repel invasion, the State shall appoint the officers. There seems to me to be a conclusive test on this whole subject. By our Constitution, Congress may declare war, *offensive* as well as *defensive.* It may acquire territory. Now, suppose that, for good cause and to right unprovoked injuries, Congress should declare war against Mexico and invade Sonora. The militia could not be called forth in such a case, the right to call it being limited "to repel invasions." Is it not plain that the law now under discussion, if passed under such circumstances, could by no possibility be aught else than a law to "raise an army"? Can one and the same law be construed into a "calling forth the militia," if the war be defensive, and a "raising of armies," if the war be offensive?

At some future day, after our independence shall have been established, it is no improbable supposition that our present enemy may be tempted to abuse his naval power by depredations on our commerce, and that we may be compelled to assert our rights by offensive war. How is it to be carried on? Of what is the army to be composed? If this Government can not call on its arms-bearing population otherwise than as militia, and if the militia can only be called forth to repel invasion, we should be utterly helpless to vindicate our honor or protect our rights. War has been well styled "the terrible litigation of nations." Have we so formed our Government that in this litigation we must never be plaintiffs? Surely this can not have been the intention of the framers of our compact.

In no respect in which I can view this law can I find just reason to distrust the propriety of my action in approving and signing it; and the question presented involves consequences, both immediate and remote, too momentous to permit me to leave your objections unanswered.

JEFFERSON DAVIS

The operation of this law was suspended in the States of Kentucky, Missouri, and Maryland, because of their occupation by the armies of the Federal Government. The opposition to it, where its execution was continued, soon became limited, and before June 1st its good effects were seen in the increased strength and efficiency of our armies. At the same time I was authorized to commission officers to form bands of "Partisan Rangers," either of infantry or cavalry, which were subsequently confined to cavalry alone. On September 27, 1862, all white men between the ages of thirty-five and forty-five were placed in the military service for three years. Authority was also given for the reception of volunteers from the States in which the law was suspended. On February 11, 1864, it was enacted by Congress that all white men between the ages of seventeen and fifty should be in the military service for the war; also, that all then in the service between the ages of eighteen and forty-five should be retained during the war. On February 17th all male free negroes between the ages of eighteen and fifty years were made liable to perform duties with the army, or in connection with the military defenses of the country. The Secretary of War was also authorized to employ for the same duties any number of negro slaves not exceeding twenty thousand.

In the operation of the military laws we found the exemption from military duty accorded by the law to all persons engaged in certain specified pursuits or professions to be unwise. In a form of government where each citizen enjoys an equality of rights and privileges, nothing can be more invidious than an unequal distribution of duties or obligations. No pursuit nor position should relieve any one who is able to do active duty from enrollment in the army, unless his functions or services are more useful to the defense of his country in another sphere. But the exemption from service of entire classes should be wholly abandoned.

The act of February 17, 1864 which authorized the employment of slaves, produced less results than had been anticipated. It, however, brought forward the question of the employment of the negroes as soldiers in the army, which was warmly advocated by some and as ardently opposed by others. My own views upon it were expressed freely and frequently in intercourse with members of Congress, and emphatically in my message of November 7, 1864, when, urging upon Congress the consideration of the propriety of a radical modification of the theory of the law, I said:

Viewed merely as property, and therefore as the subject of impressment, the service or labor of the slave has been frequently claimed for short periods in the construction of defensive works. The slave, however, bears another relation to the state—that of a person. The law of last February contemplates only the relation of the slave to the master, and limits the impressment to a certain term of service.

But, for the purposes enumerated in the act, instruction in the manner of camping, marching, and packing trains is needful, so that even in this limited employment length of service adds greatly to the value of the negro's labor. Hazard is also encountered in all the positions to which negroes can be assigned for service with the army, and the duties required of them demand loyalty and zeal.

In this aspect the relation of person predominates so far as to render it doubtful whether the private right of property can consistently and beneficially be continued, and it would seem proper to acquire for the public service the entire property in the labor of the slave, and to pay therefore due compensation, rather than to impress his labor for short terms; and this the more especially as the effect of the present law would vest this entire property in all cases where the slave might be recaptured after compensation for his loss had been paid to the private owner. Whenever the entire property in the service of a slave is thus acquired by the Government, the question is presented by what tenure he should be held.

Should he be retained in servitude, or should his emancipation be held out to him as a reward for faithful service, or should it be granted at once on the promise of such service; and if emancipated what action should be taken to secure for the freed man the permission of the State from which he was drawn to reside within its limits after the close of his public service? The permission would doubtless be more readily accorded as a reward for past faithful service, and a double motive for zealous discharge of duty would thus be offered to those employed by the Government—their freedom and the gratification of the local attachment which is so marked a characteristic of the negro and forms so powerful an incentive to his action. The policy of engaging to liberate the negro on his discharge after service faithfully rendered seems to me preferable to that of granting immediate manumission, or that of retaining him in servitude. If this policy should commend itself to the judgment of Congress, it is suggested that, in addition to the duties heretofore performed by the slave, he might be advantageously employed as a pioneer and engineer laborer, and, in that event, that the number should be augmented to forty thousand.

Beyond this limit and these employments it does not seem to me desirable under existing circumstances to go. . . .

The subject is to be viewed by us, therefore, solely in the light of policy and our social economy. When so regarded, I must dissent from those who advise a general levy and arming of the slaves for the duty of soldiers. Until our white population shall prove insufficient for the armies we require and can afford to keep in the field, to employ as a soldier the negro, who has merely been trained to labor, and, as a laborer, the white man accustomed from his youth to the use of arms, would scarcely be deemed wise or advantageous by any; and this is the question now before us. But should the alternative ever be presented of subjugation, or of the employment of the slave as a soldier, there seems no reason to doubt what should then be our decision. Whether our view embraces what would, in so extreme a case, be the sum of misery entailed by the dominion of the enemy, or be restricted solely to the effect upon the welfare and happiness of the negro-population themselves, the result would be the same. The appalling demoralization, suffering, disease, and death, which have been caused by partially substituting the invaders' system of police for the kind relation previously subsisting between the master and slave, have been a sufficient demonstration that external interference with our institution of domestic slavery is productive of evil only. If the subject involved no other consideration than the mere right of property, the sacrifices heretofore made by our people have been such as to permit no doubt of their readiness to surrender every possession in order to secure independence. But the social and political question which is exclusively under the control of the several States has a far wider and more enduring importance than that of pecuniary interest. In its manifold phases it embraces the stability of our republican institutions, resting on the actual political equality of all its citizens, and includes the fulfillment of the task which has been so happily begun—that of Christianizing and improving the condition of the Africans who have by the will of Providence been placed in our charge. Comparing the results of our own experience with those of the experiments of others who have borne similar relations to the African race, the people of the several States of the Confederacy have abundant reason to be satisfied with the past, and to use the greatest circumspection in determining their course. . . .

Subsequent events advanced my views from a prospective to a present need for the enrollment of negroes to take their place in the ranks. Strenuously I argued the question with members of Congress who called to confer with me. To a member of the Senate (the House in which we most needed a vote) I stated, as I had done to many others, the fact of having led negroes against a lawless body of armed white men, and the assurance which the experiment gave me that they might, under proper conditions, be relied on in battle, and finally used to him the expression which I believe I can repeat exactly: "If the Confederacy falls, there should be written on its tombstone, 'Died of a theory.'" General Lee was brought before a committee to state his opinion as to the probable efficiency of negroes as soldiers, and disappointed the probable expectation by his unqualified advocacy of the proposed measure.

After much discussion in Congress, a bill authorizing the President to ask for and accept from their owners such a number of able-bodied negro men as he might deem expedient subsequently passed the House, but was lost in the Senate by one vote. The Senators of Virginia opposed the measure so strongly that only legislative instruction could secure their support of it. Their Legislature did so instruct them, and they voted for it. Finally, the bill passed, with an amendment providing that not more than twenty-five per cent. of the male slaves between the ages of eighteen and forty-five should be called out. But the passage of the act had been so long delayed that the opportunity was lost. There did not remain time enough to obtain any result from its provisions.

Chapter 13

Provisional Congress;
Forts Henry and Donelson

THE THIRD SESSION of the Provisional Congress commenced
at Richmond on July 20, 1861, and ended on August 21st. At
this session of the Confederate Congress additional forces
were provided to repel invasion, by authorizing the President
to accept the services of any number of volunteers not exceeding four hundred thousand men. Authority was also given
for suitable financial measures hereafter stated, and the levy
of a tax. An act of sequestration was also adopted as a coun-
tervailing measure against the operations of the confiscation
law enacted by the Congress of the United States on August
6, 1861. This act of the United States Congress, with its complement passed in the ensuing year, will be considered further
on in these pages.

At an election on November 6, 1861, the chief executive
officers of the provisional Government were unanimously
chosen to similar positions in the permanent Government, to
be inaugurated on the ensuing 22d of February, 1862.

Important changes in the military arrangements of the
enemy were made about this time. Major-General George B.
McClellan was assigned to the chief command of his army, in
place of Lieutenant-General Scott, retired. A Department of
Ohio was constituted, embracing the States of Ohio, Michigan, Indiana, and Kentucky east of the Cumberland and
Tennessee Rivers; and Brigadier-General D. C. Buell was
assigned to its command. At the same time, General Henry
W. Halleck superseded General John C. Fremont in command of the United States Department of the West. General
W. T. Sherman was removed from Kentucky and sent to report to General Halleck. General A. S. Johnston was now
confronted by General Halleck in the West and by General
Buell in Kentucky. The former, with armies at Cairo and
Paducah, under Generals Grant and C. F. Smith, threatened
equally Columbus, the key of the lower Mississippi River,
and the water-lines of the Cumberland and the Tennessee,
with their defenses at Forts Donelson and Henry. The right
wing of General Buell also menaced Donelson and Henry,
while his center was directed against Bowling Green, and his

left was advancing against General Zollicoffer at Mill Spring, on the upper Cumberland. If the last-named position could be forced, the way seemed open to East Tennessee, by either the Jacksboro or the Jamestown routes, on the one hand, and to Nashville on the other. At the northeastern corner of Kentucky there was a force under Colonel Garfield, of Ohio, opposed to the Confederate force under General Humphrey Marshall.

When the State of Tennessee seceded measures were immediately adopted to occupy and fortify all the strong points on the Mississippi, as Memphis, Randolph, Fort Pillow, and Island No. 10. As it was our purpose not to enter the State of Kentucky and construct defenses for the Cumberland and Tennessee Rivers on her territory, they were located within the borders of Tennessee, and as near to the Kentucky line as suitable sites could be found. On these were commenced the construction of Fort Donelson on the west side of the Cumberland, and Fort Henry on the east side of the Tennessee, and about twelve miles apart. The latter stood on the low lands adjacent to the river about high-water mark, and, being just below a bend in the river and at the head of a straight stretch of two miles, it commanded the river for that distance. It was also commanded by high ground on the opposite bank of the river, which it was intended should be occupied by our troops in case of a land attack. The power of ironclad gunboats against land defenses had not yet been shown, and the low position of the fort brought the battery to the water-level, and secured the advantage of ricochet firing, the most effective against wooden ships.

Fort Donelson was placed on high ground; and, with the plunging fire from its batteries, was thereby more effective against the ironclads brought to attack it on the water side. But on the land side it was not equally strong, and required extensive outworks and a considerable force to resist an attack in that quarter.

In September, 1861, Lieutenant Dixon, of the Engineer Corps, was instructed to make an examination of the works at the two forts. He reported that Fort Henry was nearly completed. It was built, not at the most favorable position, but it was a strong work, and, instead of abandoning it and building at another place, he advised that it should be completed, and other works constructed on the high lands just above the fort on the opposite side of the river. Measures for the accomplishment of this plan were adopted as rapidly as the means at disposal would allow.

In relation to Donelson, it was his opinion that, although a better position might have been chosen for this fortification on the Cumberland, under the circumstances surrounding the command, it would be better to retain and strengthen the position chosen.

General Polk, in a report to General Johnston just previous to the battle of Shiloh, said: "The principal difficulty in the way of a successful defense of the rivers, was the want of an adequate force—a force of infantry and a force of experienced artillerists." This tells only half of the story. To match the vessels of the enemy (floating forts) we required vessels like theirs, or the means of constructing them. We had neither.

The efforts which were put forth to resist the operations on the Western rivers, for which the United States made such vast preparations, were therefore necessarily very limited. There was a lack of skilled labor, of ship-yard, and of materials for constructing ironclads, which could not be readily obtained or prepared in a beset and blockaded country. Proposals were considered both for building gunboats and for converting the ordinary side-wheel, high-pressure steamboats into gunboats. But the engineer department, though anxious to avail itself of this means of defense, decided that it was not feasible. There was not plate-iron with which to armor a single vessel, and even railroad-iron could not be spared from its uses for transportation. Unless a fleet could have been built to match the enemy's, we had to rely on land-batteries, torpedoes, and marching forces. It was thought best to concentrate the resources on what seemed practicable.

The fleet of gunboats prepared by the United States for the Mississippi and its tributaries consisted of twelve, seven of which were iron-clad, and able to resist all except the heaviest solid shot. The boats were built very wide in proportion to their length, so that in the smooth river-waters they might have almost the steadiness of land-batteries when discharging their heavy guns. This flotilla carried one hundred and forty-three guns, some sixty-four pounders, some thirty-two pounders, and some seven-inch rifled guns carrying eighty-pound shells.

On February 2d General Grant started from Cairo with seventeen thousand men on transports. Commodore Foote accompanied him with seven gunboats. On the 4th the land-

ing of the troops commenced three miles or more below
Fort Henry. General Grant took command on the east bank
with the main column, while General Charles F. Smith, with
two brigades of some five to six thousand men, landed on the
left bank, with orders to take the earthwork opposite Fort
Henry, known as Fort Hindman. On the 5th the landing was
completed, and the attack was made on the next day. The
force of General Tilghman, who was in command at Fort
Henry, was about thirty-four hundred. It is evident that on
the 5th he intended to dispute Grant's advance by land; but
on the 6th, before the attack by the gunboats, he changed
his purpose, abandoned all hope of a successful defense, and
made arrangements for the escape of his main body to Fort
Donelson, while the guns of Fort Henry should engage the
gunboats. He ordered Colonel Hindman to withdraw the command to Fort Donelson, while he himself would obtain the
necessary delay for the movement by use of the battery, and
standing a bombardment in Fort Henry. For this purpose he
retained his heavy artillery company—seventy-five men—to
work the guns, a number unequal to the strain and labor of
the defense.

Noon was the time fixed for the attack; but Grant, impeded by the overflow of water, and unwilling to expose his
men to the heavy guns of the fort, held them back to await
the result of the gunboat attack. In the mean time the Confederate troops were in retreat. Four ironclads, mounting
forty-eight heavy guns, approached and took position within
six hundred yards of the fort, firing as they advanced. About
half a mile behind these came three unarmored gunboats,
mounting twenty-seven heavy guns, which took a more distant position, and kept up a bombardment of shells that fell
within the works. Some four hundred of the formidable
missiles of the ironclad boats were also thrown into the fort.
The officers and men inside were not slow to respond, and
as many as fifty-nine of their shots were counted as striking
the gunboats. On the ironclad Essex a cannon-ball ranged
her whole length; another shot, passing through the boiler,
caused an explosion that scalded her commander, Porter, and
many of the seamen and soldiers on board.

Five minutes after the fight began, the twenty-four pounder
rifled gun, one of the most formidable in the fort, burst, disabling every man at the piece. Then a shell exploded at the
muzzle of one of the thirty-two pounders, ruining the gun,
and killing or wounding all the men who served it. About

the same moment a premature discharge occurred at one of the forty-two pounder guns, killing three men and seriously injuring others. The ten-inch columbiad, the only gun able to match the artillery of the assailants, was next rendered useless by a priming-wire that was jammed and broken in the vent. An heroic blacksmith labored for a long time to remove it, under the full fire of the enemy, but in vain. The men became exhausted and lost confidence; and Tilghman, seeing this, in person served a thirty-two pounder for some fifteen minutes. Though but four of his guns were disabled, six stood idle for want of artillerists, and but two were replying to the enemy. After an engagement of two hours and ten minutes, he ceased firing and lowered his flag. For this soldierly devotion and self-sacrifice the gallant commander and his brave band must be honored. Our casualties were five killed and sixteen wounded; those of the enemy were sixty-three of all kinds. Twelve officers and sixty-three non-commissioned officers and privates were surrendered with the fort. The Tennessee River was thus open, and a base by short lines was established against Fort Donelson.

The next movement was a combined attack by land and water upon Fort Donelson. This fort was situated on the left bank of the Cumberland, as has been stated, near its great bend, and about forty miles from the mouth of the river. It was about one mile north of the village of Dover, where the commissary and quartermaster's supplies were in depot. The fort consisted of two water-batteries on the hillside, protected by a bastioned earthwork of irregular outline on the summit, inclosing about one hundred acres. The water-batteries were admirably placed to sweep the river approaches, with an armament of thirteen guns; eight thirty-two pounders, three thirty-two pound carronade, one ten-inch columbiad, and one rifled gun of thirty-two pound caliber. The field-work, which was intended for infantry supports, occupied a plateau about one hundred feet above the river, commanding and protecting the water-batteries at close musket range. These works afforded a fair defense against gunboats; but they were not designed or adapted for resistance to a land attack or investment by an enemy.

Generals Pillow and Floyd were ordered with their separate commands to Fort Donelson. General Buckner also was sent with a division from Bowling Green; so that the Confederate effective force at the fort during the siege was between fourteen thousand five hundred and fifteen thousand men.

The force of General Grant was not less than thirty to thirty-five thousand men. On February 12th he commenced his movement across from Fort Henry, and the investment of Donelson was made without any serious opposition. On the 13th General Buckner reports that "the fire of the enemy's artillery and riflemen was incessant throughout the day; but was responded to by a well-directed fire from the intrenchments, which inflicted upon the assailant a considerable loss, and almost silenced his fire late in the afternoon." The object of the enemy undoubtedly was to discover the strength and position of our forces. The artillery-fire was continued at intervals during the night. Nearly every Confederate regiment reported a few casualties from the shot and shell which frequently fell inside of the works. Meanwhile, a gunboat of thirteen guns arrived in the morning, and, taking a position behind a headland, fired one hundred and thirty-eight shots, when our one hundred and twenty-eight pound shot crashed through one of her ports, injuring her machinery and crippling her. The enemy's fire did no damage to the fort itself, but a shot disabled a gun and killed Captain Dixon, a valuable engineer, whose loss was greatly deplored.

The weather became cold during the night, and a driving snow-storm prevailed, so that some of the soldiers were frozen, and the wounded between the lines suffered extremely. The fleet of gunboats under Commodore Foote arrived, bringing reenforcements to the enemy. These were landed during the night and the next day, which was occupied with placing them in position. Nevertheless, though no assault was made, a rambling and ineffective fire was kept up. About 3 P.M. the commander of the naval force, expecting an easy victory, like that at Fort Henry, brought his four ironclads, followed by two gunboats, up to the attack. Each of the ironclads mounted thirteen guns and the gunboats nine. Any one of them was more than a match for the guns of the fort. Their guns were eight, nine, and ten inch, three in the bow of each. Our columbiad and the rifled gun were the only two pieces effective against the ironclads. The enemy moved directly toward the water-batteries, firing with great weight of metal. It was the intention of Commodore Foote to silence these batteries, pass by, and take a position where he could enfilade the fort with broadsides. The gunboats opened at a mile and a half distance, and advanced until within three or four hundred yards. The shot and shell of the fleet tore up the earthworks, but did no further injury.

But the Confederate guns, aimed from an elevation of not less than thirty feet by cool and courageous hands, sent their shot with destructive power, and overcame all the enemy's advantages in number and weight of guns. The bolts of our two heavy guns went crashing through iron and massive timbers with resistless force, scattering slaughter and destruction through the fleet.

In consequent of reënforcements to the enemy, the plan of operations for the next day was determined by the Confederate generals about midnight. The whole of the left wing of the army except eight regiments was to move out of the trenches, attack, turn, and drive the enemy's right until Wynn's Ferry road, which led to Charlotte through a good country, was cleared, and an exit thus secured.

The troops, moving in the small hours of the night over the icy and broken roads, which wound through the obstructed area of defense, made slow progress, and delayed the projected operations. At 4 A.M. on the 15th, Pillow's troops were ready, except one brigade, which came late into action. By six o'clock, Baldwin's brigade was engaged with the enemy, only two or three hundred yards from his lines, and the bloody contest of the day had begun. At one o'clock the enemy's right was doubled back. The Wynn's Ferry road was cleared, and it only remained for the Confederates to do one of two things: The first was, to seize the golden moment and, adhering to the original purpose and plan of the sortie, move off rapidly by the route laid open by such strenuous efforts and so much bloodshed; the other depended on the inspiration of a master-mind, equal to the effort of grasping every element of the combat, and which should complete the partial victory by the utter rout and destruction of the enemy.

Three hundred prisoners, five thousand stand of small-arms, six guns, and other spoils of victory, had been won by our forces. But the enemy, cautiously advancing, gradually recovered most of his lost ground. It was about 4 P.M. when the assault on the right was made by General C. F. Smith. The enemy succeeded in carrying the advanced work, which General Buckner considered the key to his position. The loss of the enemy during the siege was four hundred killed, seventeen hundred and eighty-five wounded, and three hundred prisoners. Our losses were about three hundred and twenty-five killed and one thousand and ninety-seven wounded; including missing, it was estimated at fifteen hundred.

After nightfall a consultation of the commanding officers

was held; it was decided that a surrender was inevitable, and, that to accomplish its objects, it must be made before the assault, which was expected at daylight. The decision to surrender having been made, it remained to determine by whom it should be made. Generals Floyd and Pillow declared they would not surrender and become prisoners; the duty was therefore allotted to General Buckner. Floyd said, "General Buckner, if I place you in command, will you allow me to draw out my brigade?" General Buckner replied, "Yes, provided you do so before the enemy act upon my communication." Floyd said, "General Pillow, I turn over the command." General Pillow, regarding this as a mere technical form by which the command was to be conveyed to Buckner, then said, "I pass it." Buckner assumed the command, sent for a bugler to sound the parley, for pen, ink, and paper, and opened the negotiations for surrender.

General Pillow announced his determination to leave the post by any means available, so as to escape a surrender, and he advised Colonel N. B. Forrest, who was present, to go out with his cavalry regiment, and any others he could take with him through the overflow. General Floyd's brigade consisted of two Virginia regiments and one Mississippi regiment; these agreed that General Floyd might withdraw before the surrender. Two of the field-officers, Colonel Russell and Major Brown, of the Mississippi regiment, the twentieth, had been officers of the First Mississippi Riflemen in the war with Mexico; and the twentieth, their present regiment, was reputed to be well instructed and under good discipline. This regiment was left to be surrendered with the rest of the garrison.

Chapter 14

Movements in Tennessee;
Defense of General Johnston

THE LOSS of Forts Henry and Donelson opened the river routes to Nashville and north Alabama, and thus turned the positions both at Bowling Green and Columbus. A conference was held on February 7th by Generals Johnston, Beauregard (who had been previously ordered to report to Johnston), and Hardee, as to the future plan of campaign. It was determined, as Fort Henry had fallen and Donelson was untenable, that preparations should at once be made for a removal of the army to Nashville, in rear of the Cumberland River, a strong point some miles below that city being fortified forthwith to defend the river from the passage of gunboats and transports. From Nashville, should any further retrograde movement become necessary, it would be made to Stevenson, and thence according to circumstances.

Scarcely had the retreat to Nashville been accomplished, when the news of the fall of Donelson was received. The state of feeling which it produced is described by Colonel Munford, an aide-de-camp of General Johnston, in an address delivered in Memphis. "Dissatisfaction was general. Its mutterings, already heard, began to break out in denunciations. The demagogues took up the cry, and hounded on one another and the people in hunting down a victim. The public press was loaded with abuse. The Government was denounced for intrusting the public safety to hands so feeble. The Lower House of Congress appointed a select committee to inquire into the conduct of the war in the Western Department. The Senators and Representatives from Tennessee, with the exception of Judge Swann, waited upon the President." Their spokesman, Senator G. A. Henry, stated that they came for and in behalf of Tennessee to ask for the removal of General A. S. Johnston, and the assignment of a competent officer to the defense of their homes and people. It was further stated that they did not come to recommend any one as the successor; that it was conceded that the President was better able than they were to select a proper officer, and they only asked that he would give them a general.

Painfully impressed by this exhibition of distrust toward

254

an officer whose place, if vacated, I was sure could not be filled by his equal, yet realizing how necessary public confidence was to success, I paused under conflicting emotions, and after a time merely answered, "If Sidney Johnston is not a general, the Confederacy has none to give you."

On February 17th the rear guard from Bowling Green reached Nashville, and on the 18th General Johnston wrote to the Secretary of War at Richmond, saying:

I have ordered the army to encamp to-night midway between Nashville and Murfreesboro. My purpose is to place the force in such a position that the enemy can not concentrate his superior strength against the command, and to enable me to assemble as rapidly as possible such other troops in addition as it may be in my power to collect. The complete command which their gunboats and transports give them upon the Tennessee and Cumberland renders it necessary for me to retire my line between the rivers. I entertain the hope that this disposition will enable me to hold the enemy for the present in check, and, when my forces are sufficiently increased, to drive him back.

The fall of Fort Donelson made a speedy change of his plans necessary. General Johnston was now compelled to withdraw his forces from the north bank of the Cumberland, and to abandon the defense of Nashville; in a word, to evacuate Nashville or sacrifice the army. Not more than eleven thousand effective men were left to him with which to oppose General Buell with not less than forty thousand men, moving by Bowling Green, while another superior force, under General Thomas, was on the eastern flank; and the armies from Fort Donelson, with the gunboats and transport, had it in their power to ascend the Cumberland, so as to interrupt all communication with the south.

On February 17th and 18th the main body of the command was moved from Nashville to Murfreesboro, while a brigade remained under General Floyd to bring on the stores and property upon the approach of the enemy, all of which would have been saved except for the heavy and general rains. By the junction of the command of General Crittenden and the fugitives from Donelson, who were reorganized, the force of General Johnston was increased to seventeen thousand men. The stores not required for immediate use were ordered to Chattanooga, and those which were necessary on the march were ordered to Huntsville and Decatur. On February 28th the march was commenced for Decatur through

Shelbyville and Fayetteville. Halting at those points for the purpose, he saved his provisions and stores, removed his depots and machine-shops, obtained new arms, and finally, at the close of March, joined Beauregard at Corinth with twenty thousand men, making their aggregate force fifty thousand.

Considering the great advantage which the means of transportation upon the Tennessee and Cumberland afforded the enemy, and the peculiar topography of the State, General Johnston found that he could not with the force under his command successfully defend the whole line against the advance of the enemy. He was, therefore, compelled to elect whether the enemy should be permitted to occupy Middle Tennessee, or turn from Columbus, take Memphis, and open the valley of the Mississippi. Deciding that the defense of the valley was of paramount importance, he therefore crossed the Tennessee and united with Beauregard.

The evacuation of Nashville and the evident intention of General Johnston to retreat still further, created a panic in the public mind which spread over the whole State. Those who had refused to listen to his warning voice, when it called them to arms, were loudest in their passionate outcry at what they considered a base surrender of them to the mercies of the invader. He was accused of imbecility, cowardice, and treason. An appeal from every class was made to the President demanding his removal. Congress took the matter in hand, and, though the feeling there resulted merely in a committee of inquiry, it was evident that the case was prejudged. The Confederate House of Representatives created a special committee "to inquire into the military disasters at Fort Henry and Fort Donelson, and the surrender of Nashville to the enemy," and as to the conduct, number, and disposition of the troops under General Johnston. Great feeling was shown in the debates.

Let us now review the events which had brought such unmeasured censure on General Johnston for some months preceding this correspondence. We have seen him, with a force numerically much inferior to that of the enemy in his front, holding the position of Bowling Green, and, by active operations of detached commands, keeping up to foe and friend the impression that he had a large army in position. With self-sacrificing fortitude he remained silent under reproaches for not advancing to attack the enemy. When Forts Donelson and Henry were more immediately threatened, he gave reënforcements from his small command until his own line became more like one of skirmishers than an intrenched line of battle; and when those forts were surrendered, and his position became both untenable and useless, he withdrew in such order and with such skill that his retreat was unmolested by the enemy. Though he continued to be the subject of unreasoning vituperation, he sought not to justify himself by blaming others, or telling what he would have done if his Government had sent him the arms and munitions he asked for, but which his Government he learned did not possess.

There are yet those who, self-assured, demand why Johnston did not go himself to Donelson and Henry, and why his forces were not there concentrated. A slight inspection of the map would suffice to show that, Bowling Green abandoned, the direct road to Nashville would be open to the advance of Buell's army. Then the forts, if held, would cease to answer their purpose, and, being isolated, and also between hostile armies above and below, would be not only valueless but only temporarily tenable; and of his critics it may be asked, Who else than himself could, with the small force retained at Bowling Green, have held the enemy in check so long, and at last have retired without disaster?

The Southwestern States presented a field peculiarly favorable for the application of a new power in war. Deep rivers, with banks frequently but little elevated above the water, traverse the country. On these rivers iron-plated steamboats with heavy guns may move with a rapidity incomparably greater than that of marching armies. It is as if forts, with armaments, garrison, and stores, were endowed with locomotion more swift and enduring than that of cavalry.

The Ohio, Mississippi, Cumberland, and Tennessee Rivers all were in the field of General Johnston's operations, and at the stage of water most suited to naval purposes. Apart from the heavy guns which could thus be brought to bear at interior places upon an army having only field-artillery, the advantage of rapid transportation for troops and supplies can hardly be over-estimated. It has been seen how these advantages were utilized by the enemy at Henry and Donelson, and not less did they avail him at Shiloh.

Meantime some active operations had taken place in that part of General Johnston's command west of the Mississippi River. Detached conflicts with the enemy had been fought by the small forces under Generals Price and McCulloch, but no definite result had followed. General Earl Van Dorn had been subsequently assigned to the command, and assumed it on January 29, 1862.

General Van Dorn was now ordered to join General Johnston by the quickest route. Yet only one of his regiments arrived in time to be present at the battle of Shiloh. As has been already stated, General Beauregard left Nashville on February 14th to take charge in West Tennessee, and made his headquarters at Jackson, Tennessee, on February 17th. He was somewhat prostrated by sickness, which partially disabled him through the campaign. The two grand divisions of his army were commanded by the able Generals Bragg and Polk. On March 26th he permanently removed to Corinth. Under his orders the evacuation of Columbus by General Polk, and the establishment of a new line resting on New Madrid, Island No. 10, and Humbodlt, was completed. On March 2d Brigadier-General J. P. McCown, an "old army" officer, was assigned to the command of Island No. 10, forty miles below Columbus, whither he removed his division. A. P. Stewart's brigade was sent to New Madrid. At these points some seven thousand troops were assembled, and the remainder marched under General Cheatham to Union City. General Polk says:

In five days we moved the accumulations of six months, taking with us all our commissary and quartermaster's stores—an amount sufficient to supply my whole command for eight months—all our powder and other ammunition and ordnance stores, excepting a few shot, and gun-carriages, and every heavy gun in the fort, except two thirty-two pounders and three carronades in a remote outwork, which had been rendered useless.

The movement of the enemy up the Tennessee River commenced on March 10th. General C. F. Smith led the advance, with a new division under General Sherman. On the 13th Smith assembled four divisions at Savannah, on the west bank of the Tennessee, at the Great Bend. The ultimate design was to mass the forces of Grant and Buell against our army at Corinth. Buel was still in the occupation of Nashville. On the 16th Sherman disembarked at Pittsburg Landing, and made a reconnaissance to Monterey, nearly half-way to Corinth. On the next day General Grant took command. Two more divisions were added, and he assembled his army near Pittsburg Landing, which was the most advantageous base for a movement against Corinth. Here it lay inactive until the battle of Shiloh.

The Tennessee flows northwest for some distance, until, a little west of Hamburg, it takes its final bend to the north. Here two small streams, Owl and Lick Creeks, flowing nearly parallel, somewhat north of east, from three to five miles apart, empty into the Tennessee. Owl Creek forms the northern limit of the ridge, which Lick Creek bounds on the south. These streams, rising some ten or twelve miles back, toward Corinth, were bordered near their mouths by swamps filled with backwater from the Tennessee, and impassable except where the roads crossed them.

The inclosed space is a rolling table-land, about one hundred feet above the river-level, with its water-shed lying near Lick Creek, and either slope broken by deep and frequent ravines draining into the two streams. The acclivities were covered with forests, and often thick set with undergrowth. Pittsburg Landing, containing three or four log-cabins, was situated about midway between the mouths of the creeks, in the narrow morass that borders the Tennessee. It was three or four miles below Hamburg, six or seven above Savannah, the depot of the enemy on the right bank, and twenty-two miles from Corinth. Thus the position of the enemy was naturally strong. With few and difficult approaches, guarded on either flank by impassable streams and morasses, protected by a succession of ravines and acclivities, commanded by eminences to the rear, it seemed safe against attack, and easy to defend. No defensive works were constructed.

Chapter 15

Shiloh

GENERAL BUELL, who was to make a junction with General Grant, deemed it best that his army should march through by land, as it would facilitate the occupation of the Memphis and Charleston Railroad through north Alabama, where General Mitchell had been assigned. Accordingy, Buell commenced his march from Nashville on March 15th, with a rapid movement of cavalry, followed by a division of infantry, to seize the bridges. The bridge over Duck River being destroyed, it was the 31st before his army crossed. His advance arrived at Savannah on Saturday, April 5th, and our attack on Grant at Pittsburg Landing was made on the next day, the 6th of April. The advance of General Buell anticipated his orders by two days, and likewise the calculations of our commanders.

It had been the object of General Johnston, since falling back from Nashville, to concentrate his army at Corinth, and fight the enemy in detail—Grant first, and Buell afterward. The army of General Polk had been drawn back from Columbus. The War Department ordered General Bragg from Pensacola, with his well-disciplined army, to the aid of Johnston. A brigade was sent by General Lovell from Louisiana, and Chalmers and Walker were already on the line of the Memphis and Charleston road with considerable commands. These forces collected at Corinth, and to them were added such new levies as the Governors had in rendezvous, and a few regiments raised in response to General Beauregard's call. General Bragg, in a sketch of the battle of Shiloh, thus speaks of General Johnston's army:

. . . It was a heterogenous mass, in which there was more enthusiasm than discipline, more capacity than knowledge, and more valor than instruction. Rifles, rifled and smooth-bore muskets— some of them originally percussion, others hastily altered from flint-locks by Yankee contractors, many with the old flint and steel—and shot-guns of all sizes and patterns, held place in the same regiments. The task of organizing such a command in four weeks, and supplying it, especially with ammunition, suitable for action, was simply appalling. It was undertaken, however, with a cool, quiet self-control, calling to his [General Johnston's] aid the best knowledge and talent at his command, which not only inspired confidence, but soon yielded the natural fruits of system, order, and discipline.

This force, about forty thousand of all arms, was divided into four corps, commanded respectively by Major-Generals Polk, Bragg, and Hardee, and Brigadier-General Breckinridge. General Beauregard was second in command under General Johnston. General Beauregard says, "A want of general officers needful for the proper organization of divisions and brigades of an army brought thus suddenly together, and other difficulties in the way of effective organization, delayed the movements until the night of April 2d."

About one o'clock on the morning of April 3d preliminary orders were issued to hold the troops in readiness to move at a moment's notice, with five days' provisions and a hundred rounds of ammunition. The orders for march and battle were issued in the afternoon. At that time General Hardee led the advance, the Third Corps, from Corinth, by the northernmost route, known as the Ridge road. Bivouacking that night on the way, he arrived next morning at Mickey's, a house about eighteen miles from Corinth and four or five miles from Pittsburg. The Second Corps, under Bragg, marched by the direct road to Pittsburg through Monterey, which it reached about 11 A.M. on the 4th, and bivouacked that night near Mickey's in the rear of Hardee's corps. The First Corps, under General Polk, consisted of two divisions, under Cheatham and Clark. The latter was ordered to follow Hardee on the Ridge road at an interval of half an hour, and to halt near Mickey's, so as to allow Bragg's corps to fall in behind Hardee, at a thousand yards' interval, and form a second line of battle. Polk's corps was to form the left wing of the third line of battle; and Breckinridge's reserve the right wing. The other division of Polk, under Cheatham, was on outpost duty, at and near Bethel, on the Mobile and Ohio Railroad, about as far from Mickey's as Corinth was. He was ordered to assemble his forces at Purdy, and pursue the route to Monterey. He effected his junction on the afternoon of the 5th, and took position on the left wing of Polk's corps. Breckinridge's reserve corps moved from Burnsville early on April 4th, by way of Farmington toward Monterey, distant fourteen miles. It did not effect its junction with the other corps until late on the afternoon of Saturday the 5th, being delayed by the rains on Friday and Saturday. At daylight on the 5th Hardee moved, and by seven o'clock was sufficiently out of the way to allow Bragg to advance. Before ten o'clock Hardee's corps had reached the outposts and developed the lines of the enemy. The corps was immediately deployed into line of battle about a mile and a half west of Shiloh church, where Lick Creek and Owl Creek approach most nearly, and are about three miles apart. Gladden's brigade, of Bragg's corps, was on the right of Hardee's corps, which was not sufficiently strong to occupy the whole front. This line extended from creek to creek. Before seven o'clock Bragg's column was in motion, and the right wing of his line of battle formed about eight hundred yards in the rear of Hardee's line. But the division on the left was nowhere to be seen. Even as late as half-past twelve the missing column had not appeared, nor had any report from it been received. General Johnston, "looking first at his watch, then glancing at the position of the sun, exclaimed: 'This is not *war*! Let us have our horses!' He rode to the rear until he found the missing column standing stockstill, with its head some distance out in an open field. General Polk's reserves were ahead of it, with their wagons and artillery blocking up the road. General Johnston ordered them to clear the road, and the missing column to move forward. There was much chaffering among those implicated as to who should bear the blame. . . . It was about four o'clock when the lines were completely formed—too late, of course, to begin the battle then."

The road was not clear until 2 P.M. General Polk got Clark's division of his corps into line of battle by four o'clock; and Cheatham, who had come up on the left, promptly followed. Breckinridge's line was then formed on Polk's right. Thus was the army arrayed in three lines of battle late Saturday afternoon.

General Bragg, in a monograph, on the battle of Shiloh, says:

During the afternoon of the 5th, as the last of our troops were taking position, a casual and partly accidental meeting of general officers occurred just in rear of our second line, near the bivouac of General Bragg. The Commander-in-Chief, General Beauregard, General Polk, General Bragg, and General Breckinridge, are remembered as present. In a discussion of the causes of the delay and its incidents, it was mentioned that some of the troops, now in their third day only, were entirely out of food, though having marched with five days' rations. General Beauregard, confident our movement had been discovered by the enemy, urged its abandonment, a return to our camps for supplies, and a general change of programme. In this opinion no other seemed fully to concur; and when it was suggested that "the enemy's supplies were much nearer, and could be had for the taking," General Johnston quietly remarked, "Gentlemen, we shall attack at daylight tomorrow." The meeting then dispersed upon an invitation of the commanding general to meet at his tent that evening. At that meeting a further discussion elicited the same views, and the same firm, decided determination. The next morning, about dawn of day, the 6th, as the troops were being put in motion, several generals again met at the camp-fire of the general-in-chief. The discussion was renewed, General Beauregard again expressing his dissent; when, rapid firing in the front indicating that the attack had commenced, General Johnston closed the discussion by remarking: "The battle has opened, gentlemen; it is too late to change our dispositions." He prepared to move to the front, and his subordinates promptly joined their respective commands, inspired by his coolness, confidence, and determination. Few men have equaled him in the possession and display, at the proper time, of these great qualities of the soldier.

The results of the first day of the famous battle thus begun are very summarily presented in the following brief report of General Beauregard:

At 5 A. M., on the 6th instant, a reconnoitering party of the enemy having become engaged with our advanced pickets, the commander of the forces gave orders to begin the movement and attack as determined upon, except that Trabue's brigade of Breckinridge's division was detached and advanced to support the left of Bragg's corps and line of battle then menaced by the enemy; and the other two brigades were directed to advance by the road to Hamburg to support Bragg's right; and at the same time Maney's regiment of Polk's corps was advanced by the same road to reënforce the regiment, of cavalry and battery of four pieces, already thrown forward to watch and guard Grier's, Tanner's, and Borland's Fords of Lick Creek.

Thirty minutes after 5 A. M., our lines and columns were in motion, all animated evidently by a promising spirit. The front line was engaged at once, but advanced steadily, followed in due order, with equal resolution and steadiness, by the other lines, which were brought successively into action with rare skill, judgment, and gallantry by the several corps commanders, as the enemy made a stand with his masses rallied for the struggle for his encampments. Like an Alpine avalance our troops moved forward, despite the determined resistance of the enemy, until after

6 P. M., when we were in possession of all his encampments between Owl and Lick Creeks but one; nearly all of his field-artillery, about thirty flags, colors, and standards, over three thousand prisoners, including a division commander (General Prentiss), and several brigade commanders, thousands of small-arms, an immense supply of subsistence, forage, and munitions of war, and a large amount of means of transportation, all the substantial fruits of a complete victory—such, indeed, as rarely have followed the most successful battles, for never was an army so well provided as that of our enemy.

The remnant of his army had been driven in utter disorder to the immediate vicinity of Pittsburg, under the shelter of the heavy guns of his iron-clad gunboats, and we remained undisputed masters of his well-selected, admirably provided cantonments, after our twelve hours of obstinate conflict with his forces, who had been beaten from them and the contiguous covert, but only by the sustained onset of all the men we could bring into action.

There are two words in this report which, if they could have been truthfully omitted, it would have been worth to us the surrender of all "the subtsantial fruits of a complete victory." It says: "Our troops moved forward, despite the determined resistance of the enemy, until after 6 P.M., when we were in possession of all his encampments between Owl and Lick Creeks *but one.*" It was that "one" encampment that furnished a foothold for all the subsequent reënforcements sent by Buell, and gave occasion for the final withdrawal of our forces; whereas, if that had been captured, and the "waters of the Tennessee" reached, as General Johnston designed, it was not too much to expect that Grant's army would have surrendered; that Buell's forces would not have crossed the Tennessee; but with a skillful commander, like Johnston, to lead our troops, the enemy would have sought safety on the north bank of the Ohio; that Tennessee, Kentucky, and Missouri would have been recovered, the Northwest disaffected, and our armies filled with the men of the Southwest, and perhaps of the Northwest also.

Let us turn to reports and authorities. The author of "The Life of Gen. Albert Sidney Johnston" says:

Of the two armies, one was now an advancing, triumphant host, with arm uplifted to give the mortal blow; the other, a broken, mangled, demoralized mob, paralyzed and waiting for the stroke. While the other Confederate brigades, which had shared most actively in Prentiss's capture, were sending back the prisoners and forming again for a final attack, two brigades, under

Chalmers and Jackson, on the extreme right, had cleared away all in front of them, and, moving down the river-bank, now came upon the last point where even a show of resistance was made. Being two very bold and active brigadiers, they at once closed with the enemy in their front, crossing a deep ravine and difficult ground to get at him. Here Colonel Webster, of Grant's staff, had gathered all the guns he could find from batteries, whether abandoned or still coherent, and with stout-hearted men, picked up at random, had prepared a resistance. Some infantry, similarly constituted, had been got together; and Ammen's brigade, the van of Nelson's division of Buell's corps, had landed, and was pushing its way through the throng of pallid fugitives at the landing to take up the battle where it had fallen from the hands of Grant and Sherman. It got into position in time to do its part in checking the unsupported assaults of Chalmers and Jackson.

General Chalmers, describing this final attack in his report, says:

It was then about four o'clock in the evening, and, after distributing ammunition, we received orders from General Bragg to drive the enemy into the river. My brigade, together with that of Brigadier-General Jackson, filed to the right and formed facing the river, and endeavored to press forward to the water's edge; but in attempting to mount the last ridge we were met by a fire from a whole line of batteries, protected by infantry and assisted by shells from the gunboats.

In a subsequent memorandum General Chalmers writes:

One more resolute movement forward would have captured Grant and his whole army, and fulfilled to the letter the battle-plan of the great Confederate general, who died in the belief that victory was ours. . . .

General Hardee, who commanded the first line, says in his report:

Upon the death of General Johnston, the command having devolved upon General Beauregard, the conflict was continued until near sunset, and the advance divisions were within a few hundred yards of Pittsburg, where the enemy were huddled in confusion, when the order to withdraw was received. The troops were ordered to bivouac on the field of battle.

General Gilmer, the chief engineer of the Confederate States Army, in a letter to Colonel William Preston Johnston, dated September 17, 1872, writes as follows:

It is my well-considered opinion that if your father had survived the day he would have crushed and captured General Grant's army before the setting of the sun on the 6th. In fact, at the time your father received the mortal wound, advancing with General Breckinridge's command, the day was ours. The enemy having lost all the strong positions on that memorable field, his troops fell back in great disorder on the banks of the Tennessee. To cover the confusion, rapid fires were opened from the gunboats the enemy had placed in the river; but the shots passed entirely over our devoted men, who were exultant and eager to be led forward to the final assault, which *must* have resulted in a complete victory, owing to the confusion and general disorganization of the Federal troops. I knew the condition of General Grant's army at the moment, as I had reached a high, projecting point on the bank of the river, about a mile above Pittsburg Landing, and could see the hurried movements to get the disordered troops across to the right bank. Several thousand had already passed, and a confused mass of men crowded to the landing to get on the boats that were employed in crossing. I rode rapidly to General Bragg's position to report what I had seen, and suggested that, if he would suspend the fire of his artillery and marshal his infantry for a general advance, the enemy must surrender. General Bragg decided to make the advance, and authorized me and other officers to direct the commanders of the batteries to cease firing.

In the midst of the preparations, orders reached General Bragg from General Beauregard directing the troops to be withdrawn and placed in camp for the night—the intention being to resume the contest in the morning. This was fatal, as it enabled General Buell and General Wallace to arrive on the scene of action; that is, they came up in the course of the night. Had General Beauregard known the condition of the enemy as your father knew it when he received the fatal shot, the order for withdrawal would certainly not have been given, and, without such order, I know the enemy would have been crushed.

General Beauregard reports as follows:

It was after 6 P. M. when the enemy's last position was carried, and his force finally broke and sought refuge behind a commanding eminence covering Pittsburg Landing, not more than half a mile distant, and under the guns of the gunboats, which opened on our eager columns a fierce and annoying fire with shot and shell of the heaviest description. Darkness was close at hand. Officers and men were exhausted by a combat of over twelve hours, without food, and jaded by the march of the preceding day through mud and water; it was, therefore, impossible to collect the rich and opportune spoils of war scattered broadcast on the field left in our possession, and impracticable to make any effective dispositions for their removal to the rear.

I accordingly established my headquarters at the church of Shiloh, in the enemy's encampment, with Major-General Bragg, and directed our troops to sleep on their arms in such positions in advance and rear as corps commanders should determine, hoping, from news received by a special dispatch, that delays had been encountered by General Buell in his march from Columbia, and that his main forces, therefore, could not reach the field of battle in time to save General Grant's shattered fugitives from capture or destruction on the following day.

Such are the representations of those having the best means of information relative to the immediate causes of the failure to drive the enemy from his last foothold, and gain possession of it. Some of the more remote causes of this failure may be noticed. The first was the death of General Johnston, which is thus described by his son:

General Johnston had passed through the ordeal (the charge upon the enemy) seemingly unhurt. His noble horse was shot in four places; his clothes were pierced by missiles; his boot-sole was cut and torn by a Minié ball; but, if he himself had received any severe wound, he did not know it. At this moment Governor Harris rode up from the right, elated with his own success, and with the vindication of his Tennesseeans. After a few words, General Johnston sent him with an order to Colonel Statham, which, having delivered, he speedily returned. In the mean time knots and groups of Federal soldiers kept up an angry discharge of firearms as they retreated upon their supports, and their last line, now yielding, delivered volley after volley as they retreated. By the chance of war a Minié ball from one of these did its fatal work. As General Johnston, on horseback, sat there, knowing that he had crushed in the arch which had so long resisted the pressure of his forces, and waiting until they could collect sufficiently to give the final stroke, he received a mortal wound. It came in the moment of victory and triumph from a flying foe. It smote him at the very instant when he felt the full conviction that the day was won.

In his fall the great pillar of the Southern Confederacy was crushed, and beneath its fragments the best hope of the Southwest lay buried.

Grant's army being beaten, the next step of General Johnston's program should have followed, the defeat of Buell's and Mitchell's forces as they successively came up, and a return by our victorious army through Tennessee to Kentucky. The great embarrassment had been the want of good military weapons; these would have been largely supplied by the conquest hoped for, and, in the light of what had occurred, not unreasonably anticipated.

What great consequences would have ensued must be matter of conjecture, but that the people of Kentucky and Missouri generously sympathized with the South was then commonly admitted. Our known want of preparation for war and numerical inferiority may well have caused many to doubt the wisdom of our effort for independence, and to these a signal success would have been the makeweight deciding their course.

I believe that again in the history of war the fate of an army depended on one man; and more, that the fortunes of a country hung by the single thread of the life that was yielded on the field of Shiloh.

At the ensuing nightfall our victorious army retired from the front and abandoned its vantage-ground on the bluffs, which had been won at such a cost of blood. The enemy thereby had room and opportunity to come out from their corner, reoccupy the strong positions from which they had been driven, and dispose their troops on much more favorable ground. Called off by staff-officers, who gave no specific instructions, our brigades, according to circumstances, bivouacked on the battle-field, marched to the rear, or made themselves comfortable on the profuse spoils of the enemy's encampments. General Buell says:

Of the army of not less than fifty thousand effective men, which Grant had on the west bank of the Tennessee River, not more than five thousand were in ranks and available on the battle-field at nightfall on the 6th, exclusive of Lew Wallace's division, say eight thousand five hundred men that only came up during the night. The rest were either killed, wounded, captured, or scattered in inextricable and hopeless confusion for miles along the banks of the river.

In addition to the arrival of Wallace's division, the entire divisions of Nelson and Crittenden got across the river during the night, and by daylight that of McCook began to arrive; all but the first named belonged to Buell's army. The work of reorganization of fragments of Grant's force also occupied the night. In the morning the arrival of reënforcements to the enemy continued.

On the morning of the 7th the enemy advanced about six o'clock, and opened a heavy fire of musketry and artillery, such as gave assurance that the reënforcements had arrived, to anticipate which the battle of the 6th had been fought. A series of combats ensued, in which the Confederates showed their usual valor; but, after the junction had been effected between Grant and Buell, which Johnston's movement was made to prevent, our force was unequal to resist the combined armies, and retreat was a necessity.

The field return of the Army of Mississippi before and after the battle of Shiloh was as follows: infantry and artillery, effective before the battle, 35,953; cavalry, 4,382; total, 40,335. Infantry and artillery, effective after the battle, 25,555; cavalry, 4,081; total, 29,636. Difference, 10,699. Casualties in battle: killed, 1,728; wounded, 8,012; missing, 959.

The effective force of General Grant's army engaged in the battles of April 6th and 7th at Shiloh was 49,314; reënforcements of General Buell, 21,579; total, 70,893. The casualties in the battle of April 6th in Grant's force were as follows: killed, 1,500; wounded, 6,634; missing, 3,086; total, 11,220; leaving, for duty on the 7th, 59,673.

Chapter 16

Jackson; Shenandoah Valley

IN THE EAST, the withdrawal of our army to the Chickahominy, the abandonment of Norfolk, the destruction of the
Virginia, and opening of the lower James River, together
with the fact that McClellan's army, by changing his base to
the head of York River, was in a position to cover the approach to Washington, and thus to remove the objections
which had been made to sending the large force, retained
for the defense of that city, to make a junction with McClellan, all combined to give a new phase to our military
problem.

Soon after, General J. E. Johnston took position on the
north side of the Chickahominy; accompanied by General
Lee, I rode out to his headquarters in the field, in order that
by conversation with him we might better understand his
plans and expectations. He came in after we arrived, saying
that he had been riding around his lines to see how his position could be improved. A long conversation followed, which
was so inconclusive that it lasted until late in the night, so
late that we remained until the next morning. As we rode
back to Richmond, reference was naturally made to the conversation of the previous evening and night, when General
Lee confessed himself, as I was, unable to draw from it any
more definite purpose than that the policy was to improve
his position as far as practicable, and wait for the enemy to
leave his gunboats, so that an opportunity might be offered
to meet him on the land.

As will be seen, the operations in the Valley by General
Jackson, who there exhibited a rapidity of movement equal
to the unyielding tenacity which had in the first great battle
won for him the familiar name "Stonewall," had created
such an alarm in Washington, as, if it had been better
founded, would have justified the refusal to diminish the force
held for the protection of their capital. Indeed, our cavalry,
in observation near Fredericksburg, reported that on the 24th
McDowell's troops started southward, but General Stuart
found that night that they were returning. This indicated
that the anticipated junction was not to be made, and of this
the Prince de Joinville writes:

It needed only an effort of the will: the two armies were united, and the possession of Richmond certain! Alas! this effort was not made. I can not recall those fatal moments without a real sinking of the heart.

General McClellan, in his testimony December 10, 1862, before the court-martial in the case of General McDowell, said:

I have no doubt, for it has ever been my opinion, that the Army of the Potomac would have taken Richmond had not the corps of General McDowell been separated from it. It is also my opinion that, had the command of General McDowell joined the Army of the Potomac in the month of May, by the way of Hanover Court-House, from Fredericksburg, we would have had Richmond within a week after the junction.

Let us first inquire what was the size of this army so crippled for want of reënforcement, and then what the strength of that to which it was opposed. On the 30th of April, 1862, the official report of McClellan's army gives the aggregate present for duty as 112,392; that of the 20th of June—omitting the army corps of General Dix, then, as previously, stationed at Fortress Monroe, and including General McCall's division, which had recently joined, the strength of which was reported to be 9,514—gives the aggregate present for duty as 105,825, and the total, present and absent, as 156,838.

Two statements of the strength of our army under General J. E. Johnston during the month of May—in which General McClellan testified that he was greatly in need of McDowell's corps—give the following results: First, the official return, 21st May, 1862, total effective of all arms, 53,688; subsequently, five brigades were added, and the effective strength of the army under General Johnston on May 31, 1862, was 62,696.

I now proceed to inquire what caused the panic at Washington.

On May 23d, General Jackson, with whose force that of General Ewell had united, moved with such rapidity as to surprise the enemy, and Ewell, who was in advance, captured most of the troops at Front Royal, and pressed directly on to Winchester, while Jackson, turning across to the road from Strasburg, struck the main column of the enemy in flank and drove it routed back to Strasburg. The pursuit was continued to Winchester, and the enemy, under their commander-in-chief, General Banks, fled across the Potomac into Maryland. Two thousand prisoners were taken in the pursuit. General Banks in his report says. "There never were more grateful hearts in the same number of men, than when, at mid-day on the 26th, we stood on the opposite shore."

When the news of the attack on Front Royal, on May 23d, reached General Geary, charged with the protection of the Manassas Gap Railroad, he immediately moved to Manassas Junction. At the same time, his troops, hearing the most extravagant stories, burned their tents and destroyed a quantity of arms. General Duryea, at Catlett's Station, becoming alarmed on hearing of the withdrawal of Geary, took his three New York regiments, leaving a Pennsylvania one behind, hastened back to Centreville, and telegraphed to Washington for aid. He left behind a large quantity of army stores. The alarm spread to Washington, and the Secretary of War, Stanton, issued a call to the Governors of the "loyal" States for militia to defend that city.

This alarm at Washington, and the call for more troops for its defense, produced a most indescribable panic in the cities of the Northern States on Sunday the 25th, and two or three days afterward. The Governor of New York on Sunday night telegraphed to Buffalo, Rochester, Syracuse, and other cities, as follows:

Orders from Washington render it necessary to send to that city all the available militia force. What can you do?

E. D. MORGAN

Governor Curtin, of Pennsylvania, issued the following order:

HEADQUARTERS OF PENNSYLVANIA MILITIA,
HARRISBURG, *May 26, 1862*

On pressing requisition of the President of the United States in the present emergency, it is ordered that the several major-generals, brigadier-generals, and colonels of regiments throughout the Commonwealth muster without delay all military organizations within their respective divisions or under their control, together with all persons willing to join their commands, and proceed forthwith to the city of Washington, or such other points as may be designated by future orders. By order:

A. G. CURTIN,
Governor and Commander-in-Chief

The Governor of Massachusetts issued the following proclamation:

Men of Massachusetts!

The wily and barbarous horde of traitors to the people, to the Government, to our country, and to liberty, menace again the national capital. They have attacked and routed Major-General Banks, are advancing on Harper's Ferry, and are marching on Washington. The President calls on Massachusetts to rise once more for its rescue and defense.

The whole active militia will be summoned by a general order, issue from the office of the adjutant-general, to report on Boston Common to-morrow. They will march to relieve and avenge their brethren and friends, and to oppose, with fierce zeal and courageous patriotism, the progress of the foe. May God encourage their hearts and strengthen their arms, and may he inspire the Government, and all the people!

Given at headquarters, Boston, eleven o'clock, this (Sunday) evening, May 25, 1862.   JOHN A. ANDREW

The Governor of Ohio issued the following proclamation:

COLUMBUS, OHIO, *May 26, 1862.*

To the gallant men of Ohio.

I have the astounding intelligence that the seat of our beloved Government is threatened with invasion, and am called upon by the Secretary of War for troops to repel and overwhelm the ruthless invaders. Rally, then, men of Ohio, and respond to this call, as becomes those who appreciate our glorious Government! . . . The number wanted from each county has been indicated by special dispatches to the several military committees.

DAVID TOD, *Governor*

At the same time the Secretary of War at Washington caused the following order to be issued:

WASHINGTON, *Sunday, May 25, 1862.*

Ordered: By virtue of the authority vested by an act of Congress, the President takes military possession of all the railroads in the United States from and after this date, and directs that the respective railroad companies, their officers and servants, shall hold themselves in readiness for the transportation of troops and munitions of war, as may be ordered by the military authorities, to the exclusion of all other business.

By order of the Secretary of War:

M. C. MEIGS,
Quartermaster-General.

At the first moment of the alarm, the President of the United States issued the following order:

WASHINGTON, *May 24, 1862.*

ajor-General McDOWELL.

General Fremont has been ordered by telegraph to move to Franklin and Harrisonburg to relieve General Banks and capture or destroy Jackson's and Ewell's forces. You are instructed, laying aside for the present the movement on Richmond, to put twenty thousand men in motion at once for the Shenandoah, moving on the line or in advance of the line of the Manassas Gap Railroad. Your object will be to capture the forces of Jackson and Ewell, either in coöperation with General Fremont, or, in case want of supplies or transportation has interfered with his movement, it is believed that the force which you move will be sufficient to accomplish the object alone. The information thus far received here makes it probable that, if the enemy operates actively against General Banks, you will not be able to count upon much assistance from him, but may have even to release him. Reports received this morning are that Banks is fighting with Ewell, eight miles from Harper's Ferry.

ARBAHAM LINCOLN.

When the panic thus indicated in the headquarters of the enemy had disseminated itself through the military and social ramifications of Northern society, the excitement was tumultuous. Meanwhile, General Jackson, little conceiving the alarm his movements had caused in the departments at Washington and in the offices of the Governors of States, in addition to the diversion of McDowell from coöperation in the attack upon Richmond, after driving the enemy out of Winchester, pressed eagerly on, for he learned that the enemy had garrisons at Charlestown and Harper's Ferry, and he was resolved they should not rest on Virginia soil. General Winder's brigade in the advance found the enemy drawn up in line of battle at Charlestown. Without waiting for reënforcements, he engaged them, and after a short conflict drove them in disorder toward the Potomac. The main column then moved on near to Harper's Ferry, where General Jackson received information that Fremont was moving from the west, and the whole or a part of General McDowell's corps from the east, to make a junction in his rear and thus cut off his retreat. At this time General Jackson's effective force was about fifteen thousand men, much less than either of the two armies which were understood to be marching to form a junction against him. We now know that General McDowell had been ordered to send to the relief of General Banks in the Valley twenty to thirty thousand men. The estimated force of General Fremont when at Harrisonburg was twenty thousand. General Jackson had captured in his campaign down the Valley, a very large amount of valuable stores, over nine thousand small-arms, two pieces of artillery, many horses, and, besides the wounded and sick, who had been released on parole, was said to have twenty-three hundred prisoners. To secure these, as well as to save his army, it was necessary to retreat beyond the point where his enemies could readily unite. The amount of captured stores and other property which he was anxious to preserve were said to require a wagon-train twelve miles long. This, under the care of a regiment, was sent forward in advance of the army, which promptly retired up the Valley.

On his retreat, General Jackson received information confirmatory of the report of the movements of the enemy, and of the defeat of a small force he had left at Front Royal in charge of some prisoners and captured stores—the latter, however, had destroyed the garrison before retreating. Strasburg being General Jackson's objective point, he had farther to march to reach that position than either of the columns operating against him. The rapidity of movements which marked General Jackson's operations had given to his command the appellation of "foot cavalry"; and never had they more need to show themselves entitled to the name of Stonewall.

On the night of the 31st of May, by a forced march, General Jackson arrived with the head of his column at Strasburg, and learned that General Fremont's advance was in the immediate vicinity. To gain time for the rest of his army to arrive, General Jackson decided to check Fremont's march by an attack in the morning. This movement was assigned to General Ewell, General Jackson personally giving his attention to preserving his immense trains filled with captured stores. The repulse of Fremont's advance was so easy that General Taylor describes it as offering a temptation to go beyond General Jackson's orders and make a serious attack upon Fremont's army, but recognizes the justice of the restraint imposed by the order, "as we could not waste time chasing Fremont," for it was reported that General Shields was at Front Royal with troops of a different character from those of Fremont's army, who had been encountered near Strasburg, *id est,* the corps "commanded by General O. O. Howard, and called by both sides 'the flying Dutchmen.' " This more formidable command of General Shields therefore required immediate attention.

Leaving Strasburg on the evening of June 1st, always intent to prevent a junction of the two armies of the enemy, Jackson continued his march up the Valley. Fremont followed in pursuit, while Shields moved slowly up the Valley *via* Luray, for the purpose of reaching New Market in advance of Jackson. On the morning of the 5th Jackson reached Harrisonburg, and, passing beyond that town, turned toward the east in the direction of Port Republic. General Ashby had destroyed all the bridges between Front Royal and Port Republic, to prevent Shields from crossing the Shenandoah to join Fremont. The troops were now permitted to make shorter marches, and were allowed some halts to refresh them after their forced marches and frequent combats. Early on the 6th of June Fremont's re-enforced cavalry attacked our cavalry rear-guard under General Ashby. A sharp conflict ensued, which resulted in the repulse of the enemy and the capture of Colonel Percy Wyndham, commanding the brigade, and sixty-three others. General Ashby was in position between Harrisonburg and Port Republic, and, after the cavalry combat just described, there were indications of a more serious attack. Ashby sent a message to Ewell, informing him that cavalry supported by infantry was advancing upon his position. The Fifty-eighth Virginia and the First Maryland Regiments were sent to his support. Ashby led the Fifty-eighth Virginia to attack the enemy, who were under cover of a fence. General Ewell in the mean time had arrived, and, seeing the advantage the enemy had of position, directed Colonel Johnston to move with his regiment so as to approach the flank instead of the front of the enemy, and he was now driven from the field with heavy loss. Our loss was seventeen killed, fifty wounded, and three missing.

The main body of General Jackson's command had now reached Port Republic, a village situated in the angle formed by the junction of the North and South Rivers, tributaries of the South Fork of the Shenandoah. Over the North River was a wooden bridge, connecting the town with Harrisonburg. Over the South River there was a ford. Jackson's immediate command was encamped on the high ground north of the village and about a mile from the river. Ewell was some four miles distant, near the road leading from Harrisonburg to Port Republic. General Fremont had arrived with his forces in the vicinity of Harrisonburg, and General Shields was moving up the east side of the Shenandoah, and had reached Conrad's Store. Each was about fifteen miles distant from Jackson's position. To prevent a junction, the bridge over the river, near Shields's position, had been destroyed.

As the advance of General Shields approached on the 8th, the brigades of Taliaferro and Winder were ordered to occupy positions immediately north of the bridge. The enemy's cavalry, accompanied by artillery, then appeared, and, after directing a few shots toward the bridge, crossed South River, and, dashing into the village, planted one of their pieces at the southern entrance of the bridge. Meantime our batteries were placed in position, and, Taliaferro's brigade having approached the bridge, was ordered to dash across, capture the piece, and occupy the town. This was gallantly done, and the enemy's cavalry dispersed and driven back, abandoning another gun. A considerable body of infantry was now seen advancing, when our batteries opened with marked effect, and in a short time the infantry followed the cavalry, falling back three miles. They were pursued about a mile by our batteries on the opposite bank, when they disappeared in a wood.

This attack of Shields had scarcely been repulsed when Ewell became seriously engaged with Fremont, moving on the opposite side of the river. The enemy pushed forward, driving in the pickets, which, by gallant resistance, checked their advance until Ewell had time to select his position on a commanding ridge, with a rivulet and open ground in front, woods on both flanks, and the road to Port Republic intersecting his line. Trimble's brigade was posted on the right, the batteries of Courtney, Lusk, Brockenbrough, and Rains in the center, Stuart's brigade on the left, and Elzey's in rear of the center. Both wings were in the woods. About ten o'clock the enemy posted his artillery opposite our batteries, and a fire was kept up for several hours, with great spirit on both sides. Meantime a brigade of the enemy advanced, under cover, upon General Trimble, who reserved his fire until they reached short range, when he poured forth a deadly volley, under which they fell back; Trimble, supported by two regiments of Elzey's reserve, now advanced, with spirited skirmishing, more than a mile from his orginal line, driving the opposing force back to its former position. Ewell, finding no attack on his left was designed by the enemy, advanced and drove in their skirmishers, and at night was in position on ground previously occupied by the foe. This engagement has generally been known as the battle of Cross Keys.

As General Shields made no movement to renew the action of the 8th, General Jackson determined to attack him on the

9th. Accordingly, Ewell's forces were moved at an early hour toward Port Republic, and General Trimble was left to hold Fremont in check, or, if hard pressed, to retire across the river and burn the bridge, which subsequently was done, under orders to concentrate against Shields.

Meanwhile the enemy had taken position about two miles from Port Republic, their right on the river-bank, their left on the slope of the mountain which here threw out a spur, between which and the river was a smooth plain of about a thousand yards wide. On an elevated plateau of the mountain was placed a battery of long-range guns to sweep the plain over which our forces must pass to attack. In front of that plateau was a deep gorge, through which flowed a small stream, trending to the southern side of the promontory, so as to leave its northern point in advance of the southern. The mountain-side was covered with dense wood.

Such was the position which Jackson must assail, or lose the opportunity to fight his foe in detail—the object for which his forced marches had been made, and on which his best hopes depended.

General Winder's brigade moved down the river to attack, when the enemy's battery upon the plateau opened, and it was found to rake the plain over which we must approach for a considerable distance in front of Shields's position. Our guns were brought forward, and an attempt made to dislodge the battery of the enemy, but our fire proved unequal to theirs; whereupon General Winder, having been reënforced, attempted by a rapid charge to capture it, but encountered such a heavy fire of artillery and small-arms as to compel his command, composed of his own and another brigade, with a light battery, to fall back in disorder. The enemy advanced steadily, and in such numbers as to drive back our infantry supports and render it necessary to withdraw our guns. Ewell was hurrying his men over the bridge, and there was no fear, if human effort would avail, that he would come too late. But the condition was truly critical. General Taylor describes his chief at that moment thus: "Jackson was on the road, a little in advance of his line, where the fire was hottest with reins on his horse's neck, seemingly in prayer. Attracted by my approach, he said, in his usual voice, 'Delightful excitement.'" He then briefly gave Taylor instructions to move against the battery on the plateau, and sent a young officer from his staff as a guide. The advance of the enemy was checked by an attack on his flank by two of our regiment, under Colonel

Scott; but this was only a temporary relief, for this small command was soon afterward driven back to the woods, with severe loss. Our batteries during the check were all safely withdrawn except one six-pounder gun.

In this critical condition of Winder's command, General Taylor made a successful attack on the left and rear of the enemy, which diverted attention from the front, and led to a concentration of his force upon him. Moving to the right along the mountain acclivity, he was unseen before he emerged from the wood, just as the loud cheers of the enemy proclaimed their success in front. Although opposed by a superior force in front and flank, and with their guns in position, with a rush and shout the gorge was passed, impetuously the charge was made, and the battery of six guns fell into our hands. Three times was this battery lost and won in the desperate and determined efforts to capture and recover it, and the enemy finally succeeded in carrying off one of the guns, leaving both caisson and limber. Thus occupied with Taylor, the enemy halted in his advance, and formed a line facing to the mountain. Winder succeeded in rallying his command, and our batteries were replaced in their former positions. At the same time reënforcements were brought by General Ewell to Taylor, who pushed forward with them, assisted by the well-directed fire of our artillery.

Of this period in the battle, than which there has seldom been one of greater peril, or where danger was more gallantly met, I copy a description from the work of General Taylor:

The fighting in and around the battery was hand-to-hand, and many fell from bayonet-wounds. Even the artillerymen used their rammers in a way not laid down in the manual, and died at their guns. I called for Hayes, but he, the promptest of men, and his splendid regiment could not be found. Something unexpected had occurred, but there was no time for speculation. With a desperate rally, in which I believe the drummer-boys shared, we carried the battery for the third time, and held it. Infantry and riflemen had been driven off, and we began to feel a little comfortable, when the enemy, arrested in his advance by our attack, appeared. He had countermarched, and, with left near the river, came into full view of our situation. Wheeling to the right, with colors advanced, like a solid wall he marched straight upon us. There seemed nothing left but to set our back to the mountain and die hard. At the instant, crashing through the underwood, came Ewell, outriding staff and escort. He produced the effect of a reënforcement, and was welcomed with cheers. The line before us halted and threw forward skirmishers. A moment later a shell came shrieking along it, loud Confederate cheers reached our delighted ears, and Jackson, freed from his toils, rushed up like a whirlwind.

The enemy, in his advance, had gone in front of the plateau where his battery was placed, the elevation being sufficient to enable the guns without hazard to be fired over the advancing line; so, when he commenced retreating, he had to pass by the position of this battery, and the captured guns were effectively used against him—that dashing old soldier, "Ewell, serving as a gunner." Mention was made of the inability to find Hayes when his regiment was wanted. It is due to that true patriot to add Taylor's explanation: "Ere long my lost Seventh Regiment, sadly cut up, rejoined. This regiment was in rear of the column when we left Jackson to gain the path in the woods, and, before it filed out of the road, his thin line was so pressed that Jackson ordered Hayes to stop the enemy's rush. This was done, for the Seventh would have stopped a herd of elephants—but at a fearful cost."

The retreat of the enemy, though it was so precipitate as to cause him to leave his killed and wounded on the field, was never converted into a rout. "Shield's brave 'boys' preserved their organization to the last; and, had Shields himself, with his whole command, been on the field, we should have had tough work indeed."

The pursuit was continued some five miles beyond the battle-field, during which we captured four hundred and fifty prisoners, some wagons, one piece of abandoned artillery, and about eight hundred muskets. Some two hundred and seventy-five wounded were paroled in the hospitals near Port Republic. On the next day Fremont withdrew his forces, and retreated down the Valley. The rapid movements of Jackson, the eagle-like stoop with which he had descended upon each army of the enemy, and the terror which his name had come to inspire, created a great alarm at Washington, where it was believed he must have an immense army, and that he was about to come down like an avalanche upon the capital. Milroy, Banks, Fremont, and Shields were all moved in that direction, and peace again reigned in the patriotic and once happy Valley of the Shenandoah.

The material results of this very remarkable campaign are thus summarily stated by one who had special means of information:

In three months Jackson had marched six hundred miles, fought four pitched battles, seven minor engagements, and daily skirmishes; had defeated four armies, captured seven pieces of artillery, ten thousand stand of arms, four thousand prisoners, and a very great amount of stores, inflicting upon his adversaries a known loss of two thousand men, with a loss upon his own part comparatively small.

The general effect upon the affairs of the Confederacy was even more important, and the motives which influenced Jackson present him in a grander light than any military success could have done. Thus, on the 20th of March, 1862, he learned that the large force of the enemy before which he had retired was returning down the Valley, and, divining the object to be to send forces to the east side of the mountain to coöperate in the attack upon Richmond, General Jackson, with his small force of about three thousand infantry and two hundred and ninety cavalry, moved with his usual celerity in pursuit. He overtook the rear of the column at Kernstown, attacked a very superior force he found there, and fought with such desperation as to impress the enemy with the idea that he had a large army; therefore, the detachments, which had already started for Manassas, were recalled, and additional forces were also sent into the Valley. Nor was this all. McDowell's corps, under orders to join McClellan, was detained for the defense of the Federal capital.

Jackson's bold strategy had effected the object for which his movement was designed, and he slowly retreated to the south bank of the Shenandoah, where he remained undisturbed by the enemy, and had time to recruit his forces, which, by the 28th of April, amounted to six or seven thousand men. General Banks had advanced and occupied Harrisonburg, about fifteen miles from Jackson's position. Fremont, with a force estimated at fifteen thousand men, was reported to be preparing to join Bank's command.

The alarm at Washington had caused McDowell's corps to be withdrawn from the upper Rappahannock to Fredericksburg. Jackson, anxious to take advantage of the then divided condition of the enemy, sent to Richmond for reënforcements, but our condition there did not enable us to furnish any, except the division of Ewell, which had been left near Gordonsville in observation of McDowell, now by his withdrawal made disposable, and the brigade of Edward Johnson, which confronted Schenck and Milroy near to Staunton. Jackson, who, when he could not get what he wanted, did the best he could with what he had, called Ewell to his aid, left him to hold Banks in check, and marched to unite with Johnson; the combined forces attacked Milroy and Schenck, who, after a severe conflict, retreated in the night to join Fremont. Jackson then returned toward Harrisonburg, having ordered Ewell to join him for an attack on Banks, who in the mean time had retreated toward Winchester, where Jackson attacked and defeated him, inflicting great loss, drove him across the Potomac, and, as has been represented, filled the authorities at Washington with such dread of its capture as to disturb the previously devised plans against Richmond, and led to the operations which have already been described, and brought into full play Jackson's military genius.

Chapter 17

Seven Pines

OUR ARMY having retreated from the Peninsula, and withdrawn from the north side of the Chickahominy to the immediate vicinity of Richmond, I rode out occasionally to the lines and visited the headquarters of the commanding General. There were no visible preparations for defense, and my brief conversations with the General afforded no satisfactory information as to his plans and purposes. We had, under the supervision of General Lee, perfected as far as we could the detached works before the city, but these were rather designed to protect it against a sudden attack than to resist approaches by a great army. They were, also, so near to the city that it might have been effectually bombarded by guns exterior to them. Anxious for the defense of the ancient capital of Virginia, now the capital of the Confederate States, and remembering a remark of General Johnston, that the Spaniards were the only people who now undertook to hold fortified towns, I had written to him that he knew the defense of Richmond must be made at a distance from it. Seeing no preparation to keep the enemy at a distance, and kept in ignorance of any plan for such purpose, I sent for General R. E. Lee, then at Richmond, in general charge of army operations, and told him why and how I was dissatisfied with the condition of affairs.

He asked me what I thought it was proper to do. Recurring to a conversation held about the time we had together visited General Johnston, I answered that McClellan should be attacked on the other side of the Chickahominy before he matured his preparations for a siege of Richmond. To this he promptly assented, as I anticipated he would, for I knew it had been his own opinion. He then said: "General Johnston should of course advise you of what he expects or proposes to do. Let me go and see him, and defer this discussion until I return."

I had not doubted that General Johnston was fully in accord with me as to the purpose of defending Richmond, but I was not content with his course for that end. It had not occurred to me that he meditated a retreat which would uncover the capital, nor was it ever suspected until, in reading General Hood's book, published in 1880, the evidence was found that General Johnston, when retreating from Yorktown, told his volunteer aide, Mr. McFarland, that "he [Johnston] expected or intended to give up Richmond."

When General Lee came back, he told me that General Johnston proposed, on the next Thursday, to move against the enemy as follows: General A. P. Hill was to move down on the right flank and rear of the enemy. General G. W. Smith, as soon as Hill's guns opened, was to cross the Chickahominy at the Meadow Bridge, attack the enemy in flank, and by the conjunction of the two it was expected to double him up. Then Longstreet was to cross on the Mechanicsville Bridge and attack him in front. From this plan the best results were hoped by both of us.

On the morning of the day proposed, I hastily dispatched my office business, and rode out toward the Meadow Bridge to see the action commence. On the road I found Smith's division halted, and the men dispersed in the woods. Looking for some one from whom I could get information, I finally saw General Hood, and asked him the meaning of what I saw. He told me he did not know anything more than that they had been halted. I asked him where General Smith was; he said he believed he had gone to a farmhouse in the rear, adding that he thought he was ill. Riding on to the bluff which overlooks the Meadow Bridge, I asked Colonel Anderson, posted there in observation, whether he had seen anything of the enemy in his front. He said that he had seen only two mounted men across the bridge, and a small party of infantry on the other side of the river, some distance below, both of whom, he said, he could show me if I would go with him into the garden back of the house. There, by the use of a powerful glass, were distinctly visible two cavalry videttes at the further end of the bridge, and a squad of infantry lower down the river, who had covered themselves with a screen of green boughs. The Colonel informed me that he had not heard Hill's guns; it was, therefore, supposed he had not advanced. I then rode down the bank of the river, followed by a cavalcade of sight-seers, who, I supposed, had been attracted by the expectation of a battle. The little squad of infantry, about fifteen in number, as we approached, fled over the ridge, and were lost to sight. Near to the Mechanicsville Bridge I found General Howell Cobb, commanding the support of a battery of artillery. He pointed out to me on the opposite side of the river the only enemy he had seen, and which was evidently a light battery. Riding on to the main road which led to the Mechanicsville Bridge, I found General Longstreet, walking to and fro in an impatient, it might be said fretful, manner. Before speaking to him, he said his division had been under arms all day waiting for orders to advance, and that the day was now so far spent that he did not know what was the matter. I afterward learned from General Smith that he had received information from a citizen that the Beaver-dam Creek presented an impassable barrier, and that he had thus fortunately been saved from a disaster. Thus ended the offensive-defensive program from which Lee expected much, and of which I was hopeful.

In the meanwhile the enemy moved up, and, finding the crossing at Bottom's Bridge unobstructed, threw a brigade of the Fourth Corps across the Chickahominy as early as the 20th of May, and on the 23d sent over the rest of the Fourth Corps; on the 25th he sent over another corps, and commenced fortifying a line near to Seven Pines. In the forenoon of the 31st of May, riding out on the New Bridge road, I heard firing in the direction of Seven Pines. As I drew nearer, I saw General Whiting, with part of General Smith's division, file into the road in front of me; at the same time I saw General Johnston ride across the field from a house before which General Lee's horse was standing. I turned down to the house, and asked General Lee what the musketry-firing meant. He replied by asking whether I had heard it, and was answered in the affirmative; he said he had been under that impression himself, but General Johnston had assured him that it could be nothing more than an artillery duel. It is scarcely necessary to add that neither of us had been advised of a design to attack the enemy that day.

We then walked out to the rear of the house to listen, and were satisfied that an action, or at least a severe skirmish, must be going on. General Johnston states in his report that the condition of the air was peculiarly unfavorable to the transmission of sound.

General Lee and myself then rode to the field of battle, which may be briefly described as follows:

The Chickahominy flowing in front is a deep, sluggish, and narrow river, bordered by marshes, and covered with tangled wood. The line of battle extended along the Nine-mile road, across the York River Railroad and Williamsburg stage-road. The enemy had constructed redoubts, with long lines of rifle-pits covered by abatis, from below Bottom's Ridge to within less than two miles of New Bridge, and had constructed bridges to connect his forces on the north and south sides of the Chickahominy. The left of his forces, on the south side, was thrown forward from the river; the right was on its bank, and covered by its slope. Our main force was on the right flank of our position, extending on both sides of the Williamsburg road, near to its intersection with the Nine-mile road. This wing consisted of Hill's, Huger's, and Longstreet's divisions, with light batteries, and a small force of cavalry; the division of General G. W. Smith, less Hood's brigade ordered to the right, formed the left wing, and its position was on the Nine-mile road. There were small tracts of cleared land, but most of the ground was wooded, and much of it so covered with water as to seriously embarrass the movements of troops.

When General Lee and I riding down the Nine-mile road reached the left of our line, we found the troops hotly engaged. Our men had driven the enemy from his advanced encampment, and he had fallen back behind an open field to the bank of the river, where, in a dense wood, was concealed an infantry line, with artillery in position. Soon after our arrival, General Johnston, who had gone farther to the right, where the conflict was expected, and whither reënforcement from the left was marching, was brought back severely wounded, and, as soon as an ambulance could be obtained, was removed from the field.

Our troops on the left made vigorous assaults under most disadvantageous circumstances. They made several gallant attempts to carry the enemy's position, but were each time repulsed with heavy loss.

After a personal reconnaissance on the left of the open in our front, I sent one, then another, and another courier to General Magruder, directing him to send a force down by the wooded path, just under the bluff, to attack the enemy in flank and reverse. Impatient of delay, I had started to see General Magruder, when I met the third courier, who said he had not found General Magruder, but had delivered the message to Brigadier-General Griffith, who was moving by the path designated to make the attack.

On returning to the field, I found that the attack in front had ceased; it was, therefore, too late for a single brigade to effect anything against the large force of the enemy, and messengers were sent through the woods to direct General Griffith to go back.

The heavy rain during the night of the 30th had swollen

the Chickahominy; it was rising when the battle of Seven Pines was fought, but had not reached such height as to prevent the enemy from using his bridges; consequently, General Sumner, during the engagement, brought over his corps as a reënforcement. He was on the north side of the river, had built two bridges to connect with the south side, and, though their coverings were loosened by the upward pressure of the rising water, they were not yet quite impassable. With the true instinct of the soldier to march upon fire, when the sound of the battle reached him, he formed his corps and stood under arms waiting for an order to advance. He came too soon for us, and, but for his forethought and promptitude, he would have arrived too late for his friends. It may be granted that his presence saved the left wing of the Federal army from defeat.

As we had permitted the enemy to fortify before our attack, it would have been better to have waited another day, until the bridges should have been rendered impassable by the rise of the river.

General Lee, at nightfall, gave instructions to General Smith, the senior officer on that part of the battle-field, and left with me to return to Richmond.

Thus far I have only attempted to describe events on the extreme left of the battle-field, being that part of which I had personal observation; but the larger force and, consequently, the more serious conflict were upon the right of the line. To these I will now refer. Our force there consisted of the divisions of Major-Generals D. H. Hill, Huger, and Longstreet, the latter in chief command. In his report he writes:

Agreeably to *verbal* instructions from the commanding General, the division of Major-General D. H. Hill was, on the morning of the 31st ultimo, formed at an early hour on the Williamsburg road, as the column of attack upon the enemy's front on that road. . . . The division of Major-General Huger was intended to make a strong flank movement around the left of the enemy's position, and attack him in rear of that flank. . . . After waiting some six hours for these troops to get into position, I determined to move forward without regard to them, and gave orders to that effect to Major-General D. H. Hill. The forward movement began about two o'clock, and our skirmishers soon became engaged with those of the enemy. The entire division of General Hill became engaged about three o'clock, and drove the enemy steadily back, gaining possession of his abatis and part of his intrenched camp, General Rodes, by a movement to the right, driving in the enemy's left.

The only reënforcements on the field in hand were my own brigades, of which Anderson's, Wilcox's, and Kemper's were put in by the front on the Williamsburg road, and Colston's and Pryor's by my right flank. At the same time the decided and gallant attack made by the other brigades gained entire possession of the enemy's position, with his artillery, camp-equipage, etc. Anderson's brigade, under Colonel Jenkins, pressing forward rapidly, continued to drive the enemy till nightfall. . . . The conduct of the attack was left entirely to Major-General Hill. The entire success of the affair is sufficient evidence of his ability, courage, and skill.

This tribute to General Hill was no more than has been accorded to him by others who knew of his services on that day. The reference, made, without qualification, in General Longstreet's report, to the failure of General Huger to make the attack expected of him renders it proper that some explanation should be given of an apparent dilatoriness on the part of that veteran soldier, who after long and faithful service, now fills an honored grave.

It will be remembered that General Huger was to move by the Charles City road, so as to turn to the left of the enemy and attack him in flank. The extraordinary rain of the previous night had swollen every rivulet to the dimensions of a stream, and the route prescribed to General Huger was one especially affected by that heavy rain, as it led to the head of the White-Oak Swamp. The bridge over the stream flowing into that swamp had been carried away, and the alternatives presented to him was to rebuild the bridge or leave his artillery. He chose the former, which involved the delay that has subjected him to criticism. If any should think an excuse necessary to justify this decision, they are remanded to the accepted military maxim, that the march must never be so hurried as to arrive unfit for service; and, also, they may be reminded that Huger's specialty was artillery, he being the officer who commanded the siege-guns with which General Scott marched from Vera Cruz to the city of Mexico.

On the next day, the 1st of June, General Longstreet states that a serious attack was made on our position, and that it was repulsed. This refers to the works which Hill's division had captured the day before, and which the enemy endeavored to retake.

From the final report of General Longstreet, already cited, it appears that he was ordered to attack on the morning of the 31st, and he explains why it was postponed for six hours;

then he states that it was commenced by the division of General D. H. Hill, which drove the enemy steadily back, pressing forward until nightfall. The movement of Rodes's brigade on the right flank is credited with having contributed much to the dislodgment of the enemy from their abatis and first intrenchments. As just stated, General Longstreet reports a delay of some six hours in making this attack, because he was waiting for General Huger, and then made it successfully with Hill's division and some brigades from his own. These questions must naturally arise in the mind of the reader: Why did not our troops on the left, during this long delay, as well as during the period occupied by Hill's assault, coöperate in the attack? and Why, the battle having been preconceived, were they so far removed as not to hear the first guns? The officers of the Federal army, when called before a committee appointed by their Congress to inquire into the conduct of the war, have by their testimony made it quite plain that the divided condition of their troops and the length of time required for their concentration after the battle commenced, rendered it practicable for our forces, if united—as, taking the initiative, they well might have been—to have crushed or put to fight first Keyes' and then Heintzelman's corps before Sumner crossed the Chickahominy, between five and six o'clock in the evening.

By the official reports our aggregate loss was, "killed, wounded, and missing," 6,084, of which 4,851 were in Longstreet's command on the right, and 1,233 in Smith's command on the left.

The enemy reported his aggregate loss at 5,739. It may have been less than ours, for we stormed his successive defenses.

Our success upon the right was proved by our possession of the enemy's works, as well as by the capture of ten pieces of artillery, four flags, a large amount of camp-equipage, and more than one thousand prisoners.

Our aggregate of both wings was about 40,500. The force of the enemy confronting us may be approximated at 38,000. It thus appears that, at the commencement of the action on the 31st of May, we had a numerical superiority of about 2,500. The strength of Sumner's corps was 18,724, which would give the enemy in round numbers a force of 16,000 in excess of ours after General Sumner crossed the Chickahominy.

Both combatants claimed the victory. I have presented the

evidence in support of our claim. The withdrawal of the Confederate forces in the day after the battle from the ground on which it was fought certainly gives color to the claim of the enemy, though that was really the result of a policy much broader than the occupation of the field of Seven Pines.

On the morning of June 1st I rode out toward the position where General Smith had been left on the previous night, and where I learned from General Lee that he would remain. After turning into the Nine-mile road, and before reaching that position, I was hailed by General Whiting, who saw me at a distance, and ran toward the road to stop me. He told me I was riding into the position of the enemy, who had advanced on the withdrawal of our troops, and there, pointing, he said, "is a battery which I am surprised has not fired on you." I asked where our troops were. He said his was the advance, and the others behind him. He also told me that General Smith was at the house which had been his (Whiting's) headquarters, and I rode there to see him. To relieve both him and General Lee from any embarrassment, I preferred to make the announcement of General Lee's assignment to command previous to his arrival.

General R. E. Lee was now in immediate command, and thenceforward directed the movements of the army in front of Richmond. Laborious and exact in details, as he was vigilant and comprehensive in grand strategy, a power, with which the public had not credited him, soon became manifest in all that makes an army a rapid, accurate, compact machine, with responsive motion in all its parts. I extract the following sentence from a letter from the late Colonel R. H. Chilton, adjutant and inspector-general of the army of the Confederacy, because of his special knowledge of the subject:

I consider General Lee's exhibition of grand administrative talents and indomitable energy, in bringing up that army in so short a time to that state of discipline which maintained aggregation through those terrible seven days' fights around Richmond as probably his grandest achievement.

Chapter 18

Strategy in Virginia; Cold Harbor

DURING THE NIGHT our forces on the left had fallen back
from their position at the close of the previous day's battle,
but those on the right remained in the one they had gained,
and some combats occurred there between the opposing
forces. The enemy proceeded further to fortify his position on
the Chickahominy, covering his communication with his base
of supplies on York River. His left was on the south side of
the Chickahominy, between White-Oak Swamp and New
Bridge, and was covered by a strong intrenchment, with
heavy guns, and with abatis in front. His right wing was north
of the Chickahominy, extending to Mechanicsville, and the
approaches defended by strong works.

Our army was in line in front of Richmond, but without
intrenchments. General Lee immediately commenced the construction of an earthwork for a battery on our left flank, and
a line of intrenchment to the right, necessarily feeble because of our deficiency in tools. It seemed to be the intention
of the enemy to assail Richmond by regular approaches, which
our numerical inferiority and want of engineer troops, as well
as the deficiency of proper utensils, made it improbable that
we should be able to resist. The day after General Lee assumed command, I was riding out to the army, when I saw at
a house on my left a number of horses, and among them one
I recognized as belonging to him. I dismounted and entered
the house, where I found him in consultation with a number
of his general officers. The tone of the conversation was quite
despondent, and one, especially, pointed out the inevitable
consequence of the enemy's advance by throwing out *boyaux*,
and constructing successive parallels. I expressed, in marked
terms, my disappointment at hearing such views, and General Lee remarked that he had, before I came in, said very
much the same thing. I then withdrew and rode to the front,
where, after a short time, General Lee joined me, and entered into conversation as to what, under the circumstances, I
thought it most advisable to do. I then said to him, substantially, that I knew of nothing better than the plan he had
previously explained to me, which was to have been executed

291

by General Johnston, but which was not carried out; that the change of circumstances would make one modification necessary—that, instead, as then proposed, of bringing General A. P. Hill, with his division, on the rear flank of the enemy, it would, because of the preparation for defense made in the mean time, now be necessary to bring the stronger force of General T. J. Jackson from the Valley of the Shenandoah. So far as we were then informed, General Jackson was hotly engaged with a force superior to his own, and, before he could be withdrawn, it was necessary that the enemy should be driven out of the Valley. For this purpose, as well as to mask the design of bringing Jackson's forces to make a junction with those of Lee, a strong division under General Whiting was detached to go by rail to the Valley to join General Jackson, and, by a vigorous assault, to drive the enemy across the Potomac. As soon as he commenced a retreat which unmistakably showed that his flight would not stop within the limits of Virginia, General Jackson was instructed, with his whole force, to move rapidly on the right flank of the enemy north of the Chickahominy. The manner in which the division was detached to reënforce General Jackson was so open that it was not doubted General McClellan would soon be apprised of it, and would probably attribute it to any other than the real motive, and would confirm him in his exaggerated estimate of our strength.

By the rapidity of movement and skill with which General Jackson handled his troops, he, after several severe engagements, finally routed the enemy before the reënforcement of Whiting arrived; and he then, on the 17th of June, proceeded, with that celerity which gave to his infantry its wonderful fame and efficiency, to execute the orders which General Lee had sent to him.

Preparatory to this campaign, a light intrenchment for infantry cover, with some works for field-guns, was constructed on the south side of the Chickahominy, and General Whiting, with two brigades, as before stated, was sent to reënforce General Jackson in the Valley, so as to hasten the expulsion of the enemy, after which Jackson was to move rapidly from the Valley so as to arrive in the vicinity of Ashland by the 24th of June, and, by striking the enemy on his right flank, to aid in the proposed attack. The better to insure the success of this movement, General Lawton, who was coming with a brigade from Georgia to join General Lee, was directed to change his line of march and unite with General Jackson in the Valley.

As General Whiting went by railroad, it was expected that the enemy would be cognizant of the fact, but not, probably, assign to it the real motive; and that such was the case is shown by an unsuccessful attack of the 26th, made on the Williamsburg road, with the apparent intention of advancing by that route to Richmond.

To observe the enemy, as well as to prevent him from learning of the approach of General Jackson, General J. E. B. Stuart was sent with a cavalry force on June 8th to cover the route by which the former was to march, and to ascertain whether the enemy had any defensive works or troops in position to interfere with the advance of those forces. He reported favorably on both these points, as well as to the natural features of the country. On the 26th of June General Stuart received confidential instructions from General Lee, the execution of which is so interwoven with the seven days' battles as to be more appropriately noticed in connection with them, of which it is proposed now to give a brief account.

Our order of battle directed General Jackson to march from Ashland on the 25th toward Slash Church, encamping for the night west of the Central Railroad; to advance at 3 A.M. on the 26th, and to turn Beaver-Dam Creek. General A. P. Hill was to cross the Chickahominy at Meadow Bridge when Jackson advanced beyond that point, and to move directly upon Mechanicsville. As soon as the bridge there should be uncovered, Longstreet and D. H. Hill were to cross, the former to proceed to the support of A. P. Hill and the latter to that of Jackson.

The four commands were directed to sweep down the north side of the Chickahominy toward the York River Railroad— Jackson on the left and in advance; Longstreet nearest the river and in the rear. Huger, McLaws, and Magruder, remaining on the south side of the Chickahominy, were ordered to hold their positions as long as possible against any assault of the enemy; to observe his movements, and to follow him closely if he should retreat. General Stuart, with the cavalry, was thrown out on Jackson's left to guard his flank and give notice of the enemy's movements. Brigadier-General Pendleton was directed to employ the reserve artillery so as to resist any advance toward Richmond, to superintend that portion of it posted to aid in the operations on the north bank, and hold the remainder for use where needed. The whole of Jackson's command did not arrive in time to reach the point designated on the 25th. He had, therefore, more distance to move on the 26th, and he was retarded by the enemy.

Not until 3 P.M. did A. P. Hill begin to move. Then he crossed the river and advanced upon Mechanicsville. After a sharp conflict he drove the enemy from his intrenchments, and forced him to take refuge in his works, on the left bank of Beaver Dam, about a mile distant. This position was naturally strong, the banks of the creek in front being high and almost perpendicular, and the approach to it was over open fields commanded by the fire of artillery and infantry under cover on the opposite side. The difficulty of crossing the stream had been increased by felling the fringe of woods on its banks and destroying the bridges. Jackson was expected to pass Beaver Dam above, and turn the enemy's right, so General Hill made no direct attack. Longstreet and D. H. Hill crossed the Mechanicsville Bridge as soon as it was uncovered and could be repaired, but it was late before they reached the north bank of the Chickahominy. An effort was made by two brigades, one of A. P. Hill and the other Ripley's of D. H. Hill, to turn the enemy's left, but the troops were unable in the growing darkness to overcome the obstructions, and were withdrawn. The engagement ceased about 9 P. M. Our troops retained the ground from which the foe had been driven.

According to the published reports, General McClellan's position was regarded at this time as extremely critical. If he concentrated on the left bank of the Chickahominy, he abandoned the attempt to capture Richmond, and risked a retreat upon the White House and Yorktown, where he had no reserves, or reason to expect further support. If he moved to the right bank of the river, he risked the loss of his communications with the White House, whence his supplies were drawn by railroad. He would then have to attempt the capture of Richmond by assault, or be forced to open new communications by the James River, and move at once in that direction. There he would receive the support of the enemy's navy. This latter movement had, it appears, been thought of previously, and transports had been sent to the James River. During the night, after the close of the contest last mentioned, the whole of Porter's baggage was sent over to the right bank of the river, and united with the train that set out on the evening of the 27th for the James River.

It would almost seem as if the Government of the United

States anticipated, at this period, the failure of McClellan's expedition. On June 27th President Lincoln issued an order creating the "Army of Virginia," to consist of the forces of Fremont, in their Mountain Department; of Banks, in their Shenandoah Department; and of McDowell, at Fredericksburg. The command of this army was assigned to Major-General John Pope. This cut off all reënforcements from McDowell to McClellan.

In expectation of Jackson's arrival on the enemy's right, the battle was renewed at dawn, and continued with animation about two hours, during which the passage of the creek was attempted, and our troops forced their way to its banks, where their progress was arrested by the nature of the stream and the resistance encountered. They maintained their position while preparations were being made to cross at another point nearer the Chickahominy. Before these were completed, Jackson crossed Beaver Dam above, and the enemy abandoned his intrenchments, and retired rapidly down the river, destroying a great deal of property, but leaving much in his deserted camps.

After repairing the bridges over Beaver Dam, the several columns resumed their advance, as nearly as possible, as prescribed in the order. Jackson, with whom D. H. Hill had united, bore to the left, in order to cut off reënforcements to the enemy or intercept his retreat in that direction. Longstreet and A. P. Hill moved nearer the Chickahominy. Many prisoners were taken in their progress; and the conflagration of wagons and stores marked the course of the retreating army. Longstreet and Hill reached the vicinity of New Bridge about noon. It was ascertained that the enemy had taken a position behind Powhite Creek, prepared to dispute our progress. He occupied a range of hills, with his right resting in the vicinity of McGhee's house, and his left near that of Dr. Gaines, on a wooded bluff, which rose abruptly from a deep ravine. The ravine was filled with sharpshooters, to whom its banks gave protection. A second line of infantry was stationed on the side of the hill, overlooking the first, and protected by a breastwork of logs. A third occupied the crest, strengthened with rifle-trenches, and crowned with artillery. The approach to this position was over an open plain, about a quarter of a mile wide, commanded by a triple line of fire, and swept by the heavy batteries south of the Chickahominy. In front of his center and right the ground was generally open, bounded on the side of our approach by a wood, with dense and tangled undergrowth, and traversed by a sluggish stream, which converted the soil into a deep morass. The woods on the further side of the swamp were occupied by sharpshooters, and trees had been felled to increase the difficulty of its passage, and detain our advancing columns under the fire of infantry massed on the slopes of the opposite hills, and of the batteries on their crests.

Pressing on toward the York River Railroad, A. P. Hill, who was in advance, reached the vicinity of New Cold Harbor about 2 P. M., where he encountered the foe. He immediately formed his line nearly parallel to the road leading from that place toward McGhee's house, and soon became hotly engaged. The arrival of Jackson on our left was momentarily expected, and it was supposed that his approach would cause the extension of the opposing line in that direction. Under this impression, Longstreet was held back until this movement should commence. The principal part of the enemy's army was now on the north side of the Chickahominy. Hill's single division met this large force with impetuous courage. They drove it back, and assailed it in its strong position on the ridge. The battle raged fiercely, and with varying fortune, more than two hours. Three regiments pierced the enemy's line, and forced their way to the crest of the hill on his left, but were compelled to fall back before overwhelming numbers. This superior force, assisted by the fire of the batteries south of the Chickahominy, which played incessantly on our columns as they pressed through the difficulties that obstructed their way, caused them to recoil. Though most of the men had never been under fire until the day before, they were rallied, and in turn repelled the advance of our assailant. Some brigades were broken, others stubbornly maintained their positions, but it became apparent that the enemy was gradually gaining ground. The attack on our left being delayed by the length of Jackson's march and the obstacles he encountered, Longstreet was ordered to make a diversion in Hill's favor by a feint on the enemy's left. In making this demonstration, the great strength of the position already described was discovered, and General Longstreet perceived that, to render the diversion effectual, the feint must be converted into an attack. He resolved, with his characteristic determination, to carry the heights by assault. His column was quickly formed near the open ground, and, as his preparations were completed, Jackson arrived, and his right division—that of Whiting—took position on the left of Longstreet. At the same time, D. H. Hill formed on our extreme left, and, after a short but bloody conflict, forced his way through the morass and obstructions, and drove the foe from the woods on the opposite side. Ewell advanced on Hill's right, and became hotly engaged. The first and fourth brigades of Jackson's own division filled the interval between Ewell and A. P. Hill. The second and third were sent to the right. The arrival of these fresh troops enabled A. P. Hill to withdraw some of his brigades, wearied and reduced by their long and arduous conflict. The lines being now complete, a general advance from right to left was ordered. On the right, the troops moved forward with steadiness, unchecked by the terrible fire from the triple lines of infantry on the hill, and the cannon on both sides of the river, which burst upon them as they emerged upon the plain. The dead and wounded marked the line of their intrepid advance, the brave Texans leading, closely followed by their no less daring comrades. The enemy were driven from the ravine to the first line of breastworks, over which our impetuous column dashed up to the intrenchments on the crest. These were quickly stormed, fourteen pieces of artillery captured, and the foe driven into the field beyond. Fresh troops came to his support, and he endeavored repeatedly to rally, but in vain. He was forced back with great slaughter until he reached the woods on the banks of the Chickahominy, and night put an end to the pursuit. Long lines of dead and wounded marked each stand made by the enemy in his stubborn resistance, and the field over which he retreated was strewed with the slain. On the left, the attack was no less vigorous and successful. D. H. Hill charged across the open ground in front, one of his regiments having first bravely carried a battery whose fire enfiladed his advance. Gallantly supported by the troops on his right, he reached the crest of the ridge, and, after a sanguinary struggle, broke the enemy's line, captured several of his batteries, and drove him in confusion toward the Chickahominy, until darkness rendered further pursuit impossible. Our troops remained in undisturbed possession of the field, covered with the dead and wounded of our opponent; and his broken forces fled to the river or wandered through the wood. Owing to the nature of the country, the cavalry was unable to participate in the general engagement. It, however, rendered valuable service in guarding Jackson's flank, and took a large number of prisoners.

On the morning of the 28th it was ascertained that none

of the enemy remained in our front north of the Chickahominy. As he might yet intend to give battle to preserve his communications, the Ninth Cavalry, supported by Ewell's division, was ordered to seize the York River Railroad, and General Stuart with his main body to coöperate. When the cavalry reached Dispatch Station, the enemy retreated to the south bank of the Chickahominy, and burned the railroad-bridge. During the forenoon, columns of dust south of the river showed that he was in motion. The abandonment of the railroad and destruction of the bridge proved that no further attempt would be made to hold that line. But, from the position the enemy occupied, the roads which led toward the James River would also enable him to reach the lower bridges over the Chickahominy, and retreat down the Peninsula. In the latter event, it was necessary that our troops should continue on the north bank of the river, and, until the intention of General McClellan was discovered, it was deemed injudicious to change their disposition. Ewell was therefore ordered to proceed to Bottom's Bridge, to guard that point, and the cavalry to watch the bridges below. No certain indications of a retreat to the James River were discovered by our forces on the south side of the Chickahominy, and late in the afternoon the enemy's works were reported to be fully manned. The strength of these fortifications prevented Generals Huger and Magruder from discovering what was passing in their front. Below the enemy's works the country was densely wooded and intersected by swamps, concealing his movements and precluding reconnaissances except by the regular roads, all of which were strongly guarded. The bridges over the Chickahominy in rear of the enemy were destroyed, and their reconstruction by us was impracticable in the presence of his whole army and powerful batteries. We were therefore compelled to wait until his purpose should be developed. Generals Huger and Magruder were again directed to use the utmost vigilance, and to pursue the foe vigorously should they discover that he was retreating. During the afternoon of the 28th the signs were suggestive of a general movement, and, no indications of his approach to the lower bridges of the Chickahominy having been discovered by the pickets in observation at those points, it became inferable that General McClean was about to retreat to the James River.

Chapter 19

Raising the Siege of Richmond

DURING THE NIGHT I visited the several commands along the intrenchment on the south side of the Chickahominy. General Huger's was on the right, General McLaws's in the center, and General Magruder's on the left. The night was quite dark, especially so in the woods in front of our line, and, in expressing my opinion to the officers that the enemy would commence a retreat before morning, I gave special instructions as to the precautions necessary in order certainly to hear when the movement commenced. In the confusion of such a movement, with narrow roads and heavy trains, a favorable opportunity was offered for attack. It fell out, however, that the enemy did move before morning, and that the fact of the works having been evacuated was first learned by an officer on the north side of the river, who, the next morning, the 29th, about sunrise, was examining their works by the aid of a field-glass.

Generals Longstreet and A. P. Hill were promptly ordered to recross the Chickahominy at New Bridge, and move by the Darbytown and Long Bridge roads. General Lee, having sent his engineer, Captain Meade, to examine the condition of the abandoned works, came to the south side of the Chickahominy to unite his command and direct its movements.

Magruder and Huger found the whole line of works deserted, and large quantities of military stores of every description abandoned or destroyed. They were immediately ordered in pursuit, the former by the Charles City road, so as to take the enemy's army in flank; and the latter by the Williamsburg road, to attack his rear. Jackson was directed to cross the "Grapevine" Bridge, and move down the south side of the Chickahominy. Magruder reached the vicinity of Savage Station, where he came upon the rear-guard of the retreating army. Being informed that it was advancing, he halted and sent for reënforcements. Two brigades of Huger's division were ordered to his support, but were subsequently withdrawn, it having been ascertained that the force in Magruder's front was merely covering the retreat of the main body.

Jackson's route led to the flank and rear of Savage Station, but he was delayed by the necessity of reconstructing the "Grapevine" Bridge.

Late in the afternoon Magruder attacked the enemy with one of his divisions and two regiments of another. A severe action ensued, and continued about two hours, when night put an end to the conflict. The troops displayed great gallantry, and inflicted heavy loss; but, owing to the lateness of the hour and the small force engaged, the result was not decisive, and the enemy continued his retreat under cover of night, leaving several hundred prisoners, with his dead and wounded, in our hands. Our loss was small in numbers but great in value.

At Savage Station were found about twenty-five hundred men in hospital, and a large amount of property. Stores of much value had been destroyed, including the necessary medical supplies for the sick and wounded. The night was so dark that, before the battle ended, it was only by challenging that on several occasions it was determined whether the troops in front were friends or foes. It was therefore deemed unadvisable to attempt immediate pursuit.

Our troops slept upon their arms, and in the morning it was found that the enemy had retreated during the night, and, by the time thus gained, he was enabled to cross the White-Oak Creek, and destroy the bridge.

Early on the 30th Jackson reached Savage Station. He was directed to pursue the enemy on the road he had taken, and Magruder to follow Longstreet by the Darbytown road. As Jackson advanced, he captured so many prisoners and collected so large a number of arms, that two regiments had to be detached for their security. His progress at White-Oak Swamp was checked by the enemy, who occupied the opposite side, and obstinately resisted the rebuilding of the bridge.

Longstreet and A. P. Hill, continuing their advance, on the 30th came upon the foe strongly posted near the intersection of the Long Bridge and Charles City roads, at the place known in the military reports as Frazier's Farm.

Huger's route led to the right of this position, Jackson's to the rear, and the arrival of their commands was awaited, to begin the attack.

On the 29th General Holmes had crossed from the south side of the James River, and, on the 30th, was reënforced by a detachment of General Wise's brigade. He moved down the River road, with a view to gain, near to Malvern Hill, a position which would command the supposed route of the retreating army.

It is an extraordinary fact that, though the capital had been threatened by an attack from the seaboard on the right, though our army had retreated from Yorktown up to the Chickahominy, and, after encamping there for a time, had crossed the river and moved up to Richmond, yet, when at the close of the battles around Richmond, McClellan, retreated and was pursued toward the James River, we had no maps of the country in which we were operating; our generals were ignorant of the roads, and their guides knew little more than the way from their homes to Richmond. It was this fatal defect in preparation, and the erroneous answers of the guides, that caused General Lee first to post Holmes and Wise, when they came down the River road, at New Market, where, he was told, was the route that McClellan must pursue in his retreat to the James. Subsequently learning that there was another road, by the Willis church, which would better serve the purpose of the retreating foe, Holmes's command was moved up to a position on that road where, at the foot of a hill which concealed from view the enemy's line, he remained under the fire of the enemy's gunboats, the huge, shrieking shells from which dispersed a portion of his cavalry and artillery, though the faithful old soldier remained with the rest of his command, waiting, according to his orders, for the enemy with his trains to pass; but, taking neither of the roads pointed out to General Lee, he retreated by the shorter and better route, which led by Dr. Poindexter's house to Harrison's Landing. The dust of his advancing column caused a heavy fire from the gunboats to be opened upon him, and, in men who had never before seen the huge shells then fired, they inspired a degree of terror not justified by their effectiveness. The enemy, instead of being a straggling mass moving toward the James River, as had been reported, were found halted between West's house and Malvern Hill on ground commanding Holmes's position, with an open field between them.

General Holmes ordered his chief of artillery to commence firing upon the enemy's infantry, which immediately gave way, but a heavy fire of twenty-five or thirty guns promptly replied to our battery, and formed, with the gunboats, a cross-fire upon General Holmes's command. The numerical superiority of the opposing force, both in infantry and artillery, would have made it worse than useless to attempt an

assault unless previously reenforced, and, as no reënforcements arrived, Holmes, about an hour after nightfall, withdrew to a point somewhat in advance of the one he had held
in the morning. Though the enemy continued their cannonade
until after dark, and most of the troops were new levies,
they behaved well under the trying circumstances to which
they were exposed, except a portion of his artillery and cavalry, which gave way in disorder, probably from the effect
of the ten-inch shells, which were to them a novel imple-
ment of war; for when I met them, say half a mile from the
point they had left, and succeeded in stopping them, another
shell fell and exploded near us in the top of a wide-spreading
tree, giving a shower of metal and limbs, which soon after
caused them to resume their flight. It was after a personal
and hazardous reconnaissance that General Lee assigned
General Holmes to his last position; and when I remonstrated
with General Lee, whom I met returning from his reconnaissance, on account of the exposure to which he had subjected
himself, he said he could not get the required information
otherwise, and therefore had gone himself.

After the close of the battle of Malvern Hill, General
Holmes found that a deep ravine led up to the rear of the
left flank of the enemy's line, and expressed his regret that
it had not been known, and that he had not been ordered,
when the attack was made in front, to move up that ravine
and simultaneously assail in flank and reverse.

General Huger reported that his progress was delayed by
trees which his opponent had felled across the Willamsburg
road. In the afternoon, after passing the obstructions and
driving off the men who were still cutting down trees, they
came upon an open field (P. Williams's), where they were
assailed by a battery of rifled guns. The artillery was brought
up, and replied to the fire. In the mean time a column of
infantry was moved to the right, so as to turn the battery,
and the combat was ended. The report of this firing was
heard at Frazier's Farm, and erroneously supposed to indicate the near approach of Huger's column, and, it has been
frequently stated, induced General Longstreet to open fire
with some of his batteries as notice to General Huger where
our troops were, and that thus the engagement was brought
on. General A. P. Hill, who was in front and had made the
dispositions of our troops while hopefully waiting for the
arrival of Jackson and Huger, states that the fight commenced
by fire from the enemy's artillery, which swept down the

road, etc. This not only concurs with my recollection of the event, but is more in keeping with the design to wait for the expected reënforcements.

The detention of Huger, as above stated, and the failure of Jackson to force a passage of the White-Oak Swamp, left Longstreet and Hill, without the expected support, to maintain the unequal conflict as best they might. The superiority of numbers and advantage of position were on the side of the enemy. The battle raged furiously until 9 P. M. By that time the enemy had been driven with great slaughter from every position but one, which he maintained until he was enabled to withdraw under cover of darkness. At the close of the struggle nearly the entire field remained in our possession, covered with the enemy's dead and wounded. Many prisoners, including a general of division, were captured, and several batteries with some thousands of small-arms were taken.

After this engagement, Magruder, who had been ordered to go to the support of Holmes, was recalled, to relieve the troops of Longstreet and Hill. He arrived during the night, with the troops of his command much fatigued by the long, hot march.

In the battle of Frazier's Farm the troops of Longstreet and Hill, though disappointed in the expectation of support, and contending against superior numbers advantageously posted, made their attack successful by the most heroic courage and unfaltering determination.

Nothing could surpass the bearing of General Hill on that occasion, and I often recur with admiration to the manner in which Longstreet, when Hill's command seemed about to be overborne, steadily led his reserve to the rescue, as he might have marched on a parade. The mutual confidence between himself and his men was manifested by the calm manner in which they went into the desperate struggle.

The current of the battle which was then setting against us was reversed. That more important consequences would have followed had Huger and Jackson, or either of them, arrived in time to take part in the conflict, is unquestionable; and there is little hazard in saying that the army of McClellan would have been riven in twain, beaten in detail, and could never, as an organized body, have reached the James River.

Our troops slept on the battle-field they had that day won, and couriers were sent in the night with instructions to hasten the march of the troops who had been expected during the day. In this hour of thinned ranks and physical exhaustion, there was no thought of the expedient of retreat. This battle was in many respects one of the most remarkable of the war. Here occurred on several occasions the capture of batteries by the impetuous charge of our infantry, defying the canister and grape which plowed through their ranks, and many hand-to-hand conflicts, where bayonet-wounds were freely given and received, and men fought with clubbed muskets in the life-and-death encounter. The estimated strength of the enemy was double our own, and he had the advantage of being in position. From both causes it necessarily resulted that our loss was very heavy. During the night those who fought us at Frazier's Farm fell back to the stronger position of Malvern Hill, and by a night-march the force which had detained Jackson at White-Oak Swamp effected a junction with the other portion of the enemy. Early on the 1st of July Jackson reached the battle-field of the previous day, having forced the passage of White-Oak Swamp, where he captured some artillery and a number of prisoners. He was directed to follow the route of the enemy's retreat, but soon found him in position on a high ridge in front of Malvern Hill. Here, on a line of great natural strength, he had posted his powerful artillery, supported by his large force of infantry, covered by hastily constructed intrenchments. His left rested near Crew's house and his right near Binford's. Immediately in his front the ground was open, varying in width from a quarter to half a mile, and, sloping gradually from the crest, was completely swept by the fire of his infantry and artillery. To reach this open ground our troops had to advance through a broken and thickly wooded country, traversed nearly throughout its whole extent by a swamp passable at only a few places and difficult at these. The whole was within range of the batteries on the heights and the gunboats in the river, under whose incessant fire our movements had to be executed.

Jackson formed his line with Whiting's division on his left and D. H. Hill's on his right, one of Ewell's brigades occupying the interval. The rest of Ewell's and Jackson's own division were held in reserve. Magruder was directed to take position on Jackson's right, but before his arrival two of Huger's brigades came up and were placed next to Hill. Magruder subsequently formed on the right of these brigades, which, with a third of Huger's, were placed under his command. Longstreet and A. P. Hill were held in reserve, and took no part in the engagement. Owing to ignorance of the country, the dense forests impeding necessary communications, and the extreme difficulty of the ground, the whole line was not formed until a late hour in the afternoon. The obstacles presented by the woods and swamp made it impracticable to bring up a sufficient amount of artillery to oppose successfully the extraordinary force of that arm employed by the enemy, while the field itself afforded us few positions favorable for its use, and none for its proper concentration.

General W. N. Pendleton was in chief command of the artillery, and energetically strove to bring his long-range guns and reserve artillery into a position where they might be effectively used against the enemy, but the difficulties before mentioned were found insuperable.

Orders were issued for a general advance at a given signal, but the causes referred to prevented a proper concert of action among the troops. D. H. Hill pressed forward across the open field, and engaged the enemy gallantly, breaking and driving back his first line; but, a simultaneous advance of the other troops not taking place, he found himself unable to maintain the ground he had gained against the overwhelming numbers and numerous batteries opposed to him. Jackson sent to his support his own division and that part of Ewell's which was in reserve; but, owing to the increasing darkness and intricacy of the forest and swamp, they did not arrive in time to render the desired assistance. Hill was therefore compelled to abandon part of the ground he had gained, after suffering severe loss and inflicting heavy damage.

On the right the attack was gallantly made by Huger's and Magruder's commands. Two brigades of the former commenced the action, the other two were subsequently sent to the support of Magruder and Hill. Several determined efforts were made to storm the hill at Crew's house. The brigade advanced bravely across the open field, raked by the fire of a hundred cannon and the musketry of large bodies of infantry. Some were broken and gave way; others approached close to the guns, driving back the infantry, compelling the advance batteries to retire to escape capture, and mingling their dead with those of the enemy. For want of coöperation by the attacking columns, their assaults were too weak to break the enemy's line; and, after struggling gallantly, sustaining and inflicting great loss, they were compelled successively to retire. Night was approaching when the attack began, and it soon became difficult to distinguish friend from foe. The firing continued until after 9 P. M., but no decided result was gained.

Part of our troops were withdrawn to their original positions; others remained in the open field; and some rested within a hundred yards of the batteries that had been so bravely but vainly assailed. The lateness of the hour at which the attack necessarily began gave the foe the full advantage of his superior position, and augmented the natural difficulties of our own.

At the cessation of firing, several fragments of different commands were lying down and holding their ground within a short distance of the enemy's line, and, as soon as the fighting ceased, an informal truce was established by common consent. Numerous parties from both armies, with lanterns and litters, wandered over the field seeking for the wounded, whose groans and calls on all sides could not fail to move with pity the hearts of friend and foe.

The morning dawned with heavy rain, and the enemy's position was seen to have been entirely deserted. The ground was covered with his dead and wounded, and his route exhibited evidence of a precipitate retreat. To the fatigue of hard marches and successive battles, enough to have disqualified our troops for rapid pursuit, was added the discomfort of being thoroughly wet and chilled by rain. I sent out to the neighboring houses to buy, if it could be had, at any price, enough whisky to give to each of the men a single gill, but it could not be found.

The foe had silently withdrawn in the night by a route which had been unknown to us, but which was the most direct road to Harrison's Landing, and he had so many hours the start, that, among the general officers who expressed to me their opinion, there was but one who thought it was possible to pursue effectively. That was General T. J. Jackson, who quietly said, "They have not all got away if we go immediately after them."

During the pursuit, which has just been described, the cavalry of our army had been absent, having been detached on a service which was reported as follows: After seizing the York River Railroad, on June 28th, and driving the enemy across the Chickahominy, the force under General Stuart proceeded down the railroad to ascertain if there was any movement of the enemy in that direction. He encountered but little opposition, and reached the vicinity of the White House on the

29th. On his approach the enemy destroyed the greater part of the immense stores accumulated at that depot, and retreated toward Fortress Monroe. With one gun and some dismounted men General Stuart drove off a gunboat, which lay near the White House, and rescued a large amount of property, including more than ten thousand stand of small-arms, partially burned. General Stuart describes his march down the enemy's line of communication with the York River as one in which he was but feebly resisted. Leaving one squadron at the White House, he returned to guard the lower bridges of the Chickahominy. On the 30th he was directed to recross and coöperate with Jackson. After a long march, he reached the rear of the enemy at Malvern Hill, on the night of July 1st, at the close of the engagement.

On the 2d of July the pursuit was commenced, the cavalry under General Stuart in advance. Could our infantry, with a fair amount of artillery, during that day and the following night, have been in position on the ridge which overlooked the plain where the retreating enemy was encamped on the bank of the James River, a large part of his army must have dispersed, and the residue would have been captured. It appears, from the testimony taken before the United States Congressional Committee on the Conduct of the War, that it was not until July 3d that the heights which overlooked the encampment of the retreating army were occupied, and, from the manuscript notes on the war by General J. E. B. Stuart, we learn that he easily gained and took possession of the heights, and with his light howitzer opened fire upon the enemy's camp, producing great commotion.

General Lee was not a man of hesitation, and they have mistaken his character who suppose caution was his vice. He was prone to attack, and not slow to press an advantage when he gained it. Longstreet and Jackson were ordered to advance, but a violent storm which prevailed throughout the day greatly retarded their progress. The enemy, harassed and closely followed by the cavalry, suceeded in gaining Westover, on the James River, and the protection of his gunboats. His position was one of great natural and artificial strength, after the heights were occupied and intrenched. It was flanked on each side by a creek, and the approach in front was commanded by the heavy guns of his shipping, as well as by those mounted in his intrenchments. Under these circumstances it was deemed inexpedient to attack him; and, in view of the condition of our troops, who had been marching and fighting almost incessantly for seven days, under the most trying circumstances, it was determined to withdraw, in order to afford to them the repose of which they stood so much in need.

Several days were spent in collecting arms and other property abandoned by the enemy, and, in the mean time, some artillery and cavalry were sent below Westover to annoy his transports. On July 8th our army returned to the vicinity of Richmond. We had effected our main purpose. The siege of Richmond was raised, and the object of a campaign which had been prosecuted after months of preparation, at an enormous expenditure of men and money, was completely frustrated.

More than ten thousand prisoners, including officers of rank, fifty-two pieces of artillery, and upward of thirty-five thousand stand of small-arms were captured. The stores and supplies of every description which fell into our hands were great in amount and value, but small in comparison with those destroyed by the enemy. His losses in battle exceeded our own, as attested by the thousands of dead and wounded left on every field, while his subsequent inaction shows in what condition the survivors reached the protection of the gunboats.

A statement of the strength of the troops under General Johnston shows that on May 21, 1862, he had present for duty 53,688.

After minute inquiry, General Early estimated that "the whole force received by General Lee was about 23,000."

Taking the number given by General Early as the entire reenforcement received by General Lee after the battle of Seven Pines and before the commencement of the seven days' battles, and deducting from the 23,000 the casualties in the battle of Seven Pines (6,084), we have 16,916; if to this be added whatever number of absentees may have joined the army in anticipation of active operations, the result will be the whole increment to the army with which General Lee took the offensive against McClellan.

It appears from the official returns of the Army of the Potomac that on June 20th General McClellan had present for duty, 115,102 men. It is stated that McClellan reached the James River with "between 85,000 and 90,000 men," and that his loss in the seven days' battles was 15,249; this would make the army 105,000 strong at the commencement of the battles.

Chapter 20

Emancipation

AT THE COMMENCEMENT of the year 1862 it was the purpose of the United States Government to assail us in every manner and at every point and with every engine of destruction which could be devised. The usual methods of civilized warfare consist in the destruction of an enemy's military power and the capture of his capital. These, however, formed only a small portion of the purposes of *our* enemy. If peace with fraternity and equality in the Union, under the Constitution as interpreted by its framers, had been his aim, this was attainable without war; but, seeking supremacy at the cost of a revolution in the entire political structure, involving a subversion of the Constitution, the subjection of the States, the submission of the people, and the establishment of a union under the sword, his efforts were all directed to subjugation or extermination. Thus, while the Executive was preparing immense armies, iron-clad fleets, and huge instruments of war, with which to invade our territory and destroy our citizens, the willing aid of an impatient, enraged Congress was invoked to usurp new powers, to legislate the subversion of our social institutions, and to give the form of legality to the plunder of a frenzied soldiery.

That body had no sooner assembled than it brought forward the doctrine that the Government of the United States was engaged in a struggle for its existence, and could therefore resort to any measure which a case of self-defense would justify. The Congress next declared that our institution of slavery was the cause of all the troubles of the country, and therefore the whole power of the Government must be so directed as to remove it. If this had really been the cause of the troubles, how easily wise and patriotic statesmen might have furnished a relief. Nearly all the slaveholding States had withdrawn from the Union, therefore those who had been suffering vicariously might have welcomed their departure, as the removal of the cause which disturbed the Union, and have tried the experiment of separation. Should the trial have brought more wisdom and a spirit of conciliation to either or both, there might have arisen, as a result of the experiment, a reconstructed fraternal Union such as our fathers designed. The authors of the aggressions which had disturbed the harmony of the Union had lately acquired power on a sectional basis, and were eager for the spoil of their sectional victory. To conceal their real motive, and artfully to appeal to the prejudice of foreigners, they declared that slavery was the cause of the troubles of the country, and of the "rebellion" which they were engaged in suppressing. In his inaugural address in March, 1861, President Lincoln said: "I have no purpose, directly or indirectly, to interfere with the institution of slavery in the States where it exists. I believe I have no lawful right to do so, and I have no inclination to do so." The leader (Sumner) of the Abolition party in Congress, on February 25, 1861, said in the Senate, "I take this occasion to declare most explicitly that I do not think that Congress has any right to interfere with slavery in a State." A few months after the inaugural address above cited and the announcement of the fact above quoted were made, Congress commenced to legislate for the abolition of slavery. If it had the power now to do what it before had not, whence was it derived? There had been no addition in the interval to the grants in the Constitution; yet after July 4, 1861, it was asserted by the majority in Congress that the Government had power to interfere with slavery in the States. Whence came the change? The answer is, It was wrought by the same process and on the same plea that tyranny has ever employed against liberty and justice necessity; an excuse which is ever assumed as valid, because the usurper claims to be the sole judge of his necessity.

The formula under which it was asserted was as follows:

Whereas the laws of the United States have been for some time past and now are opposed, and the execution thereof obstructed, etc., by combinations too powerful to be suppressed by the ordinary course of judicial proceedings, etc.

Therefore, says the plea of necessity, a new power is this day found under the Constitution of the United States. This means that certain circumstances had transpired in a distant portion of the Union, and the powers of the Constitution had thereby become enlarged. The inference follows with equal reason that, when the circumstances cease to exist, the powers of the Constitution will be contracted again to their normal state; that is, the powers of the Constitution of the United

States are enlarged or contracted according to circumstances. Nevertheless, these views were adopted by the Thirty-seventh Congress of the United States, and a system of legislation was devised which embraced the following usurpations: universal emancipation in the Confederate States through confiscation of private property of all kinds; prohibition of the extension of slavery to the Territories; emancipation of slavery in all places under the exclusive control of the Government of the United States; emancipation with compensation in the border States and in the District of Columbia; practical emancipation to follow the progress of the armies; all restraints to be removed from the slaves, so that they could go free wherever they pleased, and be fed and clothed, when destitute, at the expense of the United States, literally to become a "ward of the Government."

The emancipation of slaves through confiscation in States where the United States Government had, under the Constitution, no authority to interfere with slavery, was a problem which the usurpers found it difficult legally or logically to solve, but these obstacles were less regarded than the practical difficulty in States where the Government had no physical power to enforce its edicts. The limited powers granted in the Constitution to the Government of the United States were not at all applicable to such designs, or commensurate with their execution. Now, let us see the little possibility there was for constitutional liberties and rights to survive, when intrusted to such unscrupulous hands.

In Article I, section 8, the Constitution says:

The Congress shall have power to declare war, grant letters of marque and reprisal, and make rules concerning captures on land and water; to raise and support armies; to provide and maintain a navy; to make rules for the government and regulation of the land and naval forces, etc.

This is the grant of power under which the Government of the United States makes war upon a foreign nation. If it had not been given in the Constitution, there would not have been any power under which to conduct a foreign war, such as that of 1812 against Great Britain or that of 1846 against Mexico. In such conflicts the nations engaged recognize each other as separate sovereignties and as public enemies, and use against each other all the powers granted by the law of nations. One of these powers is the confiscation of the property of the enemy. Under the law of nations of modern days this confiscation is limited in extent, made under a certain form, and for a defined object.

For the modern laws of war one must look to the usages of civilized states and to the publicists who have explained and enforced them. These usages constitute themselves the laws of war.

Mr. John Quincy Adams, in a letter to the Secretary of State, dated August 22, 1815, says:

Our object is the restoration of all the property, including slaves, which, by the usages of war among civilized nations, ought not to have been taken. All private property on shore was of that description. It was entitled by the laws of war to exemption from capture.—(4 "American State Papers," 116. etc.)

The words of the late Chief-Justice Marshall on the capture and confiscation of private property should not be omitted:

It may not be unworthy of remark that it is very unusual, even in cases of conquest, for the conqueror to do more than displace the sovereign, and assume dominion over the country. The modern usage of nations, which has become law, would be violated; that sense of justice and of right which is acknowledged and felt by the whole civilized world would be outraged, if private property should be generally confiscated and private rights annulled. The people change their allegiance; their relation to their ancient sovereign is dissolved; but their relations to each other and their rights of property remain undisturbed.—("United States *vs.* Percheman," 7 Peters, 51).

The Government of the United States recognized us as under the law of nations by attempting to use against us one of the powers of that law. Yet, if we were subject to this power, we were most certainly entitled to its protection. This was refused. The act of confiscation is a power exercised under the laws of war for the purpose of indemnifying the captor for his expense and losses. At the same time there is a mode of procedure attached to its exercise by which it is reserved from the domain of plunder and devastation. There are, under the law, exemptions of certain classes of property. It is further required that the property subject to confiscation shall be actually captured and taken possession of. It shall then be adjudicated as prize by a proper authority, then sold, and the money received must be deposited in the public

Treasury. Such are the conditions attached by the law of nations to legal confiscation.

Now, compare these conditions with the act of Congress. The act of Congress allowed no exemptions of private property, but confiscated all the property of every kind belonging to persons residing in the Confederate States who were engaged in hostilities against the United States or who were aiding or abetting those engaged in hostilities. This includes slaves as well as other property. The act provided that the slaves should go free; that is, they were exempted from capture, from being adjudicated and sold, and no proceeds of sale were to be put into the public Treasury.

By the act of the United States Congress, passed on August 6, 1861, the armies of the United States were literally authorized to invade the Confederate States, to seize all property as plunder, and to let the negroes go free. It was estimated on the floor of the House of Representatives that the aggregate amount of property within our limits subject to be acted upon by the provisions of this act would affect upward of six million people, and would deprive them of property of the value of nearly five thousand million dollars.

But this is only one feature of the confiscation act which was applied to persons who were within the Confederate States, in such a position that the ordinary process of the United States courts could not be served upon them. They could be reached only by the armies. Another feature was equally flagrant and criminal. It was extended to all that class of persons giving aid and comfort, who could be found within the United States, or in such position that the ordinary process of law could be served on them. It was derived from Article III, section 3, of the Constitution, which says:

The Congress shall have the power to declare the punishment of treason, but no attainder of treason shall work corruption of blood, or forfeiture, except during the life of the person attainted.

The mode of procedure against persons under this power was determined by other clauses of the Constitution. Article III, section 2, declared that—

The trial of all crimes, except in cases of impeachment, shall be by jury; and such trial shall be held in the State where the said crimes shall have been committed.

In section 3, of the same article, it was provided that—

No person shall be convicted of treason unless on the testimony of two witnesses to the same overt act, or on confession in open court.

This feature of the confiscation act, passed by the Congress of the United States, provided for the punishment of the owner of property, on the proof of the crime, but excluded the trial by jury, and made the forfeiture of the property absolute instead of a forfeiture for life. Heavy fines were imposed, and property was sold in fee. The property to which the act applied was not a prize under the law of nations, nor booty, nor contraband of war, nor enforced military contributions, nor used or employed in the war or in resistance to the laws. It was private property, outside of the conflict of arms, and forfeited, not because it was the instrument of offense, but as a penalty for the assertion of his rights by the owner, which was imputed to him as a crime. Such proceeding was, in effect, punishment by the forfeiture of a man's entire estate, real and personal, without trial by jury, and in utter disregard of the provisions of the Constitution. It was an attempt to get a man's property, real and personal, "silver spoons" included, into a prize court, to be tried by the laws of war.

It will be seen that we were treated by the Congress of the United States as holding the twofold relation of enemies and traitors, and that they used against us all the instruments of war, and all the penalties of municipal law which made the punishment of treason to be death. The practical operation, therefore, of these laws was that, under a Constitution which defined treason to consist in levying war against the United States, which would not suffer the traitor to be condemned except by the judgment of his peers, and, when condemned, would not forfeit his estate except during his life, the Government of the United States did proceed against six million people, without indictment, without trial by jury, without the proof of two witnesses, did adjudge our six millions of people guilty of treason in levying war, and decree to deprive us of all our estate, real and personal, for life, and in fee, being nearly five thousand million dollars. And, after we had been thus punished, without trial by jury, and by the loss in fee of our whole estate, the Government of the United States assumed the power, on the same charge of levying war, to try us and to hang us.

The first object to be secured by this act of confiscation was the emancipation of all our slaves. Upon his approval of the bill, President Lincoln sent a message to Congress, in which he said:

It is startling to say that Congress can free a slave within a State, and yet, if it were said the ownership of the slave had first been transferred to the nation, and Congress had then liberated him, the difficulty would at once vanish. And this is the real case. The traitor against the General Government forfeits his slave at least as justly as he does any other property; and he forfeits both to the Government against which he offends. The Government, so far as there can be ownership, thus owns the forfeited slaves, and the question for Congress in regard to them is, "Shall they be made free or sold to new masters?"

It is amazing to see the utter forgetfulness of all constitutional obligations and the entire disregard of the conditions of the laws of nations manifested in these words of the President of the United States. Was he ignorant of their existence, or did he seek to cover up his violation of them by a deceptive use of language? Let posterity answer the questions: Who were the revolutionists? Who were really destroying the Constitution of the United States?

The agitation of this subject brought out another still more alarming usurpation in Congress. The argument was thus framed: Assuming that the state of the "nation" was one of general hostility, and that, being so involved, it possessed the power of self-defense, the supreme power of making and conducting war was expressly placed in Congress by the Constitution. "The whole powers of war are vested in Congress." —("United States Supreme Court, Brown vs. United States," 1 Cranch.) There is no such power in the judiciary, and the Executive is simply "commander-in-chief of the army and navy"; all other powers not necessarily implied in the command of the military and naval forces are expressly given to Congress.

There is, under that view, no limit on the power of Congress; it is invested with the absolute powers of war—the civil functions of the Government are, for the time being, in abeyance when in conflict, and all State and "national" authority subordinated to the extreme authority of Congress, as the supreme power, in the peril of external or internal hostilities. The ordinary provisions of the Constitution peculiar to a state of peace, and all laws and municipal regulations, were to yield to the force of martial law, as resolved by Congress. This was designated as the "war power" of the United States Government.

Another step in the usurpations begun for the destruction of slavery was the passage by Congress of an act for the emancipation of slaves in the District of Columbia. The act emancipated all persons of African descent held to service within the District, immediately upon its passage. Those owners of slaves who had not sympathized with us were allowed ninety days to prepare and present to commissioners, appointed for that purpose, the names, ages, and personal description of their slaves, who were to be valued by commissioners. No single slave could be estimated to be worth more than three hundred dollars. One million dollars was appropriated to carry the act into effect. All claims were to be presented within ninety days after the passage of the act, and not thereafter; but there was no saving clause for minors, *femmes covert,* insane or absent persons. On his approval of the act, the Executive of the United States sent a message to Congress, in which he said:

I have never doubted the constitutional authority of Congress to abolish slavery in the District, and I have ever desired to see the national capital freed from the institution in some satisfactory way. Hence there never has been in my mind any questions upon the subject, except those of expediency, arising in view of all the circumstances.

For the previous twenty-five or thirty years the subject had again and again been presented in Congress, and was always rejected. One of the incidents that led to our withdrawal from the Union was the apprehension that it was the intention of the United States Government to violate the constitutional right of each State to adopt and maintain, to reject or abolish slavery, as it pleased. This step showed the justness of our apprehensions.

Among the rights guaranteed to every citizen of the United States, including the District of Columbia, was the right of property. No one could be deprived of his property by the Government, except in the manner prescribed and authorized by the Constitution. Its words are these:

No person shall be deprived of life, liberty, or property without due procėss of law; nor shall private property be taken for public use without just compensation. (Article V.)

Whenever it was necessary in the administration of affairs that the Government should take private property for public use, it had the right to take that private property on the condition of making compensation for it, and on no other condition. Also, it could not be taken except for public use, even by making just compensation for it; nor could it be taken to be destroyed. The simple and sole condition on which the inviolability of private property could be broken by the Government itself was that it was necessary for public use. Otherwise, there was no constitutional right on the part of the Government to take the property at all.

Again, this property, thus necessary, must be taken by due process of law. The Government had not the right to declare the mode, and arbitrarily fix the limit of price which should be paid. The negro could be taken only as other property, even admitting that he could be taken for emancipation. The due process of law required that the citizen's property should be appraised judicially. A court must proceed judicially in every case, summon a jury, appoint commissioners, and, under the supervision and sanction of the court, the valuation of the slave by them must proceed as it does in relation to any other property of the citizen that might be taken by the lawful exercise of the power of Congress or of the United States Government. Thus it will be seen that by this usurpation of power the Constitution was violated, not only by taking private property for other purposes than for public use, but in the neglect to observe the due process of law which the Constitution required.

The next step in the usurpation of power for the destruction of the right of citizens to hold property in slaves was the passage by Congress of an act which declared that, after its passage—

There shall be neither slavery nor involuntary servitude in any of the Territories of the United States now existing, or which may at any time hereafter be formed or acquired by the United States, otherwise than in the punishment of crimes, etc.

The subject had been brought forward at every session of Congress for a number of years, and was uniformly resisted by the advocates of equality among the States. We claimed an equal right with the other States to the occupation and settlement of the Territories which were the common property of the Union; and that any infringement of this right was not only a violation of the spirit of the Constitution, but destructive of that equality of the States so necessary for the maintenance of their Union. We further claimed our right under this express provision of the Constitution Article IV, section 3, clause 2:

The Congress shall have power to dispose of and make all needful rules and regulations respecting the Territory or other property belonging to the United States; and nothing in this Constitution shall be so construed as to prejudice any claims of the United States or of any particular States.

Another step taken to accomplish the emancipation of our slaves was the passage by Congress of an act making an additional article of war for the government of the army of the United States. It was in these words:

All officers or persons in the military or naval service of the United States are prohibited from employing any of the forces under their respective commands for the purpose of returning fugitives from service or labor, who may have escaped from any persons to whom such service or labor is claimed to be due; and any officer who shall be found guilty by a court-martial of violating this article shall be dismissed from the service.

The Constitution of the United States expressly declares that all such persons

Shall be delivered up on claim of the party to whom such service or labor may be due. (Article IV, section 2).

Thus an act of Congress directly forbade that which the Constitution commanded.

Another instance of the like flagrant violation of the Constitution is to be found in the ninth and tenth sections of the confiscation act previously referred to. The Constitution of the United States in Article IV, section 3, says:

No person held to service or labor in one State, under the laws thereof, escaping into another, shall, in consequence of any law or regulation therein, be discharged from such service or labor.

It will be seen, by reference to the Constitution, that the first part of the clause here referred to forbids the discharge of the fugitive, and the second part commands his delivery to the claimant. It has just been stated in what manner Congress commanded the claim for delivery to be repudiated. The "discharge from such service and labor," in consequence of any State law or regulation, is forbidden. This is a part of the Constitution, and it is thereby made the duty of the executive, legislative, and judicial departments of the United States Government to enforce the prohibition, to make sure that the fugitive is not discharged by any action of a State.

Will the friends of constitutional liberty believe our assertion that these acts, the execution of which it was so expressly made the duty of the United States Government to prevent, that Government itself did do in the most explicit and effective manner? The provisions of the act are in these words:

All slaves of persons who shall hereafter be engaged in rebellion against the Government of the United States, or who shall in any way give aid or comfort thereto, escaping from such persons and taking refuge within the lines of the army; and all slaves captured from such persons or deserted by them and coming under the control of the Government of the United States; and all slaves of such persons found or being within any place occupied by rebel forces and afterward occupied by the forces of the United States, shall be deemed captives of war, and shall be for ever free of their servitude, and not again held as slaves.

Again, the next section of the same act says:

No slave escaping into any State, Territory, or the District of Columbia from any other State, shall be delivered up, or in any way impeded or hindered of his liberty, except for crime or some offense against the laws, unless the person claiming said fugitive shall first make oath that the person, to whom the labor or service of such fugitive is alleged to be due, is his lawful owner, and has not borne arms against the United States in the present rebellion, nor in any way given aid and comfort thereto.

Perhaps it may be urged that the Confederate States were out of the Union and beyond the protection of the provisions of the Constitution. This objection can not be admitted; for there was, thus far, no act of Congress, nor proclamation of the President in existence, showing that either of them regarded the Confederate States in any other position than as States within the Union, whose citizens were subject to all the penalties contained in the Constitution, and therefore entitled to the benefit of all its provisions for their protection. Unhesitatingly it may be said, and as will be still more apparent further on in these pages, that all the conduct of the Confederate States, pertaining to the war, consisted in just efforts to preserve to themselves and their posterity rights and protections guaranteed to them in the Constitution of the United States; and that the actions of the Federal Government consisted in efforts to subvert those rights, destroy those protections, and subjugate us to compliance with its arbitrary will; and that this conduct on their part involved the subversion of the Constitution and the destruction of the fundamental principles of liberty. Who is the criminal? Let posterity answer.

Chapter 21

Emancipation (continued)

THE ATTENTION of the reader is now invited to a series of usurpations in which the President of the United States was the principal actor. On March 6, 1862, he began a direct and unconstitutional interference with slavery by sending a message to Congress recommending the adoption of a resolution which should declare that the United States ought to coöperate with any State which might adopt the gradual abolition of slavery, giving to such State pecuniary aid, to be used by such State in its discretion, to compensate for the inconvenience, public and private, produced by such change of system. He said, in explanation, that "the leaders of the existing rebellion entertain the hope that this Government will ultimately be forced to acknowledge the independence of some part of the disaffected region, and that all the slave States north of such part will then say, 'The Union for which we have struggled being already gone, we now choose to go with the Southern section.' To deprive them of this hope substantially ends the rebellion, and the initiation of emancipation deprives them of it and of all the States initiating it."

When it was asked where the power was found in the Constitution to appropriate the money of the people to carry out the purposes of the resolution, it was replied that the legislative department of the Government was competent, under these words in the preamble of the Constitution, "to provide for the general welfare," to do anything and everything which could be considered as promoting the general welfare. It was further said that this measure was to be consummated under the war power; that whatever was necessary to carry on the war to a successful conclusion might be done without restraint under the authority, not of the Constitution, but as a military necessity. It was further said that the President of the United States had thus far failed to meet the just expectations of the party which elected him to the office he held; and that his friends were to be comforted by the resolution and the message, while the people of the border slave States could not fail to observe that with the comfort to the North there was mingled an awful warning to them. It was denied by the

President that it was an interference with slavery in the States. It was an artful scheme to awaken a controversy in the slave States, and to commence the work of emancipation by holding out pecuniary aid as an inducement. In every previous declaration the President had said that he did not contemplate any interference with domestic slavery within the States. The resolution was passed by large majorities in each House.

This proposition of President Lincoln was wholly unconstitutional, because it attempted to do what was expressly forbidden by the Constitution. It proposed a contract between the State of Missouri and the Government of the United States which, in the language of the act, shall be "irrepealable without the consent of the United States." The words of the Constitution are as follows:

No State shall enter into any treaty, alliance, or confederation, grant letters of marque and reprisal, coin money, etc.*

* Article I, section 10.

This is a prohibition not only upon the power of one State to enter into a compact, alliance, confederation, or agreement with another State, but also with the Government of the United States.

Again, if the State of Missouri could enter into an irrepealable agreement or compact with the United States, that slavery should not therein exist after the acceptance on the part of Missouri of the act, then it would be an agreement on the part of that State to surrender its sovereignty and make the State unequal in its rights of sovereignty with the other States of the Union. The other States would have the complete right of sovereignty over their domestic institutions while the State of Missouri would cease to have such right. The whole system of the United States Government would be abrogated by such legislation. Again, it is a cardinal principle of the system that the people in their sovereign capacity may, from time to time, change and alter their organic law; and a provision incorporated in the Constitution of Missouri that slavery should never thereafter exist in that State could not prevent a future sovereign convention of its people from reëstablishing slavery within its limits.

Feeling itself fortified in its unlimited power from "necessity," the wheels of the revolution were now to move with accelerated velocity. Accordingly, a manifesto soon comes from the Executive on universal emancipation. On April 25, 1862, the United States Major-General Hunter, occupying a position at Hilton Head, South Carolina, issued an order declaring the States of Georgia, Florida, and South Carolina under martial law. On May 9th the same officer issued another order, declaring "the persons held as slaves in those States to be for ever free." The Executives of the United States, on May 19th, issued a proclamation declaring the order to be void, and said:

I further make known that, whether it be competent for me as commander-in-chief of the army and navy to declare the slaves of any State or States free, and whether at any time or in any case it shall have become a necessity indispensable to the maintenance of the Government to examine such supposed power, are questions which, under my responsibility, I reserve to myself, and which I can not feel justified in leaving to the decision of commanders in the field.

Speaking of this order of Major-General Hunter soon afterward, President Lincoln, in remarks on July 12, 1862, to the border States Representatives, said:

In repudiating it, I gave dissatisfaction, if not offense, to many whose support the country can not afford to lose. And this is not the end of it. The pressure in this direction is still upon me, and is increasing.

This pressure consisted in the demand of his extreme partisans that the whole authority of the Government should be exerted for the immediate and universal emancipation of the slaves.

On July 12, 1862, the President of the United States, persistent in his determination to destroy the institution of slavery, invited the Senators and Representatives of the border slave-holding States to the Executive Mansion, and addressed them on emancipation in their respective States. He said:

I intend no reproach or complaint when I assure you that, in my opinion, if you all had voted for the resolution in the gradual emancipation message of last March, the war would now be substantially ended. And the plan therein proposed is yet one of the most potent and swift means of ending it. Let the States which are in rebellion see definitely and certainly that in no event will the States you represent ever join their proposed confederacy, and they can not much longer maintain the contest. But you can not divest them of their hope to ultimately have you with them so long as you show a determination to perpetuate the institution within your own States. Beat them at elections as you have overwhelmingly done, and, nothing daunted, they still claim you as their own. You and I know what the lever of their power is. Break that lever before their faces, and they can shake you no more for ever.

He further said that the incidents of the war might extinguish the institution in their States, and added:

How much better for you as seller and the nation as buyer to sell out and buy out that without which the war could never have been, than to sink both the thing to be sold and the price of it in cutting one another's throats!

The reply of the majority, consisting of twenty of the twenty-nine Senators and Representatives, subsequently made to the President, is worthy of notice. They said that they were not of the belief that funds would be provided for the object, or that their constituents would reap the fruits of the promise held out, and added:

The right to hold slaves is a right appertaining to all the States of the Union. They have the right to cherish or abolish the institution, as their tastes or their interests may prompt, and no one is authorized to question the right, or limit its enjoyment. And no one has more clearly affirmed that right than you have. Your inaugural address does you great honor in this respect, and inspired the country with confidence in your fairness and respect for law.

After asserting that a large portion of our people were fighting because they believed the Administration was hostile to their rights, and was making war on their domestic institutions, they further said:

Remove their apprehensions; satisfy them that no harm is intended to them and their institutions; that this Government is not making war on their rights of property, but is simply defending its legitimate authority, and they will gladly return to their allegiance.

This measure of emancipation with compensation soon proved a failure. A proposition to appropriate five hundred thousand dollars to the object was voted down in the United States Senate with great unanimity. The Government was, step by step, "educating the people" up to a proclamation of emancipation, so as to make entire abolition one of the positive and declared issues of the contest.

The so-called pressure upon the President was now organized for a final onset. The Governors of fifteen States united in a request that three hundred thousand more men should be called out to fill up the reduced ranks, and it was done. The anti-slavery press then entered the arena. Charges were made against the President, in the name of

Twenty millions of people, that a great proportion of those who triumphed in his election were sorely disappointed and deeply pained by the policy he seemed to be pursuing with regard to the slaves of the rebels.

They further said:

You are strangely and disastrously remiss in the discharge of your official and imperative duty with regard to the emancipation provisions of the new confiscation act.

They further boldly added:

We complain that the Union cause has suffered, and is now suffering, immensely from mistaken deference to rebel slavery. Had you, sir, in your inaugural address, unmistakably given notice that, in case the rebellion already commenced was persisted in, and your efforts to preserve the Union and enforce the laws should be resisted by armed force, you would recognize no loyal person as rightfully held in slavery by a traitor, we believe the rebellion would therein have received a staggering if not fatal blow.

The President replied at length, saying:

I shall do less whenever I shall believe what I am doing hurts the cause, and I shall do more whenever I shall believe doing more will help the cause. I shall try to correct errors when shown to be errors; and I shall adopt new views so fast as they shall appear to be true views. I have here stated my purpose according to my view of official duty; and I intend no modification of my oft-expressed personal wish that all men everywhere could be free.

The education of the conservative portion of the Northern people up to emancipation was becoming more complete every day, notwithstanding the professed reluctance of the President. Another call for three hundred thousand men was made, but enlistments were slow, so that threats of a draft and most liberal bounties were required. The champions of emancipation sought to derive an advantage from this circumstance. They asserted that the reluctance of the people to enter the army was caused by the policy of the Government in not adopting bold emancipation measures. If such were adopted, the streets and by-ways would be crowded with volunteers to fight for the freedom of the "loyal blacks," and thrice three hundred thousand could be easily obtained. They said that slavery in the seceded States should be treated as a military question; it contributed nearly all the subsistence which supported the Southern men in arms, dug their trenches, and built their fortifications. The watchword which they now adopted was, "The abolition of slavery by the force of arms for the sake of the Union."

Meantime, on September 13th, a delegation from the so-called "Christians" in Chicago, Illinois, presented to President Lincoln a memorial, requesting him to issue a proclamation of emancipation, and urged in its favor such reasons as occurred to their minds. President Lincoln replied:

What good would a proclamation of emancipation from me do, especially as we are now situated? I do not want to issue a document that the whole world would see must necessarily be inoperative, like the Pope's bull against the comet. Would my word free the slaves, when I can not even enforce the Constitution in the rebel States? Is there a single court, or magistrate, or individual that would be influenced by it there? And what reason is there to think it would have any greater effect upon the slaves than the late law of Congress which I approved, and which offers protection and freedom to the slaves of rebel masters who come within our lines? Yet I can not learn that that law has caused a single slave to come over to us. And suppose they could be induced by a proclamation of freedom from me to throw themselves upon us, what should we do with them? How can we feed and care for such a multitude? . . .

If, now, the pressure of the war should call off our forces from New Orleans to defend some other point, what is to prevent the masters from reducing the blacks to slavery again? . . . Now, then, tell me, if you please, what possible result of good would follow the issuing of such a proclamation as you desire? I have not decided against a proclamation of liberty to the slaves, but hold the matter under advisement.

Nine days after these remarks were made—on September 22, 1862—the preliminary proclamation of emancipation was issued by the President of the United States. It declared that at the next session of Congress the proposition for emancipation in the border slaveholding States would be again recommended, and that on January 1, 1863—

All persons held as slaves within any State or designated part of a State, the people whereof shall then be in rebellion against the United States, shall be then, thenceforward, and for ever free; and the Executive Government of the United States, including the military and naval authority thereof, will recognize and maintain the freedom of such persons, and will do no act or acts to repress such persons, or any of them, in any efforts they may make for their actual freedom.

Also, all persons engaged in the military and naval service were ordered to obey and enforce the article of war and the sections of the confiscation act before mentioned. On January 1, 1863, another proclamation was issued by the President of the United States declaring the emancipation to be absolute within the Confederate States, with the exception of a few districts, "warranted . . . upon military necessity." Let us test the existence of the military necessity here spoken of by a few facts. The white male population of the Northern States was then 13,690,364. The white male population of the Confederate States was 5,449,463. The number of troops which the United States had called into the field exceeded one million men. The number of troops which the Confederate Government had then in the field was less than four hundred thousand men. The United States Government had a navy which was only third in rank in the world. The Confederate Government had a navy which at that time consisted of a single small ship on the ocean. The people of the United States had a commerce afloat all over the world. The people of the Confederate States had not a single port open to commerce. The people of the United States were the rivals of the greatest nations in all kinds of manufactures. The people of the Confederate States had few manufactures and those were of articles of inferior importance. The Government of the United States possessed the Treasury of a Union of eighty years with its vast resources. The Confederate States had to create a Treasury by the development of financial resources. The ambassadors and representatives of the former were welcomed at every court in the world. The representatives of the latter were not recognized anywhere.

Thus the consummation of the original antislavery purposes was verbally reached; but even that achievement was attended with disunion, bloodshed, and war. It is thus seen what the United States Government did, and our view of this subject would not be complete if we should omit to present their solemn declarations of that which they intended to do.

On the 22d of July, 1861, Congress passed a resolution relative to the war, from which the following is an extract:

That this war is not waged on our part in any spirit of oppression, or for any purpose of conquest or subjugation, or purpose of overthrowing or interfering with the rights or established institutions of those [Confederate] States; but to defend and maintain the supremacy of the Constitution, and to preserve the Union with all the dignity, equality, and rights of the several States unimpaired; and that, as soon as these objects are accomplished, the war ought to cease.

A single example may be cited from the declaration made by President Lincoln, under the solemnity of his oath as Chief Magistrate of the United States, on March 4, 1861:

Apprehension seems to exist among the people of the Southern States that, by the accession of a Republican Administration, their property and their peace and personal security are to be endangered. There has never been any reasonable cause for such apprehensions. Indeed, the most ample evidence to the contrary has all the while existed and been open to their inspection. It is found in nearly all the public speeches of him who now addresses you. I do but quote from one of those speeches when I declare that I have no purpose, directly or indirectly, to interfere with the institution of slavery in the States where it exists. I believe I have no lawful right to do so, and I have no inclination to do so. Those who nominated and elected me did so with full knowledge that I had made this and many similar declarations, and had never recanted them.

Nor was this declaration of the want of power or disposition to interfere with our social system confined to a state of peace. Both before and after the actual commencement of hostilities, the Executive of the United States repeated in formal official communications to the Cabinets of Great Britain and France, that it was utterly without constitutional power to do the act which it subsequently committed, and that in no possible event, whether the secession of these States resulted in the establishment of a separate Confederacy or in the restoration of the Union, was there any authority by virtue of which it could either restore a disaffected State to the Union by force of arms, or make any change in any of its institutions. I refer especially for the verification of this assertion to the dispatches addressed by the Secretary of State of the United States, under direction of the President, to the Ministers of the United States at London and Paris, under date of the 10th and 22d of April, 1861.

This emancipation proclamation was therefore received by the people of the Confederate States as the fullest vindication of their own sagacity in foreseeing the uses to which the dominant party in the United States intended from the beginning to apply their power.

In his message to Congress one year later, on December 8, 1863, the President of the United States thus boasts of his proclamation:

The preliminary emancipation proclamation, issued in September, was running its assigned period to the beginning of the new year. A month later the final proclamation came, including the announcement that colored men of suitable condition would be received into the war service. The policy of emancipation and of employing black soldiers gave to the future a new aspect, about which hope and fear and doubt contended in uncertain conflict. According to our political system, as a matter of civil administration the General Government had no lawful power to effect emancipation in any State, and for a long time it had been hoped that the rebellion could be suppressed without resorting to it as a military measure. . . . Of those who were slaves at the beginning of the rebellion, full one hundred thousand are now in the United States military service, about one half of which number actually bear arms in the ranks, thus giving the double advantage of taking so much labor from the insurgent cause, and supplying the places which otherwise must be filled with so many white men. So far as tested, it is difficult to say they are not as good soldiers as any."

Let the reader pause for a moment and look calmly at the facts presented in this statement. The forefathers of these negro soldiers were gathered from the torrid plains and malarial swamps of inhospitable Africa. Generally they were born the slaves of barbarian masters, untaught in all the useful arts and occupations, reared in heathen darkness, and, sold by heathen masters, they were transferred to shores enlightened by the rays of Christianity. There, put to servitude, they were trained in the gentle arts of peace and order and civilization; they increased from a few unprofitable savages to millions of efficient Christian laborers. Their servile instincts rendered them contented with their lot, and their patient toil blessed the land of their abode with unmeasured riches. Their strong local and personal attachment secured faithful service to those to whom their service or labor was due. A strong mutual affection was the natural result of this life-long relation, a feeling best if not only understood by those who have grown from childhood under its influence. Never was there happier dependence of labor and capital on each other. The tempter came, like the serpent in Eden, and decoyed them with the magic word of "freedom." Too many were allured by the uncomprehended and unfulfilled promises, until the highways of these wanderers were marked by corpses of infants and the aged. He put arms in their hands, and trained their humble but emotional natures to deeds of violence and bloodshed, and sent them out to devastate their benefactors. What does he boastingly announce?—"It is difficult to say they are not as good soldiers as any." Ask the bereaved mother, the desolate widow, the sonless aged sire, to whom the bitter cup was presented by those once of their own household. With double anguish they speak of its bitterness. What does the President of the United States further say?—"According to our political system, as a matter of civil administration, the General Government had no lawful power to effect emancipation in any State." And further on, as if with a triumphant gladness, he adds, "Thus giving the double advantage of taking so much labor from the insurgent cause, and supplying the places which otherwise must be filled with so many white men." A rare mixture of mafeasance with traffic in human life! It is submitted to the judgment of a Christian people how well such a boast befits the President of the United States, a federation of sovereigns under a voluntary compact for specific purposes.

Chapter 22

The Virginia and the Monitor

THE ORGANIZATION of the Navy Department comprised under its general supervision of a bureau of orders and details, one of ordnance and hydrography, one of provisions and clothing, and one of medicine and surgery. The grades of officers consisted of admirals, captains, commanders, surgeons, lieutenants, and midshipmen. Of the officers at the close of the first year there were one admiral, twelve captains, thirty commanders, and one hundred and twelve first and second lieutenants. All of the principal officers had belonged to the United States Navy. Owing to the limited number of vessels afloat, many of these officers were employed on shore-duties.

The vessels of the navy may be reduced to two classes: those intended for river and harbor defense, as ironclads, rams, floating batteries, or river-steamboats transformed into gunboats; and sea-going steamers of moderate size, some of them of great speed, but, not having been designed for war purposes, were all unsuited for a powerful armament, and could not be expected to contend successfully with ships of war.

Early in 1861 discussions and experiments were instituted by the Navy Department to determine how floating batteries and naval rams could be best constructed and protected by iron plates. Many persons had submitted plans, according to which cotton-bales might be effectively used as a shield against shot. Our deficiency in iron, and also in rolling-mills to prepare it into plates, caused cotton to be sometimes so employed; though the experiments had satisfied the Navy Department that, instead of cotton being rendered impenetrable by compression, it was really less so than in looser condition, and that iron must needs be of great thickness to resist the direct impact of heavy shot at short ranges. An officer of the navy, as skillful in ordnance as he was in seamanship, and endowed with high capacity for the investigation of new problems—Lieutenant Catesby Ap R. Jones—had conducted many of these experiments, and made efficient use of his knowledge both in construction and in battle.

After Virginia had seceded from the United States, but

before she had acceded to the Confederate States—viz., on the 19th of April, 1861—General Taliaferro, in command of Virginia forces, arrived at Norfolk. Commodore McCauley, United States Navy, and commandant of the navy-yard, held a conference with General Taliaferro, the result of which was "that none of the vessels should be removed, nor a shot fired except in self-defense." The excitement which had existed in the town was quieted by the announcement of this arrangement; but it was soon ascertained that the Germantown and Merrimac, frigates in the port, had been scuttled, and the former otherwise injured. About midnight, as elsewhere stated, a fire was started in the navy-yard, which continued to increase, involving the destruction of the ship-houses, a ship of the line, and the unfinished frame of another; several frigates, in addition to those mentioned, had been scuttled and sunk; and other property destroyed, to an amount estimated at several million dollars. The Pawnee, which arrived on the 19th, had been kept under steam, and, taking the Cumberland in tow, retired down the harbor, freighted with a great portion of valuable munitions. In the haste and secrecy of the conflagration, a large amount of material remained uninjured. The Merrimac, a beautiful frigate, in the yard for repairs, was raised by the Virginians, and the work immediately commenced, on a plan devised by Lieutenant Brooke, Confederate States Navy, to convert her hull, with such means as were available, into an iron-clad vessel. Two-inch plates were prepared, and she was covered with a double-inclined roof of four inches thickness. This armor, though not sufficiently thick to resist direct shot, sufficed to protect against a glancing ball, and was as heavy as was consistent with the handling of the ship. The shield was defective in not covering the sides sufficiently below the water-line, and the prow was unfortunately made of cast-iron; but, when all the difficulties by which we were surrounded are remembered, and the service rendered by this floating battery considered, the only wonder must be that so much was so well done under the circumstances.

Her armament consisted of ten guns, four single-banded Brooke rifles, and six nine-inch Dahlgren shell-guns. Two of the rifles, bow and stern pivots, were seven inch; the other two were six and four tenths inch, one on each broadside. The nine-inch gun on each side, nearest the furnaces, was fitted for firing hot shot. The work of construction was prosecuted with all haste, the armament and crew were put on board, and the vessel started on her trial-trip. She was our first iron-clad; her model was an experiment, and many doubted its success. Her commander, Captain (after Admiral) Franklin Buchanan, with the wisdom of age and the experience of sea-service from his boyhood, combined the daring and enterprise of youth, and with him was Lieutenant Catesby Ap R. Jones, who had been specially in charge of the battery, and other-wise thoroughly acquainted with the ship. Now the first Confederate ironclad was afloat, the Stars and Bars were given to the breeze, and she was new-christened "The Virginia." She was joined by the Patrick Henry, six guns, Commander John R. Tucker; the Jamestown, two guns, Lieutenant-commanding John N. Barney; the Beaufort, one gun, Lieutenant-commanding W. H. Parker; the Raleigh, one gun, Lieutenant-commanding J. W. Alexander; the Teaser, one gun, Lieutenant-commanding W. A. Webb.

The enemy's fleet in Hampton Roads consisted of the Cumberland, twenty-four guns; Congress, fifty guns; St. Lawrence, fifty guns; steam-frigates Minnesota and Roanoke, forty guns each. The relative force was as twenty-one guns to two hundred and four, not counting the small steamers of the enemy, though they had heavier armament than the small vessels of our fleet, which have been enumerated. The Cumberland and the Congress lay off Newport News; the other vessels were anchored about nine miles eastward, near to Fortress Monroe. Strong shore-batteries and several small steamers, armed with heavy rifled guns, protected the frigates Cumberland and Congress.

The trial-trip was at once converted into a determined attack upon the enemy. Few men, conscious as Flag-officer Buchanan was of the defects of his vessel, would have dared such unequal conflict. Slowly—about five knots an hour—he steamed down to the roads. The Cumberland and Congress, seeing the Virginia approach, prepared for action, and, from the flag-ship Roanoke, signals were given to the Minnesota and St. Lawrence to advance. The Cumberland had swung so as to give her full broadside to the Virginia, which silently and without any exhibition of her crew, moved steadily forward. The shot from the Cumberland fell thick upon her plated roof, but rebounded harmless as hailstones. At last the prow of the Virginia struck the Cumberland just forward of her starboard forechains. A dull, heavy thud was heard, but so little force was given to the Virginia that the engineer hesitated about backing her. It was soon seen, however, that a gaping breach had been made in the Cumberland, and that the sea was rushing madly in. She reeled, and, while the waves ingulfed her, her crew gallantly stood to their guns and vainly continued their fire. She went down in nine fathoms of water, and with at least one hundred of her gallant crew, her pennant still flying from her mast-head.

The Virginia then ran up stream a short distance, in order to turn and have sufficient space to get headway, and come down on the Congress. The enemy, supposing that she had retired at the sight of the vessels approaching to attack her, cheered loudly, both ashore and afloat. But, when she turned to descend upon the Congress, as she had on the Cumberland, the Congress slipped her cables and ran ashore, bows on. The Virginia took position as near as the depth of water would permit, and opened upon her a raking fire. The Minnesota was fast aground about one mile and a half below. The Roanoke and St. Lawrence retired toward the fort. The shore-batteries kept up their fire on the Virginia, as did also the Minnesota at long range, and quite ineffectually. The Congress, being aground, could but feebly reply. Several of our small vessels came up and joined the Virginia, and the combined fire was fearfully destructive to the Congress. Her commander was killed, and soon her colors were struck, and the white flag appeared both at the main and spanker gaff. The Beaufort, Lieutenant-commanding W. H. Parker, and the Raleigh, Lieutenant-commanding J. W. Alexander, tugs which had accompanied the Virginia, were ordered to the Congress to receive the surrender. The flag of the ship and the sword of its then commander were delivered to Lieutenant Parker, by whom they were subsequently sent to the Navy Department at Richmond. Other officers delivered their swords in token of surrender, and entreated that they might return to assist in getting their wounded out of the ship. The permission was granted to the officers, and they then took advantage of the clemency shown them to make their escape. In the meantime the shore-batteries fired upon the tugs, and compelled them to retire. By this fire five of their own men, our prisoners, were wounded. The crew of the Congress escaped, as did that of the Cumberland, by boats, or by swimming, and generously our men abstained from firing on them while so exposed. Flag-officer Buchanan was wounded by a rifle-ball, and had to be carried below. The executive and ordnance officer, Lieutenant Catesby Ap R. Jones, succeeded to the command. It was now so near night and the change of the tide that nothing further could be attempted on that day. The Virginia, with the smaller vessels attending her, withdrew and anchored off Sewell's Point. She had sunk the Cumberland, left the Congress on fire, had blown up a transport-steamer, sunk one schooner, and had captured another. Casualties, reported by Lieutenant Jones, were two killed and eight wounded. The prow of the Virginia was somewhat damaged, her anchor and all her flag-staffs were shot away, and her smoke-stack and steam-pipe were riddled; otherwise, the vessel was uninjured, and, as will be seen, was ready for action on the next morning. The prisoners and wounded were immediately sent up to the hospital at Norfolk.

During the night the Monitor, an iron-clad turret-steamer, of an entirely new model, came in, and anchored near the Minnesota. Like our Virginia she was an invention, and her merits and demerits were to be tested in the crucible of war. She was of light draught, and very little save the revolving turret was visible above the water; [she] was readily handled, and had good speed; but, also, like the Virginia, was not supposed by nautical men to be capable of braving rough weather at sea.

The Virginia was the hull of a frigate, modified into an iron-clad vessel. She was only suited to smooth water, and it had not been practicable to obtain for her such engines as would have given her the requisite speed. Her draught, twenty-two feet, was too great for the shoal water in the roads, and the apprehension which was excited lest she should go up to Washington might have been allayed by a knowledge of the deep water necessary to float her. Her great length, depth, and want of power, caused difficulty in handling to be anticipated. In many respects she was an experiment, and, had we possessed the means to build a new vessel, no doubt a better model could have been devised. In the morning the Virginia, with the Patrick Henry, the Jamestown, and the three little tugs, jestingly called the "mosquito fleet," returned to the scene of the previous day's combat, and to the completion of the work, the destruction of the Minnesota, which had, the evening before, been interrupted by the change of tide and the coming of night. The Monitor, which had come in during the previous night, and had been seen by the light of the burning Congress, opened fire on the Virginia when about the third of a mile distant. The Virginia sought to close with her, but the greater speed of the Monitor and the celerity with which she was handled made this impracticable. The ships passed and repassed very near each other, and frequently the Virginia delivered her broadside at close quarters, but with no perceptible effect. The Monitor fired rapidly from her revolving turret, but not with such aim as to strike successively in the same place, and the armor of the Virginia, therefore, remained unbroken. Lieutenant-commanding Catesby Jones soon discovered that the Monitor was invulnerable to his shells. He had a few solid shots, which were intended only to be fired from the nine-inch guns as hot shot, and therefore had necessarily so much windage that they would be ineffective against the shield of the Monitor. He, therefore, determined to run her down, and got all the headway he could obtain for that purpose, but the speed was so small that it merely pushed her out of the way. It was then decided to board her, and all hands were piped for that object. Then the Monitor slipped away on to shoal water where the Virginia could not approach her, and Commander Jones, after waiting a due time, and giving the usual signals of invitation to combat, without receiving any manifestation on the part of the Monitor of any intention to return to deep water, withdrew to the navy-yard.

In the two days of conflict our only casualties were from the Cumberland as she went down valiantly fighting to the last, from the men on shore when the tugs went to the Congress to receive her surrender, or from the perfidious fire from the Congress while her white flags were flying. None were killed or wounded in the fight with the Monitor.

As this was the first combat between two iron-clad vessels, it attracted great attention and provoked much speculation. Some assumed that wooden ships were henceforth to be of no use, and much has been done by the addition of armor to protect seagoing vessels; but certainly neither of the two which provoked the speculation could be regarded as seaworthy, or suited to other than harbor defense.

A new prow was put on the Virginia, she was furnished with bolts and solid shot, and slight repairs needed were promptly made. The distinguished veteran, Commodore Josiah Tatnall, was assigned to the command of the Virginia. The Virginia, as far as possible, was prepared for battle and cruise in the Roads, and, on the 11th of April, Commodore Tatnall moved down to invite the Monitor to combat. But her officers kept the Monitor close to the shore, with her steam up, and under the guns of Fortress Monroe. To provoke her to come out, the little Jamestown was sent in and pluckily captured many prizes, but the Monitor lay safe in the shoal water under the guns of the formidable fortress. After some delay, and there being no prospect of active service, the Commodore ordered the executive officer to fire a gun to windward and take the ship back to her buoy. Here, ready for service, waiting for an enemy to engage her, but never having the opportunity, she remained until the 10th of the ensuing month.

The Norfolk Navy-Yard, notwithstanding the injury done to it by conflagration, was yet the most available and equipped yard in the Confederacy. A land-force under General Huger had been placed there for its protection, and defensive works had also been constructed with a view to hold it as well for naval construction and repair as for its strategic importance in connection with the defense of the capital, Richmond. On the opposite side of the lower James, on the Peninsula between the James and York Rivers, we occupied an entrenched position of much natural strength. The two positions, Norfolk and the Peninsula, were necessary to each other, and the command of the channel between them essential to both. As long as the Virginia closed the entrance to the James River, and the intrenchment on the Peninsula was held, it was deemed possible to keep possession of Norfolk.

On the 1st of May General Johnston, commanding on the Peninsula, having decided to retreat, sent an order to General Huger to evacuate Norfolk. The Secretary of War, General Randolph, having arrived just at that time in Norfolk, assumed the authority of postponing the execution of the order "until he [General Huger] could remove such stores, munitions, and arms as could be carried off." The Secretary of the Navy, Mr. Mallory, was there also, and gave like instructions to the commandant of the yard. To the system and energy with which General Huger conducted the removal of heavy guns, machinery, stores, and munitions, we were greatly indebted in our future operations, both of construction and defense. A week was thus employed in the removal of machinery, etc., and the enemy, occupied with the retreating army on the Peninsula, did not cross the James River above, either to interrupt the transportation or to obstruct the retreat of the garrisons of the forts at Norfolk and its surroundings. When our army had been withdrawn from the Peninsula, and Norfolk had been evacuated, and the James River did not furnish depth of channel which would suffice for the Virginia to ascend it more than a few miles, her mission was ended.

It is not surprising that her brilliant career created a great desire to preserve her, and that it was contemplated to lighten her and thus try to take her up the river, but the pilots declared this to be impracticable, and the court, which subsequently investigated the matter sustained their opinion that "the only alternative was then and there to abandon and burn the ship." So, on the 10th of May, the Virginia was taken to Craney Island, one mile above, and there her crew were landed; they fell in and formed on the beach, and, in the language of an eye-witness, "then and there, on the very field of her fame, within sight of the Cumberland's topgallant-masts, all awash, within sight of that magnificent fleet still cowering on the shoal, with her laurels all fresh and green, we hauled down her drooping colors, and, with mingled pride and grief, we gave her to the flames."

Chapter 23

New Orleans

NEW ORLEANS was the most important commercial port in the Confederacy, being the natural outlet of the Mississippi Valley, as well to the ports of Europe as to those of Central and Southern America. It was the depot which, at an early period, had led to controversies with Spain, and its importance to the interior had been a main inducement to the purchase of Louisiana. It had become before 1861 the chief cotton-mart of the United States, and its defense attracted the early attention of the Confederate Government. The approaches for an attacking party were numerous. They could through several channels enter Lake Pontchartrain, to approach the city in rear for land-attack, could ascend the Mississippi from the Gulf, or descend it from the Northwest, where it was known that the enemy was preparing a formidable fleet of iron-clad gunboats. In the early part of 1862, so general an opinion prevailed that the greatest danger to New Orleans was by an attack from above, that General Lovell sent to General Beauregard a large part of the troops then in the city.

At the mouth of the Mississippi there is a bar, the greatest depth of water on which seldom exceeded eighteen feet, and it was supposed that heavy vessels of war, with their armament and supplies, would not be able to cross it. Such proved to be the fact, and the vessels of that class had to be lightened to enable them to enter the river. In that condition of affairs, an inferior fleet might have engaged them with a prospect of success. Captain Hollins, who was in command of the squadron at New Orleans, had been sent with the greater part of his fleet up the river to join the defense there being made. Two powerful vessels were under construction, the Louisiana and the Mississippi, but neither of them was finished. A volunteer fleet of transport-vessels had been fitted up by some river-men, but it was in the unfortunate condition of not being placed under the orders of the naval commander. A number of fire-rafts had been also provided, which were to serve the double purpose of lighting up the river in the event of the hostile fleet attempting to pass the forts under cover of the night, and of setting fire to any vessel with which they might become entangled

After passing the bar, there was nothing to prevent the ascent of the river until Forts Jackson and St. Philip were reached. These works, constructed many years before, were on opposite banks of the river. Their armament, as reported by General Lovell, December 5, 1861, consisted of—Fort Jackson: six forty-two-pounders, twenty-six twenty-four-pounders, two thirty-two-pounder rifles, sixteen thirty-two-pounders, three eight-inch columbiads, one ten-inch columbiad, two eight-inch mortars, one ten-inch mortar, two forty-pounder howitzers, and ten twenty-four-pounder howitzers. Fort St. Philip six forty-two-pounders, nine thirty-two-pounders, twenty-two twenty-four-pounders, four eight-inch columbiads, one eight-inch mortar, one ten-inch mortar, and three field-guns.

General Duncan reported that, on the 27th of March, he was informed by Lieutenant-Colonel Higgins, commanding Forts Jackson and St. Philip, of the coast-defenses, which were under his (General Duncan's command, that the enemy's fleet was crossing the bars, and entering the Mississippi River in force; whereupon he repaired to Fort Jackson. When the forts were attacked, the armament was one hundred and twenty-eight guns and mortars. The garrisons of Forts Jackson and St. Philip were about one thousand men on December 5, 1861; afterward, so far as I know, the number was not materially changed.

The prevailing belief that vessels of war, in a straight, smooth channel, could pass batteries, led to the construction of a raft between the two forts, which, it was supposed, would detain the ships under fire of the forts long enough for the guns to sink them, or at least to compel them to retire. The power of the river when in flood, and the drift-wood it bore upon it, broke the raft; another was constructed, which, when the drift-wood accumulated upon it, met a like fate. Whether obstructions differently arranged could have been made permanent and efficient, is a problem which need not be discussed, as the time for its application has passed from us.

The general plan for the defense of New Orleans consisted of two lines of works: an exterior one, passing through the forts near the mouth of the river, and the positions taken to defend the various water approaches; nearer to the city was the interior line, embracing New Orleans and Algiers, which was intended principally to repel an attack by land, but also, by its batteries on the river-bank, to resist approach by water. The total length of the intrenchments on this interior line was more than eight miles. When completed, it formed, in connection with impassable swamps, a very strong line of defense. At the then high stage of the river, all the land between it and the swamps was so saturated with water, that regular approaches could not have been made. The city, therefore, was at the time supposed to be doubly secure from a land-attack.

In the winter of 1861–'62 I sent one of my aides-de-camp to New Orleans to make a general inspection, and hold free conference with the commanding General. Upon his return, he reported to me that General Lovell was quite satisfied with the condition of the land-defenses—so much so as to say that his only fear was that the enemy would not make a land-attack.

Considered since the event, it may seem strange that, after the fall of Donelson and Henry, and the employment of the enemy's gunboats in the Tennessee and Cumberland, it was still generally argued that the danger to New Orleans was that the gunboats would descend the Mississippi, and applications were made to have the ship Louisiana sent up the river as soon as she was completed.

The interior lines of defense mounted more than sixty guns of various caliber, and were surrounded by wide and deep ditches. On the various water approaches, including bays and bayous on the west and east sides of the river, there were sixteen different forts, and these, together with those on the river and the batteries of the interior line, had in position about three hundred guns.

One ironclad, the Louisiana, mounting sixteen guns of heavy caliber, though she was not quite completed, was sent down to coöperate with the forts. Her defective steam-power and imperfect steering apparatus prevented her from rendering active coöperation. The steamship Mississippi, then under construction at New Orleans, was in such an unfinished condition as to be wholly unavailable when the enemy arrived. In the opinion of naval officers she would have been, if completed, the most powerful ironclad then in the world, and could have driven the enemy's fleet out of the river and raised the blockade at Mobile. There were also several small river-steamers which were lightly armed, and their bows were protected so that they could act as rams and otherwise aid in the defense of the river; but, from the reports received, they seem, with a few honorable exceptions, to have rendered little valuable service.

The means of defense, therefore, mainly relied on were the two heavy-armed forts, Jackson and St. Philip, with the obstruction placed between them: this was a raft consisting of cypress-trees, forty feet long, and averaging four or five feet at the larger end. They were placed longitudinally in the river, about three feet apart, and held together by gunwales on top, and strung upon two two-and-a-half-inch chain cables fastened to their lower sides. This raft was anchored in the river, abreast of the forts.

The fleet of the enemy below the forts consisted of seven steam sloops of war, twelve gunboats, and several armed steamers, under Commodore Farragut; also, a mortar-fleet consisting of twenty-sloops and some steam-vessels. The whole force was forty-odd vessels of different kinds, with an armament of three hundred guns of heavy caliber, of improved models.

The bombardment of the forts by the mortar-fleet commenced on April 18th, and, after six days of vigorous and constant shelling, the resisting powers of the forts was not diminished in any perceptible degree. On the 23d there were manifest preparations by the enemy to attempt the passage of the forts. This, as subsequently developed, was done in the following manner. The sloops of war and the gunboats were each formed in two divisions, and, selecting the darkest hour of the night, between 3 and 4 A.M. of the 24th, moved up the river in two columns. The commanders of the forts had vainly endeavored to have the river lighted up in anticipation of an attack by the fleet.

In the mean time, while the fleet moved up the river, there was kept up from the mortars a steady bombardment on the forts, and these opened a fire on the columns of ships and gunboats, which, from the failure to send down the fire-rafts to light up the river, was less effective than it otherwise would have been. The straight, deep channel enabled the vessels to move at their greatest speed, and thus the forts were passed.

The vessels which passed the fort anchored at the quarantine station about six miles above, and in the forenoon proceeded up the river. Batteries had been constructed where the interior line of defense touched both the right and the left bank of the river. The high stage of the river gave to its surface an elevation above that of the natural bank; but a continuous levee to protect the land from inundation existed on both sides of the river. When the ascending fleet approached these batteries, a cross-fire, which drove two of the vessels back, was opened upon it, and continued until all the ammunition was exhausted. The garrison was then withdrawn —casualties, one killed and one wounded.

On the 25th of April the enemy's gunboats and ships of war anchored in front of the city and demanded its surrender. Major-General M. Lovell, then in command, refused to comply with the summons, but, believing himself unable to make a successful defense, and in order to avoid a bombardment, agreed to withdraw his forces, and turn it over to the civil authorities. Accordingly, the city was evacuated on the same day. The forts still continued defiantly to hold their position. By assiduous exertion the damage done to the works was repaired, and the garrisons valiantly responded to the resolute determination of General Duncan and Colonel Higgins to defend the forts against the fleet still below, as well as against that which had passed and was now above. On the 26th Commodore Porter, commanding the mortar-fleet below, sent a flag-of-truce boat to demand the surrender of the forts, saying that the city of New Orleans had surrendered. To this Colonel Higgins replied, April 27th, that he had no official information that New Orleans had been evacuated, and until such notice was received he would not entertain for a moment a proposition to surrender the forts.

During the 25th, 26th, and 27th, there had been an abatement of fire on the forts, and with it had subsided the excitement which imminent danger creates in the brave. A rumor became current that the city had surrendered, and no reply had been received to inquiries sent on the 24th and 25th. About midnight on the 27th the garrison of Fort Jackson revolted *en masse,* seized upon the guard, and commenced to spike the guns. Captain S. O. Comay's company, the Louisiana Cannoneers of St. Mary's Parish, and a few others remained true to their cause and country. Under the incessant fire to which the forts had been exposed, and the rise of the water in the casemates and lower part of the works, the men had been not only deprived of sleep, but of the opportunity to prepare their food. Heroically they had braved alike dangers and discomfort; had labored constantly to repair damages; to extinguish fires caused by exploding shells; to preserve their ammunition by bailing out the water which threatened to submerge the magazine: yet, in a period of comparative repose, these men, who had been cheerful and obedient, as suddenly as unexpectedly, broke out into open mutiny. Under the circumstances which surrounded him, General Duncan had no alternative. It only remained for him to accept the proposition which had been made for a surrender of the forts. As this mutiny became known about midnight of the 27th, soon after daylight of the 28th a small boat was procured, and notice of the event was sent to Captain Mitchell, on the Louisiana, and also to Fort St. Philip. The officers of that fort concurred in the propriety of the surrender, though none of their men had openly revolted.

A flag of truce was sent to Commodore Porter to notify him of a willingness to negotiate for the surrender of the forts. The gallantry with which the defense had been conducted was recognized by the enemy, and the terms were as liberal as had been offered on former occasions. The garrisons were paroled, the officers were to retain their side-arms, and the Confederate flags were left flying over the forts until our forces had withdrawn. Captain Mitchell, commanding the Confederate States naval forces, had been notified by General Duncan of the mutiny in the forts and of the fact that the enemy had passed through a channel in rear of Fort St. Philip and had landed a force at the quarantine, some six miles above, and that, under the circumstances, it was deemed necessary to surrender the forts. As the naval forces were not under the orders of the general commanding the coast-defenses, it was optional with the naval commander to do likewise or not as to his fleet. After consultation with his officers, Captain Mitchell decided to destroy his flagship, the Louisiana, the only formidable vessel he had, rather than allow her to fall into the hands of the enemy. The crew was accordingly withdrawn, and the vessel set on fire.

Commodore Porter, commanding the fleet below, came up under a flag of truce to Fort Jackson, and, while negotiations were progressing for the surrender, the Louisiana, in flames, drifted down the river, and, when close under Fort St. Philip, exploded and sank.

The defenses afloat, except the Louisiana, consisted of tugs and river-steamers, which had been converted to war purposes by protecting their bows with iron so as to make them rams, and putting on them such armament as boats of that class would bear; and these were again divided into such as were subject to control as naval vessels, and others which, in compliance with the wish of the Governor of Louisiana and many influential citizens, were fitted out to a great extent by State and private sources, with the condition that they should be commanded by river-steamboat captains, and should not be under the control of the naval commander. This, of course, impaired the unity requisite in battle. For many other purposes they might have been used without experiencing the inconvenience felt when they were brought together to act as one force against the enemy. One of the little river-boats, the Governor Moore, commanded by Lieutenant Beverly Kennon, like the others, imperfectly protected at the bow, struck and sunk the Varuna, in close proximity to other vessels of the enemy's fleet. Such daring resulted in his losing, in killed and wounded, seventy-four out of a crew of ninety-three. Then finding that he must destroy his ship to prevent her from falling into the hands of the enemy, he set her on fire. The Manassas, Lieutenant-commanding Warley, though merely an altered "tug-boat," stoutly fought the large ships; but, being wholly unprotected, except at her bow, was perforated in many places, as soon as the guns were brought to bear upon her sides, and floated down the river a burning wreck. Another of the same class, with permission of the enemy, went up to New Orleans to convey the wounded as well from our forts as from the fleet.

On the 23d of April, 1862, General Lovell, commanding the military department, had gone down to Fort Jackson, where General Duncan, commanding the coast-defenses, then made his headquarters. The presence of the department commander did not avail to secure the full coöperation between the defenses afloat and the land-defenses, which was then of most pressing and immediate necessity.

When the enemy's fleet passed the forts, he hastened back to New Orleans, his headquarters. The confusion which prevailed in the city, when the news arrived that the forts had been passed by the enemy's fleet, shows how little it was expected. There was nothing to obstruct the ascent of the river between Forts Jackson and St. Philip and the batteries on the river where the interior line of defense rested on its right and left banks, about four miles below the city. The guns were not sufficiently numerous in these batteries to inspire much confidence; they were nevertheless well served until the ammunition was exhausted, after which the garrisons withdrew, and made their way by different routes to join the forces withdrawn from New Orleans.

Under the supposition entertained by the generals nearest to the operations, the greatest danger to New Orleans was from above, not from below, the city; therefore, most of the troops had been sent from the city to Tennessee, and Captain Hollins, with the greater part of the river-fleet, had gone up to check the descent of the enemy's gunboats.

Batteries like those immediately below the city had been constructed where the interior line touched the river above, and armed to resist an attack from that direction. Doubtful as to the direction from which, and the manner in which, an attempt might be made to capture the city, such preparations as circumstances suggested were made against many supposable dangers by the many possible routes of approach. To defend the city from the land, against a bombardment by a powerful fleet in the river before it, had not been contemplated. All the defensive preparations were properly, I think, directed to the prevention of a near approach by the enemy. To have subjected the city to bombardment by a direct or plunging fire, as the surface of the river was then higher than the land, would have been exceptionally destructive. Had the city been filled with soldiers whose families had been sent to a place of safety, instead of being filled with women and children whose natural protectors were generally in the army and far away, the attempt might have been justified to line the levee with all the effective guns and open fire on the fleet, at the expense of whatever property might be destroyed before the enemy should be driven away. The case was the reverse of the hypothesis, and nothing could have been more unjust than to censure the commanding General for withdrawing a force large enough to induce a bombardment, but insufficient to repel it. His answer to the demand for the surrender showed clearly enough the motives by which he was influenced. His refusal enabled him to withdraw the troops and most of the public property, and to use them, with the ordnance and ordnance stores thus saved, in providing for the defense of Vicksburg, but especially it deprived the enemy of any pretext for bombarding the town and sacrificing the lives of the women and children. It appears that General Lovell called for ten thousand volunteers from the citizens, but failed to get them. There were many river-steamboats at the landing, and, if the volunteers called for were intended to man these boats and board the enemy's fleet before their land-forces could arrive, it can not be regarded as utterly impracticable. The report of General Butler shows that he worked his way through one of the bayous in rear of Fort St. Philip to the Mississippi River above the forts so as to put himself in communication with the fleet at the city, and to furnish Commodore Farragut with ammunition. From this it is to be inferred that the fleet was deficient in ammunition, and the fact would have rendered boarding from river-boats the more likely to succeed. In this connection it may be remembered that, during the war, John Taylor Wood, Colonel and A. D. C. to the President, who had been an officer of high repute in the "old Navy," did in open boats attack armed vessels, board and capture them, though found with nettings up, having been warned of the probability of such an attack.

Chapter 24

Neutrality of Great Britain; Maritime Warfare

THE EXCITEMENT PRODUCED in the Northern States by the effective operations of our cruisers upon their commerce was such as to receive the attention of the United States Government. Reasonably, it might have been expected that they would send their ships of war out on the high-seas to protect their commerce by capturing or driving off our light cruisers, but, instead of this, their fleets were employed in blockading the Confederate ports, or watching those in the West Indies, from which blockade-runners were expected to sail, and, by capturing which, either on the high-seas or at the entrance of a Confederate port, a harvest of prizes might be secured. For this dereliction of duty, in the failure to protect commerce, no better reason offers itself than greed and malignity. There was, however, in this connection, a more humiliating feature in the conduct of the United States Government.

While, from its State Department, the Confederacy was denounced as an insurrection soon to be suppressed, and the cruisers, regularly commissioned by the Confederate States, were called "pirates," diplomatic demands were made upon Great Britain to prevent the so-called "pirates" from violating international law, as if it applied to pirates. Appeals to that Government were also made to prevent the sale of the materials of war to the Confederacy, and thus indirectly to aid the United States in performing what, according to the representation, was a police duty, to suppress a combination of some evil-disposed persons—gallantly claiming that they, armed *cap-a-pie*, should meet their adversary in the list, he to be without helmet, shield, or lance. If this had been all the contradictions would have been too bald to require refutation; but this would have been but half of the story. Subsequently the United States Government claimed reclamation from Great Britain for damage inflicted by vessels which had been built in her ports, and which had elsewhere been armed and equipped for purposes of war. International law recognizes the right of a neutral to sell an unarmed vessel, without reference to the use to which the purchaser might subsequently apply it. The United States Government had certainly not practiced under a different rule, but had gone even further than this—so much further as to transgress the prohibition against armed vessels.

It has already been stated that the Government of the United States, at the commencement of the war, sought to contract for the construction of iron-plated vessels in the ports of England, which were to be delivered fully armed and equipped to her. To this it may be added that her armies were recruited from almost all the countries of Europe, down almost to the last month of the war; a portion of their arms were of foreign manufacture, as well as the munitions of war; a large number of the sailors of her fleets came from the seaports of Great Britain and Germany; in a word, whatever could be of service to her in the conflict was unhesitatingly sought among neutrals, regardless of the law of nations. At the same time an effort was made on her part to make Great Britain responsible for the damage done by our cruisers, and for the warlike stores sold to our Government.

Some statements of Lord Russell on this point, in a letter to Minister Adams, dated December 19, 1862, deserve notice. He says:

It is right, however, to observe that the party which has profited by far the most by these unjustifiable practices, has been the Government of the United States, because that Government having a superiority of force by sea, and having blockaded most of the Confederate ports, has been able, on the one hand, safely to receive all the warlike supplies which it has induced British manufacturers and merchants to send to the United States ports in violation of the Queen's proclamation; and, on the other hand, to intercept and capture a great part of the supplies of the same kind which were destined from this country to the Confederate States.

If it be sought to make her Majesty's Government responsible to that of the United States because arms and munitions of war have left this country on account of the Confederate Government, the Confederate Government, as the other belligerent, may very well maintain that it has a just cause of complaint against the British Government because the United States arsenals have been replenished from British sources. Nor would it be possible to deny that, in defiance of the Queen's proclamation, many subjects of her Majesty, owing allegiance to her crown, have enlisted in the armies of the United States. Of this fact you can not be ignorant. Her Majesty's Government, therefore, has just ground for complaint against both of the belligerent parties, but most especially against the Government of the United States, for having systematically, and in disregard of the comity of nations which it was their duty to observe, induced subjects of her Majesty to violate those orders which, in conformity with her neutral position, she has enjoined all her subjects to obey.

Perhaps it may be well to inquire what is, under international law, the duty of neutral nations with regard to the construction and equipment of cruisers for either belligerent, and the supply of warlike stores. Thus the groundlessness of the claims put forth by the Government of the United States for damages to be paid by Great Britain will be more manifest, and the lawfulness of the acts of the Confederate Government demonstrated.

After the outbreak of the French Revolution in 1789, the Government of France, owing to the temporary inferiority of her naval force, openly and deliberately equipped privateers in our ports. These privateers captured British vessels in United States waters, and brought them as prizes into United States ports. These facts formed the basis of demands made upon the United States by the British plenipotentiary. The demands had reference, not to the accidental evasion of a municipal law of the United States by a particular ship, but to a systematic disregard of international law upon some of the most important points of neutral obligation.

To these demands Mr. Jefferson, then Secretary of State under President Washington, thus replied on September 3, 1793:

We are bound by our treaties with three of the belligerent nations, by all the means in our power, to protect and defend their vessels and effects in our ports or waters, or on the seas near our shores, and to recover and restore the same to the right owners when taken from them. If all the means in our power are used, and fail in this effort, we are not bound by our treaties with those nations to make compensation. Though we have no similar treaty with Great Britain, it was the opinion of the President that we should use toward that nation the same rule which, under this article, was to govern us with other nations, and even to extend it to the captures made on the high-seas and brought into our ports, if done by vessels which had been armed within them.

It will be observed that the justice of restitution, or compensation, for captures made on the high-seas and brought into our ports, is only admitted by President Washington upon one condition, which is expressed in these words: "If done by vessels which had been armed within them." In the instance of our cruisers built in the ports of England, it will be observed that they went to sea without arms or warlike stores, and, at other ports than those of Great Britain, they were converted into ships of war and put into commission by the authority of the Confederate Government. The Government of the United States asserted that they were built in the ports of Great Britain, and thereby her duty of neutrality was violated, and the Government made responsible for the damages sustained by private citizens of the United States in consequence of her captures on the seas. To this declaration of Mr. Adams, Earl Russell (he had been made an earl) replied on September 14, 1863, thus:

When the United States Government assumes to hold the Government of Great Britain responsible for the captures made by vessels which may be fitted out as vessels of war in a foreign port, because such vessels were originally built in a British port, I have to observe that such pretensions are entirely at variance with the principles of international law, and with the decisions of American courts of the highest authority; and I have only, in conclusion, to express my hope that you may not be instructed again to put forward claims which her Majesty's Government can not admit to be founded on any grounds of law or justice.

The duty of neutral nations relative to the supply of warlike stores is expressed in these words:

"It is not the practice of nations to undertake to prohibit their own subjects by previous laws from trafficking in articles contraband of war. Such trade is carried on at the risk of those engaged in it, under the liabilities and penalties prescribed by the law of nations or particular treaties." *

In accordance with these principles, President Pierce's message of December 31, 1855, contains the following passage:

The laws of the United States do not forbid their citizens to sell to either of the belligerent powers articles contraband of war, to take munitions of war or soldiers on board their private ships for transportation; and, although in so doing the individual citizen exposes his property or person to some of the hazards of war, his acts do not involve any breach of international neutrality, nor of themselves implicate the Government.

Perhaps it may not be out of place here to notice the charge of the Lord Chief Baron of the Exchequer to the jury

*Wheaton's "International Law," sixth edition, p. 571, 1855.

in the case of the Alexandra, a vessel of one hundred and twenty tones, under construction at Liverpool for our Government. The case came on for trial on June 22, 1863, in the Court of Exchequer, sitting at *nisi prius,* before the Lord Chief Baron and a special jury. After it had been summed up, the Lord Chief Baron said:

This is an information on the part of the Crown for the seizure and confiscation of a vessel that was in the course of preparation but had not been completed. It is admitted that it was not armed, and the question is, whether the preparation of the vessel in it's then condition was a violation of the Foreign Enlistment Act. The main question you will have to decide is this: Whether, under the seventh section of the act of Parliament, the vessel, as then prepared at the time of seizure, was liable to seizure? The statute was passed in 1819, and upon it no question has ever arisen in our courts of justice; but there have been exposition of a similar statute which exists in the United States. I will now read to you the opinions of some American lawyers who have contributed so greatly to make law a science. [His lordship then read a passage from Story and others]. These gentlemen are authorities which show that, when two belligerents are carrying on a war, a neutral power may supply, without any breach of international law and without a breach of the Foreign Enlistment Act, munitions of war —gunpowder, every description of arms, in fact, that can be used for the destruction of human beings.

Why should ships be an exception? I am of opinion, in point of law, they are not. The Foreign Enlistment Act was an act to prevent the enlistment or engagement of his Majesty's subject to serve in foreign armies, and to prevent the fitting out and equipping in his Majesty's dominions vessels for warlike purposes without his Majesty's license. The title of an act is not at all times an exact indication or explanation of the act, because it is generally attached after the act is passed. But, in adverting to the preamble of the act, I find that provision is made against the equipping, fitting out, furnishing, and arming of vessels, because it may be prejudicial to the peace of his Majesty's dominions.

The question I shall put to you is, Whether you think that vessel was merely in a course of building to be delivered in pursuance of a contract that was perfectly lawful, or whether there was any intention in the port of Liverpool, or any other English port, that the vessel should be fitted out, equipped, furnished, and armed, for purposes of aggression. Now, surely, if Birmingham, or any other town, may supply any quantity of munitions of war of various kinds for the destruction of life, why object to ships? Why should ships alone be in themselves contraband? I asked the Attorney-General if a man could not make a vessel intending to sell it to either of the belligerent powers that required it, and which would give the largest price for it, would not that be lawful? To my surprise, the learned Attorney-General declined to give an answer to the question, which I think a grave and pertinent one. But you gentlemen, I think, are lawyers enough to know that a man may make a vessel and offer it for sale. If a man may build a vessel for the purpose of offering it for sale to either belligerent part, may he not execute an order for it? That appears to be a matter of course. The statute is not made to provide means of protection for belligerent powers, otherwise it would have said, 'You shall not sell powder or guns, and you shall not sell arms'; and, if it had done so, all Birmingham would have been in arms against it. The object of the statute was this: that we should not have our ports in this country made the ground of hostile movements between the vessels of two belligerent powers, which might be fitted out, furnished, and armed in these ports. The Alexandra was clearly nothing more than in the course of building.

It appears to me that, if true that the Alabama sailed from Liverpool without any arms at all, as a mere ship in ballast, and that her armament was put on board at Terceira, which is not in the Majesty's dominions, then the Foreign Enlistment Act was not violated at all.

After reading some of the evidence, his lordship said:

If you think that the object was to furnish, fit out, equip, and arm that vessel at Liverpool, that is a different matter; but if you think the object really was to build a ship in obedience to an order, in compliance with a contract, leaving those who bought it to make what use they thought fit of it, then it appears to me that the Foreign Enlistment Act has not been broken.

The jury immediately returned a verdict for the defendants. An appeal was made, but the full bench decided that there was no jurisdiction. Against this decision an appeal was taken to the House of Lords, and there dismissed on some technical ground.

Sufficient has been said to show that the action of the Confederate Government relative to these cruisers is sustained and justified by international law. The complaints made by the Government of the United States against the Government of Great Britain for acts involving a breach of neutrality find no support in the letter of the law or in its principles, and were conclusively answered by the interpretations of *American jurists*. At the same time they are condemned by the antecedent acts of the United States Government.

Prescribed limits will not permit me to follow out in detail the past history of the United States as a neutral power. It must suffice to recall the memory of readers to a few significant facts in our more recent history:

The recognition of the independence of Greece in her struggle with Turkey, and the voluntary contributions of money and men sent to her; the recognition of the independence of the Spanish provinces of South America, and the war-vessels equipped and sent from the ports of the United States to Brazil during the struggle with Spain for independence; the ships sold to Russia during her war with England, France, and Turkey; the arms and munitions of war manufactured at New Haven, Connecticut, and Providence, Rhode Island, sold and shipped to Turkey to aid her in her late struggle with Russia.

One could scarcely believe, therefore, that the great crime of the Government of Great Britain in the eyes of the Government of the United States, was the recognition by the latter of the Confederate States as a belligerent power, and that a state of war existed between them and the United States. This was the constantly repeated charge against the British Government in the dispatches of the United States Government from the commencement of the war down nearly to the session of the Geneva Conference in 1872. Nevertheless, the Government of the United States, although refusing to concede belligerent rights to the Confederate States, was very ready to take advantage of such concession by other nations, whenever an opportunity offered. The voluminous correspondence of the Secretary of State of the United States Government, relative to the Confederate cruisers and their so-called "depredations," was filled with charges of violations of international law, which could be committed only by a belligerent, and which, it was alleged, had been allowed to be done in the ports of Great Britain. On this foundation was based the subsequent claim for damages, advanced by the Government of the United States against that of Great Britain; and, for the pretended lack of "due diligence" in watching the actions of this Confederate belligerent in her ports, she was mulcted in a heavy sum by the Geneva Conference, and paid it to the Government of the United States.

It is a remarkable fact that the Government of the United States, in no one instance, from the opening to the close of the war, formally spoke of the Confederate Government or States as belligerents. Although on many occasions it acted with the latter as a belligerent, yet no official designations

were ever given to them or their citizens but those of
"insurgents," or "insurrectionists." Perhaps there may be
something in the signification of the words which, combined
with existing circumstances, would express a state of affairs
that the authorities of the Government of the United States
were in no degree willing to admit, and vainly sought to
prevent from becoming manifest to the world.

With like disregard for truth, our cruisers were denounced
as *"pirates"* by the Government of the United States. A pirate,
or armed piratical vessel, is by the law of nations the enemy
of mankind, and can be destroyed by the ships of any nation.
The distinction between a lawful cruiser and a pirate is that
the former has behind it a government which is recognized
by civilized nations as entitled to the rights of war, and from
which the commander of the cruiser receives his commission
or authority, but the pirate recognizes no government, and
is not recognized by any one. That there was such a Government even the United States own courts also decided. In a
prize case (2 Black, 635), Justice Greer delivered the opinion
of the Supreme Court, saying:

It [the war] is not less a civil war, with belligerent parties in
hostile array, because it may be called an 'insurrection' by one
side, and the insurgents be considered as rebels and traitors. It is
not necessary that the independence of the revolted province or
State be acknowledged in order to constitute it a party belligerent
in a war, according to the laws of nations. Foreign nations
acknowledge it a war by a declaration of neutrality. The condition of neutrality can not exist unless there be two belligerent
parties.

The belligerent character of the Confederate States was
thus fully acknowledged by the highest judicial tribunal of
the United States. Yet the Executive Department of the
United States Government denounced our cruisers as
"pirates," our citizens as "insurgents" and "traitors," and the
action of our Government as an insurrection."

During the first months of the war all the principal ports
of the Confederacy were blockaded, and finally every inlet
was either in possession of the enemy or had one or more
vessels watching it. The steamers were independent of wind
and weather, and could hold their positions before a port day
and night. At the same time the ports of neutrals had been
closed against the prizes of our cruisers by proclamations
and orders in council. Our prizes had been sent into ports of

Cuba and Venezuela under the hope that they might gain admittance, but they were either handed over to the enemy under some fraudulent pretext, or expelled. Thus, by the action of the different nations and by the blockade with steamers, no course was left to us but to destroy the prizes, as was done in many instances under the Government of the United States Confederation.

The laws of maritime war are well known. The enemy's vessel when captured becomes the property of the captor, which he may immediately destroy; or he may take the vessel into port, have it adjudicated by an admiralty court as a lawful prize, and sold. That adjudication is the basis of title to the purchaser against all former owners. In these cases the captor sends his prizes to a port of his own country or to a friendly port for adjudication. But, if the ports of his own country are under blockade by his enemy, and the recapture of the prizes, if sent there, most probable, and if, at the same time, all friendly ports are closed against the entrance of his prizes, then there remains no alternative but to destroy the prizes by sinking or burning. Courts of admiralty are established for neutrals; not for the enemy, who has no right of appearance before them. If, therefore, any neutrals suffered during our war for want of adjudication, the fault is with their own Government, and not with our cruisers.

Many other objections were advanced by the United States Government as evidence that we committed a breach of international law with our cruisers. If the Confederate Government had been successful in taking to sea every vessel which it built, it would have swept from the oceans the commerce of the United States, would have raised the blockade of at least some of our ports, and, if by such aid our independence had been secured, there is little probability that such complaints as have been noticed would have received attention, if, indeed, they would have been uttered.

In January, 1871, the British Government proposed to the Government of the United States that a joint commission should be convened to adjust certain differences between the two nations relative to the fisheries, the Canadian boundary, etc. To this proposition the latter acceded, on condition that the so-called Alabama claims should also be considered. To this condition Great Britain assented. In the Convention the American Commissioners proposed an arbitration of these claims. The British Commissioners replied that her Majesty's Government could not admit that Great Britain had failed to discharge toward the United States the duties imposed on her by the rules of international law, or that she was justly liable to make good to the United States the losses occasioned by the acts of the cruisers to which the American Commissioners referred.

Without following the details, it may be summarily stated that the Geneva Conference ensued. That decided that "England should have fulfilled her duties as a neutral by the exercise of a diligence equal to the gravity of the danger," and that "the circumstances were of a nature to call for the exercise, on the part of her Britannic Majesty's Government, of all possible solicitude for the observance of the rights and duties involved in the proclamation of neutrality issued by her Majesty on May 13, 1861." The Conference also added: "It can not be denied that there were moments when its watchfulness seemed to fail, and when feebleness in certain branches of the public service resulted in great detriment to the United States."

The claims presented to the Conference for damages done by our several cruisers were as follows: The Alabama, $7,050,293.76; the Boston, $400; the Chickamauga, $183,-070.73; the Florida, $4,057,934.69; the Clarence, tender of the Florida, $66,736.10; the Tacony, tender of the Florida, $169,198.81; the Georgia, $431,160.72; the Jefferson Davis, $7,752; the Nashville, $108,433.95; the Retribution, $29,-018.53; the Sallie, $5,540; the Shenandoah, $6,656,838.81; the Sumter, $179,697.67; the Tallahassee, $836,841.83. Total, $19,782,917.60. Miscellaneous, $479,033; increased insurance, $6,146,219.71. Aggregate, $26,408,170.31.

The Conference rejected the claims against the Boston, the Jefferson Davis, and the Sallie, and awarded to the United States Government $15,500,000 in gold.

But the indirect damages upon the commerce of the United States produced by these cruisers were far beyond the amount of the claims presented to the Geneva Conference. The number of ships owned in the United States at the commencement of the war, which were subsequently transferred to foreign owners by a British register, was 715, and the amount of their tonnage was 480,882 tons. Such are the laws of the United States that not one of them has been allowed to resume an American register.

In the year 1860 nearly seventy per cent of the foreign commerce of the country was carried on in American ships. But, in consequence of the danger of capture by our cruisers to which these ships were exposed, the amount of this commerce carried by them had dwindled down in 1864 to forty-six per cent. It continued to decline after the war, and in 1872 it had fallen to twenty-eight and a half per cent.

Before the war the amount of American tonnage was second only to that of Great Britain, and we were competing with her for the first place. At that time the tonnage of the coasting trade, which had grown from insignificance, was 1,735,863 tons. Three years later, in 1864, it had declined to about 867,931 tons.

The damage to the articles of export is illustrated by the decline in breadstuffs exported from the Northern States. In the last four months of each of the following years the value of this export was as follows: 1861, $42,500,000; 1862, $27,842,090; 1863, $8,909,042; 1864, $1,850,819. Some of this decline resulted from good crops in England; but, in other respects, it was a consequence of causes growing out of the war.

The increase in the rates of marine insurance, in consequence of the danger of capture by the cruisers, was variable. But the gross amount so paid was presented as a claim to the Conference, as given above.

Chapter 25

Federal Subversion of Tennessee and Louisiana

ON THE CAPTURE of Nashville, on February 25, 1862, Andrew Johnson was made military Governor of Tennessee, with the rank of brigadier-general, and immediately entered on the duties of his office. This step was taken by the President of the United States under the pretense of executing that provision of the Constitution which is in these words:

The United States shall guarantee to every State in this Union a republican form of government.

The administration was conducted according to the will and pleasure of the Governor, which was the supreme law. Public officers were required to take an oath of allegiance to the United States Government, and upon refusal were expelled from office. Newspaper-offices were closed, and their publication suppressed. Subsequently the offices were sold out under the provisions of the confiscation act. All persons using "treasonable and seditious" language were arrested and required to take the oath of allegiance to the Government of the United States, and give bonds for the future, or to go into exile. Clergymen, upon their refusal to take the oath, were confined in the prisons until they could be sent away. School-teachers and editors and finally large numbers of private citizens were arrested and held until they took the oath. Conflicts became frequent in the adjacent country. Murders and the violent destruction of property ensued.

On October 21, 1862, an order for an election of members of the United States Congress in the ninth and tenth State districts was issued. Every voter was required to give satisfactory evidence of "loyalty" to the Northern Government. Two persons were chosen and admitted to seats in that body.

That portion of the State in the possession of the forces of the United States continued without change, under the authority of the military Governor, until the beginning of 1864. Measures were then commenced by the Governor for an organization of a State government in sympathy with the Government of the United States. These measures were subsequently known as the "process for State reconstruction." The Governor issued his proclamation for an election of county officers on March 5th, to be held in the various counties of the State whenever it was practicable. "It is not expected," says the Governor, "that the enemies of the United States will propose to vote, nor is it intended that they be permitted to vote or hold office." In addition to the possession of the usual qualifications, the voter was required to take the following oath:

I solemnly swear that I will henceforth support the Constitution of the United States, and defend it against the assaults of all its enemies; that I will hereafter be, and conduct myself as, a true and faithful citizen of the United States, freely and voluntarily claiming to be subject to all the duties and obligations, and entitled to all the rights and privileges, of such citizenship; that I ardently desire the suppression of the present insurrection and rebellion against the Government of the United States, the success of its armies, and the defeat of all those who oppose them; and that the Constitution of the United States, and all laws and proclamations made in pursuance thereof, may be speedily and permanently established and enforced over all the people, States, and Territories thereof; and, further, that I will hereafter aid and assist all loyal people in the accomplishment of these results.

The election was a failure, and all further efforts at reconstruction were for a time suspended. An attempt was made at the end of 1864 to obtain a so-called convention to amend the State Constitution, and a body was assembled which, without any regular authority, adopted amendments. These were submitted to the voters on February 22, 1865, and declared to be ratified by a vote of twenty-five thousand, in a State where the vote, in 1860, was one hundred and forty-five thousand. Slavery was abolished, other changes made, so-called State officers elected, and this body of voters was proclaimed as the reconstructed State of Tennessee, and one of the United States. Such was the method adopted in Tennessee to execute the provision of the Constitution which says:

The United States shall guarantee to every State in this Union a republican form of government.

The next attempt to guarantee "a republican form of government" to a State was commenced in Louisiana by the military occupation of New Orleans, on May 1, 1862. The

United States forces were under the command of Major-General Benjamin F. Butler. Martial law was declared, and Brigadier-General George F. Shepley was appointed military Governor of the State. It is unnecessary to relate in detail the hostile actions which were committed, as they had no resemblance to such warfare as is alone permissible by the rules of international law or the usages of civilization.

On December 15, 1862, Major-General N. P. Banks took command of the military forces, and Major-General Butler retired. The military Governor, early in August, had attempted to set on foot a judicial system for the city and State. For this purpose he appointed judges to two of the district courts, of which the judges were absent, and authorized a third, who held a commission dated anterior to 1861, to resume the sessions. This was an establishment of three new courts, with the jurisdiction and powers pertaining to the courts that previously bore their names, by a military officer representing the Executive of the United States. These were the only courts within the territory of the State held by the United States forces which claimed to have civil jurisdiction. But this jurisdiction was limited to citizens of the parish of Orleans as against defendants residing in the State. As to other residents of the State, outside the parish of Orleans, there was no court in which they could be sued. In this condition several parishes were held by the United States forces.

It was therefore necessary to take another step in order to enable the military power to administer civil affairs. It consisted in the publication of the following order by the President of the United States:

EXECUTIVE MANSION, WASHINGTON, *October 20, 1862.*
The insurrection which has for some time prevailed in several of the States of this Union, including Louisiana, having temporarily subverted and swept away the civil institutions of that State, including the judiciary and the judicial authorities of the Union, so that it has become necessary to hold the State in military occupation; and it being indispensably necessary that there shall be some judicial tribunal existing there capable of administering justice, I have therefore thought it proper to appoint, and I do hereby constitute a provisional court, which shall be a court of record for the State of Louisiana; and I do hereby appoint Charles A. Peabody, of New York, to be a provisional judge to hold said court, with authority to hear, try, and determine all causes civil and criminal, including causes in law, equity, revenue, and admiralty,

and particularly with all such powers and jurisdiction as belong to the District and Circuit Courts of the United States, conforming his proceedings, so far as possible, to the course of proceedings and practice which has been customary in the courts of the United States and Louisiana—his judgment to be final and conclusive. And I do hereby authorize and empower the said judge to make and establish such rules and regulations as may be necessary for the exercise of his jurisdiction, and to appoint a prosecuting attorney, marshal, and clerk of the said court, who shall perform the functions of attorney, marshal, and clerk according to such proceedings and practice as before mentioned, and such rules and regulations as may be made and established by said judge. These appointments are to continue during the pleasure of the President not extending beyond the military occupation of the city of New Orleans, or the restoration of the civil authority in that city and in the State of Louisiana. . . .

By the President: ABRAHAM LINCOLN.

W. H. SEWARD, *Secretary of State.*

This so-called court, as its judge said, "was always governed by the rules and principles of law, adhering to all the rules and forms of civil tribunals, and avoiding everything like a military administration of justice. In criminal matters it summoned a grand jury, and submitted to it all charges for examination." Yet, when its judgments and mandates were to be executed, that execution could come only from the same power by which the court was constituted, and that was the military power of the United States holding the country in military occupation. Therefore, to this end the military and naval forces were pledged. Hence it was the military power, as has been said, administering civil affairs.

The Constitution of the United States says:

The judicial power of the United States shall be vested in one Supreme Court, and in such inferior courts as the Congress may from time to time ordain and establish. (Article III, Section 1).

This provisional court was neither ordained nor established by Congress; it had not, therefore, vested in it any of the judicial power of the United States. Neither does the Constitution give to Congress any power by which it can constitute an independent State court within the limits of any State in the Union, as Louisiana was said to be.

On December 3d, in compliance with an order of the military Governor, Shepley, a so-called election was held for members of the United States Congress in the first and second State districts, each composed of about half the city of New Orleans and portions of the surrounding parishes. Those who had taken the oath of allegiance were allowed to vote. In the first district, Benjamin F. Flanders received 2,370 votes, and all others 273. In the second district, Michael Hahn received 2,799 votes, and all others 2,318. These persons presented themselves at Washington, and resolutions to admit them to seats were reported by the Committee on Elections in the House of Representatives. It was urged that the military Governor had conformed in every particular to the Constitution and laws of Louisiana, so that the election had every essential of a regular election in a time of most profound peace, with the exception of the fact that the proclamation for the election was issued by the military instead of the civil Governor of the State. The law required the proclamation to be issued by the civil Governor; so that, if these persons were admitted to seats after an election called by a military Governor, Congress thereby recognized as valid a military order of a so-called Executive that unceremoniously set aside a provision of the State civil law, and was anti-republican and a positive usurpation. Again, all the departments of the United States Government had acted on the theory that the Confederate States were in a state of insurrection, and that the Union was unbroken; under this theory, they could come back to the Union only with all the laws unimpaired which they themselves had made for their own government. Congress was as much bound to uphold the laws of Louisiana, in all their extent and in all their parts, as it was to uphold the laws of New York, or any other State, whose civil policy had not been disturbed. Both those persons, however, were admitted to seats—yeas, 92; nays, 44.

The work of constituting the State of Louisiana out of the small portion of her population and of her territory held by the forces of the United States still went on. The proposition now was to hold a so-called State Convention and frame a new Constitution, but its advocates were so few that nothing was accomplished during the year 1863. The object of the military power was to secure such civil authority as to enforce the abolition of slavery; and, until the way was clear to that result, every method of organization was held in abeyance.

Meanwhile, on December 8, 1863, the President of the United States issued a proclamation which contained his plan for making a Union State out of a fragment of a Confederate

State, and also granting an amnesty to the general mass of the people on taking an oath of allegiance.

In a message to Congress, of the same date with the preceding proclamation, the President of the United States, after explaining the objects of the proclamation, says:

In the midst of other cares, however important, we must not lose sight of the fact that the war-power is still our main reliance. To that power alone can we look, for a time, to give confidence to the people in the contested regions that the insurgent power will not again overrun them.

The intelligent reader will observe that this plan of the President of the United States to restore States to the Union, to occupy the places of those which he had been attempting to destroy, does not contain a single feature to secure a republican form of government, nor a single provision authorized by the Constitution of the United States. With his usurped war-power to sustain him in the work of destruction, he found it easy to destroy; but he was powerless to create or to restore. The whole science of a republican government is to be found in this sentence of the Declaration of Independence, made by the representatives of the United States of America, in Congress assembled, on July 4, 1776. It says:

That, to secure these rights [certain unalienable rights], governments are instituted among men—deriving their just powers from the consent of the governed; that, whenever any form of government becomes destructive of these ends, it is the right of the people to alter or abolish it, and to institute a new government, laying its foundation on such principles, and organizing its powers in such form, as to them shall seem most likely to effect their safety and happiness.

Who, then, had a right to "institute" a republican government for Louisiana? No human beings whatever but the people of Louisiana; not the strangers, not the slaves, but the manhood that knew its rights and dared to maintain them. Under what principles, then, could a citizen of Massachusetts, whether clothed in regimentals or a civilian's dress, come into Louisiana and attempt to set up a State government? Under no principles, but only by the power of the invader and the usurper. Under what principles, then, could the Government of the United States appear in Louisiana and attempt to institute a state government? As has been said above, it was the act of an invader and a usurper. Yet it proposed to "institute" a republican State government. How could an invader attempt to "institute" a republican State government? an act which can be done only by the free and unconstrained action of the people themselves. It has been charged that this and every similar act of the President of the United States was in violation of his duty to maintain and observe the requirements and restrictions of the Constitution, and to uphold in each State a republican form of government. To specify, the following is offered as an example. He did "proclaim, declare, and make known—

that, whenever any number of persons, not less than one tenth of the number of voters at the last Presidential election, shall reëstablish a State government, which shall be republican [!] and in no wise contravening said oath, such shall be recognized as the true government of the State."

One tenth of the voters can not establish a republican State government, which requires the consent of the people of the State to make its powers just, as has been shown above. Of the government thus established by one tenth of the voters, he says:

Such shall be recognized as the true government of the State, and the State shall receive thereunder the benefits of the constitutional provision which declares that "the United States shall guarantee to every State in this Union a republican form of government."

It is proper here to inquire who and what was the tenth to whom this power to rule the State was to be given. It will be seen, by reference to the proclamation, that each voter of the one tenth, in order to be qualified, is required to take an oath with certain promises in it, which are prescribed by an outside or foreign authority. This condition of itself is fatal to a republican State government, that "derives its just powers from the consent of the governed." Free consent—not cheerful consent, but unconstrained and unconditioned consent—is required that "just powers" may be derived from it. To proceed with the narration. Under the above-mentioned proclamation of the President of the United States, Major-General Banks issued at New Orleans, on January 11, 1864, a proclamation for an election of State officers, and for members of a State Constitutional Convention. The State officers, when elected, were to constitute, as the proclamation said, "the civil government of the State under the Constitution and laws of Louisiana, except so much of the said Constitution and laws as recognize, regulate, or relate to slavery, which, being inconsistent with the present condition of public affairs, and plainly inapplicable to any class of persons now existing within its limits, must be suspended." The number of votes given for State officers was 10,270. The population of the State in 1860 was 708,902. The so-called Governor-elect was inaugurated on March 4th, and on March 11th he was invested with the powers hitherto exercised by the military Governor for the President of the United States. On the same day Major-General Banks issued an order relative to the election of delegates to a so-called State Convention. The most important provisions of it defined the qualifications of voters. The delegates were elected entirely within the army lines of the forces of the United States. The so-called Convention assembled and adopted a so-called Constitution, declaring "instantaneous, universal, uncompensated, unconditional emancipation of slaves." The meager vote on the Constitution was, for its adoption, 6,836; for its rejection, 1,566. The vote of New Orleans was, yeas 4,664, nays 789. This state of affairs continued after the close of the war. Violent disputes arose as to the validity of the so-called Constitution. The so-called Legislature elected under it adopted Article XIII as an amendment to the Constitution of the United States, prohibiting the existence of slavery in the United States.

Chapter 26

Federal Subversion of Arkansas and Virginia

THE PROCEEDINGS in Arkansas to "institute" a republican State government were inaugurated by an order from the President of the United States to Major-General Steele, commanding the United States forces in Arkansas. At this time the regular government of the State, established by the consent of the people, was in full operation outside the lines of the United States army. The military order of the President, dated January 20, 1864, said:

Sundry citizens of the State of Arkansas petitioned me that an election may be held in that State, in which to elect a Governor; that it be assumed at that election, and thenceforward, that the Constitution and laws of the State, as before the rebellion, are in full force, except that the Constitution is so modified as to declare that there shall be neither slavery nor involuntary servitude, etc.

The order then directs the election to be held for State officers, prescribes the qualifications of voters and the oath to be taken, and directs the General to administer to the officers thus chosen an oath to support the Constitution of the United States, and the "modified Constitution of the State of Arkansas," when they shall be declared qualified and empowered immediately to enter upon the duties of their offices.

The reader can scarcely fail to notice the novel method here adopted to modify or amend the State Constitution. It should be called the process by "assumption"—that is, assume it to be modified, and it is so modified. Then the President orders the officers-elect to be required to swear, on their oath, to support "the modified Constitution of the State of Arkansas." Now, unless the Constitution was thus modified by assuming it to be modified, these State officers were required by oath to support that which did not exist. But it was not so modified. No Constitution or other instrument in the world containing a grant of powers can be modified by assumption, unless it be the Constitution of the United States, as shown by recent experience. Yet the chief object for which these officers were elected and qualified was to carry out these so-called modifications of the State Constitution. Meantime some persons in the northern part of Arkansas, acting under the proclamation of December 8, 1863, got together a so-called State Convention on January 8, 1864, and adopted a revised Constitution, containing the slavery prohibition, etc. This was ordered to be submitted to a popular vote, and at the same time State officers were to be elected. President Lincoln acceded to these proceedings after they had been placed under the direction of the military commander, General Steele. The election was held, the Constitution received twelve thousand votes, and the State officers were declared to be elected. Then Arkansas came forth a so-called republican State, "instituted" by military authority, and, of course, received the benefit of the constitutional provision, which declares that "the United States shall guarantee to every State in this Union a republican form of government." It should be added that Arkansas, thus "instituted" a State, was regarded by the Government of the United States as competent to give as valid a vote as New York, Massachusetts, or any other Northern State, for the ratification of Article XIII, as an amendment to the Constitution of the United States, prohibiting the existence of slavery in the United States. The vote was thus given; it was counted, and served to make up the exact number deemed by the managers to be necessary. The perversion of true republican principles was greater in Virginia than in any other State, through the coöperation of the Government of the United States. In the winter of 1860–'61 a special session of the Legislature of the State convened at Richmond and passed an act directing the people to elect delegates to a State Convention to be held on February 14, 1861. The Convention assembled, and was occupied with the subject of Federal relations and the adjustment of difficulties until the call for troops by President Lincoln was made, when an ordinance of secession was passed. The contiguity of the northwestern counties of the State of Ohio and Pennsylvania led to the manifestation of much opposition to the withdrawal of the State from the Union, and the determination to reorganize that portion into a separate State. This resulted in the assembling of a so-called convention of delegates at Wheeling on June 11th. One of its first acts was to provide for a reorganization of the State government of Virginia by declaring its offices vacant, and the appointment of new officers throughout. This new organization assumed to be the true representative of the State of Virginia, and, after various fortunes, was recognized as such by President Lincoln, as will be presently seen. The next act of the Convention was "to provide for the formation of a new State out of a portion of the territory of this State." Under this act delegates were elected to a so-called Constitutional Convention which framed a so-called Constitution for the new State of West Virginia, which was submitted to a vote of the people in April, 1862, and carried by a large majority of that section. Meantime the Governor of the reorganized government of Virginia, above mentioned, issued his proclamation calling for an election of members, and the assembling of an extra session of the so-called Legislature. This body assembled on May 6, 1862, and, adopting the new Federal process of assumption, it assumed to be the Legislature of the State of Virginia. This body, or Legislature, so called, immediately passed an act giving its consent to the formation of a new State out of the territory of Virginia. The formal act of consent and the draft of the new Constitution of West Virginia above mentioned were ordered by this so-called Legislature to be sent to the Congress of the United States, then in session, with the request that "the said new State be admitted into the Union." On December 31, 1862, the President of the United States approved an act of Congress entitled "An act for the admission of the State of West Virginia into the Union," etc. The act recited as follows:

Whereas, The Legislature of Virginia, by an act passed May 13, 1862, did give its consent to the formation of a new State within the jurisdiction of the said State of Virginia, to be known by the name of West Virginia, etc.

Again it recites:

And whereas both the Convention and the Legislature aforesaid have requested that the new State should be admitted into the Union, and the Constitution aforesaid being republican in form, Congress doth hereby consent that the said forty-eight counties may be formed into a separate and independent State.

It were well to pause for a moment and consider these proceedings in the light of fundamental republican principles. The State of Virginia was not a confederation, but a republic, or nation. Its government was instituted with the consent of the governed, and its powers, therefore, were "just powers." When the State Convention at Richmond passed an ordinance of secession, which was subsequently ratified by sixty thousand majority, it was as valid an act for the people of Virginia as was ever passed by a representative body. When, therefore, disorderly persons in the northwestern counties of the State assembled and declared the ordinance of secession "to be null and void," they rose up against the authority of the State. When they proceeded to elect delegates to a convention to resist the act of the State, and that Convention assembled and organized and proceeded to action, an insurrection against the government of Virginia was begun. When the Convention next declared the State offices to be vacant, and proceeded to fill them by the choice of Francis H. Pierpont for Governor, and other State officers, assuming itself to be the true State Convention of Virginia, it committed an act of revolution. And, when the so-called State officers elected by it entered upon their duties, they inaugurated a revolution. The subsequent organization of the State of West Virginia and its separation from the State of Virginia were acts of secession. Thus we have, in these movements, insurrection, revolution, and secession.

The reader, in his simplicity, may naturally expect to find the Government of the United States arrayed, with all its military forces, against these illegitimate proceedings. Oh, no! It made all the difference in the world, with the ministers of that Government, "whose ox it was that was gored by the bull." When the question of the admission of West Virginia was before the House of Representatives of the United States Congress, Mr. Thaddeus Stevens, of Pennsylvania, declared, with expiatory frankness, that he would not stultify himself by claiming the act to be constitutional. He said, "We know that it is not constitutional, but it is necessary."

It now became necessary for the government of Virginia, represented by Francis H. Pierpont, to emigrate; for the new State of West Virginia embraced the territory in which he was located. He therefore departed, with his carpet-bag, and located at Alexandria, on the Potomac, which became the seat of government of so-called East Virginia. On February 13, 1864, a convention, consisting of a representative from each of the ten counties in part or wholly under the control of the United States forces, assembled at Alexandria to amend the Constitution of the State of Virginia. Some sections providing for the abolition of slavery were declared to be added to the Constitution, and the so-called Convention adjourned. Nothing of importance occurred until after the occupation of Richmond by the United States forces. On May 9, 1865, President Johnson issued an "Executive order to reëstablish the authority of the United States, and execute the laws within the geographical limits known as the State of Virginia." This order recognized the factitious organization, which was begun in West Virginia and then transplanted to Alexandria, as the true government of the State of Virginia, and, by the aid of the United States Government, was now removed to Richmond and set up there. No person was allowed to take any part in this government or to vote under it unless he had previously taken the purgatorial oath above mentioned, and had not held office under the Confederate or any State government. Thus, the taking of his oath, which was prescribed by the President of the United States, became the most important of the qualifications of a voter. Such a government was not republican, for its powers were not derived from the consent of the governed. Such a State government was not in the interest of the people, but in the interest of the United States Government. Thus the voters under the State government of Virginia were required first to protect the Government of the United States, and then they were at liberty to look after their own interests through the State government.

Now, it is charged that such acts on the part of the United States Government were not only entirely unconstitutional, but they caused the complete subversion of the States. The Constitution of the United States knows States in the Union only as they are republican States. The Government of the United States violated the Constitution when it sought to place in the Union mere fictions which had not the first element of a republic. Further, it does not come within the grants of the Constitution, consequently not within the powers of the Government of the United States, to institute a republican form of government at any time or in any place. Such a government can be instituted only by the free consent of those who are to be governed by it. Any interference on the part of the United States to limit, modify, or control this consent goes directly to the nature and objects of the State government, and it ceases to be republican. To admit a State under such a government is entirely unauthorized, revolutionary, subversive of the Constitution, and destructive of the Union of States.

Chapter 27

Second Battle of Manassas

AFTER THE RETREAT of General McClellan to Westover, his army remained inactive about a month. His front was closely watched by a brigade of cavalry, and preparations made to resist a renewal of his attempt upon Richmond from his new base. The main body of our army awaited the development of his intentions, and no important event took place.

Meantime, another army of the enemy, under Major-General Pope, advanced southward from Washington, and crossed the Rappahannock as if to seize Gordonsville, and move thence upon Richmond. Contemporaneously the enemy appeared in force at Fredericksburg, and threatened the railroad from Gordonsville to Richmond, apparently for the purpose of coöperating with the movements of General Pope. To meet the advance of the latter, and restrain, as far as possible, the atrocities which he threatened to perpetrate upon our defenseless citizens, General Jackson, with his own and Ewell's division, was ordered to proceed on July 13th toward Gordonsville.

The victory of Cedar Run effectually checked the invader for the time; but it soon became apparent that his army was receiving a large increase. The corps of Major-General Burnside, from North Carolina, which had reached Fredericksburg, was reported to have moved up the Rappahannock, a few days after the battle, to unite with General Pope, and a part of General McClellan's army had left Westover for the same purpose. It therefore seemed that active operations on the James were no longer contemplated, and that the most effectual way to relieve Richmond from any danger of an attack would be to reënforce General Jackson and advance upon General Pope.

Accordingly, on August 13th, Longstreet, Anderson, and Stuart were ordered to proceed to Gordonsville. On the 16th the troops began to move from the vicinity of Gordonsville toward the Rapidan, on the north side of which, extending along the Orange and Alexandria Railroad in the direction of Culpeper Court-house, the army of invasion lay in great force. It was determined, with the cavalry, to destroy the

372

railroad-bridge over the Rappahannock in rear of the enemy, while Jackson and Longstreet crossed the Rapidan and attacked his left flank. But, the enemy becoming apprised of our design, hastily retreated beyond the Rappahannock. On the 21st our forces moved toward that river, and some sharp skirmishing ensued with our cavalry that had crossed at Beverly's Ford. As it had been determined in the mean time not to attempt the passage of the river at that point with the army, the cavalry withdrew to the south side. Soon afterward the enemy appeared in great strength on the opposite bank, and an active fire was kept up during the rest of the day between his artillery and the batteries attached to Jackson's leading division, under Brigadier-General Taliaferro.

But, as our positions on the south bank of the Rappahannock were commanded by those on the north bank, and which served to guard all the fords, General Lee determined to seek a more favorable place to cross higher up the river, and thus gain his adversary's right. Accordingly, General Longstreet was directed to leave Kelly's Ford on the 21st, and take the position in the vicinity of Beverly's Ford and the Orange and Alexandria Railroad bridge, then held by Jackson, in order to mask the movement of the latter, who was instructed to ascend the river. On the 22d Jackson proceeded up the Rappahannock, leaving Trimble's brigade near Freeman's Ford to protect his train. In the afternoon Longstreet sent General Hood with his own and Whiting's brigade to relieve Trimble. Hood had just reached the position, when he and Trimble were attacked by a considerable force which had crossed at Freeman's Ford. After a short but spirited engagement, the enemy was driven precipitately over the river with heavy loss. General Jackson attempted to cross at Warrenton Springs Ford, but was interrupted by a heavy rain, which caused the river to rise so rapidly as to be impassable for infantry and artillery, and he withdrew the troops that had reached the opposite side. General Stuart, who had been directed to cut the railroad in rear of General Pope's army, crossed the Rappahannock on the morning of the 22d, about six miles above the Springs, with parts of Lee's and Robertson's brigades. He reached Catlet's Station that night, but was prevented destroying the railroad-bridge there by the same storm that arrested Jackson's movements. He captured more than three hundred prisoners, including a number of officers. Apprehensive of the effect of the rain upon the streams, he recrossed the Rappahannock at Warrenton Springs. The rise of the river, rendering the lower fords impassable, enabled the enemy to concentrate his main body opposite General Jackson, and on the 24th Longstreet was ordered by General Lee to proceed to his support. Although retarded by the swollen condition of Hazel River and other tributaries of the Rappahannock, he reached Jeffersonton in the afternoon. General Jackson's command lay between that place and the Spring's Ford, and a warm cannonade was progressing between the batteries of General A. P. Hill's division and those in his front. The enemy was massed between Warrenton and the Springs, and guarded the fords of the Rappahannock as far above as Waterloo.

The army of General McClellan had left Westover, and a part had marched to join General Pope. It was reported that the rest would soon follow. The greater part of the army of General Cox had also been withdrawn from the Kanawha Valley for the same purpose. Two brigades of D. H. Hill's division, under General Ripley, had already been ordered from Richmond, and the remainder were to follow; also, McLaws's division, two brigades under General Walker, and Hampton's cavalry brigade. In pursuance of the plan of operations now determined upon, Jackson was directed, on the 25th, to cross above Waterloo and move around the enemy's right so as to strike the Orange and Alexandria Railroad in his rear. Longstreet, in the mean time, was to divert his attention by threatening him in front, and to follow Jackson as soon as the latter should be sufficiently advanced.

General Jackson crossed the Rappahannock on the 25th, about four miles above Waterloo, and, after sunset on the 26th, reached the railroad at Bristoe Station. At Gainesville he was joined by General Stuart, with the brigades of Robertson and Fitzhugh Lee, who continued with him during his operations, and effectually guarded both his flanks.

General Jackson was now between the large army of General Pope and Washington City, without having encountered any considerable force. At Bristoe two trains of cars were captured and a few prisoners taken. Determining, notwithstanding the darkness of the night and the long and arduous march of the day, to capture the depot of the enemy at Manassas Junction, about seven miles distant, General Trimble volunteered to proceed at once to that place with the Twenty-first North Carolina and the Twenty-first Georgia Regiments. The offer was accepted, and, to render success more certain, General Stuart was directed to accompany the expedition with part of his cavalry. About midnight the place was taken with little difficulty. Eight pieces of artillery, with their horses, ammunition, and equipments were captured; more than three hundred prisoners, one hundred and seventy-five horses, besides those belonging to the artillery, two hundred new tents, and immense quantities of commissary and quartermaster's stores, fell into our hands.

Ewell's division, with the Fifth Virginia Cavalry under Colonel Rosser, were left at Bristoe Station, and the rest of the command arrived at the Junction early on the 27th. Soon a considerable force of the enemy, under Brigadier-General Taylor, of New Jersey, approached from the direction of Alexandria, and pushed forward boldly to recover the stores. After a sharp engagement he was routed and driven back, leaving his killed and wounded on the field. The troops remained at Manassas Junction during the day, and supplied themselves with everything they required. In the afternoon, two brigades advanced against General Ewell, at Bristoe, from the direction of Warrenton Junction, but were broken and repulsed. Their place was soon supplied with fresh troops, but it was apparent that the commander had now become aware of the situation of affairs, and had turned upon General Jackson with his whole force. General Ewell, perceiving the strength of the column, withdrew and rejoined General Jackson, having first destroyed the railroad-bridge over Broad Run. The enemy halted at Bristoe. General Jackson, having a much inferior force to General Pope, retired from Manassas Junction and took a position west of the turnpike-road from Warrenton to Alexandria, where he could more readily unite with the approaching column of Longstreet. Having supplied the wants of his troops, he was compelled, through lack of transportation, to destroy the rest of the captured property. Many thousand pounds of bacon, a thousand barrels of corned beef, two thousand barrels of saltpork, and two thousand barrels of flour, besides other property of great value, were burned.

During the night of the 27th of August Taliaferro's division crossed the turnpike near Groveton and halted on the west side, near the battle-field of July 21, 1861, where it was joined on the 28th by the divisions of Hill and Ewell. During the afternoon the enemy, approaching from the direction of Warrenton down the turnpike toward Alexandria, exposed his left flank, and General Jackson determined to attack him. A fierce and sanguinary conflict ensued which continued until about 9 P.M., when he slowly fell back and left us in possession of the field. The loss on both sides was heavy. On the next morning (the 29th) the enemy had taken a position to interpose his army between General Jackson and Alexandria, and about 10 A.M. opened with artillery upon the right of Jackson's line. The troops of the latter were disposed in rear of Groveton, along the line of the unfinished branch of the Manassas Gap Railroad, and extending from a point a short distance west of the turnpike toward Sudley Mill, Jackson's division under Brigadier-General Starke being on the right, Ewell's under General Lawton in the center, and A. P. Hill on the left. The attacking columns were evidently concentrating on Jackson with the design of overwhelming him before the arrival of Longstreet. This latter officer left his position opposite Warrenton Springs on the 26th and marched to join Jackson. On the 28th, arriving at Thoroughfare Gap, he found the enemy prepared to dispute his progress. Holding the eastern extremity of the pass with a large force, the enemy directed a heavy fire of artillery upon the road leading to it and upon the sides of the mountain. An attempt was made to turn his right, but, before our troops reached their destination, he advanced to the attack, and, being vigorously repulsed, withdrew to his position at the eastern end of the Gap, keeping up an active fire of artillery until dark. He then retreated. On the morning of the 29th Longstreet's command resumed its march, the sound of cannon at Manassas announcing that Jackson was already engaged. The head of the column came upon the field in rear of the enemy's left, which had already opened with artillery upon Jackson's right, as above stated. Longstreet immediately placed some of his batteries in position, but, before he could complete his dispositions to attack the force before him, it withdrew to another part of the field. He then took position on the right of Jackson, Hood's two brigades, supported by Evans, being deployed across the turnpike and at right angles to it. These troops were supported on the left by three brigades under General Wilcox, and by a like force on the right under General Kemper. D. R. Jones's division formed the extreme right of the line, resting on the Manassas Gap Railroad. The cavalry guarded our right and left flanks, that on the right being under General Stuart in person. After the arrival of Longstreet the enemy changed his position and began to concentrate opposite Jackson's left, opening a brisk artillery-fire, which was responded to by some of A. P. Hill's batteries.

Soon afterward General Stuart reported the approach of a large force from the direction of Bristoe Station, threatening Longstreet's right. But no serious attack was made, and, after firing a few shots, that force withdrew. Meanwhile a large column advanced to assail the left of Jackson's position, occupied by the division of General A. P. Hill. The attack was received by his troops with their accustomed steadiness, and the battle raged with great fury. The enemy was repeatedly repulsed, but again pressed on the attack with fresh troops. Once he succeeded in penetrating an interval between General Gregg's brigade on the extreme left and that of General Thomas, but was quickly driven back with great slaughter by the Fourteenth South Carolina Regiment, then in reserve, and the Forty-ninth Georgia of Thomas's brigade. The contest was close and obstinate; the combatants sometimes delivered their fire at a few paces. General Gregg, who was most exposed, was reënforced by Hays's brigade under Colonel Forno. Gregg had successfully and most gallantly resisted the attack until the ammunition of his brigade was exhausted and all his field-officers but two killed or wounded. The reënforcement was of like high-tempered steel, and together in hand-to-hand fight they held their post until they were relieved, after several hours of severe fighting, by Early's brigade and the Eighth Louisiana Regiment. General Early drove the enemy back with heavy loss, and pursued about two hundred yards beyond the line of battle, when he was recalled to the position on the railroad, where Thomas, Pender, and Archer had firmly held their ground against every attack. While the battle was raging on Jackson's left, Hood and Evans were ordered by Longstreet to advance, but, before the order could be obeyed, Hood was himself attacked, and his command became at once warmly engaged. The enemy was repulsed by Hood after a severe contest, and fell back, closely followed by our troops.

The battle continued until 9 P. M., the foe retreating until he reached a strong position, which he held with a large force. Our troops remained in their advanced position until early next morning, when they were withdrawn to their first line. One piece of artillery, several stands of colors, and a number of prisoners were captured. Our loss was severe. On the morning of the 30th the enemy again advanced, and skirmishing began along the line. The troops of Jackson and Longstreet maintained their position of the previous day. At noon the firing of the batteries ceased, and all was quiet for some hours.

About 3 P. M. the enemy, having massed his troops in front of General Jackson, advanced against his position in strong force. His front line pushed forward until it was engaged at close quarters by Jackson's troops, when its progress was checked, and a fierce and bloody struggle ensued. A second and third line of great strength moved up to support the first, but in doing so came within easy range of a position a little in advance of Longstreet's left. He immediately ordered up two batteries, and, two others being thrown forward about the same time by Colonel S. D. Lee, the supporting lines were broken, and fell back in confusion under their well-directed and destructive fire. Their repeated efforts to rally were unavailing, and Jackson's troops, being thus relieved from the pressure of overwhelming numbers, began to press steadily forward, driving everything before them. The enemy retreated in confusion, suffering severely from our artillery, which advanced as he retired. General Longstreet, anticipating the order for a general advance, now threw his whole command against the center and left. The whole line swept steadily on, driving the opponents with great carnage from each successive position, until 10 P. M., when darkness put an end to the battle and the pursuit.

The obscurity of the night and the uncertainty of the fords of Bull Run rendered it necessary to suspend operations until morning, when the cavalry, being pushed forward, discovered that the retreat had continued to the strong position of Centreville, about four miles beyond Bull Run. The prevalence of a heavy rain, which began during the night, threatened to render Bull Run impassable, and to impede our movements. Longstreet remained on the battle-field to engage attention and to protect parties for the burial of the dead and the removal of the wounded, while Jackson proceeded by Sudley's Ford to the Little River turnpike to turn the enemy's right, and intercept his retreat to Washington. Jackson's progress was retarded by the inclemency of the weather and the fatigue of his troops. He reached the turnpike in the evening, and the next day (September 1st) advanced by that road toward Fairfax Court-House. The enemy in the mean time was falling back rapidly toward Washington, and had thrown a strong force to Germantown, on the Little River turnpike, to cover his line of retreat from Centreville. The advance of Jackson encountered him at Ox Hill, near Germantown, about 5 P. M. Line of battle was at once formed, and two brigades were thrown forward to attack and ascertain the strength of the position. A cold and drenching rain-storm drove in the faces of our troops as they advanced and gallantly engaged. They were subsequently supported, and the conflict was obstinately maintained until dark, when the enemy retreated, having lost two general officers, one of whom—Major-General Kearney —was left dead on the field. Longstreet's command arrived after the action was over, and the next morning it was found that the retreat had been so rapid that the attempt to intercept was abandoned. The proximity of the fortifications around Alexandria and Washington was enough to prevent further pursuit. Our army rested during the 2d near Chantilly, the retreating foe being followed only by our cavalry, who continued to harass him until he reached the shelter of his entrenchments.

In the series of engagements on the plains of Manassas more than seven thousand prisoners were taken, in addition to about two thousand wounded left in our hands. Thirty pieces of artillery, upward of twenty thousand stand of small-arms, numerous colors, and a large amount of stores, besides those taken by General Jackson at Manassas Junction, were captured.

Major-General Pope in his report says:

The whole force that I had at Centreville, as reported to me by the corps commanders, on the morning of the 1st of September, was . . . in all, 63,000 men. . . . The small fraction of 20,500 men was all of the 91,000 veteran troops from Harrison's Landing which ever drew trigger under my command.

Our losses in the engagement at Manassas Plains were considerable. The number killed was 1,090; wounded, 6,154— total, 7,244. The loss of the enemy in killed, wounded, and missing was estimated between 15,000 and 20,000.

Chapter 28

Sharpsburg (Antietam Creek)

THE ENEMY having retired to the protection of the fortifications around Washington and Alexandria, Lee's army marched, on September 3d, toward Leesburg. The armies of Generals McClellan and Pope had now been brought back to the point from which they set out on the campaign of the spring and summer. The objects of those campaigns had been frustrated, and the hostile designs against the coast of North Carolina and in western Virginia, thwarted by the withdrawal of the main body of the forces from those regions.

Northeastern Virginia was freed from the presence of the invader. His forces had withdrawn to the intrenchments of Washington. Soon after the arrival of our army at Leesburg, information was received that the hostile troops which had occupied Winchester had retired to Harper's Ferry. The war was thus transferred from the interior to the frontier, and the supplies of rich and productive districts were made accessible to our army. To prolong a state of affairs in every way desirable, and not to permit the season for active operations to pass without endeavoring to impose further check on our assailant, the best course appeared to be the transfer of our army into Maryland. Although not properly equipped for invasion, lacking much of the material of war, and deficient in transportation, the troops poorly provided with clothing, and thousands of them without shoes, it was yet believed to be strong enough to detain the opposing army upon the northern frontier until the approach of winter should render its advance into Virginia difficult, if not impracticable.

The condition of Maryland encouraged the belief that the presence of our army, though numerically inferior to that of the North, would induce the Washington Government to retain all its available force to provide against contingencies which its conduct toward the people of that State gave reason to apprehend. At the same time it was hoped that military success might afford us an opportunity to aid the citizens of Maryland in any efforts they should be disposed to make to recover their liberty. It was decided to cross the Potomac east of the Blue Ridge, in order, by threatening Washington and

Baltimore, to cause the enemy to withdraw from the south bank, where his presence endangered our communications and the safety of those engaged in the removal of our wounded and the captured property from the late battle-field. Having accomplished this result, it was proposed to move the army into western Maryland, establish our communication with Richmond through the Valley of the Shenandoah, and, by threatening Pennsylvania, induce the enemy to withdraw from our territory for the protection of his own.

The commands of Longstreet and D. H. Hill reached Sharpsburg on the morning of the 15th. General Jackson arrived early on the 16th, and General J. G. Walker came up in the afternoon. The movements of General McLaws were embarrassed by the presence of the enemy in Crampton Gap. He retained his position until the 14th, when, finding that he was not to be attacked, he gradually withdrew his command toward the Potomac, then crossed at Harper's Ferry, and marched by way of Shepardstown. His progress was slow, and he did not reach the battle-field at Sharpsburg until some time after the engagement of the 17th began.

At this time the letter, from which the following extract is made, was addressed by me to General R. E. Lee, commanding our forces in Maryland:

SIR: It is deemed proper that you should, in accordance with established usage, announce, by proclamation, to the people of Maryland, the motives and purposes of your presence among them at the head of an invading army; and you are instructed in such proclamation to make known, etc.

In obedience to instructions, General Lee issued the following address:

HEADQUARTERS, ARMY OF NORTHERN VIRGINIA,
NEAR FREDERICK,
September 8, 1862

TO THE PEOPLE OF MARYLAND: It is right that you should know the purpose that has brought the army under my command within the limits of your State, so far as that purpose concerns yourselves.

The people of the Confederate States have long watched, with the deepest sympathy, the wrongs and outrages that have been inflicted upon the citizens of a Commonwealth allied to the States of the South by the strongest social, political, and commercial ties, and reduced to the condition of a conquered province.

Under the pretense of supporting the Constitution, but in violation of its most valuable provisions, your citizens have been arrested and imprisoned upon no charge, and contrary to the forms of law. . . . The government of your chief city has been usurped by armed strangers; your Legislature has been dissolved by the unlawful arrest of its members; freedom of the press and of speech has been suppressed; words have been declared offenses by an arbitrary decree of the Federal Executive; and citizens ordered to be tried by military commissions for what they may dare to speak.

Believing that the people of Maryland possess a spirit too lofty to submit to such a Government, the people of the South have long wished to aid you in throwing off this foreign yoke, to enable you again to enjoy the inalienable rights of freemen, and restore the independence and sovereignty of your State.

In obedience to this wish, our army has come among you, and is prepared to assist you with the power of its arms in regaining the rights of which you have been so unjustly despoiled.

This, citizens of Maryland, is our mission, so far as you are concerned. No restraint upon your free-will is intended; no intimidation will be allowed within the limits of this army at least. Marylanders shall once more enjoy their ancient freedom of thought and speech. We know no enemies among you, and will protect all of you in every opinion.

It is for you to decide your destiny freely and without constraint. This army will respect your choice, whatever it may be; and while the Southern people will rejoice to welcome you to your natural position among them, they will only welcome you when you come of your own free will.

R. E. LEE, *General commanding*

The commands of Longstreet and D. H. Hill, on their arrival at Sharpsburg, were placed in position along the range of hills between the town and the Antietam, nearly parallel to the course of that stream, Longstreet on the right of the road to Boonsboro and Hill on the left. The advance of the enemy was delayed by the determined opposition he encountered from Fitzhugh Lee's cavalry, and he did not appear on the opposite side of the Antietam until about 2 P. M. During the afternoon the batteries on each side were partially engaged. On the 16th the artillery-fire became warm, and continued throughout the day. A column crossed the Antietam beyond the reach of our batteries and menaced our left. In anticipation of this movement Hood's two brigades had been transferred from the right and posted between D. H. Hill and the Hagerstown road. General Jackson was now directed to take position on Hood's left, and formed his line with his right resting on the Hagerstown road and his left extending toward the Potomac, protected by General Stuart with the cavalry and horse-artillery. General Walker with his two brigades was stationed on Longstreet's right. As evening approached, the enemy fired more vigorously with his artillery and bore down heavily with his infantry upon Hood, but the attack was gallantly repulsed. At 10 P. M. Hood's troops were relieved by the brigades of Lawton and Trimble, of Ewell's division, commanded by General Lawton. Jackson's own division, under General J. K. Jones, was on Lawton's left, supported by the remaining brigades of Ewell.

At early dawn on the 17th his artillery opened vigorously from both sides of the Antietam, the heaviest fire being directed against our left. Under cover of this fire a large force of infantry attacked General Jackson's division. They were met by his troops with the utmost resolution, and for several hours the conflict raged with intense fury and alternate success. Our troops advanced with great spirit; the enemy's lines were repeatedly broken and forced to retire. Fresh troops, however, soon replaced those that were beaten, and Jackson's men were in turn compelled to fall back. Nearly all the field officers, with a large proportion of the men, were killed or wounded. Our troops slowly yielded to overwhelming numbers, and fell back, obstinately disputing every point. General Early, in command of Ewell's division, was ordered with his brigade to take the place of Jackson's division, most of which was withdrawn, its ammunition being nearly exhausted and its numbers much reduced. The battle now raged with great violence, the small commands under Hood and Early holding their ground against many times their own infantry force and under a tremendous fire of artillery. Hood was reënforced; then the enemy's lines were broken and driven back, but fresh numbers advanced to their support, and they began to gain ground. The desperate resistance they encountered, however, delayed their progress until the troops of McLaws arrived, and those of General J. G. Walker could be brought from the right. Hood's brigade, though it had suffered extraordinary loss, only withdrew to replenish their ammunition, their supply being entirely exhausted. They were relieved by Walker's command, who immediately attacked vigorously, driving his combatant back with much slaughter. Upon the arrival of the reënforcements under McLaws, General Early attacked resolutely the large force opposed to him. McLaws advanced at the same time, and the forces before them were driven back in confusion, closely followed by our troops beyond the position occupied at the beginning of the engagement.

The attack on our left was speedily followed by one in heavy force on the center. This was met by part of Walker's division and the brigades of G. B. Anderson and Rodes, of D. H. Hill's command, assisted by a few pieces of artillery. General R. H. Anderson's division came to Hill's support, and formed in rear of his line. At this time, by a mistake of orders, Rodes's brigade was withdrawn from its position; during the absence of that command a column pressed through the gap thus created, and G. B. Anderson's brigade was broken and retired. The heavy masses moved forward, being opposed only by four pieces of artillery, supported by a few hundred of our men belonging to different brigades rallied by Hill and other officers, and parts of Walker's and R. H. Anderson's commands. Colonel Cooke, with the Twenty-seventh North Carolina Regiment, stood boldly in line without a cartridge. The firm front presented by this small force and the well-directed fire of the artillery checked the progress of the enemy, and in about an hour and a half he retired. Another attack was made soon afterward a little farther to the right, but was repulsed by Miller's guns, of the Washington Artillery, which continued to hold the ground until the close of the engagement, supported by a part of R. H. Anderson's troops. The corps designated the Washington Artillery was composed of Louisiana batteries, organized at New Orleans in the beginning of the war, under Colonel I. B. Walton. It was distinguished by its services in the first great battle of Manassas, and in nearly every important conflict, as well of the army of Virginia as that of Tennessee, to the close of the war. While the attack on the center and left was in progress, repeated efforts were made to force the passage of the bridge over the Antietam, opposite the right wing of Longstreet, commanded by Brigadier-General D. R. Jones. The bridge was defended by General Toombs with two regiments of his brigade and the batteries of General Jones. This small command repulsed five different assaults, made by a greatly superior force. In the afternoon the enemy, in large numbers, having passed the stream, advanced against General Jones, who held the ridge with less than two thousand men. After a determined and brave resistance, he was forced to give way, and the summit was gained. General A. P. Hill, having arrived from Harper's Ferry, was now ordered to reënforce General Jones. He moved to his support and attacked the force now flushed with success. Hill's batteries were thrown forward and united their fire with those of Jones, and one of D. H. Hill's also opened with good effect from the left of the Boonsboro road. The progress of the enemy was immediately arrested, and his line began to waver. At this moment General Jones ordered Toombs to charge the flank, while Archer, supported by Branch and Gregg, moved on the front of the enemy's line. After a brief resistance, he broke and retreated in confusion toward the Antietam, pursued by the troops of Hill and Jones, until he reached the protection of the batteries on the opposite side of the river.

It was now nearly dark, and McClellan had massed a number of batteries to sweep the approach to the Antietam, on the opposite side of which the corps of General Porter, which had not been engaged, now appeared to dispute our advance. Our troops were much exhausted, and greatly reduced in numbers by fatigue and the casualties of battle. Under these circumstances it was deemed injudicious to push our advantage further in the face of these fresh troops added to an army previously much exceeding the number of our own. Ours were accordingly recalled, and formed on the line originally held by General Jones. The repulse on the right ended the engagement, a protracted and sanguinary conflict in which every effort to dislodge us from our position had been defeated with severe loss. On the 18th our forces occupied the position of the preceding day, except in the center, where our line was drawn in about two hundred yards. Our ranks were increased by the arrival of a number of troops, who had not been engaged the day before, and, though still too weak to assume the offensive, Lee waited without apprehension a renewal of the attack. The day passed without any hostile demonstration. During the night of the 18th our army was withdrawn to the south side of the Potomac, crossing near Shepardstown, without loss of molestation. The enemy advanced on the next morning, but was held in check by General Fitzhugh Lee with his cavalry. The condition of our troops now demanded repose, and the army marched to the Opequan, near Martinsburg, where it remained several days, and then moved to the vicinity of Bunker Hill and Winchester. General McClellan seemed to be concentrating near Harper's Ferry, but made no forward movement.

General McClellan states, in his official report, that he had in this battle, in action, 87,164 men of all arms.

The official reports of the commanding officers of our

forces, made at the time, show our total effective infantry to have been 27,255. The estimate made for the cavalry and artillery, which is rather excessive, is 8,000. This would make General Lee's entire strength 35,255.

The official return of the Army of Northern Virginia, on September 22, 1862, after its return to Virginia, and when the stragglers had rejoined their commands, shows present for duty, 36,187 infantry and artillery; the cavalry, of which there is no report, would perhaps increase these figures to 40,000 of all arms.

The return of the United States Army of the Potomac on September 20, 1862, shows present for duty, at that date, of the commands that participated in the battle of Sharpsburg, 85,930 of all arms.

The loss of the enemy at Boonsboro and Sharpsburg was 14,794.

Chapter 29

Cotton

A CLASS of measures was adopted by the Government of the United States, the object of which was practically and effectually to plunder us of a large portion of our crop of cotton, and secure its transportation to the manufacturers of Europe. The foreign necessity for our cotton is represented in these words of her Majesty's Secretary of State for Foreign Affairs, on May 6, 1862, when speaking of the blockade of our ports:

Thousands are now obliged to resort to the poor-rates for subsistence, owing to this blockade, yet her Majesty's Government have not sought to take advantage of the obvious imperfections of this blockade, in order to declare it ineffective. They have, to the loss and detriment of the British nation, scrupulously observed the duties of Great Britain to a friendly state.

The severity of the distress thus alluded to was such, both in Great Britain and France, as to produce an intervention of the Governments of those countries to alleviate it. Instead, however, of declaring the blockade "ineffective," as it really was, they sought, through informal applications to Mr. Seward, the Secretary of State for the United States, to obtain opportunities for an increased exportation of cotton from the Confederacy. This is explained by Mr. Seward in a letter to Mr. Adams, the Minister at London, dated July 28, 1862, in which he writes as follows:

We shall speedily open all the channels of commerce, and free them from military embarrassments; and cotton, so much desired by all nations, will flow forth as freely as heretofore. We have ascertained that there are three and a half millions of bales yet remaining in the region where it was produced, though large quantities of it are yet unginned and otherwise unprepared for market. We have instructed the military authorities to favor, so far as they can consistently with the public safety, its preparation for and dispatch to the markets where it is so much wanted.

By reference to the series of measures adopted by the Government of the United States to secure possession of our cotton, it will be seen that it was inaugurated as early as

July 13, 1861. This was within ten days after the commencement of the first and extra session of Congress, under the Administration of President Lincoln. It is scarcely credible that that Government, at so early a day, foresaw the pressing demand from Europe for cotton which would ensue a year later. We must conclude that the first of these measures was the inauguration of a grand scheme for the plunder of our cotton-crop, to enrich whomsoever it might concern.

The act of the United States Congress of July 13, 1861, above mentioned, was entitled "An act to provide for the collection of duties on imports, and for other purposes." Under the "other purposes" the important features of the act are contained. Section 5 provides that—

when said insurgents claim to act under the authority of any State or States, and such claim is not disclaimed or repudiated by the persons exercising the functions of government in such State or States, or in the part or parts thereof in which said combination exists, or such insurrection suppressed by said State or States, then and in such case it may and shall be lawful for the President, by proclamation, to declare that the inhabitants of such State, or any section or part thereof, where such insurrection exists, are in a state of insurrection against the United States, and thereupon all commercial intercourse by and between the same and the citizens thereof and the citizens of the rest of the United States shall cease, and be unlawful, so long as such condition of hostility shall continue; and all goods and chattels, wares and merchandise, coming from said State or section into the other parts of the United States, and all proceeding to such State or section, by land or water, shall, together with the vessel or vehicle conveying the same, or conveying persons to or from such State or section, be forfeited to the United States.

It was provided in section 9 as follows:

Proceedings on seizures for forfeitures, under this act, may be pursued in the courts of the United States in any district into which the property so seized may be taken, and proceedings instituted.

Two effects follow this proclamation: first, the cessation of all commercial intercourse with the citizens of the United States; second, the forfeiture of all goods *in transitu*. When this condition has been reached, the act then authorizes the President, in his discretion, by license, to reopen the trade in such articles, and for such time, and by such persons, as he may think most conducive to the public interest. The articles of trade were to be chiefly cotton and tobacco; the time during which it might be continued was evidently so long as it could be used for the purpose in view; the persons were those who would most skillfully advance the end to be accomplished; and the public interest was the collection and transportation of the cotton to the European manufacturers.

One may search the Constitution of the United States in vain to find any grant of power to Congress, by which it could be authorized to pass this act; much less to find any authority conferred upon the President to approve the act. For nothing is more evident than that it is one of the powers reserved to the States to regulate the commercial intercourse between their citizens, to the extent even of the establishment of inspection and quarantine regulations. Neither did a state of war authorize the Government of the United States to interfere with the commerical intercourse between the citizens of the States, although under the law of nations it might be so justified with regard to foreign enemies. But this relation it persistently refused to concede to the Confederate States or to their citizens. It constantly asserted that they were its subjects, in a state of insurrection; and, if so, they were equally entitled to the provisions of the Constitution for their protection as well as to its penalties. Still less could the Government make an absolute forfeiture of the goods seized, as has already been shown when treating of the Confiscation Act.

But that a state of war did not enlarge the powers of the Government, as was assumed by this act, was expressly decided by Chief-Justice Taney, in a case that arose under this act. The Secretary of the Treasury issued the regulations for trade, as the act assumed the power to authorize him to do, in the section presented on a previous page. One Carpenter neglected or refused to obtain the permit required, and his goods were seized. He contested the right of seizure, and the Chief Justice gave a decision at Baltimore, in May, 1863. He said:

A civil war, or any other, does not enlarge the powers of the Federal Government over the States or the people beyond what the compact has given to it in time of war. . . . A state of war does not annul the tenth article of the amendment to the Constitution, which declares that "the powers not delegated to the United States by the Constitution, nor prohibited by it to the States, are reserved to the States respectively, or to the people.". . . Upon the whole the Court is of opinion that the regulations in question are illegal and void. . . .

The proclamation of the President required by the act was issued on August 16, 1861, declaring certain States and parts of States to be in insurrection, etc. Under it some licenses were issued to places in Kentucky and Missouri where the United States forces were located, without any fruitful results. Some strong military and naval expeditions were fitted out to invade us and occupy the ports where cotton and other valuable products were usually shipped. An advance was made up the Cumberland and Tennessee Rivers and down the Mississippi, as has been stated elsewhere. The ports of Beaufort, North Carolina, Port Royal, South Carolina, and New Orleans, Louisiana, were declared by proclamation of the President of the United States to be open for trade under the new system. Licenses were granted to foreign vessels by United States consuls and to coasting vessels by the Treasury Department, and the blockade was relaxed so far as related to those ports, except as "to persons, property, and information contraband of war." Collectors were appointed at the above-mentioned ports, and a circular was addressed to the foreign Ministers at Washington announcing the reopening of communication with conquered Southern localities.

Again, on March 3, 1863, an act was passed which authorized the Secretary of the Treasury to appoint special agents to receive and collect all abandoned or captured property in any State or portion of a State designated as in insurrection. Under this act a paper division of the whole of our territory was made into five special districts, and to each a special agent was appointed with numerous assistants. Abandoned property was defined to be that which had been deserted by the owners, or that which had been voluntarily abandoned by them to the civil or military authorities of the United States. Property which had been seized or taken from hostile possession by the military or naval forces was also to be turned over to the special agents to be sold. All property not transported in accordance with the Treasury regulations was forfeitable. All expenses incurred in relation to the property were charged upon it.

The views of General Grant on the operation of this system of measures, as tending to retard the success of subjugation, which was the object of the war, were presented to the Secretary of the United States Treasury in a letter dated at Vicksburg on July 21, 1863. He writes:

My experience in West Tennessee has convinced me that any trade whatever with the rebellious States is weakening to us at least thirty-three per cent. of our force. No matter what restrictions are thrown around trade, if any whatever is allowed, it will be made the means of supplying to the enemy what they want. Restrictions, if lived up to, make trade unprofitable, and hence none but dishonest men go into it. I will venture to say that no honest man has made money in West Tennessee in the last year, while many fortunes have been made there during the time. The people in the Mississippi Valley are now nearly subjugated. Keep trade out for a few months, and I doubt not but that the work of subjugation will be so complete that trade can be opened freely with the States of Arkansas, Louisiana, and Mississippi.

On September 11, 1863, revised regulations were issued by the Secretary which divided the country into thirteen districts, from Wheeling, West Virginia, to Natchez, on the Mississippi, and a complete system of trade and transportation was organized. In December, 1864, new regulations were issued, which authorized the purchase of our products at certain points from any person with bonds furnished by the Treasury. The products were sold, transportation was allowed, and the proceeds were made to constitute a fund for further purchases. A vigorous traffic sprang up under these regulations, which were suspended by an order of General Grant, issued on March 10, 1865, and revoked on April 11th by himself. On April 29, 1865, all restrictions upon internal, domestic, and coastwise commercial intercourse with all the country east of the Mississippi River were discontinued.

Chapter 30

Fredericksburg; Chancellorsville

ABOUT THE middle of October, 1862, General McClellan crossed the Potomac east of the Blue Ridge and advanced southward, seizing the passes of the mountains as he progressed. In the latter part of the month he began to incline eastwardly from the mountains, moving in the direction of Warrenton, about which he finally concentrated, his cavalry being thrown forward beyond the Rappahannock in the direction of Culpeper Court-House.

On November 15th the enemy was in motion. The indications were that Fredericksburg was again to be occupied. Sumner's corps had marched in the direction of Falmouth, and gunboats and transports had entered Acquia Creek.

McLaws's and Ransom's divisions were ordered to proceed to that city; and on the 21st it became apparent that the whole army—under General Burnside, who had succeeded General McClellan—was concentrating on the north side of the Rappahannock.

About November 26th Jackson was directed to advance toward Fredericksburg, and, as some of the enemy's gunboats had appeared in the river at Port Royal, and it was possible that an attempt might be made to cross in that vicinity, D. H. Hill's division was stationed near that place, and the rest of Jackson's corps so disposed as to support Hill or Longstreet, as occasion might require. The fords of the Rappahannock above Fredericksburg were closely guarded by our cavalry, and the brigade of General W. H. F. Lee was stationed near Port Royal to watch the river above and below. The interval before the advance of the foe was employed in strengthening our lines, extending from the river about a mile and a half above Fredericksburg along the range of hills in the rear of the city to the Richmond Railroad. As these hills were commanded by the opposite heights, in possession of General Burnside's force, earthworks were constructed on their crest at the most eligible positions for artillery. To prevent gunboats ascending the river, a battery, protected by epaulements, was placed on the bank four miles below the city. The plain of Fredericksburg is so completely commanded by the Stafford Heights, that no effectual opposition could be made to the passage of the river without exposing our troops to the destructive fire of the numerous batteries on the opposite heights. At the same time, the narrowness of the Rappahannock and its winding course presented opportunities for laying down pontoon-bridges at points secure from the fire of our artillery. Our position was therefore selected with a view to resist an advance after crossing, and the river was guarded by detachments of sharpshooters to impede the laying of pontoons until our army could be prepared for action.

Before dawn, on December 11th, General Burnside was in motion. About 2 A.M. he commenced preparations to throw two bridges over the Rappahannock opposite Fredericksburg, and one about a mile and a quarter below, near the mouth of Deep Run. From daybreak until 4 P.M., the troops, sheltered behind the houses on the river-bank, repelled his repeated efforts to lay bridges opposite the town, driving back his working parties and their supports with great slaughter. At the lower point, where there was no such protection, he was successfully resisted until nearly noon, when, being exposed to the severe fire of the batteries on the opposite heights and a superior force of infantry on the river-banks, our troops were withdrawn, and about 1 P.M. the bridge was completed. Soon afterward, one hundred and fifty pieces of artillery opened a furious fire upon the city, causing our troops to retire from the river-bank about 4 P.M. The enemy then crossed in boats, and proceeded rapidly to lay down the bridges. His advance into the town was bravely contested until dark, when our troops were recalled, the necessary time for concentration having been gained.

Brigadier-General William Barksdale, who commanded the force placed in Fredericksburg to resist the crossing, performed that service with his well-known gallantry. The enemy was prevented from constructing bridges, and his attempts to cross in boats, under the cover of artillery and musketry fire, were repelled until late in the afternoon, when General Barksdale was ordered to retire; he had directed Lieutenant-Colonel Fizer, commanding the Seventeenth Mississippi Regiment, of Barksdale's brigade, to select some skillful marksmen, and proceed to check the operations of the pioneers, who had commenced to lay pontoons above the city. Colonel Fizer described to me the novel and bold expedient to which he successfully resorted. He said his sharpshooters were placed in rifle-pits, on the bank opposite to that from which the bridge was started; that his men were instructed to aim only at the bridge-builders. At dawn the workmen came forward to lay the cover on the bridge; fire was opened, some were killed, and the rest of the party driven ashore. Then the enemy's batteries and riflemen opened a heavy fire on his position, when his men would sit down in the rifle-pits and remain quiet until the cannonade ceased. Probably under the supposition that our sharpshooters had been driven off, the workmen would return; our sharpshooters would arise and repeat the lesson lately given. This, he said, with intervals of about an hour, during which a continuous and heavy fire of artillery was kept up, occurred nine times, with the same result—a repulse with severe loss; and that, for twelve hours, every attempt to construct a bridge at that point was defeated. Then, under orders, they withdrew.

During the night and the succeeding day the enemy crossed in large numbers at and below the town, secured from material interruption by a dense fog. Longstreet's corps constituted our left, with Anderson's division resting on the river, and those of McLaws, Pickett, and Hood extending to the right. A. P. Hill, of Jackson's corps, was posted between Hood's right and Hamilton's Crossing, on the railroad. His front line occupied the edge of a wood. Early and Taliaferro's divisions constituted Jackson's second line, D. H. Hill's division his reserve. His artillery was distributed along his line in the most eligible positions, so as to command the open ground in front.

Shortly after 9 A.M., the partial rising of the mist disclosed a large force moving in line of battle against Jackson. Dense masses appeared in front of A. P. Hill, stretching far up the river in the direction of Fredericksburg. As they advanced, Major Pelham, of Stuart's horse-artillery, opened a rapid and well-directed enfilade fire, which arrested their progress. Four batteries immediately turned upon him, and, upon his withdrawal, the enemy extended his left down the Port Royal road, and his numerous batteries opened with vigor upon Jackson's line. Eliciting no response, his infantry moved forward to seize the position occupied by Lieutenant-Colonel Walker. The latter, reserving the fire of his fourteen pieces until their line had approached within less than eight hundred yards, opened upon it with such destructive effect as to cause it to waver and soon retreat in confusion.

About 1 P.M., the main attack on the right began by a furious cannonade, under cover of which three compact lines of infantry advanced against Hill's front. They were received as before and momentarily checked, but, soon recovering, they pressed forward, until, coming within range of our infantry, the contest became fierce and bloody. Archer and Lane, who occupied the edge of a wood, repulsed those portions of the line immediately in front of them; but, before the interval between these commands could be closed, the assailants pressed through in overwhelming numbers and turned the left of Archer and the right of Lane. Attacked in front and flank, two regiments of the former and a brigade of the latter, after a brave resistance, gave way. Archer held his line until the arrival of reënforcements. Thomas came to the relief of Lane and repulsed the column that had broken his line, and drove it back to the railroad. In the mean time a large force had penetrated the wood as far as Hill's reserve, where it was met by a fire for which it was prepared. The advancing Federals were allowed to approach quite near, when that brigade poured a withering fire into the faces of Meade's men, and Early's division from the second line swept forward, and the contest in the woods was short and decisive. The enemy was quickly routed and driven out with very heavy loss, and, though largely reënforced, was pressed back and pursued to the shelter of the railroad embankment. Here he was gallantly charged by the brigades of Hoke and Atkinson, and driven across the plain to his batteries. The attack on Hill's left was repulsed by the artillery on that part of the line, against which a hot fire from twenty-four guns was directed. The repulse of the foe on our right was decisive and the attack was not renewed, but his batteries kept up an active fire at intervals, and sharpshooters skirmished along the front during the afternoon.

While these events were transpiring on our right, the enemy, in formidable numbers, made repeated and desperate assaults upon the left of our line. About 11 A.M., having massed his troops under cover of the houses of Fredericksburg, he moved forward in strong columns to seize Marye's and Willis's Hills. All his batteries on the Stafford Heights directed their fire upon the positions occupied by our artillery, with a view to silence it, and cover the movement of the infantry. Without replying to this furious cannonade, our batteries poured a rapid and destructive fire into the dense lines of the infantry as they advanced to the attack, frequently breaking their ranks, and forcing them to retreat to the shelter of the houses. Six times did he, notwithstanding the havoc inflicted by our batteries, press on with great determination to within one hundred yards of the foot of the hill; but here, encountering the deadly fire of our infantry, his columns were broken, and fled in confusion to the town. The last assault was made shortly before dark. This effort met the fate of those that preceded it, and, when night closed in, his shattered masses had disappeared in the town, leaving the field covered with his dead and wounded.

During the night our lines were strengthened by the construction of earthworks at exposed points, and preparations made to receive the enemy on the next day. The 14th passed, however, without a renewal of the attack. The hostile batteries on both sides of the river played upon our lines at intervals, our own firing but little. On the 15th General Burnside still retained his position, apparently ready for battle, but the day passed as the preceding. But, on the morning of the 16th, it was discovered that he had availed himself of the darkness of the night and the prevalence of a violent storm of wind and rain to recross the river. The town was immediately reoccupied, and our positions on the river-bank resumed.

In the engagement we captured more than 900 prisoners and 9,000 stand of arms. A large quantity of ammunition was found in Fredericksburg. On our side 458 were killed and 3,743 wounded; total 4,201. The loss of the enemy was 1,152 killed, 9,101 wounded, and 3,234 missing; total, 13,771.

General Burnside testified before the Committee on the Conduct of the War that he "had about 100,000 men on the south side of the river, and every single man of them was under artillery-fire, and about half of them were at different times formed in columns of attack."

Less than 20,000 Confederate troops were actively engaged. This number composed about one fourth of the army under General Lee. The returns of the Army of Northern Virginia show that on the 10th of December, 1862, General Lee had present for duty 78,228, and, on December 20th, 75,524 of all arms.

Upon being asked what causes he assigned for the failure of his attack, General Burnside replied to the Committee on the Conduct of the War: "It was found impossible to get the men up to the works. The enemy's fire was too hot for them."

After the battle of Fredericksburg the Army of Northern Virginia remained encamped on the south side of the Rappahannock until the latter part of April, 1863. The Federal army occupied the north side of the river opposite Fredericksburg, extending to the Potomac. Two brigades of Anderson's division—those of Mahone and Posey—were stationed near United States Mine or Bank Mill Ford. The cavalry was distributed on both flanks—Fitzhugh Lee's brigade picketing the Rappahannock above the mouth of the Rapidan and W. H. F. Lee's near Port Royal. General Longstreet, with two divisions of his corps, was detached for service south of James River in February, and did not rejoin the army until after the battle of Chancellorsville. On April 14, 1863, the enemy's cavalry was concentrating on the upper Rappahannock, but his efforts to establish himself on the south side of the river were successfully resisted. About the 21st, small bodies of infantry appeared at Kelly's Ford and the Rappahannock Bridge; at the same time a demonstration was made opposite Port Royal. These movements indicated that the army, now commanded by Major-General Hooker, was about to resume active operations.

A brief and forcible account of the battle of Chancellorsville is given by Taylor:

A formidable force under General Sedgwick was thrown across the river below Fredericksburg, and made demonstrations of an intention to assail the Confederate front. Meanwhile, with great celerity and secrecy, General Hooker, with the bulk of his army, crossed at the upper fords, and, in an able manner and wonderfully short time, had concentrated four of his seven army corps, numbering fifty-six thousand men, at Chancellorsville, about ten miles west of Fredericksburg. His purpose was now fully developed to General Lee, who, instead of awaiting its further prosecution, immediately determined on the movement the least expected by his opponent. He neither proceeded to make strong his left against an attack from the direction of Chancellorsville nor did he move southward so as to put his army between that of General Hooker and the Confederate capital, but, leaving General Early, with about nine thousand men, to take care of General Sedgwick, he moved with the remainder of his army, numbering forty-eight thousand men, toward Chancellorsville. As soon as the advance of the enemy was encountered, it was attacked with vigor, and very soon the Federal army was on the defensive in its apparently impregnable position: It was not the part of wisdom to attempt to storm this stronghold; but Sedgwick would certainly soon be at work in the rear, and Early, with his inadequate force, could not do more than delay and harass him. It was, therefore, imperatively necessary to strike—to strike boldly, effectively, and at once. There could be no delay. Meanwhile, two more army corps had joined General Hooker, who now had about Chancellorsville ninety-one thousand men—six corps except one division of the Second Corps (Couch's), which had been left with Sedgwick at Fredericksburg. It was a critical position for the Confederate commander, but his confidence in his trusted lieutenant and brave men was such that he did not long hesitate. Encouraged by the counsel and confidence of General Jackson, he determined to still further divide his army; and, while he, with the divisions of Anderson and McLaws, less than fourteen thousand men, should hold the enemy in his front, he would hurl Jackson upon his flank and rear, and crush and crumble him as between the upper and nether millstone. The very boldness of the movement contributed much to insure its success.

The flank movement of Jackson's wing was attended with extraordinary success. On the afternoon of the 2d of May, he struck such a blow to the enemy on their extreme right as to cause dismay and demoralization to their entire army; this advantage was promptly and vigorously followed up the next day, when Generals Lee and Stuart (the latter then in command of Jackson's wing) joined elbows; and, after most heroic and determined effort, their now united forces finally succeeded in storming and capturing the works of the enemy.

Meantime Sedgwick had forced Early out of the heights at Fredericksburg, and had advanced toward Chancellorsville, thus threatening the Confederate rear. General Lee, having defeated the greater force and driven it from its stronghold, now gathered up a few of the most available of his victorious brigades and turned upon the lesser. On May 3d Sedgwick's force was encountered near Salem Church, and its further progress checked by General McLaws, with the five brigades detached by General Lee for this service, including Wilcox's, which had been stationed at Bank's Ford. On the next day, General Anderson was sent to reënforce McLaws with three additional brigades. Meanwhile, General Early had connected with these troops, and in the afternoon, so soon as dispositions could be made for attack, Sedgwick's lines were promptly assailed and broken, the main assault being made on the enemy's left by Early's troops. The situation was now a critical one for the Federal lieutenant. Darkness came to his rescue, and on the night of the 4th he crossed to the north side of the river.

On the 5th General Lee concentrated for another assault on the new line taken up by General Hooker; but on the morning of the 6th it was ascertained that the enemy, in General Lee's language, "had sought saftey beyond the Rappahannock," and the river flowed again between the hostile hosts.

The loss of the enemy, according to his own statement, was 1,512 killed and 9,518 wounded; total, 11,030. His dead and a large number of wounded were left on the field. About 5,000 prisoners, exclusive of the wounded, were taken, and 13 pieces of artillery, 19,500 stand of arms, 17 colors, and a large quantity of ammunition fell into our hands.

Our loss was much less in killed and wounded than that of the enemy, but of the number was one, a host in himself, Lieutenant-General Jackson, who was wounded, and died on May 10th. Of this great captain, General Lee, in his anguish at his death, justly said, "I have lost my right arm." As an executive officer he had no superior, and war has seldom shown an equal. Too devoted to the cause he served to have any personal motive, he shared the toils, privations, and dangers of his troops when in chief command; and in subordinate position his aim was to understand the purpose of his commander and faithfully to promote its success. He was the complement of Lee; united, they had achieved such results that the public felt secure under their shield. His place was never filled.

The official return of the Army of Northern Virginia, on March 31, 1863, shows as present for duty 57,112, of which 6,509 were cavalry and 1,621 reserve artillery. On May 20th, two weeks after the battle, and when Pickett's and Hood's divisions had rejoined the army, the total infantry force numbered but 55,261 effective men, from which, if the strength of Hood's and Pickett's divisions is deducted, there would remain 41,358 as the strength of the commands that participated in the battles of Chancellorsville.

The Army of the Potomac numbered 120,000 men, infantry and artillery, with a body of 12,000 well-equipped cavalry, and an artillery force of four hundred guns.

Chapter 31

Relations with Foreign Nations

THE PUBLIC QUESTIONS arising out of our foreign relations were too important to be overlooked. At the end of the first year of the war the Confederate States had been recognized by the leading governments of Europe as a belligerent power. This continued unchanged to the close. Mr. Mason became our representative in London, Mr. Slidell in Paris, Mr. Rost in Spain, and Mr. Mann in Belgium. They performed with energy and skill the positions, but were unsuccessful in obtaining our recognition as an independent power.

The usages of intercourse between nations require that official communication be made to friendly powers of all organic changes in the constitution of states. Each of the States was originally declared to be sovereign and independent. In this condition, at a former period, all of those then existing were severally recognized by name by the only one of the powers which had denied their right to independence. This gave to each a recognized national sovereignty. Subsequently they formed a compact of voluntary union, whereby a new organization was constituted, which was made the representative of the individual States in all general intercourse with other nations. So long as the compact continued in force, this agent represented merely the sovereignty of the States. But, when a portion of the States withdrew from the compact and formed a new one under the name of the Confederate States, they had made such organic changes in their Constitution as to require official notice in compliance with the usages of nations.

For this purpose the Provisional Government took early measures for sending to Europe Commissioners charged with the duty of visiting the capitals of the different powers and making arrangements for the opening of more formal diplomatic intercourse. Prior, however, to the arrival abroad of these Commissioners, the Government of the United States had addressed communications to the different Cabinets of Europe, in which it assumed the attitude of being sovereign over the Confederate States, and alleged that these independent States were in rebellion against the remaining States of the Union, and threatened Europe with manifestations of its displeasure if it should treat the Confederate States as having an independent existence. It soon became known that these pretensions were not considered abroad to be as absurd as they were known to be at home; nor had Europe yet learned what reliance was to be placed in the official statements of the Cabinet at Washington. Our Commissioners were met by the declaration that foreign Governments could not assume to judge between the conflicting representations of the two parties as to the true nature of their previous relations. The Governments of Great Britain and France accordingly signified their determination to confine themselves to recognizing the self-evident fact of the existence of a war, and to maintain a strict neutrality during its progress. Some of the other powers of Europe pursued the same course of policy, and it became apparent that by some understanding, express or tacit, Europe had decided to leave the initiative in all action touching the contest on this continent to the two powers just named, who were recognized to have the largest interests involved, both by reason of proximity to and of the extent of intimacy of their commercial relations with the States engaged in war.

But it was especially in relation to the so-called bockade that the policy of European powers was so shaped as to cause the greatest injury to the Confederacy, and to confer signal advantages on the United States. A few words in explanation may here be necessary.

Prior to the year 1856 the principles regulating this subject were to be gathered from the writings of eminent publicists, the decisions of admiralty courts, international treaties, and the usages of nations. The uncertainty and doubt which prevailed in reference to the true rules of maritime law, in time of war, resulting from the discordant and often conflicting principles announced from such varied and independent sources, had become a grievous evil to mankind. Whether a blockade was allowable against a port not invested by land as well as by sea, whether a blockade was valid by sea if the investing fleet was merely sufficient to render ingress to the blockaded port evidently dangerous, or whether it was further required for its legality that it should be sufficient "really to prevent access," and numerous other similar questions, had remained doubtful and undecided.

Animated by the highly honorable desire to put an end "to differences of opinion between neutrals and belligerents, which may occasion serious difficulties and even conflicts" (such was the official language), the five great powers of Europe, together with Sardinia and Turkey, adopted in 1856 the following declaration of principles:

"1. Privateering is and remains abolished.

"2. The neutral flag covers enemy's goods, with the exception of contraband of war.

"3. Neutral goods, with the exception of contraband of war, are not liable to capture under enemy's flag.

"4. Blockades, in order to be binding must be effective, that is to say, maintained by a force sufficient really to prevent access to the coast of the enemy."

This declaration contained a clause to which these powers gave immediate effect, and which provided that the states, not parties to the Congress of Paris, should be invited to accede to the declaration. Under this invitation every independent state in Europe yielded its assent; and the United States, while declining to assent to the proposition which prohibited privateering, declared that the three remaining principles were in entire accordance with their own views of international law. When, therefore, this Confederacy was formed, and when neutral powers recognized it as a belligerent power, Great Britain and France made informal proposals that their own rights as neutrals should be guaranteed by our acceding, as belligerents, to the declaration of principles made by the Congress of Paris. The request met immediate and favorable response in the resolutions of the Provisional Congress of the 13th of August, 1861, by which all the principles announced by the Congress of Paris were adopted as the guide of our conduct during the war, with the sole exception of that relative to privateering. The right to make use of privateers was reserved with entire confidence that neutral nations could not fail to perceive that just reason existed for the reservation. Nor was this confidence misplaced; for the official documents published by the British Government contained the expression of the satisfaction of that Government with the conduct of officials who conducted successfully the delicate transaction confided to their charge.

However, these solemn declarations of principle were suffered to remain inoperative against the menaces and outrages on neutral rights committed by the United States during the whole period of the war. Neutral Europe remained passive when the United States, with a naval force insufficient to blockade effectively the coast of a single State, proclaimed a paper blockade of thousands of miles of coast, extending from the Capes of the Chesapeake to those of Florida, and encircling the Gulf of Mexico from Key West to the mouth of the Rio Grande.

Repeated and formal remonstrances were made by the Confederate Government to neutral powers against the recognition of that blockade. It was shown by evidence not capable of contradiction, and which was furnished in part by the officials of neutral nations, that every prescription of maritime law and every right of neutral nations to trade with a belligerent under the sanction of principles heretofore universally respected were systematically and persistently violated by the United States. Neutral Europe received our remonstrances, and submitted in almost unbroken silence to all the wrongs that the United States chose to inflict on its commerce. The Cabinet of Great Britain, however, did not confine itself to such implied acquiescence in these breaches of international law which resulted from simple inaction, but, in a published dispatch of the Minister for Foreign Affairs, assumed to make a change in the principle enunciated by the Congress of Paris, to which the faith of the British Government was considered to be pledged. The change was so important and so prejudicial to the interests of the Confederacy that, after a vain attempt to obtain satisfactory explanations from that Government, I directed a solemn protest to be made.

In a published dispatch from her Majesty's Foreign Office to her Minister at Washington, under date of February 11th, 1862, occurred the following passage:

Her Majesty's Government, however, are of opinion that, assuming that the blockade was duly notified, and also that a number of ships is stationed and remains at the entrance of a port sufficient really to prevent access to it, *or to create an evident danger of entering it or leaving it,* and that these ships do not voluntarily permit ingress or egress, the fact that various ships may have successfully escaped through it (as in the particular instance here referred to), will not of itself prevent the blockade from being an effectual one by international law.

The importance of this change was readily illustrated by taking one of our ports as an example. There was "evident danger," in entering the port of Wilmington, from the presence of a blockading force, and by this test the blockade was effective. "Access is not really prevented" by the blockading fleet to the same port; for steamers were continually arriving and departing, so that, tried by this test, the blockade was ineffective and invalid. Thus, the neutral nations of Europe pursued a policy which, nominally impartial, was practically most favorable to our enemies and most detrimental to us.

The exercise of the neutral right of refusing entry into their ports to prizes taken by both belligerents was especially hurtful to the Confederacy. It was sternly adhered to and enforced.

The assertion of the neutral right of commerce with a belligerent, whose ports are not blockaded by fleets sufficient really to prevent access to them, would have been eminently beneficial to the Confederate States, and only thus hurtful to the United States. It was complaisantly abandoned. Perhaps it may not be out of place here to notice a correspondence between the Cabinets of France, Great Britain, and Russia, relative to a mediation between the Confederacy and the United States. On October 30, 1862, the French Minister of Foreign Affairs, Drouyn de l'Huys, addressed a note to the ambassadors of France at London and St. Petersburg. In this dispatch he stated that the Emperor had followed with painful interest the struggle which had then been going on for more than a year on this continent. Europe also had suffered in one of the principal branches of her industry, and her artisans had been subjected to most cruel trials. France and the maritime powers had, during the struggle, maintained the strictest neutrality, but the sentiments by which they were animated [seemed] to require that they should assist the two belligerent parties in an endeavor to escape from a position which appeared to have no issue. The forces of the two sides had hitherto fought with balanced success, and the latest accounts did not show any prospect of a speedy termination of the war. The Emperor of the French, therefore, proposed to her Majesty, as well as to the Emperor of Russia, that the three courts should endeavor, both at Washington and in communication with the Confederate States, to bring about a suspension of arms for six months, during which time every act of hostility, direct or indirect, should cease, at sea as well as on land. This armistice might, if necessary, be renewed for a further period.

The reply of Great Britain, through Lord John Russell, on November 13, 1862, is really contained in this extract:

. . . Her Majesty's Government are led to the conclusion that there is no ground at the present moment to hope that the Federal Government would accept the proposal suggested, and a refusal from Washington at the present time would prevent any speedy renewal of the offer.

The Russian Government, in reply said:

... We are inclined to believe that a combined step between France, England, and Russia, no matter how conciliatory, and how cautiously made, if it were taken with an official and collective character, would run the risk of causing precisely the very opposite of the object of pacification, which is the aim of the wishes of the three courts.

The unfavorable reception of the proposal was communicated by the French Minister of Foreign Affairs to the representative of France at Washington. In this communication he said:

... You will easily form an idea of our regret at seeing the initiative we have taken after mature reflection remains without results. Being also desirous of informing Mr. Dayton, the United States Minister, of our project, I confidently communicated it to him, and even read in his presence the dispatch sent to London and St. Petersburg. I could not but be surprised that the Minister of the United States should oppose his objections to the project I communicated to him, and to hear him express personally some doubts as to the reception which would be given by the Cabinet at Washington to the joint offers of the good offices of France, Russia, and Great Britain.

Perhaps it may not be out of place to present a few examples by which to show the true nature of the neutrality professed by England in this war.

In May, 1861, the Government of her Britannic Majesty assured our enemies that "the sympathies of this country [Great Britain] were rather with the North than with the South."

On June 1, 1861, the British Government interdicted the use of its ports "to armed ships and privateers, both of the United States and the so-called Confederate States," with their prizes. On the 12th of June, 1861, the United States Minister in London informed her Majesty's Minister for Foreign Affairs that the fact of his having held interviews with the Commissioners of our Government had given "great dissatisfaction, and that a protraction of this would be viewed by the United States as hostile in spirit, and to require some corresponding action accordingly." In response to this intimation her Majesty's Minister gave assurance that "he had no expectation of seeing them any more."

Further extracts will show the marked encouragement to the United States to persevere in its paper blockade, and unmistakable intimations that her Majesty's Government would not contest its validity.

On May 21, 1861, Earl Russell pointed out to the United States Minister in London that "the blockade might, no doubt, be made effective, considering the small number of harbors on the Southern coast, even though the extent of three thousand miles were comprehended in the terms of that blockade."

On May 6, 1862, so far from claiming the right of British subjects as neutrals to trade with us as belligerents, and to disregard the blockade on the ground of this explicit confession by our enemy of his inability to render it effective, her Majesty's Minister for Foreign Affairs claimed credit with the United States for friendly action in respecting it. His lordship stated that—

. . . This blockade, kept up irregularly, but, when enforced, enforced severely, has seriously injured the trade and manufactures of the United Kingdom.

Thousands are now obliged to resort to the poor-rates for subsistence owing to this blockade. Yet her Majesty's Government have never sought to take advantage of the obvious imperfections of this blockade, in order to declare it ineffective. They have, to the loss and detriment of the British nation, scrupulously observed the duties of Great Britain toward a friendly state.

The partiality of her Majesty's Government in favor of our enemies was further evinced in the marked difference of its conduct on the subject of the purchase of supplies by the two belligerents. As early as May 1, 1861, the British Minister in Washington was informed by the Secretary of State of the United States that he had sent agents to England, and that others would go to France, to purchase arms; and this fact was communicated to the British Foreign Office, which interposed no objection. Yet, in October of the same year, Earl Russell entertained the complaint of the United States Minister in London, that the Confederate States were importing contraband of war from the Island of Nassau, directed inquiry into the matter, and obtained a report from the authorities of the island denying the allegations, which report was inclosed to Mr. Adams, and received by him as satisfactory evidence to dissipate "the suspicion thrown upon the authorities by that unwarrantable act." So, too, when the Confederate Government purchased in Great Britain, as a neutral country (with strict observance both of the law of nations and the municipal law of Great Britain), vessels which were subsequently armed and commissioned as vessels of war after they had been far removed from English waters, the British Government, in violation of its own laws, and in deference to the importunate demands of the United States, made an ineffectual attempt to seize one vessel, and did actually seize and detain another which touched at the Island of Nassau, on her way to a Confederate port, and subjected her to an unfounded prosecution, at the very time when cargoes of munitions of war were openly shipped from British ports to New York, to be used in warfare against us.

Chapter 32

Vicksburg; Port Hudson

OPERATIONS IN THE WEST now claim attention. Late in the month of December General Rosecrans commenced his advance from Nashville upon the position of General Bragg at Murfreesboro. His movement began on December 26th by various routes, but such was the activity of our cavalry as to delay him four days in reaching the battle-field, a distance of twenty-six miles. On the 29th General Wheeler with his cavalry brigade gained the rear of Rosecrans's army, and destroyed several hundreds of wagons loaded with supplies and baggage. After clearing the road, he made the circuit of the enemy and joined our left. Their strength, as we have ascertained, was 65,000 men. The number of fighting men we had on the field on December 31st was 35,000, of which 30,000 were infantry and artillery.

Our line was formed about two miles from Murfreesboro, and stretched transversely across Stone River, which was fordable from the Lebanon pike on the right to the Franklin road on the left. As General Rosecrans made no demonstration on the 30th, General Bragg determined to begin the conflict early on the morning of the 31st by the advance of his left. The enemy was taken completely by surprise, and his right was steadily driven until his line was thrown entirely back at a right angle to his first position and near to the railroad, along which he had massed reserves. Their resistance after the first surprise was most gallant and obstinate. At night he had been forced from every position except the one on his extreme left, which rested on Stone River, and was strengthened by a concentration of artillery, and now seemed too formidable for assault.

On the next day (January 1st) the cannonading opened on the right center about 8 A.M., and after a short time subsided. The enemy had withdrawn from the advanced position occupied by his left flank; one or two short contests occurred on the 3d, but his line was unchanged. Our forces had now been in line of battle five days and nights, with little rest, as there were no reserves. Their tents had been packed in the wagons, which were four miles to the rear. The rain was continuous, and the cold severe. Intelligence was received that heavy reënforcements were coming to Rosecrans by a rapid transfer of all the troops from Kentucky, and for this and the reasons before stated General Bragg decided to fall back to Tullahoma, and the army was withdrawn in good order.

In the series of engagements near Murfreesboro we captured over 6,000 prisoners, 30 pieces of artillery, 6,000 small-arms, a number of ambulances, horses, and mules, and a large amount of other property. Our losses exceeded 10,000, and that of the enemy was estimated at over 25,000.

After the battle of Murfreesboro, which closed in the first days of 1863, there was a cessation of active operations in that portion of Tennessee, and attention was concentrated upon the extensive preparations which were in progress for a campaign into Mississippi, with Vicksburg as the objective point.

The campaign against Vicksburg had commenced as early as November, 1862, and reference has been made to the various attempts to capture the position both before and after General Grant arrived and took command in person. He had now by a circuitous march reached the rear of the city, established a base on the Mississippi River a few miles below, had a fleet of gunboats in the river, and controlled the navigation of the Yazoo up to Haines's Bluff, and was relieved from all danger in regard to supplying his army. We had lost the opportunity to cut his communications while he was making his long march over the rugged country between Bruinsburg and the vicinity of Vicksburg. Pemberton had by wise prevision endeavored to secure supplies sufficient for the duration of an ordinary siege, and, on the importance which he knew the Administration attached to the holding of Vicksburg, he relied for the coöperation of a relieving army to break any investment which might be made. Disappointed in the hope which I had entertained that the invading army would be unable to draw its supplies from Bruinsburg or Grand Gulf, and be driven back before crossing the Big Black, it now only remained to increase as far as possible the relieving army, and depend upon it to break the investment. The ability of the Federals to send reënforcements was so much greater than ours, that the necessity for prompt action was fully realized; therefore, when General Johnston on May 9th was ordered to proceed to Mississippi, he was directed to take from the Army of Tennessee three thousand good troops, and informed that he would find reënforcements from General

Beauregard. On May 12th a dispatch was sent to him at Jackson, stating, "In addition to the five thousand men originally ordered from Charleston [Beauregard], about four thousand more will follow. I fear more can not be spared to you." On May 22d I sent the following dispatch to General Bragg, at Tullahoma, Tennessee:

The vital issue of holding the Mississippi at Vicksburg is dependent on the success of General Johnston in an attack on the investing force. The intelligence from there is discouraging. Can you aid him?

To this he replied on the 23d of May, 1863:

Sent thity-five hundred with the General, three batteries of artillery and two thousand cavalry since; will dispatch six thousand more immediately.

On the 1st of June General Johnston telegraphed to me that the troops at his disposal available against Grant amounted to twenty-four thousand one hundred, not including Jackson's cavalry command and a few hundred irregular cavalry. Mr. Seddon, Secretary of War, replied to him stating the force to be thirty-two thousand. In another dispatch, of June 5th, the Secretary says his statement rested on official reports of numbers sent, regrets his inability to promise more, as we had drained our resources even to the danger of several points, and urged speedy action. "With the facilities and resources of the enemy time works against us." Again, on the 16th, Secretary Seddon says:

If better resources do not offer, you must hazard attack.

On the 18th, while Pemberton was inspecting the intrenchments along which his command had been placed, he received by courier a communication from General Johnston, dated "May 17, 1863, camp between Livingston and Brownsville," in answer to Pemberton's report of the result of the battles of Baker's Creek and Big Black, and the consequent evacuation of Snyder's Mills. General Johnston wrote:

If Haines's Bluff is untenable, Vicksburg is of no value and can not be held. If, therefore, you are invested in Vicksburg, you must ultimately surrender. Under such circumstances, instead of losing both troops and place, we must, if possible, save the troops. If it is not too late, evacuate Vicksburg and its dependencies, and march to the northeast.

Pemberton, in his report, remarks:

This meant the fall of Port Hudson, the surrender of the Mississippi River, and the severance of the Confederacy.

He recurs to a former correspondence with myself in which he had suggested the possibility of the investment of Vicksburg by land and water, and the necessity for ample supplies to stand a siege, and says his application met my favorable consideration, and that additional ammunition was ordered. Confident in his ability, with the preparations which had been made, to stand a siege, and firmly relying on the desire of the President and of General Johnston to raise it, he "felt that every effort would be made, and believed it would be successful." He, however, summoned a council of war, composed of all his general officers, laid before them General Johnston's communication, and desired their opinion on "the question of practicability," and on the 18th replied to General Johnston that he had placed his instructions before the general officers of the command, and that "the opinion was unanimously expressed that it was impossible to withdraw the army from this position with such *morale* and material as to be of further service to the Confederacy." He then announces his decision to hold Vicksburg as long as possible, and expresses the hope that he may be assisted in keeping this obstruction to the enemy's free navigation of the Mississippi River. While the council of war was assembled, the guns of the enemy opened on the works, and the siege proper commenced.

Making meager allowance for a reserve, it required the whole force to be constantly in the trenches, and, when they were all on duty, it did not furnish one man to the yard of the *developed line.* On the 19th two assaults were made at the center and left. Both were repulsed and heavy loss inflicted; our loss was small. At the same time the mortar-fleet of Admiral Porter from the west side of the peninsula kept up a bombardment of the city.

Vicksburg is built upon hills rising successively from the river. The intrenchments were upon ridges beyond the town, only approaching the river on the right and left flanks, so that the fire of Porter's mortar-fleet was mainly effective upon the private dwellings, and the women, the children, and other non-combatants.

The hills on which the city is built are of a tenacious calcareous clay, and caves were dug in these to shelter the women and children, many of whom resided in them during the entire siege. From these places of refuge, heroically facing the danger of shells incessantly bursting over the streets, gentlewomen hourly went forth on the mission of humanity to nurse the sick, the wounded, and to soothe the dying of their defenders who were collected in numerous hospitals. It was often remarked that, in the discharge of the pious duties assumed, they seemed as indifferent to danger as any of the soldiers who lined the trenches.

During the 20th, 21st, and the forenoon of the 22d, a heavy fire of artillery and musketry was kept up by the besiegers, as well as by the mortar- and gun-boats in the river. On the afternoon of the 22d preparation was made for a general assault. The attacking columns were allowed to approach to within good musket-range, when every available gun was opened with grape and canister, and our infantry, "rising in the trenches, poured into their ranks volley after volley with so deadly an effect that, leaving the ground literally covered in some places with their dead and wounded, they [the enemy] precipitately retreated." One of our redoubts had been breached by their artillery previous to the assault, and a lodgment made in the ditch at the foot of the redoubt, on which two colors were planted. General Stevenson says in his report:

The work was constructed in such a manner that the ditch was commanded by no part of the line, and the only means by which they could be dislodged was to retake the angle by a desperate charge, and either kill or compel the surrender of the whole party by the use of hand-grenades. A call for volunteers for this purpose was made, and promptly responded to by Lieutenant-Colonel E. W. Pettus, Twentieth Alabama Regiment, and about forty men of Waul's Texas Legion. A more gallant feat than this charge has not illustrated our arms during the war. The preparations were quietly and quickly made, but the enemy seemed at once to divine our intentions, and opened upon the angle a terrible fire of shot, shell, and musketry. Undaunted, this little band, its chivalrous commander at its head, rushed the work, and, in less time than it required to describe it, the flags were in our possession. Preparations were then quickly made for the use of hand-grenades, when the enemy in the ditch, being informed of our purpose, immediately surrendered.

From this time forward, although on several occasions their demonstrations seemed to indicate other intentions, the enemy relinquished all idea of assaulting us, and confined himself to the more cautious policy of a system of gradual approaches and mining.

His force was not less than sixty thousand men. Thus affairs continued until July 1st, when General Pemberton thus describes the causes which made capitulation necessary:

It must be remembered that, for forty-seven days and nights, those heroic men had been exposed to burning suns, drenching rains, damp fogs, and heavy dews, and that during all this period they never had, by day or by night, the slightest relief. The extent of our works required every available man in the trenches, and even then they were in many places insufficiently manned. It was not in my power to relieve any portion of the line for a single hour. Confined to the narrow limits of trench, with their limbs cramped and swollen, without exercise, constantly exposed to a murderous storm of shot and shell. . . . Is it strange that the men grew weak and attenuated? . . . They had held the place against an enemy five times their number, admirably clothed and fed, and abundantly supplied with all the appliances of war. Whenever the foe attempted an assault, they drove him back discomfited, covering the ground with his killed and wounded, and already had they torn from his grasp five stands of colors as trophies of their prowess, none of which were allowed to fall again into his hands.

Under these circumstances, he says, he became satisfied that the time had arrived when it was necessary either to evacuate the city by cutting his way out or capitulate. Inquiries were made of the division commanders respecting the ability of the troops to make the marches and undergo the fatigues necessary to accomplish a successful sortie and force their way through the enemy; all of whom reported their several commands quite unequal to the performance of such an effort. Therefore, it was resolved to seek terms of capitulation. These were obtained, and the city was surrendered on July 4th.

With an unlimited supply of provisions the garrison could not, for the reasons already given, have held out much longer. Our loss in killed, wounded, and missing, from the landing of the enemy on the east to the capitulation, was 5,632; that of the enemy, according to his own statement, was 8,875. The number of prisoners surrendered, as near as I can tell, did not exceed 28,000.

In addition to the efforts made to relieve Vicksburg by an attack on Grant's army in the rear, instructions were sent to General Kirby Smith, commanding on the west side of the river, to employ a part of his forces in coöperation with our troops on the east side. From General Richard Taylor's work, "Destruction and Reconstruction," I learn that—

the Federal army withdrew from Alexandria [a town on Red River, Louisiana] on the 13th of May, and on the 23d crossed the Mississippi and proceeded to invest Port Hudson. . . . A communication from General Kirby Smith informed me that Major-General Walker, with a division of infantry and three batteries, four thousand strong, was on the march from Arkansas, and would reach me within the next few days; and I was directed to employ Walker's force to relieve Vicksburg, now invested by General Grant, who had crossed the Mississippi on the 1st of May.

General Taylor states that his view was that this force might be best employed for the relief of Vicksburg by a movement to raise the siege of Port Hudson, which he regarded as feasible, while a direct movement toward Vicksburg he considered would be unavailing, because the peninsula opposite to that city was partially occupied by the enemy and commanded by the gunboats in the river; he states, however, that he was overruled, and proceeded with Walker's division to cross the Tensas and attack two Federal camps on the bank of the Mississippi, the one ten and the other fourteen miles above Vicksburg, but that, after driving the troops over the levee, the gunboats in the river protected them from any further assault. Then, being convinced that nothing useful could be effected in that quarter, he, in conformity with his original idea, ordered General Walker to retire to Alexandria, intending to go thence to the Têche. He says this order was countermanded and the division kept in the region between the Tensas and the Mississippi until the fall of Vicksburg. Taylor had left Moulton's and Green's brigades in the country west of the Têche, and thither he went in person. At Alexandria he found three regiments of Texan mounted men, about six hundred and fifty aggregate, under the command of Colonel (afterward Brigadier-General) Major, and these were ordered to Morgan's Ferry on the Atchafalaya. Taylor then proceeded to the camps of Moulton and Green, on the lower Têche. After giving instructions preparatory to an attack on a work which the Federals had constructed at Berwick's Bay, Taylor returned to join Colonel Major's command on the Atchafalaya, and with it moved down the Fardoche and Grossetête to Fausse Rivière, opposite to Port Hudson. Here the noise of the bombardment then in progress could be distinctly heard, and here he learned that the Federal force left in New Orleans did not exceed one thousand men.

It was now the 19th of June. He was about one hundred miles from the Federal force at Berwick's Bay. He furnished Colonel Major with guides, informed him that he must be at Berwick's Bay on the morning of the 23d, as Mouton and Green would attack at dawn on that day. Taylor then hastened to the camp of Mouton and Green. The country through which Major was to march was in possession of the enemy, therefore secrecy and celerity were alike required for success. The men carried their rations, and the wagons were sent back across the Atchafalaya. In his rapid march, Major captured seventy prisoners and burned two steamers, and the combined movements of Mouton, Green, and Major, all reached their goal at the appointed time, of which General Taylor says: "Although every precaution had been taken to exclude mistakes and insure coöperation, such complete success is not often attained in combined military movement; and I felt that sacrifices were due to fortune."

At Berwick's Bay the Federals had constructed works to strengthen a position occupied as a depot of supplies. The effective garrison was small, the principal number of those present being sick and convalescents. The works mounted twelve guns, thirty-twos and twenty-fours, and a gunboat was anchored in the bay. Our object was to capture Berwick's Bay, and thence proceed to the execution of the plan above indicated. For this purpose, having arrived on the Têche, a short distance above Berwick's Bay, some small boats (skiffs) and a number of sugar-coolers were collected, in which the men were embarked. Major Hunter, of the Texas regiment, and Major Blair, of the Second Louisiana, were placed in command, and detachments were drawn from the forces. They embarked at night, and paddled down the Têche to the Atchafalaya and Grand Lake. They had about twelve miles to go, and were expected to reach the northeast end of the island, a mile from Berwick's, before daylight, where they were to remain until they heard the guns of our force on the west side of the bay. At dawn on June 23d our guns opened on the gunboat and speedily drove it away. Fire was then directed on the earthworks, and the enemy attempted to reply, when a shout was heard in the rear, and Hunter with his party came rushing on. Resistance ceased at once. The spoils of Berwick's were of vast importance. Twelve thirty-two- and twenty-four-pounder guns, many small arms and accouterments, great quantities of quartermaster's and commissary's, ordnance, and medical stores, and seventeen hundred prisoners were taken. Then, as promptly as circumstances would permit, Taylor, with three thousand men of all arms, proceeded, with the guns and munitions he had acquired, to the execution of the object of his campaign—to raise the siege of Port Hudson, by cutting Banks's communication with New Orleans and making a demonstration which would arouse that city. "Its population of two hundred thousand was bitterly hostile to Federal rule, and the appearance of a Confederate force on the opposite bank of the river would raise such a storm as to bring Banks from Port Hudson, the garrison of which could then unite with General Joseph Johnston in the rear of General Grant."

In the first week in July, twelve guns were placed on the river below Donaldsonville. Fire was opened and one transport destroyed and several turned back. Gunboats attempted to dislodge our batteries, but were driven away by dismounted men, protected by the levee. For three days the river was closed to transports, and mounted scouts were pushed down to a point opposite Kenner, sixteen miles above New Orleans. A few hours more, and there would have been great excitement in the city. But, by the surrender of Port Hudson on July 9th, the enemy were in sufficient force, not only to arrest Taylor's movements, but to require a withdrawal from the exposed position which this little command had assumed for the great object of relieving that place, and thus giving of its garrison, perhaps about five thousand men, as a reënforcement to break the investment of Vicksburg.

Port Hudson, which thus capitulated, was situated on a bend of the Mississippi, about twenty-two miles above Baton Rouge, Louisiana, and one hundred and forty-seven above New Orleans. The defenses in front, or on the water-side, consisted of three series of batteries situated on a bluff and extending along the river above the place. Farther up was an impassable marsh forming a natural defense, and in the rear the works were strong, consisting of several lines of intrenchments and rifle-pits, with heavy trees felled in every direction. General Banks with a large force landed on May 21, 1863, and on the 27th an assault was made on the works, and repulsed. A bombardment from the river was then kept up for several days, and on June 14th another unsuccessful assault was made. This was their last assault, but the enemy, resorting to mines and regular approaches, was slowly progressing with these when the news of the surrender of Vicksburg was received. Major-General Gardner, who was in command, then made a proposal to General Banks to capitulate, which was accepted by the latter, and the position was yielded to him on the next day. The surrender included about six thousand persons all told, fifty-one pieces of artillery, and a quantity of ordnance stores. Our loss in killed and wounded in the assaults was small compared to that of the enemy, and by the fall of Vicksburg the position of Port Hudson had ceased to have much importance.

More than six weeks the garrison, which had resisted a vastly superior force attacking by both land and water, had cheerfully encountered danger and fatigue without a murmur, had borne famine and had repulsed every assault, and yielded Port Hudson only when the fall of Vicksburg had deprived the position of its importance.

I had regarded it of vast importance to hold the two positions of Vicksburg and Port Hudson. Though gunboats had passed the batteries of both, they had found it hazardous, and transport-vessels could not prudently risk it. Taylor on the 10th received intelligence of the fall of Port Hudson, and some hours later learned that Vicksburg had surrendered. His batteries and outposts were ordered in to the Lafourche, and Mouton was sent to Berwick's to cross the stores to the west side of the bay. On the 13th a force of six thousand men followed his retreat down the Lafourche; but Green, with fourteen hundred dismounted men and a battery, attacked the Federals so vigorously as to drive them into Donaldsonville, capturing two hundred prisoners, many small-arms, and two guns. Undisturbed thereafter, Taylor continued his march, removed all the stores from the fortifications at Berwick's, and on the 21st of July moved up the Têche. The pickets left at Berwick's reported that the enemy's scouts only reached the bay twenty-four hours after Taylor's troops had withdrawn.

In the recital of those events connected with the sieges of Port Hudson and Vicksburg, enough has been given to show the great anxiety of the Administration to retain those two positions as necessary to continued communication between the Confederate States on the east and west sides of the Mississippi River. General Johnston, commanding the department, and General Pemberton, the district commander, entertained quite different views. The former considered the safety of the garrisons of such paramount importance, that the position should be evacuated rather than the loss of the troops hazarded; the latter regarded the holding of Vicksburg as of such vital consequence that an army should be hazarded to maintain its possession. When General Pemberton and his forces were besieged in Vicksburg, every effort was made to supply General Johnston with an army which might raise the siege. While General Johnston was at Jackson, preparing to advance against the army investing Vicksburg, the knowledge that the enemy was receiving large reënforcements made it evident that the most prompt action was necessary for success; of this General Johnston manifested a clear perception, for on the 25th of May he sent Pemberton the following message:

Bragg is sending a division; when it comes, I will move to you.

After all the troops which could be drawn from other points had been sent to him, it was suggested that he might defeat the force investing Port Hudson, and unite the garrison with his troops at Jackson, but he replied:

We can not relieve Port Hudson without giving up Jackson, by which we should lose Mississippi.

On June 29th General Johnston reports that—

Field transportation and other supplies having been obtained, the army marched toward the Big Black, and on the evening of July 1st encamped between Brownsville and the river.

The 2d and 3d of July were spent in reconnaissance, from which the conclusion was reached that an attack on the north side of the railroad was impracticable, and examinations were commenced on the south side of the railroad. On the 3d a messenger was sent to General Pemberton that an attempt would be made about the 7th, by an attack on the enemy, to create a diversion which might enable Pemberton to cut his way out. The message was not received, and Pemberton, despairing of aid from the exterior, capitulated on the 4th.

General Grant, in expectation that an attack in his rear would be made by General J. E. Johnston, formed a provisional corps by taking brigades from several corps, and assigned General Sherman to command it. He was sent in the direction of Big Black. Colonel Wilson, then commanding the Fifteenth Illinois Cavalry, was sent to the Big Black River to watch for the expected advance of Johnston, when Sherman was to be notified, so that he might meet and hold Johnston in check until additional reënforcements should arrive. Wilson never sent the notice.

General Johnston, being informed on the 5th of the surrender of Vicksburg, fell back to Jackson, where his army arrived on the 7th. [In his words:]

On the morning of the 9th the enemy appeared in heavy force in front of the works thrown up for the defense of the place; these, consisting of a line of rifle-pits prepared at intervals for artillery, . . . were badly located and constructed, presenting but a slight obstacle to a vigorous assault.

The weather was hot; deep dust covered the country roads, and for about ten miles there was no water to supply the troops who were advancing in heavy order of battle from Clinton; and the circumstances above mentioned caused General Johnston, as he states, to expect that the enemy "would be compelled to make an immediate assault." Sherman, in command of the attacking column, did not, however, elect to assault the intrenchments, but moved the left of his line around so as to rest upon Pearl River above, and then, extending his right so as to reach the river below, commenced intrenching a line of investment. As early as May 27th Brigadier-General J. G. Rains had been directed to report to General Johnston in connection with torpedoes and sub-terra shells, and a request had been made for "all reasonable facilities and aid in the supply of men or material for the fair trial of his torpedoes and shells." There could scarcely have been presented a better opportunity for their use than that offered by the heavy column marching against Jackson, and the enemy would have been taken at great disadvantage if our troops had met them midway between Jackson and Clinton. As the defenses of Jackson had not been so corrected in location and increased in strength as to avail against anything other than a mere assault, it is greatly to be regretted that the railroad-bridge across Pearl River was not so repaired that the large equipments of the Central road might have been removed for use elsewhere and at other times. One of the serious embarrassments suffered in the last two years of the war was from the want of rolling-stock, with which to operate our railroads, as required for the transportation of troops and supplies. On the 12th of July a heavy cannonade was opened, and the missiles reached all parts of the town. An assault was also made on Major-General Breckinridge's position on our extreme left. His division, with the aid of Cobb's and Slocum's batteries, repulsed it, inflicting severe loss, and capturing two hundred prisoners, besides the wounded, and taking three regimental colors. On the 15th General Johnston was assured that the remainder of Grant's army was moving from Vicksburg to Jackson, and on the night of the 16th he successfully withdrew his army across the Pearl River, and moved toward Brandon, and continued the march as far as Morton, about thirty-five miles from Jackson. The enemy followed no further than Brandon, which was reached on the 19th, and manifested no higher purpose than that of arson, which was exhibited on a still larger scale at Jackson.

Thus, within the first half of July, our disasters had followed close upon the heels of one another. Though not defeated at Gettysburg, we had suffered a check, and an army, to which nothing was considered impossible, had been compelled to retire, leaving its opponent in possession of the field of battle. The loss of Vicksburg and Port Hudson was the surrender of the Mississippi to the enemy. It was true that gunboats had run by our batteries, but not with impunity, and some of them had been sunk in the attempt. Transports for troops, supplies, and merchandise could not, except at great risk, use the river while our batteries at those two points remained effective, and gunboats cruising between them would have but a barren field. Moreover, they needed to be very numerous to prevent intercourse between the two sides of the river, which, thus far, they had never been able to effect.

Chapter 33

Chattanooga; Chickamauga

AFTER THE BATTLE at Murfreesboro, in Tennessee, a period of inactivity ensued between the large armed forces, which was disturbed only by occasional expeditions by small bodies on each side. In September, 1863, the main body of our army was encamped near Chattanooga, while the cavalry force was recruiting from fatigue and exhaustion near Rome, Georgia. The enemy first attempted to strike Buckner in the rear, but failing, commenced a movement against our left and rear. On the last of August he had crossed his main force over the Tennessee River at Carpenter's Ferry, near Stevenson. Our effective force of infantry and artillery was about thirty-five thousand. By active reconnaissance of our cavalry, which had been brought forward, it was ascertained that Rosecrans's general movement was toward our left and rear, in the direction of Dalton and Rome, keeping Lookout Mountain between us. The want of supplies in the country and the force under Burnside on our right rendered hazardous a movement on the rear of the former with our force. General Lee, with characteristic self-denial, had consented to remain for a time on the defensive for the purpose of reënforcing Bragg's army, and General Longstreet had been detached with his corps for that purpose. These troops were to come by rail from Atlanta, and might soon be expected to arrive. It was, therefore, determined to retire toward our expected reënforcements, as well as to meet the foe in front when he should emerge from the mountain-gorges.

As we could not thus hold Chattanooga, our army, on September 7th and 8th, took position from Lee and Gordon's Mill to Lafayette, on the road leading south from Chattanooga and fronting the east slope of Lookout Mountain. The forces on the Hiawassee and at Chickamauga Station took the route by Ringgold. A small cavalry force was left in observation at Chattanooga, and a brigade of infantry at Ringgold to cover the railroad.

The enemy immediately moved the corps that threatened Buckner into Chattanooga, and, shortly after, it commenced to move on our rear by the roads to Lafayette and Ringgold. Another corps was nearly opposite the head of McLemore Cove, in Will's Valley, and one at Colonel Winston's opposite Alpine. During the 9th it was ascertained that a column, between four and five thousand, had crossed Lookout Mountain by Stevens's and Cooper's Gaps into McLemore's Cove. An effort was made by General Bragg to capture this column, with intent then to turn upon the others, and beat each in succession. But, some delay having occurred in the advance of our forces through the gaps, the enemy took advantage of it and retreated to the mountain-passes. He then withdrew his corps from the route toward Alpine to unite with the one near McLemore's Cove, which was gradually extended toward Lee and Gordon's Mills. It was not determined to turn upon the Third Corps of the enemy, approaching us from the direction of Chattanooga. The forces sent toward the Cove were accordingly withdrawn to Lafayette, and Polk's and Walker's corps were moved immediately in the direction of Lee and Gordon's Mills, Lieutenant-General Polk commanding. He was ordered to attack early the next morning, as the enemy's corps was known to be divided, and it was hoped by successive attacks to crush his army in detail; but the expectation was not realized, as his forces withdrew and formed a junction. Our trains and supplies were then put in a safe position, and all our forces were concentrated along the Chickamauga, threatening the opposing force in front. Major-General Wheeler, with two divisions of cavalry, occupied the extreme left, vacated by Hill's corps, and was directed to press the enemy in McLemore's Cove; to divert his attention from the real movement, General Forrest covered the movement on our front and right; General B. R. Johnson was moved from Ringgold to the extreme right of the line; Walker's corps formed on his left opposite Alexander's Bridge, Buckner's next, near Tedford Ford, Polk opposite Lee and Gordon's Mills, and Hill on the extreme left. Orders were issued to cross the Chickamauga at 6 A. M., commencing by the extreme right.

The movements were unexpectedly delayed by the difficulty of the roads and the resistance of the enemy's cavalry. The right column did not effect its crossing until late in the afternoon of the 18th; at this time, Major-General Hood, from the Army of Northern Virginia, arrived and assumed command of the column. General W. H. T. Walker had a severe skirmish at Alexander's Bridge, from which he finally drove the enemy, but not before he had destroyed it; General Walker, however, found a ford, crossed, and Hood united with him after night. The advance was resumed at daylight on the 19th, when Buckner's corps with Cheatham's division of Polk's corps crossed the Chickamauga, and our line of battle was thus formed: Buckner's left rested on the bank of the stream about one mile below Lee and Gordon's Mills; on his right came Hood with his own and Johnson's divisions, and Walker's formed the extreme right; Forrest with his cavalry was in advance to the right. He soon became engaged with such a large force that two brigades were sent from Walker's division to his support. Forrest, here fighting with his usual tenacity, desperately held in check the comparatively immense force which he was resisting. General Walker, being ordered to commence the attack on the right, boldly advanced, and soon developed opposing forces greatly superior to his own; he, however, drove them handsomely, capturing several batteries of artillery, by dashing charges. As he pressed back the force in his front, it rested upon such heavy masses in the rear, that he was in turn repulsed. Cheatham's division was ordered to his support; it came too late. Before it could reach him, assailed on both flanks, he had been forced back to his first position, but the two commands united, though yet greatly outnumbered, and, by a spirited attack, recovered our advantage. These movements on our right were in such direction as to create an opening between the left of Cheatham's division and the right of Hood's. To fill this, Stewart's division, the reserve of Buckner's corps, was ordered up, and soon became engaged, as now did Hood's whole front. The enemy had transferred forces from his extreme right so as to concentrate his main body on his left, acutely perceiving the probability of an effort on our part to gain his rear, and cut off his communication with his base at Chattanooga. The main part of the battle, therefore, was fought on the opposite flank from that where both armies had probably expected it. Lieutenant-General Polk was now directed to move the remainder of his corps across the stream, and to assume command in person; Hill's corps was also directed to move to our right. Stewart, by a gallant assault, broke the enemy's center, and pushed forward until he became exposed to an enfilading fire. Hood steadily advanced, driving the force in his front until night. Cleburne, of Hill's corps, immediately on reaching the right, closed so impetuously with the enemy as to create surprise, and drove him in great disorder. From prisoners and otherwise, the commanding General became satisfied that his antagonist had by marching night and day succeeded in concentrating his whole force, and that it had that day been fought on the field of Chickamauga. A part of the forces on our extreme left had not reached the field of actual conflict in time to participate in the engagement of that day; they, together with the remainder of Longstreet's corps, were brought up and put in position to renew the battle in the morning. Our troops slept upon the field they had so bravely contested. The Confederate troops engaged on the right consisted of 33,583 men.

General Wheeler with his cavalry had been in observation on the left, and for a fortnight, daily skirmishing with the enemy. On the 17th he was ordered to move into McLemore's Cove to make a demonstration in that direction, where, after a severe engagement, he developed a force too large to be dislodged. On the 18th he was directed to hold the gap in Pigeon Mountain, so as to prevent the enemy from moving on our left. As appeared subsequently, General Rosecrans, by forced marches, had made a *détour*, and formed a junction of his forces in front of ours, so that it was no longer needful to hold the passes of the Pigeon Mountain, and Wheeler with his cavalry was called to take position on the left of our line.

On the night of the 19th, the whole force having been assembled, including the five thousand effective infantry sent for temporary service from Virginia, the command was organized as two corps, the one on the right to be commanded by Lieutenant-General Polk with 22,471 men; the other, on the left, to be commanded by Lieutenant-General Longstreet with 24,850 men. The forces under Rosecrans, consisted of 64,392. On the night of the 19th General Bragg gave his instructions orally, to the general officers whom he had summoned to his camp-fire, as to the position of the different commands; and the order of battle was that the attack should commence on the right at daybreak, and be taken up successively to the left. From a combination of mishaps, it resulted that the attack was not commenced until nine or ten o'clock in the day, and, what was much more important, the troops from right to left did not in rapid succession engage, so as to have that effectiveness which would have resulted from concert of action. Prodigies of valor were performed, many partial successes were gained in the beginning of the battle, but in the first operations the troops so frequently moved to the assault without the necessary cohesion in a charging line, that nearly all early assaults by our right wing were successively repulsed with loss. Though at first invariably successful, our troops were subsequently compelled to retire before the heavy reënforcements constantly brought.

Wheeler with his cavalry struck boldly at the enemy's extreme right and center, and with such effect that, in the Federal battle reports, it appears the attack was mistaken for a flank movement by General Longstreet.

Rosecrans having transferred his main strength to our right, the attack of the left met with less resistance, and was successfully and vigorously followed up. About 4 P.M. a general assault was made by the right, and the attack was pressed from right to left until the enemy gave way at different points, and, finally, about dark, yielded along the whole line. Our army bivouacked on the ground it had so gallantly won. The foe, though driven from his lines, continued to confront us when the action closed. But it was found the next morning that he had availed himself of the night to withdraw from our front, and that his main body was soon in position within his lines at Chattanooga. We captured over eight thousand prisoners, fifty-one pieces of artillery, fifteen thousand stand of small arms, and quantities of ammunition, with wagons, ambulances, teams, and medicines with hospital stores in large quantities. From the appearance of the field the enemy's losses must have largely exceeded ours, and the victory was complete; but these results could not console us for the lives they cost. After General Rosecrans's retreat to Chattanooga, he withdrew his forces from the passes of Lookout Mountain, which covered his line of supplies from Bridgeport. These commanding positions were immediately occupied by our troops, and a cavalry force was sent across the Tennessee, which destroyed a large wagon-train in the Sequatchie Valley, captured McMinnsville and other points on the railroad, and thus temporarily cut off the source of supplies for the army at Chattanooga.

The reasons why General Bragg did not promptly pursue are stated in his report thus:

Our supplies of all kinds were greatly reduced, the railroad having been constantly occupied in transporting troops, prisoners, and our wounded, and the bridges having been destroyed to a point two miles south of Ringgold. These supplies were ordered to be replenished, and, as soon as it was seen that we could be subsisted, the army was moved forward to seize and hold the only communication the enemy had with his supplies in the rear. His important road, and the shortest by half to his depot at Bridgeport, lay along the south bank of the Tennessee. The holding of this all-important route was confided to Lieutenant-General Longstreet's command, and its possession forced the enemy to a road double the length, over two ranges of mountains, by wagon transportation. At the same time, our cavalry, in large force, was thrown across the river to operate on this long and difficult route. These dispositions, faithfully sustained, insured the enemy's speedy evacuation of Chattanooga for want of food and forage.

These reverses caused the enemy to send forward reënforcements from the army at Vicksburg, and also to assign General Grant to the command in Tennessee. As early as September 23d the Eleventh and Twelfth Corps of the Army of the Potomac were detached, and sent under General Hooker to Tennessee, and assigned to protect Rosecrans's line of communication from Bridgeport to Nashville. It was on October 23d that General Grant arrived at Chattanooga, and only in time to save their army from starvation or evacuation. The investment by General Bragg had been so close and their communications had been so destroyed that Bragg was on the point of realizing the evacuation of Chattanooga, which he had anticipated.

The first movement under Grant was, therefore, to establish a new and shorter line of supplies. For this purpose a night expedition was sent down the river from Chattanooga, which seized the range of hills at the mouth of Lookout Valley, and covered the Brown's Ferry road. By 10 A. M. a bridge was laid across the river at the ferry, which secured the end of the road nearest to our forces and the shorter line over which the enemy could move troops. General Hooker also entered Lookout Valley at Wauhatchie, and took up positions for the defense of the road from Whiteside's, over which he had marched, and also the road leading from Brown's Ferry to Kelly's Ferry. General Palmer crossed from the north side of the river opposite Whiteside's, and held the road passed over by Hooker. An unsuccessful attack was made on a portion of Hooker's troops the first night after he entered the valley. Subsequently, we lost the remaining heights held by us west of Lookout Creek.

Further operations of the enemy were delayed until the arrival of Sherman's force from Memphis. After his arrival, on November 23d, an attempt was made to feel our lines. This was done with so much force as to obtain possession of

Indian Hill and the low range of hills south of it. That night Sherman began to move to obtain a position just below the mouth of the South Chickamauga, and by daylight on the 24th he had eight thousand men on the south side of the Tennessee, and fortified in rifle-trenches. By noon pontoon-bridges were laid across the Tennessee and the Chickamauga, and the remainder of his forces crossed. During the afternoon he took possession of the whole northern extremity of Missionary Ridge nearly to the railroad-tunnel, and fortified the position equally with that held by us. A raid was also made on our line of communication, cutting the railroad at Cleveland. On the same day Hooker scaled the western slope of Lookout Mountain. On the 25th he took possession of the mountain-top with a part of his force, and with the remainder crossed Chattanooga Valley to Rossville. Our most northern point was assailed by Sherman, and the attack kept up all day. He was reënforced by a part of Howard's corps. In the afternoon the whole force of the enemy's center, consisting of four divisions, was moved to the attack. They got possession of the rifle-pits at the foot of Missionary Ridge, and commenced the ascent of the mountain from right to left, and continued it until the summit was reached, notwithstanding the volleys of grape and canister discharged at them. Our forces retreated from the ridge as the multitudinous assailants neared the thin line on the crest, and during the night withdrew from the positions on the plain below. General Grant, after advancing a short distance from Chattanooga, dispatched a portion of his forces to the relief of Burnside in East Tennessee, where he was closely besieged by General Longstreet in Knoxville. Longstreet moved east into Virginia, and ultimately joined General Lee. He had left the army of General Lee, and moved to the West with his force, on the condition that he should return when summoned. This summons had been sent to him. The loss of the enemy in the conflicts at Chattanooga was 757 killed, 4,529 wounded, and 337 missing; total, 5,616. Our loss in killed and wounded was much less than theirs.

Chapter 34

Gettysburg

IN THE SPRING of 1863 the enemy occupied his former position before Fredericksburg. He was in great strength, and, so far as we could learn, was preparing on the grandest scale for another advance against Richmond, which in political if not military circles was regarded as the objective point of the war. The consolidated report of the Army of the Potomac, then under the command of Major-General Hooker, states the force present on May 10, 1863, to be 136,704.

General Lee's forces had been reorganized into three army corps, designated the First, Second, and Third Corps. In the order named, they were commanded by Lieutenant-Generals Longstreet, Ewell, and A. P. Hill.

The zeal of our people in the defense of their country's cause had brought nearly all of the population fit for military service to the various armies then in the field, so that but little increase could be hoped for by the Army of Northern Virginia. Under these circumstances, to wait until the enemy should choose to advance was to take the desperate hazard of the great inequality of numbers, as well as ability to reënforce, which he possessed. In addition to the army under General Hooker, a considerable force occupied the lower part of the Valley of the Shenandoah.

It was decided by a bold movement to attempt to transfer hostilities to the north side of the Potomac, by crossing the river and marching into Maryland and Pennsylvania, simultaneously driving the foe out of the Shenandoah Valley. Thus, it was hoped, General Hooker's army would be called from Virginia to meet our advance toward the heart of the enemy's country. In that event, the vast preparations which had been made for an advance upon Richmond would be foiled, the plan for his summer's campaign deranged, and much of the season for active operations be consumed in the new combinations and dispositions which would be required. If, beyond the Potomac, some opportunity should be offered so as to enable us to defeat the army on which our foe most relied, the measure of our success would be full; but, if the movement only resulted in freeing Virginia from the presence of the hostile army, it was more than could fairly be expected from awaiting the attack which was clearly indicated.

On the night of the 27th information was received that General Hooker had crossed the Potomac, and was advancing northward, and that the head of the column had reached South Mountain. This menaced our communications, and it was resolved to prevent his further progress by concentrating our army on the east side of the mountain. Accordingly, the different commands were ordered to proceed to Gettysburg. This march was conducted more slowly than it would have been had the movements of Hooker been known. Heth's, the leading division of Hill's corps, met the enemy in front of Gettysburg on the morning of July 1st, driving him back to within a short distance of the town; the advance there encountered a larger force, with which two of Hill's divisions became engaged. Ewell, coming up with two of his divisions, joined in the engagement; and the opposing force was driven through Gettysburg with heavy loss, including about five thousand prisoners and several pieces of artillery.

Under the instructions given to them not to bring on a general engagement, these corps bivouacked on the ground they had won.

Preparations for a general engagement were unfortunately delayed until the afternoon, instead of being made at sunrise; then troops had been concentrated, and "Round-Top," the commanding position, unoccupied in the morning, had received the force which inflicted such disaster on our assaulting columns. The position at Gettysburg was not the choice of either side. South from the town an irregular, interrupted line of hills runs, which is sometimes called the "Gettysburg Ridge." This ridge, at the town, turns eastward and then southward. At the turn eastward is Cemetery Hill and at the turn southward Culps's Hill. From Cemetery Hill the line runs southward about three miles in a well-defined ridge, since the battle called Cemetery Ridge, and terminates in a high, rocky, and wooded peak named Round-Top, which was the key of the enemy's position, as it flanked their line. The less elevated portion, near where the crest rises into Round-Top, is termed "Little Round-Top," a rough and bold spur of the former. Thus, while Cemetery and Culps's Hills require the formation of a line of battle to face northward, the direction of Cemetery Ridge requires the line to face westward. The crest has a good slope to the rear, while to the west it falls off in a cultivated and undulating valley, which it commands. About a mile distant is a parallel crest, known as Seminary Ridge, and which our forces occupied during the battle. Longstreet, with the divisions of Hood and McLaws, faced Round-Top and a good part of Cemetery Ridge; Hill's three divisions continued the line from the left of Longstreet, fronting the remainder of Cemetery Ridge; while Ewell, with his three divisions, held a line through the town, and, sweeping round the base of Cemetery Hill, terminated the left in front of Culps's Hill.

These were the positions of the three corps after the arrival of General Longstreet's troops.

The main purpose of the movement across the Potomac was to free Virginia from the presence of the enemy. If this could be done by manœuvering merely, a most important result would be cheaply obtained. The contingency of a battle was of course deemed probable, and, with any fair opportunity, the Army of Northern Virginia was considered sure to win a victory.

It had not been intended to fight a general battle at such a distance as Gettysburg from our base, unless attacked; but, being unexpectedly confronted by the opposing army, it became a matter of difficulty to withdraw through the mountains with our large trains. At the same time the country was unfavorable for collecting supplies while in the presence of the main army of the enemy, as he was enabled to restrain our foraging parties by occupying the passes of the mountains with both regular and local troops. Encouraged by the successful issue of the engagement of the first day, and in view of the valuable results that would ensue from the defeat of the army of General Meade (who had succeeded General Hooker), General Lee thought it preferable to renew the attack.

General Meade held the high ridge above described, along which he had massed a large amount of artillery. General Ewell occupied the left of our line, General Hill the center, and General Longstreet the right. In front of General Longstreet the enemy held a position, from which, if he could be driven, it was thought that our army could gain the more elevated ground (Round-Top) beyond, and thus enable our guns to rake the crest of the ridge. That officer was directed to endeavor to carry this position, while General Ewell attacked directly the high ground on the enemy's right, which had already been partially fortified. General Hill was instructed to threaten the center of the line, in order to prevent reënforcements to either wing, and to avail himself of any opportunity that might present itself to attack. After a severe struggle Longstreet succeeded in getting possession of and holding the ground in his immediate front. Ewell also carried some of the strong positions which he assailed, and the result was such as to lead to the belief that he would ultimately be able to dislodge the force in his front. The battle ceased at dark. These partial successes determined Lee to continue the assault on the next day. Pickett, with three of his brigades, joined Longstreet on the following morning, and our batteries were moved forward to the position gained by him on the day before. The general plan of attack was unchanged, except that one division and two brigades of Hill's corps were ordered to support Longstreet.

General Meade, in the mean time, had strengthened his line with earthworks. The morning was occupied in necessary preparations, and the battle recommenced in the afternoon of the 3d, and raged with great violence until sunset. Our troops succeeded in entering the advanced works of the enemy, and getting possession of some of his batteries; but, our artillery having nearly expended its ammunition, the attacking columns became exposed to the heavy fire of the numerous batteries near the summit of the ridge, and, after a most determined and gallant struggle, were compelled to relinquish their advantage and fall back to their original positions with severe loss.

Owing to the strength of the enemy's position and the exhaustion of our ammunition, a renewal of the engagement could not be hazarded, and the difficulty of procuring supplies rendered it impossible to continue longer where we were. Such of the wounded as could be removed and a part of the arms collected on the field were ordered to Williamsport. The army remained at Gettysburg during the 4th, and at night began to retire by the road to Fairfield, carrying with it about four thousand prisoners. Nearly two thousand had been previously paroled; but the numerous wounded that had fallen into our hands after the first and second day's engagements were left behind. Little progress was made that night, owing to a severe storm, which greatly embarrassed our movements. The rear of the column did not leave its position near Gettysburg until after daylight on the 5th. The march was continued during that day without interruption by the enemy, except an unimportant demonstration upon our rear in the afternoon, when near Fairfield, which was easily checked. The army, after a tedious march, rendered more difficult by the rains, reached Hagerstown on the afternoon of the 6th and morning of the 7th of July.

The Potomac was so much swollen by the rains, that had fallen almost incessantly since our army entered Maryland as to be unfordable. A pontoon-train had been sent from Richmond, but the rise in the river gave to it a width greater than was expected, so that additional boats had to be made by the army on its retreat. Our communication with the south side was thus interrupted, and it was found difficult to procure either ammunition or subsistence, the latter difficulty being enhanced by the high water impeding the working of the mills. The trains with the wounded and prisoners were compelled to wait at Williamsport for the subsiding of the river or the construction of additional pontoon-boats. The enemy had not yet made his appearance, but, as he was in a condition to obtain large reënforcements and our want of supplies was daily becoming more embarrassing, it was deemed advisable to recross the river. By the 13th a good bridge was thrown over at Falling Waters. On the 12th Meade's army approached. A position had been previously selected to cover the Potomac from Williamsport to Falling Waters, and an attack was awaited during that and the succeeding day. This did not take place, though the two armies were in close proximity, the enemy being occupied in fortifying his own lines.

Our preparations being completed, and the Potomac, though still deep, being pronounced fordable, the army commenced to withdraw to the south side on the night of the 13th. Ewell's corps forded the river at Williamsport, those of Longstreet and Hill crossed upon the bridge. Owing to the condition of the roads the troops did not reach the bridge until after daylight on the 14th, and the crossing was not completed until 1 P. M., when the bridge was removed. General Lee said that the enemy offered no serious interruption, and the movement was attended with no loss of material except a few disabled wagons and two pieces of artillery, which the horses were unable to move through the deep mud. During the slow and tedious march to the bridge, in the midst of a violent storm of rain, some of the men lay down by the way to rest. Officers sent back for them failed to find many in the obscurity of the night, and these, with some stragglers, a few of Heth's division most remote from the bridge, were captured. On the following day the army marched to Bunker Hill, in the vicinity of which it encamped for several days. Owing to the swollen condition of the Shenandoah River, the campaign which was contemplated when the Potomac was recrossed, could not be immediately commenced. Before the waters had subsided, the movements of the enemy required us to cross the Blue Ridge and take position south of the Rappahannock.

The strength of our army at Gettysburg is stated at 62,000 of all arms. The report of the Army of the Potomac under General Meade, on June 30, 1863, states the forces present at 112,988 men. Before the Committee on the Conduct of the War, General Meade, in reference to his force at Gettysburg, said, "Including all arms of the service, my strength was a little under 100,000 men—about 95,000."

If the strength of General Lee's forces, according to the last accessible report before the movement northward, be compared with that made after his return into Virginia, there is a decrease of nineteen thousand of the brave men who had set the seal of invincibility upon the Army of Northern Virginia.

The testimony of General Meade, above mentioned, contains this statement respecting his losses:

On the evening of the 2d of July, after the battle of that day had ceased, and darkness had set in, being aware of the very heavy losses of the First and Eleventh Corps on the 1st of July, and knowing how severely the Third Corps, the Fifth Corps, and other portions of the army, had suffered in the battle of the 2d of July—in fact, as subsequently ascertained, out of the twenty-four thousand men killed, wounded, and missing, which was the amount of my losses and casualties at Gettysburg—over twenty thousand of them had been put *hors de combat* before the night of the 2d of July.

Thus closed the campaign in Pennsylvania. The wisdom of the strategy was justified by the result. The battle of Gettysburg was unfortunate. Though the loss sustained by the enemy was greater than our own, theirs could be repaired, ours could not. It was a graceful thing in President Lincoln if, as reported, when he was shown the steeps which the Northern men persistently held, he answered, "I am proud to be the countryman of the men who assailed those heights."

Chapter 35

Subjugation of Southern and Border States

THE MOST PAINFUL PAGES of this work are those which now present the subjugation of the State governments by the Government of the United States. The details in the case of Tennessee have already been stated. Let us next notice some points in the subversion of the State government of Louisiana. One of the earliest steps taken for a civil organization, after the occupation of New Orleans, was to make a registration of voters. The United States Government was in possession by military force, and the object was to secure its permanent supremacy. Therefore, the oath which was administered to the person applying for registration contained this condition:

I now register myself as a voter, freely and voluntarily, for the purpose of organizing a State government in Louisiana, loyal to the Government of the United States.

It was also announced, with the approval of the military Governor, that any person swearing falsely to any material part of the oath would be deemed to be guilty of perjury, and be liable to prosecution and punishment. The effect of this measure was to secure a registration only of persons who would maintain the supremacy of the Government of the United States. A proclamation was next issued by the commander of the United States forces for an election of State officers under the laws and Constitution of the State. It was declared that these officers, when thus elected, would constitute the so-called civil government of the State, under the Constitution and laws of Louisiana, "except so much of the said Constitution and laws as recognize, regulate, or relate to slavery," which were also declared to be inoperative and void. [A Constitutional Convention was also provided for.]

The effect of these acts was to establish a number of persons, pledged to support the Government of the United States, as the only qualified voters in the State, and to elect so-called State officers and delegates to a so-called Constitutional Convention by their ballots. Subsequently, a so-called convention was held, a so-called new Constitution adopted, complying with the views of the Government of the United States, the amendment to the Constitution of the United States as above mentioned was adopted, the State Representatives were admitted to seats in Congress, and the people acquiesced in the fraud which they had not the power to correct.

In like manner the State government of Maryland was subjugated. A military force, under the authority of the Government of the United States, occupied the city of Baltimore at a time when no invasion of the State was threatened, and when there had been no application of the Legislature, or of the Executive, for protection against domestic violence, which circumstances alone could give a constitutional authority for this organized military force to occupy the State. The commanding General, Schenck, soon issued an order, of which the following is an extract:

Martial law is declared and hereby established in the city and county of Baltimore, and in all the counties of the Western Shore of Maryland. The commanding General gives assurance that this suspension of civil government within the limits defined shall not extend beyond the necessities of the occasion. All the civil courts, tribunals, and political functionaries of State, county, or city authority, are to continue in the discharge of their duties as in times of peace, only in no way interfering with the exercise of the predominant power assumed and asserted by the military authority.

A further subversion of the State government was now commenced by an invasion and denial of some of the unalienable rights of the citizens, for the security of which that government was instituted.

Immediately upon the issue of the order of the commanding General, the arrests of citizens commenced by provost-marshals. The family residence of a lady was forced open; she was seized, put on board of a steamer, and sent to the Confederate States. A man was arrested for being "disloyal" to the United States *Government,* and held for examination. Another was charged with interfering with the enrollment; he was held for further examination. A woman charged with the attempt to resist the enrollment was arrested, and subsequently released. A man, on a charge of "disloyalty," took the oath, and was released. Another, charged with having given improper information to enrolling officers, was released on furnishing the information. Another, charged with having powder in his possession, was released on taking the oath of allegiance. Two others, charged with abuse of the negroes laboring on the fortifications, were held for examination. Another, charged with rendering assistance to wounded confederate soldiers, and expressing treasonable sentiments, took the oath of allegiance and was released. Another, charged with being a soldier in the Confederate army and paroled, was ordered to be sent across the lines. A man, charged with treasonable language, was ordered to be sent across the lines. Another, charged with receiving letters from Confederates for the purpose of delivery, took the oath of allegiance, and was discharged. Another, charged with expressing treasonable sentiments, was held for examination. Two, charged with cheering for Jefferson Davis, took the oath and were released.

One case more must be stated. On May 25, 1861 John Merryman, a most respectable citizen of the State, residing in Baltimore County, was seized in his bed by an armed force, and imprisoned in Fort McHenry. He petitioned the Chief-Justice of the United States that a writ of *habeas corpus* might be issued, which was granted. The officer upon whom it was served declined to obey the writ. An attachment was issued against the officer. The marshal was refused admittance to the fort to serve it. Upon such return being made, the Chief-Justice said:

I ordered the attachment yesterday, because upon the face of the return the detention of the prisoner was unlawful upon two grounds:

1. The President, under the Constitution and laws of the United States, can not suspend the privilege of the writ of *habeas corpus,* nor authorize any military officer to do so.

2. A military officer has no right to arrest and detain a person not subject to the rules and articles of war for an offense against the laws of the United States, except in aid of the judicial authority and subject to its control; and, if the party is arrested by the military, it is the duty of the officer to deliver him over immediately to the civil authority, to be dealt with according to law.

During the month of July arrests were made of 361 persons, on charges like the above mentioned, by the military authority. Of this number, 317 took the oath of allegiance to the Government of the United States, and were released; 5 were sent to Fort McHenry, 3 to Washington for the action of the authorities there, 11 to the North, 6 across the lines, and 19 were held for further examination.

On September 11, 1863, one of the city newspapers published the poem entitled "The Southern Cross." The publishers and editor were immediately arrested, not allowed communication with any person whatever, and on the same day sent across the lines, with the understanding that they should not return during the war. On July 2d an order was issued which forbade the citizens of Baltimore City and County to keep arms unless they were enrolled as volunteer companies. The Fifty-first Regiment of Massachusetts Volunteers was placed at the disposal of General E. B. Tyler, assisted by the provost-marshal and the chief of police. The soldiers, in concert with the police, formed into parties of three or four, and were soon diligently engaged in searching houses. Large wagons were provided, and muskets, carbines, rifles, revolvers of all kinds, sabers, bayonets, swords, and bird and ducking guns in considerable quantities were gathered. The Constitution of the United States says:

> The right of the people to keep and bear arms shall not be infringed.*

A further subversion of the State government of Maryland was next made by a direct interference with the elections. An election was to be held in the State for members of the Legislature and members of Congress on November 3, 1863. The commanding General, on October 27th, issued an order to all marshals and military officers to cause their direct interference with the voters. The Governor (Bradford) applied to the President of the United States to have the order revoked, and protested against any person who offered to vote being put to any test not found in the laws of Maryland. President Lincoln declined to interfere with the order, except in one less important point. The Governor issued a proclamation on the day preceding the election, which the military commander endeavored to suppress, and issued an order charging that the tendency of the proclamation was to invite and suggest disturbance. One or more regiments of soldiers were sent out and distributed among several of the counties to attend the places of election, in defiance of the known laws of the State prohibiting their presence. Military officers and provost-marshals were ordered to arrest voters, guilty, in their opinion, of certain offenses, and to menace judges of election with the power of the army in case this order was not respected.

But, perhaps, the forcible language of the Governor to the

* Article II, amendment.

Legislature will furnish the most undeniable statement of the facts. He says:

> The abuses commenced even before the opening of the polls. On the day preceding the election, the officer in command of the regiment which had been distributed among the counties of the Eastern Shore, and who had himself landed in Kent County, commenced his operations by arresting and sending across the bay some ten or more of the most estimable and distinguished of its citizens, including several of the most steadfast and most uncompromising loyalists of the Shore. The jail of the county was entered, the jailer seized, imprisoned, and afterward sent to Baltimore, and prisoners confined therein under indictment set at liberty. The commanding officer gave the first clew to the kind of disloyalty against which he considered himself as particularly commissioned, by printing and publishing a proclamation in which, referring to the election to take place on the next day, he invited all the truly *loyal* to avail themselves of that opportunity and establish their *loyalty*, "by giving full and ardent support to the whole Government ticket, upon the platform adopted by the Union League Convention," declaring that "none other is recognized by the Federal authorities as loyal or worthy of the support of any one who desires the peace and restoration of the Union."
>
> This Government ticket was in several, if not all, of those counties designated by its color. It was a yellow ticket, and, armed with that, a voter could safely run the gantlet of the sabers and carbines that guarded the entrance of the polls, and known sympathizers with the rebellion were allowed to vote unquestioned if they would vote that ticket, while loyal and respected citizens, ready to take the oath, were turned back by the officer in charge without even allowing them to approach the polls. In one district the military officer took his stand at the polls before they were opened, declaring that none but the "yellow ticket should be voted," and excluded all others throughout the day. In another district a similar officer caused every ballot offered to be examined, and, unless it was the favored one, the voted was required to take the oath, and not otherwise. In another district, after one vote only had been given, the polls were closed, the judges were all arrested and sent out of the county, and military occupation taken of the town. Other statements might be made.

The result was the election of a majority of members of the Legislature in favor of a State Constitutional Convention. The acts necessary for this object were passed. At the election of delegates, the military authority again interfered in order to secure a majority in favor of immediate and unconditional emancipation. The so-called Convention assembled and drafted a so-called Constitution, in which the twenty-third article of the Bill of Rights prohibited the existence of slavery in the State, and said, "All persons held to service or labor as slaves are hereby declared free."

It was urged, in objection to the adoption of the so-called Constitution by the Convention, that "the election by which the Convention was called and its members elected was not free for the legal voters of the State, but was held and conducted in clear violation of the rights of voters, in consequence of which a majority of the legal voters of the State were excluded from the polls." A rigid article on the qualifications of voters at the State elections was embodied in the Constitution, with the shameless provision that it should be in force at the election for ratification or rejection of the so-called Constitution which was to create the disabilities. The instrument also authorized a poll to be opened in each company of every Maryland regiment in the service of the United States at the quarters of the commanding officer, and that the commissioned officers of such company should act as the judges of election. The aid of the President of the United States was also obtained to help on the ratification of the new Constitution. Notwithstanding the aid of the President, of the soldiers' votes, and a most stringent oath, and the exclusion of every person who had in any manner, by word or act, aided the cause of the Confederacy, the majority for the so-called Constitution was only 375. The total vote was 59,973. In 1860 the vote of the State was 92,502.

In the State of Kentucky, the first open and direct measures taken by the Government of the United States for the subjugation of the State government and people, thereby to effect the emancipation of the slaves, consisted in an interference with the voters at the State election in August, 1863. This interference was by means of a military force stationed at the polls to sustain and enforce the action of some of the servants of the Government of the United States, the object being to overawe the judges of election, secure the administration of a rigid oath of allegiance, and thereby the rejection of as many antagonistic votes as possible. Indeed, it was intended that none but so-called "Union" men should vote—that is, men who were willing to approve of every measure which the Government of the United States might adopt to carry on the war and revolutionize the State. At the same time, no man was allowed to be a candidate or to receive any votes unless he was a well-known advocate of the Government of the United States. Meantime, on July 31, 1863, the commanding General of the Department of the Ohio issued an order declaring the State under martial law. The General in command in the western part of the State issued an order to regulate the election in that quarter, and the colonels at every post did likewise. In Louisville, on the day of election, there were ten soldiers with muskets at each voting-place who, with crossed bayonets, stood in the doors, preventing all access of voters to the polls but by their permission, and who arrested and carried to the military prison all whom they were told to arrest. Out of some eight thousand voters in the city, less than five thousand votes were taken. Very many were said to have been deterred from going to the polls through fear that they would be made the victims to personal or party malice. Similar intimidation was practiced in other parts of the State. The result was, that there was not only direct military interference with the election, but it was conducted in most of the State under the intimidation of the bayonets of the Government of the United States. The total vote was 85,695. In 1860 the vote of the State was 146,216.

The Government of the United States was now ready to move forward in its design to destroy one of the most valuable institutions of the State. Steps were taken by its officers to enroll all able-bodied male negroes in the State between the ages of twenty and forty-five years, that they might form a part of its forces. The effect of this measure was to break up the labor system of the State, and meanwhile the pseudo-philanthropists furnished food for powder, and indulged their ideas of freedom at their neighbors' expense. The excitement produced caused the Governor to visit Washington and effect agreements by which all recruiting should cease when a county's quota was full, all recruits should be removed from the State, and other similar provisions. A year later, he said to the Legislature: "Had these agreements been carried out, a very different state of feeling would have existed in Kentucky. But, instead of carrying them out, the most offensive and injurious modes were adopted to violate them."

The next step taken by the Government of the United States in the subversion of the government of Kentucky was the destruction of the unalienable right of personal liberty of the citizens, which the State was in duty bound to protect. The Union Governor of the State, whose election was aided by the United States military officers, as above stated, is the witness for the facts. In his message to the Legislature of January, 1865, he says:

> The gravest matter of military outrage has been, and yet is, the arrest, imprisonment, and banishment of loyal citizens without a hearing, and without even a knowledge of the charges against them. There have been a number of this class of arrests, merely for partisan political vengeance, and to force them to pay heavy sums to purchase their liberation. . . . For partisan political ends, General John B. Huston was arrested at midnight preceding the election, and hurried off under circumstances of shameful aggravation. He was, however, released in a few days; but that does not atone for the criminality of his malicious arrest and false imprisonment. The battle-scarred veteran, Colonel Frank Wolford, . . . is yet held in durance vile, without a hearing and without an accusation, so far as he or his friends can ascertain.
>
> Lieutenant-Governor Jacobs, whose yet unclosed wounds were received in battle for his country, was made a victim to partisan and personal enmity, and hurried without a hearing and without any known accusation through the rebel lines into Virginia. . . . Other cases might be mentioned, but these are selected because they are known to the whole country. . . .

The next step in the progress of the subjugation of the State government was taken by President Lincoln on July 5, 1864, when he issued a proclamation establishing martial law throughout the State, and the suspension of the writ of *habeas corpus*. Civil proceedings were allowed to be continued, "which did not affect the military operations or the constituted authorities of the Government of the United States." Arrests of individuals by military force soon commenced, and a large number of eminent Kentuckians of all professions and pursuits were imprisoned. A group of persons, consisting of judges, magistrates, wealthy merchants, and young women, without having been allowed a hearing, or trial, or any opportunity to vindicate themselves, were banished from the State. In this destruction of the unalienable right of personal liberty, the State government was passive; indeed, it was powerless to resist.

A State election was to be held on the first Monday of August for local officers and a Judge of the High Court of Appeals from one district. Chief-Justice Duvall was one of the two candidates. On July 29th an order was issued by the Major-General, commanding, to the sheriffs of the counties concerned, as follows:

You will not allow the name of Alvin Duvall to appear upon the poll-books as a candidate for office at the coming election.

Another name was substituted. The election of a President of the United States was to be held in November, but the Government of the United States seems to have regarded the vote of the State as unnecessary to secure the reëlection of its officials, and refrained from interference. By enlistment, over twenty-two thousand of the most valuable slaves in the State had gone into the service of the United States, and on March 3, 1865, its Congress passed an act declaring that the wives and children of all such soldiers should be free. But the final moment was near at hand when the annihilation of more than one hundred millions of property and the destruction of one of the most important institutions of the State was to take place by one of those fictions so peculiar to this administration of the Government of the United States. That was the pretended adoption of a constitutional amendment, prohibiting the existence of slavery in the United States. The subversion of the State government of Missouri by the Government of the United States was more rapid and more desperate than in the case of Kentucky. As previously stated, the Governor of the State, at the commencement of the difficulties, proposed the most conciliatory terms to the Government of the United States, which were rejected. He then, sensible of his duty to protect the rights of his people issued his proclamation calling into active service fifty thousand of the State militia, "for the purpose of repelling invasion, and for the protection of the lives, liberty, and property of the citizens." The plea of the invader was continued in an order issued from Washington to the commanding General in these words:

The President observes with concern that, notwithstanding the pledge of the State authorities to coöperate in preserving the peace of Missouri, loyal citizens in great numbers continue to be driven from their homes. . . . It will devolve on you the duty of putting a stop to them summarily by the force under your command, to be aided by such troops as you may require from Kansas, Iowa, and Illinois. . . .

In this order the only pretext put forward is that of domestic violence. But in that case the Constitution of the United States gives no authority to the United States Government to interfere except on the express conditions of an "application of the Legislature, or of the Executive, when the Legislature can not be convened." There had been no application of the Legislature or of the Executive. On the contrary, the Governor of the State, like a brave man, told the Executive of the United States to keep his hands off, and to keep his military forces without the State, and he pledged himself to preserve its peace and neutrality. However, the subjugation of the State government of Missouri to the will and designs of the Government at Washington had been determined upon, and the sovereignty of the people was to be crushed by troops from the sister States of Kansas, Iowa, and Illinois.

But the bravery of the Governor and the determination of the Legislature caused the Government of the United States to adopt bolder measures. The Governor was charged with purposes of treason and secession.

Troops were now poured into the State by the Government of the United States so rapidly as to render the successful opposition of the lawful authorities impossible, and the control of a large portion of the State was soon held by the military forces. The Governor, unable to resist, retired to the southern part of the State. Meantime, the State Convention, which had been called to consider the relations between the Government of the United States and the State of Missouri, and to adopt such measures for vindicating the sovereignty of the State as were necessary, reassembled on the call of its committee. It proceeded to declare the State offices vacant, and to elect a provisional Governor and other officers entirely subservient to the will and behests of the Administration at Washington. The commanding General now declared martial law in the State, and the emancipation of all slaves belonging to persons who had taken an active part with us. This emancipation clause was soon modified by the President as in advance of the times.

The severity of the Executive of the United States now began to be felt by the citizens of the State. All disaffected persons were silenced or arrested, prisoners of war were treated as criminals. The State government was represented by a provisional Governor; and a State Convention, that adjourned its session from year to year, after dallying periodically with the subject of the emancipation of the slaves, finally passed an ordinance for that purpose, to take effect in 1870. This was not immediate emancipation, so the disturbances were kept up in the State until, at a session of the Legislature in February, 1864, a bill was passed for a so-called State Convention to revise the State Constitution, and the election of delegates in November. It is remarkable how much the orders of the commanding General now contained relative to disorderly persons. This was preparatory to the occupation of the polls by the military force, and the exclusion of all opposition voters. The delegates were elected, and the so-called Convention assembled on January 6, 1865. An immediate emancipation ordinance was passed, and the State organization was subjugated to do the will of the usurper.

Chapter 36

Subjugation of Northern States

Now FOLLOWS the humiliating spectacle of the subjugation of the State government of New York—the "Empire" State, as she calls herself—where, with all her men and treasures, it might have been supposed that some stanch defenders of constitutional liberty would have sprung up.

To show how the laws were disregarded, and how despotically the personal liberty of the citizen was invaded, let this example bear witness: The Secretary of State at Washington, William H. Seward, a favored son of the State of New York, would "ring a little bell," which brought to him a messenger, to whom was given a secret order to arrest and confine in Fort Lafayette a person designated. This order was sent by telegraph to the United States Marshal of the district in which would be found the person who was to be arrested. The arrest being forcibly made by the marshal with armed attendants without even the form of a warrant, the prisoner without the knowledge of any charge against him was conveyed to Fort Hamilton and turned over to the commandant. An aid with a guard of soldiers then conveyed him in a boat to Fort Lafayette and delivered him to the keeper in charge, who gave a receipt for the prisoner. He was then divested of any weapons, money, valuables, or papers in his possession. His baggage was opened and searched. A soldier then took him in charge to the designated quarter, which was a portion of one of the casemates for guns, lighted only from the port-hole, and occupied by seven or eight other prisoners. All were subjected to prison fare. Some were citizens of New York, and the others of different States. This manner of imprisonment was subsequently put under the direction of the Secretary of War, and continued at intervals until the close of the war.

In the brief period between July 1 and October 19, 1861, the Secretary of State, William H. Seward, made such diligent use of his "little bell," that one hundred and seventy-five of the most respectable citizens of the country were consigned to imprisonment in Fort Lafayette, a strong fortress in the lower part of the harbor of New York.

A few instances will afford an illustration of the facts. Mr.

Pierce Butler was suspected of corresponding with persons in the Confederate States. He was arrested in Philadelphia on August 19, 1861, by order of Simon Cameron, then Secretary of War, without process of law and without any assigned cause. His trunks and drawers, wardrobe, and entire apartments were seached, and his private papers taken by the marshal and his four assistants. His office was also examined, and his books and papers taken, and within an hour he was on his way to Fort Lafayette with an armed guard. After five weeks of detention he was liberated. No reason was given for his discharge any more than for his arrest. As Mr. Cameron was about to sail as Minister to Russia, in January ensuing, he was arrested for assault and battery and false imprisonment, at the suit of Mr. Butler. The case was brought to the knowledge of the President of the United States, and on April 18, 1862, the Secretary of State, Seward, replied as follows:

The communication has been submitted to the President, and I am directed by him to say in reply that he avows the proceeding of Mr. Cameron referred to as one taken by him when Secretary of War, under the President's directions, and deemed necessary for the prompt suppression of the existing rebellion.

The writ of *habeas corpus* was issued by some of the State courts, directing the officer in command at the fort to bring some one or other of the prisoners into court for an investigation of the cause and authority for his detention. But no attention was given to these writs by the officer. Neither did the Governor of the State make any effort to enforce the processes of the courts. He, perhaps, expected that his efforts might be resisted by an overpowering force. But expectations, of whatsoever nature, do not justify or excuse the neglect of a positive duty. Thus the Constitution, the laws, the courts, the Executive of the State of New York, were subverted, turned aside from the end for which they were instituted, and all the specific arrangments were of no avail to secure this guaranteed right of its citizens. Probably every one of the prisoners was entirely innocent of any act whatever that was criminal under the laws, either of the State or of the United States.

In opinion they were opposed to the military proceedings of the Government of the United States; and these opinions they had expressed, which liberty is a part of the birthright of free-men. Indeed, Judge Nelson, of the Supreme Court of the United States, in the Circuit of New York, in an opinion delivered about this time, thus expressed himself:

Words, oral, written, or printed, however treasonable, seditious, or criminal of themselves, do not constitute an overt act of treason within the definition of the crime. When spoken, written, or printed, in relation to an act or acts which, if committed with a treasonable design, might constitute such overt act, they are admissible as evidence, tending to characterize it and show the intent with which the act was committed.

Finally, the prison in New York Harbor became so full that many prisoners were sent to Fort Warren in the harbor of Boston. At this time the Government of the United States used the Old Capitol at Washington, Fort McHenry of Baltimore, Fort Lafayette at New York, and Fort Warren at Boston, for the confinement of those whom the usurper designated as "state prisoners." Still further to relieve the fullness of the prisons, two men, John A. Dix, of the army, and Edwards Pierrepont, of civil life, were sent to investigate the cases of the prisoners, and release some who were willing to take an "oath of allegiance." Next it was made a condition precedent to an investigation that the said oath should be taken by the prisoner. As an instance, this proposal was made to two persons named Flanders, citizens of the interior of New York. The oath was as follows:

I do solemnly swear that I will support, protect, and defend the Constitution and Government of the United States against all enemies, whether domestic or foreign, and that I will bear true faith, allegiance, and loyalty to the same, any ordinance, resolution, or law of any State Convention, or Legislature, to the contrary notwithstanding; and, further, that I do this with a full determination, pledge, and purpose, without any mental reservation or evasion whatsoever; and, further, that I will well and faithfully perform all the duties which may be required of me by law.

These persons declined to take the prescribed oath. They said:

We have been guilty of no offense against the laws of our country, but have simply exercised our constitutional rights as free citizens in the open and manly expression of our opinions upon public affairs. We have been placed here without legal charges, or, indeed, any charges whatsoever being made against us, and upon no legal process, but upon an arbitrary and illegal order of the Hon. William H. Seward, Secretary of State of the United States. Every moment of our detention here is a denial of our most sacred rights. We are entitled to and hereby demand an unconditional discharge; and, while we could cheerfully take the oath prescribed by the Constitution of the United States, because we are, always have been, and ever intend to be loyal to that instrument (though at the same time protesting against the right of the Government to impose even such oath upon us as the condition of our discharge), we can not consent to take the oath now required of us, because we hold no office of any kind under the Government of the United States, and it is an oath unknown to and unauthorized by the Constitution, and commits us to the support of the Government though it may be acting in direct conflict with the Constitution, and deprives us of the right of freely discussing, and by peaceful and constitutional methods opposing its measures. . . . American citizen should voluntarily surrender. That such is the interpretation put upon this oath by the Government, and such its intended effect is plainly demonstrated by the fact that it is dictated to us as a condition of our release from an imprisonment inflicted upon us for no other cause than that we have exercised the above-specified constitutional rights.

One important fact which illustrates the flagrant outrage committed on all these prisoners should not be omitted. The Constitution of the United States declares as follows:

In all criminal prosecutions, the accused shall enjoy the right . . . to have the assistance of counsel for his defense.

On December 3, 1861, the commanding officer at Fort Lafayette came to the prisoners' quarters, and read a document, of which the following is a copy:

To the political prisoners in Fort Lafayette:
I am instructed by the Secretary of State to inform you that the Department of State of the United States will not recognize any one as an attorney for political prisoners, and will look with distrust upon all applications for release through such channels; and that such applications will be regarded as additional reasons for declining to release the prisoners.

And, further, that if such prisoners wish to make any communication to the Government, they are at liberty to make it directly to the State Department.   SETH C. HAWLEY.

In almost every Northern State the victims of this violence were to be found. At this time (November 4, 1862) the friends of the Administration of the United States Government were decisively defeated at the elections. On November 22d ensuing, the War Department issued an order releasing all except prisoners of war. The order was muffed up in a phraseology suited to hide the fact that the result of the elections had stricken home to the sensibilities of the usurpers. It said:

"Ordered—1. That all persons now in military custody, who have been arrested for discouraging volunteer enlistments, opposing the draft,* or for otherwise giving aid and comfort to the enemy, in States where the draft has been made or the quota of volunteers and militia has been furnished, shall be discharged from further military restraint."

Thus these arrests were for a short period suspended, and then vigorously renewed.

Many of these persons who had been illegally seized and imprisoned now commenced suits for damages. This led to another step on the part of the Government of the United States, by which the judiciary of the State was entirely subverted and deprived of all jurisdiction in these cases. Congress passed an act on March 3, 1863, which provided that any order of the President of the United States, or arrest made under his authority, when pleaded, should be a defense, in all courts, to any action or prosecution for any search, seizure, arrest, or imprisonment made, done, or committed, or any acts omitted to be done, under or by virtue of such order, or under color of any law of Congress. The act further provided that all actions against officers and others for torts in arrests might be removed for trial to the next Circuit Court of the United States held in the district, and said:

"It shall then be the duty of the State court to accept the surety and proceed no further in the cause or prosecution, and the bail that shall have been originally taken shall be discharged."

By the terms of this act the case could be removed to the Circuit Court when the defendant "filed a petition stating the facts verified by affidavit." Thus the jurisdiction of all the courts of the State of New York was made to terminate and cease upon the simple word of the defendant accompanied by an affidavit. But these courts were instituted by the consent

---

* The first act of Congress providing for an enrollment and draft was passed on March 3, 1863, three and a half months later than this order.

of the governed, for the protection of the personal freedom of the citizen; yet in the cases brought before them they ordered the removal on the ground that they involved the question of the constitutionality of an act of Congress, over which the courts of the United States had a jurisdiction. The absurdity of this plea is manifest; for it is founded on the presumption that the question, whether, under authority from the President of the United States, any one, without intervention of the judicial tribunals, can incarcerate a citizen, is a question which can be treated as constituting a case arising under the Constitution of the United States. Any statute authorizing such acts is palpably void, and not entitled to be a ground for a hearing under an appeal.

The subjugation of the government of the State of New York was made in another section of the same act of Congress on March 3, 1863. It declares:

That, during the present rebellion, the President of the United States, whenever in his judgment the public safety may require it, is authorized to suspend the privilege of the writ of *habeas corpus* in any case throughout the United States, or any part thereof.

Let us turn to the words of the Constitution of the United States which are contained in the grant of powers to Congress:

The privilege of the writ of *habeas corpus* shall not be suspended, unless when in cases of rebellion or invasion the public safety may require it.

It will be seen that two facts are required to exist before the Congress of the United States can suspend the privilege of this writ. Congress must, therefore, determine the existence of these facts before it has power constitutionally to act. If it finds either fact to exist and not the other, it has no power to suspend the privilege of the writ. There must be rebellion, and the public safety must require the suspension. When Congress finds these facts to exist, it can enact the suspension. It is the judgment of Congress alone that can determine that the public safety requires the suspension. This can not be delegated to the judgment of any other department of the Government. Therefore, when Congress tells the President, in the above-mentioned act, that he is authorized to suspend the privilege of this writ whenever, in his judgment, the public safety may require it, then that body undertakes to do that for which it has no authority in the Constitution. The States delegated the power solely to Congress; an act to transfer the trust to any other depository could rightfully have no force whatever.

Now, the State of New York, in which this writ was thus suspended by the Government of the United States, was one of the Northern States and a most ardent advocate of the Union. It had contributed more men and money to support the Government of the United States than any other State, and than some whole sections of States. Yet, a claim was now set up to the right to nullify the rights and immunities of every citizen, by that Government which had already nullified the powers of every court in the State. This was done by the declaration of the President that "the public safety" required the suspension of the privilege of the writ of *habeas corpus.*

The act of Congress was passed on March 3, 1863, and on September 15th the President issued his proclamation, and, referring to the authority claimed to have been granted by the act, he proceeded to say:

Whereas, In the judgment of the President, the public safety does require that the privilege of said writ shall now be suspended throughout the United States, in [enumerated] cases. . . . Therefore I do hereby proclaim and make known that the privilege of the writ of *habeas corpus* is suspended throughout the United States in the several cases before mentioned throughout the duration of said rebellion.

Another step in the subjugation of the government of the State of New York was made by the domination over it of the military power of the Government of the United States. This took place in a time of peace in the State, when the courts were all open and the civil administration of affairs was unobstructed. On July 30, 1863, the United States commanding General of that department addressed a letter to Governor Seymour, saying that the draft for New York City would "probably be resumed," and inquiring whether the military power of the State could be relied on to enforce the law, if resisted.

Governor Seymour replied on August 3d:

I have this day sent to the President of the United States a communication in relation to the draft in this State. I believe his answer will relieve you and me from the painful questions growing out of an armed enforcement of the conscription law in this patriotic State, which has contributed so largely and freely to the support of the national cause during the existing war.

On August 8th General Dix writes again:

It is from an earnest desire to avoid the necessity of employing for the purpose any of my forces, which have been placed here to garrison the forts and protect the public property, that I wished to see the draft enforced by the military power of the State, in case of armed or organized resistance to it. . . . I designed, if your coöperation could not be relied on, to ask the General Government for a force which should be adequate to insure the execution of the law and to meet any emergency growing out of it.

Meantime Governor Seymour received no answer to his letter to the President. He had asked for a suspension of the draft, on the ground that the enrollments in the city were excessive as compared with other portions of the State, and that due credit was not given for the past. He therefore replied to General Dix, saying:

As you state in your letter that it is your duty to enforce the act of Congress, and, as you apprehend its provisions may excite popular resistance, it is proposed you should know the position which will be held by the State authorities. Of course, under no circumstances, can they perform duties expressly confided to others, nor can they undertake to relieve others from their proper responsibilities. But there can be no violations of good order, or riotous proceedings, no disturbances of the public peace, which are not infractions of the law of the State; and those laws will be enforced under all circumstances. I shall take care that all the executive officers of this State perform their duties vigorously and thoroughly, and, if need be, the military power will be called into requisition. As you are an officer of the General Government, and not of the State, it does not become me to make suggestions to you with regard to your action under a law of Congress. . . .

On August 18th General Dix thus wrote to the Governor:

Not having received an answer from you, I applied to the Secretary of War on the 14th inst. for a force adequate to the object. The call was promptly responded to, and I shall be ready to meet all opposition to the draft.

The force sent by the Secretary of War, to keep the peace and subjugate the sovereignty of the people, amounted to forty-two regiments and two batteries. There was no occasion for the exertion of their powers.

Again, the subjugation of the government of the State of New York by the domination of the military power was made still more manifest by another act on the part of the Government of the United States. A spurious proclamation, seeming to have been issued by the President, calling for four hundred thousand men, by a fraudulent imposition appeared in two papers of New York City (the "Journal of Commerce" and the "World") on the morning of May 18, 1864. It was immediately contradicted by the authorities at Washington, and orders were issued, under which the offices of these papers were entered by armed men, the property of the owners seized, the premises held by force for several days, and the publications suspended. At the same time the office of the independent telegraph line was occupied by a military force in the name of the Government of the United States. The operators were taken into custody, and the proprietors of the newspapers were ordered to be arrested and imprisoned. But these orders were suspended.

Governor Seymour immediately instructed the District Attorney to proceed against the offenders.

An investigation was made by one of the city judges, and warrants were issued for the arrest of Major-General Dix and several of his officers. They voluntarily appeared by counsel on July 6th, and the argument was set down for the 9th. On that day the counsel for the defense said:

Since this warrant was issued, the President of the United States has issued another order to General Dix, which directs him that, while this civil war lasts, he "must not relieve himself from his command, or be deprived of his liberty to obey any order of a military nature which the President of the United States directs him to execute."

The result of the arguments was that the officers were held to await the action of the grand jury, who, however, took no action on the charges. The guilty person was arrested in two or three days after the appearance of the proclamation, and imprisoned in Fort Lafayette; the newspaper and telegraph offices were restored to the owners, and the publications resumed. But the government of New York never obtained any indemnification of these losses by its citizens.

Another subversion of the State government was brought about by the military interference on the part of the Government of the United States with the State election. This was in 1864, when President Lincoln and General McClellan were the candidates for the Presidency of the United States. As usual in all these cases, proceedings to work up a pretended necessity for interference on the part of the United States Government were commenced by the appearance of a grandiloquent proclamation from the commanding General, Dix, telling what horrible designs, there was reason to believe, the agents of the Confederate States in Canada had prepared to be executed on election-day, by an invasion of voters from Canada to colonize different points. Therefore, to avert these dreadful dangers and arrest the guilty parties, it was necessary that provost-marshals, sustained by a military force, should be present with authority at the polls. At the same time the State Department issued a dispatch, saying:

Information has been received from the British provinces to the effect that there is a conspiracy on foot to set fire to the principal cities in the Northern States on the day of the Presidential election.

Thus was created an apparent necessity for military force to be very active on the day of election. Governor Seymour issued a proclamation, saying:

There is no reason to doubt that the coming election will be conducted with the usual quiet and order.

Major-General Butler was sent to take command in the city, and seven thousand additional men were placed in the forts of the harbor, and proclamations were issued, threatening, by the United States Government, the severest punishment upon every person who might attempt improperly to vote at the election in the State of New York.

The State Legislature, at its previous session, had passed an act to provide for the vote of the soldiers in the field, to be taken previous to the day of election. Agents were appointed by the State government, to the localities where the soldiers were stationed, to receive the votes. The informers of the United States Government immediately brought charges of fraud against some of these agents, and they were seized by the military authorities, sent to Washington, cast into prison, and held to be tried by a military commission. The Governor of New York immediately appointed Amasa J. Parker and two other most respectable citizens as commissioners, to proceed to Washington in behalf of the State and investigate the difficulties. They informed the Governor that several hundred ballots, which had been seized, were given up, and that they visited the principal agent of the State of New York in prison, through the permission of Edwin M. Stanton, Secretary of War. They reported:

From the best investigation the undersigned have been able to make, though there may have been irregularities, they have found no evidence that any frauds, either against any elector or the elective franchise, have been committed by any person connected with the New York agency.

The commissioners then addressed a communication to the Secretary of War. A few extracts from this communication will show how utter was the subversion of the authority of the government of the State of New York. They say:

They, North, Cohn, and Jones, were not in the military or naval service of the United States, and by no law of which we are aware were they subject to the martial and military laws of the United States, or to the orders of the War Department. . . . The charges, so far as we can learn, are not for the violation of any law of the United States, but relate to acts purporting to have been done under the law of the State of New York concerning elections, and making provisions for soldiers voting in that State; it being claimed that certain irregularities have intervened which give reason to suspect that frauds and forgeries are intended, and may be consummated. These suspected and anticipated frauds have respect solely to the election laws of the State of New York, and the action of the Government in making the arrest is claimed to be justified upon the ground that, unless thus prevented, frauds will be perpetrated against the ballot-box at the approaching election in the State of New York. We . . . protest against this jurisdiction, assumed as well over the alleged offense as over the persons of the accused, who are citizens of the State, in its employ, and entitled to its protection. . . .

The demands made by the State of New York through these commissions were refused. The persons arrested were finally tried before a military commission, clearly without jurisdiction, in violation of their personal rights, and in usurpation of the just powers of the State. They were, however, acquitted and discharged, glad to get off no worse.

The proposed limits will not permit me further to present the details relative to the subjugation of the State government of New York by the Government of the United States. Neither can space be spared to relate the details of the subjugation of the government of each Northern State. In many the events were similar to those in New York; in others they arose under dissimilar circumstances; but, in all, the sovereignty of the people was entirely disregarded, and the operation of the institutions which had been established for the protection of their rights was suspended, or nullified, by a military force of the Government of the United States.

A military domination was established in all of the Northern States, under the pretext of securing the arrest of deserters from the army. This was accomplished on September 24, 1862, by the appointment of a Provost-Marshal-General of the War Department at Washington, and in each State one or more special provost-marshals, who were required to report to and receive instructions from the Provost-Marshal-General.

To enable these marshals to perform their duties efficiently, they were authorized to call on any available military force within their respective districts, or else to employ the assistance of citizens, constables, sheriffs, or police officers, so far as might be necessary. No trial was allowed to any person thus arrested except before a military commission consisting of military officers designated for the purpose; the prosecutor was the Judge Advocate, and the punishments were exemplary, unusual, and too often such as were unknown to the laws. The State governments within whose domains the courts were open, the civil institutions in quiet operation, and the transactions of peaceful life uniform and constant, were powerless to protect their citizens.

The country was filled with horror during 1865 by two trials held before a military commission in the city of Washington. The first commenced on May 13th, and ended on June 29th. The specification was—

That David E. Harold, Edward Spangler, Lewis Payne, John H. Surratt, Michael O'Loughlin, Samuel Arnold, George A. Atzerott, Samuel A. Mudd, and Mary E. Surratt, did on April 15, 1865, combine, confederate, and conspire together to murder President Abraham Lincoln, Vice-President Andrew Johnson, Lieutenant-General U. S. Grant, and Secretary of State William H. Seward.

President Lincoln had been shot, and Secretary Seward was badly wounded with a knife. The others were uninjured.

The sentence of the commission was that David E. Harold, G. A. Atzerott, Lewis Payne, and Mary E. Surratt, be hanged by the proper military authority, under the direction of the Secretary of War, on July 7, 1865. The others were sentenced to imprisonment at hard labor for a term of years or for life. With only one day's delay, the sentences were carried into execution. John H. Surratt escaped before trial. He was sought for by the spies of the War Department half round the world, and after a long time was found serving as a soldier in the corps of Papal Zouaves at Rome. He was brought back to Washington, tried, and acquitted.

The insertion of my name with those of others, honorable gentlemen, as "inciting and encouraging" these acts, served as an exhibition of the malignant spirit with which justice was administered by the authorities in Washington at that time. The case of Mrs. Surratt, at whose house some of these persons had boarded, awakened much sympathy. She was spoken of by her counsel, Reverdy Johnson, of Maryland, as "a devout Christian, ever kind, affectionate, and charitable," which was confirmed by evidence and uncontradicted. On the day of execution, her daughter, who was quite a devoted and affectionate person, sought to obtain an audience with President Johnson to implore at least a brief suspension of the sentence of her mother. She was obstructed and prevented from seeing the President by ex-Senator Preston King, of New York, and Senator James H. Lane, of Kansas, who were reported to have been at the Executive Mansion to keep guard over President Johnson. Each of these Senators at a later period committed suicide.

The trial of Major Henry Wirz was the next in importance which came before a military commission. In April, 1865, President Johnson issued a proclamation, stating that, from evidence in possession of the "Bureau of Military Justice," it appeared that I, Jefferson Davis, was implicated in the assassination of President Lincoln, and for that reason he offered a reward of one hundred thousand dollars for my capture. That testimony was subsequently found to be entirely false, having been a mere fabrication. The manner in which this was done will be presently stated. Meantime, certain persons of influence and public position at that time, either aware of the fabricated character of this testimony or convinced of its insufficiency to secure my conviction on a trial, sought to find ample material to supply this deficiency, in the great mortality of the soldiers we had captured during the war and imprisoned at Andersonville.*

Orders were therefore issued by the authorities of the United States Government to arrest a subaltern officer,

* See chapter on exchange of prisoners.

Captain Henry Wirz, a foreigner by birth, poor, friendless, and wounded, and held as a prisoner of war. He had been included in the surrender of General J. E. Johnston. On May 7th he was placed in the "Old Capitol" Prison at Washington. The poor man was doomed before he was heard, and the permission to be heard according to law was denied him. Captain Wirz had been in command at the Confederate prison at Andersonville. The first charge alleged against him was that of conspiring with myself, Secretary Seddon, General Howell Cobb, General Winder, and others, to cause the death of thousands of the prisoners through cruelty, etc. The second charge was alleged against himself for murder in violation of the laws and customs of war. The so-called trial lasted for three months, but no evidence whatsoever was produced showing the existence of such a conspiracy as had been charged. Wirz was, however, pronounced guilty, and, in accordance with the sentence of the commission, he was executed on November 10, 1865.

On April 4, 1867, Mr. Louis Schade, of Washington, and the attorney for Wirz on the trial, published a vindication of his character. The following is an extract from this publication:

On the night previous to the execution of the prisoner, some parties came to the confessor of Wirz (Rev. Father Boyle) and also to me. One of them informed me that a high Cabinet officer wished to assure Wirz that, if he would implicate Jefferson Davis with the atrocities committed at Andersonville, his sentence should be commuted. He (the messenger, whoever he was) requested me to inform Wirz of this. In presence of Father Boyle, I told him next morning what had happened. The Captain simply and quietly replied: "Mr. Schade, you know that I have always told you that I do not know anything about Jefferson Davis. He had no connection with me as to what was done at Andersonville. If I knew anything of him, I would not become a traitor against him or anybody else to save my life." Thus ended the attempt to suborn Captain Wirz against Jefferson Davis.

In the other case of the fabrication of evidence by some of the authorities in Washington relative to myself, it will be sufficient here to present what others have said and done. Three principal measures were resorted to for the accomplishment of this object: the charge in the case of Wirz, above mentioned; the fabrications in the case now under consideration; and the cruel and inhuman treatment inflicted upon me while a prisoner in Fortress Monroe.

At the session of Congress of 1865-'66, a committee was appointed in the House of Representatives "to inquire into and report upon the alleged complicity of Jefferson Davis with the assassination of the late President Lincoln," or words to that effect. George S. Boutwell was chairman of the committee, and the majority of the members were extreme advocates of the war. The charge emanated from the "Bureau of Military Justice," as it was designated—a similar institution to the "Secret Committee" of the French Revolution. Of this institution Judge-Advocate Joseph Holt was the chief. After an investigation continuing through several months, a majority of the committee made their report to Congress.

That report not only failed to establish the charge, but the committee were forced to confess in it that the witnesses, on whose testimony Holt had affected to reply, were wholly untrustworthy. Shortly after this report was presented to the House, Mr. A. J. Rogers, of the committee, a very respectable member from New Jersey, made a minority report. He asserted that much of the evidence was altogether suppressed, and that the witnesses, who had received large sums of money from Holt for testifying to the criminality of Mr. Davis, recanted their evidence before the committee, and acknowledged that they had perjured themselves by testifying to a mass of falsehoods.

Chapter 37

The Wilderness

IT WAS in March, 1864, that Major-General Ulysses S. Grant, having been appointed lieutenant-general, assumed command of the armies of the United States. He subsequently proceeded to Culpeper and assumed personal command of the Army of the Potomac, although nominally that army remained under the command of General Meade. Reënforcements were gathered from every military department of the United States and sent to that army.

On May 3d General Lee held the south bank of the Rapidan River, with his right resting near the mouth of Mine Run and his left extending to Liberty Mills, on the road from Gordonsville to the Shenandoah Valley. Ewell's corps was on the right, Hill's on the left, and two divisions of Longstreet's corps, having returned from East Tennessee, were encamped in the rear near Gordonsville. The army of General Grant had occupied the north bank of the Rapidan, with the main body encamped in Culpeper County and on the Rappahannock River.

While Grant with his immense and increasing army was thus posted, Lee, with a comparatively small force, and to which few reënforcements could be furnished, confronted him on a line stretching from near Somerville Ford to Gordonsville. To Grant was left the choice to move directly on Lee and attempt to defeat his army, the only obstacle to the capture of Richmond, and which his vast means rendered supposable, or to cross the Rapidan above or below Lee's position. The second would fulfill the condition, so imperatively imposed on McClellan, of covering the United States capital; the third would be in the more direct line toward Richmond. Of the three he chose the last, and so felicitated himself on his unopposed passage of the river as to suppose that he had, unobserved, turned the flank of Lee's army, got between it and Richmond, and necessitated the retreat of the Confederates to some point where they might resist his further advance. So little could he comprehend the genius of Lee, that he expected him to be surprised, as appears from his arrangements contemplating only combats with the rear-guard covering the retreat. Lee, dauntless as he was sagacious, seized the opportunity, which the movement of his foe offered, to meet him where his artillery would be least available, where his massive columns would be most embarrassed in their movements, and where Southern individuality and self-reliance would be specially effective. Grant's object was to pass through "the Wilderness" to the roads between Lee and Richmond. Lee resolved to fight him in those pathless woods. In order to cross the Rapidan, Grant's army moved on May 3d toward Germania Ford, which was ten or twelve miles from our right. He succeeded in seizing the ford and crossing. The direct road from this ford to Richmond passed by Spottsylvania Court-House, and, when Grant had crossed the river, he was nearer than General Lee to Richmond. From Orange Court-House there are two nearly parallel roads running eastwardly to Fredericksburg. The one nearest the river is called the "Stone Turnpike," and the other the "Plank-road." The road from the ford to Spottsylvania Court-House crosses the Old Stone Turnpike at the "Old Wilderness Tavern," and, two or three miles farther on, it crosses the plank-road.

As soon as Grant's movement was known, Lee's troops were put in motion. Ewell's corps moved on the Stone Turnpike, and Hill's corps on the plank-road, into which Longstreet's force also came from his camp near Gordonsville. Ewell's corps crossed Mine Run, and encamped at Locust Grove, four miles beyond, on the afternoon of the 4th. On the morning of the 5th it was again in motion, and encountered Grant's troops in heavy force at a short distance from the Old Wilderness Tavern, and Jones's and Battle's brigades were driven back in some confusion. Early's division was ordered up, formed across the pike, and moved forward. It advanced through a dense pine-thicket, and, with other brigades of Rodes's division, drove the enemy back with heavy loss, capturing several hundred prisoners and gaining a commanding position on the right. Meantime, Johnson's division, on the left of the pike, and extending across the road to Germania Ford, was heavily engaged in front, and Hays's brigade was sent to his left to participate in a forward movement. It advanced, encountered a large force, and, not meeting with the expected coöperation, was drawn back. Subsequently, Pegram's brigade took position on Hays's left, and just before night an attack was made on their front, which was repulsed with severe loss to the enemy. During the afternoon there was hot skirmishing along the whole line, and several attempts were made by the foe to regain the position from which he had been driven. At the close of the day, Ewell's corps had captured over a thousand prisoners, besides inflicting on the enemy very severe losses in killed and wounded. Two pieces of artillery had been abandoned and were secured by our troops.

A. P. Hill, on the 4th, with Heth's and Wilcox's divisions of his corps, moved eastwardly along the plank-road. They bivouacked at night near Verdiersville, and resumed their march on the 5th with Heth in advance. About 1 P. M. musketry firing was heard in front; the sound indicated the presence of a large body of infantry. Kirkland's brigade deployed on both sides of the plank-road, and the column proceeded to form in line of battle on its flanks. Hill's advance had followed the plank-road, while Ewell's pursued the Stone turnpike. These parallel movements were at this time from three to four miles apart. The country intervening and round about for several miles is known as the "Wilderness," and, having very little open ground, consists almost wholly of a forest of dense undergrowth of shrubs and small trees. In order to open communication with Ewell, Wilcox's division moved to the left, and effected a junction with Gordon's brigade on Ewell's extreme right. The line of battle thus completed extended from the right of the plank-road through a succession of open fields and dense forest to the left of the Stone turnpike. It presented a line of six miles, and the thicket that lay along the whole front of our army was so impenetrable as to exclude the use of artillery save only at the roads. Heth's skirmishers were driven in about 3 P. M. by a massive column that advanced, firing rapidly. The struggle thus commenced in Hill's front continued for two or three hours unabated. Heth's ranks were greatly reduced, when Wilcox was ordered to his support, but the bloody contest continued until night closed over our force in the position it had originally taken. This stubborn and heroic resistance was made by the divisions of Heth and Wilcox, of Hill's corps, fifteen thousand strong, against the repeated and desperate assaults of five divisions—four divisions of Hancock's and one of Sedgwick's corps, numbering about forty-five thousand men. Our forces completely foiled their adversaries, and inflicted upon them most serious loss. During the day the Ninth Corps of the enemy under General Burnside, had come on the field. The third division of Hill's corps, under General Anderson, and the two divisions of Longstreet's corps, did not reach the scene of conflict until dawn of day on the morning of the 6th. Simultaneously the attack on Hill was renewed with great vigor. In addition to the force he had so successfully resisted on the previous day, a fresh division of the enemy's Fifth Corps had secured position on Hill's flank, and coöperated with the column assaulting in front. After a severe contest, the left of Heth's division and the right of Wilcox's were overpowered before the advance of Longstreet's column reached the ground, and were compelled to retire. The repulsed portions of the divisions were in considerable disorder. General Lee now came up, and, fully appreciating the impending crisis, dashed amid the fugitives, calling on the men to rally and follow him.

The soldiers, seeing General Lee's manifest purpose to advance with them, and realizing the great danger in which he then was, begged him to go to the rear, promising that they would soon have matters rectified. The General waved them on with some words of cheer.

The assault was checked.

Longstreet, having come up with two divisions, deployed them in line of battle, and gallantly advanced to recover the lost ground. The enemy was driven back over the ground he had gained by his assault on Hill's line, but reformed in the position previously held by him. About mid-day an attack on his left flank and rear was ordered by Longstreet. For this purpose three brigades were detached, and, moving forward, were joined by General J. R. Davis's brigade, which had been the extreme right of Hill's line. Making a sufficient *détour* to avoid observation, and, rushing precipitately to attack the foe in flank and reverse while he was preparing to resist the movement in his front, he was taken completely by surprise. The assault resulted in his utter rout, with heavy loss on that part of his line.

Preparations were now made to follow up the advantages gained by a forward movement of the whole line under General Longstreet's personal direction. When advancing at the head of Jenkins's brigade, with that officer and others, a body of Confederates in the wood on the roadside, supposing the column to be a hostile force, fired into it, killing General Jenkins, and severely wounding General Longstreet. The valuable services of General Longstreet were thus lost to the army at a critical moment, and this caused the suspension of a movement which promised the most important results; and time was thus afforded to the enemy to rally, reënforce, and find shelter behind his intrenchments. Under these circumstances the commanding General deemed it unadvisable to attack.

On the morning of the 6th the contest was renewed on the left, and a very heavy attack was made on the front, occupied by Pegram's brigade, but it was handsomely repulsed, as were several subsequent attacks at the same point. In the afternoon an attack was made on the enemy's right flank, resting in the woods, when Gordon's brigade, with Johnson's in the rear and followed by Pegram's, succeeded in throwing it into great confusion, doubling it up and forcing it back some distance, capturing two brigadier-generals and several hundred prisoners. Darkness closed the contest. On the 7th an advance was made which disclosed the fact that Grant had given up his line of works on his right. During the day there was some skirmishing, but no serious fighting. The result of these battles was the infliction of severe loss upon the foe, the gain of ground, and the capture of prisoners, artillery, and other trophies. The cost to us, however, was so serious as to enforce, by additional considerations, the policy of Lee to spare his men as much as was possible.

A rapid flank movement was next made by Grant to secure possession of Spottsylvania Court-House. General Lee comprehended his purpose, and on the night of the 7th a division of Longstreet's corps was sent as the advance to that point. Stuart, then in observation on the flank, and ever ready to work or to fight as the one or the other should best serve the cause of his country, dismounted his troopers, and, by felling trees, obstructed the roads so as materially to delay the march of the enemy. The head of the opposing forces arrived almost at the same moment on the 8th; theirs, being a little in advance, drove back our cavalry, but in turn was quickly driven from the strategic point by the arrival of our infantry. On the 9th the two armies, each forming on its advance as a nucleus, swung round and confronted each other in line of battle.

The 10th and 11th passed in comparative quiet. On the morning of the 12th the enemy made a very heavy attack on Ewell's front, and broke the line where it was occupied by Johnson's division. At this time and place the scene occurred of which Mississippians are justly proud. Colonel Venable, of General Lee's staff, states that, on the receipt of one of the

messages from General Rodes for more troops, he was sent
by General Lee to bring Harris's Mississippi brigade from the
extreme right; that General Lee met the brigade and rode at
its head until under fire, when a round shot passed so near to
him that the soldiers invoked him to go back; and when he
said, "If you will promise me to drive those people from our
works, I will go back," the brigade shouted the promise, and
Colonel Venable says:

As the column of Mississippians came up at a double quick
an aide-de-camp came up to General Rodes with a message from
Ramseur that he could hold out only a few minutes longer unless
assistance was at hand. Your brigade was thrown instantly into
the fight, the column being formed into line under a tremendous
fire and on very difficult ground. Never did a brigade go into
fiercer battle under greater trials; never did a brigade do its duty
more nobly.

A portion of the attacking force swept along Johnson's
line to Wilcox's left, and was checked by a prompt movement
on that flank. Several brigades sent to Ewell's assistance were
carried into action under his orders, and they all suffered
severely. Subsequently, on the same day, some brigades were
thrown to the front, for the purpose of moving to the left and
attacking the flank of the column which broke Ewell's line, to
relieve the pressure on him, and recover the part of the line
which had been lost. These, as they moved, soon encountered
the Ninth Corps, under Burnside, advancing to the attack.
They captured over three hundred prisoners and three battle-
flags, and their attack on the enemy's flank, taking him by
surprise, contributed materially to his repulse.

Taylor, in his "Four Years with General Lee," says that
Lee, having detected the weakness of "the salient" occupied
by the division of General Edward Johnson, of Ewell's corps,
directed a second line to be constructed across its base, to
which he proposed to move the troops occupying the angle.
Suspecting another flank movement by Grant, before these
arrangements were quite completed, he ordered most of the
artillery at this portion of the lines to be withdrawn so as to
be available. Toward dawn on the 12th, Johnson, discovering
indications of an impending assault, ordered the immediate
return of the artillery, and made other preparations for
defense. But the unfortunate withdrawal was so partially and
tardily restored that a spirited assault at daybreak overran that

portion of the lines before the artillery was put in position, and captured most of the division, including its brave commander.

The above-mentioned attacking column advanced, under cover of a pine-thicket, to within a very short distance of a salient defended by Walker's brigade. A heavy fire of musketry and artillery, from a considerable number of guns on Heth's line, opened with tremendous effect upon the column, and it was driven back with severe loss, leaving its dead in front of our works.

Several days of comparative quiet ensued. During this time the army of General Grant was heavily reënforced from Washington.

In numerical strength his army so much exceeded that under General Lee that, after covering the entire Confederate front with double lines of battle, he had in reserve a large force with which to extend his flank and compel a corresponding movement on the part of his adversary, in order to keep between him and his coveted prize—the capital of the Confederacy.

On the 18th another assault was made upon our lines, but it produced no impression. On the 20th of May, after twelve days of skirmish and battle at Spottsylvania against a superior force, General Lee's information led him to believe that the enemy was about to attempt another flanking movement, and interpose his army between the Confederate capital and its defenders. To defeat this purpose Longstreet was ordered to move at midnight in the direction of Hanover Junction, and on the following day and night Ewell's and Hill's corps marched for the same point.

The Confederate commander, divining that Grant's objective point was the intersection of the two railroads leading to Richmond at a point two miles south of the North Anna River, crossed his army over that stream and took up a line of battle which frustrated the movement.

Grant began his flanking movement on the night of the 20th, marching in two columns, the right, under General Warren, crossing the North Anna at Jericho Ford without opposition. On the 23rd the left, under General Hancock, crossing four miles lower down, at the Chesterfield or County Bridge, was obstinately resisted by a small force, and the passage of the river was not made until the 24th. After crossing the North Anna, Grant dicovered that his movement was a blunder, and that his army was in a position of much peril.

The Confederate commander established his line of battle on the south side of the river, both wings retracted so as to form an obtuse angle, with the apex resting on the river between the two points of the enemy's crossing, Longstreet's and Hill's corps forming the two sides, and Little River and the Hanover marshes the base. Ewell's corps held the apex or center.

The hazard of Grant's position appears not to have been known to him until he attempted to unite his two columns, which were four miles apart, by establishing a connecting line along the river. Foiled in the attempt, he discovered that the Confederate army was interposed between his two wings, which were also separated by the North Anna, and that the one could give no support to the other except by a double crossing of the river. That the Confederate commander did not seize the opportunity to strike his embarrassed foe and avail himself of the advantage which his superior generalship had gained, may have been that, concluding from past observation of Grant's tactics, he felt assured that the "continuous hammering" process was to be repeated without reference to circumstances or position. If Lee acted on this supposition, he was mistaken, as the Federal commander, profiting by the severe lessons of Spottsylvania and the Wilderness, with cautious, noiseless movement, withdrew under cover of the night of the 26th to the north side of the North Anna, and moved eastward down to the Pamunkey River.

At Hanover Junction General Lee was joined by Picket's division of Longstreet's corps, which had been on detached service in North Carolina, and by a small force under General Breckinridge from southwestern Virginia, twenty-two hundred strong. Hoke's brigade, of Early's division, twelve hundred strong, which had been on detached duty at the Junction, here also rejoined its division. On the 29th the whole of Grant's army was across the Pamunkey, while General Lee's army on the next day was in line of battle with his left at Atlee's Station. By another movement eastward the two armies were brought face to face at Cold Harbor on June 3d. Here fruitless efforts were made by General Grant to pierce or drive back the forces of General Lee. Our troops were protected by temporary earthworks, and while under cover of these were assailed by the enemy:

But in vain. The assault was repulsed along the whole line, and the carnage on the Federal side was fearful. I well recall having received a report, after the assault, from General Hoke—whose division reached the army just previous to this battle—to the effect that the ground in his entire front, over which the enemy had charged, was literally covered with their dead and wounded; and that up to that time he had not had a single man killed. No wonder that, when the command was given to renew the assault, the Federal soldiers sullenly and silently declined. "The order was issued through the officers to their subordinate commanders, and from them descended through the wonted channels; but no man stirred, and the immobile lines pronounced a verdict, silent yet emphatic, against further slaughter. The loss on the Union side in this sanguinary action was over thirteen thousand, while on the part of the Confederates it is doubtful whether it reached that many hundreds." After some disingenuous proposals, General Grant finally asked a truce to enable him to bury his dead. Soon after this he abandoned his chosen line of operations, and moved his army so as to secure a crossing to the south side of James River. The struggle from the Wilderness to this point covered a period of over one month, during which time there had been an almost daily encounter of arms, and the Army of Northern Virginia had placed *hors de combat,* of the army under General Grant, a number exceeding the entire numerical strength, at the commencement of the campaign, of Lee's army, which, notwithstanding its own heavy losses and the reënforcements received by the enemy, still presented an impregnable front to its opponent.

By the report of the United States Secretary of War (Stanton), Grant had, on the 1st of May, 1864, two days before he crossed the Rapidan, 141,160 men. To meet this vast force, Lee had on the Rapidan less than 50,000 men. By the same authority it appears that Grant had a reserve upon which he could draw of 137,672. Lee had practically no reserve, for he was compelled to make detachments from his army for the protection of West Virginia and other points, about equal to all the reënforcements which he received. In the "Southern Historical Papers," vol. vi, page 144, upon the very reliable authority of the editor, there appears the following statement:

Grant says he lost, in the campaign from the Wilderness to Cold Harbor, 39,000 men; but Swinton puts his loss at over 60,000, and a careful examination of the figures will show that his real loss was nearer 100,000. In other words, he lost about twice as many men as Lee had, in order to take a position which he could have taken at first without firing a gun or losing a man.

Chapter 38

Atlanta; Sherman's March to the Sea

On December 16, 1863, I directed General J. E. Johnston to transfer the command of the Department of Mississippi and East Louisiana to Lieutenant-General Polk, and repair to Dalton, Georgia, to assume command of the Army of Tennessee, representing at that date an effective total of 43,094. My information led me to believe that the condition of that army, in all that constitutes efficiency, was satisfactory, and that the men were anxious for an opportunity to retrieve the loss of prestige sustained in the disastrous battle of Missionary Ridge. I was also informed that the enemy's forces, then occupying Chattanooga, Bridgeport, and Stevenson, with a detached force at Knoxville, were weaker in numbers that at any time since the battle of Missionary Ridge, and that they were especially deficient in cavalry and in artillery and train-horses. I desired, therefore, that prompt and vigorous measures be taken to enable our troops to commence active operations against the enemy as early as practicable. It was important to guard against the injurious results to the *morale* of the troops, which always attend a prolonged season of inactivity; but the recovery of the territory in Tennessee and Kentucky, which we had been compelled to abandon, and on the supplies of which the proper subsistence of our armies mainly depended, imperatively demanded an onward movement. I believed that, by a rapid concentration of our troops between the scattered forces of the enemy, without attempting to capture his intrenched positions, we could compel him to accept battle in the open field, and that, should we fail to draw him out of his intrenchments, we could move upon his line of communications. The Federal force at Knoxville depended mainly for support on its connection with that at Chattanooga, and both were wholly dependent on uninterrupted communication with Nashville. Could we, then, by interposing our force, separate these two bodies of the enemy, and cut off his communication from Nashville to Chattanooga by destroying the railroad, both conditions were fulfilled. Of the practicability of this movement I had little doubt; of its expediency, if practicable, there could be none. I impressed repeatedly upon General Johnston by letter, and by officers of my staff and others, sent to him by me for the purpose of putting him in possession of these views, the importance of a prompt aggressive movement by the Army of Tennessee. The following were among the considerations presented to General Johnston, at my request, by Brigadier-General W. N. Pendleton, chief of artillery of the Army of Northern Virginia, on April 16, 1864:

1. To take the enemy at disadvantage while weakened, it is believed, by sending troops to Virginia, and having others still absent on furlough.

2. To break up his plans by anticipating and frustrating his combinations.

3. So to press him in his present position as to prevent his heavier massing in Virginia.

4. To defeat him in battle, and gain great consequent strength in supplies, men, and productive territory.

5. To prevent the waste of the army incident to inactivity.

6. To inspirit the troops and the country by success, and to discourage the enemy.

7. To obviate the necessity of falling back, which might probably occur if our antagonist be allowed to consummate his plans without molestation.

General Johnston cordially approved of an aggressive movement, and informed me of his purpose to make it as soon as reënforcements and supplies, then on the way, should reach him. He did not approve the proposed advance into Tennessee. He believed that the Federal forces in Tennessee were not weaker, but if anything stronger, than at Missionary Ridge; that defeat beyond the Tennessee would probably prove ruinous to us, resulting in the loss of his army, the occupation of Georgia by the enemy, the "piercing of the Confederacy in its vitals," and the loss of all the southwestern territory. He proposed, therefore, to stand on the defensive until strengthened, "to watch, prepare, and strike" as soon as possible. As soon as reënforced, he declared his purpose to advance to Ringgold, attack there, and, if successful, as he expected to be, to strike at Cleveland, cut the railroad, control the river, and thus isolate East Tennessee, and, as a consequence, force his antagonist to give battle on this side of the Tennessee River. Simultaneously with, and in aid of, this movement, General

Johnston proposed that a large cavalry force should be sent to Middle Tennessee, in the rear of the enemy. These operations, he thought, would result in forcing the Federal army to evacuate the Tennessee Valley, and make an advance into the heart of the State safely practicable.

The irreparable loss of time in making any forward movement as desired having sufficed for the combinations which rendered an advance across the Tennessee River no longer practicable, I took prompt measures to enable General Johnston to carry out immediately his own proposition to strike first at Ringgold and then at Cleveland, proposing that General Buckner should threaten Knoxville, General Forrest advance into or threaten Middle Tennessee, and General Roddy hold the enemy in northern Alabama, and thus prevent his concentration in our front. This movement, although it held out no such promise as did the plan of advance before the enemy had had time to make his combinations, might have been attended with good results had it been promptly executed. But no such movement was made or even attempted. General Johnston's belief that General Grant would be ready to assume the offensive before he could be prepared to do so, proved too well founded, while his purpose, if the Federal army did not attack, that we should prepare and take the initiative ourselves, was never carried out.*

On the morning of May 2, 1864, General Johnston discovered that the enemy, under the command of General Sherman, was advancing against him, and two days subsequently it was reported that he had reached Ringgold (about fifteen miles north of Dalton) in considerable force.

At this date the official returns show that the effective strength of the Army of Tennessee, counting the troops actually in position at Dalton and those in the immediate rear of that place, was about fifty thousand. When to these is added General Polk's command (then *en route*), and the advance of which joined him at Resaca, the effective strength of General Johnston's army was not less than 68,620 men of all arms, ex-

---

* It was during this time, i.e., in March and April, 1864, that Forrest made his extraordinary expedition from north Mississippi across Tennessee to Paducah, Kentucky, and continued his operations against depots of supplies, lines of communication, and troops moving to reënforce Sherman—having, on June 11th, a severe action in Tishemingo with a force estimated at eight or nine thousand, supposed to be on their way to join Sherman. The energy, strategy, and high purposes of Forrest, during all this period, certainly entitle him to higher military rank than that of a partisan, and enroll him in the list of great cavalry commanders. Some of his other expeditions are elsewhere mentioned in these pages.

cluding from the estimate the thousands of men employed on extra duty, amounting, as General Hood states, to ten thousand when he assumed command of the army.

To enable General Johnston to repulse the hostile advance and assume the offensive, no effort was spared on the part of the Government. Almost all the available military strength of the south and west, in men and supplies, was pressed forward and placed at his disposal. The supplies of the commissary, quartermaster, and ordnance departments of his army were represented as ample and suitably located. The troops, encouraged by the large accessions of strength which they saw arriving daily, and which they knew were marching rapidly to their support, were eager to advance, and confident in their power to achieve victory and recover the territory which they had lost. Their position was such as to warrant the confident expectation of successful resistance at least. Long Mountain-ranges, penetrated by few and difficult roads and paths, and deep and wide rivers, seemed to render our position one from which we could not be dislodged or turned, while that of the enemy, dependent for his supplies upon a single line of railroad from Nashville to the point where he was operating, was manifestly perilous. The whole country shared the hope which the Government entertained, that a decisive victory would soon be won in the mountains of Georgia which would free the south and west from invasion, would open to our occupation and the support of our armies the productive territory of Tennessee and Kentucky, and so recruit our army in the West as to render it impracticable for the enemy to accumulate additional forces in Virginia.

But the universal expectations were disappointed. General Johnston withdrew his forces successively from Dalton to Resaca, from Resaca to Adairsville, from Adairsville to Alatoona (involving by the evacuation of Kingston the loss of Rome, with its valuable mills, foundries, and large quantities of military stores), from Alatoona to Kenesaw, from Kenesaw to the Chattahoochee, and then to Atlanta; retreat followed retreat, during seventy-four days of anxious hope and bitter disappointment, until at last the Army of Tennessee fell back within the fortifications of Atlanta. The Federal army soon occupied the arc of a circle extending from the railroad between Atlanta and the Chattahoochee River to some miles south of the Georgia Railroad (from Atlanta to Augusta) in a direction north and northeast of Atlanta. We had suffered a disastrous loss of territory.

When it became known that the Army of Tennessee had been successively driven from one strong position to another, until finally it had reached the earthworks constructed for the exterior defense of Atlanta, the popular disappointment was extreme. The possible fall of the "Gate City," with its important railroad communication, vast stores, factories for the manufacture of all sorts of military supplies, rolling-mill and foundries, was now contemplated for the first time at its full value, and produced intense anxiety far and wide. From many quarters, came delegations, petitions, and letters, urging me to remove General Johnston from the command of the army, and assign that important trust to some officer who would resolutely hold and defend Atlanta. While sharing in the keen sense of disappointment at the failure of the campaign which pervaded the whole country, I was perhaps more apprehensive than others of the disasters likely to result from it, because I was in a position to estimate more accurately their probable extent. On the railroads threatened with destruction, the armies then fighting the main battles of the war in Virginia had for some time to a great degree depended for indispensable supplies. Yet I did not respond to the wishes of those who came in hottest haste for the removal of General Johnston; for here again, more fully than many others, I realized how serious it was to change commanders in the presence of the enemy. I only issued the order relieving him from command when I became satisfied that his declared purpose to occupy the works at Atlanta with militia levies and withdraw his army into the open country for freer operations would inevitably result in the loss of that important point, and where the retreat would cease could not be foretold. If the Army of Tennessee was found to be unable to hold positions of great strength like those at Dalton, Resaca, Etowah, Kenesaw, and on the Chattahoochee, I could not reasonably hope that it would be more successful in the plains below Atlanta, where it would find neither natural nor artificial advantages of position. As soon as the Secretary of War showed me the answer which he had just received in reply to his telegram to General Johnston, requesting positive information as to the General's plans and purposes, I gave my permission to issue the order relieving General Johnston and directing him to turn over to General Hood the command of the Army of Tennessee.

General Hood assumed command on the 18th of July. In his report of the operations of the army while under his command, he states that the effective strength of his force on that day was forty-eight thousand seven hundred and fifty men of all arms. Feeling that the only chance of holding Atlanta consisted in assuming the offensive by forcing the enemy to accept battle, General Hood determined, on the 20th of July, to attack the corps of Generals Thomas and Schofield, who were in the act of crossing Peachtree Creek, hoping to defeat Thomas before he could fortify himself, then to fall on Schofield, and finally to attack McPherson's corps, which had reached Decatur, on the Georgia Railroad, driving the enemy back to the creek and into the narrow space included between that stream and the Chattahoochee River. Owing to an unfortunate misapprehension of the order of battle and the consequent delay in making the attack, the movement failed. On the 21st, finding that McPherson's corps was threatening his communications, General Hood resolved to attack him at or near Decatur, in front and on flank, turn his left, and then, following up the movement from the right to the left with his whole army, force the enemy down Peachtree Creek. This engagement was the hottest of the campaign, but it failed to accomplish any other favorable result than to check General McPherson's movement upon the communications of our army, while it cost heavily in the loss of many officers and men.

No movement of special importance took place between July 22d and August 26th, at which latter date it was discovered that Sherman was marching his main body to the south and southwest of Atlanta, to use it, as he himself has expressed it, "against the communications of Atlanta, instead of against its entrenchments." On the 30th, it being known that he was moving on Jonesboro, the county town of Clayton County, about twenty miles south of Atlanta, General Hood sent two corps under General Hardee to confront him at that point, in the hope that he could drive him across Flint River, oblige him to abandon his works on the left, and then be able to attack him successfully in flank. The attack at Jonesboro was unsuccessful. General Hardee was obliged, on September 1st, to fall back to Lovejoy's, seven miles south of Jonesboro, on the Macon and Western Railroad. Thus, the main body of the Federal army was between Hardee and Atlanta, and the immediate evacuation of that city became a necessity. There was an additional and cogent reason for that movement. Owing to the obstinately cruel policy which the United States Government had pursued for some time, of refusing on any terms to exchange prisoners of war, upward of thirty thousand prisoners were at Andersonville in southwestern Georgia at this time. To guard against the release and arming of these prisoners, General Hood thought it necessary to place our army between them and the enemy, and abandon the project, which he thought feasible, of moving on Sherman's communications and destroying his depots of supplies at Marietta.

Upon abandoning Atlanta, Hood marched his army in a westerly direction, and formed a junction with the two corps which had been operating at Jonesboro and Lovejoy's under General Hardee.

General Sherman, desisting from any further aggressive movement in the field, returned to Atlanta, which had been formally surrendered by the Mayor on September 2d, with the promise, as reported, on the part of the Federal commander, that non-combatants and private property should be respected. Shortly after his arrival, the commanding General of the Federal forces, forgetful of this promise, and on the pretense that the exigencies of the service required that the place should be used exclusively for military purposes, issued an order directing all civilians living in Atlanta, male and female, to leave the city within five days from the date of the order (September 5th). Since Alva's atrocious cruelties to the noncombatant population of the Low Countries in the sixteenth century, the history of war records no instance of such barbarous cruelty as that which this order designed to perpetrate. It involved the immediate expulsion from their homes and only means of subsistence of thousands of unoffending women and children, whose husbands and fathers were either in the army, in Northern prisons, or had died in battle. In vain did the Mayor and corporate authorities of Atlanta appeal to Sherman to revoke or modify this inhuman order, representing in piteous language "the woe, the horror, and the suffering, not to be described by words," which its execution would inflict on helpless women and infant children. His only reply was:

I give full credit to your statements of the distress that will be occasioned by it, and yet shall not revoke my order, because my orders are not designed to meet the humanities of the case.

At the time appointed, the women and children were expelled from their houses, and, before they were passed within our lines, complaint was generally made that the Federal officers and men who were sent to guard them had robbed them of the few articles of value they had been permitted to take from their homes. The cowardly dishonesty of its executioners was in perfect harmony with the temper and spirit of the order.

Thomas having been sufficiently reënforced in Tennessee to enable him to hold Hood in check, and Sherman relieved from the necessity of defending himself against an active army, and of protecting a long line of railroad communication with a fortified base in his rear, resolved upon his march to the sea, abandoning Atlanta, after having first utterly destroyed that city by fire. Not a single house was spared, not even a church. Similar acts of vandalism marked the progress of the Federal army at Rome, Kingston, Acworth, Marietta, and every town or village along its route, thus carrying out General Sherman's order "to enforce a devastation more or less relentless" along the line of his march, where he only encountered helpless women and children. The arson of the dwelling-houses of non-combatants and the robbery of their property, extending even to the trinkets worn by women, made the devastation as relentless as savage instincts could suggest.

On November 16th Sherman left his entrenchments around Atlanta, and, dividing his army into two bodies, each from twenty-five to thirty thousand strong, the one followed the Georgia Railroad in the direction of Augusta, and the other took the line of the Macon and Western Railroad to Jonesboro. Avoiding Macon and Augusta, they passed through central Georgia, taking Milledgeville on the way, marching in compact column, and advancing with extreme caution, although only opposed by detachments of Wheeler's cavalry and a few hastily formed regiments of raw militia. Partial efforts were made to obstruct and destroy the roads in the front and on the flanks of the invading army, and patriotic appeals by prominent citizens were made to the people, to remove all provisions from its path, but no formidable opposition was made, except at the railroad-bridge over the Oconee, where Wheeler, with a portion of his command and a few militia, held the enemy in check for two or three days. With his small force, General Wheeler daringly and persistently harassed, and, when practicable, delayed the enemy's advance, attacking and defeating exposed detachments, deterring his foragers from venturing far from the main body, defending all cities and towns along the railroad lines, and affording protection to depots of supplies, arsenals, and other important Government works. The report of his operations from November 14th to December 20th displays a dash, activity, vigilance, and consummate skill, which justly entitle him to a prominent place on the roll of great cavalry leaders. Operating on all sides of Sherman's columns, he was enabled to keep the Government and commanders of our troops advised of the enemy's movements. It soon became manifest that Savannah was General Sherman's objective point. That city was occupied by General W. J. Hardee with about eighteen thousand men, a considerable portion of which was composed of militia, local troops, reserves, and hastily organized regiments and battalions made up of convalescents from the hospitals and artisans from the Government shops. On the 10th of December the enemy's columns reached the immediate vicinity of Savannah, and on the 12th they occupied a semicircular line extending from the Savannah River to the Savannah and Gulf Railroad. The defenses of the city were strong, the earthworks and other fortifications were flanked by inundated rice-swamps extending across the peninsula formed by the Savannah and Ogeechee Rivers, and the causeways leading through them were well fortified by works mounting heavy guns. With a sufficient force to occupy his long lines of defense, General Hardee could have sustained a protracted siege. The city was amply supplied, and its lines of communication were still open. Although Sherman had reached Savannah, he had not yet opened communication with the Federal fleet. Fort McAllister, situated on the right bank of the Ogeechee, about six miles from Ossabaw Sound, was a serious obstacle in his way, as it was a work of considerable strength, mounting twenty-one heavy guns, a deep and wide ditch extending along its front, with every avenue of approach swept by the guns mounted upon its bastions. The fort was held by a garrison of two hundred and fifty men under the command of experienced officers. The work was attacked on the evening of the 13th, and carried by assault after a short and feeble resistance. In consequence of the loss of this fort, Sherman speedily opened communication with the fleet, and became perfectly secure against any future want of supplies. This also enabled him to obtain heavy ordnance for use against the city. He proceeded immediately to take measures to invest Savannah, and in a few days had succeeded in doing so on every side of the city except that fronting the river. While Hardee's troops had not yielded a single position or lost a foot of ground, with the exception of Fort McAllister, when, on December 20th, he discovered that Sherman had put heavy siege-guns in position near enough to bombard the city, and that the enemy was threatening Union Causeway, which extends across the large swamps that lie between Savannah and Charleston, and offered the only practicable line of retreat, he determined to evacuate the place rather than expose the city and its inhabitants to bombardment. He also thought holding it had ceased to be of any special importance, and that his troops could do more valuable service in the field. Accordingly, on the night of December 20th, having destroyed the navy-yard, the iron-clads, and other Government property, and razed the fortifications below the city, he withdrew his army and reached Hardeeville on the evening of the 22d, without hindrance or molestation on the part of the enemy.

The following account of the campaign of Hood's army in Tennessee after the fall of Atlanta relies on General Hood's official account:

He reported the arrival of his army at Gadsden on the 20th of October, 1864, where he was joined by General P. G. T. Beauregard, commanding the military department. He writes that, after withdrawing from Atlanta, his hope had been that Sherman in following might offer an opportunity to strike him in detail, but in this he was disappointed. Hood reported that the *morale* of his army, though improved, was not such as, in the opinion of his corps commanders, would justify a general engagement while the enemy remained united. At Gadsden he found a thorough supply of shoes and other stores, but, after a full and free conference with General Beauregard at Tuscumbia, he decided to cross the Tennessee and move against Thomas, who with his corps had been detached by Sherman and sent into Middle Tennessee. General Beauregard had sent orders to General Forrest to move with his cavalry into Tennessee; the main body of Hood's cavalry had been sent to follow Sherman. As the orders to Forrest were accidentally delayed, and Hood had not cavalry enough to protect his trains, he was compelled to wait for the coming of Forrest, and, to hasten the meeting, moved down the river as far as Florence, where he arrived on the 31st of October. This unfortunate delay gave the enemy time to repair the railroad to Chattanooga, and accumulate supplies at Atlanta for a march thence toward the Atlantic coast. Forrest's cavalry joined on the 21st of November, and the movement began.

The enemy's forces at that time were concentrated at Pulaski and at Lawrenceburg. Hood endeavored to place his army between these forces and Nashville, but our cavalry, having driven off the enemy at Lawrenceburg, gave notice of our advance, and on the 23d he evacuated Pulaski and moved rapidly by the turnpike and railroad to Columbia. On the evening of the 27th of November our army took position in front of the works at that place. During the night the town was evacuated, and a strong position was taken on the opposite side of the river, about a mile and a half distant. On the evening of the 28th General Forrest crossed Duck River a few miles above Columbia, and in the morning of the 29th Stewart's and Cheatham's corps followed the cavalry, leaving Lieutenant-General Stephen D. Lee's corps confronting the enemy at Columbia. The cavalry and the two infantry corps moved in light marching order, the object being, by advancing rapidly on roads parallel to the Columbia and Franklin turnpike at or near Spring Hill, to cut off that portion of the foe at Columbia. The movement having been discovered after Hood's forces had got well on the flank of the enemy, he began to retreat along the turnpike toward Spring Hill. About noon of that day the cavalry attacked his trains, but found them too strongly guarded to be captured. The retreat was rapidly conducted along the turnpike, with flankers thrown out to protect the main column. Near Spring Hill Major-General Cheatham, being in the advance, commenced to come in contact with the retreating column about two miles from Spring Hill. He was ordered to attack vigorously, and get possession of the turnpike. This was so feebly executed that he failed to attain the object, and the enemy passed on toward Spring Hill. Though the golden opportunity had passed with daylight, Hood did not abandon the hope of effecting by a night movement the end he sought. Accordingly, Lieutenant-General Stewart was furnished with a guide, and ordered to move his corps beyond Cheatham's, and place it across the road beyond Spring Hill. In the dark and confusion, he did not succeed in getting the position desired. About midnight, ascertaining that the enemy was moving in disorder, with artillery, wagons, and troops intermixed, Hood sent instructions to General Cheatham to advance a heavy line of skirmishers, still further to impede the retreat. "This was not accomplished. The enemy continued to move along the road in hurry and confusion nearly all the night. Thus was lost a great opportunity for striking him for which we had labored so long—the greatest this campaign had offered, and one of the greatest during the war. Lieutenant-General S. D. Lee, left in front of the enemy at Columbia, was instructed to press him the moment he abandoned his position at that point. He did not abandon his works until dark, showing that his trains obstructed the road for fifteen miles during the day and a great part of the night." At daylight Hood pursued the enemy so rapidly as to compel him to burn a number of his wagons. On the hills about four miles south of Franklin, he made demonstration as if to give battle, but, when our forces deployed for the attack, he retired to Franklin.

From dispatches captured at Spring Hill, Hood learned that Schofield was instructed by Thomas to hold that position until Franklin could be made secure, and thus knew that it was important to attack Schofield promptly, and concluded that, if he should escape at Franklin, he would gain the fortifications about Nashville. Hood reports that "the nature of the position was such as to render it inexpedient to attempt any other flank movement, and I therefore determined to attack him in front and without delay."

As this was one of the bloodiest battles of the war, and its results materially affected the future, before entering on an account of it, I pause for some general reflections. It is not quite easy to determine what my gallant friend Hood meant by the expression, "the nature of the position." It may have referred to the probability that the enemy, if he attempted a flank movement, would retreat rapidly, as he had done from Columbia, and it is now known that a part of his troops and a large part of his train had already been sent across the Harpeth River. Thomas's dispatch indicated a purpose to hold Franklin; and its relation to Murfreesboro, where a garrison was maintained, would seem to render this a probable part of a plan to maintain communication with Chattanooga. Franklin had to us, as a mere *military* question, no other value than that the road to Nashville led through it. Whether it would have been possible to turn the position so promptly as to strike the enemy's line of retreat is a question which no doubt General Hood considered and decided in the negative, otherwise he would surely have preferred to attack the enemy on the march rather than in his intrenchments, especially as these were so near to the town that Hood was restrained from using his artillery on account of the women and children resident in it. The position itself was favorable for defense; the Harpeth River by a short bend flows on two sides of the town, and the works in front had the center so boldly salient, their flanks resting on the river, as to inclose the town in something like a square, two sides being river and two sides intrenchment. The exterior line of defense had been recently and hastily constructed; the interior line was much stronger. Behind the town there were two bridges, one on the main road leading through it, and the other a pontoon-bridge a short distance above it. Hood had served with distinction under Lee and Jackson, and his tactics were of that school. If he had, by an impetuous attack, crushed Schofield's army, without too great a loss to his own, and Forrest could have executed his orders to capture the trains when Schofield's army was crushed, we should never have heard complaint because Hood attacked at Franklin, and these were the hopes with which he made his assault.

On the 30th of November he formed his line of battle. At 4 P.M. he gave the order to advance; his troops moved gallantly forward, carried the first line, and advanced against the interior works; here the engagement was close and fierce; the combatants occupied the opposite sides of the intrenchments, our men carrying them in some places, many being killed entirely inside the enemy's work. Some of the Tennesseans, after years of absence, saw again their homes, and strove with desperation to expel the invader from them; the contest continued till near midnight, when the enemy abandoned his works and crossed the river, leaving his dead and wounded behind him. We had won a victory, but it was purchased at fearful cost. General Hood, in his letter of December 11, 1864, written near Nashville, reported his entire loss was about four thousand five hundred. Hood reported that the number of dead left on the field by the enemy indicated that his loss was equal to or near our own; that those of our men who were captured were inside the enemy's works.

Chapter 39

Exchange of Prisoners

PERHAPS THERE WAS no question in the treatment of which the true character and intentions of the Government of the United States was so clearly exposed as in the exchange of prisoners. That we should dare to resort to arms for the preservation of our rights, and "to secure the blessings of liberty to ourselves and our posterity," was regarded by our enemies as most improbable. Their aspirations for dominion and sovereignty, through the Government of the Union, had become so deep-seated and apparently real as to cause that Government, at its first step, to assume the haughtiness and imperiousness of an absolute sovereign. "I appeal to all loyal citizens to favor, facilitate, and aid this effort to maintain the honor, the integrity, and the existence of our national Union," said President Lincoln, in the first proclamation, calling for seventy-five thousand men. The term "loyal" has no signification except as applied to the sovereign of an empire or kingdom. In a republic the people are the sovereign, and the term "loyal" or its opposite can have no signification except in relation to the true sovereign. The Government of the United States is now the sovereign here, says President Lincoln in this proclamation, and loyalty consists in the maintenance of that sovereignty against all its foes. The sovereignty of the people and of the several and distinct States, in his mind, was only a weakness and enthusiasm of the fathers. The States and the people thereof had become consolidated into a national Union. The Confederate States not only refused to aid, but they took up arms to defeat the consummation of such a monstrous usurpation of popular rights and popular sovereignty.

This was the adversary with whom we had to struggle, and this was the issue for which we fought. We were denounced as "rebels." It was asserted that those of us "who were captured should be hung as rebels taken in the act."

On April 17, 1861, I issued a proclamation in which I offered to grant letters of marque and reprisal to seamen. On April 19th President Lincoln issued a counter-proclamation, declaring that, "if any person, under the pretended authority of said States, or under any other pretense, shall molest a vessel of the United States, or the persons or cargo on board of her, such person shall be held amenable to the laws of the United States for the prevention and punishment of piracy," which was death.

Some small vessels obtained these letters of marque and were captured. Their officers and crew constituted the first prisoners that fell into the hands of the enemy. They were immediately imprisoned, and held for trial as pirates. The trial came on later in the year. A report of it states that "the views of all the judges seemed to center upon the one point, that these men were taken in arms against the Government of the United States, and that, inasmuch as the laws of that Government did not recognize the authority under which the men acted, there was no course but to condemn them." As early as July 6, 1861, I sent by a special messenger a communication to President Lincoln, as follows:

Having learned that the schooner Savannah, a private armed vessel in the service and sailing under a commission issued by the authority of the Confederate States of America, had been captured by one of the vessels forming the blockading squadron off Charleston Harbor, I directed a proposition to be made to the commanding officer of the squadron for an exchange of officers and crew of the Savannah for prisoners of war held by this Government, "according to number and rank.". . . It now appears, by statements made without contradiction in newspapers published in New York, that the prisoners above mentioned were conveyed to that city, and have been treated not as prisoners of war, but as criminals; that they have been put in irons, confined in jail, brought before courts of justice on charges of piracy and treason; and it is even rumored that they have been convicted of the offenses charged, for no other reason than that they bore arms in defense of the rights of this Government and under the authority of its commission. . . . It is the desire of this Government so to conduct the war now existing as to mitigate its horrors as far as may be possible, and, with this intent, its treatment of the prisoners captured by its forces has been marked by the greatest humanity and leniency consistent with public obligation. Some have been permitted to return home on parole, others to remain at large, under similar conditions, within this Confederacy, and all have been furnished with rations for their subsistence, such as are allowed to our own troops. It is only since the news has been received of the treatment of the prisoners taken on the Savannah, that I have been compelled to withdraw these indulgences, and to hold the prisoners taken by us in strict confinement. . . . Painful as will be the necessity, this Government will deal out to the prisoners held by it the same treatment and the same fate as shall be experienced by those captured on the Savannah; and, if driven to the terrible necessity of retaliation by your execution of any of the officers or crew of the Savannah, that retaliation will be extended so far as shall be requisite to secure the abandonment of a practice unknown to the warfare of civilized man, and so barbarous as to disgrace the nation which shall be guilty of inaugurating it.

. . . I now renew the proposition made to the commander of the blockading squadron, to exchange for the prisoners taken on the Savannnah an equal number of those now held by us according to rank.

No answer ever came. We were compelled to select by lot from among the prisoners in our hands a number to whom we proposed to mete out the same fate which might await the crew of the Savannah. These measures of retaliation arrested the cruel and illegal purposes of the enemy.

Meantime, as early as May 21, 1861, the Confederate Congress passed an act which provided that—

All prisoners of war taken, whether on land or sea, during the pending hostilities with the United States, shall be transferred by the captors from time to time, and as often as convenient, to the Department of War; and it shall be the duty of the Secretary of War, with the approval of the President, to issue such instructions to the quartermaster-general and his subordinates as shall provide for the safe custody and sustenance of prisoners of war, and the rations furnished prisoners of war shall be the same in quantity and quality as those furnished to enlisted men in the army of the Confederacy.

This law of Congress was embodied in the orders issued from the War Department and from the headquarters in the field, and no order was ever issued in conflict with its humane provisions.

Nevertheless, the Government of the United States, forgetful of the conduct of Great Britain toward her revolted colonies, apparently refused all consideration of the question of exchange of prisoners, as if impressed with the idea that it would derogate from the dignity of its position to accept any interchange of courtesy. An exchange was therefore occasionally made by the various commanders of troops under flags of truce, while the Federal Government made the paltry pretense of not knowing it. We released numbers at different points on parole, and the matter was compromised in various ways. A proposition made in the Confederate

Congress to return the prisoners captured by us at first Manassas, without any formality whatever, would doubtless have prevailed but for the difficulty in reference to the crew of the Savannah.

But this determination of the United States Government, not to meet us on the equal footing consistent with the modern usages of war and exchange prisoners, thus far prevented any general arrangement for that object. In consequence, however, of the clamors of the Northern people for the restoration of their friends, both Houses of Congress united in a request to President Lincoln to take immediate steps for a general exchange. Instead of complying with this request, two respectable commissioners were, however, appointed to visit the prisoners we held, relieve their necessities, and provide for their comfort at the expense of the United States. It is impossible to conceive any reason for such conduct, unless it was to exasperate and "fire up the Northern heart," as it was expressed, and thus cause the people to make greater efforts for our devastation. This action on the part of the Government was at a later day known by the expression "waving the bloody shirt."

The commissioners arrived at Norfolk, Virginia, but were not allowed to proceed any farther. A readiness on our part to negotiate for a general exchange was manifested, and agreed to by them. This was subsequently approved at Washington. Shortly afterward, on February 14, 1862, an arrangement was made between General Howell Cobb on our part and General Wool, the commander at Fortress Monroe, by the terms of which the prisoners of war in the hands of each Government were to be exchanged man for man, the officers being assimilated as to rank; our privateersmen were to be exchanged on the footing of prisoners of war; any surplus remaining on either side was to be released; and during the continuance of hostilities prisoners taken on either side should be paroled. The exchange proceeded, and about three hundred in excess had been delivered, when it was discovered that not one of our privateersmen had been released, and that our men taken prisoners at Fort Donelson, instead of being paroled, had been sent into the interior. Some of the hostages we held for our privateersmen had gone forward, but the remainder were retained. Being informed of this state of affairs, I recommended to Congress that all of our men who had been paroled by the United States Government should be released from the obligations of their parole so as to bear arms in our defense, in consequence of this breach of good faith on the part of that Government. It was subsequently said, on behalf of the United States Government, that the detention of our privateersmen had been intended to be only temporary, to make it certain that the hostages were coming forward.

The negotiations between Generals Wool and Cobb were abruptly broken off, and the matter left where it was before. After these negotiations had begun, the capture of Forts Henry and Donelson had given to the United States a considerable preponderance in the number of prisoners held by them, and they at once returned to their original purpose of unequal treatment.

A suspension of exchange for some months ensued. Finally, a storm of indignation beginning to arise among the Northern people at the conduct of their Government, it was forced to yield its absurd pretensions, and, on July 22, 1862, a cartel for the exchange of prisoners was executed, based on the cartel of 1812 between the United States and Great Britain. In accordance with these terms an exchange commenced, and by the middle of August most of the officers of rank on either side, who had been for any long period in captivity, were released.

On the same day on which the cartel was signed, an order was issued by the Secretary of War, in Washington, under instructions from President Lincoln, empowering the military commanders in Virginia and elsewhere "to seize and use any property, real or personal, which may be necessary or convenient for their several commands for supplies or for other military purposes," and "to keep accounts sufficiently accurate and in detail to show quantities and amounts and from whom it shall come, as a basis upon which compensation can be made in proper cases." This was simply a system of plunder, for no compensation would be made to any person unless he could prove his fidelity to the Government of the United States.

On the next day, Major-General Pope, in command of the United States forces near Washington, issued a general order directing the murder of our peaceful inhabitants as spies, if found quietly tilling the farms in his rear, even outside of his lines; and one of his brigadier-generals seized upon innocent and peaceful inhabitants to be held as hostages, to the end that they might be murdered in cold blood if any of his soldiers were killed by some unknown persons, whom he designated as "bushwhackers." Under this state of facts, I issued a general order, recognizing General Pope and his commissioned officers to be in the position which they had chosen for themselves—that of robbers and murderers, and not that of public enemies, entitled, if captured, to be considered as prisoners of war. We renounced our right of retaliation on the innocent, and continued to treat the soldiers of General Pope's army as prisoners of war, confining our repressive measures to the punishment only of commissioned officers as were willing participants in such crimes. General Pope was soon afterward removed from command.

In August a letter involving similar principles was addressed by General R. E. Lee to the commanding General at Washington, General Halleck, making inquiries as to the truth of the case of William B. Mumford, reported to have been murdered at New Orleans by Major-General Benjamin F. Butler, and of Colonel John Owens, reported to have been murdered in Missouri by order of Major-General Pope. I had also been credibly informed that numerous other officers of the army of the United States within the Confederacy had been guilty of felonies and capital offenses. Inquiries were made by letter relative to a few of the best-authenticated cases. It was announced that Major-General Hunter had armed slaves for the murder of their masters, and had thus done all in his power to inaugurate a servile war, which is worse than that of the savage, inasmuch as it super-adds other horrors to the indiscriminate slaughter of all ages, sexes, and conditions.

Brigadier-General Phelps was reported to have initiated at New Orleans the example set by General Hunter in South Carolina. General Lee was further directed by me to say that, if a reply was not received in fifteen days, it would be assumed that the alleged facts were true, and were sanctioned by the Government of the United States, and on that Government would rest the responsibility of retaliatory measures. The reply of the commanding General (Halleck) at Washington was in these words:

As these papers are couched in language insulting to the Government of the United States, I most respectfully decline to receive them.

On August 21, 1862, I issued an order which directed that Major-General Hunter and Brigadier-General Phelps should be no longer held and treated as public enemies of the Confederate States, but as outlaws; and that in the event of the capture of either of them, or that of any other commissioned officer employed in drilling, organizing, or instructing slaves, with a view to their armed service in this war, he should not be regarded as a prisoner of war, but held in close confinement for execution as a felon, at such time and place as may be ordered.

In the case of William B. Mumford, I had received evidence fully establishing the fact that the said Mumford, a citizen of the Confederacy, was actually and publicly executed in cold blood by hanging after the occupation of New Orleans by the forces under General Benjamin F. Butler, when said Mumford was an unresisting and non-combatant captive, and for no offenses even alleged to have been committed by him subsequent to the date of the occupation of the city. The silence of the Government of the United States and its maintenance of Butler in high office afforded evidence too conclusive that it sanctioned his conduct, and was determined that he should remain unpunished for these crimes. I therefore pronounced and declared the said Butler a felon, deserving capital punishment, and ordered that he be no longer considered and treated as a public enemy of the Confederate States, but as an outlaw and common enemy of mankind; and that, in the event of his capture, the officer in command should cause him to be immediately executed by hanging.

At length, so many difficulties were raised, and so many complaints made in the execution of the cartel, that, for the sake of the unfortunate prisoners, I resolved to seek an adjustment through the authorities at Washington. For this purpose Vice-President Stephens offered his services as a commissioner.

On July 3, 1863, Mr. Stephens proceeded down the James River under a flag of truce, and when near Newport News his further progress was arrested by the orders of the Admiral of the enemy's fleet. The object of his mission, with a request for permission to go to Washington, was made known to that officer, who, by telegraph, communicated with the Government at Washington. The reply of that Government was:

The request is inadmissible. The customary agents and channels are adequate for all needful military communications and conference between the United States forces and the insurgents.

From the correspondence of our exchange commissioner, Judge Ould, it appears that, from the date of the cartel on July 22, 1862, until the summer of 1863, we had an excess of prisoners. During the interval deliveries were made as fast as the enemy furnished transportation. Indeed, upon more than one occasion they were urged to send increased means of transportation. It was never alleged that we failed or neglected to make prompt deliveries of prisoners who were not held under charges when they had the excess. On the other hand, the cartel was openly and notoriously violated by the Washington authorities. Officers and men were kept in confinement, sometimes in irons or doomed to cells, without charge or trial. Many officers were kept in confinement even after the notices published by the enemy had declared them to be exchanged.

In the summer of 1863 the authorities at Washington insisted upon exchanges limited to such as were held in confinement on either side. This was resisted as in violation of the cartel. Such a construction not only kept in confinement the excess on either side, but ignored all paroles which were held by the Confederate Government. These were very many, being the paroles of officers and men who had been released on capture. The authorities at Washington at that time held few or no paroles. They had all, or nearly all, been surrendered. We gave prisoners as an equivalent for them. As long as we had the excess of prisoners, matters went on smoothly enough, but, as soon as the posture of affairs in that respect was changed, the cartel could no longer be observed. So long as the United States Government held the paroles of Confederate officers and men, they were respected and made the basis of exchange; but when equivalents were obtained for them, and no more were in hand, they would not recognize the paroles which were held by us. In consequence of the position thus assumed by the Government of the United States, the requirement of the cartel that all prisoners should be delivered within ten days was practically nullified. The deliveries which were afterward made were the results of special agreements.

The wish of the Confederate Government, which it was hoped had been accomplished by the cartel, was the prompt release of all prisoners on both sides, either by exchange or parole. When, in 1864, the cartel was so disregarded by the enemy as to indicate that prisoners would be held long in confinement, Andersonville, in Georgia, was selected for the location of a principal prison. The site was chosen because of its supposed security from raids, together with its salubrity, the abundance of water and timber, and the productive farming country around it. General Howell Cobb, then commanding in Georgia, employed a large number of negro laborers in the construction of a stockade and temporary shelter for the number of prisoners it was expected would be assembled there. The number, however, rapidly increased, and, by the middle of May, gangrene and scurvy made their appearance. General John H. Winder, who had been stationed in Richmond in charge of the police and local guards, as well as the general control of prisoners, went to Andersonville in June, and found disease prevailing to such an extent that, to abate the pestilence, he immediately advised the removal of prisoners to other points. As soon as arrangements could be made, he was instructed to disperse them to Millen and elsewhere, as in his judgment might be best for their health, comfort, and safety. In July he made arrangements to procure vegetables, recommended details of men to cultivate gardens, and that hospital accommodations should be constructed outside of the prison; all of which recommendations were approved, and as far as practicable executed. In September General Winder, with the main body of the prisoners, removed first to Millen, Georgia, and then to Florence, South Carolina.

Major Wirz thereafter remained in command at Andersonville, and the testimony of Chief-Surgeon Stevenson, of the hospital at Andersonville, bears testimony to the success with which Wirz improved the post, and the good effect produced upon the health of the prisoners. This unfortunate man—who, under the severe temptation to which he was exposed before his execution, exhibited honor and fidelity strongly in contrast with his tempters and persecutors—it now appears, was the victim of men whom, in his kindness, he paroled to take care of their sick comrades, and who, after having violated their parole, appeared to testify against him.

In like manner has calumny pursued the memory of General John H. Winder, a man too brave to be cruel to anything within his power, too well bred and well born to be influenced by low and sordid motives. I have referred only to a few of the facts illustrative of his kindness to the prisoners after he went to Georgia, and they were in keeping with his conduct toward the prisoners at Richmond. This latter fact, together with his sterling integrity and soldierly character, had caused his selection for the chief control of Confederate prisons.

In January, 1864, and even earlier, it became manifest that, in consequence of the complication in relation to exchanges, the large mass of prisoners on both sides would remain in captivity for many long and weary months, if not for the duration of the war. In order to alleviate the hardships of confinement on both sides, our commissioner, on January 24, 1863, addressed a communication to General E. A. Hitchcock, United States commissioner of exchange, in which he proposed that all prisoners on each side should be attended by a proper number of their own surgeons, who, under rules to be established, should be permitted to take charge of their health and comfort.

It was also proposed that these surgeons should act as commissaries, with power to receive and distribute such contributions of money, food, clothing, and medicines as might be forwarded for the relief of the prisoners. It was further proposed that these surgeons should be selected by their own Government, and that they should have full liberty at any and all times, through the agents of exchange, to make reports, not only of their own acts, but of any matters relating to the welfare of the prisoners.

To this communication no reply of any kind was ever made.

Again, Commissioner Ould, in a communication published in August, 1868, further says:

About the last of March, 1864, I had several conferences with General B. F. Butler, then agent of exchange at Fortress Monroe, in relation to the difficulties attending the exchange of prisoners, and we reached what we both thought a tolerably satisfactory basis. The day that I left there General Grant arrived. General Butler says he communicated to him the state of the negotiations, and "most emphatic verbal directions were received from the Lieutenant-General not to take any step by which another able-bodied man should be exchanged until further orders from him"; and that on April 30, 1864, he received a telegram from General Grant "to receive all the sick and wounded the Confederate authorities may send you, but send no more in exchange." Unless my recollection fails me, General Butler also, in an address to his constituents, substantially declared that he was directed, in his management of the question of exchange with the Confederate authorities, to put the matter *offensively, for the purpose of preventing an exchange.*

The signification of the word "offensively," in the preceding line, relates to the exchange of negro soldiers. The Government of the United States contended that the slaves in their ranks were such no longer; that it was bound to accord to them, when made prisoners, the same protection that it gave all other soldiers. We asserted the slaves to be property, under the Constitution of the United States and that of the Confederate States, and that property recaptured from the enemy in war reverts to its owner, if he can be found, or it may be disposed of by its captor.

On October 1st, when the number of prisoners was large on either side, General Lee addressed a note to General Grant, saying:

With a view of alleviating the sufferings of our soldiers, I have the honor to propose an exchange of the prisoners of war belonging to the armies operating in Virginia, man for man, or upon the basis established by the cartel.

On the next day General Grant replied:

I could not of a right accept your proposition further than to exchange those prisoners captured within the last three days, and who have not yet been delivered to the commanding General of prisoners. Among those lost by the armies operating against Richmond were a number of colored troops. Before further negotiations are had upon the subject, I would ask if you propose delivering these men the same as white soldiers.

On the next day General Lee said, in rejoinder:

In my propsition . . . I intended to include all captured soldiers of the United States, of whatever nation and color, under my control. Deserters from our service and negroes belonging to our citizens are not considered subjects of exchange, and were not included in my proposition. If there are any such among those stated by you to have been captured around Richmond, they can not be returned.

On October 20th General Grant finally answered, saying:

I shall always regret the necessity of retaliating for wrong done our soldiers, but regard it my duty to protect all persons received into the army of the United States, regardless of color or nationality; when acknowledged soldiers of the Government are captured, they must be treated as prisoners of war, or such treatment as they receive inflicted upon an equal number of prisoners held by us.

In a dispatch from General Grant to General Butler, dated City Point, August 18, 1864, the former says:

On the subject of exchange, however, I differ from General Hitchcock. It is hard on our men held in Southern prisons not to exchange them, but it is humanity to those left in the ranks to fight our battles. Every man released on parole, or otherwise, becomes an active soldier against us at once, either directly or indirectly. If we commence a system of exchange, which liberates all prisoners taken, we will have to fight on until the whole South is exterminated. If we hold those caught, they amount to no more than dead men. At this particular time to release all rebel prisoners North would insure Sherman's defeat, and would compromise our safety here.

We now proposed to the Government of the United States to exchange the prisoners respectively held, officer for officer and man for man. We had previously declined this proposal, and insisted on the terms of the cartel, which required the delivery of the excess on either side on parole. At the same time we sent a statement of the mortality prevailing among the prisoners at Andersonville.

This offer, which would have released every soldier of the United States confined in our prisons, was not even noticed. Indeed, the United States Government had, at that time, a large excess of prisoners, and the effect of the proposal, if carried out, would have been to release all the prisoners belonging to it, while a large number of ours would have remained in prison awaiting the chances of the capture of their equivalents.

Thus, having ascertained that exchanges could not be made, either on the basis of the cartel, or officer for officer and man for man, we offered to the United States Government their sick and wounded without requiring any equivalents. On these terms, we agreed to deliver from ten to fifteen thousand at the mouth of the Savannah River; and we further added that, if the number for which transportation might be sent could not be readily made up from sick and wounded, the difference should be supplied with well men. Although the offer was made in the summer, the transportation did not arrive until November. And as the sick and wounded were at points distant from Georgia, and could not be brought to Savannah within a reasonable time, five thousand well men were substituted. In return, some three thousand sick and wounded were delivered to us at the same place. The original rolls showed that some thirty-five hundred had started from Northern prisons and that death had reduced the number during the passage to about three thousand.

On two occasions we were specially asked to send the very sick and desperately wounded prisoners, and a particular request was made for men who were so seriously sick that it was doubtful whether they would survive a removal a few miles down James River. Accordingly, some of the worst cases, contrary to the judgment of our surgeons, but in compliance with the piteous appeals of the sick prisoners, were sent away, and after being delivered they were taken to Annapolis, Maryland, and there photographed as specimen prisoners. The photographs at Annapolis were terrible indeed, but the misery they portrayed was surpassed by some of those we received in exchange at Savannah. Why was there this delay between the summer and November in sending vessels for the transportation of sick and wounded, for whom no equivalents were asked? Were Federal prisoners left to suffer, and afterward photographed "to aid in firing the popular heart of the North"?

In the summer of 1864, in consequence of certain information communicated to our commissioner, Mr. Ould, by the Surgeon-General of the Confederate States, as to the deficiency of medicines, Mr. Ould offered to make purchases of medicines from the United States authorities, to be used exclusively for the relief of the Union prisoners. He offered to pay gold, cotton, or tobacco for them, and even two or three prices if required. At the same time he gave assurances that the medicines would be used exclusively for the treatment of Union prisoners; and moreover agreed, on behalf of the Confederate States, if it were insisted on, that such medicines might be brought into the Confederate lines by the United States surgeons, and dispensed by them. Incredible as it may appear, it is, nevertheless, strictly true that no reply was ever received to this offer.

One final effort was now made to obtain an exchange. This consisted in my sending a delegation from the prisoners at Andersonville to plead their cause before the authorities at Washington. It was of no avail. President Lincoln refused to see them. They were made to understand that the interests of the Government of the United States required that they should return to prison and remain there. They carried back the sad tidings that their Government held out no hope of their release.

At any hour perfect arrangements could have been made with us for the restoration to it of all its soldiers held as prisoners by us, if its authorities at Washington had consented so to do. On them rests the criminality for the sufferings of these prisoners.

Further, the Government of the United States, in order to effect our subjugation, devastated our fields, destroyed our crops, broke up our railroads, and thus interrupted our means of transportation, and reduced our people, our armies, and consequently their soldiers, who were our prisoners, all alike, to the most straitened condition for food. Our medicines for the sick were exhausted, and, contrary to the usage of civilized nations, they were made, by our enemy, contraband of war. After causing these and other distressing events, this Government of the United States turned to the Northern people, and, charging us with atrocious cruelties to their sons, who were our prisoners, appealed to them again and again to recruit the armies and take vengeance upon us by our abject subjugation or entire extermination.

During all this time, Northern prisons were full of our brave and heroic soldiers, of whom there were about sixty thousand. The privations which they suffered, the cruelties inspired by the malignant spirit of the Government, which were inflicted upon them, surpass any records of modern history: yet we have had no occasion to seek out a Wirz for public trial before an illegal court, that we might conceal behind him our own neglect and cruel sacrifice of them. That we might clothe our brave men in the prisons of the United States Government, I made an application for permission to send cotton to Liverpool, and therewith purchase the supplies which were necessary. The request was granted, but only on condition that the cotton should be sent to New York and the supplies bought there. This was done by our agent, General Beale. The suffering of our men in Northern prisons caused the application; that it was granted, refutes the statement that our men were comfortably maintained.

Finally, to the bold allegations of ill-treatment of prisoners on our side, and humane treatment and adequate supplies on that of our opponents, it is only necessary to offer two facts: First, the report of the Secretary of War, E. M. Stanton, made on July 19, 1866, shows that, of all the prisoners in our hands during the war, only 22,576 died; while, of the prisoners on our opponents' hands, 26,246 died. Second, the official report of Surgeon-General Barnes, an officer of the United States Government, states that, in round numbers, the number of Confederate States prisoners in their hands amounted to 220,000, the number of United States prisoners in our hands amounted to 270,000. Thus, out of the 270,000 in our hands, 22,000 died; while of the 220,000 of our soldiers in their hands, 26,000 died. Thus, more than twelve per cent of the prisoners in our opponents' hands died, and less than nine per cent of the prisoners in our hands died.

When, in this connection, it is remembered how much our resources were reduced, that our supply of medicines required in summer diseases was exhausted, and that Northern men when first residing at the South must undergo acclimation, and that these conditions in the Northern States were the reverse in each particular—the fact that greater mortality existed in Northern than in Southern prisons can only be accounted for by the kinder treatment received in the latter.

Chapter 40

Peace Negotiations

THAT IT WAS the purpose of the Government of the United States to subjugate the Southern States and the Southern people, under the pretext of a restoration of the Union, is established by the terms and conditions offered to us in all the conferences relative to a settlement of differences. All were comprehended in one word, and that was subjugation. If the purpose had been an honorable and fraternal restoration of the Union as was avowed, methods for the adjustment of difficulties would have been presented and discussed; propositions for reconciliation with concessions and modifications for grievances would have been kindly offered and treated; and a way would have been opened for a mutual and friendly intercourse. How unlike this were all the propositions offered to us, will be seen.

Several efforts were made by us to communicate with the authorities at Washington without success. Commissioners were sent before hostilities were begun, and the Government of the United States refused to receive them, or hear what they had to say. A second time I sent a military officer with a communication addressed by myself to President Lincoln. The letter was received by General Scott, who did not permit the officer to see Mr. Lincoln, but promised that an answer would be sent. No answer was ever received. The third time a gentleman was sent whose position, character, and reputation were such as to insure his reception, if the enemy had not been determined to receive no proposals whatever from our Government. Vice-President Stephens made a patriotic tender of his services, in the hope of being able to promote the cause of humanity. The enemy refused to let him pass through their lines or to hold any conference with him. He was stopped before he reached Fortress Monroe.

If we would break up our Government, dissolve the Confederacy, disband our armies, emancipate our slaves, take an oath of allegiance, binding ourselves to obedience to it and to disloyalty to our own States, the Government of the United States proposed to pardon us, and not to deprive us of anything more than the property already robbed from us, and such slaves as still remained. In order to render the proposals so insulting as to secure their rejection, the President of the United States joined to them a promise to support with his army one tenth of the people of any State who would attempt to set up a government over the other nine tenths.

The next movement relating to the accommodation of differences occurred in July, 1864, and consisted in the appearance at Richmond of Colonel James F. Jacques, of the Seventy-eighth Illinois Infantry, and James R. Gilmore, of Massachusetts, soliciting an interview with me. They stated that they had no official character or authority, "but were fully possessed of the views of the United States Government, relative to an adjustment of the differences existing between the North and the South," and did not doubt that a free interchange of views would open the way to official negotiations, etc. They had crossed our lines through a letter of General Grant to Colonel Ould, commissioner for the exchange of prisoners. Mr. Gilmore addressed me, and in a few minutes conveyed the information that the two gentlemen had come to Richmond impressed with the idea that the Confederate Government would accept a peace on the basis of a reconstruction of the Union, the abolition of slavery, and the grant of an amnesty to the people of the States as repentant criminals. In order to accomplish the abolition of slavery, it was proposed that there should be a general vote of all the people of both federations, in mass, and the majority of the vote thus taken was to determine that as well as all other disputed questions. These were stated to be Mr. Lincoln's views. The impudence of the remarks could only be extenuated because of the ignorance displayed and the profuse avowal of the kindest motives and intentions.

I answered that, as these proposals had been prefaced by the remark that the people of the North were a majority, and that a majority ought to govern, the offer was, in effect, a proposal that the Confederate States should surrender at discretion, admit that they had been wrong from the beginning of the contest, submit to the mercy of their enemies, and avow themselves to be in need of pardon for their crimes; that extermination was preferable to dishonor. I stated that, if they were themselves so unacquainted with the form of their own government as to make such propositions, Mr. Lincoln ought to have known, when giving them his views, that it was out of the power of the Confederate Government to act on the subject of the domestic institutions of the several

States, each State having exclusive jurisdiction on that point, still less to commit the decision of such a question to the vote of a foreign people. Having no disposition to discuss questions of state with such persons, especially as they bore no credentials, I terminated the interview, and they withdrew with Mr. Benjamin.

The opening of the spring campaign of 1864 was deemed a favorable conjuncture for the employment of the resources of diplomacy. To approach the Government of the United States directly would have been in vain. Repeated efforts had already demonstrated its inflexible purpose—not to negotiate with the Confederate authorities. Political developments at the North, however, favored the adoption of some action that might influence popular sentiment in the hostile section. The aspect of the peace party was quite encouraging, and it seemed that the real issue to be decided in the Presidential election of that year, was the continuance or cessation of the war. A commission of three persons, eminent in position and intelligence, was accordingly appointed to visit Canada, with a view to negotiation with such persons in the North as might be relied upon to aid the attainment of peace. The commission was designed to facilitate such preliminary conditions as might lead to formal negotiations between the two Governments, and they were expected to make judicious use of any political opportunity that might be presented.

The commissioners—Messrs. Clay, of Alabama; Holcombe, of Virginia; and Thompson, of Mississippi—established themselves at Niagara Falls in July, and on the 12th commenced a correspondence with Horace Greeley, of New York. Through him they sought a safe-conduct to Washington. Mr. Lincoln at first appeared to favor an interview, but finally refused on the ground that the commissioners were not authorized to treat for peace. His final announcement to them was the following:

EXECUTIVE MANSION, WASHINGTON, D. C., *July 18, 1864*
To whom it may concern:
Any proposition which embraces the restoration of peace, the integrity of the whole union, and the abandonment of slavery, and which comes by and with an authority that can control the armies now at war against the United States, will be received and considered by the Executive Government of the United States, and will be met by liberal terms on other substantial and collateral points, and the bearer or bearers thereof shall have safe conduct both ways.   ABRAHAM LINCOLN

This movement, like all others which had preceded it, was a failure.

On December 30, 1864, I received a request from Mr. Francis P. Blair, a distinguished citizen of Montgomery County, Maryland, for permission to visit Richmond for certain personal objects, which was conceded to him. On January 12, 1865, he visited me, and the following statement of our interview was immediately afterward prepared:

RICHMOND, VIRGINIA, *January 12, 1865*
Memorandum of a confidential conversation held this day with
F. P. BLAIR, *of Montgomery County, Maryland.*

Mr. Blair stated that, not receiving an answer to his application for permission to visit Richmond, which had been sent from the headquarters of General Grant's army, he returned to Washington and there received the reply which had been made to his application, but by some means had been withheld from him and been forwarded after having been opened; that he had originally obtained permission to visit Richmond from Mr. Lincoln, after stating to him that he (Mr. Blair) had for many years held friendly relations with myself. Mr. Lincoln stopped him, though he afterward gave him permission to visit me. He stated [that] his views . . . were to be regarded merely as his own. . . . He had recognized the difference of our positions as not entitling him to a response from me to the arguments and suggestions which he desired to offer. I . . . allowed him to read without comment on my part. When he had finished, I inquired as to his main proposition, the cessation of hostilities and the union of the military forces for the common purpose of maintaining the "Monroe doctrine"—how that object was to be reached. He said that both the political parties of the United States asserted the Monroe doctrine as a cardinal point of their creed; that there was a general desire to apply it to the case of Mexico: For that purpose a secret treaty might be made, etc. I called his attention to my past efforts for negotiation, and my inability to see—unless Mr. Lincoln's course in that regard should be changed—how we were to take the first step. He expressed the belief that Mr. Lincoln would now receive commissioners, but subsequently said he could not give any assurance on that point, and proposed to return to Washington to explain his project to Mr. Lincoln, and notify me, if his hope proved well founded, that Mr. Lincoln would now agree to a conference for the purpose of entering into negotiations. He affirmed that Mr. Lincoln did not sympathize with the radical men who desired the devastation and subjugation of the Southern States, but that he was unable to control the extreme party, which now had great power in the Congress, and would at the next session have still more; referred to the existence of two parties in the Cabinet, to the reluctant nomination of Mr. Chase to be Chief-Justice, etc. . . .

It was evident that he counted on the disintegration of the Confederate States if the war continued, and that in any event he regarded the institution of slavery as doomed to extinction. I thought any remark by me on the first proposition would lead to intimations in connection with public men which I preferred not more distinctly to hear than as manifested in his general remarks; on the latter point, for the reason stated, the inequality of his responsibility and mine, I preferred to have no discussion. The only difficulty which he spoke of as insurmountable was that of existing engagements between European powers and the Confederate States. This point . . . was met by me with a statement that we had now no such complication, were free to act as to us should seem best, and desired to keep state policy and institutions free from foreign control. Throughout the conference Mr. Blair . . . claimed no other power than that of serving as a medium of communication between those who had thus far had no intercourse, and were therefore without the co-intelligence which might secure an adjustment of their controversy. . . . Our conference ended with no other result than an agreement that he would learn whether Mr. Lincoln would adopt his (Mr. Blair's) project, and send or receive commissioners to negotiate for a peaceful solution of the question at issue; that he would report to him my readiness to enter upon negotiations, and that I knew of no insurmountable obstacle to such a treaty of peace as would secure greater advantage to both parties than any result which arms could achieve.

The following letter was given by me to Mr. Blair:

RICHMOND, VIRGINIA, *January 12, 1865.*
F. P. BLAIR, Esq.

SIR: I have deemed it proper and probably desirable to you to give you in this form the substance of remarks made by me to be repeated by you to President Lincoln, etc, etc.

I have no disposition to find obstacles in forms, and am willing now, as heretofore, to enter into negotiations for the restoration of peace, am ready to send a commission whenever I have reason to suppose it will be received, or to receive a commission if the United States Government shall choose to send one. That, notwithstanding the rejection of our former offers, I would, if you could promise that a commissioner, minister, or other agent would be received, appoint one immediately, and renew the effort to enter into conference with a view to secure peace to the two countries.

Yours, etc., JEFFERSON DAVIS

WASHINGTON, *January 18, 1865*

F. P. BLAIR, Esq.

SIR: You having shown me Mr. Davis's letter to you of the 12th instant, you may say to him that I have constantly been, am now, and shall continue ready to receive any agent whom he or any other influential person now resisting the national authority may informally send to me with the view of securing peace to the people of our one common country.

Yours, etc.,   A. LINCOLN

When Mr. Blair returned and gave me this letter of Mr. Lincoln of January 18th, it being a response to my note to Mr. Blair of the 12th, he said it had been a fortunate thing that I gave him that note, as it had created greater confidence in Mr. Lincoln regarding his efforts at Richmond. Further reflection, he said, had modified the views he formerly presented to me, and that he wanted to have my attention for a different mode of procedure. He then unfolded to me the embarrassment of Mr. Lincoln on account of the extreme men in Congress and elsewhere, who wished to drive him into harsher measures than he was inclined to adopt; whence it would not be feasible for him to enter into any arrangement with us by the use of political agencies; that, if anything beneficial could be effected, it must be done without the intervention of the politicians. He, therefore, suggested that Generals Lee and Grant might enter into an arrangement by which hostilities would be suspended, and a way paved for the restoration of peace. I responded that I would willingly entrust to General Lee such negotiation as was indicated.

To report to Mr. Lincoln the result of his visit, Mr. Blair returned to Washington. He subsequently informed me that the idea of a military convention was not favorably received at Washington, so it only remained for me to act upon the letter of Mr. Lincoln.

I determined to send, as commissioners or agents for the informal conference, Messrs. Alexander H. Stephens, R. M. T. Hunter, and John A. Campbell. The letter of Mr. Lincoln expressing a willingness to receive any agent I might send to Washington City, a commission was appointed to go there; but it was not allowed to proceed farther than Hampton Roads, where Mr. Lincoln, accompanied by Mr. Seward, met the commissioners. Seward craftily proposed that the conference should be confidential, and the commissioners regarded this so binding on them as to prevent them from including in their report the discussion which occurred. This enabled Mr. Seward to give his own version of it in a dispatch to the United States Minister to the French Government, which was calculated to create distrust of, if not hostility to, the Confederacy on the part of the power in Europe most effectively favoring our recognition.

The report of the commissioners, dated February 5, 1865, was as follows:

To the President of the Confederate States:

SIR: . . . The conference . . . took place on the 30th ult., on board of a steamer anchored in Hampton Roads, where we met President Lincoln and the Hon. Mr. Seward, Secretary of State of the United States. It continued for several hours, and was both full and explicit. We learned from them that the message of President Lincoln to the Congress of the United States, in December last, explains clearly and distinctly his sentiments as to the terms, conditions, and method of proceeding by which peace can be secured to the people, and we were not informed that they would be modified or altered to obtain that end. We understood from him that no terms or proposals of any treaty, or agreement looking to an ultimate settlement, would be entertained or made by him with the authorities of the Confederate States, because that would be a recognition of their existence as a separate power, which under no circumstances would be done; and, for a like reason, that no such terms would be entertained by him for the States separately; that no extended truce or armistice (as at present advised) would be granted or allowed without a satisfactory assurance in advance of the complete restoration of the authority of the Constitution and laws of the United States over all places within the States of the Confederacy; that whatever consequences may follow from the reëstablishment of that authority must be accepted; but that individuals subject to pains and penalties under the laws of the United States might rely upon a very liberal use of the power confided to him to remit those pains and penalties if peace be restored.

During the conference, the proposed amendment to the Constitution of the United States adopted by Congress on the 31st ultimo was brought to our notice.

This amendment provides that neither slavery nor involuntary servitude, except for crime, should exist within the United States, or any place within their jurisdiction, and that Congress should have power to enforce this amendment by appropriate legislation. Very respectfully, etc.,

ALEXANDER H. STEPHENS,
R. M. T. HUNTER,
JOHN A. CAMPBELL.

Thus closed the conference, and all negotiations with the

Government of the United States for the establishment of peace. Says Judge Campbell, in his memoranda:

In conclusion, Mr. Hunter summed up what seemed to be the result of the interview: that there could be no arrangements by treaty between the Confederate States and the United States, or any agreements between them; that there was nothing left for them but unconditional submission.

By reference to the message of President Lincoln of December 6, 1864, which is mentioned in the report, it appears that the terms of peace therein stated were as follows:

In presenting the abandonment of armed resistance to the national authority on the part of the insurgents, as the only indispensable condition to ending the war on the part of the Government, I retract nothing heretofore said as to slavery. I repeat the declaration made a year ago, that "while I remain in my present position I shall not attempt to retract or modify the emancipation proclamation, nor shall I return to slavery any person who is free by the terms of that proclamation, or by any act of Congress." If the people should, by whatever mode or means, make it an executive duty to reënslave such persons, another, and not I, must be their instrument to perform it.

The first section of the fourth article of the Constitution of the United States is in these words:

No person held to service or labor in one State, under the laws thereof, escaping into another, shall, in consequence of any law or regulation therein, be discharged from such service or labor, but shall be delivered up on claim of the party to whom such service or labor may be due.

The intelligent reader will observe that the words of this section, "in consequence of any law or regulation therein," embrace a President's emancipation proclamation, as well as any other regulation therein. Thus the Constitution itself nullified Mr. Lincoln's proclamation, and made it of no force whatever. Yet he assumed and maintained, with all the military force he could command, that it set every slave free.

Again he says:

Nor shall I return to slavery any person who is free by the terms of that proclamation or by an act of Congress.

But the Constitution says he shall return them—

> but shall be delivered up on claim of the party to whom such service is due.

Was it thus obeyed by Mr. Lincoln as the supreme law of the land? It was not obeyed, but set aside, subverted, overturned by him, despite his oath of office.

Again the report says:

> We understood from him that no terms or proposals of any treaty or agreement looking to an ultimate settlement would be entertained or made by him with the authorities of the Confederate States, because that would be a recognition of their existence as a separate power, which under no circumstances would be done; and, for a like reason, that no such terms would be entertained by him for the States separately.

Now the Constitution of the United States says, in Article X:

> The powers not delegated to the United States by the Constitution, nor prohibited by it to the States, are reserved to the States respectively, or to the people.

Within the purview of this article of the Constitution the States are independent, distinct, and sovereign bodies—that is, in their reserved powers they are as sovereign, separate, and supreme as the Government of the United States in its delegated powers. One of these reserved powers is the right of the people to alter or abolish any form of government, and to institute a new one such as to them shall seem most likely to effect their safety and happiness; that power is neither "delegated to the United States by the Constitution nor prohibited by it to the States." On the contrary, it is guaranteed to the States by the Constitution itself in these words:

> The powers not delegated to the United States by the Constitution, nor prohibited by it to the States, are reserved to the States respectively, or to the people.

It has been stated above that the conditions offered to our soldiers whenever they proposed to capitulate, were only those of subjugation. When General Buckner, on February 16, 1862, asked of General Grant to appoint commissioners to agree upon terms of capitulation, he replied:

No terms, except unconditional and immediate surrender, can be accepted.

When General Lee asked the same question, on April 9, 1865, General Grant replied:

The terms upon which peace can be had are well understood. By the South laying down their arms, they will hasten that most desirable event, save thousands of human lives and hundreds of millions of property not yet destroyed.

When General Sherman made an agreement with General Johnston for formal disbandment of the army of the latter, it was at once disapproved by the Government of the United States, and Sherman therefore wrote to Johnston:

I demand the surrender of your army on the same terms as were given to General Lee at Appomattox, on April 9th, purely and simply.

It remains to be stated that the Government which spurned all these proposals for peace, and gave no terms but unconditional and immediate surrender, was instituted and organized for the purposes and objects expressed in the following extract, and for no others:

We, the people of the United States, in order to form a more perfect union, establish justice, insure domestic tranquility, provide for the common defense, promote the general welfare, and secure the blessings of liberty to ourselves and our posterity, do ordain and establish this Constitution for the United States of America.

Chapter 41

Charleston

AFTER THE EVACUATION of Savannah by General Hardee, it soon became known that General Sherman was making preparations to march northward through the Carolinas with the supposed purpose of uniting his forces with those of General Grant before Richmond. General Hardee, having left detachments at proper points to defend the approaches to Charleston and Augusta, Georgia, withdrew the rest of his command to the first-named city. General Wheeler's cavalry held all the roads northward, and, by felling trees and burning bridges, obstructed considerably the enemy's advance, which in the early part of January was still further impeded by the heavy rains which had swollen the rivers and creeks far beyond their usual width and depth.

The seriously impaired condition of our railroad communications in Georgia and Alabama, the effect of the winter rains on the already poor and ill-constructed country roads, the difficulty in collecting and transporting supplies, so impeded the concentration of our available forces, that Generals Beauregard and Hardee—the former at Columbia, South Carolina, and the latter at Charleston—could only retard, not prevent, the onward march of the enemy. At the outset of his movement the Salkehatchie River presented a very strong line of defense. Its swollen condition at that time, and the wide, deeply inundated swamps on both sides, rendered it almost impossible to force or outflank the position if adequately defended. It might have been better if we had then abandoned the attempt to hold cities of no strategic importance, and concentrated their garrisons at this point, where the chances of successful resistance were greater than at any subsequent period of the campaign. For, even if our expectation had been disappointed, and had the superior numerical force of the enemy compelled us to withdraw from this line, the choice of several good positions was open to us, any one of which, by moving upon converging lines, we could reach sooner than was possible to Sherman, whose passage of the river must have been much encumbered and delayed by his trains. Of these defensive positions, Branchville and Orangeburg may be regarded as eligible: had Sherman headed his columns toward Charleston, our forces would have been in position to attack him in front and on the flank. Had his objective point been Augusta, he would have had our army in his rear; and had, as proved to be the case, Columbia been the place at which he aimed, our army would have been able to reach there sooner than he could.

General Sherman left Savannah January 22, 1865, and reached Pocotaligo on the 24th. On February 3d he crossed the Salkehatchie with slight resistance at River's and Beaufort bridges, and thence pushed forward to the South Carolina Railroad at Midway, Bamberg, and Graham's. After thoroughly destroying the railroad between these places, which occupied three or four days, he advanced slowly along the line of the railroad, threatening Branchville, the junction of the railroads from Augusta to Columbia and Charleston. For a short time it was doubtful whether he proposed to attack Augusta, Georgia, where it was well known we had our principal powder-mill, many important factories and shops, and large stores of army supplies; but on the 11th it was found that he was moving north to Orangeburg, on the road from Branchville to Columbia, the latter city being the objective point of his march. Early on the morning of the 16th the head of his columns reached the congaree opposite Columbia. The bridge over that stream had been burned by our retreating troops, but a pontoon bridge, built by the enemy under cover of strong detachments who had crossed higher up at Saluda Factory, enabled the main body to pass the river and enter the city on the morning of the 17th, the Confederate troops having previously evacuated it. On the same day the Mayor formally surrendered the city to Colonel Stone, commanding a brigade of the Fifteenth Corps, and claimed for its citizens the protection which the laws of civilized war always accord to non-combatants. In infamous disregard not only of the established rules of war, but of the common dictates of humanity, the defenseless city was burned to the ground, after the dwelling-houses had been robbed of everything of value, and their helpless inmates subjected to outrage and insult. Hypocrisy is the tribute which vice pays to virtue; therefore General Sherman has endeavored to escape the reproaches for the burning of Columbia by attributing it to General Hampton's order to burn the cotton in the city, that it might not fall into the hands of the enemy. General Hampton has proved circumstantially that General Sherman's statement is untrue; hundreds of unimpeachable witnesses have testified that the burning of Columbia was the deliberate act of the Federal soldiery, and that it was certainly permitted, if not ordered, by the commanding General.

Were this the only instance of such barbarity perpetrated by General Sherman's army, his effort to escape the responsibility might be more successful, because more plausible; but when the eulogists of his exploits note exultingly that "widespreading columns of smoke rose wherever the army went," when it is incontrovertibly true that the line of his march could be traced by the burning dwelling-houses and by the wail of women and children pitilessly left to die from starvation and exposure in the depth of winter, his plea of "not guilty" in the case of the city of Columbia can not free him from the reprobation which outraged humanity must attach to an act of cruelty which only finds a parallel in the barbarous excesses of Wallenstein's army in the Thirty Years' War, and which, even at that period of the world's civilization, sullied the fame of that otherwise great soldier.

In consequence of General Sherman's movements, it was considered advisable to evacuate Charleston (February 17th), that General Hardee's command might become available for service in the field; and thus that noble city and its fortresses, which the combined military and naval forces of the United States, during an eighteen months' siege, had failed to reduce, were, on February 21st, without resistance, occupied by the Federal forces under General Q. A. Gillmore.

Fort Sumter, though it now presented the appearance of a ruin, was really better proof against bombardment than when first subjected to fire. The upper tier of masonry, from severe battering, had fallen on the outer wall, and shot and shell served only to solidify and add harder material to the mass. Over its rampart the Confederate flag defiantly floated until the city of Charleston was evacuated.

On the 9th of April the Confederate forces took up the line of march to Raleigh, and reached that city early in the afternoon of the same day closely followed by the Federal army.

Chapter 42

Fort Fisher; Petersburg

WHEN THE CAMPAIGN OPENED on the Rapidan, General Lee's effective strength was in round numbers sixty thousand of all arms; that of General Grant at the same time one hundred and forty thousand. In the many battles fought before the close of the campaign, Grant's loss had been a multiple of that sustained by Lee; but the large reënforcements he had received, both before and after he crossed the James River, repaired his losses, and must have increased the numerical disparity between the two armies; yet, notwithstanding the great superiority in the number of his force, the long-projected movement for the reduction of Fort Fisher and the capture of Wilmington was delayed, because of Grant's unwillingness to detach any of his troops for that purpose until after active operations had been suspended before Petersburg.

It was proposed to make a combined land and naval attack —Major-General B. F. Butler to command the land-forces, and Admiral D. D. Porter the fleet. The enemy seems about this time to have conceived a new means of destroying forts; it was, to place a large amount of powder in a ship, and, having anchored off the fort, to explode the powder and so destroy the works and incapacitate the garrison as to enable a storming party to capture them. How near to Fort Fisher it was expected to anchor the ship I do not know, nor have I learned how far it was supposed the open atmosphere could be made to act as a projectile. General Whiting, who was in command of the defenses of Wilmington, stated that the powder-ship did not come nearer to Fort Fisher than twelve or fifteen hundred yards. He further stated that he heard the report of the explosion at Wilmington, and sent a telegram to Colonel Lamb, the commanding officer at the fort, to inquire what it meant, and was answered, "Enemy's gunboat blown up." No effect, as might have been anticipated, was produced on the fort. From the same source it is learned that the combined force of this expedition was about six thousand five hundred land-troops and fifty vessels of war of various sizes and classes, several ironclads, and the ship charged with two hundred and thirty-five tons of powder. Some of the troops landed, but after a reconnaissance of the fort, which then had a garrison of about six thousand five hundred men, the troops were reëmbarked, and thus the expedition ended.

On January 15, 1865, the attempt was renewed with a larger number of troops, amounting, after the arrival of General Schofield, to twenty-odd thousand. Porter's fleet also received additional vessels, making the whole number fifty-eight engaged in the attack. The garrison of Fort Fisher had been increased to about double the number of men there on the 24th of December. The iron-clad vessels of the enemy approached nearer the fort than on a former occasion, and the fire of the fleet was more concentrated and vastly more effective. Many of the guns in the fort were dismounted, and the parapets seriously injured, by the fire. The garrison stood bravely to their guns, and, when the assault was made, fought with such determined courage as to repulse the first column, and obstinately contended with another approaching from the land-side, continuing the fight long after they had got into the fort. Finally, overwhelmed by numbers, and after the fort and its armament had been mainly destroyed by a bombardment—I believe greater than ever before concentrated upon a fort—the remnant of the garrison surrendered. General Whiting was mortally, and the commander of the fort, Colonel Lamb, was seriously, wounded. They both fell into the hands of the enemy. General Hoke had been ordered down to support the garrison, and under the directions of General Bragg, commanding the department, had advanced to attack the investing force, but a reconnaissance convinced them both that his command was too weak to effect the object. The other forts, of necessity, fell with the main work, Fisher, and were abandoned. Hoke with his small force retiring through Wilmington, after destroying the public vessels and property, to prevent them from falling into the hands of the enemy, slowly fell back, fighting at several points, and seeking to find in the separation of the vastly superior army which was following him an opportunity to attack a force the number of which should not greatly exceed his own, and finally made a junction with General Johnston, then opposing Sherman's advance through North Carolina.

The fixed purpose of General Grant's campaign of 1864 was the capture of Richmond, the Confederate capital. For this he had assembled the large army with which he crossed the Rapidan and fought the numerous battles between there and the James River. For this he had moved against Petersburg, the capture of which was only valuable because it was on the line of communication with the more southern States, and offered another approach to Richmond. In his attack upon Petersburg it will be seen from the events already described that he adopted neither of the two plans which were open to him: the one, the concentration of all his efforts to break the line covering Petersburg; the other, to move his army round it and seize the Weldon and Southside Railroads, so as to cut off the supplies of Lee's army and compel the evacuation of both Petersburg and Richmond. Had there been approximate equality between his army and that of Lee, he could not wisely have ventured upon the latter movement against a soldier so able as his antagonist; but the vast numerical superiority of Grant's army might well have induced him to invite Lee to meet him in the open field. He did, however, neither the one nor the other, but something of both.

In the opening of the campaign of 1865, he continued, as he had done in 1864, to extend his line to the left, seeking, after having gained the Weldon Railroad, to reach still farther to that connecting Petersburg with the Richmond and Danville Railroad. Lee, with a well-deserved confidence in his troops and his usual intrepidity, drew from his lines of defense men enough to enable him for a long time to defeat the enemy in these efforts, by extension to turn his right flank. After Grant's demonstration on the north side of the James by sending over Hancock's corps had been virtually abandoned by its withdrawal, Longstreet's corps, which had been sent to oppose it, remained for a long time on the north side of the James. Finally, General Ewell with a few troops, the Richmond reserves, and a division of the navy under Admiral Semmes, held the river and land defenses on the east side of Richmond.

General A. R. Lawton, who had become the quartermaster-general of the Confederate army, ably supported by Lewis E. Harvie, President of the Richmond and Danville Railroad, increased the carrying capacity of that line so as to compensate for our loss of the use of the Weldon Railroad. At the same time, General St. John, chief of the commissariat, by energetic efforts and the use of the Virginia Canal, kept up the supplies of General Lee's army, so as to secure from him the complimentary acknowledgment, made about a month before the evacuation of Petersburg, that the army there had not been so well supplied for many months.

During the months of February and March, Lee's army was materially reduced by the casualties of battle and the frequency of absence without leave. I will not call these absentees deserters, because they did not leave to join the enemy, and again, because in some instances where the facts were fully developed, they had gone to their necessitous families with intent to return and resume their places in the line of battle. His cavalry force had been also diminished by the absence of General Hampton's division, to which permission had been given to go to their home, South Carolina, to get fresh horses, and also to fill up their ranks. Long, arduous, and distant service had rendered both necessary.

In the early part of March, as well as my memory can fix the date, General Lee held with me a long and free conference. He stated that the circumstances had forced on him the conclusion that the evacuation of Petersburg was but a question of time. He had early and fully appreciated the embarrassment which would result from losing the workshops and foundry at Richmond, which had been our main reliance for the manufacture and repair of arms as well as the preparation of ammunition. The importance of Richmond in this regard was, however, then less than it had been by the facilities which had been created for these purposes at Augusta, Selma, Fayetteville, and some smaller establishments; also by the progress which was being made for a large armory at Macon, Georgia. To my inquiry whether it would not be better to anticipate the necessity by withdrawing at once, he said that his artillery and draught horses were too weak for the roads in their then condition, and that he would have to wait until they became firmer. There naturally followed the consideration of the line of retreat. General Lee's program was to retire to Danville, at which place supplies should be collected and a junction made with the troops under General J. E. Johnston, the combined force to be hurled upon Sherman in North Carolina, with the hope of defeating him before Grant could come to his relief. Then the more southern States, freed from pressure and encouraged by this success, it was expected, would send large reënforcements to the army, and Grant, drawn far from his base of supplies into the midst of a hostile population, it was hoped, might yet be defeated, and Virginia be delivered from the invader. Efforts were energetically continued to collect supplies in depots where they would be available, and, in furtherance of the suggestion of General Lee as to the necessary improvement in the condition of his horses, the quartermaster-general was instructed to furnish larger rations of corn to the quartermaster at Petersburg.

On the 27th of March the main part of Grant's forces confronting Richmond were moved over to the lines before Petersburg, and his left was on the same day joined by Sheridan's division of cavalry. Lee had sent Longstreet to the north side of the James as soon as he discovered that Grant had sent a corps across with the supposed purpose of attacking Richmond from that side. It was intended that Longstreet should return whenever the enemy withdrew his main force from the north side of the James; but it appears that this was so secretly done as to conceal the fact from General Longstreet, and that both Hancock and Ord had joined Grant, to swell his forces by two corps before our troops returned to join Lee. Grant, thus strengthened, made a more determined movement to gain the right of Lee's position; before, however, he was ready to make his assault, Lee marched with a comparatively very small force, took the initiative, and on the 31st struck the enemy's advance, and repulsed him in great confusion, following until confronted by the heavy masses formed in open ground in the rear, when Lee withdrew his men back to their intrenchments.

A strategic position of recognized importance was that known as Five Forks. Lee had stationed there Major-General Pickett with his division, and some additional force. On the next day, the 1st of April, this position was assaulted, and our troops were driven from it in confusion. The unsettled question of time was now solved.

Grant's massive columns, advancing on right, left, and center, compelled our forces to retire to the inner line of defense, so that, on the morning of the 2d, the enemy was in a condition to besiege Petersburg in the true sense of that term. Battery Gregg made an obstinate defense, and, with a garrison of about two hundred and fifty men, held a corps in check for a large part of the day. The arrival of Longstreet's troops, and the strength of the shorter line now held by Lee, enabled him to make several attempts to dislodge his assailant from positions he had gained.

Retreat was now a present necessity. All that could be done was to hold the inner lines during the day, and make needful preparations to withdraw at night. In the forenoon of Sunday, the 2d, I received, when in church, a telegram announcing that the army would retire from Petersburg at night, and I went to my office to give needful directions for the evacuation of Richmond, the greatest difficulty of which was the withdrawal of the troops who were on the defenses east of the city, and along the James River.

At nightfall our army commenced crossing the Appomattox, and, before dawn, was far on its way toward Amelia Court-House, Lee's purpose being, as previously agreed on in conference with me, to march to Danville, Virginia. By a reference to the map, it will be seen that General Grant, starting from the south side of the Appomattox, had a shorter line to Danville than that which General Lee must necessarily follow, and, if Grant directed his march so as to put his forces between Danville and those of Lee, it was quite possible for him to effect it. This was done, and thus Lee was prevented from carrying out his original purpose, and directed his march toward Lynchburg. The enemy, having first placed himself across the route to Danville, at Jetersville, subsequently took up the line of Lee's retreat. His large force of cavalry, and the exhausted condition of the horses of our small number of that arm, gave the pursuing foe a very great advantage; but, worn and reduced in numbers as Lee's army was, the spirit it had always shown flashed out whenever it was pressed. A division would turn upon a corps and drive it; and General Fitzhugh Lee, with a brigade of our emaciated cavalry, would drive a division of their pursuers. These scenes were repeatedly enacted during the long march from Petersburg to Appomattox Court-House.

Lee had never contemplated surrender. He had, long before, in language similar to that employed by Washington during the Revolution, expressed to me the belief that in the mountains of Virginia he could carry on the war for twenty years, and, in directing his march toward Lynchburg, it may well be that as an alternative he hoped to reach those mountains, and, with the advantage which the topography would give, yet to baffle the hosts which were following him. On the evening of the 8th General Lee decided, after conference with his corps commanders, that he would advance the next morning beyond Appomattox Court-House, and, if the force reported to be there should prove to be only Sheridan's cavalry, to disperse it and continue the march toward Lynchburg; but, if infantry should be found in large force, the attempt to break through it was not to be made, and the correspondence which General Grant had initiated on the previous day should be reopened by a flag, with propositions for an interview to arrange the terms of capitulation. Gordon, whose corps formed the rear-guard from Petersburg, and who had fought daily for the protection of the trains, had now been transferred to the front. On the next morning, before daylight, Lee sent Colonel Venable, one of his staff, to Gordon, commanding the advance, to learn his opinion as to the chances of a successful attack, to which Gordon replied, "My old corps is reduced to a frazzle, and, unless I am supported by Longstreet heavily, I do not think we can do anything more." When Colonel Venable returned with this answer to General Lee, he said, "Then there is nothing left me but to go and see General Grant."

At that time Longstreet, covering the rear, was threatened by Meade, so that there was no ability to reënforce Gordon, and thus to explain why General Lee then realized that the emergency had arisen for the surrender of his army which, in his note to General Grant of the previous day, he had said he did not believe to exist. Colonel Venable, at early dawn, had left Gordon with about five thousand infantry, and Fitzhugh Lee with about fifteen hundred cavalry, and Colonel Carter's battalion of artillery, forming his line of battle to attack the enemy, which, so far as then known, consisted of Sheridan's cavalry, which had got in front of our retreating column. The assault was made with such vigor and determination as to drive Sheridan for a considerable distance; and, if this had been the only obstacle, the road would have been opened for Lee to resume his march toward Lynchburg. After Gordon had advanced nearly a mile, he was confronted by a large body of infantry, subsequently ascertained to be about eighty thousand. To attack that force was, of course, hopeless, and Gordon commenced falling back, and simultaneously the enemy advanced, but suddenly came to a halt. Lee had sent a flag to Grant, who had consequently ordered a suspension of hostilities.

A leader less resolute, an army less heroically resisting fatigue, constant watching, and starvation, would long since have reached the conclusion that surrender was a necessity. Lee had left Petersburg with not more than twenty thousand infantry, five thousand cavalry, and four thousand artillery. Men and horses all reduced below the standard of efficiency by exposure and insufficient supplies of clothing, food, and forage, only the mutual confidence between the men and their commander could have sustained either under the trials to which they were subjected. It is not a matter of surprise that the army had wasted away to a mere remnant, but rather that it had continued to exist as an organized body still willing to do battle.

General Grant, in response to the communication under a white flag made by General Lee came to Appomattox, where a suitable room was procured for their conference, and, the two generals being seated at a small table, General Lee opened the interview thus:

General, I deem it due to proper candor and frankness to say at the very beginning of this interview that I am not willing even to discuss any terms of surrender inconsistent with the honor of my army, which I am determined to maintain to the last.

General Grant replied:

I have no idea of proposing dishonorable terms, General, but I would be glad if you would state what you consider honorable terms.

General Lee then briefly stated the terms upon which he would be willing to surrender. Grant expressed himself as satisfied with them, and Lee requested that he would formally reduce the propositions to writing. The following exchange is self-explanatory:

APPOMATTOX COURT-HOUSE, *April 9, 1865*

General R. E. LEE, *commanding Confederate States Army:*

In accordance with the substance of my letter to you of the 8th inst., I propose to receive the surrender of the Army of Northern Virginia on the following terms, to wit:

Rolls of all the officers and men to be made in duplicate, one copy to be given to an officer designated by me, the other to be retained by such officers as you may designate.

The officers to give their individual parole not to take arms against the Government of the United States until properly exchanged, and each company or regimental commander to sign a like parole for the men of their commands.

The arms, artillery, and public property to be parked and stacked and turned over to the officers appointed by me to receive them.

This will not embrace the side-arms of the officers, nor their private horses or baggage.

This done, each officer and man will be allowed to return to their homes, not to be disturbed by the United States authority so long as they observe their parole and the laws in force where they may reside.

Very respectfully,

U. S. GRANT, *Lieutenant-General.*

HEADQUARTERS ARMY OF NORTHERN VIRGINIA, *April 9, 1865*

GENERAL: I have received your letter of this date containing the terms of surrender of the Army of Northern Virginia, as proposed by you. As they are substantially the same as those expressed in your letter of the 8th inst., they are accepted. I will proceed to designate the proper officers to carry the stipulations into effect.

Very respectfully, your obedient servant,

R. E. LEE.

Chapter 43

Surrender and Capture

AT THIS CRITICAL MOMENT, I invited General Johnston for a conference,

GREENSBORO, NORTH CAROLINA, *April 11, 1865—12 M.*
GENERAL J. E. JOHNSTON, *headquarters, via Raleigh:*
The Secretary of War did not join me at Danville. Is expected here this afternoon.

As your situation may render best, I will go to your headquarters immediately after the arrival of the Secretary of War, or you can come here; in the former case our conference must be without the presence of General Beauregard. I have no official report from General Lee. The Secretary of War may be able to add to information heretofore communicated.

The important question first to be solved is, At what point shall concentration be made, in view of the present position of the two columns of the enemy, and the routes which they may adopt to engage your forces before a proposed junction with General Walker and others. Your more intimate knowledge of the data for the solution of the problem deters me from making a specific suggestion on that point.   JEFFERSON DAVIS.

General J. E. Johnston came up from Raleigh to Greensboro, and with General Beauregard met me and most of my Cabinet at my quarters. Though I was fully sensible of the gravity of our position, seriously affected as it was by the evacuation of the capital, the surrender of the Army of Northern Virginia, and the consequent discouragement which these events would produce, I did not think we should despair. We still had effective armies in the field, and a vast extent of rich and productive territory both east and west of the Mississippi, whose citizens had evinced no disposition to surrender. Ample supplies had been collected in the railroad depots, and much still remained to be placed at our disposal when needed by the army in North Carolina.

The failure of several attempts to open negotiations with the Federal Government, and notably the last by comissioners who met President Lincoln at Hampton Roads, convinced me of the hopelessness under existing circumstances to obtain better terms than were then offered, i.e., a surrender at discretion. My motive, therefore, in holding an interview with the senior generals of the army in North Carolina was not to learn their opinion as to what might be done by negotiation with the United States Government, but to derive from them information in regard to the army under their command, and what it was feasible and advisable to do as a military problem.

The members of my Cabinet were already advised as to the object of the meeting, and, when the subject was introduced to the generals in that form, General Johnston was very reserved, and seemed far less than sanguine. His first significant expression was that of a desire to open correspondence with General Sherman, to see if he would agree to a suspension of hostilities, the object being to permit the civil authorities to enter into the needful arrangements to terminate the existing war. Confident that the United States Government would not accept a proposition for such negotiations, I distinctly expressed my conviction on that point, and presented as an objection to such an effort that, so far as it should excite delusive hopes and expectations, its failure would have a demoralizing effect both on the troops and the people. Neither of them had shown any disposition to surrender, or had any reason to suppose that their Government contemplated abandoning its trust—the maintenance of the Constitution, freedom, and independence of the Confederate States. From the inception of the war, the people had generally and at all times expressed their determination to accept no terms of peace that did not recognize their independence; and the indignation manifested when it became known that Mr. Lincoln had offered to our commissioners at Hampton Roads a surrender at discretion as the only alternative to a continuance of the war assured me that no true Confederate was prepared to accept peace on such terms. During the last years of the war the main part of the infantry in the Army of Northern Virginia was composed of men from the farther South. Many of these, before the evacuation of Petersburg and especially about the time of Lee's surrender, had absented themselves to go homeward, and, it was reported, made avowal of their purpose to continue the struggle. I had reason to believe that the spirit of the army in North Carolina was unbroken, for, though surrounded by circumstances well calculated to depress and discourage them, I had learned that they earnestly protested to their officers against the surrender which rumor informed them was then in contemplation.

But if, taking the gloomiest view, the circumstances were

such as to leave no hope of maintaining the independence of the Confederate States—if negotiations for peace must be on the basis of reunion and the acceptance of the war legislation —it seemed to me that certainly better terms for our country could be secured by keeping organized armies in the field than by laying down our arms and trusting to the magnanimity of the victor.

It was not at all hopeful of any success in the attempt to provide for negotiations between the civil authorities of the United States and those of the Confederacy, believing that, even if Sherman should agree to such a proposition, his Government would not ratify it; but, after having distinctly announced my opinion, I yielded to the judgment of my constitutional advisers, of whom only one held my views, and consented to permit General Johnston, as he desired, to hold a conference with General Sherman for the purpose above recited.

Then, turning to what I supposed would soon follow, I invited General Johnston to an expression of his choice of a line of retreat toward the southwest. He declared a preference for a different route from that suggested by me, and, yielding the point, I informed him that I would have depots of supplies for his army placed on the rote he had selected. The commissary-general, St. John, executed the order.

Referring to the period which followed the surrender of the Army of Northern Virginia, General I. M. St. John, Commissary-General Confederate States Army, writes:

The bureau headquarters were continued in North Carolina until the surrender of that military department. During the interval preparations were made for the westward movement of forces as then contemplated. In these arrangements the local depots were generally found so full and supplied so well in hand, from Charlotte southwest, that the commissary-general was able to report to the Secretary of War that the requisitions for which he was notified to prepare could all be met. The details of this service were executed, and very ably, by Major J. H. Claiborne, then, and until the end, assistant commissary-general."

Major Claiborne, in his report, writes:

Being placed under orders as assistant commissary-general, I forwarded supplies from South Carolina to General J. E. Johnston's army, and also collected supplies at six or seven named points in that State for the supposed retreat of General Johnston's army through the South. This duty, with a full determination at the evacuation of this city [Richmond] to follow the fortunes of our cause, gave me opportunity of ascertaining the resources of the country for my department. The great want was that of transportation, and specially was it felt by all collecting commissaries for a few months before the surrender.

After it had been decided that General Johnston should attempt negotiation with General Sherman, he left for his army headquarters; and I, expecting that he would soon take up his line of retreat, which his superiority in cavalry would protect from harassing pursuit, proceeded with my Cabinet and staff toward Charlotte, North Carolina. While on the way, a dispatch was received from General Johnston announcing that General Sherman had agreed to a conference, and asking that the Secretary of War, General J. C. Breckinridge, should return to coöperate in it. The application was complied with, and the Postmaster-General, John H. Reagan, also went at my request. He, however, was not admitted to the conference.

We arrived at Charlotte on April 18, 1865, and I there received, at the moment of dismounting, a telegram from General Breckinridge announcing, on information received from General Sherman, that President Lincoln had been assassinated. An influential citizen of the town, who had come to welcome me, was standing near me, and, after remarking to him in a low voice that I had received sad intelligence, I handed the telegram to him. Some troopers encamped in the vicinity had collected to see me; they called to the gentleman who had the dispatch in his hand to read it, no doubt supposing it to be army news. He complied with their request, and a few, only taking in the fact, but not appreciating the evil it portended, cheered, as was natural at news of the fall of one they considered their most powerful foe. The man who invented the story of my having read the dispatch with exultation, had free scope for his imagination, as he was not present.

For an enemy so relentless in the war for our subjugation, we could not be expected to mourn; yet, in view of its political consequences, it could not be regarded otherwise than as a great misfortune to the South. He had power over the Northern people, and was without personal malignity toward the people of the South; his successor was without power in the North, and the embodiment of malignity toward the Southern people, perhaps the more so because he had betrayed and deserted them in the hour of their need. The war had now shrunk into narrow proportions, but the important consideration remained to so conduct it that, if failing to secure our independence, we might obtain a treaty or *quasi*-treaty of peace which would secure to the Southern States their political rights, and to the people thereof immunity from the plunder of their private property.

I found some cavalry at Charlotte, and soon had the satisfaction to increase them to five brigades. They had been on detached service, and were much reduced in numbers. Among the troopers who assembled there was the remnant of the command which had spread terror north of the Ohio, under the command of General John Hunt Morgan. Their present chief was General Basil Duke.

On April 13, 1865, General Johnston wrote to General Sherman as follows:

The results of the recent campaign in Virginia have changed the relative military condition of the belligerents. I am therefore induced to address you, in this form, the inquiry whether, to stop the further effusion of blood and the devastation of property, you are willing to make a temporary suspension of active operations; . . . the object being to permit the civil authorities to enter into the needful arrangements to terminate the existing war.

General Sherman replied, on the 14th:

I am fully empowered to arrange with you any terms for the suspension of hostilities between the armies commanded by you and those commanded by myself, and will be willing to confer with you to that end, etc., etc.

General Sherman describes an interview with Mr. Lincoln, held at City Point on the 27th and 28th of March preceding, in which he says:

Mr. Lincoln distinctly authorized me to assure Governor Vance and the people of North Carolina that, as soon as the rebel armies laid down their arms, and resumed their civil pursuits, they would at once be guaranteed all their rights as citizens of a common country; and that, to avoid anarchy, the State governments then in existence, with their civil functionaries, would be recognized by him as the government *de facto* till Congress could provide others.

In regard to the memorandum or basis of agreement, Sherman states that, while in consultation with General Johnston, a messenger brought him a parcel of papers from Mr. Reagan,

Postmaster-General; that Johnston and Breckinridge looked over them, and handed one of them to him, which he found inadmissible, and proceeds:

Then, recalling the conversation with Mr. Lincoln at City Point, I sat down at the table and wrote off the terms which I thought concisely expressed his views and wishes.

But, while these matters were progressing, Mr. Lincoln had been assassinated, and a vindicative policy had been substituted for his, which avowedly was, to procure a speedy surrender of the army upon *any terms*. His evident wish was to stop the further shedding of blood; that of his successors to extract all which it was possible to obtain. From the memoranda of the interview between Mr. Lincoln and Sherman it is clearly to be inferred that, but for the untimely death of Mr. Lincoln, the following agreement between Generals Sherman and Johnston would have been ratified; and the wounds inflicted on civil liberty by the "reconstruction" measures might not have left their shameful scars on the United States.

Memorandum, or basis of agreement, made this 18th day of April, A. D. 1865, near Durham Station, and in the State of North Carolina, by and between General Joseph E. Johnston, commanding the Confederate army, and Major-General W. T. Sherman, commanding the army of the United States in North Carolina, both present:

1. The contending armies now in the field to maintain their *status quo,* until notice is given by the commanding General of either one to its opponents, and reasonable time, say forty-eight hours, allowed.

2. The Confederate armies now in existence to be disbanded and conducted to the several State capitals, there to deposit their arms and public property in the State Arsenal, and each officer and man to execute and file an agreement to cease from acts of war, and abide the action of both Federal and State authorities. The number of arms and munitions of war to be reported to the chief of ordnance at Washington City, subject to future action of the Congress of the United States, and in the mean time to be used solely to maintain peace and order within the borders of the States respectively.

3. The recognition by the Executive of the United States of the several State governments, on their officers and Legislatures taking the oath prescribed by the Constitution of the United States; and, where conflicting State governments have resulted from the war, the legitimacy of all shall be submitted to the Supreme Court of the United States.

4. The reëstablishment of all Federal courts in the several States, with powers as defined by the Constitution and laws of Congress.

5. The people and inhabitants of all States to be guaranteed, so far as the Executive can, their political rights and franchises, as well as their rights of person and property, as defined by the Constitution of the United States and of the States respectively.

6. The Executive authority of the Government of the United States not to disturb any of the people by reason of the late war, so long as they live in peace and quiet, abstain from acts of armed hostility, and obey laws in existence at any place of their residence.

7. In general terms, war to cease, a general amnesty, so far as the Executive power of the United States can command, or on condition of the disbandment of the Confederate armies, the distribution of arms, and resumption of peaceful pursuits by officers and men, as hitherto composing said armies. Not being fully empowered by our respective principals to fulfill these terms, we individually and officially pledge ourselves to promptly obtain necessary authority, and to carry out the above programme.

W. T. SHERMAN, *Major-General, etc., etc.*
J. E. JOHNSTON, *General, etc., etc.*

The proposition for a suspension of hostilities to allow the civil authorities to negotiate, was not even entertained; the agreement was, in fact, a military convention, in which all reference to the civil authorities was excluded, except by the admission that the negotiators respectively had principals from whom they must obtain authority, i.e., ratification of the agreement into which they had entered. There seemed to be a special dread on the part of the United States officials lest they should do something which would be construed as the recognition of the existence of a government which for four years they had been vainly trying to subdue. In consideration of the disbandment of our armies it provided for the recognition of the several State governments, guaranteed to the people of the States their political rights and franchises, as well as their rights of person and property as defined by the Constitution of the United States and other States respectively; promised not to disturb any of the people by reason of the late war, and generally indicated that the United States Government was to be restricted to the exercise of the powers delegated in the Constitution.

Though this convention, if ratified, would not have all the binding force of a treaty, it secured to our people the political rights and safety from pillage, to obtain which I proposed to continue the war. I, therefore, with the concurrence of my constitutional advisers, addressed General Johnston as follows:

CHARLOTTE, NORTH CAROLINA, *April 24, 1865.*
General J. E. JOHNSTON, *Greensboro, North Carolina.*

The Secretary of War has delivered to me the copy you handed to him of the basis of an agreement between yourself and General Sherman. Your action is approved. You will so inform General Sherman; and, if the like authority be given by the Government of the United States to complete the arrangement, you will proceed on the basis adopted.

Further instructions will be given after the details of the negotiation and the methods of executing the terms of agreement when notified by you of the readiness on the part of the General commanding United States forces to proceed with the arrangement.   JEFFERSON DAVIS.

From the terms of this letter it will be seen that I doubted whether the agreement would be ratified by the United States Government. The opinion I entertained in regard to President Johnson and his venomous Secretary of War, Stanton, did not permit me to expect that they would be less vindictive after a surrender of our army had been proposed than when it was regarded as a formidable body defiantly holding its position in the field. Whatever hope others entertained that the existing war was about to be peacefully terminated, was soon dispelled by the rejection of the basis of agreement on the part of the Government of the United States, and a notice from General Sherman of termination of the armistice in forty-eight hours after noon of the 24th of April, 1865.

General Johnston communicated to me the substance of the above information received by him from General Sherman, and asked for instructions. My reply was that he should retire with his cavalry, and as many infantry as could be mounted upon draught-horses, and some light artillery, the rest of the infantry to be disbanded, and a place of rendezvous appointed. It was unnecessary to say anything of the route, as that had been previously agreed on, and supplies placed on it for his retreating army. This order was disobeyed, and he sought another interview with Sherman, to renew his attempt to reach an agreement for a termination of hostilities. Meantime, General Hampton, commanding the cavalry of Johnston's army, came to me at Charlotte, told me that he feared the army was to be surrendered, and wished permission to withdraw his part of it and report to me. I gave the permission, extending it to all the cavalry, which was in accordance with the instructions I had sent to General Johnston. He returned immediately, but I have since learned from him that the cavalry had been included in a proposition to surrender, before he reached them.

After the expiration of the armistice, I rode out of Charlotte, attended by the members of my Cabinet (except Attorney-General Davis, who had gone to see his family, residing in that section, and the Secretary of the Treasury, Mr. Trenholm, who was too ill to accompany me), my personal staff, and the cavalry which had been concentrated from different, and some of them distant, fields of detached service. The number was about two thousand, and they represented six brigade organizations; though so much reduced in numbers, they were in a good state of efficiency, and among their officers were some of the best in our service. General Hampton, finding his troops had been included in the surrender, endeavored to join me to offer his individual service, and to share my fate whatever it might be. He accidentally failed to meet me.

On the 26th, the day on which the armistice terminated, General Johnston again met General Sherman, who offered the same terms which had been made with General Lee, and he says, "General Johnston, without hesitation, agreed to, and we executed the following," which was the surrender of General Johnston's troops, with the condition of their being paroled and the officers being permitted to retain their side-arms, private horses, and baggage.

It is true that these were the terms accepted by Lee, but the condition of the two armies was very different. Lee's supplies had been cut off, his men were exhausted by fatigue and hunger; he had no reënforcements in view; notwithstanding the immense superiority in numbers and equipments of the enemy pursuing, he had from point to point fought them in rear and on both flanks, and had, the day before his line of retreat was closed, rejected the demand for surrender, and only yielded to it after his starving little army had been surrounded by masses through which he tried to, but could not, cut his way.

Johnston's line of retreat was open, and supplies had been placed upon it. His cavalry was superior to that of the enemy, as had been proved in every conflict between them. Maury and Forrest and Taylor still had armies in the field—not large, but strong enough to have collected around them the men who had left Johnston's army and gone to their homes to escape a surrender, as well as those who under similar circumstances had left Lee. The show of continued resistance, I then believed, as I still do, would have overcome the depression which was spreading like a starless night over the country, and that the exhibition of a determination not to leave our political future at the mercy of an enemy which had for four years been striving to subjugate the States would have led the United States authorities to do, as Mr. Lincoln had indicated —give any terms which might be found necessary speedily to terminate the existing war.

I had left Charlotte with no other sure reliance against any cavalry movement of the enemy than the force which was with me; that, however, I believed to be sufficient for any probable exigency, if the reënforcements hoped for should not join us on the way. We proceeded at easy stages; some of the command thought we went too slow. After making two halts of about half a day each, we reached the Savannah River. I crossed early in the morning of the 4th of May, with a company, which had been detailed as my escort, and rode some miles to a farmhouse, where I halted to get breakfast and have our horses fed. Here I learned that a regiment of the enemy were moving upon Washington, Georgia, which was one of our depots of supplies, and I sent back a courier with a pencil-note addressed to General Vaughn, or the officer commanding the advance, requestioning him to come on and join me immediately. After waiting a considerable time, I determined to move on with my escort, trusting that the others would overtake us, and that, if not, we should arrive in Washington in time to rally the citizens to its defense. When I reached there, scouts were sent out on the different roads, and my conclusion was that we had had a false alarm. The Secretary of State, Mr. Benjamin, being unaccustomed to traveling on horseback, parted from me, at the house where we stopped to breakfast, to take another mode of conveyance and a different route from that which I was pursuing, with intent to rejoin me in the trans-Mississippi Department. At Washington, the Secretary of the Navy, Mr. Mallory, left me temporarily to attend to the needs of his family. The Secretary of War, Mr. Breckinridge, had remained with the cavalry at the crossing of the Savannah River. During the night after my arrival in Washington, he sent in an application for authority to draw from the treasure, under the protection of the troops, enough to make to them a partial payment. I authorized the acting

Secretary of the Treasury to meet the requisition by the use of the silver coin in the train. When the next day passed without the troops coming forward, I sent a note to the Secretary of War, showing the impolicy of my longer delay, having there heard that General Upton had passed within a few miles of the town on his way to Augusta to receive the surrender of the garrison and military material at that place, in conformity with orders issued by General Johnton. This was my first positive information of his surrender. Not receiving an immediate reply to the note addressed to the Secretary of War, General Breckinridge, I spoke to Captain Campbell, of Kentucky, commanding my escort, explained to him the condition of affairs, and telling him that his company was not strong enough to fight, and too large to pass without observation, asked him to inquire if there were ten men who would volunteer to go with me without question wherever I should choose. He brought back for answer that the whole company volunteered on the terms proposed. Gratifying as this manifestation was, I felt it would expose them to unnecessary hazard to accept the offer, and told him, in any manner he might think best, to form a party of ten men. With these, Captain Campbell, Lieutenant Barnwell, of South Carolina, Colonels F. R. Lubbock, John Taylor Wood, and William Preston Johnston, of my personal staff, I left Washington. Secretary Reagan remained for a short time to transfer the treasure in his hands, except a few thousand dollars, and then rejoined me on the road. This transfer of the treasure was made to Mr. Semple, a bonded officer of the navy, and his assistant, Mr. Tidball, with instructions, as soon as it could be safely done, to transport it abroad and deliver it to the commercial house which had acted as the financial agent of the Confederate Government, and was reported to have incurred liabilities on its account.

Mr. Reagan overtook me in a few hours, but I saw no more of General Breckinridge, and learned subsequently that he was following our route, with a view to overtake me, when he heard of my capture, and, turning to the east, reached the Florida coast unmolested. On the way he met J. Taylor Wood, and, in an open boat, they crossed the straits to the West Indies. No report reached me at that time, or until long afterward, in regard to the cavalry command left at the Savannah River; then it was to the effect that paroled men from Johnston's army brought news of its surrender, and that the condition of returning home and remaining unmolested embraced all the men of the department who would give their parole, and that this had exercised a great influence over the troops, inclining them to accept those terms.

When I left Washington, Georgia, with my small party, my object was to go to the south far enough to pass below the points reported to be occupied by Federal troops, and then turn to the west, cross the Chattahoochie, and then go on to meet the forces still supposed to be in the field in Alabama. If, as now seemed probable, there should be no prospect of a successful resistance east of the Mississippi, I intended then to cross to the trans-Mississippi Department, where I believed Generals E. K. Smith and Magruder would continue to uphold our cause. That I was not mistaken in the character of these men, I extract from the order issued by General E. K. Smith to the soldiers of the trans-Mississippi Army on the 21st of April, 1865:

Great disasters have overtaken us. The Army of Northern Virginia and our General-in-Chief are prisoners of war. With you rest the hopes of our nation, and upon you depends the fate of our people. . . . Prove to the world that your hearts have not failed in the hour of disaster. . . . Stand by your colors—maintain your discipline. The great resources of this department, its vast extent, the numbers, the discipline, and the efficiency of the army, will secure to our country terms that a proud people can with honor accept.

General Magruder, with like determination, invoked the troops and people of Texas not to be despondent, and pointed out their ability in the interior of that vast State to carry on the war indefinitely.

General D. H. Maury, after his memorable defense of Mobile, withdrew his forces on the 12th of April, at the last moment, and moved toward Meridian. Commodore Farrand, commanding our navy at Mobile Bay, withdrew his armed vessels and steamers up the Tombigbee River, and planted torpedoes in the Alabama below. Forrest and Maury had about eight thousand men, but these were veterans, tried in many hard engagements, and trained to the highest state of efficiency. Before Maury withdrew from Mobile, news had been received of Lee's surrender. Taylor says the news was soon disseminated through his army, but that the men remained steadfast, and manifested a determination to maintain the honor of our arms to the last. In his book, he gives an account of the intelligence received of the Johnston-Sherman convention of the 18th of April, and of the meeting between Canby and himself to arrange terms for his army, and an agreement that there should be an armistice; but he says, two days after that meeting, news was received of Johnston's surrender, and the capture of President Davis. The latter was untrue, and he does not say who communicated it, but that he was at the same time notified that the Johnston-Sherman convention had been disavowed by the United States Government, and notice given for the termination of the armistice. Under these circumstances he asked General Canby to meet him again, and on the 8th of May, two days before I was actually captured, but which he supposed had already occurred, he agreed with Canby on terms for the surrender of the land and naval forces in Mississippi and Alabama. These terms were similar to those made between Johnston and Sherman; the mounted men were to retain their horses, being their private property.

On the 26th of May, the chief of staff of General E. Kirby Smith, and the chief of staff of General Canby, at Baton Rouge, arranged similar terms for the surrender of the troops in the trans-Mississippi Department. On May 11th, after the last army east of the Mississippi had surrendered, but before Kirby Smith had entered into terms, the enemy sent an expedition from the Brazos Santiago against a little Confederate encampment some fifteen miles above. The camp was captured and burned, but, in the zeal to secure the fruits of victory, they remained so long collecting the plunder, that General J. E. Slaughter heard of the expedition, moved against it, and drove it back with considerable loss, sustaining very little injury to his command. This was, I believe, the last armed conflict of the war, and, though very small in comparison to its great battles, it deserves notice as having closed the long struggle—as it opened—with a Confederate victory.

The total number of prisoners paroled at Greensboro, North Carolina, as reported by General Schofield, was 36,817; in Georgia and Florida, as reported by General Wilson, 52,543; aggregate surrender under the capitulation of General J. E. Johnston, 89,270. How many of this last number were men who left General Johnston's army to avoid the surrender, or were on detached service from the armies of Virginia and North Carolina, I have no means of ascertaining.

The total number in the Department of Alabama and Mississippi paroled by General Canby, under agreement with General Richard Taylor, of the 8th of May, 1865, as reported, was 42,293, to which may be added of the navy a small force —less than 150. The number surrendered by General E. Kirby Smith, commanding the trans-Mississippi Department, as reported, was 17,686. To this small dimension had General Smith's army been reduced when he accepted the terms to which a reference has already been made. This reduction resulted from various causes, but it is believed was mainly due to the reluctance of a large part of his army to accept a parole, preferring to take whatever hazard belonged to absenting themselves without leave and continuing their character of belligerents. A few, but so far as I know very few, even went to the extent of expatriating themselves, and joined Maximilian in Mexico. Against no one as much as myself did the hostility of our victorious enemy manifest itself, but I was never willing to seek the remedy of exile, and always advised those who consulted me against that resort. The mass of our people could not go; the few who were able to do so were most needed to sustain the others in the hour of a common adversity. The example of Ireland after the Treaty of Limerick, and of Canada after its conquest by Great Britain, were instructive as to the duty of the influential men to remain and share the burden of a common disaster.

With General E. K. Smith's surrender the Confederate flag no longer floated on the land; but one gallant sailor still unfurled it on the Pacific. Captain Waddell, commanding the Confederate cruiser Shenandoah, swept the ocean from Australia nearly to Behring's Straits, making many captures in the Okhobak Sea and Arctic Ocean. In August, 1865, he learned from the captain of a British ship that the Confederacy, as an independent Government, had ceased to exist. With the fall of his Government his right to cruise was of course terminated; he therefore sailed for the coast of England, entered the Mersey, and on November 6, 1865, and in due form, surrendered his vessel to the British Government. She was accepted and subsequently transferred to the United States.

After leaving Washington I overtook a commissary and quartermaster's train, having public papers of value in charge, and, finding that they had no experienced woodsman with it, I gave them four of the men of my small party, and went on with the rest. On the second or third day after leaving Washington, I heard that a band of marauders, supposed to be stragglers and deserters from both armies, were in pursuit of my family, whom I had not seen since they left Richmond, but of whom I heard, at Washington, that they had gone with my private secretary and seven paroled men, who generously offered their services as an escort, to the Florida coast. Their route was to the east of that I was pursuing, but I immediately changed direction and rode rapidly across the country to overtake them. About nightfall the horses of my escort gave out, but I pressed on with Secretary Reagan and my personal staff. It was a bright moonlight night, and just before day, as the moon was sinking below the treetops, I met a party of men in the road, who answered my questions by saying they belonged to an Alabama regiment; that they were coming from a village not far off, on their way homeward. Upon inquiry being made, they told me they had passed an encampment of wagons, with women and children, and asked me if we belonged to that party. Upon being answered in the affirmative, they took their leave. After a short time I was hailed by a voice which I recognized as that of my private secretary, who informed me that the marauders had been hanging around the camp, and that he and others were on post around it, and were expecting an assault as soon as the moon went down. A silly story had got abroad that it was a treasure-train, and the *auri sacra fames* had probably instigated these marauders, as it subsequently stimulated General J. H. Wilson, to send out a large cavalry force to capture the same train. For the protection of my family I traveled with them two or three days, when, believing that they had passed out of the region of marauders, I determined to leave their encampment at nightfall, to execute my original purpose. My horse and those of my party proper were saddled preparatory to a start, when one of my staff, who had ridden into the neighboring village, returned and told me that he had heard that a marauding party intended to attack the camp that night. This decided me to wait long enough to see whether there was any truth in the rumor, which I supposed would be ascertained in a few hours. My horse remained saddled and my pistols in the holsters, and I lay down, fully dressed, to rest. Nothing occurred to rouse me until just before dawn, when my coachman, a free colored man, who faithfully clung to our fortunes, came and told me there was firing over the branch, just behind our encampment. I stepped out of my wife's tent and saw some horsemen, whom I immediately recognized as cavalry, deploying around the encampment. I turned back and told my wife these were not the expected marauders, but regular troopers. She implored me to leave her at once. I hesitated, from unwillingness to do so, and lost a few precious moments before yielding to her importunity. My horse and arms were near the road on which I expected to leave, and down which the cavalry approached; it was therefore impracticable to reach them. I was compelled to start in the opposite direction. As it was quite dark in the tent, I picked up what was to be my "raglan," a water-proof, light overcoat, without sleeves; it was subsequently found to be my wife's, so very like my own as to be mistaken for it; as I started, my wife thoughtfully threw over my head and shoulders a shawl. I had gone perhaps fifteen or twenty yards when a trooper galloped up and ordered me to halt and surrender, to which I gave a defiant answer, and, dropping the shawl and raglan from my shoulders, advanced toward him; he leveled his carbine at me, but I expected, if he fired, he would miss me, and my intention was in that event to put my hand under his foot, tumble him off on the other side, spring into his saddle, and attempt to escape. My wife, who had been watching, when she saw the soldier aim his carbine at me, ran forward and threw her arms around me. Success depended on intantaneous action, and recognizing that the opportunity had been lost, I turned back, and, the morning being damp and chilly, passed on to a fire beyond the tent. Our pursuers had taken different roads, and approached our camp from opposite directions; they encountered each other and commenced firing, both supposing they had met our armed escort, and some casualties resulted from their conflict with an imaginary body of Confederate troops. During the confusion, while attention was concentrated upon myself, except by those who were engaged in pillage, one of my aides, Colonel J. Taylor Wood, with Lieutenant Barnwell, walked off unobserved. His daring exploits on the sea had made him, on the part of the Federal Government, an object of special hostility, and rendered it quite proper that he should avail himself of every possible means of escape. Colonel Pritchard went over to their battle-field, and I did not see him for a long time, surely more than an hour after my capture. He subsequently claimed credit, in a conversation with me, for the forbearance shown by his men in not shooting me when I refused to surrender.

On our way to Macon we received the proclamation of President Andrew Johnson offering a reward for my apprehension as an accomplice in the assassination of the late President A. Lincoln. Some troops by the wayside had the proclamation, which was displayed with vociferous demon-

strations of exultation over my capture. When we arrived at
Macon I was conducted to the hotel where General Wilson
had his quarters. A strong guard was in front of the entrance,
and, when I got down to pass in, it opened ranks, facing in-
ward, and presented arms.

A commodious room was assigned to myself and family.
After a while the steward of the hotel called and inquired
whether I would dine with General Wilson or have dinner
served with myself and family in my room. I chose the latter.
After dinner I received a message from General Wilson,
asking whether he should wait upon me, or whether I would
call upon him. I rose and accompanied the messenger to
General Wilson's presence. We had met at West Point when
he was a cadet, and I a commissioner sent by the Congress
to inquire into the affairs of the Academy. After some conversation in regard to former times and our common acquaintance, he referred to the proclamation offering a reward for
my capture. Taking it for granted that any significant remark
of mine would be reported to his Government, and fearing
that I might never have another opportunity to give my opinion to A. Johnson, I told him there was one man in the
United States who knew that proclamation to be false. He
remarked that my expression indicated a particular person.
I answered that I did, and the person was the one who signed
it, for he at least knew that I preferred Lincoln to himself.
Some other conversation then occurred in regard to the
route on which we were to be carried. Having several small
children, one of them an infant, I expressed a preference for
the easier route by water, supposing then, as he seemed to do,
that I was to go to Washington City. He manifested a courteous, obliging temper, and either by the authority with which
he was invested or by obtaining it from a higher power, my
preference as to the route was accorded. I told him that some
of the men with me were on parole, and that they all were
riding their own horses—private property—that I would be
glad they should be permitted to retain them, and I have a
distinct recollection that he promised me it should be done;
but I have since learned that they were all deprived of their
horses, and some who were on parole, who had not violated
their obligations of parole, but had been captured because
they were found voluntarily traveling with my family to
protect them from marauders, were sent with me as prisoners
of war, and all incarcerated, in disregard of the protection
promised when they surrendered. At Augusta we were put on

a steamer, and there met Vice-President Stephens; Hon. C. C. Clay, who had voluntarily surrendered himself upon learning that he was included in the proclamation for the arrest of certain persons charged with complicity in the assassination of Mr. Lincoln; General Wheeler, the distinguished cavalry officer, and his adjutant, General Ralls. My private secretary, Burton N. Harrison, had refused to be left behind, and, though they would not allow him to go in the carriage with me, he was resolved to follow my fortunes, as well from sentiment as the hope of being useful. His fidelity was rewarded by a long and rigorous imprisonment. At Port Royal we were transferred to a sea-going vessel, which, instead of being sent to Washington City, was brought to anchor at Hampton Roads. One by one all my companions in misfortune were sent away, we knew not whither, leaving on the vessel only Mr. Clay and his wife and myself and family. After some days' detention, Clay and myself were removed to Fortress Monroe, and there incarcerated in separate cells. Not knowing that the Government was at war with women and children, I asked that my family might be permitted to leave the ship and go to Richmond or Washington City, or to some place where they had acquaintances, but this was refused. I then requested that they might be permitted to go abroad on one of the vessels lying at the Roads. This was also denied; finally, I was informed that they must return to Savannah on the vessel by which we came. This was an old transport-ship, hardly seaworthy. My last attempt was to get for them the privilege of stopping at Charleston, where they had many personal friends. This also was refused—why, I did not then know, have not learned since, and unwilling to make a supposition, as none could satisfactorily account for such an act of inhumanity. My daily experience as a prisoner shed no softer light on the transaction, but only served to intensify my extreme solicitude. Bitter tears have been shed by the gentle, and stern reproaches have been made by the magnanimous, on account of the needless torture to which I was subjected, and the heavy fetters riveted upon me, while in a stone casemate and surrounded by a strong guard; but all these were less excruciating than the mental agony my captors were able to inflict. It was long before I was permitted to hear from my wife and children, and this, and things like this, was the power which education added to savage cruelty.

Chapter 44

Northern Conduct of the War

ON APRIL 25TH, at Raleigh, North Carolina, General J. E. Johnston capitulated to General Sherman, as has been stated, and his army was disbanded. On May 4th General R. Taylor capitulated with the last of our forces east.

The number of men brought into the field by the Government of the United States during the war, according to the official returns in the Adjutant-General's office, Washington, was 2,678,967. In addition to these, 86,724 paid a commutation.

Of the manner in which our adversaries conducted the war I had frequent occasion to remark. Those observations made at the time present a more correct representation of facts than could be given in more recent statements. In a message to Congress on August 15, 1862, I said:

. . . Rapine and wanton destruction of private property, war upon non-cambatants, murder of captives, bloody threats to avenge the death of an invading soldiery by the slaughter of unarmed citizens, orders of banishment against peaceful farmers engaged in the cultivation of the soil, are some of the means used by our ruthless invaders to enforce the submission of a free people to a foreign sway. Confiscation bills, of a character so atrocious as to insure, if executed, the utter ruin of the entire population of these States, are passed by their Congress and approved by their Executive. The moneyed obligations of the Confederate Government are counterfeited by citizens of the United States, and publicly advertised for sale in their cities, with a notoriety that sufficiently attests the knowledge of their Government; and the soldiers of the invading armies are found supplied with large quantities of these forged notes as a means of despoiling the country people by fraud out of such portions of their property as armed violence may fail to reach. Two at least of the generals of the United States are engaged, unchecked by their Government, in exciting servile insurrection, and in arming and training slaves for warfare against their masters, citizens of the Confederacy.

The war, which in its inception was waged for forcing us back into the Union, having failed to accomplish that purpose, passed into a second stage, in which it was attempted to conquer and rule our States as dependent provinces. Defeated in this design, our enemies entered upon another, which could have no other purpose than revenge and plunder of private property. In May, 1864, it was still characterized by the barbarism with which it had been previously conducted. Aged men, helpless women and children appealed in vain to the humanity which should be inspired by their condition, for immunity from arrest, incarceration, or banishment from their homes. Plunder and devastation of the property of non-cambatants, destruction of private dwellings, and even of edifices devoted to the worship of God, expeditions organized for the sole purpose of sacking cities, consigning them to the flames, killing the unarmed inhabitants, and inflicting horrible outrages on women and children, were some of the constantly recurring atrocities of the invader.

On June 19, 1864, Major-General Hunter began his retreat from before Lynchburg down the Shenandoah Valley. Lieutenant-General Early, who followed in pursuit, thus describes the destruction he witnessed along the route:

Houses had been burned, and helpless women and children left without shelter. The country had been stripped of provisions, and many families left without a morsel to eat. Furniture and bedding had been cut to pieces, and old men and women and children robbed of all the clothing they had, except that on their backs. Ladies' trunks had been rifled, and their dresses torn to pieces in mere wantonness. Even the negro girls had lost their little finery. At Lexington he had burned the Military Institute with all its contents, including its library and scientific apparatus. Washington College had been plundered, and the statue of Washington stolen. The residence of ex-Governor Letcher at that place had been burned by orders, and but a few minutes given Mrs. Letcher and her family to leave the house. In the county a most excellent Christian gentleman, a Mr. Creigh, had been hung, because, on a former occasion, he had killed a straggling and marauding Federal soldier while in the act of insulting and outraging the ladies of his family.

A letter dated Charleston, September 14, 1865, written by Rev. Dr. John Bachman, then pastor of the Lutheran Church in that city, presents many facts respecting the devastation and robberies by the enemy in South Carolina. So much as relates to the march of Sherman's army through parts of the State is here presented:

When Sherman's army came sweeping through Carolina, leaving a broad track of desolation for hundreds of miles, whose steps were accompanied with fire, and sword, and blood, reminding us of the tender mercies of the Duke of Alva, I happened to be at Cash's Depot, six miles from Cheraw. The owner was a widow, Mrs. Ellerbe, seventy-one years of age. Her son, Colonel Cash, was absent. I witnessed the barbarities inflicted on the aged, the widow, and young and delicate females. Officers, high in command, were engaged tearing from the ladies their watches, their ear and wedding rings, the daguerreotypes of those they loved and cherished. A lady of delicacy and refinement, a personal friend, was compelled to strip before them, that they might find concealed watches and other valuables under her dress. A system of torture was practiced toward the weak, unarmed, and defenseless, which, as far as I know and believe, was universal throughout the whole course of that invading army. Before they arrived at a plantation, they inquired the names of the most faithful and trustworthy family servants; these were immediately seized, pistols were presented at their heads; with the most terrific curses, they were threatened to be shot if they did not assist them in finding buried treasures. If this did not succeed, they were tied up and cruelly beaten. Several poor creatures died under the infliction. The last resort was that of hanging, and the officers and men of the triumphant army of General Sherman were engaged in erecting gallows and hanging up these faithful and devoted servants. They were strung up until life was nearly extinct, when they were let down, suffered to rest awhile, then threatened and hung up again. It is not surprising that some should have been left hanging so long that they were taken down dead. Coolly and deliberately these hardened men proceeded on their way, as if they had perpetuated no crime, and as if the God of heaven would not pursue them with his vengeance. But it was not alone the poor blacks (to whom they professed to come as liberators) that were thus subjected to torture and death. Gentlemen of high character, pure and honorable and gray-headed, unconnected with the military, were dragged from their fields or their beds, and subjected to this process of threats, beating, and hanging. Along the whole track of Sherman's army, traces remain of the cruelty and inhumanity practiced on the aged and the defenseless. Some of those who were hung up died under the rope, while their cruel murderers have not only been left unreproached and unhung, but have been hailed as heroes and patriots. The list of those martyrs whom the cupidity of the officers and men of Sherman's army sacrificed to their thirst for gold and sliver, is large and most revolting. If the editors of this paper will give their consent to publish it, I will give it in full, attested by the names of the purest and best men and women of our Southern land.

I, who have been a witness to these acts of barbarity that are revolting to every feeling of humanity and mercy, was doomed to feel in my own person the effects of the avarice, cruelty, and despotism which characterized the men of that army. I was the only male guardian of the refined and delicate females who had fled there for shelter and protection. I soon ascertained the plan that was adopted in this wholesale system of plunder, insult, blasphemy, and brutality. The first party that came was headed by officers, from a colonel to a lieutenant, who acted with seeming politeness, and told me that they only came to secure our firearms, and when these were delivered up nothing in the house should be touched. Out of the house, they said, they were authorized to press forage for their large army. I told them that along the whole line of the march of Sherman's army, from Columbia to Cheraw, it had been ascertained that ladies had been robbed and personally insulted. I asked for a guard to protect the females. They said that there was no necessity for this, as the men dare not act contrary to orders. If any did not treat the ladies with proper respect, I might blow their brains out. "But," said I, "you have taken away our arms, and we are defenseless." They did not blush much, and made no reply. Shortly after this came the second party, before the first had left. They demanded the keys of the ladies' drawers, took away such articles as they wanted, then locked the drawers and put the keys in their pockets. In the mean time, they gathered up the spoons, knives, forks, towels, table-cloths, etc. As they were carrying them off, I appealed to the officers of the first party; they ordered the men to put back the things; the officers of the second party said he would see them d——d first; and, without further ado, packed them up, and they glanced at each other and smiled. The elegant carriage and all the vehicles on the premises were seized and filled with bacon and other plunder. The smoke-houses were emptied of their contents and carried off. Every head of poultry was seized and flung over their mules, and they presented the hideous picture in some of the scenes in "Forty Thieves." Every article of harness they did not wish was cut in pieces.

By this time the first and second parties had left, and a third appeared on the field. They demanded the keys of the drawers, and, on being informed that they had been carried off, coolly and deliberately proceeded to break open the locks, took what they wanted, and when we uttered words of complaint were cursed. Every horse, mule, and carriage, even to the carts, was taken away, and, for hundreds of miles, the last animal that cultivated the widow's corn-field, and the vehicles that once bore them to the house of worship, were carried off or broken into pieces and burned.

The first party that came promised to leave ten days' provisions, the rest they carried off. An hour afterward, other hordes of marauders from the same army came and demanded the last pound of bacon and the last quart of meal. On Sunday, the negroes were dressed in their best suits. They were kicked, and knocked down and robbed of all their clothing, and they came to us in their shirt-sleeves, having lost their hats, clothes, and shoes. Most of our own clothes had been hid in the woods. The negroes who had assisted in removing them were beaten and threatened with death, and compelled to show them where they were concealed. They cut open the trunks, threw my manuscripts and devotional books into a mud-hole, stole the ladies' jewelry, hair ornaments, etc., tore many garments into tatters, or gave the rest to the negro women to bribe them into criminal intercourse. These women afterward returned to us those articles that, after the mutilations, were scarcely worth preserving. The plantation, of one hundred and sixty negroes, was some distance from the house, and to this place successive parties of fifty at a time resorted for three long days and nights, the husbands and fathers being fired at and compelled to fly to the woods.

Now commenced scenes of licentiousness, brutality, and ravishment that have scarcely had an equal in the ages of heathen barbarity. I conversed with aged men and women, who were witnesses of these infamous acts of Sherman's unbridled soldiery, and several of them, from the cruel treatment they had received, were confined to their beds for weeks afterward. The time will come when the judgment of Heaven will await these libidinous, beastly barbarians. During this time, the fourth party, whom, I was informed by others, we had the most reason to dread, had made their appearance. They came, as they said, in the name of the great General Sherman, who was next to God Almighty. They came to burn and lay in ashes all that was left. They had burned bridges and depots, cotton-gins, mills, barns, and stables. They swore they would make the d——d rebel women pound their corn with rocks, and eat their raw meal without cooking. They succeeded in thousands of instances. I walked out at night, and the innumerable fires that were burning as far as the eye could reach, in hundreds of places, illuminated the whole heavens, and testified, to the vindictive barbarity of the foe. I presume they had orders not to burn occupied houses, but they strove all in their power to compel families to fly from their houses that they might afterward burn them. The neighborhood was filled with refugees who had been compelled to fly from their plantations on the seaboard. As soon as they had fled, the torch was applied, and, for hundreds of miles, those elegant mansions, once the ornament and pride of our inland country, were burned to the ground.

All manner of expedients were now adopted to make the residents leave their homes for the second time. I heard them saying, "This is too large a house to be left standing, we must contrive to burn it." Canisters of powder were placed all around the house, and an expedient resorted to that promised almost certain success. The house was to be burned down by firing the outbuildings.

These were so near each other that the firing of the one would lead to the destruction of all. I had already succeeded in having a few bales of cotton rolled out of the building, and hoped, if they had to be burned, the rest would also be rolled out, which could have been done in ten minutes by several hundred men who were looking on, gloating over the prospect of another elegant mansion in South Carolina being left in ashes. The torch was applied, and soon the large storehouse was on fire. This communicated to several other buildings in the vicinity, which, one by one, were burned to the ground. At length the fire reached the smoke-house, where they had already carried off the bacon of two hundred and fifty hogs. This was burned, and the fire was now rapidly approaching the kitchen, which was so near the dwelling-house that, should the former burn, the destruction of the large and noble edifice would be inevitable.

A captain of the United States service, a native of England, whose name I would like to mention here, if I did not fear to bring down upon him the censure of the abolitionists as a friend to the rebels, mounted the roof, and the wet blankets we sent up to him prevented the now smoking roof from bursting into flames. I called for help to assist us in procuring water from a deep well; a young lieutenant stepped up, condemned the infamous conduct of the burners, and called on his company for aid; a portion of them came cheerfully to our assistance; the wind seemed almost by a miracle to subside; the house was saved, and the trembling females thanked God for their deliverance. All this time, about one hundred mounted men were looking on, refusing to raise a hand to help us; laughing at the idea that no efforts of ours could save the house from the flames.

My trials, however, were not yet over. I had already suffered much in a pecuniary point of view. I had been collecting a library on natural history during a long life. The most valuable of these books had been presented by various societies in England, France, Germany, Russia, etc., who had honored me with membership, and they or the authors presented me with these works, which had never been for sale, and could not be purchased. My herbarium, the labor of myself and the ladies of my house for many years, was also among these books. I had left them as a legacy to the library of the Newbury College, and concluded to send them at once. They were detained in Columbia, and there the torch was applied, and all were burned. The stealing and burning of books appear to be one of the programmes on which the army acted. I had assisted in laying the foundation and dedicating the Lutheran Church at Columbia, and there, near its walls, had recently been laid the remains of one who was dearer to me than life itself. To set that brick church on fire from below was impossible. The building stood by itself on a square but little built up. One of Sherman's burners was sent up to the roof. He was seen applying the torch to the cupola. The church was burned to the ground, and the grave of my loved one desecrated. The story circulated, that the citizens had set their own city on fire, is utterly untrue, and only reflects dishonor on those who vilely perpetrated it. General Sherman had his army under control. The burning was by his orders, and ceased when he gave the command.

I was now doomed to experience in person the effects of avarice and barbarous cruelty. The robbers had been informed in the neighborhood that the family which I was protecting had buried one hundred thousand dollars in gold and silver. They first demanded my watch, which I had effectually secured from their grasp. They then asked me where the money had been hid. I told them I knew nothing about it, and did not believe there was a thousand dollars worth in all, and what there was had been carried off by the owner, Coloner Cash. All this was literally true. They then concluded to try an experiment on me which had proved so successful in hundreds of other instances. Coolly and deliberately they prepared to inflict torture on a defenseless, gray-headed old man. They carried me behind a stable, and once again demanded where the money was buried, or "I should be sent to hell in five minutes." They cocked their pistols and held them to my head. I told them to fire away. One of them, a square-built, broad-faced, large-mouthed, clumsy lieutenant, who had the face of a demon, and who did not utter five words without an awful blasphemy, now kicked me in the stomach until I fell breathless and prostrate. As soon as I was able, I rose again. He once more asked me where the silver was. I answered as before, "I do not know." With his heavy, elephant foot he now kicked me on my back until I fell again. Once more I arose, and he put the same question to me. I was nearly breathless, but answered as before. Thus was I either kicked or knocked down seven or eight times. I then told him it was perfectly useless for him to continue his threats or his blows. He might shoot me if he chose. I was ready and would not budge an inch, but requested him not to bruise and batter an unarmed, defenseless old man. "Now," said he, "I'll try a new plan. How would you like to have both your arms cut off?" He did not wait for an answer, but, with his heavy sheathed sword, struck me on my left arm, near the shoulder. I heard it crack; it hung powerless by my side, and I supposed it was broken. He then repeated the blow on the other arm. The pain was most excruciating, and it was several days before I could carve my food or take my arm out of a sling, and it was black and blue for weeks. (I refer to Dr. Kollock, of Cheraw.) At that moment the ladies, headed by my daughter, who had only then been made aware of the brutality practiced upon me, rushed from the house, and came flying to my rescue. "You dare not murder my father," said my child; "he has been a minister in the same church for fifty years, and God has always protected, and will protect him." "Do you believe in a God, miss?" said one of the brutal wretches; "I don't believe in a God, a heaven, nor a hell." "Carry me," said I, "to your General." I did not intend to go to General Sherman, who was at Cheraw, from whom, I was informed, no redress could be obtained, but to a general in the neighborhood, said to be a religious man. Our horses and carriages had all been taken away, and I was too much bruised to be able to walk. The other young officers came crowding around me very officiously, telling me that they would represent the case to the General, and that they would have him shot by ten o'clock the next morning. I saw the winks and glances that were interchanged between them. Every one gave a different name to the officers. The brute remained unpunished, as I saw him on the following morning, as insolent and as profane as he had been on the preceding day.

As yet, no punishment had fallen on the brutal hyena, and I strove to nurse my bruised body and heal my wounds, and forget the insults and injuries of the past. A few weeks after this I was sent for to perform a parochial duty at Mars Bluff, some twenty miles distant. Arriving at Florence in the vicinity, I was met by a crowd of young men connected with the militia. They were excited to the highest pitch of rage, and thirsted for revenge. They believed that among the prisoners that had just arrived on the railroad-car, on their way to Sumter, were the very men who committed such horrible outrages in the neighborhood. Many of their houses had been laid in ashes. They had been robbed of every means of support. Their horses had been seized; their cattle and hogs bayoneted; their mothers and sisters had been insulted, and robbed of their watches, ear and wedding rings. Some of their parents had been murdered in cold blood. The aged pastor, to whose voice they had so often listened, had been kicked and knocked down by repeated blows, and his hoary head had been dragged about in the sand. They entreated me to examine the prisoners and see whether I could identify the men that had inflicted such barbarities on me. I told them I would do so, provided they would remain where they were and not follow me. The prisoners saw me at a distance, held down their guilty heads, and trembled like aspen-leaves. All cruel men are cowards. One of my arms was still in a sling. With the other I raised some of their hats. They all begged for mercy. I said to them, "The other day you were tigers—you are sheep now." But a hideous object soon arrested my attention. *There sat my brutal enemy*—the vulgar, swaggering lieutenant, who had ridden up to the steps of the house, insulted the ladies, and beaten me most unmercifully. I approached him slowly, and, in a whisper asked him: "Do you know me, sir?—the old man whose pockets you first searched, to see whether he might not have a penknife to defend himself, and then kicked and knocked him down with your fist and heavy scabbard?" He presented the picture of an arrant coward, and in a trembling voice implored me to have mercy: "Don't let me be shot; have pity! Old man, beg for me! I won't do it again! For God's sake, save me! O God, help me!" "Did you not tell my daughter there was no God? Why call on him now?" "Oh, I have changed my mind; I believe in a God now." I turned and saw the impatient, flushed, and indignant crowd approaching. "What are they going to do with me?" said he. "Do you hear that sound—click, click?" "Yes" said he, "they are cocking their pistols." "True," said I; "and if I raise a finger you will have a dozen bullets through your brain." "Then I will go to hell; don't let them kill me. Lord, have mercy!" "Speak low," said I, "and don't open your lips." The men advanced. Already one had pulled me by the coat. "Show us the men." I gave no clew by which the guilty could be identified. I walked slowly through the car, sprang into the waiting carriage, and drove off.

Chapter 45

Reconstruction

WHEN THE CONFEDERATE soldiers laid down their arms and went home, all hostilities against the power of the Government of the United States ceased. The powers delegated in the compact of 1787 by these States to a central organization to promote their general welfare, had been used for their devastation and subjugation. It was conceded, as the result of the contest, that the United States Government was stronger in resources than the Confederate Government, and that the Confederate States had not achieved their independence.

Nothing remained to be done but for the sovereigns, the people of each State, to assert their authority and restore order. If the principle of the sovereignty of the people, the cornerstone of all our institutions, had survived and was still in force, it was necessary only that the people of each State should reconsider their ordinances of secession, and again recognize the Constitution of the United States as the supreme law of the land. This simple process would have placed the Union on its original basis, and have restored that which had ceased to exist, the Union by consent. Unfortunately, such was not the intention of the conqueror. Henceforth there was to be established a Union of force. Sovereignty was to pass from the people to the Government of the United States, and to be upheld by those who had furnished the money and the soldiers for the war.

The first step required, therefore, in the process for the reconstruction of the new and forced Union, was to prepare those who had been the late champions of the sovereignty of the people to become suitable subjects under the new sovereign. Standing defenseless, stripped of their property, and exposed, as it was asserted, to the penalties of insurrection on the one hand, and that of treason on the other, the President of the United States, Mr. Andrew Johnson, who, as Vice-President, became President after the death of Mr. Lincoln, on May 29, 1865, thus addressed them:

To the end, therefore, that the authority of the Government of the United States may be restored, and that peace, order, and freedom may be reëstablished, I, Andrew Johnson, President of the United States, do proclaim and declare that I hereby grant to all persons who have directly or indirectly participated in the existing rebellion, except as hereinafter excepted, amnesty and pardon, with restoration of all rights of property, except as to slaves, and except in cases where legal proceedings under the laws of the United States providing for the confiscation of property of persons engaged in the rebellion have been instituted; but on the condition, nevertheless, that every such person shall take and subscribe the following oath or affirmation, and thenceforward keep and maintain said oath inviolate; and which oath shall be registered for permanent preservation, and shall be of the tenor and effect following, to wit:

I ⸺ ⸺, do solemnly swear, or affirm, in presence of Almighty God, that I will henceforth faithfully support and defend the Constitution of the United States and the Union thereunder, and that I will, in like manner, abide by and faithfully support all laws and proclamations which have been made during the existing rebellion with reference to the emancipation of slaves, so help me God.

The permission to take this oath was withheld from large classes of citizens. It will be seen that there are two stipulations in this oath, the first faithfully to support the Constitution of the United States and the Union thereunder. This comprises obedience to the laws made in conformity to the Constitution, and is all that is requisite in the simple oath of allegiance of an American citizen. The second stipulation is:

To abide by and faithfully support all laws and proclamations which have been made during the existing rebellion with reference to the emancipation of slaves.

What need was there of this second stipulation? Because the laws were not enacted, nor the proclamation issued under any grant of power in the Constitution or under its authority. Now, the exercise of a power by Government, for which it has no constitutional authority, is not only a usurpation, but it destroys the sanction of all written instruments of government. Also, what has become of the unalienable right of property, which all the State governments were created to protect and preserve? Where was the sovereignty of the people under these proceedings? Yet the Confederate citizen was required to bind himself by an oath to abide by and faithfully support all these usurpations; the alternative being to resist the Government, or to aid and abet a violation of the Constitution.

Meanwhile, each of the late Confederate States was occupied by a military force of the Government of the United States and military orders were the supreme law; and that Government thereby proceeded to establish a State organization based on the principle of its own sovereignty. In the first place, the President of the United States issued a proclamation in such terms as to bè applicable to each of the Confederate States wherever its affairs were in such process of subjugation as to permit the commencement of the proposed organization. This proclamation begins by setting forth four propositions as the basis of his authority: First, the Constitution declares that the United States shall guarantee to every State in the Union a republican form of government, and protect each against invasion and domestic violence. Second, the President is Commander-in-Chief of the Army and Navy, as well as chief civil executive officer, and bound to take care that the laws be faithfully executed. Third, the rebellion, in its revolutionary progress, deprived the people of all civil government. Fourth, it becomes necessary and proper to enforce and carry out the obligations of the United States to the people of the State in securing it in the enjoyment of a republican form of government. Therefore, etc.

These propositions call for a notice as well because of their fallacy as their enormity. The third declares that the so-called rebellion, in its progress, deprived the people of each Confederate State of all civil goverment. There was a government over each Confederate State, then existing and in full operation. It was, in all its internal relations, the same government which existed when the State was a member of the Union, whereby it was recognized by the Government of the United States and by the other States as a lawful and republican State government. It had been created by the free consent of the people of the State, and they had defended it with their lives and their fortunes. It had been denied by the Government of the United States that any one of the Confederate States was a foreign state or outside the Union by its secession. There was, therefore, neither in law nor in fact, any foundation for the assertion that the so-called rebellion had deprived the people of each Confederate State of all civil government.

Having thus stripped each Confederate State of all civil government, it was asserted that the Constitution declares that the United States shall guarantee to each State a republican form of government. But to guarantee is not to create, to organize, or to bring into existence. This can be done for a State government only by the free and unconstrained action of the whole people of a State. The creation of such a government is beyond the powers of the Government of the United States. After a republican government has been instituted by the people, the Constitution requires the United States to guarantee its existence, and thereby forbids them or their Government to overthrow it and set up a creature of its own. The duty to guarantee commands the preservation of that which already exists. Such were the governments of the Confederate States before the war and after the war. Thus the power granted in the Constitution to preserve and guarantee State governments was perverted to overthrow and destroy republican governments, and to erect in their places military Governors, Legislatures, and judicial tribunals.

The third proposition is that the President is Commander-in-Chief of the Army and Navy and the chief civil executive. His troops already occupied each of these States, and held the people in subjection. His proclamation was therefore merely a military order from the hand of the conqueror. Everything which he can do under such a character partakes of the nature, simply and solely, of martial law. Therefore he proceeds under the fourth proposition, wherein it "becomes necessary and proper to carry out the obligations of the United States to the people" of each Confederate State, "in securing them in the enjoyment of a republican form of government." The American people were now about to witness, on an extensive scale, the tyrannical experiment of instituting republican governments by the processes of martial law. [In the Declaration of Independence,] they had declared it to be a self-evident truth that it was "the right of the people to alter or to abolish it [their government], and to institute a new government, laying its foundation on such principles, and organizing its powers in such form, as to them shall seem most likely to effect their safety and happiness." This principle of the sovereignty of the people was now rejected, and the sovereignty of fleets and armies was substituted.

It will be here noticed that all the proceeding are undertaken for the sake of the "loyal" persons in the State. Who is to decide what persons are "loyal"? He who issues the military order—the President and his agent the provisional Governor; and they naturally will decide those to be loyal who support and obey their orders. The free assent and dissent which are the basis of the validity of every political action under our system, are unknown in this case.

It is declared that the so-called rebellion, "deprived the people of the State of all civil government"; but here it is made the first duty of the provisional Governor to procure a convention of "loyal" persons "to alter and amend the Constitution" of the State. Thus it seems that there was a State in existence, and a Constitution in full vigor, notwithstanding the above declaration of the President to the contrary. This was that Constitution of the State which was in force during that long and peaceful period through which the Constitution of the United States was observed, and constitutional laws enacted. Now it was to be altered and amended from what the sovereign people of those days had ordained it to be, at the command, and to conform to the views, of another sovereign. The nature of those alterations and amendments will be stated hereafter.

This convention was to possess the authority to exercise all the powers necessary "to restore the State to its constitutional relations with the Federal Government." It was further provided that no person should vote unless he had taken the amnesty oath mentioned on a previous page, and was a qualified voter previous to the secession of the State. The convention or the subsequent Legislature was to prescribe the qualification of all voters afterward—"a power," says the President, "the people of the several States composing the Federal Union have rightfully exercised from the origin of the Government to the present time."

The first movement for the restoration of the Confederate States to the Union under subjugation was commenced in Virginia. Richmond was occupied by the forces of the United States Government, and the authority of all State officers elected during the war was annulled. Affairs remained in this position until May 9, 1865, when the President of the United States issued an order declaring all the acts and proceedings of the political, military, and civil organizations in the State which had been in insurrection against the United States to be null and void; and that all persons who should attempt to exercise any authority as under the late State or Confederate officers, should be deemed and taken as in rebellion, etc. At this time Francis H. Pierpont, who had assumed to exercise the office of Governor of Virginia over ten counties around Alexandria, was recognized by the President as the true Governor of the State. He was aided to remove the seat of his government from Alexandria to Richmond, and there maintained by the military force. No hostile opposition, however, was anywhere manifested, while at Alexandria delegates from the ten counties had assembled in convention and assumed to amend the State Constitution, and the little so-called legislative body had undertaken to pass various acts of importance. The so-called Governor, in presenting a summary of them, concluded by saying, "Thus, State sovereignty—the *status* of the African race—the armed resistance to the Government of the United States—are disposed of." An election for a new Legislature and State officers was held on October 12th. All were allowed to vote who had not held office under the State government or the Confederacy during the war, after they had taken the amnesty oath. The so-called Legislature assembled and entered upon the regulation of all the affairs of the State. A general act of vagrancy was passed, whereupon the major-general in command issued an order "that no magistrate, civil officer, or other person shall, in any way or manner, apply, or attempt to apply, the provisions of the said statute to any colored person in this department." At the municipal election in Richmond, the Mayor, Attorney, and Superintendent of the Poor, elected, were persons who had held office under the Confederate States. They were not allowed by the military authority to qualify, and subsequently declined.

In 1865 the Congress of the United States passed an act which provided that the following amendment to the Constitution should be submitted to the Legislatures of the several States for ratification or rejection:

SECTION 1. Neither slavery nor involuntary servitude, except as a punishment for crime, whereof the party shall have been duly convicted, shall exist within the United States, or any place subject to its jurisdiction.

SECTION 2. Congress shall have full power to enforce this article by appropriate legislation.

One Dr. James L. Watson was tried for killing a negro in Rockbridge County, and acquitted. Major-General Schofield, in command of the military forces of the department, immediately ordered his arrest and trial by a military commission. On the assembling of the commission a writ of *habeas corpus* was issued out of the Circuit Court of Richmond in behalf of Watson, and served on the General. In his answer, he declined compliance with the writ, saying:

Dr. Watson is held for trial by military commission, under the authority of the act of Congress of July 16, 1866, which act directs and requires the President, through the commissioner and officers of the Freedman's Bureau, to exercise military jurisdiction over all cases and questions concerning the free enjoyment of the right to have full and equal benefit of all laws and proceedings concerning personal liberty, personal security, etc., by all citizens, without respect to race or color, or previous condition of slavery, of the States whose constitutional relations to the Government of the United States have been discontinued by the rebellion, and have not been restored.

In the mean time, the United States Attorney-General having examined the case, and reported that, in his opinion, the military commission had not competent jurisdiction, the President thereupon directed that the commission be dissolved and the prisoner discharged without delay.

Meantime Congress had passed an act, known as the Civil Rights Bill, and a case came before the Circuit Court, at Alexandria, in which one of the parties offered to produce negro evidence. The Judge (Thomas) ruled that, inasmuch as the State laws of Virginia forbade the introduction of negro testimony in civil suits to which white men alone were parties, the evidence of the negro was inadmissible; and that Congressional legislation could not impair the right of the States to decide what classes of persons were competent to testify in her courts.

A storm was now brewing which was soon to involve the President and Congress in open conflict. During the period in which these proceedings took place in Virginia, similar ones occurred in all the remaining Confederate States. Not only in Virginia, but in several of the other States, some persons had been voted for as members of Congress, but in no case had they been admitted to seats. This was one of the measures taken by Congress to indicate its disapproval of the President's plan for the treatment of the late Confederate States.

The difficulties that now arose between the President and Congress had reference entirely to the affairs of the Confederate States. The plan of the President left the negroes to the care of the States alone after the establishment of their emancipation. Congress desired them to be made American citizens, secure in all the rights of freemen and voters. The refusal to admit Senators and Representatives to Congress from the Confederate States served to arrest the operation of the President's plans to hold these States in abeyance.

No compromise could be made between the two. Each appealed to the Constitution, forgetful that each had sustained all its ruthless violations during the last four years. Congress, therefore, commenced an independent action, and in its reckless course sought, unsuccessfully, to rid itself of the President by impeachment. Its first act, at the commencement of the session, in December, 1865, was the appointment, by a large majority in each House, of a joint Committe of Fifteen, to which was referred all questions relating to the conditions and manner in which Congress would recognize the late Confederate States as members of the Union. Meantime the credentials of all persons sent as Representatives and Senators from them were laid upon the table in each House, there to remain until the final action of the Committee of Fifteen. This was followed by the passage, in February, 1866, of "an act to establish a bureau for the relief of freedmen, refugees, and abandoned lands." It proposed to establish military jurisdiction over all parts of the United States containing refugees and freedmen. This bill was vetoed by the President, and passed over his veto.

In March an act was passed "to protect all persons in the United States in their civil rights, and furnish the means of their vindication." The first section declared all persons born in the United States, and not subject to any foreign power, excluding Indians not taxed, to be citizens of the United States, and enumerates the rights to be enjoyed by those so declared to be citizens. The second section affords discriminating protection to colored persons in the full enjoyment of all the rights secured to them by the preceding section. This bill was vetoed by the President, and passed over his veto.

On June 8, 1866, a majority and a minority report were made by the Committee of Fifteen. Meanwhile, a report had been made from the same committee, in the form of an amendment to the Constitution, which was debated and amended in each House, and finally passed by the requisite majority in each. Thus was to be secured the political support and votes of the negroes, who were expected to be the controlling citizens of the late Confederate States.

The amendment to the Constitution was now submitted to the Legislatures of all the States, to be valid as a part of the Constitution, when ratified by three fourths, in the following form:

ARTICLE—, SECTION 1. All persons born or naturalized in the

United States, and subject to the jurisdiction thereof, are citizens of the United States, and of the State wherein they reside. No State shall make or enforce any law which shall abridge the privileges or immunities of citizens of the United States; nor shall any State deprive any person of life, liberty, or property, without due process of law, nor deny to any person within its jurisdiction the equal protection of the laws.

SECTION 2. Representatives shall be apportioned among the several States according to their respective numbers, counting the whole number of persons in each State, excluding Indians not taxed. But, when the right to vote at any election for the choice of electors for President and Vice-President of the United States, Representatives in Congress, the executive and judicial officers of a State, or the members of the Legislature thereof, is denied to any of the male inhabitants of such State, being twenty-one years of age, and citizens of the United States, or in any way abridged, except for participation in rebellion or other crime, the basis of representation therein shall be reduced in the proportion which the number of such male citizens shall bear to the whole number of male citizens twenty-one years of age in such State.

SECTION 3. No person shall be a Senator or Representative in Congress, or elector of President and Vice-President, or hold any office, civil or military, under the United States, or under any State, who having previously taken an oath as a member of Congress, or as an officer of the United States, or as a member of any State Legislature, or as an executive or judicial officer of any State, to support the Constitution of the United States, shall have engaged in insurrection or rebellion against the same, or given aid or comfort to the enemies thereof. But Congress may by a vote of two thirds of each House remove such disability.

SECTION 4. The validity of the public debt of the United States, authorized by law, including debts incurred for payment of pensions and bounties for services in suppressing insurrection or rebellion, shall not be questioned. But the United States shall neither assume nor pay any debt or obligation incurred in aid of insurrection or rebellion against the United States, or any claim for the loss or emancipation of any slave; but all such debts, obligations, and claims shall be held illegal and void.

SECTION 5. The Congress shall have power to enforce, by appropriate legislation, the provisions of this article.

It may here be stated that the restoration of the late Confederate States to all the rights and privileges of States as co-equal members of the Union, under the plan of President Johnson, received the approval of the executive and judicial branches of the Government soon after the cessation of hostilities. Congress, however, not only withheld its assent, but, during its session in 1866, required as a condition precedent to a recognition of any one of these States, and the admission of its Representatives and Senators to seats, the adoption by its Legislature of the above-mentioned amendment. The question really involved in this amendment was the admission to citizenship and the ballot of the negroes in these States. The amendment itself, in its second section, recognized the authority to grant or withhold the elective franchise as existing in the State governments.

This amendment was submitted to the Legislatures of the States immediately after its adoption by Congress in June, 1866, and by March 30, 1867, it had been ratified by twenty States, including West Virginia, Maryland, Missouri, and Tennessee, and rejected by thirteen, including Delaware and Kentucky, and eleven of the late Confederate States. There were thirty-four States at that time, and thirty had voted. A ratification by three fourths was required to make it valid.

When this amendment was presented for ratification to the Legislature of Virginia at its session commencing December, 1866, it was rejected in the Senate by a unanimous vote, and in the House by a vote of seventy-four to one. Meantime the Freedmen's Bureau was organized and put in operation in the State, but the military occupation continued, and the condition of affairs remained unchanged during the proceedings of Congress to construct its plan for subjugation.

After the vote of the States up to March, 1867, it was manifest that no real advance had been made in the extension of the franchise to the negro population of the States. In this position of affairs Congress, on March 2d, adopted an entirely new system of measures relative to the late Confederate States. The fiction upon which these measures were based is thus expressed in the preamble of the first act:

Whereas, No legal State governments, or adequate protection for life or property, now exists in the rebel States of Virginia, North Carolina, South Carolina, Georgia, Alabama, Mississippi, Louisiana, Florida, Texas, and Arkansas; and *whereas,* it is necessary that peace and good order should be enforced in said States, until loyal and republican State governments can be legally established: therefore, *be it enacted,* etc.

These States were then divided into five military districts, and it was further provided:

Until the people of the said rebel States shall by law be admitted to representation to the Congress of the United States, all civil governments that may exist therein shall be deemed provisional only, and shall be in all respects subject to the paramount authority of the United States, at any time to abolish, modify, control, and supersede the same, and in all elections to any office under such provisional governments, all persons shall be entitled to vote under the provisions of the fifth section of this act.

Thus these States, when held by military force as conquered territory, with the sovereignty of the people extinct, were not allowed to claim to possess any rights under the Federal Constitution, or any other than such as might be granted by the will of the conqueror. It was asserted that the right to regulate the elective franchise, recognized as belonging to the States in the Union, could not attach to those out of the Union, and having only provisional political institutions. Congress then proceeded to declare, in the fifth section of the bill, the terms upon which a late Confederate State could become a member of the Union:

SECTION 5. That, when the people of any one of said rebel States shall have formed a Constitution of government in conformity with the Constitution of the United States in all respects, framed by a convention of delegates elected by the male citizens of said State, twenty-one years old and upward, of whatever race, color, or previous condition, who have been resident in said State for one year previous to the day of such election, except such as may be disfranchised for participation in the rebellion or for felony at common law, and when such Constitution shall provide that the elective franchise shall be enjoyed by all such persons as have the qualifications herein stated for electors of delegates, and when such Constitution shall be ratified by a majority of the persons voting on the question of ratification who are qualified as electors for delegates, and when such Constitution shall have been submitted to Congress for examination and approval, and Congress shall have approved the same, and when said State, by a vote of its Legislature elected under said Constitution, shall have adopted the amendment to the Constitution of the United States, proposed by the Thirty-ninth Congress, and known as Article XIV, and when said article shall have become a part of the Constitution of the United States, said State shall be declared entitled to representation in Congress, and Senators and Representatives shall be admitted therefrom on their taking the oath prescribed by law, and then and thereafter the preceding sections of this act shall be inoperative in said State, etc.

The bill became a law, notwithstanding the veto of the President.

On March 4th a new Congress commenced its session, and on March 23d a supplement to the preceding act was passed. It ordered a registration to be made of the qualified voters in each military sub-district of the State, an election to be held for the State Convention to draft a Constitution for the State, and for delegates to such convention; and that such Constitution should be submitted to the voters for adoption or rejection, and upon its adoption a State government should be organized, etc. The registration was required to be made of all citizens as defined by the "act to protect all persons in the United States in their civil rights," etc. Many disqualifications of voters, arising from participation in the war, were also expressed. This act also became a law, notwithstanding the objections of the President.

It will be seen that this act contemplated two distinct governments in each of the ten States—the one military and the other civil. Both were provisional, and both were to continue until the new State Constitution was framed, and the State was admitted to representation in Congress. The two were to be carried on together, and the people were made subject to both and obliged to obey both. The law was next put in operation by constituting the districts, as follows: 1. Virginia, commander, Major-General Schofield; 2. North Carolina and South Carolina, commander, Major-General Sickles; 3. Georgia, Florida, and Alabama, commander, Major-General John Pope; 4. Mississippi and Arkansas, commander, Major-General Ord; 5. Louisiana and Texas, commander, Major-General Sheridan.

Previous to adjournment, on July 19, 1867, Congress passed an additional supplement to the act of March 2d and the supplement of March 23d. It declared the intent and meaning of the previous acts to have been: that the civil governments of the ten States were not legal governments, and, if continued, were to be subject in all respects to the military commanders and the paramount authority of Congress. It made the acts of the military commanders subject only to the disapproval of General of the Army U. S. Grant, and authorized them to remove any person from office under the State government. It further defined the classes disfranchised, and directed that no district commander should be bound in his action by any opinion of any civil officer of the United States.

The President vetoed the bill, and in his message said:

Thus, over all these ten States, this military government is now declared to have unlimited authority. It is no longer confined to the preservation of the public peace, the administration of criminal law, the registration of voters, and the superintendence of elections; but, "in all respects," is asserted to be paramount to the existing civil governments. It is impossible to conceive any state of society more intolerable than this, and yet it is to this condition that twelve millions of American citizens are reduced by the Congress of the United States. . . .

Congress having thus completed its plan of operations, the crushing wheels of subjugation began to move forward. Let us proceed with the narration of affairs in Virginia.

On the appearance of Major-General Schofield at Richmond, all the proceedings of the so-called civil government, for the organization and restoration of the State to the Union, at once ceased, and he assumed command. A board of army officers was named by the commanding General for the purpose of selecting suitable persons for appointment as registering officers throughout the State. In making the selections, the preference was given, first, to officers of the army and of the Freedmen's Bureau, on duty in the State; second, to persons who had been discharged from the Federal army, after "meritorious" services during the war; third, to "loyal" citizens of the country or city where they were to serve. On April 2d an order appeared from the major-general, suspending all elections, whether State, county, or municipal, "under the provisional government," until after the registration was completed. A lecture on the "Chivalry of the South," advertised to be delivered in Lynchburg, was suppressed by the order of the post commander at that place. A warning was given by the major-general to the editor of the Richmond "Times," which said, "The efforts of your paper to foster enmity, create disorder, and lead to violence, can no longer be tolerated." On the refusal of five magistrates of the Corporation Council of Norfolk to receive the testimony of a negro, they were arrested on a process issued under the Civil Rights Bill, and held to bail to appear before the District Court. All armed organizations in the State were disbanded. Inflammatory messages of freedmen and those who sought their political alliance were held in different parts of the State.

Military commissioners were appointed over sub-districts for the suppression of disorder and violence, for the protection of all persons in their so-called rights of person and property, and clothed with all the powers of justices of a county or police magistrates of a city. The State was also divided into sub-districts, and commanders appointed over the same. These officers were empowered to exercise a general supervision over the military commissioners, and to furnish them, when necessary, with sufficient military force to enable them to discharge their duties. Further orders relative to the qualification of voters were issued by the major-general, in which it was declared that "all persons who voluntarily joined the rebel army, and all persons in that army, whether volunteers or conscripts, who committed voluntarily any hostile act, were thereby engaged in insurrection or rebellion; and all who voted for the ordinance of secession, gave aid and comfort to the enemy. Also all who voluntarily furnished supplies of food, or clothing, arms, ammunition, horses, or mules, or any other material of war, participated in the rebellion," and were disfranchised. The whole number registered was 116,982 whites and 104,772 blacks. The vote for the Convention was 14,835 whites and 92,507 blacks; against the Convention, 61,249 whites and 638 blacks.

The Convention assembled on December 3d and adjourned on April 17, 1868. The Bill of Rights adopted declared that—

The State shall ever remain a member of the United States of America, and the people thereof a part of the American nation, and all attempts, from whatever source, and upon whatever pretext, to dissolve said Union, or to sever said Union, are unauthorized, and ought to be resisted with the whole power of the State.

The Constitution of the United States, and the laws of Congress passed in pursuance thereof, constitute the supreme law of the land, to which paramount allegiance and obedience are due from every citizen, anything in the Constitution, ordinances, or laws of any State to the contrary notwithstanding.

Suffrage was granted to every male citizen twenty-one years of age. All officers of the State were required to take the following oath:

I, —— ——, do solemnly swear that I will support and maintain the Constitution and laws of the United States and the Constitution and laws of the State of Virginia; and that I recognize and accept the civil and political equality of all men before the law, etc.

In addition, all State, city, and county officers were required to take the test-oath prescribed by Congress on July 2, 1862, as follows:

I do solemnly swear that I have never borne arms against the United States since I have been a citizen thereof; that I have voluntarily given no aid, countenance, counsel, or encouragement to persons engaged in armed hostility thereto; that I have never sought or accepted, nor attempted to exercise the functions of any office whatever, under any authority, or pretended authority, in hostility to the United States; that I have not yielded a voluntary support to any pretended government, authority, power, or Constitution within the United States, hostile, or inimical thereto; and I do further swear that, to the best of my knowledge and ability, I will support and defend the Constitution of the United States against all enemies, foreign and domestic; that I will bear true faith and allegiance to the same; that I will take this obligation freely, without any mental reservation or purpose of evasion; and that I will well and faithfully discharge the duties of the office on which I am about to enter.

Major-General Schofield, in an address to the Convention in opposition to these stringent provisions, said:

You can not find in some of the counties a sufficient number of men who are capable of filling the offices, and who can take the oath you have prescribed here, I have no hesitation in saying that I believe it impossible to inaugurate a government upon that basis.

Meantime the so-called Constitution was adopted by the Convention, and June 2d fixed for the popular vote upon it. But no appropriation was made for the expenses of the election, and it was not held. Major-General Stoneman now succeeded Major-General Schofield.

The utter subjugation of the sovereign people of Virginia was now manifest. Not a public act of the least importance could they do without the consent of the military chief who ruled over them, and who was a stranger in their State. Finding the provisions of this Constitution were so restrictive as to exclude from the elective franchise nearly all of the most intelligent and best-educated citizens, on account of their participation in the late war, a movement was commenced for a modification of these clauses or their entire omission. The sovereignty of the people was extinct, so no relief could be secured except through the action of the sovereign sitting in Washington. Congress, therefore, passed an act authorizing the President (Grant), at such time as he might deem best, to submit the Constitution to the registered voters of Virginia, and also submit to a separate vote such provisions of the Constitution as he thought proper. The act also required the Legislature that should be elected to ratify the fourteenth and fifteenth amendments to the Constitution of the United States, as a condition precedent "to the readmission of the State into the Union."

The fifteen article of amendment to the Constitution was passed by Congress in February, 1869, and submitted to the Legislatures of the States. It was as follows:

SECTION 1. The right of citizens of the United States to vote shall not be denied or abridged by the United States, or by any State, on account of race, color, or previous condition of servitude.

SECTION 2. The Congress shall have power to enforce this article by appropriate legislation.

On the passage of the amendment by the United States Senate, Senator Garrett Davis, of Kentucky, said:

Sir, your amendments to the Constitution are all void; they are of no effect. They were proposed by a mutilated Congress; they were proposed by a mutilated House of Representatives and Senate.

In the preceding chapter the reader will find a narration of the series of measures, adopted by the Government of the United States, to complete the final subjugation of the State of Virginia. The same series of measures was applied, in the same order, to each of the Confederate States. It is, therefore, unnecessary to repeat the narration of these details in their application to the other States.

This overthrow of the rights of freemen and the establishment of such new relations required a complete revolution in the principle of the government of the United States, the subversion of the State governments, the subjugation of the people, and the destruction of the fraternal Union. The work has been done. Will it stand?

Conclusion

My first object in this work was to prove, by historical authority, that each of the States, as sovereign parties to the compact of Union, had the reserved power to secede from it whenever it should be found not to answer the ends for which it was established. If this has been done, it follows that the war was, on the part of the United States Government, one of aggression and usurpation, and, on the part of the South, was for the defense of an inherent, unalienable right.

My next purpose was to show, by the gallantry and devotion of the Southern people, in their unequal struggle, how thorough was their conviction of the justice of their cause; that, by their humanity to the wounded and captives, they proved themselves the worthy descendants of chivalric sires, and fit to be free; and that, in every case, as when our army invaded Pennsylvania, by their respect for private rights, their morality and observance of the laws of civilized war, they showed that they are entitled to the confidence and regard of mankind.

In asserting the right of secession, it has not been my wish to incite to its exercise: I recognize the fact that the war showed it to be impracticable, but this did not prove it to be wrong; and, now that it may not be again attempted, and that the Union may promote the general welfare, it is needful that the truth, the whole truth, should be known, so that crimination and recrimination may for ever cease, and then, on the basis of fraternity and faithful regard for the rights of the States, there may be written on the arch of the Union, *Esto perpetua.*

INDEX

Index

563